SILVER RING T
COVENANT

In signing this covenant before God Almighty, I

Emily
____

agree to wear a silver ring as a sign of my pledge to abstain from sexual behavior that is inconsistent with Biblical standards. On my wedding day, I will present my silver ring to my spouse, representing my faithful commitment to the marriage covenant.

"God wants you to be holy, so you should keep clear of all sexual sin. Then each of you will control your body and live in holiness and honor."

1 Thessalonians 4:3-4

Emily Potter 11/15/08
____
STUDENT SIGNATURE DATE

____
ACCOUNTABILITY PARTNER SIGNATURE DATE

Denny Pattyn
SILVER RING THING
FOUNDER AND PRESIDENT

Debra Ott
SILVER RING THING
BIBLE PROJECT COORDINATOR

CONTRIBUTORS

Greg Laurie, General Editor
Karen Dagher, Harvest Ministries Editor
Danny Bond, Harvest Ministries Assistant Editor
Steve Benson, Tyndale House Editor
Timothy R. Botts and David Riley Associates, Graphic Designers

Greg Laurie is not only an evangelist and pastor, but he is the president of Harvest Ministries as well. Harvest Ministries sponsors Harvest Crusades. These crusades are public evangelistic events intended to present the message of Jesus Christ to people in a nonreligious environment. Begun in 1990, Harvest Crusades are known for their informal atmosphere, contemporary music, and simple, straightforward messages by Greg Laurie. To date, some 1.5 million people have attended the nondenominational Harvest Crusades. If you would like more information on Harvest Ministries and/or their crusades, write to Harvest Ministries, P.O. Box 4000, Riverside, CA 92514-4000. Or call (951) 687-6595. On the internet, type http://www.harvest.org.

Denny Pattyn, Silver Ring Thing General Editor
Debra Ott, Silver Ring Thing Editor
Kelli Watson, Silver Ring Thing Assistant Editor
Cover design and Silver Ring Thing notes design by Greg Pytlik of Pytlik Design Associates, Pittsburgh, Pennsylvania

ISBN-13: 978-0-8423-5541-4
ISBN-10: 0-8423-5541-3

Printed in the United States of America

12 11 10 09 08 07
10 9 8 7

Tyndale House Publishers and Wycliffe Bible Translators share the vision for an understandable, accurate translation of the Bible for every person in the world. Each sale of the *Holy Bible,* New Living Translation, benefits Wycliffe Bible Translators. Wycliffe is working with partners around the world to accomplish Vision 2025—an initiative to start a Bible translation program in every language group that needs it by the year 2025.

Ring Stuff

I Lost My Ring!!!

And other issues you may encounter

1. I LOST MY RING! WHAT DO I DO?

Easy! Just send a check for $20 (made out to Silver Ring Thing) and a note telling us what show you attended, size you need, and your address. Send it to:

Silver Ring Thing
544 Moon Clinton Road
Moon Township, PA 15108

2. I NEED A NEW SIZE!

We're happy to let you purchase a new size. No, you don't need to wait until a show to do this. Simply send a check for $20 and a note telling us what size you want, your address and mail it to the above address.

3. MY RING TARNISHED!!!

If your skin reacts to the ring by turning green, don't be alarmed! This is a common reaction to sterling silver (happens 33% of the time). Simply paint the inside of the ring with clear nail polish once a year.

4. WANT A SILVER ONLY RING?

You can remove the black background from the ring by soaking it in acetone nail polish remover and scrubbing it with a toothbrush with hard bristles.

EVERYDAY:

No excuses — wear the ring everyday! Wear this ring like you'll wear your wedding ring — it is a promise to the person you will marry.

GREAT IDEA!

Let the ring be a reminder for you to pray for your future spouse everyday.

Table of Contents

"God wants you to be holy, so you should keep clear of all sexual sin. Then each of you will control your body and live in holiness and honor."

1 Thessalonians 4:3–4

Prepared by

Silver Ring Thing Abstinence Programs
544 Moon Clinton Road
Moon Township, PA 15108

www.silverringthing.com
e-mail: info@silverringthing.com

Silver Ring Thing

14-Day Reading Plan

Living an abstinent lifestyle and avoiding pre-marital sex requires dynamic faith. Therefore, using the page numbers listed below, read one of the selections called "**Cornerstones**" every day for two weeks. Allow God to teach you what it means to daily live a life that is faithful to Him.

Cornerstones

"The key ingredient to effective prevention is dynamic faith."

Denny Pattyn

First Steps

For New Believers

1. UNDERSTANDING YOUR DECISION

After deciding to accept Jesus Christ as Lord and Savior of your life, many questions emerge! For instance... What do I do now? What's the next step? How do I begin talking to a God I can't even see? These are real questions that demand real answers. So let us help you. Read on.....

First of all, do you truly understand the depth and meaning of the life-changing decision you recently made? Are you aware of the effect it will have on the rest of your life? Probably not.

Dig deeper: Take some quiet time (maybe 15 minutes) to read and reflect on pages A1 – A9, "How You Can Know God." This will help you better understand this BIG faith decision you made and why it's such a BIG deal to God.

2. UNDERSTANDING YOUR DISCIPLINE

As a new believer, it is crucial that you begin to develop a personal relationship with Jesus Christ. This will happen when you take some time each day to read from the Bible and talk with God in prayer. Therefore, using the page numbers listed below, read one of the "**First Steps**" selections every day for two weeks. God will bless you.

First Steps

New Believers' 14-Day Reading Plan

Know About the

Silver Ring Thing

Introduction and History

The Silver Ring Thing is the fastest growing teen abstinence program in the United States and is rapidly gaining international recognition for its high-tech presentation style incorporating music, video, cameras, laser lights, humor, and most importantly, the Good News of the Gospel of Jesus Christ. Through this program teens are able to understand that abstinence until marriage is not only the way to avoid contracting a sexually transmitted disease but is also the way to enjoy a richer and more blessed marital life. By reaching out with the gospel message of forgiveness and new beginnings, the program also ministers to those teens who have already been pressured into becoming sexually active and offers an opportunity to embrace a "second virginity."

The Silver Ring Thing program was created in 1996 by Denny and Amy Pattyn as a Christian response to the escalating numbers of teen pregnancies in Yuma, Arizona. In 2000, the Silver Ring Thing was expanded and relocated to its national headquarters in Pittsburgh, Pennsylvania and incorporated into the John Guest Team. In 2004, The John Guest Team Board decided to make Silver Ring Thing its sole mission and promoted Denny Pattyn to President.

The growing demand for the program is demonstrated by the fact that in the first four years 1,400 teenagers attended an SRT event, while in the next 5 1/2 years over 75,000 young people attended Silver Ring Thing events. A key objective of the Silver Ring Thing is to lead children to make a commitment to Christ, a commitment that will result in **behavioral change**, including a reduction in teen pregnancies.

Therefore, the Silver Ring Thing promotes abstinence until marriage as an achievable and desirable life style, and presents a personal relationship with Jesus Christ as the best way to discipline a teenager's free will resulting in a fulfilling and sexually pure life.

Section 1

10 Key Helps From The Silver Ring Thing

"What are YOU waiting for?"

That's the question the Silver Ring Thing New Testament is designed to help you answer. God has a plan for your sex life! His plan is awesome. God invented sex, invented abstinence, invented marriage and invented how it all works together. The key is to know what you're waiting for and the plan God has for your life.

Turn the page. Let us help...

Help #1

Accountability Partners/Groups

Who should I pick to be my accountability partner? Please choose a person of the same sex: guys... choose a guy; girls... choose a girl.

What if they move, "change", or we are no longer friends and therefore can no longer be my partner? It's OK to have a list of more than one accountability partner! Just make sure you get a new partner if you have lost your old one, and have them sign the front page of your Bible. You can have as many as you need – get it?

6 Suggestions For Accountability Partners/Groups

1. **Get One!** — Have them sign the covenant page of this Bible.
2. **Meet Regularly** — whether it's in person, on the phone, once a week, or once a month...stay in touch on a regular basis.
3. **Ask Tough Questions** — you can find some suggested questions on www.silverringthing.com.
4. **Support each other** when things get tough. Your help can make a world of difference!
5. **GO THROUGH THE 4 BIBLE STUDIES** we've provided for you in the SRT 434 section.
6. **Quiz each other** on "Top 10 Ingredients of Abstinence" and "When It Comes to Dating..." on the next page.

Remember — the goal is to support your accountability partner all the way to the day they get married.

Help #2

Remember Your Promise

Report Card Alert:
Review this summary when you receive your report card. What's your grade in abstinence? Go for an "A"!

Top 10 Ingredients Of Abstinence

1. Develop your personal relationship with Jesus Christ
2. Communicate with your parents about your decision
3. Meet and talk regularly with your accountability partner
4. Date people with the same "high values" you vowed to keep
5. Be honest and be upfront about your commitment to abstinence
6. Always respect the other person
7. Stay out of compromising situations
8. Remember, your past does NOT determine your future
9. Dress, act, and speak in the way that you want to be treated
10. Decide **TODAY**, not in the middle of temptation

When It Comes To Dating

1. Write down your standards and limits before you start dating
2. Develop a strong friendship before you decide to date
3. Keep Jesus at the center of a dating relationship
4. Make sure your dates are planned out
5. Plan dates for public places (restaurant, mall, park, etc.)
6. Go out on group dates whenever possible
7. Don't put yourself in a tempting or compromising situation
8. Know that you never have to prove yourself
9. Avoid the horizontal (i.e. lying on a sofa watching a video)
10. Keep clothes on, in, buttoned and zipped
11. Never compromise your standards, not for anyone
12. Drugs, alcohol, and sleepiness will make you more vulnerable

Five Honest Questions To Ask Yourself

1. **Do I believe what God says to me about sexual purity?**
2. **Do I believe God's blessings are worth waiting for?**
3. **Am I ready to stay abstinent when my friends are not?**
4. **How do I plan to say No? Write it out!**
5. **How will I answer questions about my commitment?**

Help #3
Talk About Your Experience

Read Some E-mails From Your Peers Who Are Wearing Silver Rings

God has really changed my life.

And I just want to thank you guys for all of this. I keep my ring on all the time whether it's in the shower or in bed or whether I'm wearing gold or silver. This has really changed my life AND FOR THE BETTER!
Thanks so much! — *Casey*

I loved the show.

You touched my friends and everyone around. I was so impressed the way that the message was put through the skits! It was great. I know my friend had some problems and the show touched him. I just want to thank all of you at SILVER RING THING. — *Damon*

I went to the Silver Ring Thing with my youth group.

The next day, the phone rings and it's my boyfriend, Chris. I started to tell him about it. That's when God took over. After I told him about my vow he said to me, "That is so awesome." He said, "You know we really do need to calm things down. I know that we talked about it but it's time that we just stop before we do something that we are going to regret. God wants us to be pure. You took a vow to Him and that is important." Thank you!!
— *Emily*

I just wanted to encourage you for what you are doing.

Silver Ring Thing really changed my life and gave me a lot of hope.
I will not compromise, and I'm free to serve God better in my relationships and in life in general. It was like a breath of fresh air to get the truth about sex for once. Every place I look I am hit with lies and messages about sex. It was so good to get the truth and clear up the confusion.
This generation needs the truth desperately. — *Mike*

Help #4

Join The Team

More than a ring...JOIN THE LEADERSHIP TEAM!

Silver Ring Thing is "teen-driven." Therefore, we need YOU to be part of our Leadership Team. There are 3 ways to join our team:

CREW — Sign up on our website to be on the student leadership team. CREW training can be done online or in a city near you. If you want to make a difference in your school and be part of the SRT shows, this is the place to start.

Details: **www.silverringthing.com/signup.html**

High School Internships — We offer internships to high school students to get some real-life ministry experience and consider whether God may be calling you to a career in ministry.

Details: **www.silverringthing.com**

College Internship — These internships are for college students who want to get some hands-on experience. We're looking for interns with a heart for outreach (including road trips) and a desire for a challenge. You WILL grow spiritually as a part of our young & dynamic Christian leadership team. SRT will tailor internships to meet the requirements for your major. (6 tracks available)

Details: **www.silverringthing.com/college.html**

Help #5
Know the Truth

STDs, Pregnancy, and the Spiritual Challenge

The young people of America are in trouble. They are the heirs of the sexual revolution that began in the sixties; a revolution that changed the face of the USA and is felt throughout the world. Statistics concerning teen pregnancy rates, welfare roles, abortions and sexually transmitted diseases reveal the disastrous impact that teenage promiscuity has on the nation.*

- **840,000** teenage girls become pregnant each year
- **33%** of teen pregnancies end in abortion
- **65 million** people in the US have an incurable STD like HIV, HPV, and Herpes
- **80%** of mothers who are under 18 years old will raise their children in poverty

From the Christian's perspective, even more harm is done to the souls of our young people. A lifestyle based on the popular culture's belief in easy sex leads to cynicism about life, reliance upon feelings as a moral guide, the abuse of drugs and alcohol, and an attitude that devalues human life; an attitude that can even lead to suicide. Clearly, this is not God's plan for His creation.

The Physical Problem

The current teen lifestyle has experienced an epidemic of sexually transmitted diseases (STDs) in which teens are disproportionately affected. Teens represent 10% of the US population and yet they incur 25% of the STDs. This epidemic is not limited to HIV/AIDS. In the 1960s the medical profession recognized only two major sexually transmitted diseases: gonorrhea and syphilis. Today they have identified nearly 30!

In the USA this year alone

- **3.75 million** teenagers will be newly infected with a one or more STDs
- **20%** of people over the age of 12 will be infected with incurable genital herpes
- **1 in 10** teenage girls will have chlamydia
- More than **4,000** women will die from cervical cancer as a direct result of an STD called human papilloma virus (HPV)

*All sources available at www.silverringthing.com

Help #6

Second Chances

I Messed Up! Can I Start Over Again?

Dear Silver Ring Thing,

I don't know how to start this e-mail, so I guess I'll just come right out and ask — What if I messed up? Can I start over again?

Please write back soon,
Matt

Dear Matt,

Yes! There are always second chances. Thank you for being strong enough to let us know that you need to start over. Did you take your ring off? If so, thank you for not messing up while wearing your ring. We appreciate your respect! Next, I want you to call us because we would like to walk you through putting your ring back on your finger. Follow the steps below and we look forward to hearing from you very soon!

1. Decide that you WANT to start over again.
2. Read John 8:1–11 on page 115 and focus especially on what Jesus says to the person caught in adultery at the end — "Go and sin no more."
3. Take a moment just to chill and spend some quiet time with God. Tell Him what's on your heart, what you did wrong, and ask Him to forgive you. Ask Him for help as you put your ring back on your finger.
4. Call our office and we'll pray with you to put your ring back on.
5. Fight the temptation and wait until you are married to have sex!

To find some helpful, practical dating suggestions...check out SRT 11.

Help #7

Fully Invested

From Start To Finish: The Entire SRT Experience

12 Step Follow-up Program

1. **The Ring** — the symbol and namesake of the Silver Ring Thing. The ring is a constant reminder of the commitment made and sends a profound message to everyone who sees it.

2. **SRT Bible** — abstinence study Bible with support material specific to students. A distinct connection between the Bible and e-mail follow-up provides depth and further understanding of the decision made.

3. **The Vow** — a public promise to remain abstinent until marriage pledged by each student in a group setting. The Vow is signed and dated on the first page of the SRT Bible as a reminder and constant source of encouragement and support.

4. **A Faith Decision** — in accepting the ring, the student accepts the reason for wearing it. The student understands that God has a plan for his or her life, and a plan for his or her sexuality. When the decision is faith-based, the student has the power of God working within them.

5. **Accountability Partner** — within 48 hours, every student is asked to name an accountability partner of the same sex to encourage, share, and support his or her decision.

6. **E-mail** — SRT team members initiate e-mail contact with all students in an exhaustive effort to remain present in the daily lives of students. E-mails go out twice a week for four months and help guide and direct students through the SRT Bible and through daily circumstances.

12 Step Follow-up Program (continued)

7. **SRT 434 Program - Student Edition** — Once you have completed Silver Ring Thing, the SRT 434 Program - Student Edition (on pages SRT 21-SRT 40) is the best way to help your friends get a ring and for you to strengthen your decision.

8. **CREW/Leadership training** — SRT is a teen and peer-driven organization. Students are taught leadership skills that strengthen the willpower to keep the vow and are given technical training of SRT systems and equipment. Joining Crew strengthens the abstinence commitment.

9. **Youth Group** — using contact information, students are encouraged and "plugged-in" to local youth networks for support and discipleship.

10. **Website** — our website, **www.silverringthing.com**, provides information for upcoming shows, current issues, latest SRT news, pictures, etc. The "SRT Helpline" provides honest answers to real-life questions to challenge and help teenagers understand the importance of an abstinence commitment.

11. **Abstinence Saturated Communities** — SRT is aggressively expanding its national and international reach as students become part of an ever-growing peer group who will strengthen each other's commitment. The goal is to perform 20–30 events per year in each Hub city, where students can attend numerous shows and receive constant encouragement and positive peer pressure.

12. **Internship/Staff Opportunities** — High school and college intern positions are available along with full-time staff positions in each developing Hub city. These positions provide strong bonds and fellowship, adding an additional level of accountability.

Help #8

Key Players on the Abstinence Team

Stay plugged in! You are not alone in your decision to wait. There are people and organizations all over that want to support you. Here are some great resources to help you stay strong in your decision.

Silver Ring Thing
www.silverringthing.com

Silver Ring Thing **(South Carolina)**
www.silverringthing.sc

Silver Ring Thing **(South Africa)**
www.silverringthing.co.za

Silver Ring Thing **(United Kingdom)**
www.silverringthing.org.uk

1. The Medical Institute
www.medinstitute.org
2. Love Matters
www.lovematters.com
3. True Love Waits
www.truelovewaits.com
4. Friends First
www.friendsfirst.org
5. AC Green
www.clubac.com
6. Passion and Principles
www.passionandprinciples.com
7. Great To Wait
www.greattowait.com
8. Sex Can Wait
www.sexcanwait.com
9. Project SOS
www.projectsos.com
10. Not Me Not Now
www.notmenotnow.org
11. Choosing the Best
www.choosingthebest.org
12. Pam Stenzel
www.pamstenzel.com
13. Institute for Youth Development
www.youthdevelopment.org
14. Why kNOw?
www.whyknow.org
15. Pregnancy Care Center
www.pregnancycenters.org
16. Just Wait
www.justwait.com

Help #9

Help Friends in Trouble

Helping Your Friends with Pregnancy Questions

An unplanned pregnancy is a hard thing to face.

If a friend is facing an unplanned pregnancy, there is hope — they are not alone. In many communities, there are pregnancy centers where people can go to talk to somebody about what they are facing. In fact, there is even a 24-hour, seven days a week phone line called the **Option Line (1-800-395-HELP)**, where trained phone consultants are available to take your calls. In addition, there is a website, **www.pregnancycenters.org**, to help locate a pregnancy center nearby and answer e-mail questions. These centers offer many services, including free pregnancy tests, peer counseling, post-abortion help, and information about pregnancy symptoms, fetal development, abortion procedures, abortion risks, and pregnancy options.

They are not alone.

Each year, millions of women facing unplanned pregnancies feel alone and scared. The message to these women from abortion clinics is, "You **ARE** alone. There is no one to help you." The truth is, there is always someone out there who will care, listen, and help. Each year, hundreds of thousands of women find this someone at a pregnancy center in their community and discover they are not alone.

Real choices.

Nine out of ten women who have had abortions say that they wish they had been given more information and positive options. Women deserve to be given more than one choice — the sad choice of abortion.

Pregnancy resource centers are places for women to discover the hope that is within them. If you know a friend has questions or needs to talk to someone about these issues, contact the **Option Line at 1-800-395-HELP**, or go to **www.pregnancycenters.org**.

The Option Line call center is located in Columbus, Ohio and is owned and operated by Care Net and Heartbeat International.

Help #10

SRT 434: Worldwide Program

This Bible is fully equipped with **SRT 434 abstinence study materials** to be used as:

- A tool for the **SRT 434 Abstinence Program - Student Edition**
- A follow-up to the Silver Ring Thing Programs and other national and international abstinence programs

All over the world, students can now make a vow of abstinence and wear the silver ring by participating in this program.

The Worldwide **SRT 434 Program** is exactly that... WORLDWIDE! With most of the materials needed located directly in this abstinence study Bible, the heart of the Silver Ring Thing Abstinence Program can now be taken with you wherever you go.

SRT 434 is shaped for your home groups, youth groups, college ministries, or any type of small group. It can also be used in Christian, Catholic, and Sunday school classrooms. It may also be used as a resource for national or international mission trips.

Because the Silver Ring is more than a ring, this is more than a Bible study. **SRT 434** reinforces what was heard at the Silver Ring Thing High-Tech program to support an exciting, committed life of sexual abstinence. The **SRT 434 Student Edition** can also be used as a stand-alone program for those who cannot get to a live Silver Ring Thing show.

SRT 434 Program – Parent Edition - Silver Ring Thing has designed a program just for parents. The purpose of the program is to educate, motivate, and equip parents to effectively support their child's decision to remain sexually abstinent until married.

Available now:

SRT 434 Leader's Materials
SRT 434 Student's Materials
SRT 434 Parent's Materials

Order the SRT 434 Programs at: **www.silverringthing.com**

Section 2

SRT 434 Program – Student Edition

Turn the page. Let's get started...

Section 2

The SRT 434 Program – Student Edition

Student Edition

The SRT 434 Program - Student Edition offers four segments in which a leader or parent facilitates DVD-enhanced Bible study sessions. These sessions have been designed to thoroughly train a large or small group of students in God's plan for purity and marriage. Students will view DVD program highlights, participate in group discussions and receive valuable information about waiting and sexual purity. Upon completion of all four sessions, students will be given the opportunity to wear the silver ring as a constant reminder of their decision to remain abstinent until marriage. A handcrafted silver ring is provided with this program as part of the student materials. A 12-step follow-up plan is a critical piece of this program and includes an accountability partner, eight weekly e-mails, a devotional/journal, leadership opportunities and much, much more.

Get Started

Gather your group, get your materials, and get started! Each group must have a minimum of 3 participants, and the leader. To order more Leader or Student Materials, please visit www.silverringthing.com today.

Students interested in ordering a silver ring must complete all four sessions with a qualified leader who will teach all of the **SRT 434** materials.

Session #1

Temptation

1. Complete the Bible Study on pages SRT 24–25.
2. Watch the DVD session. Read through the brochure designed for this session.
3. Read "Rejoice Because Victory is Yours in Christ Jesus" on page 209 of your SRT Bible. Discuss how you plan to depend on God to help you with temptation.
4. Answer and discuss each question below:

   1. Who experiences temptation?

   2. What are some practical ways to overcome sexual temptation?

   3. What is the greatest display of Christ's love for us?

   4. If someone gives into temptation, how do they get back on track with God?

   5. What is justification?

Group Bible Study #1

Temptation

Temptation is a part of everyone's life. It's very real. Nobody can go through life without being tempted — not even Jesus. It's something you simply can not avoid. You might even say temptation is uncontrollable — you can't do a thing about it. Right? **WRONG!** There is a way out. There is a way to deal with temptation, even sexual temptation.

Take control. Determine today how you will react to temptation and remain strong. Rely on the Holy Spirit to give you the conviction and strength to overcome temptation. Do not accept half-truths about pre-marital sex. Simply put, many more teenagers practice abstinence on a daily basis than those who engage in pre-marital sex. Everyone you know practices abstinence at least 90% of the time. The trick to living an abstinent life is to live it **CONSISTENTLY**. That means being abstinent all the time. Therefore, to overcome temptation on a daily basis, you'll need help from the Lord.

The key is to ask Him for help!

Abstinence is totally possible, and you are not on your own. God knows exactly what you're going through. Nobody was faced with more temptation than Jesus. How did he deal with it? He defeated both Satan and temptation by quoting Scripture and by relying on the truth. Satan got frustrated and went away. Jesus showed us the way out and promises to provide a way out for you as well. Remember, He never breaks His promises. **The key is to ask Him for HELP!**

Read these:

Matthew 4:1–11, 19:26
1 Corinthians 10:13
Hebrews 4:15
I Peter 5:6–10
"First Steps," page 243
"First Steps," page 303

Group Bible Study #1 Questions

Temptation

Take 10 minutes and discuss how you were tempted this week. Did you ask God for help? How does He answer us when we ask? Take 10 more minutes and check out these questions:

- **Why does God allow us to be tempted?**

- **How can you encourage others who are being tempted?**

- **List 12 ways to escape temptations when they're "in your face."**

Important extras for

Temptation

So many people have seen my ring and asked me what it is about and stuff. With this ring on it opens up so many doors. I've been through a lot in my life recently and I am really struggling but when I feel my ring there or look at it I get this feeling that there really is someone who is there for me that cares for me and nothing will ever come between us. He is trying to help me through this hard time but I am pushing him away trying to convince myself and those around me that I am a strong person. I don't know what to do, I don't even want to ask for help although I want it and need it SO bad!!! — **student, USA** (The largest Silver Ring Thing event to date)

Wow! Thanks for sending us e-mail - especially about God being there when we're tempted. I know He loves me and so far I think I'm on the right track.

I have definitely been sticking to the commitment I made at the Silver Ring Thing. Sometimes it's hard but I have a great support group - SRT, my awesome youth group, my awesome youth leaders and my great church.

Every thing is fine in my life right now but you give excellent advice so when something goes wrong I will tell you about it!!!!!!!!!! — **student, South Africa** (3,500 attended in Johannesburg, South Africa)

I JUST THOUGHT I WOULD DROP YOU A LINE AND SAY THANK YOU FOR "THE SILVER RING THING." I GUESS LIKE ALL GUYS MY AGE, I WAS ALWAYS ANXIOUS TO HAVE SEX, BUT NOW I KNOW THAT IT IS A SPECIAL THING ONLY YOU AND YOUR SPOUSE SHOULD DO. I AM STILL A VIRGIN THOUGH MANY TIMES I HAVE BEEN TEMPTED TO HAVE SEX. BUT NOW THAT I UNDERSTAND WHAT SEX IS ALL ABOUT I CAN LIVE MY LIFE KNOWING THAT MY WIFE IS GOING TO BE THE ONE AND ONLY PERSON I WILL EVER DO THAT WITH. PLUS, NOW THAT I HAVE A RING I CAN HAVE A REMINDER ON MY FINGER EVERY DAY. THANK YOU FOR ALL THAT YOU HAVE DONE AND WILL DO. — **student, USA**

How do you handle temptation? E-mail us at info434@silverringthing.com and speak your mind!

Student Action Tip: Create your own plan to handle temptation BEFORE you find yourself in a situation where you are tempted to compromise your commitment. Wearing your ring as a daily reminder is a great start, but make sure you know how to stay away from situations where you will need to say NO.

Session #2

How Far Can I Go?

1. Complete the Bible Study on pages SRT 28–29.
2. Watch the DVD session. Read through the brochure designed for this session.
3. Read the Cornerstone, "Live to Please God" (Romans 8:5–8) on page 184.
4. Reflect on the Cornerstone, "Keep an Eternal Perspective" (2 Peter 3:10–11) on page 316 and write out the three verses listed in your own words.
5. On the back inside cover of the SRT Bible, write a prayer to the Lord about the joy you anticipate will come into your life as you commit to sexual abstinence until marriage.
6. Answer and discuss each question below:
    1. **How can disciplining your sex drive make a difference in your life?**
    2. **Instead of focusing on what you are not allowed to do, what should your mindset be?**
    3. **Read Romans 8:5–8 and Live to Please God on page 184. What does it mean for you to be a "servant by choice" when it comes to your abstinence decision?**
    4. **What is the literal definition of the word pure?**
    5. **How can you keep your focus on the Eternal Perspective?**

Group Bible Study #2

How Far Can I Go?

Think of a glass of water. It's sparkling, fresh, and clear. Pure. What happens when you add a drop of food coloring? It's not pure anymore. What happens when you add 2 drops of food coloring? It's less pure. How about 3 drops of food coloring? Even less pure. Whether you add 1 drop or 4,128,395 drops, one thing is still the same — it's not pure.

Purity is a way of life. It has to do with the way you dress, the way you act, what you think, what you look at, what you lust after and what you say. How far you go sexually is not about what **you cannot do** but rather about **treasuring who you are becoming**. The important point here is to develop a mindset of purity that seeks freedom vs. limitations. Jesus himself said, "You are my disciples if you obey my teachings. And you will know the truth and the truth will set you free" (John 8:31–32). This freedom allows you to find what great relationships are all about. If the truth be known, to practice purity means to do nearly the opposite of everything you are being taught to believe on TV. When you know God's truth, you are set free to reject the insanity of "sex without consequences."

Take 10 minutes and discuss the concept of purity. Write a one sentence definition of purity.

List 5 actions a teenager might do in a dating relationship that you think go "too far" and 5 actions that you think do not go "too far." Discuss your answers.

Read these:

1 Thessalonians 4:3–4
2 Timothy 2:22
Matthew 5:27–32
"Cornerstone," page 276

Group Bible Study #2 Questions

How Far Can I Go?

Take 10 more minutes and check out these questions:

- **How can disciplining your sex drive make a difference in your life?**

- **What is the difference between purity and abstinence? Explain.**

- **What does God say about your purity? (Clue: read Galatians 5:19–26)**

BIG DEAL! Now that you know all this stuff...what's next? Write out an action plan from a "freedom" perspective describing how you will discipline your sexual thoughts, desires and actions.

Important extras for

How Far Can I Go?

Just in case you needed some more good reasons **WHY** to practice self-control and wait until you're married to have sex, here are some great reasons **WHY** abstinence is the best choice:

It's your choice. It's your life.

Abstinence is risk free
Your wedding night is worth waiting for
Abstinence works every time
Abstinence is smart
YOU are worth waiting for
Abstinence is never too late
Abstinence is worry free
STDs can kill
You are valuable
STDs are painful
Abstinence is responsible
Abstinence is honest
Abstinence is bold
Abstinence doesn't leave scars
Some STDs are forever
AIDS doesn't discriminate
Abstinence shows patience
Abstinence shows independence
Virginity is given, not lost
Sex isn't a preview for marriage. It's an act of love

This is my story....

Silver Ring Thing was awesome. I went with 3 other friends from school. I pretty much always thought that I wanted to wait until marriage, but I never made a decision. I'm glad I went to SRT because it made me make a final decision, and one that I wanted to stick to. I really appreciate the way your crew relates to people our age. With your real life situations, many people knew that they were not alone in past decisions or actions. I was so excited in school today telling all of my other friends about my ring and what it means. I read the introduction to my Bible, and look forward to continue with that.

I tend to think that only girls want to wait for marriage and that guys don't care, but this started to prove me wrong. I realized there are just as many guys that care about this. My accountability partner is my friend who I went with to SRT on Saturday. We attend the same high school and do a lot together, so I know I will always have someone to support me and help me stay away from situations where I might go "too far." Thanks and see you soon!

What are your thoughts about how far you can go – got any advice to share?
E-mail us at **info434@silverringthing.com** and speak your mind!

Student Action Tip: What are your standards? Write your standards in pen (not pencil) on a piece of paper and share it with family and friends. Ask them to help keep you accountable to those standards.

Session #3

Consequences

1. Complete the Bible Study on pages SRT 32–33.
2. Ask Students to discuss the abstinence summary on page SRT 11.
3. Watch the DVD session. Read through the brochure designed for this session.
4. Read over "Accountability" under Cornerstones on pages A22–A23.
5. Read I John 1:5–10 & write out each verse in your own words.
6. Answer and discuss each question below:

   1. Read 1 John 1:5–10. What do these verses teach you about the Truth?

   2. How will you be held accountable for this responsibility?

   3. What is the great responsibility that we acquire once we become a Christian?

   4. What do you think these verses have to do with the consequences you discussed earlier in the Bible study on pages 32-33?

   5. We know from 1 John 1:9 that if we confess our sins, God will forgive us. What do you need to confess and ask God to forgive you for?

Group Bible Study #3

Consequences

Saying "yes" or "no" to abstinence will definitely affect your life. **Your** decision determines the consequences. Saying "yes" to abstinence means you agree with God's truth and therefore receive His promises in this area of your life. Saying "no" to abstinence means you have bought into Satan's BIG lie. You dare God to look the other way simply because you want to "do it" your way. Sooner or later the consequences become a reality, catch up with you, and determine who you are.

The choice is YOURS and the consequences are real.

Take a closer look at the POSITIVE consequences of abstinence:

- You know God will bless you and your future marriage
- Your future spouse will be incredibly special to you
- You won't have to worry about running into past partners
- You can give your future spouse a gift no one else can — YOU
- You can speak to your future kids about your life with integrity
- You can live worry-free: no pregnancy, AIDS, or STDs
- No one else will have a part of you
- You can encourage others who practice an abstinent lifestyle

Take a closer look at the negative consequences of pre-marital sex:

- You have an estranged relationship with God
- You ruin the #1 gift you can give to your future spouse — purity
- You run the risk of contracting diseases (AIDS, HIV, STDs)
- You may bring embarrassing STDs or AIDS into the marriage bed
- You can cause unwanted pregnancies and possibly abortions
- You suffer emotional stress and scarred memories
- You will experience feelings of guilt
- You risk losing the trust of your parents
- According to statistics your relationship won't last

Read these:

1 Thessalonians 4:1–8
John 8:1–11
2 Corinthians 6:14–7:1
"First Steps," page 191

Group Bible Study #3 Questions

Consequences

Write down the consequences (either awesome or awful) you've experienced from choices you've made. What have you seen in the lives of others (your own family, friends, etc.) from the choices they've made?

	AWESOME	AWFUL
YOU		
FAMILY		
FRIENDS		

Important extras for

Consequences

Hi! I went to "The Silver Ring Thing" in Alabama. I loved it!! I've heard about it before and was so excited when I heard that it was coming to my town. I've been dating a guy for a little over a month that goes to church with me, and going to the show really helped me through some things that I had been thinking about. I had been hurt so many times in the past because of failed relationships, but I felt like a load had been lifted off me when I left the show. I realized that I wasn't the only one that had been through things when I heard your story about starting over after you gave your virginity to your ex-boyfriend. I've never had sex, but came close a few times because of bad situations and the SRT really helped me start over. I talked to my boyfriend and we have set boundaries that we are going to go by. I'm so glad that I came to the show. Thank you so much!!! — **student, USA**

Hi Denny
I have noticed the change in the people I meet when they have also been to the SRT. I have learned some new things... like God will help you "renew" your heart once you have "gone to far." {I haven't of course} Thanx a lot — **student, South Africa**

HEY — I went to the silver ring thing in April. First I wanted to say that SRT is awesome. It was amazing because it really showed me that it wasn't just for virgins and that waiting is the best option. It was really cool to hear about starting over. I know that guys aren't supposed to care about this stuff, but we really do. I needed to start over and wasn't sure what to do, but then I asked God to forgive me and put on my silver ring. That was my starting over night. So I started over with my new virginity, and it feels awesome. SO THANKS, and of course gotta give glory to God.— **student, USA**

What are your thoughts about consequences?
E-mail us at **info434@silverringthing.com** and speak your mind!

Student Action Tip: Choosing abstinence brings positive consequences. Remember that there are consequences to every single decision we make. You have the freedom to decide if you want the positive consequences of abstinence or the negative consequences of pre-marital sex. Make a list of the positive consequences which you expect to experience by choosing abstinence today.

Session #4

How To Give GOD Control

1. Complete the Bible Study on pages SRT 36–37.
2. Discuss the five questions on the bottom of page SRT 11.
3. Watch the DVD session. Read through the brochure designed for this session.
4. Read over "Seek God's Will" under First Steps on page A30.
5. Write down 10 reasons why "Waiting to have sex with your future spouse" is one of the biggest decisions you will ever make in your life.
6. Answer and discuss each question below:

   1. **What will be your biggest challenge in giving God control of your life?**

   2. **What practical steps can you take in order to ensure that you don't keep taking back the control?**

   3. **What is the "inside track" in discovering God's will for your life? Explain why.**

   4. **Why is it important to wear the ring?**

   5. **How does putting on the ring fit into God's will for your life?**

7. Watch final session on DVD. After watching this, follow the steps on SRT 39 to get your ring.

Group Bible Study #4

How to Give GOD Control

Giving God control is probably one of the hardest things to do. The first step is to accept Jesus Christ as your Lord and Savior. Then it gets a little bit more challenging...you have to "Walk the Talk." (ref. Cornerstones, p.12)

When it comes to abstinence, either **you** or **God** will be in control. If **you** say God is in control, but **you** make decisions that put **you** in compromising situations, then **you** have not honestly given God control. Giving God control means trusting **Him** for what **you** know to be true even when **you** feel like doing something else.

What are some basic ways to start living with God in control? Start with these ideas, discuss them, and add your own:

1. Pray regularly and build a solid friendship with God
2. Be real and admit your temptations, then ask for help
3. Share your feelings with your accountability partner
4. Spend quality time with others who wear the silver ring
5. Memorize & reflect on the Silver Ring Thing verses I Thess. 4:3–4
6. Worship God, go to church, get involved in a youth group, etc.
7. Keep your vow to abstinence at ALL cost

Read these:

Luke 11:28
1 John 2:3–6
1 John 2:15
"Cornerstones," page 16

Group Bible Study #4 Questions

How to Give GOD Control

Take 10 minutes and discuss whether you have really given God control of your life. How can you tell? List several ways, and discuss them.

What are some ways to make sure that He stays in control?

Read "Rededicating your life to Jesus Christ" and "What God has done for you" on pages A7–A8. Discuss how God is willing to forgive us when we confess our sin before Him.

Important extras for

How To Give GOD Control

We wanted to encourage you with testimony from other students who decided that they needed to give God control while they were at a Silver Ring Thing show. Here is what they had to say:

Hi Denny
From the time I went to Soweto to the SRT, I made a decision to put the ring on my finger as a symbol of purity. Things changed for me from then. I learned to respect my body and say no to sex before marriage. The SRT group has taught me a lot. Firstly, the Bible has taught me to keep my body pure and holy until I am married. I know now the greatest gift you can give your husband is your virginity. I keep the ring on all the time. I also had an opportunity to tell my friends about the SRT and how important it is to say no. Thank you SRT for showing me sex is not cool before marriage. Please pray for me that I will be strong and grounded in the word of God. I do have a boyfriend and I would like you to pray for me so the will of God can be done in my life. God Bless you. — **student, South Africa**

I play basketball, softball and I cheer. I am an average student and I love life. I consider myself really lucky when it comes down to popularity because I am one of those people who no matter what I have a smile on my face and always seem to have fit in. So picture me sitting along with hundreds of other people my age that night at SRT and you all practically acting out what I am going through. It hit me like a rock. Because I am that student who has the pressures of what I should do and not do and if it will affect my "popularity." I did "stuff" because everyone else said it would make me look good. And it worked until I realized it wasn't for me.

I sat there just listening to the words that were being spoken and hearing them talk about the silver ring... well honestly I just thought I would get the ring and wear it for a while and lose it. But I made a promise to myself that "Hey, I can do this."

And I learned who I really was. For the past years I've been the one to do lots of Christian-ish stuff, but I have been hiding behind this mask because I was still cussing and being a different person around other people who just pretended to be my friends when I wasn't at church. Some stuff happened and they decided they didn't like me anymore. But I realized that no matter what I still have one true friend and his name is Jesus. Please... I've prayed for months to God telling him I'll go where ever he wants me to go and be who ever he wants me to be. I want people to know what I know...that my life is at its best when God is in control.
— student, USA

What are your experiences in giving God control?
E-mail us at **info434@silverringthing.com** and speak your mind!

Student Action Tip: Giving God control means trusting Him and following Him every day, but we all need help. Find people who will support and encourage you in your decision to let God be in control of your life. Make sure you are actively and regularly going to church and other activities that build you up in your faith.

The Silver Ring Thing SRT 434 Program

Make Your Pledge

Silver Ring Thing Sexual Abstinence Covenant

1. Print your first name on the line below "COVENANT" on the inside front cover of this SRT Bible.
2. With your group leader, read out loud the Covenant Agreement to God to pledge to abstain from sexual behavior until marriage.
3. Sign your name below the Covenant agreement and date it.
4. Within 48 hours, find an accountability partner of the same sex who will sign your covenant page and agree to help you keep your abstinence commitment.
5. Put on your Silver Ring. Read and memorize I Thess. 4:3–4 which is written on the first page of your SRT Bible and is inscribed on your SRT Ring.
6. Have your leader e-mail the Silver Ring Thing office (**info434@silverringthing.com**) to confirm that you have completed the program.
7. Have your leader take a picture of your group and e-mail it to the Silver Ring Thing office (e-mail above). Look for your picture on **www.silverringthing.com**.

You have now officially completed the program.

CONGRATULATIONS!!!!

NOW, find friends to join you in your decision.

SRT 434 Next Steps

If you are serious about giving GOD control of your life, start by giving Him each day — one day at a time. Get into His Word and learn how it applies to your life. These steps are to help you get started:

1. Start your Silver Ring Thing reading plan! On page SRT 6 there is a 14-day reading plan which the SRT Team handpicked for you to read. Start today and read one each day.

2. Once you've finished the 14-day reading plan in this SRT Abstinence Study Bible, start reading the daily devotional/journal that also came with your student materials. You will start reading your devotional/journal the day after you finish your 14-day reading plan.

3. Check your e-mail. Expect to receive an e-mail once a week for 2 months as part of our follow-up program.

4. We want to hear back from you. E-mail our team and tell us how you are doing! Send e-mails to **info434@silverringthing.com** and answer the questions below. (***Please Note***: in e-mailing us, you are giving us permission to share your e-mail with others. We will change names to keep confidentiality.)

   - **Which of the 4 sessions in SRT 434 did you like best? Why?**

   - **How are you doing?**

   - **Share your story with us. As part of this program, you have read some of the e-mails we have received from students just like you. Let your story be an encouragement to others!**

Visit our website regularly: www.silverringthing.com

Section 3

SRT 434 Program – Parent Edition

SRT 434 Program — Parent Edition

Mission Statement: To educate, motivate, and equip parents to effectively support their child's decision to remain sexually abstinent until married.

Why the SRT 434 Program — Parent Edition was created

When asked what is the most influential factor in teenagers' sexual decision-making, teens reported that their parents are the single most influential factor. Adults wrongly assume that their children's friends have the greatest influence. That simply is not true. Therefore, the more that parents are educated on this topic, the easier it will be for them to discuss a sexually pure lifestyle with their teens. Open communication is the key to providing a healthy parent-teen relationship.

This four session DVD-enhanced program is designed to equip parents to become more effective and supportive in helping their children make the best choices regarding sexual purity.

Introduction

Prepare to be involved

Congratulations on choosing to be more educated about your child's sexual purity! By the end of the following four sessions, you will be more comfortable in discussing sexual issues with your teen.

Watch the Introductory DVD — At this time, watch the DVD (Chapter 1) provided with this program explaining the **SRT 434 Program — Parent Edition**. Return to this page after watching the DVD and continue reading the introduction below.

Parents of 21st century teenagers often claim to feel powerless as their children develop their own attitudes and values about sex. Despite the way media and peer influence bombard teens with sexual messages, you are still the **#1 factor** in your teen's sexual decision making. Reflect on the following excuses:

"I'm too busy." You can not be too busy, or too tired for that matter. You need to stay alert and be well informed on this subject.

"I'm too embarrassed to talk about sex with my child." By the end of this program you will be equipped with resources so that you will be more confident and less embarrassed to discuss sex with your teenager.

"I feel like a hypocrite." You can not allow your past mistakes to disqualify you from parenting duties. There are no perfect parents.

"They won't listen to me." Don't mistakenly think that your child is not listening. Surveys clearly indicate that you make the most significant difference in your teenager's sexual decision-making.

Just for the record, consider the following statistics:*

- Today there are 25 significant sexually transmitted diseases (STDs), as opposed to only two being dealt with in the 1960s - gonorrhea and syphilis.
- In the 1970s, one teen in 47 contracted an STD. At the dawning of the 21st century, the figure is one in four.
- A British study found that the human papilloma virus (HPV) infects 46% of teenage girls after their first sexual intercourse.
- HPV is directly linked to more than 90% of all cervical cancers in women.
- Nearly 80% of teens with STDs show no symptoms and are therefore less likely to receive medical attention.
- In America, nearly 1 million teenage girls become pregnant each year.

*All sources available at www.silverringthing.com

Considering these brief statistics, this is no time to have a sexually active teenager. The good news is, after you have completed the **SRT 434 Program — Parent Edition**, you will be better equipped for the task of helping your child make the best choices regarding sexual abstinence. Given the serious threat of STDs and teen pregnancy, you will learn to overcome your discomfort, embarrassment, or lack of knowledge, and step up to your parenting responsibilities.

Program Overview

STEP 1

Pick one day a week over the next four weeks, in which you will spend 1.5 hours with each of the four sessions (It is highly recommended to complete each session the same day as your child is also completing the session to make it easier for you to discuss what they are learning).

STEP 2

Seriously consider ordering the items on the next page before officially beginning this program. The two books will better educate you about your child's journey (the books are referenced throughout this program). Wearing the ring will encourage and remind you to effectively pray for your teenager.

STEP 3

Begin with Session #1 on your scheduled start date. A DVD player will be needed in order to watch a selected video for each session. Continue on until you have completed the remaining three sessions.

STEP 4

Session #3 is designed to be a group session where you will meet with other parents whose children are also participating in this program. Speak with the leader who is in charge of the **SRT 434 program — Student Edition** to help you organize your parents group session. Schedule a two hour meeting time, place, and date as soon as possible to avoid conflicts. Your group will need to select one of the parents to be the group facilitator to lead your group through the Session #3 materials. Ask one of the parents to volunteer to be the facilitator or pick the parent with the earliest birthday month/day.

STEP 5

In each session you will review some of the same information your child is learning in order for you to be better equipped to discuss that particular information with your teen when he/she returns home.

STEP 6

In sessions #1, #2, and #4, you will be instructed to read through selected readings in the parenting brochure provided with your materials.

STEP 7

When you have finished Session #4, follow the ***Next Steps*** section on the bottom of page 52. This is your follow-up program.

Suggested Reading before starting this program:
(Read chapter 2; "The Epidemic Is Real" in Dr. Meeker's book described below)

OPTIONAL MATERIALS :

(Strongly suggested to enhance this program)

1. Order **"YOUR" Silver Ring** today.
   Why? As a constant reminder to:
   - Pray for your teen everyday
   - Pray for his/her future spouse everyday
   - Pray for your purity everyday

   Cost $20.00 + s/h

2. Order *Parenting Teenagers* by Denny Pattyn. This is an interactive workbook designed to be your parenting roadmap.
   Retail $17.99
   Your price $12.95 + s/h

3. Order *Epidemic: How Teen Sex is Killing Our Kids* by Dr. Meg Meeker. The book informs parents of the reality and dangers of teen sex.
   Retail $24.95
   Your price $17.95 + s/h

Order today at **www.silverringthing.com** or call: 1-866-449-RING
(Visa and MasterCard accepted)

Session #1
Getting started

Parents influence their children like no other. Unfortunately, many obstacles keep parents from effectively communicating with their children about sexual purity and dating.

1. ***Parents Brochure*: Read "Parents of the 21st Century Teens" starting on page one in the provided brochure.

   You as a parent need to make sure you are up to date on what is going on in the sex-obsessed culture your child lives in every day. The risks are real and need to be clearly understood.

2. ***Parents Brochure*: Read "Educate Yourself" on page two of the provided brochure.

3. **Condoms and the "safe-sex" myth!** For the past 20+ years, the "safe-sex" method has been taught, promoting condom usage. However, the question is, do condoms offer safety? New scientific data* reveals that condoms, even when used 100% of the time, failed to reduce the risk of some of the most common and potentially dangerous STDs to an **acceptable** level. (The Medical Institute for Sexual Health, Oct. 2002)

   - Less than $^1/_2$ of sexually active adolescents report that they use condoms correctly.
   - The more partners a person has, the less likely they are to use condoms.
   - Even 100% condom use does not **eliminate** the risk of any STD including HIV.
   - Among adults who knew their partner had HIV, only 56% used condoms every time.
   - With 100% condom use, there still is a 15% relative risk of contracting HIV.
   - There is no evidence that condoms reduce the risk of contracting human papilloma virus (HPV).

Grow Deeper!

Read "Condoms and the Myth of Safe Sex" (chapter 7) in Dr. Meeker's book.

*All sources available at www.silverringthing.com

4. Connect with your child

- Review what your child is learning in Session #1, "Temptation" on pages SRT 23-26.
  - Watch the DVD (Session #1) for students.

5. Summary

- Your child is living in a sex-obsessed culture. It is important to understand what is at stake.
- You are the most influential factor in helping your child deal with temptations and issues that relate to his/her sexual decisions.
- Reflect on the following verse as God promises His protection on your child:

  "But remember that the temptations that come into your life are no different from what others experience. And God is Faithful. He will keep the temptation from becoming so strong that you can't stand up against it. When you are tempted, He will show you a way out so that you will not give in to it." (1 Corinthians 10:13 NLT)

6. Reflection

Pray right now for your child and his/her friends and ask God to use this time to help them overcome the temptations of this sex-obsessed culture.

Parent Action Tip

If your child and his/her friends ever feel uncomfortable in a situation outside the home, make sure they know they can always call you to come get them with no questions asked and no speeches made. This is a way of saying that you love them unconditionally.

Session #2

Take a stand

There is nothing more valuable than face-to-face communication between a parent and a child. This session is designed to help you shape your thoughts and standards to communicate with your teen.

1. Communication is more that just talking. It is highly recommended to use these three steps in conversation with your teen.

TELL

- Your standards
- How you plan to support him/her
- That you are proud of him/her for making this decision
- That you love him/her no matter what

ASK

- Do you understand what I expect of you?
- Can you help me understand the temptations and struggles that you are facing in school and in your life?
- What is the best way for me to support you? (pray for you, talk about everything, ask tough questions, etc.)

LISTEN

- Ask your teenager to share and do not interrupt.
- For what is really being said.
- For tone of voice and non-verbal communication.

Grow Deeper!
Read, "Communication" (chapter 6) in Denny Pattyn's Workbook

2. ***Parents Brochure*:** Read "Firm Up Your Position on Teen Sex", "Deliver a Clear Message to Your Teens", and "Integrate Your Values Into Discussions" on page three and four in the provided brochure.

3. Write a clear message on what your expectations are for your child's morals and sexual decisions (in five sentences or less).

____

____

____

____

4. Active Participation

- Schedule a time to have "the sex talk" with your teen after you and your child have completed all four sessions. Make sure you have prayed and reviewed all your resources beforehand. Find a place where you will not be interrupted.
- Remember: if you do not talk to your teen about sex, somebody else will do it for you, and not necessarily in the manner of which you would approve!
- Clearly communicate your standards, values, and morals.
- Let your child know that you love him/her unconditionally and that he/she can always be honest with you.

5. Connect with your child

- Review what your child is learning in Session #2,"How Far Can I Go" on pages SRT 27-30.
- Watch the DVD (Session #2) for students.

6. Summary

- Do not be hesitant to take a strong stand due to guilt from past behaviors.
- Teenagers will "wait" longer if their parents deliver a clear message about the risks of sex and the rewards of abstinence.
- The best way to communicate with your child may be through empathetic listening.
- "*The Key Ingredient to Effective Prevention is Dynamic Faith*" — Denny Pattyn

7. Reflection

It takes a community to raise a child. Next week will be your group session. Call the other parents to remind them about the meeting. Think through ideas on how your group can build a support network around your children. Be prepared to share your ideas during the group session.

Parents Action Tip

Be sensitive to the fact that your child may have already experienced some sort of sexual activity of which you may not be aware. Your teen may have a strong need to start over but may not know how. In Session # 3, he/she will be considering the option to start over. Be praying for your child throughout this week concerning this important decision.

Session #3

Group Session

Please note: It is very important to get together as a group of parents and discuss the issues of sexual purity. Make every effort to organize the group session. However, if you are unable to form a group, skip to **#4 Discussion Questions** and write out your answers on a separate piece of paper and watch the selected DVD for session #3.

1. If not previously decided upon, select one of the parents to lead this group session. Choose a volunteer or pick the parent with the earliest birthday month/day.

2. The group leader should then open the meeting with prayer.

3. The group leader should ask each person to share a bit about their lives and their teens' lives (possibly sharing about their teens' dating lives or lack thereof).

4. Discussion Questions (the group leader should ask parents to discuss the following):

- What have been your teenager's greatest challenges in regards to sex (i.e. media influence, internet, dating situations, friends' influences, etc.)?
- Share some success stories.
- What are the differences in the dangers of being sexually active today as opposed to when you were young?
- Discuss what you have been learning thus far in Sessions #1 and #2.
- Strategize about how you can support each other and your children.

5. Connecting with your children

- As a group, review what your children are learning in Session #3, "Consequences" on pages SRT 31-34.
- Watch as a group the DVD (Session #3) for students.
- Discuss the physical, spiritual, and emotional consequences a teenager experiences when giving up his/her virginity before marriage (based on the personal story shared on the DVD).
- Discuss if starting over ("second virginity") is possible.

6. Summary

- Healing and forgiveness is available for any sexually active teenager. Read the verse below as a source of strength.

  "Jesus returned to the Mount of Olives, but early the next morning he was back again at the Temple. A crowd soon gathered, and he sat down and taught them. As he was speaking, the teachers of religious law and Pharisees brought a woman they had caught in the act of adultery. They put her in front of the crowd. "Teacher," they said to Jesus, "this woman was caught in the very act of adultery. The law of Moses says to stone her. What do you say?" They were trying to trap him into saying something they could use against him, but Jesus stooped down and wrote in the dust with his finger. They kept demanding an answer, so he stood up again and said, "All right, stone her. But let those who have never sinned throw the first stones!" Then he stooped down again and wrote in the dust. When the accusers heard this, they slipped away one by one, beginning with the oldest, until only Jesus was left in the middle of the crowd with the woman. Then Jesus stood up again and said to her, "Where are your accusers? Didn't even one of them condemn you?" "No, Lord," she said. And Jesus said, "Nether do I. Go and sin no more." (John 8:1-11 NLT)

- Starting over is a critical decision for a sexually involved teenager living in the 21st century.
- Sexually transmitted diseases are extremely widespread and have severe and sometimes deadly consequences.

Parents Action Tip

Ask each parent to strongly consider forming an accountability partnership with one other member of the group (if not participating in a group session, seek out a friend who will commit to be your accountability partner).

Session #4
Putting it all together

Effective Influencing — It is a mistake to think that teaching sexual purity is best handled by schools alone. Think about it! Schools cannot integrate your faith and family values and, in most cases, they may actually oppose them. Never assume your children are better off hearing it from someone else. Remember, you are the "#1 influencer" in your child's sexual decision-making.

1. ***Parents Brochure*:** Read "How can you become more effective at influencing your teen's sexual decision making?" on page four in the provided brochure.

2. **Set boundaries** for your teen and stick to them
   - Determine boundaries before the time when the boundary should be applied.
     (Example: Tell your child the age they can start dating (one-on-one) two or three years before they reach that age)
   - Before a boundary is broken, make the consequences known.
     (Example: If you break the curfew of 11:00 p.m., your curfew will be held at 9:00 p.m. for one month)
   - Be sure to adjust boundaries so they remain age-appropriate.
   - Reward responsible behavior and communicate to your teen when they have earned your trust.

Grow Deeper!
Read "Rules Not Made to Be Broken" (chapter 2) in Denny Pattyn's Workbook.

3. **Connect with your child**
   - Review what your child is learning in Session #4, "How to Give God Control" on pages SRT 35-38.
   - Watch the DVD (Session #4) for students.

4. Summary

- God needs to be the center of your discussions as you continue to communicate with your child about sexual purity.
- You and your child should be growing actively in your faith which will allow God to be the inner-convicting voice in your lives.
- Your child should now be better equipped and capable to resist sexual activity.

Parents Action Tip

The prayers of parents are potent and powerful. Write your child's name on a post-it note. Stick it on your mirror as a reminder to pray for him/her each time you brush your teeth.

Next Steps

1. **Purchase a Ring!** It is strongly recommended that you purchase a ring for yourself to remind you to:
    - Pray for your child everyday
    - Pray for his/her future spouse everyday
    - Pray for yourself everyday
2. **Talk to your child** about his/her sexual decision-making
3. **Dig into God's word!** Commit to using the **daily devotional/journal** that comes with this program. Share with your child what you are reading and ask to hear about what he/she is reading as well. It is encouraged that you and your child do a devotion together, possibly once a week (the devotional/journal that you and your child received are similar and designed for occasional cooperative reading).
4. **Share** the Silver Ring Thing and **SRT 434** programs with your friends. Encourage them to bring a Silver Ring Thing or **SRT 434** program to their community.

Order YOUR Silver Ring ($20.00 + s/h) and/or other materials today at **www.silverringthing.com** or **1-866-449-RING**
(Visa and MasterCard accepted)

HOW YOU CAN KNOW GOD

What Is Missing in Our Lives?

Purpose, meaning, a reason for living—these are all things we desire and search for in life. Despite steps each one of us takes to find purpose and meaning in life, we still feel empty, unfulfilled. That is because there is a spiritual emptiness in each of our lives. We each have a hole in our heart, a spiritual vacuum deep within our soul—a "God-shaped blank." Possessions won't fill this hole, nor will success. Relationships alone cannot satisfy this emptiness, and morality, in and of itself, falls miserably short of occupying this space. In fact, even religion cannot fill the void in our heart.

There is only one way to effectively fill that void. This way will not only help us to have a life that is full and rich on this earth, but—more important—will give us the absolute hope of spending eternity in the presence of God. Before we can truly appreciate this good news though, we need to understand the bad news, which is a serious problem we all have.

THE PROBLEM: SIN

The Bible clearly identifies our serious problem as sin. Sin is not just an act but the actual nature of our being. In other words, we are not sinners because we sin. Rather, we sin because we are sinners! We are born with a nature to do wrong. King David, the Old Testament Israelite ruler, wrote, "For I was born a sinner—yes, from the moment my mother conceived me" (Psalm 51:5). Because we are born sinners, sinning comes to all of us naturally. That is why it is futile to think that the answer to all of life's problems comes from "within." According to the Bible, the *problem* is within! Scripture tells us, "The human heart is most deceitful and desperately wicked. Who really knows how bad it is?" (Jeremiah 17:9).

We are not basically good—we are basically sinful. This sinfulness spills out into everything we do. Every problem we experience in our society today can be traced back to our refusal to live God's way. Clear back to the Garden of Eden, Adam made his choice, and he suffered the consequences of it, setting the pattern that all humanity would follow. The Bible explains, "When Adam sinned, sin entered the entire human race. Adam's sin brought death, so death spread to everyone, for everyone sinned. . . . Yes, Adam's one sin brought condemnation upon everyone" (Romans 5:12, 18).

"That's not fair!" you may protest. Why should we suffer because of what someone else has done? Yet, given the opportunity, each one of us would have done the same thing as Adam. In fact, not a single day passes that we do not face the same test that was set before Adam. God has given us the freedom to choose between two separate paths: the path that leads to life and the path that leads to death. The Bible says, "Today, I have given you the choice between life and death, between blessings and curses. I call on heaven and earth to witness the choice you make, Oh, that you would choose life, that you and your descendants might live!" (Deuteronomy 30:19).

WITHOUT A LEG TO STAND ON

Someone may say, "But I live a good life. I try to be kind and considerate to others. I live by the Ten Commandments." But the truth of the matter is that the Ten Commandments, or the law, as they are called in the Bible, were not given to make us good but to show us how bad we are. The Bible tells us, "No one can ever be made right in God's sight by doing what his law commands. For the more we know God's law, the clearer it becomes that we aren't obeying it" (Romans 3:20). The purpose of the law is to make us realize how sinful we are. You might say that God's law was given to "shut our mouths" and show us that we desperately need his help and forgiveness for our terminal condition as sinners.

Look at the passages below to get a better understanding of the nature and seriousness of sin.

1. **We Have All Missed the Mark** (see Romans 3:23, p. 178). Romans 3:23 says, we have *all* sinned. For those that would claim to be the sole exception to this eternal truth, verse ten of this chapter plainly says, "No one is good—not even one (Romans 3:10). Another word for *good* is *righteous*. The word *righteous* means, "One who is as he or she ought to be." When the Bible says that no one is righteous, or good, it is not so much referring to behavior but to inner character.

   What exactly is "God's glorious standard" that Romans 3:23 says we have failed to meet? God's "glorious standard" is absolute perfection. Jesus said, "But you are to be perfect, even as your Father in heaven is perfect" (Matthew 5:48). In other words, anyone who is not as good as God is not acceptable to him.

   One definition of *sin*, derived from the Greek word *hamartia,* is to "miss the mark." As far as the mark of perfection goes, we miss it by a mile. Although our sinful nature makes it impossible for us to live up to God's standard, we cannot blame sin on our nature alone. Sin is also a deliberate act.
2. **Sin Is a Deliberate Act** (see Ephesians 2:1-3, p. 238). Another word for *sins* in Ephesians 2:1 is *transgressions* or *trespasses.* This word speaks of a lapse or deviation from truth. In contrast to simply "missing the mark," this is a deliberate action. Because sin is a deliberate action, we cannot blame our sin on our society or our environment or our mental or physical state. Everyone has chosen to do what was wrong. If we protest this point, "we are only fooling ourselves and refusing to accept the truth" (1 John 1:8).

3. **The Ultimate Penalty for Sin Is Death** (see Romans 6:23, p. 182). According to the Bible, we have offended a Holy God. We have not done this once or twice, but so many times that we are unable to keep count. Romans 6:23 says, "The *wages* of sin is death. . . ." Wages are something that you are paid for work rendered. In other words, you earn your wages. Because we have all repeatedly sinned, we have earned the penalty of death, which is eternal torment and punishment in a place called hell.

Amid all this talk about sin and death, there is some good news. God has given us a way to escape the penalty of our sin. He has made it possible for us to have a relationship with him and enjoy the hope of eternal life without punishment.

The Solution: Jesus Christ

God understood our problem and knew that we could do nothing about it. Because God loves us, he sent his own Son, Jesus Christ, to earth to bridge the chasm of sin that separates us from him.

WHY JESUS CAN BRIDGE THE GAP

There has never been anyone like Jesus. For starters, Jesus was not conceived in the womb of his mother through natural means. Rather, he was supernaturally conceived in the womb of a young virgin named Mary. Because of his supernatural conception, Jesus, who is wholly God, also became wholly human.

Though Jesus is God, he chose to lay aside the privileges of his deity to live on earth as a man. The Bible, describing the sacrifice Christ made in becoming a man, says that Jesus "made himself nothing; he took the humble position of a slave and appeared in human form. And in human form he obediently humbled himself even further by dying a criminal's death on a cross" (Philippians 2:7-8). It is extremely important to note that Jesus did not cease to be God when he came to earth. He simply laid aside his divine privileges and walked the earth as a man. In doing so, he was personally able to experience the gamut of human emotions, ranging from happiness to deep sorrow. He felt what it was like to be tired, cold, and hungry.

Moreover, he came to this earth with a clear objective in mind: to bridge that gap between us and God.

When the Israelites of the Old Testament sinned, they would have the high priest go into the Temple and offer an animal sacrifice to God to atone for their sins. In a symbolic sense, this was a way of putting one's sins on the animal, which stood in the place of the guilty person. The Bible teaches, "Without the shedding of blood, there is no forgiveness of sins" (Hebrews 9:22).

The sacrificial rituals carried out by the Israelites in the Old Testament foreshadowed what Jesus would do when he came to this earth. He took the sin of the world upon himself when he hung on the cross so many years ago.

Numerous Old Testament prophecies pointed not only to his birth and life but also to his death, including the way in which he would die.

Jesus knew from the beginning that he had come expressly to die for the sins of humanity. He also knew that this sacrifice would be made on a Roman cross. He began his final journey to the cross of Calvary at a place called Caesarea Philippi, and he often spoke of his impending death with his disciples. Scripture records, "From then on Jesus began to tell his disciples plainly that he had to go to Jerusalem, and he told them what would happen to him there. He would suffer at the hands of the leaders and the leading priests and the teachers of religious law. He would be killed, and he would be raised on the third day" (Matthew 16:21).

He was eventually arrested on false charges after Judas Iscariot, one of his own disciples, betrayed him. But it was no accident. If humanity was going to be put in touch with God and have the barrier that separated them removed, something drastic had to be done. In essence, with one hand Jesus took hold of a Holy God, and with the other hand he took hold of the sinful human race. As crude nails were pounded into his hands, he bridged the gap for us!

We must not forget, however, that three days after his crucifixion, Jesus rose from the dead! If it is true that "you can't keep a good man down," then it is even truer that you can't keep the "God-man" down.

WE PUT JESUS ON THE CROSS

The necessity of the death of Jesus Christ on the cross shows just how radical our situation was as fallen people. It's been said that you can tell the depth of a well by how much rope is lowered. When we look at "how much rope was lowered" from heaven, we realize how grave our situation really was.

For that reason, don't blame the people of that day for putting Jesus on the cross. We are just as guilty as they. In reality, it was not the Roman soldiers who put him on the cross, nor was it the Jewish leaders: it was our sins that made it necessary for Jesus to volunteer for this torturous and humiliating death.

Read the verses and notes below to see exactly what Jesus did for us.

1. **The Greatest Demonstration of Love** (see Romans 5:6-8, p. 180). Jesus did not die for us while we were his friends, but while we were his enemies, opposing him by our sinfulness. Yet, in spite of all of this, God demonstrated his love for us by dying on the cross. In this verse, the Apostle Paul explains that Jesus did not simply die for humanity as a whole, but that he died for us as individuals. Elsewhere, Paul writes, "[Christ] loved me and gave himself for me" (Galatians 2:20).

   Whenever you are tempted to doubt God's love for you, take a long look at the cross on which Jesus died. Then realize that, for all practical purposes, it was not nails that held him to the cross, but love.

2. **Forsaken That We Might Be Forgiven** (see Luke 23:32-49, p. 104). Many of us have heard this story at some point in our lives. Yet the significance behind this heart-wrenching scene is often missed or misunderstood. This was not simply some "good teacher" being crucified for his beliefs. It was God in human form who hung on that cross, bridging the gap between sinful people and a holy God.

   Matthew's Gospel tells us that when Jesus hung on that cross, he cried out, "My God, my God, why have you forsaken me?" (Matthew 27:46). Many Bible scholars believe that those words marked the precise moment at which God placed the sins of the world upon his Son. The Bible, speaking of God, says, "You are of purer eyes than to behold evil, and cannot look on wickedness" (Habakkuk 1:13, NKJV). For that reason, the holy Father had to "turn his face" and pour out his wrath upon his own Son. On the cross, Jesus received the wages that were due us. He was not heard that we might be heard. The ear of God was closed to Jesus for a time that it might never be closed to us.

3. **Christ, the Sole Mediator** (see 1 Timothy 2:5-6, p. 270). Why is there only one mediator who is qualified to bridge the gap between God and people? Haven't there been other religious leaders who have claimed to have *the* way to God? Haven't some of them also died as a result of their message?

While the answers to these questions may be yes, the truth is that not one of these other leaders was fully God and fully human. That is why Jesus is uniquely qualified to deal with sin. Jesus said, "I am the way, the truth, and the life. No one can come to the Father except through me" (John 14:6). Acts 4:12 tells us, "There is salvation in no one else! There is no other name in all of heaven for people to call on to save them." And, most important, Jesus Christ rose from the dead!

Though it is true that you must believe Jesus died on the cross for your sins in order to receive eternal life and be a true Christian, there is still something else you must do.

The Response: Accept God's Offer

To know Jesus Christ personally and have your sins forgiven, you must believe that you are a sinner separated from God and that your only hope is Jesus Christ, the Son of God, who came and died for your sins. To stop here, however, would be to stop short of salvation.

There are two things you must now do to enter into a relationship with the God from whom you have been separated.

1. TURN FROM YOUR SINS

As Jesus began his public ministry, his first message was "Turn from your sins" (Mark 1:15). In essence, Jesus was tellling the people to repent—to acknowledge their sinning, change their minds, and change the direction of their lives.

Look at it this way. In the past, we have been blinded by our sins, causing us to run from God. As we repent, we do a "U-turn" and start running toward him. It is not enough just to be sorry for our sins. We must also change our lifestyle, for the Bible teaches that "God can use sorrow in our lives to help us turn away from sin" (2 Corinthians 7:10). In other words, if you are really sorry for something, it will result in a change in your actions.

The apostle Paul summed up this change succinctly when he quoted Jesus, who had said that people must "turn from darkness to light, and from the power of Satan to God. Then they will receive forgiveness for their sins and be given a place among God's people, who are set apart by faith in me (Acts 26:18).

You see, there are some things only God can do and some things only you can do. Only God can remove your sins and give you the gift of eternal life, but only you can turn from your sins and receive Jesus as your Savior. That brings up the second thing you must do to respond to God's offer.

2. BELIEVE IN JESUS CHRIST AND RECEIVE HIM INTO YOUR LIFE

Having seen the enormity of your sin and having decided to turn from it, you then must believe in and receive Jesus Christ as your Lord and Savior. Becoming a Christian, however, is far more than following a creed or trying to live by certain standards. Jesus said that you must be "born again," or more literally, "born from above" (John 3:3). This spiritual rebirth happens when we personally believe in Jesus Christ, receive him by inviting him into our lives, and turn from our sins. In other words, we ask Jesus to come and take residence in our lives, making the changes he deems necessary. A person must take this all-important step in order to become a child of God.

Notice that this offer is yours for the asking, and it is free. You don't have to work for it, trying to clean up your life before you make this life-changing decision. The Bible says, "The free gift of God is eternal life through Christ Jesus our Lord" (Romans 6:23).

Being a Christian also means having a relationship with the living God. In Revelation 3:20, Jesus said, "Look! Here I stand at the door and knock. If you hear me calling and open the door, I will come in, and we will share a meal as friends." To better understand the meaning of this verse, it is important to understand the culture at the time it was written. Eating together in Bible times was a long, drawn-out affair. People would not sit on chairs behind tables in a formal setting as we do, but they would sit on the floor, reclining on pillows around a low table. The relaxed atmosphere made meals a time when you would not only satisfy your appetite but also receive a gratifying serving of enjoyable table conversation. You would share your heart and life with those who sat beside you.

Consequently, when Jesus says that he will "share a meal" with us, it implies intimacy, closeness, and friendship. He offers this to us, but we must first "hear him calling" us.

To hear God calling us, we must know how he speaks. One way in which God speaks to us is described in the Bible as a "still, small voice." This could be described in another way as that tug you may have felt on your heart from the Holy Spirit showing you your need for Jesus. He may even be speaking to you right now! It is at that point that you must "open the door." Only you can do that. Jesus will not force his way in.

RECEIVING JESUS CHRIST INTO YOUR HEART

If you are ready to turn from your sins and believe in Jesus Christ so that you can receive the forgiveness of sin and the hope of eternal life, then take a moment to bow your head and pray a prayer like this one right now:

> God, I'm sorry for my sin. I turn from it right now. I thank you for sending Jesus Christ to die on the cross for my sin.
>
> Jesus, I ask you to come into my heart and life right now. Be my Lord, Savior, and friend. Help me to follow you all the days of my life as your disciple.
>
> Thank you for forgiving and receiving me right now. Thank

you that my sin is forgiven and that I am going to heaven. In Jesus' name I pray, amen.

REDEDICATING YOUR LIFE TO JESUS CHRIST

Perhaps you are already a Christian but you have strayed from Jesus Christ. You have been a prodigal son or daughter. God will forgive you right now if you will return to him. He tells us in Scripture, "My wayward children, come back to me and I will heal your wayward hearts" (Jeremiah 3:22). If you would like to return to God and rededicate your life to him right now, you may want to pray something like this:

> God, I am sorry for my sin. I am sorry that I have strayed from you. I ask you to forgive me now as I repent of my sin. I don't want to live like a prodigal any longer.
>
> Renew and revive me as I once again follow you as my God. Thank you for your forgiveness. In Jesus' name I pray, amen.

Whether you prayed to make a first time commitment or a recommitment, you have made the right decision. God has forgiven and received you if you really meant it. Know that your relationship with Jesus Christ will bring radical and dramatic changes in your life. Describing this, the Bible says, "Those who become Christians become new persons. They are not the same anymore, for the old life is gone. A new life has begun!" (2 Corinthians 5:17). Now that is good news! But more importantly, God has changed your eternal destiny. Instead of fearing a eternal punishment in a place called hell, you will spend peaceful eternity in his presence in heaven.

Read the next section to see what else God has done for you now that you have taken this step.

What God Has Done for You

What actually happens when Jesus Christ comes into your life? First, he saves you from your sins and the punishment you deserve as a result of them—eternity in hell. This is called salvation, or regeneration, and has to do with what takes place in your heart: God gives you new life.

Second, he justifies you. Justification has to do with your standing before God and includes the complete removal and forgiveness of your sins. Think about it! When you receive Jesus Christ into your life, you are completely forgiven. God's Word tells us, "Brothers, listen! In this man Jesus there is forgiveness for your sins! Everyone who believes in him is freed from all guilt and declared right with God [justified]—something the Jewish law could never do" (Acts 13:38-39). Speaking of our sins, God says, "I will never again remember [your] sins and lawless deeds" (Hebrews 10:17). What a wonderful promise!

Justification, however, is more than just the forgiveness and removal of the guilt and condemnation that accompany sin. While God has removed your sins and forgiven you of them, he has also placed the perfect righteousness of Jesus Christ "into your account," so to speak. You don't have to earn it or try to achieve it. It is yours as a gracious gift from the God who loves you. To understand justification more fully, read the following Scripture passages and notes below.

1. **God Promises Us His Gracious Forgiveness** (see 1 John 1:9, p. 317). The word *confess* means "to say the same thing as another" or "to agree with." To confess means that we are agreeing with God about our sin. We are seeing it as he does. We know that God hates sin. Therefore, to truly confess our sin means that we essentially feel the same way God feels about what we have done. After committing that sin, we will be determined to put it out of our lives and never do it again. That is true confession in the biblical sense. The reason many believers are not experiencing the forgiveness and joy they desire is because they have not yet truly confessed! Once we have met God's conditions, however, we will know his gracious forgiveness. We may not "feel" forgiven, but we are. We have his word on it.
2. **God Has Balanced Our Moral and Spiritual Budget** (see Romans 5:1-2, p. 180). When God makes us right in his sight, he does so by placing all of the righteousness of Christ to our credit. This balances the moral and spiritual budget for us. We now have sufficient "capital of character" to get on with the business of living.

   Up to this point, salvation has been God's responsibility. From this point on, it continues to be his responsibility except that we are responsible for the wise investment of our "capital of character"—that is, we are responsible for living as God desires us to. It is as if your checking account were empty, but then someone made a $100,000 deposit. What you do with that money is up to you.
3. **God Calls Us His Children** (see Luke 15:11-32, p. 91). This incredible story illustrates what happens when a person turns from sin and returns to God. First, notice that the father in the story did not give this prodigal son what he deserved—banishment. In the same way, we do not receive from God what we deserve—punishment for sin. Second, the young man was given what he did not deserve—the rights and privileges of full sonship. Likewise, although we are not worthy to be called children of God, he calls us sons and daughters. In summary, he doesn't give us what we deserve (judgment). He gives us what we don't deserve (forgiveness and justification).

Speaking of sons and daughters, read on to see how God has adopted you into his family.

Adopted and Assured

We have looked at what happens when we are regenerated (when Christ comes into our lives) and when we are justified (when God forgives our sin and puts his righteousness in its place). Now let us look at another incredible thing God has done for us. He has adopted us into his family as his children!

Adoption means "to be given the rights of a son." In essence, you have been given the full rights of sonship in the family of God as though you were born that way. The story of the Prodigal Son illustrates this (Luke 15:11-32). The wayward son thought that after leaving home, he would no longer be considered a son but would instead be treated as a hired servant. Much to his surprise, when he made the long journey home, his father welcomed him and smothered him with kisses. He then gave orders to bring out the best robe and to put a ring on his finger, signifying full rights as a son. That is exactly what God has done for you! Take some time now to examine three Scripture passages that assure you of your adoption into God's family.

1. **God Disciplines His Children** (see Hebrews 12:5-9, p. 297). Recognizing you are now a child of God is not some distant hope but a present reality. One of the ways God will remind you of this is by correcting you and bringing you back into line like a loving father when you stray away from him.

   Before we were believers, we may have felt no sense of guilt for certain things we did or did not do. But now that we are Christians, God's Holy Spirit shows us the way to live, which includes correcting us. He does this not because he hates us, but because he loves us as his own dear children. Understanding this truth should help us in the way we behave.
2. **You Have an Approachable Father** (see Galatians 4:6, p. 232). The Aramaic word translated "dear Father" is *abba,* which is a word of affection that a young child would use endearingly toward his or her father. A western equivalent of that phrase would be "papa" or "daddy." God does not want to be viewed as some distant, disinterested father, but as a loving, approachable father to whom you can turn at any time because you are his child.
3. **His Promises Are Not Based upon Your Feelings** (see 1 John 5:11-13, p. 323). There will be times as a Christian when you may not "feel" God's presence. You may even be tempted to doubt that he has come into your life. But 1 John 5:13 does not say, "I write this to you who believe in the Son of God so that you may *feel* you have eternal life." This is because feelings come and go. They fluctuate. Nor does the Bible say, "I write this so that you may *hope*—if God is in a really good mood—that you have eternal life." It says, "so that you may *know.* . . ." Eternal life is yours! Stand on God's promise to you. You are forgiven, justified, adopted into his family, and assured of salvation. Now that is reason to rejoice!

To find out more about God, turn to "Who Is God?" p. A11, in the Cornerstones section.

CORNERSTONES

FOUNDATIONAL TRUTHS OF THE FAITH

Who Is God?

Thousands of years ago, Pharaoh, the Egyptian ruler, posed a question people are still asking today: "Who is the LORD that I should listen to him?" That's a good question, but it is not an easy subject to tackle. It is difficult for our limited minds to grasp the limitless, eternal God. It has been said, "If God were small enough for your minds, he wouldn't be big enough for your needs." For that reason, don't be exasperated if you can't fully understand who God is or why he does certain things. One day, Scripture promises, everything about God and his character will be made perfectly clear to us (1 Corinthians 13:12). But until then, we will find everything we need to know about him in his Word. Look up the following notes and passages to find out who God is.

1. **God Is All-Knowing, Ever Present, and All-Powerful.** The Creator of the Universe knows every intimate detail of his creation (see Matthew 10:29-31, p.15).
2. **God Is Holy.** God's incomparable holiness merits our worship (see Revelation 15:2-4, p. 343).
3. **God Is Loving and Just.** God's justice is tempered by his love (see 2 Peter 3:3-9, p. 314).
4. **God Is Personal.** This characteristic of God sets him apart from the so-called "gods" of other religions (see Acts 17:22-31, p. 162).
5. **God Is in Control.** It is important to remember that God is still in control, even if things around us seem to be in chaos (see Romans 11:33-36, p. 191).
6. **The God of the Bible Is the One True God.** While some insist on the existence of many gods, only the God of the Bible is the true, living God, worthy of our devotion (see 1 Corinthians 8:4-6, p. 206).

Who Is Jesus?

Throughout history many people have attempted to answer this question. Some have done so accurately, but many have not. Our best source for answering this question is—once again—God's own Word. The Bible presents us with some inescapable truths about Jesus that demand a response. Anyone who seriously studies Scripture to learn more about Jesus must answer two probing questions: (1) What do you think of Jesus Christ? and (2) Who is he? The writer C. S. Lewis made this observation: "You must make your choice. Either this man was, and is, the Son of God: or else a madman or something worse. You can shut Him up for a fool, you can spit at Him and kill Him as a demon; or you can fall at His feet and call Him Lord and God. But let us not come with any patronising nonsense about His being a great human teacher. He has not left that open to us. He did not intend to" (*Mere Christianity,* rev. ed. [New York: Macmillan, 1952], 41).

Jesus was not just a good man. He was—and is—the God-man. Let's examine what the Bible has to say about Jesus.

1. **Jesus Is Human.** Jesus became our supreme example as God in human form (see Philippians 2:5-11, p. 248).
2. **Jesus Is Divine.** Even though Jesus became human, he still remained God (see Colossians 1:15-20, p. 254).
3. **Jesus Had a Specific Mission to Accomplish.** Jesus came to save humankind from sin (see Luke 4:16-21, p. 70).
4. **Jesus Made the Ultimate Sacrifice.** Jesus endured tremendous pain so that we could enjoy eternity with him (see 1 Peter 2:24, p. 307).
5. **Jesus Has Great Power to Transform People.** Jesus can change the most unlikely person into one of the most powerful witnesses on his behalf (see Acts 4:13, p. 140).
6. **Jesus Has an Eternal Dominion.** Jesus' Kingdom extends beyond the boundaries of space and time (see Revelation 1:4-8, p. 332).

Who Is the Holy Spirit?

The Holy Spirit is the most mysterious member of the Trinity, which includes God the Father, God the Son (Jesus Christ), and God the Spirit (or the Holy Spirit). Many struggle with the idea of God being three persons, yet one. Quite honestly, we will never fully grasp the concept this side of heaven.

Some, however, have wrongly thought of the Holy Spirit as more of an "it" than a "him." That is probably due in part to biblical descriptions of him as being like the wind or coming upon Jesus in the form of a dove, among other comparisons.

Yet these descriptions must be balanced with the descriptions of the other members of the Trinity. For instance, Jesus referred to himself as "the bread of life" and "the good shepherd." In the same way, God the Father is referred to as "a refuge" and "a consuming fire." Does this mean that Jesus is a loaf of bread or a sheep farmer, or that the Father is a pile of rocks or a blast furnace? Of course not! These are simply metaphors used in Scripture to help communicate God's character. Likewise, the unique descriptions attributed to the Holy Spirit do not imply that the Holy Spirit is merely some "force" or "power." Jesus said this about the Holy Spirit: "When the Spirit of truth comes, he will guide you into all truth. . . . He will tell you about the future" (John 16:13). Note the use of the pronoun *he*. The Holy Spirit has a distinct personality, and he also has specific work that he wants to do in our lives as followers of Jesus Christ. Explore what the Bible says about him.

1. **Who the Holy Spirit Helps.** The Holy Spirit strengthens and empowers followers of Christ (see Acts 2:1-40, p. 136).
2. **How the Holy Spirit Works with the Father and the Son.** The Holy Spirit works alongside God the Father and Jesus, God's Son, to make our lives pleasing to God (see 1 Peter 1:2, p. 306).
3. **Why God Gives Us the Holy Spirit.** The Holy Spirit's presence in our lives is God's mark of ownership (see Ephesians 1:13-14, p. 238).
4. **How the Holy Spirit Works in Our Lives.** The Holy Spirit draws us to Christ, enters our life at conversion, and empowers us as we allow him to work in our life (see John 14:15-17, p. 126).
5. **When the Holy Spirit Can Be Sinned Against.** There are six specific ways we can sin against the Holy Spirit (see Acts 5:1-10, p. 142).
6. **Why Christians Need the Holy Spirit.** Living the Christian life is impossible without the Holy Spirit's help (see Galatians 5:16-26, p. 230).

Who Is the Devil?

What is the Devil like? Does he really look like the red-suited, pitchfork-holding cartoon caricature seated on a throne in hell? Or does he roam through the earth disguised as an angel of light?

Unfortunately, far too many people do not have an accurate view of who the Devil is. Many underestimate him and his prowess, even going as far as to doubt his very existence. Someone once asked the great evangelist Charles Finney, "Mr. Finney, do you believe in a literal Devil?" Finney replied, "You try opposing him for a while, and you see if he's literal or not." You will find out how literal the Devil is the moment you make a commitment to Jesus Christ.

The Bible clearly shows us just how active and conniving the Devil really is. At the same time, Scripture also lets us know about the Devil's limitations and ultimate demise. The more we understand the tactics of this intelligent spirit being, the better equipped we will be to ward off his attacks. Below are some key passages of Scripture that answer some of the most commonly asked questions about the Devil—who is also referred to as Satan.

1. **Where Did Satan Come From?** Satan's pride led to his fall from heaven (see Revelation 12:7-9, p. 340).
2. **What Are Satan's Abilities?** Satan does have the power and access to do certain things in this world (see 2 Corinthians 4:3-4, p. 220).
3. **What Are Satan's Limitations?** While we should not underestimate Satan's power, we should realize that it is limited (see 2 Timothy 4:18, p. 278).
4. **How Does Satan Attack People?** Satan masterfully uses manipulation and distortion to deceive people (see 2 Corinthians 11:13-15, p. 226).
5. **Who Can Thwart Satan's Agenda?** Those who lay down their lives for Christ will defeat this evil foe (see Revelation 12:10-12, p. 340).

According to recent surveys, most people believe in the existence of angels. A glut of books on the subject fill bookstore shelves. Still, our only reliable source on angels and their activity is the Bible. Just who are these mysterious creatures? What do they look like? Do they wear long, flowing robes and have large birdlike wings? And what is their purpose?

You might call angels "God's secret agents." They basically work undercover. Most of the time these secret agents remain invisible—except on those special occasions when God allows people to see them. No doubt God realized that if we were allowed to see them all of the time, they would become an object of our worship, which is to be reserved for God alone. Let's take some time to see what the Bible has to say about angels and their role in this world.

1. **Why Did God Create Angels?** God created angels as unique spiritual beings who worship Christ and care for his followers (see Hebrews 1:4-14, p. 286).
2. **What Do Angels Do in the Life of a Christian?** God has ordered the angels to protect his followers and keep them from harm (see Acts 27:23-24, p. 171).
3. **How Are Angels Involved in Our Prayers?** Our prayers can trigger spiritual warfare (see Luke 22:42-44, p. 101).
4. **What Role Will Angels Play in the End Times?** Angels will play a strategic role in spreading the everlasting gospel (see Revelation 14:6-7, p. 342).

What Are Demons?

Just as there are angels who look out for your welfare, there are angels who are bent upon your destruction. The Bible teaches that when Satan fell from heaven, he took one-third of the angels with him (Revelation 12:4). Although we do not know their exact number, Scripture tells us there are multitudes (Luke 2:13) and legions (Matthew 26:53) of angels. So Satan has a sizable, highly organized force under his control. These fallen angels, also known as demons, help Satan accomplish his purpose, which, in the words of Christ, is to steal, kill, and destroy. While the Bible does not give us specific details as to how demons work, we can be confident that everything we need to know about them is found in Scripture. We do not need to look elsewhere for insights into the spiritual world. See what God's Word has to say about these evil agents.

1. **What Do Demons Believe?** Strange as it may seem, demons acknowledge that there is only one God (see James 2:19, p. 304).
2. **Can Demons Personally Harm You?** Those people who have a true relationship with Christ cannot be overcome by demons; those who do not are "fair game" for these servants of Satan (see Acts 19:13-20, p. 164).
3. **What Makes Demons Powerless?** The name of Jesus used by the followers of Jesus makes the demons tremble (see Luke 10:1-20, p. 82).

What Is Heaven?

The Bible gives us wonderful, vivid descriptions of heaven. From Scripture we know that heaven's streets are made of gold, and that pain, fear, and sorrow are not present there. But even with all of this detail, we still fall short of understanding "the big picture." That is because it is difficult for us to grasp the absolute perfection and glory of heaven.

All splendor aside, though, what truly makes heaven spectacular is that we will be forever in God's presence. As the psalmist so poignantly expressed, "You will show me the way of life, granting me the joy of your presence and the pleasures of living with you forever" (Psalm 16:11).

While we may not be able to have all of our questions about heaven answered here on earth, the Bible does answer some of our most probing questions.

1. **Who Will Enter Heaven?** Heaven is a place for those who have received Jesus Christ as Lord (see John 14:1-6, p. 124).
2. **When Does a Christian Enter Heaven?** When we take our last breath on earth, we will take our first breath in heaven (see 2 Corinthians 5:6-9, p. 222).
3. **Will We Recognize People in Heaven?** While our heavenly bodies may resemble our earthly bodies, we will in some ways be like the angels (see Matthew 22:23-33, p. 30).
4. **What Will Life in Heaven Be Like?** Our lives in heaven will no longer be consumed by the cares of this life, but we will be filled with joy being in the presence of our heavenly Father (see Revelation 7:13-17, p. 336).

What Is Hell?

According to the Bible, you have two options to choose from when it comes to deciding where you will spend your life after death. One option is heaven. The other is hell. Interestingly enough, while there seems to be an increased belief in a place called hell, most people don't believe that they are headed there. Instead, they believe that hell is reserved for only the most hardened of criminals and other "evil" elements of our society. But God's Word judges people by a different set of criteria. You are not sent to hell for being a bad person any more than you are sent to heaven for being a good person. We all deserve to spend eternity in hell (Romans 3:22-23).

While God clearly says that those who reject the salvation offered through his Son, Jesus Christ, will spend eternity in this place of torment, he repeatedly gives each person ample opportunity to choose life—abundant life on earth and eternal life in heaven (2 Peter 3:9). If you haven't made that choice yet, or if you have decided and want a better understanding of what your nonbelieving friends will have to face, consider these facts about hell from the pages of Scripture.

1. **What Is Hell Like?** Hell is a place of unending, isolated torment (see Luke 16:19-31, p. 92).
2. **Who Will Go to Hell?** Those whose names do not appear in the Book of Life are destined to everlasting punishment (see Revelation 20:11-15, p. 346).
3. **What Is the Worst Punishment of Hell?** Hell's worst punishment is everlasting separation from God's presence (see 2 Thessalonians 1:7-10, p. 266).

On one occasion Jesus was asked what commandment was the most important. He replied, "The most important commandment is this: 'Hear, O Israel! The Lord our God is the one and only Lord. And you must love the Lord your God with all your heart, all your soul, all your mind, and all your strength.' The second is equally important: 'Love your neighbor as yourself'" (Mark 12:29-31).

These are the two most important commandments because if you truly love God with all your heart, soul, mind, and strength, you will want to do what pleases him. In the same way, if you really love others as much as you love yourself, you will be concerned for their welfare and will treat them accordingly. Before you can effectively love God, however, you must first realize how much he loves you.

Scripture explains that God showed his great love for us by sending Christ to die for us while we were still sinners who had no relationship with him (Romans 5:8). The more we realize this wonderful truth, the more our love for God will grow. The Bible correctly recognizes that our love for God comes as a result of his loving us first (1 John 4:19). These Scripture passages explore some different facets of the love we should have for God and for others.

1. **God Should Be the Greatest Love of Our Life.** Before we can fully love one another, however, we must fully love God and understand his love for us (see Matthew 22:37-38, p. 32).
2. **Christ's Love Sets the Standard.** Our love for others should model Christ's love for us (see Ephesians 5:1-2, p. 244).
3. **Love Surpasses All Spiritual Gifts.** A Christian who understands what love truly means and shows love in his or her life is the greatest testimony to others (see 1 Corinthians 13:1-13, p. 214).
4. **Our Love for God Prepares Us for Service.** The depth of our love for God directly affects our ability to minister to others (see John 21:15-17, p. 132).
5. **Our Love for Others Mirrors the Condition of Our Heart.** The love we have for those around us is an indication of the strength of our Christian walk (see 1 John 2:9-11, p. 318).
6. **Our Love Should Grow.** The closer we grow to God, the more our love for others should increase (see 1 Thessalonians 3:12-13, p. 260).

One of the great principles of the Christian life is forgiveness. Jesus modeled this principle for us when he hung on the cross and prayed for the very people who had put him there (see Luke 23:34, p. 104). His words were so powerful and unexpected that they brought about the conversion of one of the thieves hanging on a cross next to him.

Because Jesus completely forgave us, he wants us to follow his example by forgiving others. As Scripture says: "Be kind to each other, tenderhearted, forgiving one another, just as God through Christ has forgiven you. Follow God's example in everything you do, because you are his dear children" (Ephesians 4:32–5:1). The Bible gives us several important characteristics of the forgiveness we should have for others.

1. **Forgiveness First Comes from God.** Our forgiveness of others should flow from God's forgiveness of us (see Mark 11:25, p. 56).
2. **Forgiveness Knows No Limits.** For a Christian, no wrong is too great or too small to forgive (see Matthew 18:21-35, p. 26).
3. **Forgiveness Is Not Selective.** You can't choose to forgive some people and not forgive others (see Matthew 5:43-48, p. 10).
4. **Forgiveness Breaks Down Walls.** When you choose to forgive, you experience true freedom (see Colossians 3:12-15, p. 257).

Purity

Purity is a quality we hear too little about today. Usually when we do hear something about purity, it is in reference to sexual purity. But purity goes beyond this to include wholesome thoughts, a sincere desire to do what is right, and a commitment to obey God's Word. Jesus alluded to the importance of purity by promising that those whose hearts were pure would see God (Matthew 5:8). In using the word heart, Jesus was saying that the center of our being—our will, our emotions, and our thought processes—needs to be cleansed of sin. The Bible texts below examine the idea of purity and how it affects us as followers of Jesus Christ.

1. **Don't Place Yourself in the Way of Unnecessary Temptation.** Know your moral weaknesses and avoid situations where the temptation to sin would be irresistible (see James 1:14-15, p. 299).
2. **Guard the Content of Your Thoughts.** Don't fill your mind with the world's moral filth (see 2 Timothy 2:22, p. 276).
3. **Beware of the Sins of the Heart.** The person who commits adultery in his heart is just as guilty as the person who actually carries it out (see Matthew 5:27-30, p. 8).
4. **Avoid Adulterous Relationships.** God specifically warns us against living in immoral relationships (see 1 Thessalonians 4:1-8, p. 262).
5. **If You Fall, Ask God to Forgive You and Purify Your Heart and Desires.** Only God can forgive you, restore your joy, and fill you with the right desires (see 1 John 1:9, p. 317).
6. **Keep an Eternal Perspective.** Don't waste your time chasing after earthly pleasures (see 2 Peter 3:10-11, p. 316).

7. Live to Please God. Surrendering your life to the leading of the Holy Spirit is the only way to live a life that is pleasing to God (see Romans 8:5-8, p. 184).

Perseverance

There will be times in your Christian walk when you will feel emotionally "down." You may think that God has forgotten about you. Or you might become discouraged as you see others who have professed faith in Jesus Christ lose interest in spiritual things and fall away. You may begin to wonder whether you are next on the Devil's "hit list." But God will not allow you to be hit with more than you can handle spiritually. In fact, it is during times of trouble that you will actually be strengthened, not weakened.

As you read your Bible, you will come across words like *endurance* and *perseverance.* These words are often used when the Bible compares the Christian life to a race. The race referred to is a marathon, not a fifty-yard dash. Because the Christian life is a long-distance run, you need to pace yourself, to persevere, and most of all, to *finish* the race. Look up the following passages that describe how and why you need to persevere through the inevitable struggles of life.

1. Perseverance Produces Results. As you steadily grow in your understanding of God's Word and apply it to your life, you will win others to the Lord (see Luke 8:15, p. 78).

2. Life's Trials Will Make You Stronger. You shouldn't view difficulties as obstacles to your faith, but as opportunities for spiritual growth (see James 1:2-4, p. 300).

3. Christ Endured Great Pain for Us. Jesus modeled the ultimate in endurance so that we would be encouraged to keep our faith strong in the race of life (see Hebrews 12:1-3, p. 294).

4. God Honors Those Who Persevere. A wholehearted commitment to God will enable you to "finish well" with your faith intact (see 2 Timothy 4:7-8, p. 278).

Honesty and Integrity

Honesty and integrity seem to be in short supply these days. Yet the Bible tells us that they are a part of the godly man's or woman's life. Unfortunately, the world tends to gloss over that aspect of the Christian life. It wants to characterize Christians as people who are out of touch with reality. But the Christian is simply someone who allows God to influence every aspect of his or her life—down to the practical, everyday dealings of business, finances, and relationships. The following passages examine how honesty and integrity should characterize our lives.

1. **We Should Be above Criticism.** A faithful and honest lifestyle will cause others to be more receptive to your message (see 2 Corinthians 7:2, p. 222).
2. **Our Conduct Should Cause Others to Glorify Christ.** Living a good, honest life around our unbelieving neighbors will ultimately bring glory to God (see 1 Peter 2:9-12, p. 310).
3. **We Need to Set an Example for Others.** We must seriously pursue a life of integrity in order to be a solid example for our fellow Christians (see Titus 2:6-8, p. 280).

When a person truly comes to Jesus Christ, this relationship will dramatically transform his or her life. We may see this transformation more immediately in the lives of some than others. For those whose lives are characterized by pronounced bad habits and blatant immoral living, the change in lifestyle will show others that something profound has indeed happened within that person's life. For others who may not be known for blatantly sinful living, the change may not be as outwardly pronounced, but it is just as significant. Remember, all of us were separated from God by sin, which was dealt with and atoned for at the cross of Jesus.

Our conversion will show itself in both fruit and works. This concept of "bearing fruit" is used often in Scripture to describe the results of someone's commitment to Jesus Christ. If we do not bear fruit, then it is apparent we have not really come to know Jesus Christ as Lord and Savior. Bearing fruit is not an option. It is the natural result of a person coming into union with God. Sometimes there is confusion in this area of fruit bearing, or works. See what the Bible has to say about the issue.

1. **Our Lives Should Show That God Is at Work in Our Hearts.** God desires that we demonstrate our spiritual growth through our outward actions (see Romans 7:4, p. 182).
2. **We Must Live Out Our Faith.** Faith without deeds is incomplete (see James 2:14-18, p. 302).
3. **God Saved Us for a Purpose.** While God himself gave us salvation, he planned that our salvation would lead to good works (see Ephesians 2:10, p. 240).
4. **Our Walk Should Match Our Talk.** God isn't as concerned with what we *say* we believe as with how we *live* what we believe (see Matthew 7:21-23, p. 12).

Discernment

An inspector who worked for Scotland Yard in the counterfeit department was once asked if he spent a lot of time handling counterfeit money. He said, "No." He then explained that he spent so much time handling the "real thing" that he could immediately detect the counterfeit. In the same way, as we become knowledgeable about God's Word, we, too, will be able to detect teachings and concepts that are contrary to Scripture. Make no mistake—counterfeit "truth" is out there in force. Look at the following Scripture passages to find out how you can keep from falling prey to false teachings.

1. **Beware of Satan's Clever Imitations.** Satan's work and agents may appear godly, but in the end they will be exposed for what they really are (see Matthew 13:24-30, p. 20).
2. **Recognize Satan's Strategies.** Lies and deceit are Satan's two main strategies to lead people away from the truth (see 1 Timothy 4:1-2, p. 270).
3. **Understand the Difference between the True Gospel and a False Gospel.** Scripture provides us with a "litmus test" to distinguish between truth and error (see 1 John 4:1-3, p. 320).
4. **Use God's Word to Evaluate Someone's Teachings.** The best way to detect a counterfeit is to become more familiar with the "real thing" (see Acts 17:11, p. 160).

Peace

Peace of mind—it seems almost elusive in a day when murders are commonplace, job security is nonexistent, and the moral fabric of society is tearing apart at the seams. Yet Jesus has promised that each one of us can experience true peace: "I am leaving you with a gift—peace of mind and heart. And the peace I give isn't like the peace the world gives. So don't be troubled or afraid" (John 14:27).

Unfortunately, some people are so caught up in the "pursuit of peace," that they have forgotten that Jesus has already given it to them. They have simply left that gift "unopened." And we cannot find peace outside of the parameters God has given us. As Augustine said many years ago, "Our souls are restless until they find their rest in God." Begin to "unwrap" this precious gift by examining what God's Word has to say about it.

1. **Peace Begins When We Relinquish Control of Our Lives to God.** When we give Jesus our burdens and allow him to guide us, we find rest (see Matthew 11:28-30, p. 16).

2. **Perfect Peace Builds upon Total Trust.** As God becomes a regular part of our daily lives, our worries begin to disappear (see John 16:33, p. 128).
3. **Our Peace Continues As We Follow the Holy Spirit.** We must stop allowing our old, sinful nature to control us before we can really experience peace (see Romans 8:5-8, p. 188).
4. **God's Peace Needs to Rule in Our Hearts.** We must constantly keep other things from crowding out God's peace in our lives (see Colossians 3:15, p. 256).

Joy

One noticeable change that takes place in a new believer's life is the inner joy he or she receives. In fact, joy is listed as part of the "fruit of the Spirit" that should be evident in a believer's life (see Galatians 5:22). But this joy is different from the fleeting and temporary "happiness" that is usually dependent upon "good things" happening in someone's life. While sorrows will come a believer's way, the Holy Spirit gives him or her an inner joy and peace that cannot be taken away. Below are some of the ways in which you can experience God's joy in your life.

1. **Studying God's Word Helps Us to Experience His Joy.** As we study God's Word and honor God with our lives, we experience his joy in our lives (see 1 Thessalonians 1:6, p. 259).
2. **Knowing and Trusting God Is the Source of Inexpressible Joy.** The greatest joy we can experience comes only from a personal relationship with Jesus Christ (see 1 Peter 1:8, p. 308).
3. **Sharing Your Faith Results in Joy.** While laboring to introduce people to Jesus is difficult work, the end result will give you much to celebrate (see John 4:36, p. 111).
4. **Overlooking Petty Issues Frees Us to Experience Joy.** God wants us to experience his joy in our lives and to avoid those things that could hamper that joy (see 1 Corinthians 1:10-17, p. 198).
5. **Knowing Whom You Belong to and What the Future Holds Brings True Joy.** Realizing that you are a child of God and that you will spend eternity in heaven with him will bring you joy (see Romans 15:13, p. 196).

Accountability

Once you receive Jesus Christ into your life as your personal Lord and Savior, not only do you obtain the privileged gift of eternal life, but you immediately acquire a great responsibility. You have been entrusted with the message of the gospel and are responsible for what you do with it in your life. In the end, we know that what we have done on this earth for Christ will be examined before almighty God and displayed before the rest of the world. The question we must all ask is this: Will what I am doing for Christ and his Kingdom stand the test of time? Those who have done much with what God has given them will be greatly rewarded. Take some time to see what God's Word has to say on this subject.

1. **The More We Know, the Greater Our Responsibility Will Be.** The Lord holds those who have been given positions of spiritual leadership to a higher accountability for what they do (see Luke 12:48, p. 88).
2. **We Are Responsible for Our Own Sins and Mistakes.** We cannot pass blame onto others for our own failings (see Romans 3:23, p. 178).
3. **We Need to Invest Our Abilities and Resources in God's Kingdom.** God has graciously given us abilities and resources to invest in the expansion of his Kingdom (see Luke 19:11-26, p. 96).
4. **The Value of Our Work on Earth Will Be Tested.** On Judgment Day, the quality of our faith and the work we have done for Jesus Christ will be revealed and rewarded accordingly (see 1 Corinthians 3:10-15, p. 200).

What to do after you have accepted Christ . . .

You might say that the Bible is the "user's manual of life" we have all been searching for. Everything we need to know about God and living a life that pleases him is found in its pages.

Tragically, some of us go through life without so much as picking up this amazing book, whose words were inspired by God. Yet, success or failure in the Christian life is determined by how much of the Bible we get into our hearts and minds and how obedient we are to the principles and teachings found within it. Just as we need to continually breathe oxygen to survive, we need to regularly study the Bible to grow and flourish spiritually. Here are some important reasons why we need to spend time in this life-changing book.

1. **Studying the Bible Is Necessary for Our Spiritual Growth.** The Bible performs three functions to help us mature spiritually (see 2 Timothy 3:16-17, p. 277).
2. **Studying the Bible Keeps Us Spiritually Strong.** The more we get into this book and apply its teachings, the more we will be able to stand our ground in the storms and trials of life (see Matthew 7:24-27, p. 12).
3. **Studying the Bible Makes Scripture a Central Part of Our Lives.** God desires that we make the Bible an integral part of our lives (see Colossians 3:16, p. 257).
4. **Studying the Bible Helps Us Apply Its Truth to Our Lives.** We will notice positive changes in our lives as we apply what we read in Scripture (see 2 Timothy 3:16-17, p. 277).

Pray

The idea of talking to God can be intimidating. But it doesn't have to be. In fact, prayer can be a wonderful experience if we know how to do it God's way. Fortunately, we have God's Word to teach us how to pray. The Bible instructs us to pray at all times, in any posture, in any place, for any reason. In addition, it does not matter whether you pray in King James English or the most contemporary jargon. God only desires that you pray from a pure and sincere heart.

The disciples observed the profound effect prayer had in Jesus' life and ministry. They witnessed how Jesus would often go off by himself to spend time in prayer with his heavenly Father. They saw the power, peace, and tranquillity that emanated from his life, giving him the ability to stay calm in troubled circumstances. Jesus' prayer life so impressed these men that they asked him to teach them to pray (Luke 11:1-13). Certainly if the perfect Son of God often took time to pray during his life here on earth, how much more do we, mere men and women, need to pray?

Because prayer is an essential ingredient to walking with Jesus Christ, we need to examine its elements found in God's Word.

1. **Prayer Was Modeled for Us by Christ.** Jesus took the time to show his followers how to pray (see Matthew 6:5-15, p. 9).
2. **Prayer Is Not a Solitary Experience.** God has given us his Holy Spirit to aid us in prayer, even when we do not know what to pray (see Romans 8:26-27, p. 183).
3. **Prayer Allows Us to Voice Our Requests to God.** Prayer is God's appointed way for us to relate our concerns and present our needs to him (see James 4:2-3, p. 301).
4. **Prayer Enables Us to Seek Forgiveness.** When we pray sincerely for forgiveness, God will hear our prayers and restore us (see James 5:15-16, p. 304).
5. **Prayer Helps Us Overcome Worry.** In the midst of troubles, we can receive God's peace through prayer (see Philippians 4:6-7, p. 251).
6. **Prayer Increases Our Spiritual Knowledge and Maturity.** God will give us greater spiritual understanding through prayer (see Colossians 1:9, p. 253).

Look for and Attend the Right Church

One of the essential building blocks of spiritual growth is fellowship with other believers by becoming part of a local church. The church (meaning the entire body of Christians) is not really an organization so much as an organism. It thrives by keeping its members spiritually active and well fed. The church provides you with spiritual instruction from God's Word, allows you to worship God with other believers, enables you to use your God-given gifts and abilities as God intended, and makes you accountable to spiritual leadership. Some people think they can get enough spiritual input from Christian television, radio programs, and books. While those things do have value, nothing can replace the need to become an active member of a church. Think about it—if joining in fellowship with other believers was not important, why did Jesus establish the church? (see Matthew 16:18). The Bible has plenty to say about the characteristics of a healthy, vibrant church and the necessity of Christian fellowship. Here are four helpful insights from God's Word on looking for and attending the right church.

1. **What to Look for in a Church.** You should look for a church that has the qualities and characteristics of the first century church (see Acts 2:42, 44-47, p. 139).
2. **Why We Need Fellowship with Other Believers.** Fellowship with other Christians sharpens your spiritual discernment and prepares you for Christ's return (see Hebrews 10:25, p. 293).
3. **Why the Church Needs You.** Not only will you benefit from the church, but the church will benefit from you and your God-given abilities (see Ephesians 4:11-16, p. 239).
4. **You Have a Place in the Church.** God has given each one of us a unique role to play in our place of fellowship (see 1 Corinthians 12:12-31, p. 213).

Obey God

The real evidence of a true Christian is a changed life. The great British preacher Charles Haddon Spurgeon once said, "Of what value is the grace I profess to receive if it does not dramatically change the way that I live? If it doesn't change the way that I live, it will never change my eternal destiny."

A changed life begins with obedience to God. This means that you will have to stop doing certain things and start doing others. While God begins to change your heart and desires once you have surrendered your life to him, he still gives you the freedom to decide just how much of your life you will let him control. But know this: Whatever you give up to follow Jesus Christ will pale in comparison to what he will give you in return. For example, when you give up sinful behaviors for God, he will replace your sin with forgiveness and a clear conscience. With this incentive for obedience, look at six specific ways the Bible instructs us to obey God.

1. **Recognize That You Are a New Creation.** When you understand what God has done in your life, obedience becomes more of a desire than a mere duty (see 2 Corinthians 5:14-17, p. 223).
2. **Follow God Wholeheartedly.** When you follow God completely, you will finish the race of life well (see Hebrews 12:1-3, p. 296).

3. **Offer God More than Lip Service.** God looks at your heart more than your religious actions (see Matthew 23:25-28, p. 33).
4. **Live in God's Love.** Discover the secret of true and lasting joy (see John 15:9-11, p. 127).
5. **Put on God's Armor.** Obedience prepares you for the battles of life (see Romans 13:11-14, p. 191).
6. **Let God Occupy Your Thoughts.** Your thoughts will affect your actions (see Colossians 3:1-4, p. 255).

Resist Temptation

Now that you are a follower of Jesus Christ, Satan is going to try to draw you away by tempting you to disobey God's Word. It is not a sin to be tempted—even Jesus was tempted (see Luke 4:1-13). We sin when we give in to that temptation. The good news is that God will never let a temptation become so strong that we can't handle it. In addition, he has given us specific ways to handle temptation. Here are three things to remember when dealing with temptation.

1. **Realize Who Is Tempting You.** Satan is the mastermind behind all of your temptations (see Ephesians 6:10-12, p. 243).
2. **Resist the Devil.** The Bible says that if you resist Satan's enticements, he will flee from you (see James 4:7-8, p. 303).
3. **Rejoice Because Victory Is Yours in Christ Jesus.** God promises that he will always provide a way of escape (see 1 Corinthians 10:13, p. 209).

Live in God's Power

Some people look at the Christian life and say, "I couldn't begin to live that way and hold to those standards. It is too hard!" This is true. It is not hard to be a Christian—it is impossible (that is without the help of the Holy Spirit). You see, God has given you power to live the Christian life. The moment you asked Jesus Christ into your heart, he gave you the gift of his Holy Spirit (see "Who Is the Holy Spirit?" p. A12).

The Holy Spirit not only takes up residence in your heart, but he empowers you to live a holy life and to be an effective witness for Jesus Christ. The Holy Spirit's power is much like an investment. You need to draw upon his power daily to live out your faith. To find out more about how the Holy Spirit can empower and strengthen your Christian walk, look up the following passages of Scripture.

1. **God's Spirit Will Guide You.** The Holy Spirit will help you understand the truths of Scripture and the character of God (see John 16:13-15, p. 129).
2. **God's Spirit Will Empower Your Witness.** The Holy Spirit will give you greater courage and an increased ability to share your faith (see Acts 1:8, p. 137).
3. **God's Spirit Will Encourage You to Be Obedient.** You will have a Holy Spirit-inspired desire to obey God's commands (see Romans 8:13-14, p. 184).
4. **God's Spirit Will Help You Overcome Sin.** Sin will no longer have the power over you it had before you accepted Christ into your life (see Romans 8:9-14, p. 181).

Share Your Faith

Next to personally knowing Jesus and walking with him, one of the greatest blessings of the Christian life is to actually lead someone to Jesus Christ. The good news is that God wants to use you—not just pastors, missionaries, and evangelists—as his instrument to speak to others.

Jesus gave us this very commission in Mark 16:15, where he says, "Go into all the world and preach the Good News to everyone, everywhere." This wonderful charge is known as the "great commission." But the way some Christians follow it, you would think it was the "great suggestion." Sharing our faith, however, is something that Jesus wants—and commands—us to do! How do we do this? First Peter 3:15-16 tells us to be ready to give an answer to anyone who asks us about the hope we have in Jesus. Here are five passages from God's Word that will help you to share your faith.

1. **You Don't Need Any Training to Share.** A changed heart is all you need to begin sharing your faith with others (see John 9:1-41, p. 117).
2. **Be Open to God's Leading.** Effectively sharing your faith begins with a willing heart (see Acts 8:4-8, 26-38, p. 147).
3. **Understand the Simplicity of the Gospel.** The message of the gospel is simple yet powerful (see 1 Corinthians 2:1-5, p. 199).
4. **Share Your Own Story.** Never underestimate the strength of your personal testimony (see Acts 26:1-23, p. 171).

Seek God's Will

Have you ever wondered about the future? Have you pondered the answers to such important, life-changing decisions as whom you should marry or what career path you should pursue? More than likely, most of us have asked these questions and wondered if God has a definite plan or opinion in the matter. With that in mind, here is some good news: God is vitally interested in your life, and he does want to lead you in your decisions.

Jesus called his followers friends (see John 15:15). As God's friend you already have an "inside track" in discovering God's will for your life. It is called the Bible. There you will find God's general will for your life (such as putting God first in all you do and following God's guidelines for marriage), as well as some principles to follow when seeking his specific direction for your life. In the end, finding God's will comes down to living out what you read in the Bible and then living by faith. Here are six steps you can take as you seek God's will.

1. **Unconditionally Surrender Your Life.** Certain conditions must be met if you want to know God's will for your life (see Romans 12:1-2, p. 185).
2. **Realize That God Has a Plan for Your Life.** Your life has purpose and meaning, and God wants to reveal it to you (see Ephesians 1:7-9, p. 237).
3. **Act upon What God Has Already Revealed in Scripture.** God has already given us some specific guidelines to follow in his Word (see 1 Thessalonians 4:1-8, p. 261).
4. **Trust God Completely.** There is nothing more reassuring than entrusting an unknown future to a known God (see Philippians 4:6-7, p. 250).
5. **Listen for God's Voice.** Sometimes God speaks to us in a quiet voice (see John 10:27, p. 119).

Live as a Disciple

When you hear the word *disciple,* do you immediately think of the Twelve who followed Jesus during his ministry on earth? Many people do not realize that Jesus still has disciples in this day and age. While every disciple is a believer, not every believer is necessarily a disciple. A disciple is someone who has made a wholehearted commitment to follow Jesus Christ as Savior and Lord. In one sense, you might call discipleship "radical Christian living." When you truly make a commitment to be Christ's disciple, you will be living the Christian life as it was meant to be lived. Anything short of discipleship is settling for less than what God desires. Here are four passages from the Bible that explain what it means to truly be a disciple of Jesus.

1. **A Disciple Takes Up His or Her Cross and Follows Christ.** Being a disciple takes work and commitment (see Luke 9:23-25, p. 81).
2. **A Disciple Counts the Cost.** Jesus' disciples are willing to give up everything to follow him (see Luke 14:25-33, p. 91).
3. **A Disciple Abides in Christ.** The source of a disciple's strength comes from his or her closeness to Christ (see John 15:1-17, p. 125).
4. **A Disciple Walks as Jesus Walked.** Disciples pattern their lives after Jesus, the ultimate example of how to live (see 1 John 2:3-6, p. 319).

Money is such an important topic in the Bible that it is the main subject of nearly *half* the parables Jesus told. In addition, one out of every seven verses in the New Testament deals with the topic. To give you an idea of how this compares with other topics, Scripture offers about five hundred verses on prayer and fewer than five hundred on faith, while there are more than *two thousand* verses on money!

You may be wondering what money has to do with your faith. Now that Jesus Christ has come into your life, he wants to be Lord (to be in command) of every aspect of it. That includes your finances. Martin Luther astutely observed, "There are three conversions necessary: the conversion of the heart, the mind, and the purse [or wallet]." When we experience this "conversion of the purse" and give freely of our finances to the Lord's work (to our church, a missionary, or a ministry), we will make the best investment possible—an investment with eternal dividends. With that in mind, here are five questions to consider about wealth and giving.

1. **Why Should You Give a Portion of Your Financial Resources to God?** God wants to prove his faithfulness through your regular giving, or tithes (see 2 Corinthians 9:6-11, p. 225).
2. **How Much Should You Give?** God encourages us to give sacrificially (see Mark 12:41-44, p. 59).
3. **What Happens When You Give?** When you give with the right motives, you will experience joy and God's generous blessings (see 2 Corinthians 9:6-14, p. 227).
4. **How Should You View Material Wealth?** Accumulating wealth should never be a high priority because it is eternally worthless (see Matthew 6:19-34, p. 11).
5. **Can You Enjoy Wealth?** God may bless you materially, but you are responsible for using your material blessings wisely (see 1 Timothy 6:17-19, p. 271).

Have Courage in Trials

Many Christians have the mistaken idea that once they make a commitment to Jesus Christ, life will be smooth sailing from that day forward. This is certainly not the case. While it is true that walking with Christ will help us avoid many of the problems we used to face, we are still going to experience what the Bible calls "trials."

Trials may come in the form of a crisis, a sudden illness, the loss of a loved one, or some drastic change in your life. You may go through a difficult time when you don't feel God's presence, when church may not be as exciting as it once was for you, or your prayers seem to go no higher than the ceiling. This may cause you to wonder if you have angered God or if he has left you. But God does not allow us to experience trials because he wants to see us suffer. Rather, he allows these difficulties into our lives to help us grow spiritually—to learn to live by faith, not by feelings. Look up the following passages to see the role trials play in our lives. Notice also God's promise to be with us during these times of trouble.

1. **Trials Sharpen Our Faith.** Hardships develop our character and purify our faith (see 1 Peter 1:3-7, p. 307).
2. **Trials Help Us Comfort Others.** Experiencing suffering deepens our compassion for others who suffer (see 2 Corinthians 1:3-7, p. 219).
3. **Trials Are Survivable.** We must keep our eternal perspective through the tough times (see 2 Corinthians 4:7-18, p. 221).
4. **Trials Test Our Foundation.** When we ground our lives in Christ, we can weather any storm (see Luke 6:47-49, p. 75).
5. **Jesus Is with Us in Life's Storms.** We are never outside of God's watchful eye and his abiding presence (see Mark 4:35-41, p. 47).
6. **God Gives Hope to Our Troubled Hearts.** We can have peace of mind in the middle of our greatest trials (see John 14:1-7, p. 123).

The
NEW
Testament

Matthew

CHAPTER 1

The Record of Jesus' Ancestors

This is a record of the ancestors of Jesus the Messiah, a descendant of King David and of Abraham:

2 Abraham was the father of Isaac.
Isaac was the father of Jacob.
Jacob was the father of Judah and his brothers.
3 Judah was the father of Perez and Zerah (their mother was Tamar).
Perez was the father of Hezron.
Hezron was the father of Ram.*
4 Ram was the father of Amminadab.
Amminadab was the father of Nahshon.
Nahshon was the father of Salmon.
5 Salmon was the father of Boaz (his mother was Rahab).
Boaz was the father of Obed (his mother was Ruth).
Obed was the father of Jesse.
6 Jesse was the father of King David.
David was the father of Solomon (his mother was Bathsheba, the widow of Uriah).
7 Solomon was the father of Rehoboam.
Rehoboam was the father of Abijah.
Abijah was the father of Asaph.*
8 Asaph was the father of Jehoshaphat.
Jehoshaphat was the father of Jehoram.*
Jehoram was the father* of Uzziah.
9 Uzziah was the father of Jotham.
Jotham was the father of Ahaz.
Ahaz was the father of Hezekiah.
10 Hezekiah was the father of Manasseh.
Manasseh was the father of Amos.*
Amos was the father of Josiah.
11 Josiah was the father of Jehoiachin* and his brothers (born at the time of the exile to Babylon).
12 After the Babylonian exile:
Jehoiachin was the father of Shealtiel.
Shealtiel was the father of Zerubbabel.
13 Zerubbabel was the father of Abiud.
Abiud was the father of Eliakim.
Eliakim was the father of Azor.
14 Azor was the father of Zadok.
Zadok was the father of Akim.
Akim was the father of Eliud.
15 Eliud was the father of Eleazar.
Eleazar was the father of Matthan.
Matthan was the father of Jacob.
16 Jacob was the father of Joseph, the husband of Mary.
Mary was the mother of Jesus, who is called the Messiah.

17All those listed above include fourteen generations from Abraham to King David, and fourteen from David's time to the Babylonian exile,
and fourteen from the Babylonian exile to the
Messiah.

The Birth of Jesus the Messiah

18Now this is how Jesus the Messiah was born.
His mother, Mary, was engaged to be married to
Joseph. But while she was still a virgin, she
became pregnant by the Holy Spirit. 19Joseph,
her fiancé, being a just man, decided to break
the engagement quietly, so as not to disgrace her
publicly.

20As he considered this, he fell asleep, and an
angel of the Lord appeared to him in a dream.

1:3 Greek *Aram;* also in 1:4. See 1 Chr 2:9-10. 1:7 *Asaph* is the same person as Asa; also in 1:8. See 1 Chr 3:10. 1:8a Greek *Joram.* See 1 Kgs 22:50 and note at 1 Chr 3:11. 1:8b Or *ancestor;* also in 1:11. 1:10 *Amos* is the same person as Amon. See 1 Chr 3:14. 1:11 Greek *Jeconiah;* also in 1:12. See 2 Kgs 24:6 and note at 1 Chr 3:16.

"Joseph, son of David," the angel said, "do not
be afraid to go ahead with your marriage to
Mary. For the child within her has been conceived by the Holy Spirit. 21And she will have a
son, and you are to name him Jesus,* for he will
save his people from their sins." 22All of this
happened to fulfill the Lord's message through
his prophet:

23 "Look! The virgin will conceive a child!
She will give birth to a son,
and he will be called Immanuel*
(meaning, God is with us)."

24When Joseph woke up, he did what the angel
of the Lord commanded. He brought Mary
home to be his wife, 25but she remained a virgin
until her son was born. And Joseph named him
Jesus.

CHAPTER 2

The Visit of the Wise Men

Jesus was born in the town of Bethlehem in
Judea, during the reign of King Herod. About
that time some wise men* from eastern lands
arrived in Jerusalem, asking, 2"Where is the
newborn king of the Jews? We have seen his star
as it arose,* and we have come to worship him."

3Herod was deeply disturbed by their question, as was all of Jerusalem. 4He called a meeting of the leading priests and teachers of
religious law. "Where did the prophets say the
Messiah would be born?" he asked them.

5"In Bethlehem," they said, "for this is what
the prophet wrote:

6 'O Bethlehem of Judah,
you are not just a lowly village in Judah,
for a ruler will come from you
who will be the shepherd for my people
Israel.'* "

7Then Herod sent a private message to the
wise men, asking them to come see him. At this
meeting he learned the exact time when they
first saw the star. 8Then he told them, "Go to
Bethlehem and search carefully for the child.
And when you find him, come back and tell me
so that I can go and worship him, too!"

9After this interview the wise men went their
way. Once again the star appeared to them, guid-
ing them to Bethlehem. It went ahead of them
and stopped over the place where the child was.
10When they saw the star, they were filled with
joy! 11They entered the house where the child
and his mother, Mary, were, and they fell down
before him and worshiped him. Then they
opened their treasure chests and gave him gifts
of gold, frankincense, and myrrh. 12But when it
was time to leave, they went home another way,
because God had warned them in a dream not
to return to Herod.

The Escape to Egypt

13After the wise men were gone, an angel of the
Lord appeared to Joseph in a dream. "Get up
and flee to Egypt with the child and his mother,"
the angel said. "Stay there until I tell you to
return, because Herod is going to try to kill the
child." 14That night Joseph left for Egypt with
the child and Mary, his mother, 15and they
stayed there until Herod's death. This fulfilled
what the Lord had spoken through the prophet:
"I called my Son out of Egypt."*

16Herod was furious when he learned that the
wise men had outwitted him. He sent soldiers to
kill all the boys in and around Bethlehem who
were two years old and under, because the wise
men had told him the star first appeared to them
about two years earlier.* 17Herod's brutal action
fulfilled the prophecy of Jeremiah:

18 "A cry of anguish is heard in Ramah—
weeping and mourning unrestrained.
Rachel weeps for her children,
refusing to be comforted—for they are
dead."*

The Return to Nazareth

19When Herod died, an angel of the Lord appeared in a dream to Joseph in Egypt and told
him, 20"Get up and take the child and his
mother back to the land of Israel, because those
who were trying to kill the child are dead." 21So
Joseph returned immediately to Israel with Jesus
and his mother. 22But when he learned that the
new ruler was Herod's son Archelaus, he was
afraid. Then, in another dream, he was warned
to go to Galilee. 23So they went and lived in a
town called Nazareth. This fulfilled what was
spoken by the prophets concerning the Messiah:
"He will be called a Nazarene."

CHAPTER 3

John the Baptist Prepares the Way

In those days John the Baptist began preaching
in the Judean wilderness. His message was,

1:21 *Jesus* means "The LORD saves." 1:23 Isa 7:14; 8:8, 10. 2:1 Or *royal astrologers;* Greek reads *Magi;* also in 2:7, 16. 2:2 Or *in the east.* 2:6 Mic 5:2; 2 Sam 5:2. 2:15 Hos 11:1. 2:16 Or *according to the time he calculated from the wise men.* 2:18 Jer 31:15.

2 "Turn from your sins and turn to God, because the Kingdom of Heaven is near.*" 3 Isaiah had spoken of John when he said,

"He is a voice shouting in the wilderness:
'Prepare a pathway for the Lord's coming!
Make a straight road for him!'"*

4 John's clothes were woven from camel hair, and he wore a leather belt; his food was locusts and wild honey. 5 People from Jerusalem and from every section of Judea and from all over the Jordan Valley went out to the wilderness to hear him preach. 6 And when they confessed their sins, he baptized them in the Jordan River.

7 But when he saw many Pharisees and Sadducees coming to be baptized, he denounced them. "You brood of snakes!" he exclaimed. "Who warned you to flee God's coming judgment? 8 Prove by the way you live that you have really turned from your sins and turned to God. 9 Don't just say, 'We're safe—we're the descendants of Abraham.' That proves nothing. God can change these stones here into children of Abraham. 10 Even now the ax of God's judgment is poised, ready to sever your roots. Yes, every tree that does not produce good fruit will be chopped down and thrown into the fire.

11 "I baptize with* water those who turn from their sins and turn to God. But someone is coming soon who is far greater than I am—so much greater that I am not even worthy to be his slave.* He will baptize you with the Holy Spirit and with fire.* 12 He is ready to separate the chaff from the grain with his winnowing fork. Then he will clean up the threshing area, storing the grain in his barn but burning the chaff with never-ending fire."

The Baptism of Jesus

13 Then Jesus went from Galilee to the Jordan River to be baptized by John. 14 But John didn't want to baptize him. "I am the one who needs to be baptized by you," he said, "so why are you coming to me?"

15 But Jesus said, "It must be done, because we must do everything that is right.*" So then John baptized him.

16 After his baptism, as Jesus came up out of the water, the heavens were opened and he saw the Spirit of God descending like a dove and settling on him. 17 And a voice from heaven said, "This is my beloved Son, and I am fully pleased with him."

CHAPTER 4

The Temptation of Jesus

Then Jesus was led out into the wilderness by the Holy Spirit to be tempted there by the Devil. 2 For forty days and forty nights he ate nothing and became very hungry. 3 Then the Devil* came and said to him, "If you are the Son of God, change these stones into loaves of bread."

4 But Jesus told him, "No! The Scriptures say,

'People need more than bread for their life;
they must feed on every word of God.'*"

5 Then the Devil took him to Jerusalem, to the highest point of the Temple, 6 and said, "If you are the Son of God, jump off! For the Scriptures say,

'He orders his angels to protect you.
And they will hold you with their hands
to keep you from striking your foot on a stone.'*"

7 Jesus responded, "The Scriptures also say, 'Do not test the Lord your God.'*"

8 Next the Devil took him to the peak of a very high mountain and showed him the nations of the world and all their glory. 9 "I will give it all to you," he said, "if you will only kneel down and worship me."

10 "Get out of here, Satan," Jesus told him. "For the Scriptures say,

'You must worship the Lord your God;
serve only him.'*"

11 Then the Devil went away, and angels came and cared for Jesus.

The Ministry of Jesus Begins

12 When Jesus heard that John had been arrested, he left Judea and returned to Galilee. 13 But instead of going to Nazareth, he went to Capernaum, beside the Sea of Galilee, in the region of Zebulun and Naphtali. 14 This fulfilled Isaiah's prophecy:

15 "In the land of Zebulun and of Naphtali,
beside the sea, beyond the Jordan River—
in Galilee where so many Gentiles live—
16 the people who sat in darkness
have seen a great light.
And for those who lived in the land where
death casts its shadow,
a light has shined."*

17 From then on, Jesus began to preach, "Turn

3:2 Or *has come* or *is coming soon.* **3:3** Isa 40:3. **3:11a** Or *in.* **3:11b** Greek *to carry his sandals.* **3:11c** Or *in the Holy Spirit and in fire.* **3:15** Or *we must fulfill all righteousness.* **4:3** Greek *the tempter.* **4:4** Deut 8:3. **4:6** Ps 91:11-12. **4:7** Deut 6:16. **4:10** Deut 6:13. **4:15-16** Isa 9:1-2.

from your sins and turn to God, because the
Kingdom of Heaven is near.*"

The First Disciples

18One day as Jesus was walking along the shore
beside the Sea of Galilee, he saw two brothers—Simon, also called Peter, and Andrew—fishing with a
net, for they were commercial fishermen. 19Jesus
called out to them, "Come, be my disciples, and I
will show you how to fish for people!" 20And they
left their nets at once and went with him.

21A little farther up the shore he saw two other
brothers, James and John, sitting in a boat with their
father, Zebedee, mending their nets. And he called
them to come, too. 22They immediately followed
him, leaving the boat and their father behind.

The Ministry of Jesus in Galilee

23Jesus traveled throughout Galilee teaching in the
synagogues, preaching everywhere the Good News
about the Kingdom. And he healed people who had
every kind of sickness and disease. 24News about
him spread far beyond the borders of Galilee so that
the sick were soon coming to be healed from as far
away as Syria. And whatever their illness and pain,
or if they were possessed by demons, or were epilep-
tics, or were paralyzed—he healed them all. 25Large
crowds followed him wherever he went—people
from Galilee, the Ten Towns,* Jerusalem, from all
over Judea, and from east of the Jordan River.

CHAPTER 5

The Sermon on the Mount

One day as the crowds were gathering, Jesus
went up the mountainside with his disciples and
sat down to teach them.

The Beatitudes

2This is what he taught them:

3 "God blesses those who realize their need
for him,*
for the Kingdom of Heaven is given to
them.
4 God blesses those who mourn,
for they will be comforted.
5 God blesses those who are gentle and lowly,
for the whole earth will belong to them.
6 God blesses those who are hungry and
thirsty for justice,
for they will receive it in full.
7 God blesses those who are merciful,
for they will be shown mercy.
8 God blesses those whose hearts are pure,
for they will see God.
9 God blesses those who work for peace,
for they will be called the children of
God.
10 God blesses those who are persecuted
because they live for God,
for the Kingdom of Heaven is theirs.

11"God blesses you when you are mocked
and persecuted and lied about because you are
my followers. 12Be happy about it! Be very glad!
For a great reward awaits you in heaven. And
remember, the ancient prophets were persecuted, too.

Teaching about Salt and Light

13"You are the salt of the earth. But what good
is salt if it has lost its flavor? Can you make it
useful again? It will be thrown out and trampled
underfoot as worthless. 14You are the light of the
world—like a city on a mountain, glowing in

4:17 Or *has come* or *is coming soon.* 4:25 Greek *Decapolis.* 5:3 Greek *the poor in spirit.*

OFF AND RUNNING

We Need to Recognize Our True Condition

Read MATTHEW 5:3-5

Jesus shows us the way to true happiness in this text. Interestingly, not a word is said about seeking "personal fulfillment." Here Jesus gives us a three-step prescription to spiritual health and happiness:

1. See Yourself as You Really Are. When you realize your need for God (verse 3), you see yourself as you really are: a sinner, in desperate need of God's forgiveness. This is the first "rung on the ladder." The phrase "need for God" in this verse comes from a verb meaning "to shrink, cower, or cringe," as beggars often did in that day. It speaks of someone who is destitute and completely dependent on others for help. Therefore, to "realize your need for God" is to admit that you are spiritually destitute apart from God.

2. Take Action. Another way to translate verse 4 is "happy are the unhappy." Because we see ourselves as we really are, we mourn over, or are sorry for, our condition. This leads us to begin making changes in our

the night for all to see. 15Don't hide your light
under a basket! Instead, put it on a stand and let
it shine for all. 16In the same way, let your good
deeds shine out for all to see, so that everyone
will praise your heavenly Father.

Teaching about the Law

17"Don't misunderstand why I have come. I did
not come to abolish the law of Moses or the
writings of the prophets. No, I came to fulfill
them. 18I assure you, until heaven and earth
disappear, even the smallest detail of God's law
will remain until its purpose is achieved. 19So if
you break the smallest commandment and
teach others to do the same, you will be the least
in the Kingdom of Heaven. But anyone who
obeys God's laws and teaches them will be great
in the Kingdom of Heaven.

20"But I warn you—unless you obey God
better than the teachers of religious law and the
Pharisees do, you can't enter the Kingdom of
Heaven at all!

Teaching about Anger

21"You have heard that the law of Moses says,
'Do not murder. If you commit murder, you are
subject to judgment.'* 22But I say, if you are
angry with someone,* you are subject to judgment! If you call someone an idiot,* you are in
danger of being brought before the high council. And if you curse someone,* you are in
danger of the fires of hell.

23"So if you are standing before the altar in
the Temple, offering a sacrifice to God, and you
suddenly remember that someone has something against you, 24leave your sacrifice there
beside the altar. Go and be reconciled to that
person. Then come and offer your sacrifice to
God. 25Come to terms quickly with your enemy
before it is too late and you are dragged into
court, handed over to an officer, and thrown in
jail. 26I assure you that you won't be free again
until you have paid the last penny.

Teaching about Adultery

27"You have heard that the law of Moses says, 'Do
not commit adultery.'* 28But I say, anyone who even
looks at a woman with lust in his eye has already
committed adultery with her in his heart. 29So if
your eye—even if it is your good eye*—causes you
to lust, gouge it out and throw it away. It is better for
you to lose one part of your body than for your
whole body to be thrown into hell. 30And if your
hand—even if it is your stronger hand*—causes
you to sin, cut it off and throw it away. It is better for
you to lose one part of your body than for your
whole body to be thrown into hell.

Teaching about Divorce

31"You have heard that the law of Moses says, 'A
man can divorce his wife by merely giving her a
letter of divorce.'* 32But I say that a man who
divorces his wife, unless she has been unfaithful,
causes her to commit adultery. And anyone who
marries a divorced woman commits adultery.

Teaching about Vows

33"Again, you have heard that the law of Moses
says, 'Do not break your vows; you must carry out
the vows you have made to the Lord.'* 34But I say,

5:21 Exod 20:13; Deut 5:17. 5:22a Greek *your brother;* also in 5:23. Some manuscripts add *without cause.* 5:22b Greek uses an Aramaic term of contempt: *If you say to your brother, 'Raca.'* 5:22c Greek *if you say, 'You fool.'* 5:27 Exod 20:14; Deut 5:18. 5:29 Greek *your right eye.* 5:30 Greek *your right hand.* 5:31 Deut 24:1. 5:33 Num 30:2.

lives. Scripture tells us, "For God can use sorrow in our lives to help us turn away from sin and seek salvation. We will never regret that kind of sorrow. But sorrow without repentance is the kind that results in death" (2 Corinthians 7:10). Our true sorrow will lead to joy—salvation in Jesus Christ. But without that sorrow, there will be no joy.

3. Pursue Meekness. Seeing ourselves as we really are produces two vital spiritual qualities: gentleness and lowliness (verse 5). We are no longer inflated with pride. We have an accurate and honest assessment of ourselves that, in turn, affects how we approach others. This contradicts the world's way of thinking, which advocates standing up for your rights and asserting yourself in order to get "your piece of the pie." The meekness Jesus describes here is not some sort of weakness or cowardice, but rather "power under constraint," much like a powerful stallion submitting to the control of the bit.

The more we humble ourselves and admit our weaknesses, the more we will rely on God's grace—and the happier we will be with ourselves and others.

Beware of the Sins of the Heart Read MATTHEW 5:27-30

Some people have the mistaken notion that unless you commit the act of adultery, you have not really sinned. They think it is OK to fantasize about or look at someone, so long as you don't become involved in a sinful relationship with that person. But Jesus "cuts to the chase" in this passage. He lets us know that even a lustful glance is as sinful as committing the act of adultery.

In the original Greek, one of the meanings for the word Jesus uses for "look" is intentional and repeated gazing. Jesus' remedy for someone who has a problem in this area seems rather harsh, but you really have to look at the context and the culture of the day to understand this radical but important statement.

In the Jewish culture, the right eye and the right hand were thought of as the best one had. The right eye represented one's best vision and the right hand represented one's best skills. In essence, Jesus is saying that you should be willing to give up whatever is necessary to keep you from falling into this sin. That may mean terminating a relationship, canceling a cable channel or magazine subscription, or changing how or where you spend your spare time. In other words, remove yourself from those things that can have a spiritually destructive effect on your life. Then take practical steps to fill your mind with the things of God: "Fix your thoughts on what is true and honorable and right. Think about things that are pure and lovely and admirable. Think about things that are excellent and worthy of praise" (Philippians 4:8).

CORNERSTONES

don't make any vows! If you say, 'By heaven!' it is
a sacred vow because heaven is God's throne.
35And if you say, 'By the earth!' it is a sacred vow
because the earth is his footstool. And don't swear,
'By Jerusalem!' for Jerusalem is the city of the great
King. 36Don't even swear, 'By my head!' for you
can't turn one hair white or black. 37Just say a
simple, 'Yes, I will,' or 'No, I won't.' Your word is
enough. To strengthen your promise with a vow
shows that something is wrong.*

Teaching about Revenge

38"You have heard that the law of Moses says, 'If an
eye is injured, injure the eye of the person who did
it. If a tooth gets knocked out, knock out the tooth
of the person who did it.'* 39But I say, don't resist an
evil person! If you are slapped on the right cheek,
turn the other, too. 40If you are ordered to court and
your shirt is taken from you, give your coat, too. 41If
a soldier demands that you carry his gear for a mile,*
carry it two miles. 42Give to those who ask, and
don't turn away from those who want to borrow.

Teaching about Love for Enemies

43"You have heard that the law of Moses says,
'Love your neighbor'* and hate your enemy.
44But I say, love your enemies!* Pray for those
who persecute you! 45In that way, you will be
acting as true children of your Father in
heaven. For he gives his sunlight to both the
evil and the good, and he sends rain on the
just and on the unjust, too. 46If you love only
those who love you, what good is that? Even
corrupt tax collectors do that much. 47If you
are kind only to your friends,* how are you
different from anyone else? Even pagans do
that. 48But you are to be perfect, even as your
Father in heaven is perfect.

CHAPTER 6

Teaching about Giving to the Needy

"Take care! Don't do your good deeds publicly,
to be admired, because then you will lose the
reward from your Father in heaven. 2When you
give a gift to someone in need, don't shout
about it as the hypocrites do—blowing trumpets in the synagogues and streets to call attention to their acts of charity! I assure you, they
have received all the reward they will ever get.
3But when you give to someone, don't tell your
left hand what your right hand is doing. 4Give

5:37 Or *Anything beyond this is from the evil one.* 5:38 Greek *'An eye for an eye and a tooth for a tooth.'* Exod 21:24; Lev 24:20; Deut 19:21. 5:41 Greek *milion* [4,854 feet or 1,478 meters]. 5:43 Lev 19:18. 5:44 Some manuscripts add *Bless those who curse you, do good to those who hate you.* 5:47 Greek *your brothers.*

your gifts in secret, and your Father, who knows
all secrets, will reward you.

Teaching about Prayer and Fasting

5"And now about prayer. When you pray,
don't be like the hypocrites who love to pray
publicly on street corners and in the synagogues where everyone can see them. I assure
you, that is all the reward they will ever get.
6But when you pray, go away by yourself, shut
the door behind you, and pray to your Father
secretly. Then your Father, who knows all secrets, will reward you.

7"When you pray, don't babble on and on
as people of other religions do. They think
their prayers are answered only by repeating
their words again and again. 8Don't be like
them, because your Father knows exactly what
you need even before you ask him! 9Pray like
this:

Our Father in heaven,
may your name be honored.
10 May your Kingdom come soon.
May your will be done here on earth,
just as it is in heaven.
11 Give us our food for today,*
12 and forgive us our sins,
just as we have forgiven those who have
sinned against us.
13 And don't let us yield to temptation,
but deliver us from the evil one.*

14"If you forgive those who sin against you,
your heavenly Father will forgive you. 15But if
you refuse to forgive others, your Father will not
forgive your sins.

16"And when you fast, don't make it obvious, as the hypocrites do, who try to look pale
and disheveled so people will admire them for
their fasting. I assure you, that is the only
reward they will ever get. 17But when you fast,
comb your hair and wash your face. 18Then no
one will suspect you are fasting, except your
Father, who knows what you do in secret. And
your Father, who knows all secrets, will reward
you.

Teaching about Money and Possessions

19"Don't store up treasures here on earth, where
they can be eaten by moths and get rusty, and
where thieves break in and steal. 20Store your
treasures in heaven, where they will never become moth-eaten or rusty and where they will

6:11 Or *for tomorrow.* 6:13 Or *from evil.* Some manuscripts add *For yours is the kingdom and the power and the glory forever. Amen.*

Prayer Was Modeled for Us by Christ

Read MATTHEW 6:5-15

You have probably heard what has been called "the Lord's Prayer." Jesus gave us this particular prayer to show us *how* to pray. Incidentally, just because we call this prayer "the Lord's Prayer" does not mean that Jesus prayed it for himself. He had no reason to ask for forgiveness because he never sinned. Instead, it is more accurate to call this prayer "the Disciples' Prayer," for it was given by Jesus as a response to the disciples' request, "Lord, teach us how to pray."

To better understand this prayer, we can break it down into two sets of petitions:

The first three petitions focus on the glory of God.

- "Our Father in heaven": Recognize that you are addressing a holy God who sees you as his child.
- "May your name be honored": Begin your prayers with reverence and praise to God for who he is. This will enable you to put your needs or problems in their proper perspective.
- "May your Kingdom come soon. May your will be done here on earth, just as it is in heaven": Ask God for his will to reign supreme in your life. You cannot pray "your Kingdom come" until you pray "my kingdom go."

The second three petitions focus on our personal needs.

- "Give us our food for today": Make your physical and personal needs known to God. Remember, Scripture tells us that God will provide for all of our needs (see Philippians 4:19, p. 251).
- "And forgive us our sins, just as we have forgiven those who have sinned against us": Confess your sins to God. Psalm 66:18 says, "If I had not confessed the sin in my heart, my Lord would not have listened." If you are clinging to some sin, your prayer life will come to a screeching halt.
- "And don't let us yield to temptation, but deliver us from the evil one": Recognize your inclination to fall into sin, and pray that the opportunity to sin and the desire to do so will never coincide.

Make it a point to include these important aspects in your personal prayers. By doing so, you will begin to understand how immense your God is and how small your problems are in comparison to him.

FIRST STEPS

Forgiveness Is Not Selective Read MATTHEW 5:43-48

As one Bible commentator has put it, "To return evil for good is devilish; to return good for good is human. To return good for evil is divine." Although we are not divine, we, as believers, do not have the liberty to choose whom we will forgive and not forgive. This means that we must do as Jesus has commanded and not only forgive our enemies, but love them as well.

Loving our enemies is certainly something that does not come easily—or naturally. In fact, if we wait for some feeling of love to suddenly overtake us, it simply won't happen. We must begin to pray for our enemies even before we are conscious of loving them. This is absolutely impossible to do apart from the help of the Holy Spirit. If you feel you fall short in the area of forgiveness, take heart. The Bible is full of examples of that "divine" ability to forgive, which can only come from the working of the Holy Spirit in our lives:

- God's Spirit enabled Abraham to give the best land to his traveling partner and nephew, Lot (Genesis 13:1-12).
- God's Spirit gave Joseph the ability to embrace and kiss the very brothers who had sold him into slavery (Genesis 45:1-15).
- God's Spirit kept David from taking advantage of an opportunity to kill King Saul, who was then seeking David's life (1 Samuel 24).
- God's Spirit caused Stephen (the first Christian martyr) to pray for those who were stoning him to death (see Acts 7:59-60, p. 147).

The ultimate example of forgiving one's enemies, however, comes from Jesus. He clearly modeled this principle for us when, while hanging on the cross, he prayed, "Father, forgive these people, because they don't know what they are doing" (see Luke 23:34, p. 104). If the cruel torture of crucifixion would not silence Jesus' prayer for his enemies, what pain, prejudice, or unfair treatment could justify the silencing of our prayers for our enemies? Just as God's Spirit worked in the lives of the individuals above, he will enable you to love, pray, and do good to those who hate and hurt you.

CORNERSTONES

be safe from thieves. 21Wherever your treasure is,
there your heart and thoughts will also be.
22"Your eye is a lamp for your body. A
pure eye lets sunshine into your soul. 23But
an evil eye shuts out the light and plunges
you into darkness. If the light you think you
have is really darkness, how deep that darkness will be!
24"No one can serve two masters. For you will
hate one and love the other, or be devoted to one
and despise the other. You cannot serve both
God and money.
25"So I tell you, don't worry about everyday
life—whether you have enough food, drink, and
clothes. Doesn't life consist of more than food
and clothing? 26Look at the birds. They don't
need to plant or harvest or put food in barns
because your heavenly Father feeds them. And
you are far more valuable to him than they are.
27Can all your worries add a single moment to
your life? Of course not.
28"And why worry about your clothes? Look
at the lilies and how they grow. They don't work
or make their clothing, 29yet Solomon in all his
glory was not dressed as beautifully as they are.
30And if God cares so wonderfully for flowers
that are here today and gone tomorrow, won't he
more surely care for you? You have so little faith!
31"So don't worry about having enough
food or drink or clothing. 32Why be like the
pagans who are so deeply concerned about
these things? Your heavenly Father already
knows all your needs, 33and he will give you all
you need from day to day if you live for him
and make the Kingdom of God your primary
concern.
34"So don't worry about tomorrow, for tomorrow will bring its own worries. Today's
trouble is enough for today.

CHAPTER 7

Don't Condemn Others

"Stop judging others, and you will not be
judged. 2For others will treat you as you treat
them.* Whatever measure you use in judging
others, it will be used to measure how you are
judged. 3And why worry about a speck in your
friend's eye* when you have a log in your own?
4How can you think of saying, 'Let me help you
get rid of that speck in your eye,' when you can't
see past the log in your own eye? 5Hypocrite!
First get rid of the log from your own eye; then
perhaps you will see well enough to deal with
the speck in your friend's eye.

6"Don't give what is holy to unholy people.*
Don't give pearls to swine! They will trample the
pearls, then turn and attack you.

Effective Prayer

7"Keep on asking, and you will be given what
you ask for. Keep on looking, and you will find.
Keep on knocking, and the door will be opened.
8For everyone who asks, receives. Everyone who
seeks, finds. And the door is opened to everyone
who knocks. 9You parents—if your children ask
for a loaf of bread, do you give them a stone
instead? 10Or if they ask for a fish, do you give
them a snake? Of course not! 11If you sinful
people know how to give good gifts to your
children, how much more will your heavenly
Father give good gifts to those who ask him.

The Golden Rule

12"Do for others what you would like them to
do for you. This is a summary of all that is taught
in the law and the prophets.

The Narrow Gate

13"You can enter God's Kingdom only through
the narrow gate. The highway to hell* is broad,
and its gate is wide for the many who choose the
easy way. 14But the gateway to life is small, and
the road is narrow, and only a few ever find it.

The Tree and Its Fruit

15"Beware of false prophets who come disguised as
harmless sheep, but are really wolves that will tear
you apart. 16You can detect them by the way they act,
just as you can identify a tree by its fruit. You don't
pick grapes from thornbushes, or figs from thistles.
17A healthy tree produces good fruit, and an unhealthy tree produces bad fruit. 18A good tree can't

7:2 Or *For God will treat you as you treat others;* Greek reads *For with the judgment you judge you will be judged.* 7:3 Greek *your brother's eye;* also in 7:5. 7:6 Greek *Don't give the sacred to dogs.* 7:13 Greek *The way that leads to destruction.*

How Should You View Material Wealth? Read MATTHEW 6:19-34

This passage is part of Jesus' famous Sermon on the Mount. Here Jesus deals with possibly the greatest distraction to following him wholeheartedly: wealth. This series of verses gives us at least three warnings about wealth and one prescription to overcome its enslaving effects:

1. We Must Watch How and What We Store. Verse 19 says that we should not "store up treasures." The idea here is not simply saving, but stockpiling. Jesus is not condemning saving your resources or providing for your family (see 1 Timothy 5:8, p. 272). He is condemning the accumulation of possessions to flaunt or to impress others. We need to be able to enjoy what God has given us without making those possessions our primary ambition.

2. We Must Keep Our Vision Clear. While we can enjoy what God gives us, we need to understand that the material things of this world are only temporary. Our personal possessions and investments can be devalued by inflation or deflation, destroyed by natural disasters, or stolen by thieves. That is the problem with making the accumulation of "things" your life's passion. It is so fleeting, temporary, unfulfilling, and even enslaving. When we don't have this perspective, we can become easily enslaved to consumption and accumulation. Then we are no longer serving God but money, and our vision is dark, shutting out the light of God's Word (verses 22-24).

3. We Should Not Worry about Material Things. Worry is a powerful force that can divide or distract us. You can worry about your future, your job, your health, or even about what others think about you. But Jesus tells you to stop worrying, because God will *always* meet your needs (verses 25-30). Quite simply, worry is a waste of your valuable time as his servant on earth.

4. We Must Put God First in Our Lives Our main concern should not be the acquiring of material possessions or prestige. Our primary pursuit should be seeking the reign of Jesus Christ in our lives above all else (verses 31-34). It makes a lot of sense to place your temporary needs and worries in the hands of an eternal God.

Our Walk Should Match Our Talk Read MATTHEW 7:21

In this verse, Jesus gets down to the heart of every person's belief. He states that calling him "Lord" is not enough to get into heaven. That is because anyone can say the word but not mean it. What counts is a person's changed life—a life of obedience to God's will.

Regarding the Christian life, it has been said, "It is not how high you can jump that matters, but how straight you can walk when you hit the ground again." You may be able to say all of the "right things," but if your faith does not impact the way you live, it is meaningless—even offensive. In truth, you do not have a real relationship with God.

An engraving on a cathedral wall in Germany bears these soul-searching words:

Thus speaketh Christ our Lord to us,
"You call me Master and obey me not;
You call me light and see me not;
You call me the Way and walk me not;
You call me life and live me not;
You call me wise and follow me not;
You call me fair and love me not;
You call me rich and ask me not;
You call me eternal and seek me not;
If I condemn you, blame me not."

The more we learn about what God has done for us, the more we will want to know what we can do for him. In addition, our motives will come from a pure heart, not from selfish ambition. God is looking for genuine believers whose walk matches their talk. Can you be counted as one?

CORNER STONES

produce bad fruit, and a bad tree can't produce good
fruit. 19So every tree that does not produce good
fruit is chopped down and thrown into the fire.
20Yes, the way to identify a tree or a person is by the
kind of fruit that is produced.

True Disciples

21"Not all people who sound religious are really
godly. They may refer to me as 'Lord,' but they still
won't enter the Kingdom of Heaven. The decisive
issue is whether they obey my Father in heaven.
22On judgment day many will tell me, 'Lord, Lord,
we prophesied in your name and cast out demons
in your name and performed many miracles in
your name.' 23But I will reply, 'I never knew you.
Go away; the things you did were unauthorized.*'

Building on a Solid Foundation

24"Anyone who listens to my teaching and obeys
me is wise, like a person who builds a house on
solid rock. 25Though the rain comes in torrents
and the floodwaters rise and the winds beat
against that house, it won't collapse, because it is
built on rock. 26But anyone who hears my teaching and ignores it is foolish, like a person who
builds a house on sand. 27When the rains and
floods come and the winds beat against that
house, it will fall with a mighty crash."

28After Jesus finished speaking, the crowds
were amazed at his teaching, 29for he taught as
one who had real authority—quite unlike the
teachers of religious law.

CHAPTER 8

Jesus Heals a Man with Leprosy

Large crowds followed Jesus as he came down
the mountainside. 2Suddenly, a man with leprosy approached Jesus. He knelt before him,
worshiping. "Lord," the man said, "if you
want to, you can make me well again."

3Jesus touched him. "I want to," he said. "Be

7:23 Or *unlawful.*

healed!" And instantly the leprosy disappeared. 4Then Jesus said to him, "Go right over to the priest and let him examine you. Don't talk to anyone along the way. Take along the offering required in the law of Moses for those who have been healed of leprosy, so everyone will have proof of your healing."

Faith of the Roman Officer

5When Jesus arrived in Capernaum, a Roman officer came and pleaded with him, 6"Lord, my young servant lies in bed, paralyzed and racked with pain."

7Jesus said, "I will come and heal him."

8Then the officer said, "Lord, I am not worthy to have you come into my home. Just say the word from where you are, and my servant will be healed! 9I know, because I am under the authority of my superior officers and I have authority over my soldiers. I only need to say, 'Go,' and they go, or 'Come,' and they come. And if I say to my slaves, 'Do this or that,' they do it."

10When Jesus heard this, he was amazed. Turning to the crowd, he said, "I tell you the truth, I haven't seen faith like this in all the land of Israel! 11And I tell you this, that many Gentiles will come from all over the world and sit down with Abraham, Isaac, and Jacob at the feast in the Kingdom of Heaven. 12But many Israelites—those for whom the Kingdom was prepared—will be cast into outer darkness, where there will be weeping and gnashing of teeth."

13Then Jesus said to the Roman officer, "Go on home. What you have believed has happened." And the young servant was healed that same hour.

Jesus Heals Many People

14When Jesus arrived at Peter's house, Peter's mother-in-law was in bed with a high fever. 15But when Jesus touched her hand, the fever left her. Then she got up and prepared a meal for him.

16That evening many demon-possessed people were brought to Jesus. All the spirits fled when he commanded them to leave; and he healed all the sick. 17This fulfilled the word of the Lord through Isaiah, who said, "He took our sicknesses and removed our diseases."*

The Cost of Following Jesus

18When Jesus noticed how large the crowd was growing, he instructed his disciples to cross to the other side of the lake.

19Then one of the teachers of religious law said to him, "Teacher, I will follow you no matter where you go!"

20But Jesus said, "Foxes have dens to live in, and birds have nests, but I, the Son of Man, have no home of my own, not even a place to lay my head."

21Another of his disciples said, "Lord, first let me return home and bury my father."

22But Jesus told him, "Follow me now! Let those who are spiritually dead care for their own dead."*

Jesus Calms the Storm

23Then Jesus got into the boat and started across the lake with his disciples. 24Suddenly, a terrible storm came up, with waves breaking into the boat. But Jesus was sleeping. 25The disciples went to him and woke him up, shouting, "Lord, save us! We're going to drown!"

26And Jesus answered, "Why are you afraid? You have so little faith!" Then he stood up and rebuked the wind and waves, and suddenly all was calm. 27The disciples just sat there in awe. "Who is this?" they asked themselves. "Even the wind and waves obey him!"

Jesus Heals Two Demon-Possessed Men

28When Jesus arrived on the other side of the lake in the land of the Gadarenes,* two men who were possessed by demons met him. They lived in a cemetery and were so dangerous that no one could go through that area. 29They began screaming at him, "Why are you bothering us, Son of God? You have no right to torture us before God's appointed time!" 30A large herd of pigs was feeding in the distance, 31so the demons begged, "If you cast us out, send us into that herd of pigs."

32"All right, go!" Jesus commanded them. So the demons came out of the men and entered the pigs, and the whole herd plunged down the steep hillside into the lake and drowned in the water. 33The herdsmen fled to the nearby city, telling everyone what happened to the demon-possessed men. 34The entire town came out to meet Jesus, but they begged him to go away and leave them alone.

CHAPTER 9

Jesus Heals a Paralyzed Man

Jesus climbed into a boat and went back across the lake to his own town. 2Some people brought

8:17 Isa 53:4. 8:22 Greek *Let the dead bury their own dead.* 8:28 Some manuscripts read *Gerasenes;* other manuscripts read *Gergesenes.* See Mark 5:1; Luke 8:26.

to him a paralyzed man on a mat. Seeing their faith, Jesus said to the paralyzed man, "Take heart, son! Your sins are forgiven."

3"Blasphemy! This man talks like he is God!" some of the teachers of religious law said among themselves.

4Jesus knew what they were thinking, so he asked them, "Why are you thinking such evil thoughts? 5Is it easier to say, 'Your sins are forgiven' or 'Get up and walk'? 6I will prove that I, the Son of Man, have the authority on earth to forgive sins." Then Jesus turned to the paralyzed man and said, "Stand up, take your mat, and go on home, because you are healed!"

7And the man jumped up and went home! 8Fear swept through the crowd as they saw this happen right before their eyes. They praised God for sending a man with such great authority.

Jesus Calls Matthew

9As Jesus was going down the road, he saw Matthew sitting at his tax-collection booth. "Come, be my disciple," Jesus said to him. So Matthew got up and followed him.

10That night Matthew invited Jesus and his disciples to be his dinner guests, along with his fellow tax collectors and many other notorious sinners. 11The Pharisees were indignant. "Why does your teacher eat with such scum*?" they asked his disciples.

12When he heard this, Jesus replied, "Healthy people don't need a doctor—sick people do." 13Then he added, "Now go and learn the meaning of this Scripture: 'I want you to be merciful; I don't want your sacrifices.'* For I have come to call sinners, not those who think they are already good enough."

A Discussion about Fasting

14One day the disciples of John the Baptist came to Jesus and asked him, "Why do we and the Pharisees fast, but your disciples don't fast?"

15Jesus responded, "Should the wedding guests mourn while celebrating with the groom? Someday he will be taken from them, and then they will fast. 16And who would patch an old garment with unshrunk cloth? For the patch shrinks and pulls away from the old cloth, leaving an even bigger hole than before. 17And no one puts new wine into old wineskins. The old skins would burst from the pressure, spilling the wine and ruining the skins. New wine must be stored in new wineskins. That way both the wine and the wineskins are preserved."

Jesus Heals in Response to Faith

18As Jesus was saying this, the leader of a synagogue came and knelt down before him. "My daughter has just died," he said, "but you can bring her back to life again if you just come and lay your hand upon her."

19As Jesus and the disciples were going to the official's home, 20a woman who had had a hemorrhage for twelve years came up behind him. She touched the fringe of his robe, 21for she thought, "If I can just touch his robe, I will be healed."

22Jesus turned around and said to her, "Daughter, be encouraged! Your faith has made you well." And the woman was healed at that moment.

23When Jesus arrived at the official's home, he noticed the noisy crowds and heard the funeral music. 24He said, "Go away, for the girl isn't dead; she's only asleep." But the crowd laughed at him. 25When the crowd was finally outside, Jesus went in and took the girl by the hand, and she stood up! 26The report of this miracle swept through the entire countryside.

Jesus Heals the Blind and Mute

27After Jesus left the girl's home, two blind men followed along behind him, shouting, "Son of David, have mercy on us!"

28They went right into the house where he was staying, and Jesus asked them, "Do you believe I can make you see?"

"Yes, Lord," they told him, "we do."

29Then he touched their eyes and said, "Because of your faith, it will happen." 30And suddenly they could see! Jesus sternly warned them, "Don't tell anyone about this." 31But instead, they spread his fame all over the region.

32When they left, some people brought to him a man who couldn't speak because he was possessed by a demon. 33So Jesus cast out the demon, and instantly the man could talk. The crowds marveled. "Nothing like this has ever happened in Israel!" they exclaimed.

34But the Pharisees said, "He can cast out demons because he is empowered by the prince of demons."

The Need for Workers

35Jesus traveled through all the cities and villages of that area, teaching in the synagogues

9:11 Greek *with tax collectors and sinners.* **9:13** Hos 6:6.

and announcing the Good News about the Kingdom. And wherever he went, he healed people
of every sort of disease and illness. 36He felt great
pity for the crowds that came, because their
problems were so great and they didn't know
where to go for help. They were like sheep without a shepherd. 37He said to his disciples, "The
harvest is so great, but the workers are so few.
38So pray to the Lord who is in charge of the
harvest; ask him to send out more workers for
his fields."

CHAPTER 10

Jesus Sends Out the Twelve Apostles

Jesus called his twelve disciples to him and gave
them authority to cast out evil spirits and to heal
every kind of disease and illness. 2Here are the
names of the twelve apostles:

first Simon (also called Peter),
then Andrew (Peter's brother),
James (son of Zebedee),
John (James's brother),
3 Philip,
Bartholomew,
Thomas,
Matthew (the tax collector),
James (son of Alphaeus),
Thaddaeus,
4 Simon (the Zealot*),
Judas Iscariot (who later betrayed him).

5Jesus sent the twelve disciples out with these
instructions: "Don't go to the Gentiles or the
Samaritans, 6but only to the people of Israel—
God's lost sheep. 7Go and announce to them
that the Kingdom of Heaven is near.* 8Heal the
sick, raise the dead, cure those with leprosy, and
cast out demons. Give as freely as you have
received!

9"Don't take any money with you. 10Don't
carry a traveler's bag with an extra coat and
sandals or even a walking stick. Don't hesitate to
accept hospitality, because those who work deserve to be fed.* 11Whenever you enter a city or
village, search for a worthy man and stay in his
home until you leave for the next town. 12When
you are invited into someone's home, give it
your blessing. 13If it turns out to be a worthy
home, let your blessing stand; if it is not, take
back the blessing. 14If a village doesn't welcome
you or listen to you, shake off the dust of that
place from your feet as you leave. 15I assure you,
the wicked cities of Sodom and Gomorrah will
be better off on the judgment day than that place
will be.

16"Look, I am sending you out as sheep
among wolves. Be as wary as snakes and harmless as doves. 17But beware! For you will be
handed over to the courts and beaten in the
synagogues. 18And you must stand trial before
governors and kings because you are my followers. This will be your opportunity to tell them
about me—yes, to witness to the world. 19When
you are arrested, don't worry about what to say
in your defense, because you will be given the
right words at the right time. 20For it won't be
you doing the talking—it will be the Spirit of
your Father speaking through you.

21"Brother will betray brother to death,
fathers will betray their own children, and children will rise against their parents and cause
them to be killed. 22And everyone will hate you
because of your allegiance to me. But those who
endure to the end will be saved. 23When you are
persecuted in one town, flee to the next. I assure
you that I, the Son of Man, will return before you
have reached all the towns of Israel.

24"A student is not greater than the teacher. A
servant is not greater than the master. 25The
student shares the teacher's fate. The servant
shares the master's fate. And since I, the master
of the household, have been called the prince of
demons,* how much more will it happen to
you, the members of the household! 26But don't
be afraid of those who threaten you. For the time
is coming when everything will be revealed; all
that is secret will be made public. 27What I tell
you now in the darkness, shout abroad when
daybreak comes. What I whisper in your ears,
shout from the housetops for all to hear!

28"Don't be afraid of those who want to kill
you. They can only kill your body; they cannot
touch your soul. Fear only God, who can destroy
both soul and body in hell. 29Not even a sparrow, worth only half a penny, can fall to the
ground without your Father knowing it. 30And
the very hairs on your head are all numbered.
31So don't be afraid; you are more valuable to
him than a whole flock of sparrows.

32"If anyone acknowledges me publicly here
on earth, I will openly acknowledge that person
before my Father in heaven. 33But if anyone
denies me here on earth, I will deny that person
before my Father in heaven.

34"Don't imagine that I came to bring peace
to the earth! No, I came to bring a sword. 35I

10:4 Greek *the Cananean.* **10:7** Or *has come* or *is coming soon.* **10:10** Or *the worker is worthy of support.* **10:25** Greek *Beelzeboul.*

Peace Begins When We Relinquish Control of Our Lives to God Read MATTHEW 11:28-30

In this passage, Jesus teaches us three things we must do in order to find true peace, or "rest." Yet, for some odd reason, we sometimes find these things difficult to do:

1. Come to Christ. If you have already accepted Jesus Christ as Lord and Savior in your life, you have already completed this step. If you are still searching, you might be right at the door. But know this: You will not find peace from anyone or anything else. Sure, you may have temporary peace of mind when you feel financially secure or if you think you have discovered that "perfect" relationship. But when the bottom falls out, what happens then? Only Christ can guarantee you unending peace.

2. Exchange Your Yoke for His Yoke. A yoke is a heavy wooden harness that is placed over the neck of one or more oxen in order to help pull a wagon or other piece of equipment. It enables a farmer to direct the oxen. Shifting the analogy to humans, our "heavy yoke" could be the weight of guilt, or the burden of keeping God's commands and trying to please him through our own good works. Jesus wants you to exchange that load for his lighter load—God's grace. You can rest in knowing that you do not have to work for God's favor; you need only to accept his Son.

3. Let Jesus Lead. This is undoubtedly one of the hardest parts of this promise. That is because we want to be in control. But God says that we need to give him the reins so that he can "teach" us. Are you ready and willing to leave your abilities, your future, and your problems in God's hands? Then—and only then—will you experience God's promised "rest" for your soul.

CORNER STONES

have come to set a man against his father, and a daughter against her mother, and a daughter-in-law against her mother-in-law. 36Your enemies will be right in your own household! 37If you love your father or mother more than you love me, you are not worthy of being mine; or if you love your son or daughter more than me, you are not worthy of being mine. 38If you refuse to take up your cross and follow me, you are not worthy of being mine. 39If you cling to your life, you will lose it; but if you give it up for me, you will find it.

40"Anyone who welcomes you is welcoming me, and anyone who welcomes me is welcoming the Father who sent me. 41If you welcome a prophet as one who speaks for God,* you will receive the same reward a prophet gets. And if you welcome good and godly people because of their godliness, you will be given a reward like theirs. 42And if you give even a cup of cold water to one of the least of my followers, you will surely be rewarded."

CHAPTER 11

Jesus and John the Baptist

When Jesus had finished giving these instructions to his twelve disciples, he went off teaching and preaching in towns throughout the country.

2John the Baptist, who was now in prison, heard about all the things the Messiah was doing. So he sent his disciples to ask Jesus, 3"Are you really the Messiah we've been waiting for, or should we keep looking for someone else?"

4Jesus told them, "Go back to John and tell him about what you have heard and seen—5the blind see, the lame walk, the lepers are cured, the deaf hear, the dead are raised to life, and the Good News is being preached to the poor. 6And tell him: 'God blesses those who are not offended by me.*'"

7When John's disciples had gone, Jesus began talking about him to the crowds. "Who is this man in the wilderness that you went out to see? Did you find him weak as a reed, moved by every breath of wind? 8Or were you expecting to see a

10:41 Greek *welcome a prophet in the name of a prophet.* **11:6** Or *who don't fall away because of me.*

man dressed in expensive clothes? Those who
dress like that live in palaces, not out in the
wilderness. 9Were you looking for a prophet?
Yes, and he is more than a prophet. 10John is the
man to whom the Scriptures refer when they say,

'Look, I am sending my messenger before
you,
and he will prepare your way before you.'*

11"I assure you, of all who have ever lived, none
is greater than John the Baptist. Yet even the
most insignificant person in the Kingdom of
Heaven is greater than he is! 12And from the
time John the Baptist began preaching and baptizing until now, the Kingdom of Heaven has
been forcefully advancing, and violent people
attack it.* 13For before John came, all the teachings of the Scriptures looked forward to this
present time. 14And if you are willing to accept
what I say, he is Elijah, the one the prophets said
would come.* 15Anyone who is willing to hear
should listen and understand!

16"How shall I describe this generation?
These people are like a group of children playing
a game in the public square. They complain to
their friends, 17'We played wedding songs, and
you weren't happy, so we played funeral songs,
but you weren't sad.' 18For John the Baptist
didn't drink wine and he often fasted, and you
say, 'He's demon possessed.' 19And I, the Son of
Man, feast and drink, and you say, 'He's a glut-
ton and a drunkard, and a friend of the worst
sort of sinners!' But wisdom is shown to be right
by what results from it."

Judgment for the Unbelievers

20Then Jesus began to denounce the cities where
he had done most of his miracles, because they
hadn't turned from their sins and turned to God.
21"What horrors await you, Korazin and Bethsaida! For if the miracles I did in you had been
done in wicked Tyre and Sidon, their people
would have sat in deep repentance long ago,
clothed in sackcloth and throwing ashes on their
heads to show their remorse. 22I assure you, Tyre
and Sidon will be better off on the judgment day
than you! 23And you people of Capernaum, will
you be exalted to heaven? No, you will be
brought down to the place of the dead.* For if
the miracles I did for you had been done in
Sodom, it would still be here today. 24I assure
you, Sodom will be better off on the judgment
day than you."

Jesus' Prayer of Thanksgiving

25Then Jesus prayed this prayer: "O Father, Lord
of heaven and earth, thank you for hiding the
truth from those who think themselves so wise
and clever, and for revealing it to the childlike.
26Yes, Father, it pleased you to do it this way!

27"My Father has given me authority over
everything. No one really knows the Son except
the Father, and no one really knows the Father
except the Son and those to whom the Son
chooses to reveal him."

28Then Jesus said, "Come to me, all of you
who are weary and carry heavy burdens, and I
will give you rest. 29Take my yoke upon you. Let
me teach you, because I am humble and gentle,
and you will find rest for your souls. 30For my
yoke fits perfectly, and the burden I give you is
light."

CHAPTER **12**

Controversy about the Sabbath

At about that time Jesus was walking through
some grainfields on the Sabbath. His disciples
were hungry, so they began breaking off heads of
wheat and eating the grain. 2Some Pharisees saw
them do it and protested, "Your disciples
shouldn't be doing that! It's against the law to
work by harvesting grain on the Sabbath."

3But Jesus said to them, "Haven't you ever
read in the Scriptures what King David did when
he and his companions were hungry? 4He went
into the house of God, and they ate the special
bread reserved for the priests alone. That was
breaking the law, too. 5And haven't you ever
read in the law of Moses that the priests on duty
in the Temple may work on the Sabbath? 6I tell
you, there is one here who is even greater than
the Temple! 7But you would not have condemned those who aren't guilty if you knew the
meaning of this Scripture: 'I want you to be
merciful; I don't want your sacrifices.'* 8For I,
the Son of Man, am master even of the Sabbath."

9Then he went over to the synagogue, 10where
he noticed a man with a deformed hand. The
Pharisees asked Jesus, "Is it legal to work by
healing on the Sabbath day?" (They were, of
course, hoping he would say yes, so they could
bring charges against him.)

11And he answered, "If you had one sheep,
and it fell into a well on the Sabbath, wouldn't
you get to work and pull it out? Of course you

11:10 Mal 3:1. **11:12** Or *until now, eager multitudes have been pressing into the Kingdom of Heaven.* **11:14** See Mal 4:5. **11:23** Greek *to Hades.* **12:7** Hos 6:6.

would. 12And how much more valuable is a
person than a sheep! Yes, it is right to do good
on the Sabbath." 13Then he said to the man,
"Reach out your hand." The man reached out
his hand, and it became normal, just like the
other one. 14Then the Pharisees called a meeting
and discussed plans for killing Jesus.

Jesus, God's Chosen Servant

15But Jesus knew what they were planning. He
left that area, and many people followed him.
He healed all the sick among them, 16but he
warned them not to say who he was. 17This
fulfilled the prophecy of Isaiah concerning him:

18 "Look at my Servant,
whom I have chosen.
He is my Beloved,
and I am very pleased with him.
I will put my Spirit upon him,
and he will proclaim justice to the
nations.
19 He will not fight or shout;
he will not raise his voice in public.
20 He will not crush those who are weak,
or quench the smallest hope,
until he brings full justice with his final
victory.
21 And his name will be the hope
of all the world."*

Jesus and the Prince of Demons

22Then a demon-possessed man, who was both
blind and unable to talk, was brought to Jesus.
He healed the man so that he could both speak
and see. 23The crowd was amazed. "Could it be
that Jesus is the Son of David, the Messiah?"
they wondered out loud.

24But when the Pharisees heard about the
miracle, they said, "No wonder he can cast out
demons. He gets his power from Satan,* the
prince of demons."

25Jesus knew their thoughts and replied,
"Any kingdom at war with itself is doomed. A
city or home divided against itself is doomed.
26And if Satan is casting out Satan, he is fighting
against himself. His own kingdom will not survive. 27And if I am empowered by the prince of
demons,* what about your own followers? They
cast out demons, too, so they will judge you for
what you have said. 28But if I am casting out
demons by the Spirit of God, then the Kingdom
of God has arrived among you. 29Let me illustrate this. You can't enter a strong man's house
and rob him without first tying him up. Only
then can his house be robbed!* 30Anyone who
isn't helping me opposes me, and anyone who
isn't working with me is actually working
against me.

31"Every sin or blasphemy can be forgiven—
except blasphemy against the Holy Spirit, which
can never be forgiven. 32Anyone who blasphemes against me, the Son of Man, can be
forgiven, but blasphemy against the Holy Spirit
will never be forgiven, either in this world or in
the world to come.

33"A tree is identified by its fruit. Make a tree
good, and its fruit will be good. Make a tree bad,
and its fruit will be bad. 34You brood of snakes!
How could evil men like you speak what is good
and right? For whatever is in your heart determines what you say. 35A good person produces
good words from a good heart, and an evil
person produces evil words from an evil heart.
36And I tell you this, that you must give an
account on judgment day of every idle word you
speak. 37The words you say now reflect your fate
then; either you will be justified by them or you
will be condemned."

12:18-21 Isa 42:1-4. 12:24 Greek *Beelzeboul.* 12:27 Greek *by Beelzeboul.* 12:29 Or *One cannot rob Satan's kingdom without first tying him up. Only then can his demons be cast out.*

OFF AND RUNNING

Refrain from Idle Talk Read MATTHEW 12:35-37

The verse preceding this text says, "For whatever is in your heart determines what you say." Your speech mirrors the condition of your heart. Your heart represents your innermost thoughts, desires, and emotions. If your heart is filled with bitterness, your speech will be tainted by it. If it is filled with the love of God, your words will also express that love.

If we take seriously Jesus' warning about being held accountable for our idle words, then we should not only weigh our words, but we should also examine our hearts—the source of our speech. Here is a good rule to apply before you speak: THINK.

The Sign of Jonah

38One day some teachers of religious law and Pharisees came to Jesus and said, "Teacher, we want you to show us a miraculous sign to prove that you are from God."

39But Jesus replied, "Only an evil, faithless generation would ask for a miraculous sign; but the only sign I will give them is the sign of the prophet Jonah. 40For as Jonah was in the belly of the great fish for three days and three nights, so I, the Son of Man, will be in the heart of the earth for three days and three nights. 41The people of Nineveh will rise up against this generation on judgment day and condemn it, because they repented at the preaching of Jonah. And now someone greater than Jonah is here—and you refuse to repent. 42The queen of Sheba* will also rise up against this generation on judgment day and condemn it, because she came from a distant land to hear the wisdom of Solomon. And now someone greater than Solomon is here—and you refuse to listen to him.

43"When an evil spirit leaves a person, it goes into the desert, seeking rest but finding none. 44Then it says, 'I will return to the person I came from.' So it returns and finds its former home empty, swept, and clean. 45Then the spirit finds seven other spirits more evil than itself, and they all enter the person and live there. And so that person is worse off than before. That will be the experience of this evil generation."

The True Family of Jesus

46As Jesus was speaking to the crowd, his mother and brothers were outside, wanting to talk with him. 47Someone told Jesus, "Your mother and your brothers are outside, and they want to speak to you."

48Jesus asked, "Who is my mother? Who are my brothers?" 49Then he pointed to his disciples and said, "These are my mother and brothers. 50Anyone who does the will of my Father in heaven is my brother and sister and mother!"

12:42 Greek *The queen of the south.*

CHAPTER 13

Story of the Farmer Scattering Seed

Later that same day, Jesus left the house and went down to the shore, 2where an immense crowd soon gathered. He got into a boat, where he sat and taught as the people listened on the shore. 3He told many stories such as this one:

"A farmer went out to plant some seed. 4As he scattered it across his field, some seeds fell on a footpath, and the birds came and ate them. 5Other seeds fell on shallow soil with underlying rock. The plants sprang up quickly, 6but they soon wilted beneath the hot sun and died because the roots had no nourishment in the shallow soil. 7Other seeds fell among thorns that shot up and choked out the tender blades. 8But some seeds fell on fertile soil and produced a crop that was thirty, sixty, and even a hundred times as much as had been planted. 9Anyone who is willing to hear should listen and understand!"

10His disciples came and asked him, "Why do you always tell stories when you talk to the people?"

11Then he explained to them, "You have been permitted to understand the secrets of the Kingdom of Heaven, but others have not. 12To those who are open to my teaching, more understanding will be given, and they will have an abundance of knowledge. But to those who are not listening, even what they have will be taken away from them. 13That is why I tell these stories, because people see what I do, but they don't really see. They hear what I say, but they don't really hear, and they don't understand. 14This fulfills the prophecy of Isaiah, which says:

T— Is it true?
H—Is it helpful?
I— Is it inspiring?
N—Is it necessary?
K—Is it kind?

If the content of what you want to say doesn't pass this test, you really do not need to say it. Otherwise, you will have to give an explanation when you stand before the Lord.

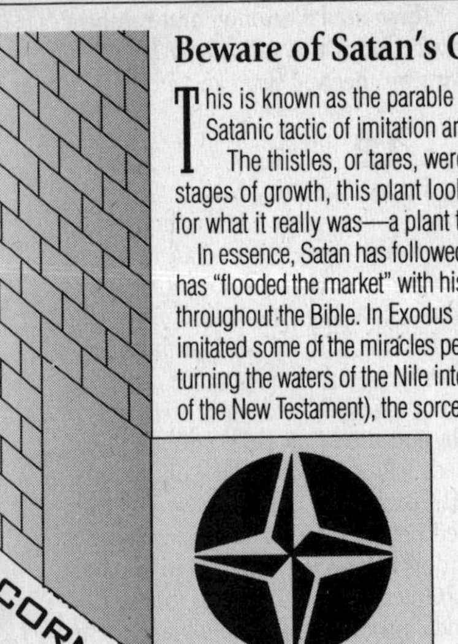

Beware of Satan's Clever Imitations Read MATTHEW 13:24-30

This is known as the parable of the wheat and the tares. Jesus gave this illustration to expose the Satanic tactic of imitation and infiltration.

The thistles, or tares, were actually a plant that came from the darnel seed. In the initial stages of growth, this plant looked exactly like wheat. But in time the wild weed would show itself for what it really was—a plant that actually uprooted the wheat.

In essence, Satan has followed the pattern of the darnel seed in his attacks against the church. He has "flooded the market" with his imitations of the real thing. There are numerous examples of this throughout the Bible. In Exodus (the second book of the Old Testament), the Egyptian magicians imitated some of the miracles performed by God through Moses—like turning a rod into a snake, turning the waters of the Nile into blood, and bringing forth a plague of frogs. In Acts (the fifth book of the New Testament), the sorcerer Simon imitated Philip (see Acts 8:9-24, pp. 147-148).

In fact, whenever the church has experienced a great revival, a false movement has grown up by its side proclaiming half-truths and deceptions.

Satan knows that half of a truth is more dangerous than a lie. For those who have modified the truth have always injured the truth more than those who have denied it openly. Therefore we must guard against falling for half-truths and gospel imitations at all costs.

'You will hear my words,
but you will not understand;
you will see what I do,
but you will not perceive its meaning.
15 For the hearts of these people are hardened,
and their ears cannot hear,
and they have closed their eyes—
so their eyes cannot see,
and their ears cannot hear,
and their hearts cannot understand,
and they cannot turn to me
and let me heal them.'*

16"But blessed are your eyes, because they see;
and your ears, because they hear. 17I assure you,
many prophets and godly people have longed to
see and hear what you have seen and heard, but
they could not.

18"Now here is the explanation of the story I
told about the farmer sowing grain: 19The seed
that fell on the hard path represents those who
hear the Good News about the Kingdom and
don't understand it. Then the evil one comes
and snatches the seed away from their hearts.
20The rocky soil represents those who hear the
message and receive it with joy. 21But like young
plants in such soil, their roots don't go very
deep. At first they get along fine, but they wilt as
soon as they have problems or are persecuted
because they believe the word. 22The thorny
ground represents those who hear and accept
the Good News, but all too quickly the message
is crowded out by the cares of this life and the
lure of wealth, so no crop is produced. 23The
good soil represents the hearts of those who
truly accept God's message and produce a huge
harvest—thirty, sixty, or even a hundred times as
much as had been planted."

Story of the Wheat and Weeds

24Here is another story Jesus told: "The Kingdom of Heaven is like a farmer who planted
good seed in his field. 25But that night as everyone slept, his enemy came and planted weeds
among the wheat. 26When the crop began to
grow and produce grain, the weeds also grew.
27The farmer's servants came and told him, 'Sir,
the field where you planted that good seed is full
of weeds!'

28" 'An enemy has done it!' the farmer exclaimed.

" 'Shall we pull out the weeds?' they asked.

29"He replied, 'No, you'll hurt the wheat if
you do. 30Let both grow together until the harvest. Then I will tell the harvesters to sort out the
weeds and burn them and to put the wheat in
the barn.' "

13:14-15 Isa 6:9-10.

Illustration of the Mustard Seed
31Here is another illustration Jesus used: "The
Kingdom of Heaven is like a mustard seed
planted in a field. 32It is the smallest of all seeds,
but it becomes the largest of garden plants and
grows into a tree where birds can come and find
shelter in its branches."

Illustration of the Yeast
33Jesus also used this illustration: "The Kingdom of
Heaven is like yeast used by a woman making bread.
Even though she used a large amount* of flour, the
yeast permeated every part of the dough."
34Jesus always used stories and illustrations
like these when speaking to the crowds. In fact,
he never spoke to them without using such parables. 35This fulfilled the prophecy that said,

"I will speak to you in parables.
I will explain mysteries hidden since the
creation of the world."*

The Wheat and Weeds Explained
36Then, leaving the crowds outside, Jesus went
into the house. His disciples said, "Please explain the story of the weeds in the field."
37"All right," he said. "I, the Son of Man, am
the farmer who plants the good seed. 38The field
is the world, and the good seed represents the
people of the Kingdom. The weeds are the
people who belong to the evil one. 39The enemy
who planted the weeds among the wheat is the
Devil. The harvest is the end of the world, and
the harvesters are the angels.
40"Just as the weeds are separated out and
burned, so it will be at the end of the world. 41I, the
Son of Man, will send my angels, and they will
remove from my Kingdom everything that causes
sin and all who do evil, 42and they will throw them
into the furnace and burn them. There will be weeping and gnashing of teeth. 43Then the godly will
shine like the sun in their Father's Kingdom. Anyone
who is willing to hear should listen and understand!

Illustration of the Hidden Treasure
44"The Kingdom of Heaven is like a treasure that
a man discovered hidden in a field. In his excitement, he hid it again and sold everything he
owned to get enough money to buy the field—
and to get the treasure, too!

Illustration of the Pearl Merchant
45"Again, the Kingdom of Heaven is like a pearl
merchant on the lookout for choice pearls.
46When he discovered a pearl of great value, he
sold everything he owned and bought it!

Illustration of the Fishing Net
47"Again, the Kingdom of Heaven is like a fishing net that is thrown into the water and gathers
fish of every kind. 48When the net is full, they
drag it up onto the shore, sit down, sort the good
fish into crates, and throw the bad ones away.
49That is the way it will be at the end of the
world. The angels will come and separate the
wicked people from the godly, 50throwing the
wicked into the fire. There will be weeping and
gnashing of teeth. 51Do you understand?"
"Yes," they said, "we do."
52Then he added, "Every teacher of religious
law who has become a disciple in the Kingdom
of Heaven is like a person who brings out of the
storehouse the new teachings as well as the old."

Jesus Rejected at Nazareth
53When Jesus had finished telling these stories,
he left that part of the country. 54He returned to
Nazareth, his hometown. When he taught there
in the synagogue, everyone was astonished and
said, "Where does he get his wisdom and his
miracles? 55He's just a carpenter's son, and we
know Mary, his mother, and his brothers—
James, Joseph, Simon, and Judas. 56All his sisters
live right here among us. What makes him so
great?" 57And they were deeply offended and
refused to believe in him.
Then Jesus told them, "A prophet is honored
everywhere except in his own hometown and
among his own family." 58And so he did only a
few miracles there because of their unbelief.

CHAPTER 14

The Death of John the Baptist
When Herod Antipas* heard about Jesus, 2he
said to his advisers, "This must be John the
Baptist come back to life again! That is why he
can do such miracles." 3For Herod had arrested
and imprisoned John as a favor to his wife Herodias (the former wife of Herod's brother
Philip). 4John kept telling Herod, "It is illegal
for you to marry her." 5Herod would have executed John, but he was afraid of a riot, because
all the people believed John was a prophet.
6But at a birthday party for Herod, Herodias's
daughter performed a dance that greatly
pleased him, 7so he promised with an oath to

13:33 Greek *3 measures.* 13:35 Ps 78:2. 14:1 Greek *Herod the tetrarch.* He was a son of King Herod and was ruler over one of the four districts in Palestine.

give her anything she wanted. 8At her mother's
urging, the girl asked, "I want the head of John
the Baptist on a tray!" 9The king was sorry, but
because of his oath and because he didn't want
to back down in front of his guests, he issued
the necessary orders. 10So John was beheaded
in the prison, 11and his head was brought on a
tray and given to the girl, who took it to her
mother. 12John's disciples came for his body
and buried it. Then they told Jesus what had
happened.

Jesus Feeds Five Thousand

13As soon as Jesus heard the news, he went off
by himself in a boat to a remote area to be alone.
But the crowds heard where he was headed and
followed by land from many villages. 14A vast
crowd was there as he stepped from the boat,
and he had compassion on them and healed
their sick.

15That evening the disciples came to him and
said, "This is a desolate place, and it is getting
late. Send the crowds away so they can go to the
villages and buy food for themselves."

16But Jesus replied, "That isn't necessary—
you feed them."

17"Impossible!" they exclaimed. "We have
only five loaves of bread and two fish!"

18"Bring them here," he said. 19Then he told
the people to sit down on the grass. And he took
the five loaves and two fish, looked up toward
heaven, and asked God's blessing on the food.
Breaking the loaves into pieces, he gave some of
the bread and fish to each disciple, and the
disciples gave them to the people. 20They all ate
as much as they wanted, and they picked up
twelve baskets of leftovers. 21About five thousand men had eaten from those five loaves, in
addition to all the women and children!

Jesus Walks on Water

22Immediately after this, Jesus made his disciples get back into the boat and cross to the other
side of the lake while he sent the people home.
23Afterward he went up into the hills by himself
to pray. Night fell while he was there alone.
24Meanwhile, the disciples were in trouble far
away from land, for a strong wind had risen, and
they were fighting heavy waves.

25About three o'clock in the morning* Jesus
came to them, walking on the water. 26When the
disciples saw him, they screamed in terror,
thinking he was a ghost. 27But Jesus spoke to
them at once. "It's all right," he said. "I am here!
Don't be afraid."

28Then Peter called to him, "Lord, if it's really
you, tell me to come to you by walking on
water."

29"All right, come," Jesus said.

So Peter went over the side of the boat and
walked on the water toward Jesus. 30But when
he looked around at the high waves, he was
terrified and began to sink. "Save me, Lord!" he
shouted.

31Instantly Jesus reached out his hand and
grabbed him. "You don't have much faith,"
Jesus said. "Why did you doubt me?" 32And
when they climbed back into the boat, the wind
stopped.

33Then the disciples worshiped him. "You
really are the Son of God!" they exclaimed.

34After they had crossed the lake, they landed
at Gennesaret. 35The news of their arrival spread
quickly throughout the whole surrounding area,
and soon people were bringing all their sick to
be healed. 36The sick begged him to let them
touch even the fringe of his robe, and all who
touched it were healed.

CHAPTER 15

Jesus Teaches about Inner Purity

Some Pharisees and teachers of religious law
now arrived from Jerusalem to interview Jesus.
2"Why do your disciples disobey our age-old
traditions?" they demanded. "They ignore our
tradition of ceremonial hand washing before
they eat."

3Jesus replied, "And why do you, by your
traditions, violate the direct commandments of
God? 4For instance, God says, 'Honor your
father and mother,' and 'Anyone who speaks
evil of father or mother must be put to death.'*
5But you say, 'You don't need to honor your
parents by caring for their needs if you give the
money to God instead.' 6And so, by your own
tradition, you nullify the direct commandment
of God. 7You hypocrites! Isaiah was prophesying about you when he said,

8 'These people honor me with their lips,
 but their hearts are far away.
9 Their worship is a farce,
 for they replace God's commands with
  their own man-made teachings.'* "

10Then Jesus called to the crowds and said,
"Listen to what I say and try to understand.

14:25 Greek *In the fourth watch of the night.* 15:4 Exod 20:12; 21:17; Lev 20:9; Deut 5:16. 15:8-9 Isa 29:13.

11You are not defiled by what you eat; you are
defiled by what you say and do.*"
12Then the disciples came to him and asked,
"Do you realize you offended the Pharisees by
what you just said?"
13Jesus replied, "Every plant not planted by
my heavenly Father will be rooted up, 14so ignore them. They are blind guides leading the
blind, and if one blind person guides another,
they will both fall into a ditch."
15Then Peter asked Jesus, "Explain what you
meant when you said people aren't defiled by
what they eat."
16"Don't you understand?" Jesus asked him.
17"Anything you eat passes through the stomach
and then goes out of the body. 18But evil words
come from an evil heart and defile the person
who says them. 19For from the heart come evil
thoughts, murder, adultery, all other sexual immorality, theft, lying, and slander. 20These are
what defile you. Eating with unwashed hands
could never defile you and make you unacceptable to God!"

The Faith of a Gentile Woman

21Jesus then left Galilee and went north to the
region of Tyre and Sidon. 22A Gentile* woman
who lived there came to him, pleading, "Have
mercy on me, O Lord, Son of David! For my
daughter has a demon in her, and it is severely
tormenting her."
23But Jesus gave her no reply—not even a
word. Then his disciples urged him to send her
away. "Tell her to leave," they said. "She is bothering us with all her begging."
24Then he said to the woman, "I was sent
only to help the people of Israel—God's lost
sheep—not the Gentiles."
25But she came and worshiped him and
pleaded again, "Lord, help me!"
26"It isn't right to take food from the children
and throw it to the dogs," he said.
27"Yes, Lord," she replied, "but even dogs are
permitted to eat crumbs that fall beneath their
master's table."
28"Woman," Jesus said to her, "your faith is
great. Your request is granted." And her daughter
was instantly healed.

Jesus Heals Many People

29Jesus returned to the Sea of Galilee and
climbed a hill and sat down. 30A vast crowd
brought him the lame, blind, crippled, mute,
and many others with physical difficulties, and
they laid them before Jesus. And he healed them
all. 31The crowd was amazed! Those who hadn't
been able to speak were talking, the crippled
were made well, the lame were walking around,
and those who had been blind could see again!
And they praised the God of Israel.

Jesus Feeds Four Thousand

32Then Jesus called his disciples to him and said,
"I feel sorry for these people. They have been
here with me for three days, and they have nothing left to eat. I don't want to send them away
hungry, or they will faint along the road."
33The disciples replied, "And where would
we get enough food out here in the wilderness
for all of them to eat?"
34Jesus asked, "How many loaves of bread do
you have?"
They replied, "Seven, and a few small fish."
35So Jesus told all the people to sit down on the
ground. 36Then he took the seven loaves and the
fish, thanked God for them, broke them into
pieces, and gave them to the disciples, who distributed the food to the crowd.
37They all ate until they were full, and when
the scraps were picked up, there were seven large
baskets of food left over! 38There were four
thousand men who were fed that day, in addition to all the women and children. 39Then Jesus
sent the people home, and he got into a boat
and crossed over to the region of Magadan.

CHAPTER 16

Leaders Demand a Miraculous Sign

One day the Pharisees and Sadducees came to
test Jesus' claims by asking him to show them a
miraculous sign from heaven.
2He replied, "You know the saying, 'Red sky
at night means fair weather tomorrow, 3red sky
in the morning means foul weather all day.' You
are good at reading the weather signs in the sky,
but you can't read the obvious signs of the
times!* 4Only an evil, faithless generation
would ask for a miraculous sign, but the only
sign I will give them is the sign of the prophet
Jonah." Then Jesus left them and went away.

Yeast of the Pharisees and Sadducees

5Later, after they crossed to the other side of the
lake, the disciples discovered they had forgotten
to bring any food. 6"Watch out!" Jesus warned

15:11 Or *what comes out of the mouth defiles a person.* 15:22 Greek *Canaanite.* 16:2-3 Several manuscripts do not include any of the words in 16:2-3 after *He replied.*

them. "Beware of the yeast of the Pharisees and Sadducees."

7They decided he was saying this because they hadn't brought any bread. 8Jesus knew what they were thinking, so he said, "You have so little faith! Why are you worried about having no food? 9Won't you ever understand? Don't you remember the five thousand I fed with five loaves, and the baskets of food that were left over? 10Don't you remember the four thousand I fed with seven loaves, with baskets of food left over? 11How could you even think I was talking about food? So again I say, 'Beware of the yeast of the Pharisees and Sadducees.'"

12Then at last they understood that he wasn't speaking about yeast or bread but about the false teaching of the Pharisees and Sadducees.

Peter's Declaration about Jesus

13When Jesus came to the region of Caesarea Philippi, he asked his disciples, "Who do people say that the Son of Man is?"

14"Well," they replied, "some say John the Baptist, some say Elijah, and others say Jeremiah or one of the other prophets."

15Then he asked them, "Who do you say I am?"

16Simon Peter answered, "You are the Messiah, the Son of the living God."

17Jesus replied, "You are blessed, Simon son of John,* because my Father in heaven has revealed this to you. You did not learn this from any human being. 18Now I say to you that you are Peter,* and upon this rock I will build my church, and all the powers of hell* will not conquer it. 19And I will give you the keys of the Kingdom of Heaven. Whatever you lock on earth will be locked in heaven, and whatever you open on earth will be opened in heaven." 20Then he sternly warned them not to tell anyone that he was the Messiah.

Jesus Predicts His Death

21From then on Jesus began to tell his disciples plainly that he had to go to Jerusalem, and he told them what would happen to him there. He would suffer at the hands of the leaders and the leading priests and the teachers of religious law. He would be killed, and he would be raised on the third day.

22But Peter took him aside and corrected him. "Heaven forbid, Lord," he said. "This will never happen to you!"

23Jesus turned to Peter and said, "Get away from me, Satan! You are a dangerous trap to me. You are seeing things merely from a human point of view, and not from God's."

24Then Jesus said to the disciples, "If any of you wants to be my follower, you must put aside your selfish ambition, shoulder your cross, and follow me. 25If you try to keep your life for yourself, you will lose it. But if you give up your life for me, you will find true life. 26And how do you benefit if you gain the whole world but lose your own soul* in the process? Is anything worth more than your soul? 27For I, the Son of Man, will come in the glory of my Father with his angels and will judge all people according to their deeds. 28And I assure you that some of you standing here right now will not die before you see me, the Son of Man, coming in my Kingdom."

16:17 Greek *Simon son of Jonah;* see John 1:42; 21:15-17. **16:18a** *Peter* means "stone" or "rock." **16:18b** Greek *and the gates of Hades.* **16:26** Or *your life.*

OFF AND RUNNING

We Must Surrender Our Dreams and Seek God's Will

Read MATTHEW 16:24-26

Jesus' words in this passage may seem extremely harsh. Yet in reality they are compassionate, because they point the way to real life. Anyone who wants this real life must become a disciple of Jesus. That means obeying Jesus' commands and adopting an attitude of self-denial. This text makes three points on what it means to adopt that attitude and follow Jesus:

1. We Must "Lose Our Life." We "find life" not in seeking it but in coming into a proper alignment with God and his plan for us. As you "lose your life," you find it again. This "life" Jesus speaks of not only includes life after death, but also "life during life." Jesus tells us that he came to "give life in all its fullness" (John 10:10). You should never be afraid to trust an unknown future to a known God. God's plan for you is good. In fact, it is better than any plan you may have for yourself.

CHAPTER 17

The Transfiguration

Six days later Jesus took Peter and the two brothers,
James and John, and led them up a high mountain.
2As the men watched, Jesus' appearance changed so
that his face shone like the sun, and his clothing
became dazzling white. 3Suddenly, Moses and Elijah appeared and began talking with Jesus. 4Peter
blurted out, "Lord, this is wonderful! If you want me
to, I'll make three shrines,* one for you, one for
Moses, and one for Elijah."

5But even as he said it, a bright cloud came
over them, and a voice from the cloud said,
"This is my beloved Son, and I am fully pleased
with him. Listen to him." 6The disciples were
terrified and fell face down on the ground.

7Jesus came over and touched them. "Get
up," he said, "don't be afraid." 8And when they
looked, they saw only Jesus with them. 9As they
descended the mountain, Jesus commanded
them, "Don't tell anyone what you have seen
until I, the Son of Man, have been raised from
the dead."

10His disciples asked, "Why do the teachers of
religious law insist that Elijah must return before
the Messiah comes*?"

11Jesus replied, "Elijah is indeed coming first to
set everything in order. 12But I tell you, he has
already come, but he wasn't recognized, and he was
badly mistreated. And soon the Son of Man will also
suffer at their hands." 13Then the disciples realized
he had been speaking of John the Baptist.

Jesus Heals a Demon-Possessed Boy

14When they arrived at the foot of the mountain,
a huge crowd was waiting for them. A man came
and knelt before Jesus and said, 15"Lord, have
mercy on my son, because he has seizures and
suffers terribly. He often falls into the fire or into
the water. 16So I brought him to your disciples,
but they couldn't heal him."

17Jesus replied, "You stubborn, faithless
people! How long must I be with you until you
believe? How long must I put up with you? Bring
the boy to me." 18Then Jesus rebuked the demon in the boy, and it left him. From that
moment the boy was well.

19Afterward the disciples asked Jesus privately, "Why couldn't we cast out that demon?"

20"You didn't have enough faith," Jesus told
them. "I assure you, even if you had faith as
small as a mustard seed you could say to this
mountain, 'Move from here to there,' and it
would move. Nothing would be impossible."*

Jesus Again Predicts His Death

22One day after they had returned to Galilee,
Jesus told them, "The Son of Man is going to be
betrayed. 23He will be killed, but three days later
he will be raised from the dead." And the disciples' hearts were filled with grief.

Payment of the Temple Tax

24On their arrival in Capernaum, the tax collectors for the Temple tax came to Peter and asked
him, "Doesn't your teacher pay the Temple tax?"

25"Of course he does," Peter replied. Then he
went into the house to talk to Jesus about it.

But before he had a chance to speak, Jesus
asked him, "What do you think, Peter*? Do
kings tax their own people or the foreigners they
have conquered?"

17:4 Or *shelters;* Greek reads *tabernacles.* 17:10 Greek *that Elijah must come first.* 17:20 Some manuscripts add verse 21, *But this kind of demon won't leave unless you have prayed and fasted.* 17:25 Greek *Simon.*

---

2. We Must Deny Ourselves. To "deny ourselves" means that we put the will and purposes of God above our own. We discover God's will for our lives as we search, study, and obey God's Word.

3. We Must Take Up Our Cross. This speaks of "dying" to our own will and selfish ambition. Don't let this passage frighten you. It is through this dying to ourselves that we find God's plan and purpose for our lives.

The Christian life is not one of morbid misery and hyper self-examination. It is a life of peace and joy as we walk in harmony with the God who made us. Paul sums it up perfectly when he writes, "I have been crucified with Christ. I myself no longer live, but Christ lives in me. So I live my life in this earthly body by trusting in the Son of God, who loved me and gave himself for me" (Galatians 2:19-20). It is only when the bulb of a tulip goes into the ground and dies that a beautiful flower can grow in its place. Be willing to entrust yourself to God's plan for your life. You won't regret it.

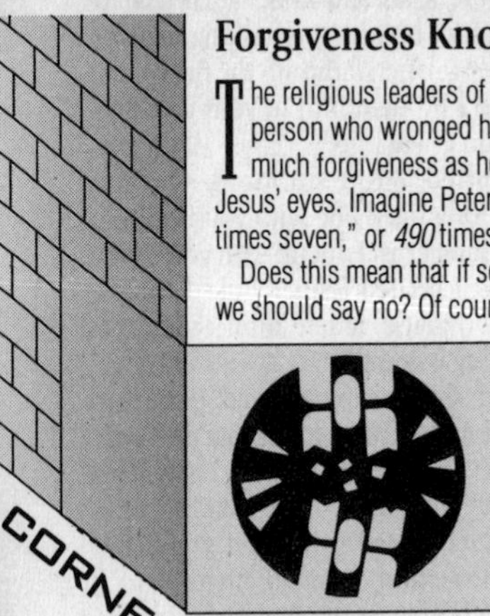

Forgiveness Knows No Limits Read MATTHEW 18:21-35

The religious leaders of that day taught that one who had been wronged was to forgive the person who wronged him two to three times—at the most! In this text, Peter, mustering up as much forgiveness as he could, wondered if forgiving someone seven times would be enough in Jesus' eyes. Imagine Peter's shock when Jesus told him that he should forgive up to "seventy times seven," or *490* times.

Does this mean that if someone needed forgiveness after the four-hundred-ninety-first time that we should say no? Of course not. Rather, Jesus was teaching that we should extend unlimited forgiveness to others. He then went on to tell this dramatic story of a man who was forgiven for so much (possibly $10 million), yet was unwilling to even work out terms with a person who owed him far less (around two thousand dollars). The point of Jesus' message is that we, as sinners, have been forgiven much. Therefore, we ought to forgive those who have hurt us, no matter how badly. For they owe us little, compared to what we had owed to God.

26"They tax the foreigners," Peter replied.
"Well, then," Jesus said, "the citizens are free!
27However, we don't want to offend them, so go
down to the lake and throw in a line. Open the
mouth of the first fish you catch, and you will find a
coin. Take the coin and pay the tax for both of us."

CHAPTER **18**

The Greatest in the Kingdom

About that time the disciples came to Jesus and
asked, "Which of us is greatest in the Kingdom
of Heaven?"
2Jesus called a small child over to him and put
the child among them. 3Then he said, "I assure
you, unless you turn from your sins and become
as little children, you will never get into the Kingdom of Heaven. 4Therefore, anyone who becomes
as humble as this little child is the greatest in the
Kingdom of Heaven. 5And anyone who welcomes
a little child like this on my behalf is welcoming
me. 6But if anyone causes one of these little ones
who trusts in me to lose faith, it would be better
for that person to be thrown into the sea with a
large millstone tied around the neck.
7"How terrible it will be for anyone who
causes others to sin. Temptation to do wrong is
inevitable, but how terrible it will be for the
person who does the tempting. 8So if your hand
or foot causes you to sin, cut it off and throw it
away. It is better to enter heaven* crippled or
lame than to be thrown into the unquenchable
fire with both of your hands and feet. 9And if
your eye causes you to sin, gouge it out and throw
it away. It is better to enter heaven half blind than
to have two eyes and be thrown into hell.
10"Beware that you don't despise a single one
of these little ones. For I tell you that in heaven
their angels are always in the presence of my
heavenly Father.*

Story of the Lost Sheep

12"If a shepherd has one hundred sheep, and one
wanders away and is lost, what will he do? Won't
he leave the ninety-nine others and go out into the
hills to search for the lost one? 13And if he finds it,
he will surely rejoice over it more than over the
ninety-nine that didn't wander away! 14In the
same way, it is not my heavenly Father's will that
even one of these little ones should perish.

Correcting a Fellow Believer

15"If another believer* sins against you, go privately and point out the fault. If the other person
listens and confesses it, you have won that person back. 16But if you are unsuccessful, take one
or two others with you and go back again, so
that everything you say may be confirmed by
two or three witnesses. 17If that person still refuses to listen, take your case to the church. If the
church decides you are right, but the other person won't accept it, treat that person as a pagan
or a corrupt tax collector. 18I tell you this: Whatever you prohibit on earth is prohibited in

18:8 Greek *enter life;* also in 18:9. 18:10 Some manuscripts add verse 11, *And I, the Son of Man, have come to save the lost.* 18:15 Greek *your brother*

heaven, and whatever you allow on earth is allowed in heaven.

19"I also tell you this: If two of you agree down here on earth concerning anything you ask, my Father in heaven will do it for you. 20For where two or three gather together because they are mine,* I am there among them."

Story of the Unforgiving Debtor

21Then Peter came to him and asked, "Lord, how often should I forgive someone* who sins against me? Seven times?"

22"No!" Jesus replied, "seventy times seven!*

23"For this reason, the Kingdom of Heaven can be compared to a king who decided to bring his accounts up to date with servants who had borrowed money from him. 24In the process, one of his debtors was brought in who owed him millions of dollars.* 25He couldn't pay, so the king ordered that he, his wife, his children, and everything he had be sold to pay the debt. 26But the man fell down before the king and begged him, 'Oh, sir, be patient with me, and I will pay it all.' 27Then the king was filled with pity for him, and he released him and forgave his debt.

28"But when the man left the king, he went to a fellow servant who owed him a few thousand dollars.* He grabbed him by the throat and demanded instant payment. 29His fellow servant fell down before him and begged for a little more time. 'Be patient and I will pay it,' he pleaded. 30But his creditor wouldn't wait. He had the man arrested and jailed until the debt could be paid in full.

31"When some of the other servants saw this, they were very upset. They went to the king and told him what had happened. 32Then the king called in the man he had forgiven and said, 'You evil servant! I forgave you that tremendous debt because you pleaded with me. 33Shouldn't you have mercy on your fellow servant, just as I had mercy on you?' 34Then the angry king sent the man to prison until he had paid every penny.

35"That's what my heavenly Father will do to you if you refuse to forgive your brothers and sisters* in your heart."

CHAPTER 19

Discussion about Divorce and Marriage

After Jesus had finished saying these things, he left Galilee and went southward to the region of Judea and into the area east of the Jordan River. 2Vast crowds followed him there, and he healed their sick.

3Some Pharisees came and tried to trap him with this question: "Should a man be allowed to divorce his wife for any reason?"

4"Haven't you read the Scriptures?" Jesus replied. "They record that from the beginning 'God made them male and female.'* 5And he said, 'This explains why a man leaves his father and mother and is joined to his wife, and the two are united into one.'* 6Since they are no longer two but one, let no one separate them, for God has joined them together."

7"Then why did Moses say a man could merely write an official letter of divorce and send her away?"* they asked.

8Jesus replied, "Moses permitted divorce as a concession to your hard-hearted wickedness, but it was not what God had originally intended. 9And I tell you this, a man who divorces his wife and marries another commits adultery—unless his wife has been unfaithful.*"

10Jesus' disciples then said to him, "Then it is better not to marry!"

11"Not everyone can accept this statement," Jesus said. "Only those whom God helps. 12Some are born as eunuchs, some have been made that way by others, and some choose not to marry for the sake of the Kingdom of Heaven. Let anyone who can, accept this statement."

Jesus Blesses the Children

13Some children were brought to Jesus so he could lay his hands on them and pray for them. The disciples told them not to bother him. 14But Jesus said, "Let the children come to me. Don't stop them! For the Kingdom of Heaven belongs to such as these." 15And he put his hands on their heads and blessed them before he left.

The Rich Young Man

16Someone came to Jesus with this question: "Teacher,* what good things must I do to have eternal life?"

17"Why ask me about what is good?" Jesus replied. "Only God is good. But to answer your question, you can receive eternal life if you keep the commandments."

18"Which ones?" the man asked.

And Jesus replied: " 'Do not murder. Do not commit adultery. Do not steal. Do not testify

18:20 Greek *gather together in my name.* 18:21 Greek *my brother.* 18:22 Or *77 times.* 18:24 Greek *10,000 talents.* 18:28 Greek *100 denarii.* A denarius was the equivalent of a full day's wage. 18:35 Greek *your brother.* 19:4 Gen 1:27; 5:2. 19:5 Gen 2:24. 19:7 Deut 24:1. 19:9 Some manuscripts add *And the man who marries a divorced woman commits adultery.* 19:16 Some manuscripts read *Good Teacher.*

falsely. 19Honor your father and mother. Love your neighbor as yourself.'* "

20"I've obeyed all these commandments," the young man replied. "What else must I do?"

21Jesus told him, "If you want to be perfect, go and sell all you have and give the money to the poor, and you will have treasure in heaven. Then come, follow me." 22But when the young man heard this, he went sadly away because he had many possessions.

23Then Jesus said to his disciples, "I tell you the truth, it is very hard for a rich person to get into the Kingdom of Heaven. 24I say it again—it is easier for a camel to go through the eye of a needle than for a rich person to enter the Kingdom of God!"

25The disciples were astounded. "Then who in the world can be saved?" they asked.

26Jesus looked at them intently and said, "Humanly speaking, it is impossible. But with God everything is possible."

27Then Peter said to him, "We've given up everything to follow you. What will we get out of it?"

28And Jesus replied, "I assure you that when I, the Son of Man, sit upon my glorious throne in the Kingdom,* you who have been my followers will also sit on twelve thrones, judging the twelve tribes of Israel. 29And everyone who has given up houses or brothers or sisters or father or mother or children or property, for my sake, will receive a hundred times as much in return and will have eternal life. 30But many who seem to be important now will be the least important then, and those who are considered least here will be the greatest then.*

CHAPTER 20

Story of the Vineyard Workers

"For the Kingdom of Heaven is like the owner of an estate who went out early one morning to hire workers for his vineyard. 2He agreed to pay the normal daily wage* and sent them out to work.

3"At nine o'clock in the morning he was passing through the marketplace and saw some people standing around doing nothing. 4So he hired them, telling them he would pay them whatever was right at the end of the day. 5At noon and again around three o'clock he did the same thing. 6At five o'clock that evening he was in town again and saw some more people standing around. He asked them, 'Why haven't you been working today?'

7"They replied, 'Because no one hired us.'

"The owner of the estate told them, 'Then go on out and join the others in my vineyard.'

8"That evening he told the foreman to call the workers in and pay them, beginning with the last workers first. 9When those hired at five o'clock were paid, each received a full day's wage. 10When those hired earlier came to get their pay, they assumed they would receive more. But they, too, were paid a day's wage. 11When they received their pay, they protested, 12'Those people worked only one hour, and yet you've paid them just as much as you paid us who worked all day in the scorching heat.'

13"He answered one of them, 'Friend, I haven't been unfair! Didn't you agree to work all day for the usual wage? 14Take it and go. I wanted to pay this last worker the same as you. 15Is it against the law for me to do what I want with my money? Should you be angry because I am kind?'

16"And so it is, that many who are first now will be last then; and those who are last now will be first then."

Jesus Again Predicts His Death

17As Jesus was on the way to Jerusalem, he took the twelve disciples aside privately and told them what was going to happen to him. 18"When we get to Jerusalem," he said, "the Son of Man will be betrayed to the leading priests and the teachers of religious law. They will sentence him to die. 19Then they will hand him over to the Romans to be mocked, whipped, and crucified. But on the third day he will be raised from the dead."

Jesus Teaches about Serving Others

20Then the mother of James and John, the sons of Zebedee, came to Jesus with her sons. She knelt respectfully to ask a favor. 21"What is your request?" he asked.

She replied, "In your Kingdom, will you let my two sons sit in places of honor next to you, one at your right and the other at your left?"

22But Jesus told them, "You don't know what you are asking! Are you able to drink from the bitter cup of sorrow I am about to drink?"

"Oh yes," they replied, "we are able!"

23"You will indeed drink from it," he told them. "But I have no right to say who will sit on

19:18-19 Exod 20:12-16; Lev 19:18; Deut 5:16-20. **19:28** Greek *in the regeneration.* **19:30** Greek *But many who are first will be last; and the last, first.* **20:2** Greek *a denarius,* the payment for a full day's labor; also in 20:9, 10, 13.

the thrones next to mine. My Father has prepared those places for the ones he has chosen."

24When the ten other disciples heard what James and John had asked, they were indignant. 25But Jesus called them together and said, "You know that in this world kings are tyrants, and officials lord it over the people beneath them. 26But among you it should be quite different. Whoever wants to be a leader among you must be your servant, 27and whoever wants to be first must become your slave. 28For even I, the Son of Man, came here not to be served but to serve others, and to give my life as a ransom for many."

Jesus Heals Two Blind Men

29As Jesus and the disciples left the city of Jericho, a huge crowd followed behind. 30Two blind men were sitting beside the road. When they heard that Jesus was coming that way, they began shouting, "Lord, Son of David, have mercy on us!" 31The crowd told them to be quiet, but they only shouted louder, "Lord, Son of David, have mercy on us!"

32Jesus stopped in the road and called, "What do you want me to do for you?"

33"Lord," they said, "we want to see!" 34Jesus felt sorry for them and touched their eyes. Instantly they could see! Then they followed him.

CHAPTER 21

The Triumphal Entry

As Jesus and the disciples approached Jerusalem, they came to the town of Bethphage on the Mount of Olives. Jesus sent two of them on ahead. 2"Go into the village over there," he said, "and you will see a donkey tied there, with its colt beside it. Untie them and bring them here. 3If anyone asks what you are doing, just say, 'The Lord needs them,' and he will immediately send them." 4This was done to fulfill the prophecy,

5 "Tell the people of Israel,*
'Look, your King is coming to you.
He is humble, riding on a donkey—
even on a donkey's colt.'"*

6The two disciples did as Jesus said. 7They brought the animals to him and threw their garments over the colt, and he sat on it.*

8Most of the crowd spread their coats on the road ahead of Jesus, and others cut branches from the trees and spread them on the road. 9He was in the center of the procession, and the crowds all around him were shouting,

"Praise God* for the Son of David!
Bless the one who comes in the name of the Lord!
Praise God in highest heaven!"*

10The entire city of Jerusalem was stirred as he entered. "Who is this?" they asked.

11And the crowds replied, "It's Jesus, the prophet from Nazareth in Galilee."

Jesus Clears the Temple

12Jesus entered the Temple and began to drive out the merchants and their customers. He knocked over the tables of the money changers and the stalls of those selling doves. 13He said, "The Scriptures declare, 'My Temple will be called a place of prayer,' but you have turned it into a den of thieves!"*

14The blind and the lame came to him, and he healed them there in the Temple. 15The leading priests and the teachers of religious law saw these wonderful miracles and heard even the little children in the Temple shouting, "Praise God for the Son of David." But they were indignant 16and asked Jesus, "Do you hear what these children are saying?"

"Yes," Jesus replied. "Haven't you ever read the Scriptures? For they say, 'You have taught children and infants to give you praise.'* " 17Then he returned to Bethany, where he stayed overnight.

Jesus Curses the Fig Tree

18In the morning, as Jesus was returning to Jerusalem, he was hungry, 19and he noticed a fig tree beside the road. He went over to see if there were any figs on it, but there were only leaves. Then he said to it, "May you never bear fruit again!" And immediately the fig tree withered up.

20The disciples were amazed when they saw this and asked, "How did the fig tree wither so quickly?"

21Then Jesus told them, "I assure you, if you have faith and don't doubt, you can do things like this and much more. You can even say to this mountain, 'May God lift you up and throw you into the sea,' and it will happen. 22If you believe, you will receive whatever you ask for in prayer."

The Authority of Jesus Challenged

23When Jesus returned to the Temple and began teaching, the leading priests and other leaders

21:5a Greek *Tell the daughter of Zion.* Isa 62:11. **21:5b** Zech 9:9. **21:7** Greek *over them, and he sat on them.* **21:9a** Greek *Hosanna,* an exclamation of praise that literally means "save now"; also in 21:9b, 15. **21:9b** Pss 118:25-26; 148:1. **21:13** Isa 56:7; Jer 7:11. **21:16** Ps 8:2.

Will We Recognize People in Heaven? Read MATTHEW 22:23-33

A number of the people in Jesus' day had some aberrant views of life after death. The particular group of religious leaders mentioned here, the Sadducees, did not believe in life beyond the grave. So when Jesus answered their question (which they had asked to test him), he immediately addressed the error of their teaching: "Your problem is that you don't know the Scriptures, and you don't know the power of God" (verse 29). In refuting the error and arrogance of the Sadducees, Jesus revealed these three insights about life in heaven:

1. We Will Not Be Married. We will not participate in the same activities we do now, such as marriage and family life. In fact, it would appear that the majority of our time will be spent worshiping God (see Revelation 19:5, p. 345).

2. We Will Recognize One Another. Jesus said that we will be as the angels. We won't become angels, but we will probably have some of the same capabilities or characteristics. We will not simply be a spirit, but we will actually have a resurrected body. While no specific passage of Scripture guarantees that we will recognize one another in heaven, many verses suggest that we will. Jesus' disciples were able to recognize his resurrected body, so he must have retained certain physical characteristics. In the parable of Lazarus and the rich man (see Luke 16:19-31, p. 93), both men retained their identity. The Bible also says that we will have increased knowledge in heaven: "Now we see things imperfectly as in a poor mirror, but then we will see everything with perfect clarity. All that I know now is partial and incomplete, but then I will know everything completely, just as God knows me now" (1 Corinthians 13:12). With that kind of knowledge, we will probably recognize more people in heaven than we do here on earth!

3. We Will Have a Distinct Personality. Notice that at the end of the text Jesus refers to the Old Testament passage that says, "I *am* the God of Abraham, the God of Isaac, and the God of Jacob." Not only does this verse give great proof for a bodily resurrection, but it also refers to these men by name. When we read that God writes our names in the Book of Life, it indicates that we are distinct personalities in heaven. God didn't write a number—he wrote your *name.*

Some day, "in the blinking of an eye," Christ will call us home to heaven, and our bodies will be transformed into "heavenly bodies that will never die" (see 1 Corinthians 15:50-53, p. 215).

To live forever in these present bodies of ours would be a curse. But to live forever in new bodies—free of sickness and pain—in the presence of God will be a blessing.

CORNER STONES

came up to him. They demanded, "By whose
authority did you drive out the merchants from
the Temple?* Who gave you such authority?"
24"I'll tell you who gave me the authority to
do these things if you answer one question,"
Jesus replied. 25"Did John's baptism come from
heaven or was it merely human?"

They talked it over among themselves. "If we
say it was from heaven, he will ask why we didn't
believe him. 26But if we say it was merely human, we'll be mobbed, because the people think
he was a prophet." 27So they finally replied, "We
don't know."

And Jesus responded, "Then I won't answer your question either.

Story of the Two Sons

28"But what do you think about this? A man
with two sons told the older boy, 'Son, go out
and work in the vineyard today.' 29The son answered, 'No, I won't go,' but later he changed his
mind and went anyway. 30Then the father told
the other son, 'You go,' and he said, 'Yes, sir, I
will.' But he didn't go. 31Which of the two was
obeying his father?"

They replied, "The first, of course."

21:23 Or *By whose authority do you do these things?*

Then Jesus explained his meaning: "I assure
you, corrupt tax collectors and prostitutes will
get into the Kingdom of God before you do.
32For John the Baptist came and showed you the
way to life, and you didn't believe him, while tax
collectors and prostitutes did. And even when
you saw this happening, you refused to turn
from your sins and believe him.

Story of the Evil Farmers

33"Now listen to this story. A certain landowner
planted a vineyard, built a wall around it, dug a
pit for pressing out the grape juice, and built a
lookout tower. Then he leased the vineyard to
tenant farmers and moved to another country.
34At the time of the grape harvest he sent his
servants to collect his share of the crop. 35But the
farmers grabbed his servants, beat one, killed
one, and stoned another. 36So the landowner
sent a larger group of his servants to collect for
him, but the results were the same.

37"Finally, the owner sent his son, thinking,
'Surely they will respect my son.'

38"But when the farmers saw his son coming,
they said to one another, 'Here comes the heir to
this estate. Come on, let's kill him and get the
estate for ourselves!' 39So they grabbed him, took
him out of the vineyard, and murdered him.

40"When the owner of the vineyard returns,"
Jesus asked, "what do you think he will do to
those farmers?"

41The religious leaders replied, "He will put
the wicked men to a horrible death and lease the
vineyard to others who will give him his share of
the crop after each harvest."

42Then Jesus asked them, "Didn't you ever
read this in the Scriptures?

'The stone rejected by the builders
has now become the cornerstone.
This is the Lord's doing,
and it is marvelous to see.'*

43What I mean is that the Kingdom of God
will be taken away from you and given to a nation
that will produce the proper fruit. 44Anyone who
stumbles over that stone will be broken to pieces,
and it will crush anyone on whom it falls.*"

45When the leading priests and Pharisees
heard Jesus, they realized he was pointing at
them—that they were the farmers in his story.
46They wanted to arrest him, but they were
afraid to try because the crowds considered Jesus
to be a prophet.

CHAPTER 22

Story of the Great Feast

Jesus told them several other stories to illustrate
the Kingdom. He said, 2"The Kingdom of
Heaven can be illustrated by the story of a king
who prepared a great wedding feast for his son.
3Many guests were invited, and when the banquet was ready, he sent his servants to notify
everyone that it was time to come. But they all
refused! 4So he sent other servants to tell them,
'The feast has been prepared, and choice meats
have been cooked. Everything is ready.
Hurry!' 5But the guests he had invited ignored
them and went about their business, one to his
farm, another to his store. 6Others seized his
messengers and treated them shamefully, even
killing some of them.

7"Then the king became furious. He sent out
his army to destroy the murderers and burn their
city. 8And he said to his servants, 'The wedding
feast is ready, and the guests I invited aren't
worthy of the honor. 9Now go out to the street
corners and invite everyone you see.'

10"So the servants brought in everyone they
could find, good and bad alike, and the banquet
hall was filled with guests. 11But when the king
came in to meet the guests, he noticed a man
who wasn't wearing the proper clothes for a
wedding. 12'Friend,' he asked, 'how is it that you
are here without wedding clothes?' And the man
had no reply. 13Then the king said to his aides,
'Bind him hand and foot and throw him out
into the outer darkness, where there is weeping
and gnashing of teeth.' 14For many are called,
but few are chosen."

Taxes for Caesar

15Then the Pharisees met together to think of a
way to trap Jesus into saying something for
which they could accuse him. 16They decided to
send some of their disciples, along with the
supporters of Herod, to ask him this question:
"Teacher, we know how honest you are. You
teach about the way of God regardless of the
consequences. You are impartial and don't play
favorites. 17Now tell us what you think about
this: Is it right to pay taxes to the Roman government or not?"

18But Jesus knew their evil motives. "You
hypocrites!" he said. "Whom are you trying to
fool with your trick questions? 19Here, show me
the Roman coin used for the tax." When they
handed him the coin,* 20he asked, "Whose picture and title are stamped on it?"

21:42 Ps 118:22-23. **21:44** This verse is omitted in some early manuscripts. **22:19** Greek *a denarius.*

21"Caesar's," they replied.
"Well, then," he said, "give to Caesar what
belongs to him. But everything that belongs to
God must be given to God." 22His reply amazed
them, and they went away.

Discussion about Resurrection

23That same day some Sadducees stepped forward—a group of Jews who say there is no
resurrection after death. They posed this question: 24"Teacher, Moses said, 'If a man dies without children, his brother should marry the
widow and have a child who will be the brother's heir.'* 25Well, there were seven brothers.
The oldest married and then died without children, so the second brother married the widow.
26This brother also died without children, and
the wife was married to the next brother, and so
on until she had been the wife of each of them.
27And then she also died. 28So tell us, whose
wife will she be in the resurrection? For she was
the wife of all seven of them!"
29Jesus replied, "Your problem is that you
don't know the Scriptures, and you don't know
the power of God. 30For when the dead rise, they
won't be married. They will be like the angels in
heaven. 31But now, as to whether there will be a
resurrection of the dead—haven't you ever read
about this in the Scriptures? Long after Abraham, Isaac, and Jacob had died, God said,* 32'I
am the God of Abraham, the God of Isaac, and
the God of Jacob.'* So he is the God of the
living, not the dead."
33When the crowds heard him, they were
impressed with his teaching.

The Most Important Commandment

34But when the Pharisees heard that he had
silenced the Sadducees with his reply, they
thought up a fresh question of their own to ask
him. 35One of them, an expert in religious law,
tried to trap him with this question: 36"Teacher,
which is the most important commandment in
the law of Moses?"
37Jesus replied, " 'You must love the Lord
your God with all your heart, all your soul, and
all your mind.'* 38This is the first and greatest
commandment. 39A second is equally important: 'Love your neighbor as yourself.'* 40All the
other commandments and all the demands of
the prophets are based on these two commandments."

Whose Son Is the Messiah?

41Then, surrounded by the Pharisees, Jesus
asked them a question: 42"What do you think
about the Messiah? Whose son is he?"
They replied, "He is the son of David."
43Jesus responded, "Then why does David,
speaking under the inspiration of the Holy
Spirit, call him Lord? For David said,

44 'The LORD said to my Lord,
Sit in honor at my right hand
until I humble your enemies beneath
your feet.'*

45Since David called him Lord, how can he be
his son at the same time?"
46No one could answer him. And after that,
no one dared to ask him any more questions.

CHAPTER 23

Jesus Warns the Religious Leaders

Then Jesus said to the crowds and to his disciples, 2"The teachers of religious law and the
Pharisees are the official interpreters of the
Scriptures. 3So practice and obey whatever
they say to you, but don't follow their example. For they don't practice what they teach.
4They crush you with impossible religious demands and never lift a finger to help ease the
burden.

22:24 Deut 25:5-6. 22:31 Greek *in the Scriptures? God said.* 22:32 Exod 3:6. 22:37 Deut 6:5. 22:39 Lev 19:18. 22:44 Ps 110:1.

OFF AND RUNNING

We Will Find Happiness in Loving God and Others

Read MATTHEW 22:37-39

In two commands Jesus summarized the entire Old Testament law. His summarization shows us what is important for us as his followers to do: to love God wholeheartedly and to love our neighbors as ourselves. When we do these two things, we will not only please God by our obedience, but we will also experience real happiness.

Ironically, real happiness is not found in fulfilling our own appetites and desires. Rather, it is found in loving God and others. This is not by chance, either. God designed it that way. He knew the value of loving

5 "Everything they do is for show. On their
arms they wear extra wide prayer boxes with
Scripture verses inside,* and they wear extra
long tassels on their robes. 6 And how they love
to sit at the head table at banquets and in the
most prominent seats in the synagogue! 7 They
enjoy the attention they get on the streets, and
they enjoy being called 'Rabbi.'* 8 Don't ever let
anyone call you 'Rabbi,' for you have only one
teacher, and all of you are on the same level as
brothers and sisters.* 9 And don't address anyone here on earth as 'Father,' for only God in
heaven is your spiritual Father. 10 And don't let
anyone call you 'Master,' for there is only one
master, the Messiah. 11 The greatest among you
must be a servant. 12 But those who exalt themselves will be humbled, and those who humble
themselves will be exalted.

13 "How terrible it will be for you teachers of
religious law and you Pharisees. Hypocrites! For
you won't let others enter the Kingdom of
Heaven, and you won't go in yourselves.* 15 Yes,
how terrible it will be for you teachers of religious
law and you Pharisees. For you cross land and sea
to make one convert, and then you turn him into
twice the son of hell as you yourselves are.

16 "Blind guides! How terrible it will be for
you! For you say that it means nothing to swear
'by God's Temple'—you can break that oath.
But then you say that it is binding to swear 'by
the gold in the Temple.' 17 Blind fools! Which is
greater, the gold, or the Temple that makes the
gold sacred? 18 And you say that to take an oath
'by the altar' can be broken, but to swear 'by the
gifts on the altar' is binding! 19 How blind! For
which is greater, the gift on the altar, or the altar
that makes the gift sacred? 20 When you swear 'by
the altar,' you are swearing by it and by everything on it. 21 And when you swear 'by the
Temple,' you are swearing by it and by God, who
lives in it. 22 And when you swear 'by heaven,'
you are swearing by the throne of God and by
God, who sits on the throne.

23 "How terrible it will be for you teachers of
religious law and you Pharisees. Hypocrites! For
you are careful to tithe even the tiniest part of
your income,* but you ignore the important
things of the law—justice, mercy, and faith. You
should tithe, yes, but you should not leave undone the more important things. 24 Blind
guides! You strain your water so you won't acci-
dentally swallow a gnat; then you swallow a
camel!

25 "How terrible it will be for you teachers of
religious law and you Pharisees. Hypocrites! You
are so careful to clean the outside of the cup and
the dish, but inside you are filthy—full of greed
and self-indulgence! 26 Blind Pharisees! First
wash the inside of the cup, and then the outside
will become clean, too.

27 "How terrible it will be for you teachers of
religious law and you Pharisees. Hypocrites! You
are like whitewashed tombs—beautiful on the
outside but filled on the inside with dead
people's bones and all sorts of impurity. 28 You
try to look like upright people outwardly, but
inside your hearts are filled with hypocrisy and
lawlessness.

29 "How terrible it will be for you teachers of
religious law and you Pharisees. Hypocrites! For
you build tombs for the prophets your ancestors
killed and decorate the graves of the godly
people your ancestors destroyed. 30 Then you
say, 'We never would have joined them in killing
the prophets.'

31 "In saying that, you are accusing yourselves
of being the descendants of those who murdered
the prophets. 32 Go ahead. Finish what they

23:5 Greek *They enlarge their phylacteries.* 23:7 *Rabbi,* from Aramaic, means "master" or "teacher." 23:8 Greek *brothers.* 23:13 Some manuscripts add verse 14, *How terrible it will be for you teachers of religious law and you Pharisees. Hypocrites! You shamelessly cheat widows out of their property, and then, to cover up the kind of people you really are, you make long prayers in public. Because of this, your punishment will be the greater.* 23:23 Greek *to tithe the mint, the dill, and the cumin.*

---

others even before he proved his love for us on the cross. He also knew how self-absorbed we are as humans and that we would fill our lives with empty pursuits in search of happiness if he didn't command us to love him and to love others.

As Paul tells us, all of our works will be tested by fire on Judgment Day (see 1 Corinthians 3:13, p. 200). Those works that were done out of selfishness will not last. But those works done out of love for God and others will. Because this love—and the works motivated by it—are everlasting, we will find real meaning in doing them. In addition, we will experience real joy in giving of ourselves to God and others out of love. It is in giving that we find purpose in life. From purpose we gain true happiness.

started. 33Snakes! Sons of vipers! How will you
escape the judgment of hell? 34I will send you
prophets and wise men and teachers of religious
law. You will kill some by crucifixion and whip
others in your synagogues, chasing them from
city to city. 35As a result, you will become guilty
of murdering all the godly people from righteous
Abel to Zechariah son of Barachiah, whom you
murdered in the Temple between the altar and
the sanctuary. 36I assure you, all the accumulated
judgment of the centuries will break upon the
heads of this very generation.

Jesus Grieves over Jerusalem

37"O Jerusalem, Jerusalem, the city that kills the
prophets and stones God's messengers! How
often I have wanted to gather your children
together as a hen protects her chicks beneath her
wings, but you wouldn't let me. 38And now
look, your house is left to you, empty and desolate. 39For I tell you this, you will never see me
again until you say, 'Bless the one who comes in
the name of the Lord!'* "

CHAPTER **24**

Jesus Foretells the Future

As Jesus was leaving the Temple grounds, his
disciples pointed out to him the various Temple
buildings. 2But he told them, "Do you see all
these buildings? I assure you, they will be so
completely demolished that not one stone will
be left on top of another!"

3Later, Jesus sat on the slopes of the Mount of
Olives. His disciples came to him privately and
asked, "When will all this take place? And will
there be any sign ahead of time to signal your
return and the end of the world*?"

4Jesus told them, "Don't let anyone mislead
you. 5For many will come in my name, saying,
'I am the Messiah.' They will lead many astray.
6And wars will break out near and far, but don't
panic. Yes, these things must come, but the end
won't follow immediately. 7The nations and
kingdoms will proclaim war against each other,
and there will be famines and earthquakes in
many parts of the world. 8But all this will be
only the beginning of the horrors to come.

9"Then you will be arrested, persecuted, and
killed. You will be hated all over the world because of your allegiance to me. 10And many will
turn away from me and betray and hate each
other. 11And many false prophets will appear
and will lead many people astray. 12Sin will be
rampant everywhere, and the love of many will
grow cold. 13But those who endure to the end
will be saved. 14And the Good News about the
Kingdom will be preached throughout the
whole world, so that all nations will hear it; and
then, finally, the end will come.

15"The time will come when you will see what
Daniel the prophet spoke about: the sacrilegious
object that causes desecration* standing in the
Holy Place"—reader, pay attention! 16"Then
those in Judea must flee to the hills. 17A person
outside the house* must not go inside to pack.
18A person in the field must not return even to
get a coat. 19How terrible it will be for pregnant
women and for mothers nursing their babies in
those days. 20And pray that your flight will not be
in winter or on the Sabbath. 21For that will be a
time of greater horror than anything the world
has ever seen or will ever see again. 22In fact,
unless that time of calamity is shortened, the
entire human race will be destroyed. But it will be
shortened for the sake of God's chosen ones.

23"Then if anyone tells you, 'Look, here is the
Messiah,' or 'There he is,' don't pay any attention. 24For false messiahs and false prophets will
rise up and perform great miraculous signs and
wonders so as to deceive, if possible, even God's
chosen ones. 25See, I have warned you.

26"So if someone tells you, 'Look, the Messiah is out in the desert,' don't bother to go and
look. Or, 'Look, he is hiding here,' don't believe
it! 27For as the lightning lights up the entire sky,
so it will be when the Son of Man comes. 28Just
as the gathering of vultures shows there is a
carcass nearby, so these signs indicate that the
end is near.*

29"Immediately after those horrible days end,

> the sun will be darkened,
>   the moon will not give light,
> the stars will fall from the sky,
>   and the powers of heaven will be
>   shaken.*

30And then at last, the sign of the coming of the
Son of Man will appear in the heavens, and there
will be deep mourning among all the nations of
the earth. And they will see the Son of Man
arrive on the clouds of heaven with power and
great glory.* 31And he will send forth his angels
with the sound of a mighty trumpet blast, and
they will gather together his chosen ones from
the farthest ends of the earth and heaven.

23:39 Ps 118:26. **24:3** Or *the age.* **24:15** Greek *the abomination of desolation.* See Dan 9:27; 11:31; 12:11. **24:17** Greek *on the roof.* **24:28** Greek *Wherever the carcass is, the vultures gather.* **24:29** See Isa 13:10; 34:4; Joel 2:10. **24:30** See Dan 7:13.

32"Now learn a lesson from the fig tree. When its buds become tender and its leaves begin to sprout, you know without being told that summer is near. 33Just so, when you see the events I've described beginning to happen, you can know his return is very near, right at the door. 34I assure you, this generation* will not pass from the scene before all these things take place. 35Heaven and earth will disappear, but my words will remain forever.

36"However, no one knows the day or the hour when these things will happen, not even the angels in heaven or the Son himself.* Only the Father knows.

37"When the Son of Man returns, it will be like it was in Noah's day. 38In those days before the Flood, the people were enjoying banquets and parties and weddings right up to the time Noah entered his boat. 39People didn't realize what was going to happen until the Flood came and swept them all away. That is the way it will be when the Son of Man comes.

40"Two men will be working together in the field; one will be taken, the other left. 41Two women will be grinding flour at the mill; one will be taken, the other left. 42So be prepared, because you don't know what day your Lord is coming.

43"Know this: A homeowner who knew exactly when a burglar was coming would stay alert and not permit the house to be broken into. 44You also must be ready all the time. For the Son of Man will come when least expected.

45"Who is a faithful, sensible servant, to whom the master can give the responsibility of managing his household and feeding his family? 46If the master returns and finds that the servant has done a good job, there will be a reward. 47I assure you, the master will put that servant in charge of all he owns. 48But if the servant is evil and thinks, 'My master won't be back for a while,' 49and begins oppressing the other servants, partying, and getting drunk—50well, the master will return unannounced and unexpected. 51He will tear the servant apart and banish him with the hypocrites. In that place there will be weeping and gnashing of teeth.

CHAPTER 25

Story of the Ten Bridesmaids

"The Kingdom of Heaven can be illustrated by the story of ten bridesmaids* who took their lamps and went to meet the bridegroom. 2Five of them were foolish, and five were wise. 3The five who were foolish took no oil for their lamps, 4but the other five were wise enough to take along extra oil. 5When the bridegroom was delayed, they all lay down and slept. 6At midnight they were roused by the shout, 'Look, the bridegroom is coming! Come out and welcome him!'

7"All the bridesmaids got up and prepared their lamps. 8Then the five foolish ones asked the others, 'Please give us some of your oil because our lamps are going out.' 9But the others replied, 'We don't have enough for all of us. Go to a shop and buy some for yourselves.'

10"But while they were gone to buy oil, the bridegroom came, and those who were ready went in with him to the marriage feast, and the door was locked. 11Later, when the other five bridesmaids returned, they stood outside, calling, 'Sir, open the door for us!' 12But he called back, 'I don't know you!'

13"So stay awake and be prepared, because you do not know the day or hour of my return.

Story of the Three Servants

14"Again, the Kingdom of Heaven can be illustrated by the story of a man going on a trip. He called together his servants and gave them money to invest for him while he was gone. 15He gave five bags of gold* to one, two bags of gold to another, and one bag of gold to the last—dividing it in proportion to their abilities—and then left on his trip. 16The servant who received the five bags of gold began immediately to invest the money and soon doubled it. 17The servant with two bags of gold also went right to work and doubled the money. 18But the servant who received the one bag of gold dug a hole in the ground and hid the master's money for safekeeping.

19"After a long time their master returned from his trip and called them to give an account of how they had used his money. 20The servant to whom he had entrusted the five bags of gold said, 'Sir, you gave me five bags of gold to invest, and I have doubled the amount.' 21The master was full of praise. 'Well done, my good and faithful servant. You have been faithful in handling this small amount, so now I will give you many more responsibilities. Let's celebrate together!'

22"Next came the servant who had received the two bags of gold, with the report, 'Sir, you

24:34 Or *this age,* or *this nation.* 24:36 Some manuscripts omit the phrase *or the Son himself.* 25:1 Or *virgins;* also in 25:7, 11.
25:15 Greek *talents;* also throughout the story. A talent is equal to 75 pounds or 34 kilograms.

gave me two bags of gold to invest, and I have doubled the amount.' 23The master said, 'Well done, my good and faithful servant. You have been faithful in handling this small amount, so now I will give you many more responsibilities. Let's celebrate together!'

24"Then the servant with the one bag of gold came and said, 'Sir, I know you are a hard man, harvesting crops you didn't plant and gathering crops you didn't cultivate. 25I was afraid I would lose your money, so I hid it in the earth and here it is.'

26"But the master replied, 'You wicked and lazy servant! You think I'm a hard man, do you, harvesting crops I didn't plant and gathering crops I didn't cultivate? 27Well, you should at least have put my money into the bank so I could have some interest. 28Take the money from this servant and give it to the one with the ten bags of gold. 29To those who use well what they are given, even more will be given, and they will have an abundance. But from those who are unfaithful,* even what little they have will be taken away. 30Now throw this useless servant into outer darkness, where there will be weeping and gnashing of teeth.'

The Final Judgment

31"But when the Son of Man comes in his glory, and all the angels with him, then he will sit upon his glorious throne. 32All the nations will be gathered in his presence, and he will separate them as a shepherd separates the sheep from the goats. 33He will place the sheep at his right hand and the goats at his left. 34Then the King will say to those on the right, 'Come, you who are blessed by my Father, inherit the Kingdom prepared for you from the foundation of the world. 35For I was hungry, and you fed me. I was thirsty, and you gave me a drink. I was a stranger, and you invited me into your home. 36I was naked, and you gave me clothing. I was sick, and you cared for me. I was in prison, and you visited me.'

37"Then these righteous ones will reply, 'Lord, when did we ever see you hungry and feed you? Or thirsty and give you something to drink? 38Or a stranger and show you hospitality? Or naked and give you clothing? 39When did we ever see you sick or in prison, and visit you?' 40And the King will tell them, 'I assure you, when you did it to one of the least of these my brothers and sisters,* you were doing it to me!'

41"Then the King will turn to those on the left and say, 'Away with you, you cursed ones, into the eternal fire prepared for the Devil and his demons! 42For I was hungry, and you didn't feed me. I was thirsty, and you didn't give me anything to drink. 43I was a stranger, and you didn't invite me into your home. I was naked, and you gave me no clothing. I was sick and in prison, and you didn't visit me.'

44"Then they will reply, 'Lord, when did we ever see you hungry or thirsty or a stranger or naked or sick or in prison, and not help you?' 45And he will answer, 'I assure you, when you refused to help the least of these my brothers and sisters, you were refusing to help me.' 46And they will go away into eternal punishment, but the righteous will go into eternal life."

CHAPTER 26

The Plot to Kill Jesus

When Jesus had finished saying these things, he said to his disciples, 2"As you know, the Passover celebration begins in two days, and I, the Son of Man, will be betrayed and crucified."

3At that same time the leading priests and other leaders were meeting at the residence of Caiaphas, the high priest, 4to discuss how to capture Jesus secretly and put him to death. 5"But not during the Passover," they agreed, "or there will be a riot."

Jesus Anointed at Bethany

6Meanwhile, Jesus was in Bethany at the home of Simon, a man who had leprosy. 7During supper, a woman came in with a beautiful jar* of expensive perfume and poured it over his head. 8The disciples were indignant when they saw this. "What a waste of money," they said. 9"She could have sold it for a fortune and given the money to the poor."

10But Jesus replied, "Why berate her for doing such a good thing to me? 11You will always have the poor among you, but I will not be here with you much longer. 12She has poured this perfume on me to prepare my body for burial. 13I assure you, wherever the Good News is preached throughout the world, this woman's deed will be talked about in her memory."

Judas Agrees to Betray Jesus

14Then Judas Iscariot, one of the twelve disciples, went to the leading priests 15and asked, "How much will you pay me to betray Jesus to you?" And they gave him thirty pieces of silver.

25:29 Or *who have nothing.* 25:40 Greek *my brothers.* 26:7 Greek *an alabaster jar.*

16From that time on, Judas began looking for
the right time and place to betray Jesus.

The Last Supper

17On the first day of the Festival of Unleavened
Bread, the disciples came to Jesus and asked,
"Where do you want us to prepare the Passover
supper?"

18"As you go into the city," he told them,
"you will see a certain man. Tell him, 'The
Teacher says, My time has come, and I will eat
the Passover meal with my disciples at your
house.'" 19So the disciples did as Jesus told
them and prepared the Passover supper there.

20When it was evening, Jesus sat down at the
table with the twelve disciples. 21While they
were eating, he said, "The truth is, one of you
will betray me."

22Greatly distressed, one by one they began
to ask him, "I'm not the one, am I, Lord?"

23He replied, "One of you who is eating with
me now* will betray me. 24For I, the Son of Man,
must die, as the Scriptures declared long ago. But
how terrible it will be for my betrayer. Far better
for him if he had never been born!"

25Judas, the one who would betray him, also
asked, "Teacher, I'm not the one, am I?"

And Jesus told him, "You have said it yourself."

26As they were eating, Jesus took a loaf of
bread and asked God's blessing on it. Then he
broke it in pieces and gave it to the disciples,
saying, "Take it and eat it, for this is my body."
27And he took a cup of wine and gave thanks to
God for it. He gave it to them and said, "Each of
you drink from it, 28for this is my blood, which
seals the covenant* between God and his
people. It is poured out to forgive the sins of
many. 29Mark my words—I will not drink wine
again until the day I drink it new with you in my
Father's Kingdom." 30Then they sang a hymn
and went out to the Mount of Olives.

Jesus Predicts Peter's Denial

31"Tonight all of you will desert me," Jesus told
them. "For the Scriptures say,

'God* will strike the Shepherd,
and the sheep of the flock will be
scattered.'*

32But after I have been raised from the dead, I
will go ahead of you to Galilee and meet you
there."

33Peter declared, "Even if everyone else deserts you, I never will."

34"Peter," Jesus replied, "the truth is, this very
night, before the rooster crows, you will deny me
three times."

35"No!" Peter insisted. "Not even if I have to
die with you! I will never deny you!" And all the
other disciples vowed the same.

Jesus Prays in Gethsemane

36Then Jesus brought them to an olive grove
called Gethsemane, and he said, "Sit here while
I go on ahead to pray." 37He took Peter and
Zebedee's two sons, James and John, and he
began to be filled with anguish and deep distress. 38He told them, "My soul is crushed with
grief to the point of death. Stay here and watch
with me."

39He went on a little farther and fell face
down on the ground, praying, "My Father! If it
is possible, let this cup of suffering be taken away
from me. Yet I want your will, not mine." 40Then
he returned to the disciples and found them
asleep. He said to Peter, "Couldn't you stay
awake and watch with me even one hour?
41Keep alert and pray. Otherwise temptation will
overpower you. For though the spirit is willing
enough, the body is weak!"

42Again he left them and prayed, "My Father!
If this cup cannot be taken away until I drink it,
your will be done." 43He returned to them again
and found them sleeping, for they just couldn't
keep their eyes open.

44So he went back to pray a third time, saying
the same things again. 45Then he came to the
disciples and said, "Still sleeping? Still resting?*
Look, the time has come. I, the Son of Man, am
betrayed into the hands of sinners. 46Up, let's be
going. See, my betrayer is here!"

Jesus Is Arrested

47And even as he said this, Judas, one of the
twelve disciples, arrived with a mob that was
armed with swords and clubs. They had been
sent out by the leading priests and other leaders
of the people. 48Judas had given them a prearranged signal: "You will know which one to
arrest when I go over and give him the kiss of
greeting." 49So Judas came straight to Jesus.
"Greetings, Teacher!" he exclaimed and gave
him the kiss.

50Jesus said, "My friend, go ahead and do
what you have come for." Then the others

26:23 Or *The one who has dipped his hand in the bowl with me.* 26:28 Some manuscripts read *the new covenant.* 26:31a Greek *I.*
26:31b Zech 13:7. 26:45 Or *Sleep on, take your rest.*

grabbed Jesus and arrested him. 51One of the men with Jesus pulled out a sword and slashed off an ear of the high priest's servant.

52"Put away your sword," Jesus told him. "Those who use the sword will be killed by the sword. 53Don't you realize that I could ask my Father for thousands* of angels to protect us, and he would send them instantly? 54But if I did, how would the Scriptures be fulfilled that describe what must happen now?"

55Then Jesus said to the crowd, "Am I some dangerous criminal, that you have come armed with swords and clubs to arrest me? Why didn't you arrest me in the Temple? I was there teaching every day. 56But this is all happening to fulfill the words of the prophets as recorded in the Scriptures." At that point, all the disciples deserted him and fled.

Jesus before the Council

57Then the people who had arrested Jesus led him to the home of Caiaphas, the high priest, where the teachers of religious law and other leaders had gathered. 58Meanwhile, Peter was following far behind and eventually came to the courtyard of the high priest's house. He went in, sat with the guards, and waited to see what was going to happen to Jesus.

59Inside, the leading priests and the entire high council* were trying to find witnesses who would lie about Jesus, so they could put him to death. 60But even though they found many who agreed to give false witness, there was no testimony they could use. Finally, two men were found 61who declared, "This man said, 'I am able to destroy the Temple of God and rebuild it in three days.'"

62Then the high priest stood up and said to Jesus, "Well, aren't you going to answer these charges? What do you have to say for yourself?" 63But Jesus remained silent. Then the high priest said to him, "I demand in the name of the living God that you tell us whether you are the Messiah, the Son of God."

64Jesus replied, "Yes, it is as you say. And in the future you will see me, the Son of Man, sitting at God's right hand in the place of power and coming back on the clouds of heaven."*

65Then the high priest tore his clothing to show his horror, shouting, "Blasphemy! Why do we need other witnesses? You have all heard his blasphemy. 66What is your verdict?"

"Guilty!" they shouted. "He must die!"

67Then they spit in Jesus' face and hit him with their fists. And some slapped him, 68saying, "Prophesy to us, you Messiah! Who hit you that time?"

Peter Denies Jesus

69Meanwhile, as Peter was sitting outside in the courtyard, a servant girl came over and said to him, "You were one of those with Jesus the Galilean."

70But Peter denied it in front of everyone. "I don't know what you are talking about," he said.

71Later, out by the gate, another servant girl noticed him and said to those standing around, "This man was with Jesus of Nazareth."

72Again Peter denied it, this time with an oath. "I don't even know the man," he said.

73A little later some other bystanders came over to him and said, "You must be one of them; we can tell by your Galilean accent."

74Peter said, "I swear by God, I don't know the man." And immediately the rooster crowed. 75Suddenly, Jesus' words flashed through Peter's mind: "Before the rooster crows, you will deny me three times." And he went away, crying bitterly.

CHAPTER 27

Judas Hangs Himself

Very early in the morning, the leading priests and other leaders met again to discuss how to persuade the Roman government to sentence Jesus to death. 2Then they bound him and took him to Pilate, the Roman governor.

3When Judas, who had betrayed him, realized that Jesus had been condemned to die, he was filled with remorse. So he took the thirty pieces of silver back to the leading priests and other leaders. 4"I have sinned," he declared, "for I have betrayed an innocent man."

"What do we care?" they retorted. "That's your problem." 5Then Judas threw the money onto the floor of the Temple and went out and hanged himself. 6The leading priests picked up the money. "We can't put it in the Temple treasury," they said, "since it's against the law to accept money paid for murder." 7After some discussion they finally decided to buy the potter's field, and they made it into a cemetery for foreigners. 8That is why the field is still called the Field of Blood. 9This fulfilled the prophecy of Jeremiah that says,

26:53 Greek *12 legions.* 26:59 Greek *the Sanhedrin.* 26:64 See Ps 110:1; Dan 7:13.

"They took* the thirty pieces of silver—
the price at which he was valued by the
people of Israel—
10 and purchased the potter's field,
as the Lord directed.*"

Jesus' Trial before Pilate

[11]Now Jesus was standing before Pilate, the Roman governor. "Are you the King of the Jews?"
the governor asked him.

Jesus replied, "Yes, it is as you say."

[12]But when the leading priests and other
leaders made their accusations against him,
Jesus remained silent. [13]"Don't you hear their
many charges against you?" Pilate demanded.
[14]But Jesus said nothing, much to the governor's
great surprise.

[15]Now it was the governor's custom to release
one prisoner to the crowd each year during the
Passover celebration—anyone they wanted.
[16]This year there was a notorious criminal in
prison, a man named Barabbas.* [17]As the
crowds gathered before Pilate's house that
morning, he asked them, "Which one do you
want me to release to you—Barabbas, or Jesus
who is called the Messiah?" [18](He knew very
well that the Jewish leaders had arrested Jesus
out of envy.)

[19]Just then, as Pilate was sitting on the judgment seat, his wife sent him this message:
"Leave that innocent man alone, because I had
a terrible nightmare about him last night."

[20]Meanwhile, the leading priests and other
leaders persuaded the crowds to ask for Barabbas to be released and for Jesus to be put to
death. [21]So when the governor asked again,
"Which of these two do you want me to release
to you?" the crowd shouted back their reply:
"Barabbas!"

[22]"But if I release Barabbas," Pilate asked
them, "what should I do with Jesus who is called
the Messiah?"

And they all shouted, "Crucify him!"

[23]"Why?" Pilate demanded. "What crime has
he committed?"

But the crowd only roared the louder, "Crucify him!"

[24]Pilate saw that he wasn't getting anywhere
and that a riot was developing. So he sent for a
bowl of water and washed his hands before the
crowd, saying, "I am innocent of the blood of
this man. The responsibility is yours!"

[25]And all the people yelled back, "We will
take responsibility for his death—we and our
children!"*

[26]So Pilate released Barabbas to them. He
ordered Jesus flogged with a lead-tipped whip,
then turned him over to the Roman soldiers to
crucify him.

The Soldiers Mock Jesus

[27]Some of the governor's soldiers took Jesus into
their headquarters and called out the entire battalion. [28]They stripped him and put a scarlet
robe on him. [29]They made a crown of long,
sharp thorns and put it on his head, and they
placed a stick in his right hand as a scepter. Then
they knelt before him in mockery, yelling, "Hail!
King of the Jews!" [30]And they spit on him and
grabbed the stick and beat him on the head with
it. [31]When they were finally tired of mocking
him, they took off the robe and put his own
clothes on him again. Then they led him away to
be crucified.

The Crucifixion

[32]As they were on the way, they came across a
man named Simon, who was from Cyrene,* and
they forced him to carry Jesus' cross. [33]Then they
went out to a place called Golgotha (which
means Skull Hill). [34]The soldiers gave him wine
mixed with bitter gall, but when he had tasted it,
he refused to drink it.

[35]After they had nailed him to the cross, the
soldiers gambled for his clothes by throwing
dice.* [36]Then they sat around and kept guard as
he hung there. [37]A signboard was fastened to the
cross above Jesus' head, announcing the charge
against him. It read: "This is Jesus, the King of
the Jews."

[38]Two criminals were crucified with him,
their crosses on either side of his. [39]And the
people passing by shouted abuse, shaking their
heads in mockery. [40]"So! You can destroy the
Temple and build it again in three days, can you?
Well then, if you are the Son of God, save yourself and come down from the cross!"

[41]The leading priests, the teachers of religious
law, and the other leaders also mocked Jesus.
[42]"He saved others," they scoffed, "but he can't
save himself! So he is the king of Israel, is he? Let
him come down from the cross, and we will
believe in him! [43]He trusted God—let God
show his approval by delivering him! For he

27:9 Or *I took.* 27:9-10 Greek *as the Lord directed me.* Zech 11:12-13; Jer 32:6-9. 27:16 Some manuscripts read *Jesus Barabbas;* also in 27:17. 27:25 Greek *"His blood be on us and on our children."* 27:32 *Cyrene* was a city in northern Africa. 27:35 Greek *by casting lots.* A few late manuscripts add *This fulfilled the word of the prophet: "They divided my clothes among themselves and cast lots for my robe."* See Ps 22:18.

said, 'I am the Son of God.' " 44And the criminals who were crucified with him also shouted the same insults at him.

The Death of Jesus

45At noon, darkness fell across the whole land until three o'clock. 46At about three o'clock, Jesus called out with a loud voice, *"Eli, Eli, lema sabachthani?"* which means, "My God, my God, why have you forsaken me?"*

47Some of the bystanders misunderstood and thought he was calling for the prophet Elijah. 48One of them ran and filled a sponge with sour wine, holding it up to him on a stick so he could drink. 49But the rest said, "Leave him alone. Let's see whether Elijah will come and save him."*

50Then Jesus shouted out again, and he gave up his spirit. 51At that moment the curtain in the Temple was torn in two, from top to bottom. The earth shook, rocks split apart, 52and tombs opened. The bodies of many godly men and women who had died were raised from the dead 53after Jesus' resurrection. They left the cemetery, went into the holy city of Jerusalem, and appeared to many people.*

54The Roman officer and the other soldiers at the crucifixion were terrified by the earthquake and all that had happened. They said, "Truly, this was the Son of God!"

55And many women who had come from Galilee with Jesus to care for him were watching from a distance. 56Among them were Mary Magdalene, Mary (the mother of James and Joseph), and Zebedee's wife, the mother of James and John.

The Burial of Jesus

57As evening approached, Joseph, a rich man from Arimathea who was one of Jesus' followers, 58went to Pilate and asked for Jesus' body. And Pilate issued an order to release it to him. 59Joseph took the body and wrapped it in a long linen cloth. 60He placed it in his own new tomb, which had been carved out of the rock. Then he rolled a great stone across the entrance as he left. 61Both Mary Magdalene and the other Mary were sitting nearby watching.

The Guard at the Tomb

62The next day—on the first day of the Passover ceremonies*—the leading priests and Pharisees went to see Pilate. 63They told him, "Sir, we remember what that deceiver once said while he was still alive: 'After three days I will be raised from the dead.' 64So we request that you seal the tomb until the third day. This will prevent his disciples from coming and stealing his body and then telling everyone he came back to life! If that happens, we'll be worse off than we were at first."

65Pilate replied, "Take guards and secure it the best you can." 66So they sealed the tomb and posted guards to protect it.

CHAPTER 28

The Resurrection

Early on Sunday morning,* as the new day was dawning, Mary Magdalene and the other Mary went out to see the tomb. 2Suddenly there was a great earthquake, because an angel of the Lord came down from heaven and rolled aside the stone and sat on it. 3His face shone like lightning, and his clothing was as white as snow. 4The guards shook with fear when they saw him, and they fell into a dead faint.

5Then the angel spoke to the women. "Don't be afraid!" he said. "I know you are looking for Jesus, who was crucified. 6He isn't here! He has been raised from the dead, just as he said would happen. Come, see where his body was lying. 7And now, go quickly and tell his disciples he has been raised from the dead, and he is going ahead of you to Galilee. You will see him there. Remember, I have told you."

8The women ran quickly from the tomb. They were very frightened but also filled with great joy, and they rushed to find the disciples to give them the angel's message. 9And as they went, Jesus met them. "Greetings!" he said. And they ran to him, held his feet, and worshiped him. 10Then Jesus said to them, "Don't be afraid! Go tell my brothers to leave for Galilee, and they will see me there."

The Report of the Guard

11As the women were on their way into the city, some of the men who had been guarding the tomb went to the leading priests and told them what had happened. 12A meeting of all the religious leaders was called, and they decided to bribe the soldiers. 13They told the soldiers, "You must say, 'Jesus' disciples came during the night

27:46 Ps 22:1. 27:49 Some manuscripts add *And another took a spear and pierced his side, and out came water and blood.* 27:51-53 Or *The earth shook, rocks split apart, tombs opened, and the bodies of many godly men and women who had died were raised from the dead. After Jesus' resurrection, they left the cemetery, went into the holy city of Jerusalem, and appeared to many people.* 27:62 Or *On the next day, which is after the Preparation.* 28:1 Greek *After the Sabbath, on the first day of the week.*

while we were sleeping, and they stole his body.'
14If the governor hears about it, we'll stand up
for you and everything will be all right." 15So the
guards accepted the bribe and said what they
were told to say. Their story spread widely
among the Jews, and they still tell it today.

The Great Commission

16Then the eleven disciples left for Galilee, going
to the mountain where Jesus had told them to
go. 17When they saw him, they worshiped
him—but some of them still doubted!

18Jesus came and told his disciples, "I have
been given complete authority in heaven and on
earth. 19Therefore, go and make disciples of all
the nations, baptizing them in the name of the
Father and the Son and the Holy Spirit. 20Teach
these new disciples to obey all the commands I
have given you. And be sure of this: I am with
you always, even to the end of the age."

Mark

CHAPTER 1

John the Baptist Prepares the Way

Here begins the Good News about Jesus the Messiah, the Son of God.*

2In the book of the prophet Isaiah, God said,

"Look, I am sending my messenger before you,
and he will prepare your way.*
3 He is a voice shouting in the wilderness:
'Prepare a pathway for the Lord's coming!
Make a straight road for him!'* "

4This messenger was John the Baptist. He lived in the wilderness and was preaching that people should be baptized to show that they had turned from their sins and turned to God to be forgiven.* 5People from Jerusalem and from all over Judea traveled out into the wilderness to see and hear John. And when they confessed their sins, he baptized them in the Jordan River. 6His clothes were woven from camel hair, and he wore a leather belt; his food was locusts and wild honey. 7He announced: "Someone is coming soon who is far greater than I am—so much greater that I am not even worthy to be his slave.* 8I baptize you with* water, but he will baptize you with the Holy Spirit!"

The Baptism of Jesus

9One day Jesus came from Nazareth in Galilee, and he was baptized by John in the Jordan River. 10And when Jesus came up out of the water, he saw the heavens split open and the Holy Spirit descending like a dove on him. 11And a voice came from heaven saying, "You are my beloved Son, and I am fully pleased with you."

The Temptation of Jesus

12Immediately the Holy Spirit compelled Jesus to go into the wilderness. 13He was there for forty days, being tempted by Satan. He was out among the wild animals, and angels took care of him.

The First Disciples

14Later on, after John was arrested by Herod Antipas, Jesus went to Galilee to preach God's Good News. 15"At last the time has come!" he announced. "The Kingdom of God is near! Turn from your sins and believe this Good News!"

16One day as Jesus was walking along the shores of the Sea of Galilee, he saw Simon* and his brother, Andrew, fishing with a net, for they were commercial fishermen. 17Jesus called out to them, "Come, be my disciples, and I will show you how to fish for people!" 18And they left their nets at once and went with him.

19A little farther up the shore Jesus saw Zebedee's sons, James and John, in a boat mending their nets. 20He called them, too, and immediately they left their father, Zebedee, in the boat with the hired men and went with him.

Jesus Casts Out an Evil Spirit

21Jesus and his companions went to the town of Capernaum, and every Sabbath day he went into the synagogue and taught the people. 22They were amazed at his teaching, for he taught as one who had real authority—quite unlike the teachers of religious law.

23A man possessed by an evil spirit was in the synagogue, 24and he began shouting, "Why are you bothering us, Jesus of Nazareth? Have you come to destroy us? I know who you are—the Holy One sent from God!"

25Jesus cut him short. "Be silent! Come out of the man." 26At that, the evil spirit screamed

1:1 Some manuscripts do not include *the Son of God.* 1:2 Mal 3:1. 1:3 Isa 40:3. 1:4 Greek *preaching a baptism of repentance for the forgiveness of sins.* 1:7 Greek *to stoop down and untie his sandals.* 1:8 Or *in.* 1:16 *Simon* is called *Peter* in 3:16 and thereafter.

and threw the man into a convulsion, but then he left him.

27Amazement gripped the audience, and they began to discuss what had happened. "What sort of new teaching is this?" they asked excitedly. "It has such authority! Even evil spirits obey his orders!" 28The news of what he had done spread quickly through that entire area of Galilee.

Jesus Heals Many People

29After Jesus and his disciples left the synagogue, they went over to Simon and Andrew's home, and James and John were with them. 30Simon's mother-in-law was sick in bed with a high fever. They told Jesus about her right away. 31He went to her bedside, and as he took her by the hand and helped her to sit up, the fever suddenly left, and she got up and prepared a meal for them.

32That evening at sunset, many sick and demon-possessed people were brought to Jesus. 33And a huge crowd of people from all over Capernaum gathered outside the door to watch. 34So Jesus healed great numbers of sick people who had many different kinds of diseases, and he ordered many demons to come out of their victims. But because they knew who he was, he refused to allow the demons to speak.

Jesus Preaches in Galilee

35The next morning Jesus awoke long before daybreak and went out alone into the wilderness to pray. 36Later Simon and the others went out to find him. 37They said, "Everyone is asking for you."

38But he replied, "We must go on to other towns as well, and I will preach to them, too, because that is why I came." 39So he traveled throughout the region of Galilee, preaching in the synagogues and expelling demons from many people.

Jesus Heals a Man with Leprosy

40A man with leprosy came and knelt in front of Jesus, begging to be healed. "If you want to, you can make me well again," he said.

41Moved with pity,* Jesus touched him. "I want to," he said. "Be healed!" 42Instantly the leprosy disappeared—the man was healed. 43Then Jesus sent him on his way and told him sternly, 44"Go right over to the priest and let him examine you. Don't talk to anyone along the way. Take along the offering required in the law of Moses for those who have been healed of leprosy, so everyone will have proof of your healing."

45But as the man went on his way, he spread the news, telling everyone what had happened to him. As a result, such crowds soon surrounded Jesus that he couldn't enter a town anywhere publicly. He had to stay out in the secluded places, and people from everywhere came to him there.

CHAPTER 2

Jesus Heals a Paralyzed Man

Several days later Jesus returned to Capernaum, and the news of his arrival spread quickly through the town. 2Soon the house where he was staying was so packed with visitors that there wasn't room for one more person, not even outside the door. And he preached the word to them. 3Four men arrived carrying a paralyzed man on a mat. 4They couldn't get to Jesus through the crowd, so they dug through the clay roof above his head. Then they lowered the sick man on his mat, right down in front of Jesus. 5Seeing their faith, Jesus said to the paralyzed man, "My son, your sins are forgiven."

6But some of the teachers of religious law who were sitting there said to themselves, 7"What? This is blasphemy! Who but God can forgive sins!"

8Jesus knew what they were discussing among themselves, so he said to them, "Why do you think this is blasphemy? 9Is it easier to say to the paralyzed man, 'Your sins are forgiven' or 'Get up, pick up your mat, and walk'? 10I will prove that I, the Son of Man, have the authority on earth to forgive sins." Then Jesus turned to the paralyzed man and said, 11"Stand up, take your mat, and go on home, because you are healed!"

12The man jumped up, took the mat, and pushed his way through the stunned onlookers. Then they all praised God. "We've never seen anything like this before!" they exclaimed.

Jesus Calls Levi (Matthew)

13Then Jesus went out to the lakeshore again and taught the crowds that gathered around him. 14As he walked along, he saw Levi son of Alphaeus sitting at his tax-collection booth. "Come, be my disciple," Jesus said to him. So Levi got up and followed him.

15That night Levi invited Jesus and his disciples to be his dinner guests, along with his fel-

1:41 Some manuscripts read *Moved with anger.*

low tax collectors and many other notorious sinners. (There were many people of this kind among the crowds that followed Jesus.) 16But when some of the teachers of religious law who were Pharisees* saw him eating with people like that, they said to his disciples, "Why does he eat with such scum*?"

17When Jesus heard this, he told them, "Healthy people don't need a doctor—sick people do. I have come to call sinners, not those who think they are already good enough."

A Discussion about Fasting

18John's disciples and the Pharisees sometimes fasted. One day some people came to Jesus and asked, "Why do John's disciples and the Pharisees fast, but your disciples don't fast?"

19Jesus replied, "Do wedding guests fast while celebrating with the groom? Of course not. They can't fast while they are with the groom. 20But someday he will be taken away from them, and then they will fast. 21And who would patch an old garment with unshrunk cloth? For the new patch shrinks and pulls away from the old cloth, leaving an even bigger hole than before. 22And no one puts new wine into old wineskins. The wine would burst the wineskins, spilling the wine and ruining the skins. New wine needs new wineskins."

A Discussion about the Sabbath

23One Sabbath day as Jesus was walking through some grainfields, his disciples began breaking off heads of wheat. 24But the Pharisees said to Jesus, "They shouldn't be doing that! It's against the law to work by harvesting grain on the Sabbath."

25But Jesus replied, "Haven't you ever read in the Scriptures what King David did when he and his companions were hungry? 26He went into the house of God (during the days when Abiathar was high priest), ate the special bread reserved for the priests alone, and then gave some to his companions. That was breaking the law, too." 27Then he said to them, "The Sabbath was made to benefit people, and not people to benefit the Sabbath. 28And I, the Son of Man, am master even of the Sabbath!"

CHAPTER 3

Jesus Heals on the Sabbath

Jesus went into the synagogue again and noticed a man with a deformed hand. 2Since it was the Sabbath, Jesus' enemies watched him closely. Would he heal the man's hand on the Sabbath? If he did, they planned to condemn him. 3Jesus said to the man, "Come and stand in front of everyone." 4Then he turned to his critics and asked, "Is it legal to do good deeds on the Sabbath, or is it a day for doing harm? Is this a day to save life or to destroy it?" But they wouldn't answer him. 5He looked around at them angrily, because he was deeply disturbed by their hard hearts. Then he said to the man, "Reach out your hand." The man reached out his hand, and it became normal again! 6At once the Pharisees went away and met with the supporters of Herod to discuss plans for killing Jesus.

Crowds Follow Jesus

7Jesus and his disciples went out to the lake, followed by a huge crowd from all over Galilee, Judea, 8Jerusalem, Idumea, from east of the Jordan River, and even from as far away as Tyre and Sidon. The news about his miracles had spread far and wide, and vast numbers of people came to see him for themselves.

9Jesus instructed his disciples to bring around a boat and to have it ready in case he was crowded off the beach. 10There had been many healings that day. As a result, many sick people were crowding around him, trying to touch him. 11And whenever those possessed by evil spirits caught sight of him, they would fall down in front of him shrieking, "You are the Son of God!" 12But Jesus strictly warned them not to say who he was.

Jesus Chooses the Twelve Apostles

13Afterward Jesus went up on a mountain and called the ones he wanted to go with him. And they came to him. 14Then he selected twelve of them to be his regular companions, calling them apostles.* He sent them out to preach, 15and he gave them authority to cast out demons. 16These are the names of the twelve he chose:

Simon (he renamed him Peter),
17 James and John (the sons of Zebedee, but Jesus nicknamed them "Sons of Thunder"*),
18 Andrew,
Philip,
Bartholomew,
Matthew,

2:16a Greek *the scribes of the Pharisees.* **2:16b** Greek *with tax collectors and sinners.* **3:14** Some manuscripts do not include *calling them apostles.* **3:17** Greek *whom he named Boanerges, which means Sons of Thunder.*

Thomas,
James (son of Alphaeus),
Thaddaeus,
Simon (the Zealot*),
19 Judas Iscariot (who later betrayed him).

Jesus and the Prince of Demons

20When Jesus returned to the house where he
was staying, the crowds began to gather again,
and soon he and his disciples couldn't even find
time to eat. 21When his family heard what was
happening, they tried to take him home with
them. "He's out of his mind," they said.

22But the teachers of religious law who had
arrived from Jerusalem said, "He's possessed by
Satan,* the prince of demons. That's where he
gets the power to cast out demons."

23Jesus called them over and said to them by
way of illustration, "How can Satan cast out
Satan? 24A kingdom at war with itself will collapse. 25A home divided against itself is
doomed. 26And if Satan is fighting against himself, how can he stand? He would never survive.
27Let me illustrate this. You can't enter a strong
man's house and rob him without first tying
him up. Only then can his house be robbed!*

28"I assure you that any sin can be forgiven,
including blasphemy; 29but anyone who blasphemes against the Holy Spirit will never be
forgiven. It is an eternal sin." 30He told them
this because they were saying he had an evil
spirit.

The True Family of Jesus

31Jesus' mother and brothers arrived at the
house where he was teaching. They stood outside and sent word for him to come out and talk
with them. 32There was a crowd around Jesus,
and someone said, "Your mother and your
brothers and sisters* are outside, asking for
you."

33Jesus replied, "Who is my mother? Who are
my brothers?" 34Then he looked at those
around him and said, "These are my mother and
brothers. 35Anyone who does God's will is my
brother and sister and mother."

CHAPTER 4

Story of the Farmer Scattering Seed

Once again Jesus began teaching by the
lakeshore. There was such a large crowd along
the shore that he got into a boat and sat down
and spoke from there. 2He began to teach the
people by telling many stories such as this one:

3"Listen! A farmer went out to plant some
seed. 4As he scattered it across his field, some
seed fell on a footpath, and the birds came and
ate it. 5Other seed fell on shallow soil with
underlying rock. The plant sprang up quickly,
6but it soon wilted beneath the hot sun and died
because the roots had no nourishment in the
shallow soil. 7Other seed fell among thorns that
shot up and choked out the tender blades so that
it produced no grain. 8Still other seed fell on
fertile soil and produced a crop that was thirty,
sixty, and even a hundred times as much as had
been planted." Then he said, 9"Anyone who is
willing to hear should listen and understand!"

10Later, when Jesus was alone with the twelve
disciples and with the others who were gathered
around, they asked him, "What do your stories
mean?"

11He replied, "You are permitted to understand the secret about the Kingdom of God. But
I am using these stories to conceal everything
about it from outsiders, 12so that the Scriptures
might be fulfilled:

'They see what I do,
  but they don't perceive its meaning.
They hear my words,
  but they don't understand.
So they will not turn from their sins
  and be forgiven.'*

13"But if you can't understand this story, how
will you understand all the others I am going to
tell? 14The farmer I talked about is the one who
brings God's message to others. 15The seed that
fell on the hard path represents those who hear
the message, but then Satan comes at once and
takes it away from them. 16The rocky soil represents those who hear the message and receive it
with joy. 17But like young plants in such soil,
their roots don't go very deep. At first they get
along fine, but they wilt as soon as they have
problems or are persecuted because they believe
the word. 18The thorny ground represents those
who hear and accept the Good News, 19but all
too quickly the message is crowded out by the
cares of this life, the lure of wealth, and the
desire for nice things, so no crop is produced.
20But the good soil represents those who hear
and accept God's message and produce a huge
harvest—thirty, sixty, or even a hundred times as
much as had been planted."

3:18 Greek *the Cananean.* 3:22 Greek *Beelzeboul.* 3:27 Or *One cannot rob Satan's kingdom without first tying him up. Only then can his demons be cast out.* 3:32 Some manuscripts do not include *and sisters.* 4:12 Isa 6:9-10.

Illustration of the Lamp
21Then Jesus asked them, "Would anyone light a
lamp and then put it under a basket or under a
bed to shut out the light? Of course not! A lamp
is placed on a stand, where its light will shine.
22"Everything that is now hidden or secret
will eventually be brought to light. 23Anyone
who is willing to hear should listen and understand! 24And be sure to pay attention to what
you hear. The more you do this, the more you
will understand—and even more, besides. 25To
those who are open to my teaching, more understanding will be given. But to those who are not
listening, even what they have will be taken
away from them."

Illustration of the Growing Seed
26Jesus also said, "Here is another illustration of
what the Kingdom of God is like: A farmer
planted seeds in a field, 27and then he went on
with his other activities. As the days went by, the
seeds sprouted and grew without the farmer's
help, 28because the earth produces crops on its
own. First a leaf blade pushes through, then the
heads of wheat are formed, and finally the grain
ripens. 29And as soon as the grain is ready, the
farmer comes and harvests it with a sickle."

Illustration of the Mustard Seed
30Jesus asked, "How can I describe the Kingdom
of God? What story should I use to illustrate it? 31It
is like a tiny mustard seed. Though this is one of
the smallest of seeds, 32it grows to become one of
the largest of plants, with long branches where
birds can come and find shelter."
33He used many such stories and illustrations
to teach the people as much as they were able to
understand. 34In fact, in his public teaching he
taught only with parables, but afterward when
he was alone with his disciples, he explained the
meaning to them.

Jesus Calms the Storm
35As evening came, Jesus said to his disciples,
"Let's cross to the other side of the lake." 36He
was already in the boat, so they started out,
leaving the crowds behind (although other
boats followed). 37But soon a fierce storm arose.
High waves began to break into the boat until it
was nearly full of water.
38Jesus was sleeping at the back of the boat
with his head on a cushion. Frantically they
woke him up, shouting, "Teacher, don't you
even care that we are going to drown?"
39When he woke up, he rebuked the wind
and said to the water, "Quiet down!" Suddenly
the wind stopped, and there was a great calm.
40And he asked them, "Why are you so afraid?
Do you still not have faith in me?"

Jesus Is with Us in Life's Storms Read MARK 4:35-41

This story illustrates how God is with us and in control of even the most desperate of circumstances. Here we find the disciples, several of whom were seasoned fishermen and sailors, frantically worried that they would perish in this storm. Although Jesus was with them in the middle of it, they thought he was oblivious to the severity of their situation. Yet Jesus wanted them to discover three important lessons.

1. Jesus Is Aware of Your Situation. Although Jesus, being human, needed physical sleep for his weary body, he was still fully aware of the disciples' predicament. The moment one of them cried to him, he responded immediately and powerfully. Though the shrieking of the storm did not wake him, the cry of one of his disciples did. Matthew 10:29 says, "Not even a sparrow . . . can fall to the ground without your Father knowing it."

2. Jesus Will Answer Your Call for Help. The Lord will do the same for you in the midst of your trials. Sometimes he just lets us reach the point of desperation so we will recognize that he is our only hope. He wants us to remember that he is "on board" with us, so to speak.

3. You Can Make It Through. Every one of us is going to face hardship. But only the child of God has the promise that God's presence is with him or her in the midst of the storm. As surely as Jesus said to the disciples, "Let's cross to the other side of the lake" (verse 35), God has promised to finish the work he has begun in your life. He will not leave you stranded in the middle of your problem. Although he didn't promise smooth sailing, he did promise safe passage. Paul reminds us that "I am sure that God, who began the good work within you, will continue his work until it is finally finished on that day when Christ Jesus comes back again" (Philippians 1:6).

41And they were filled with awe and said
among themselves, "Who is this man, that even
the wind and waves obey him?"

CHAPTER 5

Jesus Heals a Demon-Possessed Man

So they arrived at the other side of the lake, in
the land of the Gerasenes.* 2Just as Jesus was
climbing from the boat, a man possessed by an
evil spirit ran out from a cemetery to meet him.
3This man lived among the tombs and could
not be restrained, even with a chain. 4Whenever
he was put into chains and shackles—as he
often was—he snapped the chains from his
wrists and smashed the shackles. No one was
strong enough to control him. 5All day long and
throughout the night, he would wander among
the tombs and in the hills, screaming and hitting
himself with stones.

6When Jesus was still some distance away, the
man saw him. He ran to meet Jesus and fell
down before him. 7He gave a terrible scream,
shrieking, "Why are you bothering me, Jesus,
Son of the Most High God? For God's sake, don't
torture me!" 8For Jesus had already said to the
spirit, "Come out of the man, you evil spirit."

9Then Jesus asked, "What is your name?"

And the spirit replied, "Legion, because there
are many of us here inside this man." 10Then the
spirits begged him again and again not to send
them to some distant place. 11There happened
to be a large herd of pigs feeding on the hillside
nearby. 12"Send us into those pigs," the evil
spirits begged. 13Jesus gave them permission. So
the evil spirits came out of the man and entered
the pigs, and the entire herd of two thousand
pigs plunged down the steep hillside into the
lake, where they drowned.

14The herdsmen fled to the nearby city and
the surrounding countryside, spreading the
news as they ran. Everyone rushed out to see for
themselves. 15A crowd soon gathered around
Jesus, but they were frightened when they saw
the man who had been demon possessed, for he
was sitting there fully clothed and perfectly sane.
16Those who had seen what happened to the
man and to the pigs told everyone about it,
17and the crowd began pleading with Jesus to go
away and leave them alone.

18When Jesus got back into the boat, the man
who had been demon possessed begged to go,
too. 19But Jesus said, "No, go home to your
friends, and tell them what wonderful things the
Lord has done for you and how merciful he has
been." 20So the man started off to visit the Ten
Towns* of that region and began to tell everyone
about the great things Jesus had done for him;
and everyone was amazed at what he told them.

Jesus Heals in Response to Faith

21When Jesus went back across to the other side
of the lake, a large crowd gathered around him
on the shore. 22A leader of the local synagogue,
whose name was Jairus, came and fell down
before him, 23pleading with him to heal his
little daughter. "She is about to die," he said in
desperation. "Please come and place your hands
on her; heal her so she can live."

24Jesus went with him, and the crowd
thronged behind. 25And there was a woman in
the crowd who had had a hemorrhage for twelve
years. 26She had suffered a great deal from many
doctors through the years and had spent everything she had to pay them, but she had gotten
no better. In fact, she was worse. 27She had heard
about Jesus, so she came up behind him
through the crowd and touched the fringe of his
robe. 28For she thought to herself, "If I can just
touch his clothing, I will be healed." 29Immedi-
ately the bleeding stopped, and she could feel
that she had been healed!

30Jesus realized at once that healing power
had gone out from him, so he turned around in
the crowd and asked, "Who touched my
clothes?"

31His disciples said to him, "All this crowd is
pressing around you. How can you ask, 'Who
touched me?' "

32But he kept on looking around to see who
had done it. 33Then the frightened woman,
trembling at the realization of what had happened to her, came and fell at his feet and told
him what she had done. 34And he said to her,
"Daughter, your faith has made you well. Go in
peace. You have been healed."

35While he was still speaking to her, messengers arrived from Jairus's home with the message, "Your daughter is dead. There's no use
troubling the Teacher now."

36But Jesus ignored their comments and said
to Jairus, "Don't be afraid. Just trust me." 37Then
Jesus stopped the crowd and wouldn't let anyone go with him except Peter and James and
John. 38When they came to the home of the
synagogue leader, Jesus saw the commotion and
the weeping and wailing. 39He went inside and

5:1 Some manuscripts read *Gadarenes;* others read *Gergesenes.* See Matt 8:28; Luke 8:26. 5:20 Greek *Decapolis.*

spoke to the people. "Why all this weeping and commotion?" he asked. "The child isn't dead; she is only asleep."

40The crowd laughed at him, but he told them all to go outside. Then he took the girl's father and mother and his three disciples into the room where the girl was lying. 41Holding her hand, he said to her, "Get up, little girl!"* 42And the girl, who was twelve years old, immediately stood up and walked around! Her parents were absolutely overwhelmed. 43Jesus commanded them not to tell anyone what had happened, and he told them to give her something to eat.

CHAPTER 6

Jesus Rejected at Nazareth

Jesus left that part of the country and returned with his disciples to Nazareth, his hometown. 2The next Sabbath he began teaching in the synagogue, and many who heard him were astonished. They asked, "Where did he get all his wisdom and the power to perform such miracles? 3He's just the carpenter, the son of Mary and brother of James, Joseph,* Judas, and Simon. And his sisters live right here among us." They were deeply offended and refused to believe in him.

4Then Jesus told them, "A prophet is honored everywhere except in his own hometown and among his relatives and his own family." 5And because of their unbelief, he couldn't do any mighty miracles among them except to place his hands on a few sick people and heal them. 6And he was amazed at their unbelief.

Jesus Sends Out the Twelve Apostles

Then Jesus went out from village to village, teaching. 7And he called his twelve disciples together and sent them out two by two, with authority to cast out evil spirits. 8He told them to take nothing with them except a walking stick—no food, no traveler's bag, no money. 9He told them to wear sandals but not to take even an extra coat. 10"When you enter each village, be a guest in only one home," he said. 11"And if a village won't welcome you or listen to you, shake off its dust from your feet as you leave. It is a sign that you have abandoned that village to its fate."

12So the disciples went out, telling all they met to turn from their sins. 13And they cast out many demons and healed many sick people, anointing them with olive oil.

The Death of John the Baptist

14Herod Antipas, the king, soon heard about Jesus, because people everywhere were talking about him. Some were saying,* "This must be John the Baptist come back to life again. That is why he can do such miracles." 15Others thought Jesus was the ancient prophet Elijah. Still others thought he was a prophet like the other great prophets of the past. 16When Herod heard about Jesus, he said, "John, the man I beheaded, has come back from the dead." 17For Herod had sent soldiers to arrest and imprison John as a favor to Herodias. She had been his brother Philip's wife, but Herod had married her. 18John kept telling Herod, "It is illegal for you to marry your brother's wife." 19Herodias was enraged and wanted John killed in revenge, but without Herod's approval she was powerless. 20And Herod respected John, knowing that he was a good and holy man, so he kept him under his protection. Herod was disturbed whenever he talked with John, but even so, he liked to listen to him.

21Herodias's chance finally came. It was Herod's birthday, and he gave a party for his palace aides, army officers, and the leading citizens of Galilee. 22Then his daughter, also named Herodias,* came in and performed a dance that greatly pleased them all. "Ask me for anything you like," the king said to the girl, "and I will give it to you." 23Then he promised, "I will give you whatever you ask, up to half of my kingdom!"

24She went out and asked her mother, "What should I ask for?"

Her mother told her, "Ask for John the Baptist's head!"

25So the girl hurried back to the king and told him, "I want the head of John the Baptist, right now, on a tray!"

26Then the king was very sorry, but he was embarrassed to break his oath in front of his guests. 27So he sent an executioner to the prison to cut off John's head and bring it to him. The soldier beheaded John in the prison, 28brought his head on a tray, and gave it to the girl, who took it to her mother. 29When John's disciples heard what had happened, they came for his body and buried it in a tomb.

5:41 Greek text uses Aramaic *"Talitha cumi"* and then translates it as "Get up, little girl." **6:3** Greek *Joses;* see Matt 13:55. **6:14** Some manuscripts read *He was saying.* **6:22** Some manuscripts read *the daughter of Herodias herself.*

Jesus Feeds Five Thousand

30The apostles returned to Jesus from their ministry tour and told him all they had done and what they had taught. 31Then Jesus said, "Let's get away from the crowds for a while and rest." There were so many people coming and going that Jesus and his apostles didn't even have time to eat. 32They left by boat for a quieter spot. 33But many people saw them leaving, and people from many towns ran ahead along the shore and met them as they landed. 34A vast crowd was there as he stepped from the boat, and he had compassion on them because they were like sheep without a shepherd. So he taught them many things.

35Late in the afternoon his disciples came to him and said, "This is a desolate place, and it is getting late. 36Send the crowds away so they can go to the nearby farms and villages and buy themselves some food."

37But Jesus said, "You feed them."

"With what?" they asked. "It would take a small fortune* to buy food for all this crowd!"

38"How much food do you have?" he asked. "Go and find out."

They came back and reported, "We have five loaves of bread and two fish." 39Then Jesus told the crowd to sit down in groups on the green grass. 40So they sat in groups of fifty or a hundred.

41Jesus took the five loaves and two fish, looked up toward heaven, and asked God's blessing on the food. Breaking the loaves into pieces, he kept giving the bread and fish to the disciples to give to the people. 42They all ate as much as they wanted, 43and they picked up twelve baskets of leftover bread and fish. 44Five thousand men had eaten from those five loaves!

Jesus Walks on Water

45Immediately after this, Jesus made his disciples get back into the boat and head out across the lake to Bethsaida, while he sent the people home. 46Afterward he went up into the hills by himself to pray.

47During the night, the disciples were in their boat out in the middle of the lake, and Jesus was alone on land. 48He saw that they were in serious trouble, rowing hard and struggling against the wind and waves. About three o'clock in the morning* he came to them, walking on the water. He started to go past them, 49but when they saw him walking on the water, they screamed in terror, thinking he was a ghost. 50They were all terrified when they saw him. But Jesus spoke to them at once. "It's all right," he said. "I am here! Don't be afraid." 51Then he climbed into the boat, and the wind stopped. They were astonished at what they saw. 52They still didn't understand the significance of the miracle of the multiplied loaves, for their hearts were hard and they did not believe.

53When they arrived at Gennesaret on the other side of the lake, they anchored the boat 54and climbed out. The people standing there recognized him at once, 55and they ran throughout the whole area and began carrying sick people to him on mats. 56Wherever he went—in villages and cities and out on the farms—they laid the sick in the market plazas and streets. The sick begged him to let them at least touch the fringe of his robe, and all who touched it were healed.

CHAPTER 7

Jesus Teaches about Inner Purity

One day some Pharisees and teachers of religious law arrived from Jerusalem to confront Jesus. 2They noticed that some of Jesus' disciples failed to follow the usual Jewish ritual of hand washing before eating. 3(The Jews, especially the Pharisees, do not eat until they have poured water over their cupped hands,* as required by their ancient traditions. 4Similarly, they eat nothing bought from the market unless they have immersed their hands in water. This is but one of many traditions they have clung to—such as their ceremony of washing cups, pitchers, and kettles.*) 5So the Pharisees and teachers of religious law asked him, "Why don't your disciples follow our age-old customs? For they eat without first performing the hand-washing ceremony."

6Jesus replied, "You hypocrites! Isaiah was prophesying about you when he said,

7 'These people honor me with their lips,
but their hearts are far away.
Their worship is a farce,
for they replace God's commands with
their own man-made teachings.'*

8For you ignore God's specific laws and substitute your own traditions."

9Then he said, "You reject God's laws in order

6:37 Greek *200 denarii.* A denarius was the equivalent of a full day's wage. 6:48 Greek *About the fourth watch of the night.* 7:3 Greek *washed with the fist.* 7:4 Some Greek manuscripts add *and dining couches.* 7:7 Isa 29:13.

to hold on to your own traditions. 10For instance, Moses gave you this law from God: 'Honor your father and mother,' and 'Anyone who speaks evil of father or mother must be put to death.'* 11But you say it is all right for people to say to their parents, 'Sorry, I can't help you. For I have vowed to give to God what I could have given to you.'* 12You let them disregard their needy parents. 13As such, you break the law of God in order to protect your own tradition. And this is only one example. There are many, many others."

14Then Jesus called to the crowd to come and hear. "All of you listen," he said, "and try to understand. 15You are not defiled by what you eat; you are defiled by what you say and do!*"

17Then Jesus went into a house to get away from the crowds, and his disciples asked him what he meant by the statement he had made. 18"Don't you understand either?" he asked. "Can't you see that what you eat won't defile you? 19Food doesn't come in contact with your heart, but only passes through the stomach and then comes out again." (By saying this, he showed that every kind of food is acceptable.)

20And then he added, "It is the thought-life that defiles you. 21For from within, out of a person's heart, come evil thoughts, sexual immorality, theft, murder, 22adultery, greed, wickedness, deceit, eagerness for lustful pleasure, envy, slander, pride, and foolishness. 23All these vile things come from within; they are what defile you and make you unacceptable to God."

The Faith of a Gentile Woman

24Then Jesus left Galilee and went north to the region of Tyre.* He tried to keep it secret that he was there, but he couldn't. As usual, the news of his arrival spread fast. 25Right away a woman came to him whose little girl was possessed by an evil spirit. She had heard about Jesus, and now she came and fell at his feet. 26She begged him to release her child from the demon's control.

Since she was a Gentile, born in Syrian Phoenicia, 27Jesus told her, "First I should help my own family, the Jews.* It isn't right to take food from the children and throw it to the dogs."

28She replied, "That's true, Lord, but even the dogs under the table are given some crumbs from the children's plates."

29"Good answer!" he said. "And because you have answered so well, I have healed your daughter." 30And when she arrived home, her little girl was lying quietly in bed, and the demon was gone.

Jesus Heals a Deaf and Mute Man

31Jesus left Tyre and went to Sidon, then back to the Sea of Galilee and the region of the Ten Towns.* 32A deaf man with a speech impediment was brought to him, and the people begged Jesus to lay his hands on the man to heal him. 33Jesus led him to a private place away from the crowd. He put his fingers into the man's ears. Then, spitting onto his own fingers, he touched the man's tongue with the spittle. 34And looking up to heaven, he sighed and commanded, "Be opened!"* 35Instantly the man could hear perfectly and speak plainly!

36Jesus told the crowd not to tell anyone, but the more he told them not to, the more they spread the news, 37for they were completely amazed. Again and again they said, "Everything he does is wonderful. He even heals those who are deaf and mute."

CHAPTER 8

Jesus Feeds Four Thousand

About this time another great crowd had gathered, and the people ran out of food again. Jesus called his disciples and told them, 2"I feel sorry for these people. They have been here with me for three days, and they have nothing left to eat. 3And if I send them home without feeding them, they will faint along the road. For some of them have come a long distance."

4"How are we supposed to find enough food for them here in the wilderness?" his disciples asked.

5"How many loaves of bread do you have?" he asked.

"Seven," they replied. 6So Jesus told all the people to sit down on the ground. Then he took the seven loaves, thanked God for them, broke them into pieces, and gave them to his disciples, who distributed the bread to the crowd. 7A few small fish were found, too, so Jesus also blessed these and told the disciples to pass them out.

8They ate until they were full, and when the scraps were picked up, there were seven large baskets of food left over! 9There were about four thousand people in the crowd that day, and he

7:10 Exod 20:12; 21:17; Lev 20:9; Deut 5:16. 7:11 Greek *'What I could have given to you is Corban' (that is, a gift).* 7:15 Some manuscripts add verse 16, *Anyone who is willing to hear should listen and understand.* 7:24 Some Greek manuscripts add *and Sidon.* 7:27 Greek *Let the children eat first.* 7:31 Greek *Decapolis.* 7:34 Greek text uses Aramaic *"Ephphatha"* and then translates it as "Be opened."

sent them home after they had eaten. 10Immedi-
ately after this, he got into a boat with his disciples and crossed over to the region of
Dalmanutha.

Pharisees Demand a Miraculous Sign

11When the Pharisees heard that Jesus had arrived, they came to argue with him. Testing him
to see if he was from God, they demanded,
"Give us a miraculous sign from heaven to prove
yourself."

12When he heard this, he sighed deeply and
said, "Why do you people keep demanding a
miraculous sign? I assure you, I will not give this
generation any such sign." 13So he got back into
the boat and left them, and he crossed to the
other side of the lake.

Yeast of the Pharisees and Herod

14But the disciples discovered they had forgotten to bring any food, so there was only one loaf
of bread with them in the boat. 15As they were
crossing the lake, Jesus warned them, "Beware of
the yeast of the Pharisees and of Herod."

16They decided he was saying this because
they hadn't brought any bread. 17Jesus knew
what they were thinking, so he said, "Why are
you so worried about having no food? Won't
you ever learn or understand? Are your hearts
too hard to take it in? 18'You have eyes—can't
you see? You have ears—can't you hear?'* Don't
you remember anything at all? 19What about the
five thousand men I fed with five loaves of
bread? How many baskets of leftovers did you
pick up afterward?"

"Twelve," they said.

20"And when I fed the four thousand with
seven loaves, how many large baskets of leftovers did you pick up?"

"Seven," they said.

21"Don't you understand even yet?" he asked
them.

Jesus Heals a Blind Man

22When they arrived at Bethsaida, some people
brought a blind man to Jesus, and they begged
him to touch and heal the man. 23Jesus took the
blind man by the hand and led him out of the
village. Then, spitting on the man's eyes, he laid
his hands on him and asked, "Can you see
anything now?"

24The man looked around. "Yes," he said, "I
see people, but I can't see them very clearly. They
look like trees walking around."

25Then Jesus placed his hands over the man's
eyes again. As the man stared intently, his sight
was completely restored, and he could see everything clearly. 26Jesus sent him home, saying,
"Don't go back into the village on your way
home."

Peter's Declaration about Jesus

27Jesus and his disciples left Galilee and went up
to the villages of Caesarea Philippi. As they were
walking along, he asked them, "Who do people
say I am?"

28"Well," they replied, "some say John the
Baptist, some say Elijah, and others say you are
one of the other prophets."

29Then Jesus asked, "Who do you say I am?"

Peter replied, "You are the Messiah." 30But
Jesus warned them not to tell anyone about him.

Jesus Predicts His Death

31Then Jesus began to tell them that he, the Son
of Man, would suffer many terrible things and
be rejected by the leaders, the leading priests,
and the teachers of religious law. He would be
killed, and three days later he would rise again.
32As he talked about this openly with his disciples, Peter took him aside and told him he
shouldn't say things like that.*

33Jesus turned and looked at his disciples and
then said to Peter very sternly, "Get away from
me, Satan! You are seeing things merely from a
human point of view, not from God's."

34Then he called his disciples and the crowds
to come over and listen. "If any of you wants to
be my follower," he told them, "you must put
aside your selfish ambition, shoulder your cross,
and follow me. 35If you try to keep your life for
yourself, you will lose it. But if you give up your
life for my sake and for the sake of the Good
News, you will find true life. 36And how do you
benefit if you gain the whole world but lose your
own soul* in the process? 37Is anything worth
more than your soul? 38If a person is ashamed
of me and my message in these adulterous and
sinful days, I, the Son of Man, will be ashamed
of that person when I return in the glory of my
Father with the holy angels."

CHAPTER 9

Jesus went on to say, "I assure you that some of
you standing here right now will not die before
you see the Kingdom of God arrive in great
power!"

8:18 Jer 5:21. 8:32 Or *and began to correct him.* 8:36 Or *your life;* also in 8:37.

The Transfiguration

2Six days later Jesus took Peter, James, and John
to the top of a mountain. No one else was there.
As the men watched, Jesus' appearance changed,
3and his clothing became dazzling white, far
whiter than any earthly process could ever make
it. 4Then Elijah and Moses appeared and began
talking with Jesus.

5"Teacher, this is wonderful!" Peter exclaimed. "We will make three shrines*—one for
you, one for Moses, and one for Elijah." 6He
didn't really know what to say, for they were all
terribly afraid.

7Then a cloud came over them, and a voice
from the cloud said, "This is my beloved Son.
Listen to him." 8Suddenly they looked around,
and Moses and Elijah were gone, and only Jesus
was with them. 9As they descended the mountainside, he told them not to tell anyone what
they had seen until he, the Son of Man, had risen
from the dead. 10So they kept it to themselves,
but they often asked each other what he meant
by "rising from the dead."

11Now they began asking him, "Why do the
teachers of religious law insist that Elijah must
return before the Messiah comes?"

12Jesus responded, "Elijah is indeed coming
first to set everything in order. Why then is it
written in the Scriptures that the Son of Man
must suffer and be treated with utter contempt?
13But I tell you, Elijah has already come, and he
was badly mistreated, just as the Scriptures predicted."

Jesus Heals a Boy Possessed by an Evil Spirit

14At the foot of the mountain they found a great
crowd surrounding the other disciples, as some
teachers of religious law were arguing with
them. 15The crowd watched Jesus in awe as he
came toward them, and then they ran to greet
him. 16"What is all this arguing about?" he
asked.

17One of the men in the crowd spoke up and
said, "Teacher, I brought my son for you to heal
him. He can't speak because he is possessed by
an evil spirit that won't let him talk. 18And
whenever this evil spirit seizes him, it throws
him violently to the ground and makes him
foam at the mouth and grind his teeth and
become rigid.* So I asked your disciples to cast
out the evil spirit, but they couldn't do it."

19Jesus said to them, "You faithless people!
How long must I be with you until you believe?
How long must I put up with you? Bring the boy
to me." 20So they brought the boy. But when the
evil spirit saw Jesus, it threw the child into a
violent convulsion, and he fell to the ground,
writhing and foaming at the mouth. 21"How
long has this been happening?" Jesus asked the
boy's father.

He replied, "Since he was very small. 22The
evil spirit often makes him fall into the fire or
into water, trying to kill him. Have mercy on us
and help us. Do something if you can."

23"What do you mean, 'If I can'?" Jesus asked.
"Anything is possible if a person believes."

24The father instantly replied, "I do believe,
but help me not to doubt!"

25When Jesus saw that the crowd of onlookers was growing, he rebuked the evil spirit.
"Spirit of deafness and muteness," he said, "I
command you to come out of this child and
never enter him again!" 26Then the spirit
screamed and threw the boy into another violent convulsion and left him. The boy lay there
motionless, and he appeared to be dead. A murmur ran through the crowd, "He's dead." 27But
Jesus took him by the hand and helped him to
his feet, and he stood up.

28Afterward, when Jesus was alone in the
house with his disciples, they asked him, "Why
couldn't we cast out that evil spirit?"

29Jesus replied, "This kind can be cast out
only by prayer.*"

Jesus Again Predicts His Death

30Leaving that region, they traveled through Galilee. Jesus tried to avoid all publicity 31in order
to spend more time with his disciples and teach
them. He said to them, "The Son of Man is going
to be betrayed. He will be killed, but three days
later he will rise from the dead." 32But they
didn't understand what he was saying, and they
were afraid to ask him what he meant.

The Greatest in the Kingdom

33After they arrived at Capernaum, Jesus and
his disciples settled in the house where they
would be staying. Jesus asked them, "What
were you discussing out on the road?" 34But
they didn't answer, because they had been arguing about which of them was the greatest.
35He sat down and called the twelve disciples
over to him. Then he said, "Anyone who wants
to be the first must take last place and be the
servant of everyone else."

36Then he put a little child among them.
Taking the child in his arms, he said to them,

9:5 Or *shelters;* Greek reads *tabernacles.* 9:18 Or *become weak.* 9:29 Some manuscripts add *and fasting.*

37“Anyone who welcomes a little child like this on my behalf welcomes me, and anyone who welcomes me welcomes my Father who sent me.”

Using the Name of Jesus

38John said to Jesus, “Teacher, we saw a man using your name to cast out demons, but we told him to stop because he isn’t one of our group.”

39“Don’t stop him!” Jesus said. “No one who performs miracles in my name will soon be able to speak evil of me. 40Anyone who is not against us is for us. 41If anyone gives you even a cup of water because you belong to the Messiah, I assure you, that person will be rewarded.

42“But if anyone causes one of these little ones who trusts in me to lose faith, it would be better for that person to be thrown into the sea with a large millstone tied around the neck. 43If your hand causes you to sin, cut it off. It is better to enter heaven* with only one hand than to go into the unquenchable fires of hell with two hands.* 45If your foot causes you to sin, cut it off. It is better to enter heaven with only one foot than to be thrown into hell with two feet.* 47And if your eye causes you to sin, gouge it out. It is better to enter the Kingdom of God half blind than to have two eyes and be thrown into hell, 48‘where the worm never dies and the fire never goes out.’*

49“For everyone will be purified with fire.* 50Salt is good for seasoning. But if it loses its flavor, how do you make it salty again? You must have the qualities of salt among yourselves and live in peace with each other.”

CHAPTER 10

Discussion about Divorce and Marriage

Then Jesus left Capernaum and went southward to the region of Judea and into the area east of the Jordan River. As always there were the crowds, and as usual he taught them.

2Some Pharisees came and tried to trap him with this question: “Should a man be allowed to divorce his wife?”

3“What did Moses say about divorce?” Jesus asked them.

4“Well, he permitted it,” they replied. “He said a man merely has to write his wife an official letter of divorce and send her away.”*

5But Jesus responded, “He wrote those instructions only as a concession to your hard-hearted wickedness. 6But God’s plan was seen from the beginning of creation, for ‘He made them male and female.’* 7‘This explains why a man leaves his father and mother and is joined to his wife,* 8and the two are united into one.’* Since they are no longer two but one, 9let no one separate them, for God has joined them together.”

10Later, when he was alone with his disciples in the house, they brought up the subject again. 11He told them, “Whoever divorces his wife and marries someone else commits adultery against her. 12And if a woman divorces her husband and remarries, she commits adultery.”

Jesus Blesses the Children

13One day some parents brought their children to Jesus so he could touch them and bless them, but the disciples told them not to bother him.

9:43a Greek *enter life;* also in 9:45. 9:43b Some manuscripts add verse 44 (which is identical with 9:48). 9:45 Some manuscripts add verse 46 (which is identical with 9:48). 9:48 Isa 66:24. 9:49 Greek *salted with fire.* Some manuscripts add *and every sacrifice will be salted with salt.* 10:4 Deut 24:1. 10:6 Gen 1:27; 5:2. 10:7 Some manuscripts do not include *and is joined to his wife.* 10:7-8 Gen 2:24.

OFF AND RUNNING

Divorce Is Not Part of God’s Plan Read MARK 10:2-12

At the time Jesus was asked this question about divorce, some people had a liberal attitude toward it. Much like today, one could dissolve a marriage for practically any reason. But Jesus reminded the people of God’s original plan for marriage (verses 6-9). God desires that a man and woman make a lifelong commitment to each other. Divorce should not even be a consideration.

Perhaps one of the greatest deterrents for divorce is to see how much God really hates it:

“You cry out, ‘Why has the LORD abandoned us?’ I’ll tell you why! Because the LORD witnessed the vows you and your wife made to each other on your wedding day when you were young. But you have been disloyal to her, though she remained your faithful companion, the wife of your marriage vows. Didn’t the LORD make you one with your wife? In body and spirit you are his. And what does he want? Godly children from your union. So guard yourself; remain loyal to the wife of your youth. ‘For I hate divorce!’” (Malachi 2:14-16).

14 But when Jesus saw what was happening, he
was very displeased with his disciples. He said to
them, "Let the children come to me. Don't stop
them! For the Kingdom of God belongs to such
as these. 15 I assure you, anyone who doesn't
have their kind of faith will never get into the
Kingdom of God." 16 Then he took the children
into his arms and placed his hands on their
heads and blessed them.

The Rich Man

17 As he was starting out on a trip, a man came
running up to Jesus, knelt down, and asked,
"Good Teacher, what should I do to get eternal
life?"

18 "Why do you call me good?" Jesus asked.
"Only God is truly good. 19 But as for your question, you know the commandments: 'Do not
murder. Do not commit adultery. Do not steal.
Do not testify falsely. Do not cheat. Honor your
father and mother.'*"

20 "Teacher," the man replied, "I've obeyed all
these commandments since I was a child."

21 Jesus felt genuine love for this man as he
looked at him. "You lack only one thing," he
told him. "Go and sell all you have and give the
money to the poor, and you will have treasure in
heaven. Then come, follow me." 22 At this, the
man's face fell, and he went sadly away because
he had many possessions.

23 Jesus looked around and said to his disciples, "How hard it is for rich people to get into
the Kingdom of God!" 24 This amazed them. But
Jesus said again, "Dear children, it is very hard*
to get into the Kingdom of God. 25 It is easier for
a camel to go through the eye of a needle than
for a rich person to enter the Kingdom of God!"

26 The disciples were astounded. "Then who
in the world can be saved?" they asked.

27 Jesus looked at them intently and said,
"Humanly speaking, it is impossible. But not
with God. Everything is possible with God."

28 Then Peter began to mention all that he
and the other disciples had left behind. "We've
given up everything to follow you," he said.

29 And Jesus replied, "I assure you that everyone who has given up house or brothers or
sisters or mother or father or children or property, for my sake and for the Good News, 30 will
receive now in return, a hundred times over,
houses, brothers, sisters, mothers, children, and
property—with persecutions. And in the world
to come they will have eternal life. 31 But many
who seem to be important now will be the least
important then, and those who are considered
least here will be the greatest then.*"

Jesus Again Predicts His Death

32 They were now on the way to Jerusalem, and
Jesus was walking ahead of them. The disciples
were filled with dread and the people following
behind were overwhelmed with fear. Taking the
twelve disciples aside, Jesus once more began to
describe everything that was about to happen to
him in Jerusalem. 33 "When we get to Jerusalem," he told them, "the Son of Man will be
betrayed to the leading priests and the teachers
of religious law. They will sentence him to die
and hand him over to the Romans. 34 They will
mock him, spit on him, beat him with their

10:19 Exod 20:12-16; Deut 5:16-20. 10:24 Some manuscripts add *for those who trust in riches.* 10:31 Greek *But many who are first will be last; and the last, first.*

Just as one should count the cost of getting married, one should also count the cost of getting divorced. Not only does it devastate the "companionship" God desires between a husband and wife, but it will also greatly affect any children they may have. As God says here, he wants his people to bring up godly children from the union between husband and wife. When a home is broken by divorce, it can become more difficult to raise children in obedience to the Lord.

Does God ever permit divorce? While the Bible cites two instances (adultery, and if a nonbelieving spouse chooses to leave a believing spouse), God's will is that a married couple stay together. Any confusion about the subject arises when we try to accommodate the divine standard to the lack of standards in our contemporary morality.

Winston Churchill astutely observed, "Victory is not obtained through evacuation." If you are married, ask God to strengthen your marriage today. Remember that God has joined you and your spouse together. Stand by your commitment. Don't retreat from your problems, but ask God to help you face and overcome them. Cultivate "oneness" and friendship in your marriage, and get back to God's original design.

Forgiveness First Comes from God Read MARK 11:25

As verse 25 of this passage implies, an attitude of unforgiveness can actually hinder our prayer life.

In verse 25, Jesus is not saying that God's forgiveness is dependent upon your forgiveness of others. God's acceptance and forgiveness is entirely dependent upon what he did for you at the cross. He is simply stressing that if you are truly a forgiven person, you—of all people—should be willing to forgive others. At the same time, if you are not willing to forgive others, one would wonder if you personally know anything of God's forgiveness.

Don't let unforgiveness rob you of your joy. Forgive as Christ forgave you.

CORNERSTONES

whips, and kill him, but after three days he will
rise again."

Jesus Teaches about Serving Others

35Then James and John, the sons of Zebedee,
came over and spoke to him. "Teacher," they
said, "we want you to do us a favor."

36"What is it?" he asked.

37"In your glorious Kingdom, we want to sit
in places of honor next to you," they said, "one
at your right and the other at your left."

38But Jesus answered, "You don't know what
you are asking! Are you able to drink from the
bitter cup of sorrow I am about to drink? Are you
able to be baptized with the baptism of suffering
I must be baptized with?"

39"Oh yes," they said, "we are able!"

And Jesus said, "You will indeed drink from
my cup and be baptized with my baptism, 40but
I have no right to say who will sit on the thrones
next to mine. God has prepared those places for
the ones he has chosen."

41When the ten other disciples discovered
what James and John had asked, they were indignant. 42So Jesus called them together and
said, "You know that in this world kings are
tyrants, and officials lord it over the people beneath them. 43But among you it should be quite
different. Whoever wants to be a leader among
you must be your servant, 44and whoever wants
to be first must be the slave of all. 45For even I,
the Son of Man, came here not to be served but
to serve others, and to give my life as a ransom
for many."

Jesus Heals Blind Bartimaeus

46And so they reached Jericho. Later, as Jesus and
his disciples left town, a great crowd was following. A blind beggar named Bartimaeus (son of
Timaeus) was sitting beside the road as Jesus was
going by. 47When Bartimaeus heard that Jesus
from Nazareth was nearby, he began to shout
out, "Jesus, Son of David, have mercy on me!"

48"Be quiet!" some of the people yelled at
him.

But he only shouted louder, "Son of David,
have mercy on me!"

49When Jesus heard him, he stopped and
said, "Tell him to come here."

So they called the blind man. "Cheer up,"
they said. "Come on, he's calling you!" 50Barti-
maeus threw aside his coat, jumped up, and
came to Jesus.

51"What do you want me to do for you?"
Jesus asked.

"Teacher," the blind man said, "I want to
see!"

52And Jesus said to him, "Go your way. Your
faith has healed you." And instantly the blind
man could see! Then he followed Jesus down
the road.*

CHAPTER 11

The Triumphal Entry

As Jesus and his disciples approached Jerusalem,
they came to the towns of Bethphage and Bethany, on the Mount of Olives. Jesus sent two of
them on ahead. 2"Go into that village over
there," he told them, "and as soon as you enter
it, you will see a colt tied there that has never

10:52 Or *on the way.*

been ridden. Untie it and bring it here. 3If anyone asks what you are doing, just say, 'The Lord needs it and will return it soon.'"

4The two disciples left and found the colt standing in the street, tied outside a house. 5As they were untying it, some bystanders demanded, "What are you doing, untying that colt?" 6They said what Jesus had told them to say, and they were permitted to take it. 7Then they brought the colt to Jesus and threw their garments over it, and he sat on it.

8Many in the crowd spread their coats on the road ahead of Jesus, and others cut leafy branches in the fields and spread them along the way. 9He was in the center of the procession, and the crowds all around him were shouting,

"Praise God!*
Bless the one who comes in the name of the Lord!
10 Bless the coming kingdom of our ancestor David!
Praise God in highest heaven!"*

11So Jesus came to Jerusalem and went into the Temple. He looked around carefully at everything, and then he left because it was late in the afternoon. Then he went out to Bethany with the twelve disciples.

Jesus Curses the Fig Tree

12The next morning as they were leaving Bethany, Jesus felt hungry. 13He noticed a fig tree a little way off that was in full leaf, so he went over to see if he could find any figs on it. But there were only leaves because it was too early in the season for fruit. 14Then Jesus said to the tree, "May no one ever eat your fruit again!" And the disciples heard him say it.

Jesus Clears the Temple

15When they arrived back in Jerusalem, Jesus entered the Temple and began to drive out the merchants and their customers. He knocked over the tables of the money changers and the stalls of those selling doves, 16and he stopped everyone from bringing in merchandise. 17He taught them, "The Scriptures declare, 'My Temple will be called a place of prayer for all nations,' but you have turned it into a den of thieves."*

18When the leading priests and teachers of religious law heard what Jesus had done, they began planning how to kill him. But they were afraid of him because the people were so enthusiastic about Jesus' teaching. 19That evening Jesus and the disciples* left the city.

20The next morning as they passed by the fig tree he had cursed, the disciples noticed it was withered from the roots. 21Peter remembered what Jesus had said to the tree on the previous day and exclaimed, "Look, Teacher! The fig tree you cursed has withered!"

22Then Jesus said to the disciples, "Have faith in God. 23I assure you that you can say to this mountain, 'May God lift you up and throw you into the sea,' and your command will be obeyed. All that's required is that you really believe and do not doubt in your heart. 24Listen to me! You can pray for anything, and if you believe, you will have it. 25But when you are praying, first forgive anyone you are holding a grudge against, so that your Father in heaven will forgive your sins, too.*"

The Authority of Jesus Challenged

27By this time they had arrived in Jerusalem again. As Jesus was walking through the Temple area, the leading priests, the teachers of religious law, and the other leaders came up to him. They demanded, 28"By whose authority did you drive out the merchants from the Temple?* Who gave you such authority?"

29"I'll tell who gave me authority to do these things if you answer one question," Jesus replied. 30"Did John's baptism come from heaven or was it merely human? Answer me!"

31They talked it over among themselves. "If we say it was from heaven, he will ask why we didn't believe him. 32But do we dare say it was merely human?" For they were afraid that the people would start a riot, since everyone thought that John was a prophet. 33So they finally replied, "We don't know."

And Jesus responded, "Then I won't answer your question either."

CHAPTER 12

Story of the Evil Farmers

Then Jesus began telling them stories: "A man planted a vineyard, built a wall around it, dug a pit for pressing out the grape juice, and built a lookout tower. Then he leased the vineyard to tenant farmers and moved to another country.

11:9 Greek *Hosanna,* an exclamation of praise that literally means "save now"; also in 11:10. **11:9-10** Pss 118:25-26; 148:1. **11:17** Isa 56:7; Jer 7:11. **11:19** Greek *they;* some manuscripts read *he.* **11:25** Some manuscripts add verse 26, *But if you do not forgive, neither will your Father who is in heaven forgive your sins.* **11:28** Or *By whose authority do you do these things?*

2At grape-picking time he sent one of his servants to collect his share of the crop. 3But the farmers grabbed the servant, beat him up, and sent him back empty-handed.

4"The owner then sent another servant, but they beat him over the head and treated him shamefully. 5The next servant he sent was killed. Others who were sent were either beaten or killed, 6until there was only one left—his son whom he loved dearly. The owner finally sent him, thinking, 'Surely they will respect my son.'

7"But the farmers said to one another, 'Here comes the heir to this estate. Let's kill him and get the estate for ourselves!' 8So they grabbed him and murdered him and threw his body out of the vineyard.

9"What do you suppose the owner of the vineyard will do?" Jesus asked. "I'll tell you—he will come and kill them all and lease the vineyard to others. 10Didn't you ever read this in the Scriptures?

'The stone rejected by the builders
has now become the cornerstone.
11 This is the Lord's doing,
and it is marvelous to see.'* "

12The Jewish leaders wanted to arrest him for using this illustration because they realized he was pointing at them—they were the wicked farmers in his story. But they were afraid to touch him because of the crowds. So they left him and went away.

Taxes for Caesar

13The leaders sent some Pharisees and supporters of Herod to try to trap Jesus into saying something for which he could be arrested. 14"Teacher," these men said, "we know how honest you are. You are impartial and don't play favorites. You sincerely teach the ways of God. Now tell us—is it right to pay taxes to the Roman government or not? 15Should we pay them, or should we not?"

Jesus saw through their hypocrisy and said, "Whom are you trying to fool with your trick questions? Show me a Roman coin,* and I'll tell you." 16When they handed it to him, he asked, "Whose picture and title are stamped on it?"

"Caesar's," they replied.

17"Well, then," Jesus said, "give to Caesar what belongs to him. But everything that belongs to God must be given to God." This reply completely amazed them.

Discussion about Resurrection

18Then the Sadducees stepped forward—a group of Jews who say there is no resurrection after death. They posed this question: 19"Teacher, Moses gave us a law that if a man dies, leaving a wife without children, his brother should marry the widow and have a child who will be the brother's heir.* 20Well, there were seven brothers. The oldest of them married and then died without children. 21So the second brother married the widow, but soon he too died and left no children. Then the next brother married her and died without children. 22This continued until all the brothers had married her and died, and still there were no children. Last of all, the woman died, too. 23So tell us, whose wife will she be in the resurrection? For all seven were married to her."

24Jesus replied, "Your problem is that you don't know the Scriptures, and you don't know the power of God. 25For when the dead rise, they won't be married. They will be like the angels in heaven. 26But now, as to whether the dead will be raised—haven't you ever read about this in the writings of Moses, in the story of the burning bush? Long after Abraham, Isaac, and Jacob had died, God said to Moses,* 'I am the God of Abraham, the God of Isaac, and the God of Jacob.'* 27So he is the God of the living, not the dead. You have made a serious error."

The Most Important Commandment

28One of the teachers of religious law was standing there listening to the discussion. He realized that Jesus had answered well, so he asked, "Of all the commandments, which is the most important?"

29Jesus replied, "The most important commandment is this: 'Hear, O Israel! The Lord our God is the one and only Lord. 30And you must love the Lord your God with all your heart, all your soul, all your mind, and all your strength.'* 31The second is equally important: 'Love your neighbor as yourself.'* No other commandment is greater than these."

32The teacher of religious law replied, "Well said, Teacher. You have spoken the truth by saying that there is only one God and no other. 33And I know it is important to love him with all my heart and all my understanding and all my strength, and to love my neighbors as myself. This is more important than to offer all of

12:10-11 Ps 118:22-23. **12:15** Greek *a denarius.* **12:19** Deut 25:5-6. **12:26a** Greek *in the story of the bush? God said to him.* **12:26b** Exod 3:6. **12:29-30** Deut 6:4-5. **12:31** Lev 19:18.

the burnt offerings and sacrifices required in the law."

34Realizing this man's understanding, Jesus said to him, "You are not far from the Kingdom of God." And after that, no one dared to ask him any more questions.

Whose Son Is the Messiah?

35Later, as Jesus was teaching the people in the Temple, he asked, "Why do the teachers of religious law claim that the Messiah will be the son of David? 36For David himself, speaking under the inspiration of the Holy Spirit, said,

'The LORD said to my Lord,
Sit in honor at my right hand
until I humble your enemies beneath
your feet.'*

37Since David himself called him Lord, how can he be his son at the same time?" And the crowd listened to him with great interest.

38Here are some of the other things he taught them at this time: "Beware of these teachers of religious law! For they love to parade in flowing robes and to have everyone bow to them as they walk in the marketplaces. 39And how they love the seats of honor in the synagogues and at banquets. 40But they shamelessly cheat widows out of their property, and then, to cover up the kind of people they really are, they make long prayers in public. Because of this, their punishment will be the greater."

The Widow's Offering

41Jesus went over to the collection box in the Temple and sat and watched as the crowds dropped in their money. Many rich people put in large amounts. 42Then a poor widow came and dropped in two pennies.* 43He called his disciples to him and said, "I assure you, this poor widow has given more than all the others have given. 44For they gave a tiny part of their surplus, but she, poor as she is, has given everything she has."

CHAPTER 13

Jesus Foretells the Future

As Jesus was leaving the Temple that day, one of his disciples said, "Teacher, look at these tremendous buildings! Look at the massive stones in the walls!"

2Jesus replied, "These magnificent buildings will be so completely demolished that not one stone will be left on top of another."

3Later, Jesus sat on the slopes of the Mount of Olives across the valley from the Temple. Peter, James, John, and Andrew came to him privately and asked him, 4"When will all this take place? And will there be any sign ahead of time to show us when all this will be fulfilled?"

5Jesus replied, "Don't let anyone mislead you, 6because many will come in my name, claiming to be the Messiah.* They will lead many astray. 7And wars will break out near and far, but don't panic. Yes, these things must come, but the end won't follow immediately. 8Nations and kingdoms will proclaim war against each other, and there will be earth-

12:36 Ps 110:1. 12:42 Greek *2 lepta, which is a kodrantes.*

13:6 Greek *name, saying, 'I am.'*

How Much Should You Give?

Read MARK 12:41-44

Generosity is not measured by the size of the gift itself, but by the motivation. In this story, we see how Jesus valued the small offering of this poor widow over the large sums of money from the wealthy people. Jesus knew that she had given all she had. He could see that her heart was in the right place.

The great psalmist, David, king of Israel, said he would not give to the Lord that which cost him nothing. In other words, we are not to give our "leftovers" to God, but our best. When you think about it, is that really too much to ask? After all, he gave his best to us when he sent us his own dear Son to die in our place.

Our attitude toward giving should be like that of the generous believers in Macedonia, who eagerly came to the aid of the church in Jerusalem during its time of need: "For I can testify that they gave not only what they could afford but far more. And they did it of their own free will. They begged us again and again for the gracious privilege of sharing in the gift for the Christians in Jerusalem" (2 Corinthians 8:3-4).

When you question how much of your income should be spent on God's work, remember this promise: "God loves the person who gives cheerfully. And God will generously provide all you need" (2 Corinthians 9:7-8).

FIRST STEPS

quakes in many parts of the world, and famines. But all this will be only the beginning of
the horrors to come. 9But when these things
begin to happen, watch out! You will be
handed over to the courts and beaten in the
synagogues. You will be accused before governors and kings of being my followers. This will
be your opportunity to tell them about me.*
10And the Good News must first be preached to
every nation. 11But when you are arrested and
stand trial, don't worry about what to say in
your defense. Just say what God tells you to.
Then it is not you who will be speaking, but the
Holy Spirit.

12"Brother will betray brother to death,
fathers will betray their own children, and children will rise against their parents and cause
them to be killed. 13And everyone will hate you
because of your allegiance to me. But those who
endure to the end will be saved.

14"The time will come when you will see the
sacrilegious object that causes desecration*
standing where it should not be"—reader, pay
attention! "Then those in Judea must flee to the
hills. 15A person outside the house* must not
go back into the house to pack. 16A person in
the field must not return even to get a coat.
17How terrible it will be for pregnant women
and for mothers nursing their babies in those
days. 18And pray that your flight will not be in
winter. 19For those will be days of greater horror than at any time since God created the
world. And it will never happen again. 20In fact,
unless the Lord shortens that time of calamity,
the entire human race will be destroyed. But for
the sake of his chosen ones he has shortened
those days.

21"And then if anyone tells you, 'Look, here is
the Messiah,' or, 'There he is,' don't pay any
attention. 22For false messiahs and false prophets
will rise up and perform miraculous signs and
wonders so as to deceive, if possible, even God's
chosen ones. 23Watch out! I have warned you!

24"At that time, after those horrible days end,

the sun will be darkened,
  the moon will not give light,
25 the stars will fall from the sky,
  and the powers of heaven will be
    shaken.*

26Then everyone will see the Son of Man arrive
on the clouds with great power and glory.*
27And he will send forth his angels to gather
together his chosen ones from all over the
world—from the farthest ends of the earth and
heaven.

28"Now, learn a lesson from the fig tree.
When its buds become tender and its leaves
begin to sprout, you know without being told
that summer is near. 29Just so, when you see the
events I've described beginning to happen, you
can be sure that his return is very near, right at
the door. 30I assure you, this generation* will
not pass from the scene until all these events
have taken place. 31Heaven and earth will disappear, but my words will remain forever.

32"However, no one knows the day or hour
when these things will happen, not even the
angels in heaven or the Son himself. Only the
Father knows. 33And since you don't know
when they will happen, stay alert and keep
watch.*

34"The coming of the Son of Man can be
compared with that of a man who left home to
go on a trip. He gave each of his employees
instructions about the work they were to do, and
he told the gatekeeper to watch for his return.
35So keep a sharp lookout! For you do not know
when the homeowner will return—at evening,
midnight, early dawn, or late daybreak. 36Don't
let him find you sleeping when he arrives without warning. 37What I say to you I say to everyone: Watch for his return!"

CHAPTER 14

Jesus Anointed at Bethany

It was now two days before the Passover celebration and the Festival of Unleavened Bread. The
leading priests and the teachers of religious law
were still looking for an opportunity to capture
Jesus secretly and put him to death. 2"But not
during the Passover," they agreed, "or there will
be a riot."

3Meanwhile, Jesus was in Bethany at the
home of Simon, a man who had leprosy. During
supper, a woman came in with a beautiful jar of
expensive perfume.* She broke the seal and
poured the perfume over his head. 4Some of
those at the table were indignant. "Why was this
expensive perfume wasted?" they asked. 5"She
could have sold it for a small fortune* and given
the money to the poor!" And they scolded her
harshly.

13:9 Or *This will be your testimony against them.* 13:14 Greek *the abomination of desolation.* See Dan 9:27; 11:31; 12:11. 13:15 Greek *on the roof.* 13:24-25 See Isa 13:10; 34:4; Joel 2:10. 13:26 See Dan 7:13. 13:30 Or *this age,* or *this nation.* 13:33 Some manuscripts add *and pray.* 14:3 Greek *an alabaster jar of expensive ointment, pure nard.* 14:5 Greek *300 denarii.* A denarius was the equivalent of a full day's wage.

6 But Jesus replied, "Leave her alone. Why berate her for doing such a good thing to me? 7 You will always have the poor among you, and you can help them whenever you want to. But I will not be here with you much longer. 8 She has done what she could and has anointed my body for burial ahead of time. 9 I assure you, wherever the Good News is preached throughout the world, this woman's deed will be talked about in her memory."

Judas Agrees to Betray Jesus

10 Then Judas Iscariot, one of the twelve disciples, went to the leading priests to arrange to betray Jesus to them. 11 The leading priests were delighted when they heard why he had come, and they promised him a reward. So he began looking for the right time and place to betray Jesus.

The Last Supper

12 On the first day of the Festival of Unleavened Bread (the day the Passover lambs were sacrificed), Jesus' disciples asked him, "Where do you want us to go to prepare the Passover supper?"

13 So Jesus sent two of them into Jerusalem to make the arrangements. "As you go into the city," he told them, "a man carrying a pitcher of water will meet you. Follow him. 14 At the house he enters, say to the owner, 'The Teacher asks, Where is the guest room where I can eat the Passover meal with my disciples?' 15 He will take you upstairs to a large room that is already set up. That is the place; go ahead and prepare our supper there." 16 So the two disciples went on ahead into the city and found everything just as Jesus had said, and they prepared the Passover supper there.

17 In the evening Jesus arrived with the twelve disciples. 18 As they were sitting around the table eating, Jesus said, "The truth is, one of you will betray me, one of you who is here eating with me."

19 Greatly distressed, one by one they began to ask him, "I'm not the one, am I?"

20 He replied, "It is one of you twelve, one who is eating with me now.* 21 For I, the Son of Man, must die, as the Scriptures declared long ago. But how terrible it will be for my betrayer. Far better for him if he had never been born!"

22 As they were eating, Jesus took a loaf of bread and asked God's blessing on it. Then he broke it in pieces and gave it to the disciples, saying, "Take it, for this is my body."

23 And he took a cup of wine and gave thanks to God for it. He gave it to them, and they all drank from it. 24 And he said to them, "This is my blood, poured out for many, sealing the covenant* between God and his people. 25 I solemnly declare that I will not drink wine again until that day when I drink it new in the Kingdom of God." 26 Then they sang a hymn and went out to the Mount of Olives.

Jesus Predicts Peter's Denial

27 "All of you will desert me," Jesus told them. "For the Scriptures say,

'God* will strike the Shepherd,
 and the sheep will be scattered.'*

28 But after I am raised from the dead, I will go ahead of you to Galilee and meet you there."

29 Peter said to him, "Even if everyone else deserts you, I never will."

30 "Peter," Jesus replied, "the truth is, this very night, before the rooster crows twice, you will deny me three times."

31 "No!" Peter insisted. "Not even if I have to die with you! I will never deny you!" And all the others vowed the same.

Jesus Prays in Gethsemane

32 And they came to an olive grove called Gethsemane, and Jesus said, "Sit here while I go and pray." 33 He took Peter, James, and John with him, and he began to be filled with horror and deep distress. 34 He told them, "My soul is crushed with grief to the point of death. Stay here and watch with me."

35 He went on a little farther and fell face down on the ground. He prayed that, if it were possible, the awful hour awaiting him might pass him by. 36 "Abba,* Father," he said, "everything is possible for you. Please take this cup of suffering away from me. Yet I want your will, not mine."

37 Then he returned and found the disciples asleep. "Simon!" he said to Peter. "Are you asleep? Couldn't you stay awake and watch with me even one hour? 38 Keep alert and pray. Otherwise temptation will overpower you. For though the spirit is willing enough, the body is weak."

39 Then Jesus left them again and prayed, repeating his pleadings. 40 Again he returned to

14:20 Or *one who is dipping bread into the bowl with me.* **14:24** Some manuscripts read *the new covenant.* **14:27a** Greek *I.* **14:27b** Zech 13:7. **14:36** *Abba* is an Aramaic term for "father."

them and found them sleeping, for they just couldn't keep their eyes open. And they didn't know what to say.

41When he returned to them the third time, he said, "Still sleeping? Still resting?* Enough! The time has come. I, the Son of Man, am betrayed into the hands of sinners. 42Up, let's be going. See, my betrayer is here!"

Jesus Is Betrayed and Arrested

43And immediately, as he said this, Judas, one of the twelve disciples, arrived with a mob that was armed with swords and clubs. They had been sent out by the leading priests, the teachers of religious law, and the other leaders. 44Judas had given them a prearranged signal: "You will know which one to arrest when I go over and give him the kiss of greeting. Then you can take him away under guard."

45As soon as they arrived, Judas walked up to Jesus. "Teacher!" he exclaimed, and gave him the kiss. 46Then the others grabbed Jesus and arrested him. 47But someone pulled out a sword and slashed off an ear of the high priest's servant.

48Jesus asked them, "Am I some dangerous criminal, that you come armed with swords and clubs to arrest me? 49Why didn't you arrest me in the Temple? I was there teaching every day. But these things are happening to fulfill what the Scriptures say about me."

50Meanwhile, all his disciples deserted him and ran away. 51There was a young man following along behind, clothed only in a linen nightshirt. When the mob tried to grab him, 52they tore off his clothes, but he escaped and ran away naked.

Jesus before the Council

53Jesus was led to the high priest's home where the leading priests, other leaders, and teachers of religious law had gathered. 54Meanwhile, Peter followed far behind and then slipped inside the gates of the high priest's courtyard. For a while he sat with the guards, warming himself by the fire.

55Inside, the leading priests and the entire high council* were trying to find witnesses who would testify against Jesus, so they could put him to death. But their efforts were in vain. 56Many false witnesses spoke against him, but they contradicted each other. 57Finally, some men stood up to testify against him with this lie: 58"We heard him say, 'I will destroy this Temple made with human hands, and in three days I will build another, made without human hands.'" 59But even then they didn't get their stories straight!

60Then the high priest stood up before the others and asked Jesus, "Well, aren't you going to answer these charges? What do you have to say for yourself?" 61Jesus made no reply. Then the high priest asked him, "Are you the Messiah, the Son of the blessed God?"

62Jesus said, "I am, and you will see me, the Son of Man, sitting at God's right hand in the place of power and coming back on the clouds of heaven."*

63Then the high priest tore his clothing to show his horror and said, "Why do we need other witnesses? 64You have all heard his blasphemy. What is your verdict?" And they all condemned him to death.

65Then some of them began to spit at him, and they blindfolded him and hit his face with their fists. "Who hit you that time, you prophet?" they jeered. And even the guards were hitting him as they led him away.

Peter Denies Jesus

66Meanwhile, Peter was below in the courtyard. One of the servant girls who worked for the high priest 67noticed Peter warming himself at the fire. She looked at him closely and then said, "You were one of those with Jesus, the Nazarene."

68Peter denied it. "I don't know what you're talking about," he said, and he went out into the entryway. Just then, a rooster crowed.*

69The servant girl saw him standing there and began telling the others, "That man is definitely one of them!" 70Peter denied it again.

A little later some other bystanders began saying to Peter, "You must be one of them because you are from Galilee."

71Peter said, "I swear by God, I don't know this man you're talking about." 72And immediately the rooster crowed the second time. Suddenly, Jesus' words flashed through Peter's mind: "Before the rooster crows twice, you will deny me three times." And he broke down and cried.

CHAPTER 15

Jesus' Trial before Pilate

Very early in the morning the leading priests, other leaders, and teachers of religious law—the entire high council*—met to discuss their next step. They bound Jesus and took him to Pilate, the Roman governor.

14:41 Or *Sleep on, take your rest.* 14:55 Greek *the Sanhedrin.* 14:62 See Ps 110:1; Dan 7:13. 14:68 Some manuscripts do not include *Just then, a rooster crowed.* 15:1 Greek *the Sanhedrin;* also in 15:43.

2Pilate asked Jesus, "Are you the King of the Jews?"

Jesus replied, "Yes, it is as you say."

3Then the leading priests accused him of many crimes, 4and Pilate asked him, "Aren't you going to say something? What about all these charges against you?" 5But Jesus said nothing, much to Pilate's surprise.

6Now it was the governor's custom to release one prisoner each year at Passover time—anyone the people requested. 7One of the prisoners at that time was Barabbas, convicted along with others for murder during an insurrection. 8The mob began to crowd in toward Pilate, asking him to release a prisoner as usual. 9"Should I give you the King of the Jews?" Pilate asked. 10(For he realized by now that the leading priests had arrested Jesus out of envy.) 11But at this point the leading priests stirred up the mob to demand the release of Barabbas instead of Jesus. 12"But if I release Barabbas," Pilate asked them, "what should I do with this man you call the King of the Jews?"

13They shouted back, "Crucify him!"

14"Why?" Pilate demanded. "What crime has he committed?"

But the crowd only roared the louder, "Crucify him!"

15So Pilate, anxious to please the crowd, released Barabbas to them. He ordered Jesus flogged with a lead-tipped whip, then turned him over to the Roman soldiers to crucify him.

The Soldiers Mock Jesus

16The soldiers took him into their headquarters* and called out the entire battalion. 17They dressed him in a purple robe and made a crown of long, sharp thorns and put it on his head. 18Then they saluted, yelling, "Hail! King of the Jews!" 19And they beat him on the head with a stick, spit on him, and dropped to their knees in mock worship. 20When they were finally tired of mocking him, they took off the purple robe and put his own clothes on him again. Then they led him away to be crucified.

The Crucifixion

21A man named Simon, who was from Cyrene,* was coming in from the country just then, and they forced him to carry Jesus' cross. (Simon is the father of Alexander and Rufus.) 22And they brought Jesus to a place called Golgotha (which means Skull Hill). 23They offered him wine drugged with myrrh, but he refused it. 24Then they nailed him to the cross. They gambled for his clothes, throwing dice* to decide who would get them.

25It was nine o'clock in the morning when the crucifixion took place. 26A signboard was fastened to the cross above Jesus' head, announcing the charge against him. It read: "The King of the Jews." 27Two criminals were crucified with him, their crosses on either side of his.* 29And the people passing by shouted abuse, shaking their heads in mockery. "Ha! Look at you now!" they yelled at him. "You can destroy the Temple and rebuild it in three days, can you? 30Well then, save yourself and come down from the cross!"

31The leading priests and teachers of religious law also mocked Jesus. "He saved others," they scoffed, "but he can't save himself! 32Let this Messiah, this king of Israel, come down from the cross so we can see it and believe him!" Even the two criminals who were being crucified with Jesus ridiculed him.

The Death of Jesus

33At noon, darkness fell across the whole land until three o'clock. 34Then, at that time Jesus called out with a loud voice, "*Eloi, Eloi, lema sabachthani?*" which means, "My God, my God, why have you forsaken me?"*

35Some of the bystanders misunderstood and thought he was calling for the prophet Elijah. 36One of them ran and filled a sponge with sour wine, holding it up to him on a stick so he could drink. "Leave him alone. Let's see whether Elijah will come and take him down!" he said.

37Then Jesus uttered another loud cry and breathed his last. 38And the curtain in the Temple was torn in two, from top to bottom. 39When the Roman officer who stood facing him saw how he had died, he exclaimed, "Truly, this was the Son of God!"

40Some women were there, watching from a distance, including Mary Magdalene, Mary (the mother of James the younger and of Joseph*), and Salome. 41They had been followers of Jesus and had cared for him while he was in Galilee. Then they and many other women had come with him to Jerusalem.

The Burial of Jesus

42This all happened on Friday, the day of preparation,* the day before the Sabbath. As evening

15:16 Greek *the courtyard, which is the praetorium.* **15:21** *Cyrene* was a city in northern Africa. **15:24** Greek *casting lots.* See Ps 22:18. **15:27** Some manuscripts add verse 28, *And the Scripture was fulfilled that said, "He was counted among those who were rebels."* See Isa 53:12. **15:34** Ps 22:1. **15:40** Greek *Joses;* also in 15:47. See Matt 27:56. **15:42** Greek *on the day of preparation.*

approached, 43an honored member of the high
council, Joseph from Arimathea (who was waiting for the Kingdom of God to come), gathered
his courage and went to Pilate to ask for Jesus'
body. 44Pilate couldn't believe that Jesus was
already dead, so he called for the Roman military officer in charge and asked him. 45The officer confirmed the fact, and Pilate told Joseph he
could have the body. 46Joseph bought a long
sheet of linen cloth, and taking Jesus' body
down from the cross, he wrapped it in the cloth
and laid it in a tomb that had been carved out of
the rock. Then he rolled a stone in front of the
entrance. 47Mary Magdalene and Mary the
mother of Joseph saw where Jesus' body was
laid.

CHAPTER 16

The Resurrection

The next evening, when the Sabbath ended,
Mary Magdalene and Salome and Mary the
mother of James went out and purchased
burial spices to put on Jesus' body. 2Very early
on Sunday morning,* just at sunrise, they
came to the tomb. 3On the way they were
discussing who would roll the stone away
from the entrance to the tomb. 4But when they
arrived, they looked up and saw that the
stone—a very large one—had already been
rolled aside. 5So they entered the tomb, and
there on the right sat a young man clothed in
a white robe. The women were startled, 6but
the angel said, "Do not be so surprised. You
are looking for Jesus, the Nazarene, who was
crucified. He isn't here! He has been raised
from the dead! Look, this is where they laid his
body. 7Now go and give this message to his
disciples, including Peter: Jesus is going ahead
of you to Galilee. You will see him there, just
as he told you before he died!" 8The women
fled from the tomb, trembling and bewildered,
saying nothing to anyone because they were
too frightened to talk.*

[Shorter Ending of Mark]

Then they reported all these instructions briefly to Peter and his companions. Afterward Jesus himself sent them out from east to west with the sacred and unfailing message of salvation that gives eternal life. Amen.

[Longer Ending of Mark]

9It was early on Sunday morning when Jesus rose
from the dead, and the first person who saw him
was Mary Magdalene, the woman from whom he
had cast out seven demons. 10She went and found
the disciples, who were grieving and weeping. 11But
when she told them that Jesus was alive and she had
seen him, they didn't believe her.

12Afterward he appeared to two who were
walking from Jerusalem into the country, but
they didn't recognize him at first because he had
changed his appearance. 13When they realized
who he was, they rushed back to tell the others,
but no one believed them.

14Still later he appeared to the eleven disciples
as they were eating together. He rebuked them for
their unbelief—their stubborn refusal to believe
those who had seen him after he had risen.

15And then he told them, "Go into all the
world and preach the Good News to everyone,
everywhere. 16Anyone who believes and is baptized will be saved. But anyone who refuses to
believe will be condemned. 17These signs will
accompany those who believe: They will cast out
demons in my name, and they will speak new
languages.* 18They will be able to handle snakes
with safety, and if they drink anything poisonous, it won't hurt them. They will be able to
place their hands on the sick and heal them."

19When the Lord Jesus had finished talking
with them, he was taken up into heaven and sat
down in the place of honor at God's right hand.
20And the disciples went everywhere and
preached, and the Lord worked with them, con-
firming what they said by many miraculous signs.

16:2 Greek *on the first day of the week;* also in 16:9. 16:8 The most reliable early manuscripts conclude the Gospel of Mark at verse 8. Other manuscripts include various endings to the Gospel. Two of the more noteworthy endings are printed here. 16:17 Or *new tongues.* Some manuscripts omit *new.*

Luke

CHAPTER 1

Introduction

Most honorable Theophilus:
Many people have written accounts about the
events that took place* among us. 2They used as
their source material the reports circulating
among us from the early disciples and other
eyewitnesses of what God has done in fulfillment
of his promises. 3Having carefully investigated all
of these accounts from the beginning, I have
decided to write a careful summary for you, 4to
reassure you of the truth of all you were taught.

The Birth of John the Baptist Foretold

5It all begins with a Jewish priest, Zechariah,
who lived when Herod was king of Judea. Zechariah was a member of the priestly order of Abijah. His wife, Elizabeth, was also from the
priestly line of Aaron. 6Zechariah and Elizabeth
were righteous in God's eyes, careful to obey all
of the Lord's commandments and regulations.
7They had no children because Elizabeth was
barren, and now they were both very old.

8One day Zechariah was serving God in the
Temple, for his order was on duty that week. 9As
was the custom of the priests, he was chosen by
lot to enter the sanctuary and burn incense in the
Lord's presence. 10While the incense was being
burned, a great crowd stood outside, praying.

11Zechariah was in the sanctuary when an
angel of the Lord appeared, standing to the right
of the incense altar. 12Zechariah was overwhelmed with fear. 13But the angel said, "Don't
be afraid, Zechariah! For God has heard your
prayer, and your wife, Elizabeth, will bear you a
son! And you are to name him John. 14You will
have great joy and gladness, and many will rejoice with you at his birth, 15for he will be great
in the eyes of the Lord. He must never touch
wine or hard liquor, and he will be filled with
the Holy Spirit, even before his birth.* 16And he
will persuade many Israelites to turn to the Lord
their God. 17He will be a man with the spirit and
power of Elijah, the prophet of old. He will
precede the coming of the Lord, preparing the
people for his arrival. He will turn the hearts of
the fathers to their children, and he will change
disobedient minds to accept godly wisdom."*

18Zechariah said to the angel, "How can I
know this will happen? I'm an old man now,
and my wife is also well along in years."

19Then the angel said, "I am Gabriel! I stand in
the very presence of God. It was he who sent me
to bring you this good news! 20And now, since you
didn't believe what I said, you won't be able to
speak until the child is born. For my words will
certainly come true at the proper time."

21Meanwhile, the people were waiting for
Zechariah to come out, wondering why he was
taking so long. 22When he finally did come out,
he couldn't speak to them. Then they realized
from his gestures that he must have seen a vision
in the Temple sanctuary.

23He stayed at the Temple until his term of
service was over, and then he returned home.
24Soon afterward his wife, Elizabeth, became
pregnant and went into seclusion for five
months. 25"How kind the Lord is!" she exclaimed. "He has taken away my disgrace of
having no children!"

The Birth of Jesus Foretold

26In the sixth month of Elizabeth's pregnancy,
God sent the angel Gabriel to Nazareth, a village
in Galilee, 27to a virgin named Mary. She was
engaged to be married to a man named Joseph,

1:1 Or *have been fulfilled.* 1:15 Or *even from birth.* 1:17 See Mal 4:5-6.

a descendant of King David. 28Gabriel appeared
to her and said, "Greetings, favored woman!
The Lord is with you!*"
29Confused and disturbed, Mary tried to
think what the angel could mean. 30"Don't be
frightened, Mary," the angel told her, "for God
has decided to bless you! 31You will become
pregnant and have a son, and you are to name
him Jesus. 32He will be very great and will be
called the Son of the Most High. And the Lord
God will give him the throne of his ancestor
David. 33And he will reign over Israel* forever;
his Kingdom will never end!"
34Mary asked the angel, "But how can I have
a baby? I am a virgin."
35The angel replied, "The Holy Spirit will
come upon you, and the power of the Most
High will overshadow you. So the baby born to
you will be holy, and he will be called the Son
of God. 36What's more, your relative Elizabeth
has become pregnant in her old age! People
used to say she was barren, but she's already in
her sixth month. 37For nothing is impossible
with God."
38Mary responded, "I am the Lord's servant,
and I am willing to accept whatever he wants.
May everything you have said come true." And
then the angel left.

Mary Visits Elizabeth

39A few days later Mary hurried to the hill country of Judea, to the town 40where Zechariah
lived. She entered the house and greeted Elizabeth. 41At the sound of Mary's greeting, Elizabeth's child leaped within her, and Elizabeth
was filled with the Holy Spirit.
42Elizabeth gave a glad cry and exclaimed to
Mary, "You are blessed by God above all other
women, and your child is blessed. 43What an
honor this is, that the mother of my Lord should
visit me! 44When you came in and greeted me,
my baby jumped for joy the instant I heard your
voice! 45You are blessed, because you believed
that the Lord would do what he said."

The Magnificat: Mary's Song of Praise

46Mary responded,

"Oh, how I praise the Lord.
47 How I rejoice in God my Savior!
48 For he took notice of his lowly servant girl,
and now generation after generation
will call me blessed.
49 For he, the Mighty One, is holy,
and he has done great things for me.
50 His mercy goes on from generation to
generation,
to all who fear him.
51 His mighty arm does tremendous things!
How he scatters the proud and haughty
ones!
52 He has taken princes from their thrones
and exalted the lowly.
53 He has satisfied the hungry with good things
and sent the rich away with empty hands.
54 And how he has helped his servant Israel!
He has not forgotten his promise to be
merciful.
55 For he promised our ancestors—Abraham
and his children—
to be merciful to them forever."

56Mary stayed with Elizabeth about three
months and then went back to her own home.

The Birth of John the Baptist

57Now it was time for Elizabeth's baby to be
born, and it was a boy. 58The word spread
quickly to her neighbors and relatives that the
Lord had been very kind to her, and everyone
rejoiced with her.
59When the baby was eight days old, all the
relatives and friends came for the circumcision
ceremony. They wanted to name him Zechariah,
after his father. 60But Elizabeth said, "No! His
name is John!"
61"What?" they exclaimed. "There is no one
in all your family by that name." 62So they asked
the baby's father, communicating to him by
making gestures. 63He motioned for a writing
tablet, and to everyone's surprise he wrote, "His
name is John!" 64Instantly Zechariah could
speak again, and he began praising God.
65Wonder fell upon the whole neighbor-
hood, and the news of what had happened
spread throughout the Judean hills. 66Everyone
who heard about it reflected on these events and
asked, "I wonder what this child will turn out to
be? For the hand of the Lord is surely upon him
in a special way."

Zechariah's Prophecy

67Then his father, Zechariah, was filled with the
Holy Spirit and gave this prophecy:

68 "Praise the Lord, the God of Israel,
because he has visited his people and
redeemed them.

1:28 Some manuscripts add *Blessed are you among women.* 1:33 Greek *over the house of Jacob.*

Is the Bible Believable? Read LUKE 1:1-4

In writing this Gospel, Luke took painstaking efforts to confirm the accuracy of his work. He made it clear that he meticulously put this book together, going so far as to "recheck" the disciples' accounts "from the beginning."

Although Luke and other writers of the books of the Bible have taken great pains to accurately record the events within, some people have tried to point out alleged contradictions or inconsistencies in the Bible. These same people argue that the Bible is not credible based on what they believe to be contradictions. But here are three reasons why the Bible is believable:

1. God Is the Author. Despite the fact that the Bible was written by more than forty authors, we must recognize one important fact: The people who put the pen to the paper were but instruments in the hand of God. The real author of the Bible is God. As the apostle Paul wrote, "All Scripture is inspired by God" (2 Timothy 3:16). God chose to speak through these different people much like an artist uses different brushes to paint on a canvas. Each one had his own unique style, but the truth was the same.

2. The Main Story of the Bible Is Too Complex to Be a Hoax. The renowned historian Will Durant, who devoted his life to the study of records of antiquity, made this observation concerning the accounts of Jesus and the early church in Scripture: "That a few simple men should in one generation have invented so powerful and appealing a personality, so lofty an ethic, and so inspiring a vision of human brotherhood, would be a miracle far more incredible than any recorded in the Gospels. After two centuries of Higher Criticism the outlines of life, character, and teaching of Christ remain reasonably clear, and constitute the most fascinating feature in the history of Western man" [*Caesar and Christ,* in The Story of Civilization, vol. 3 (New York: Simon & Schuster, 1944), p. 557].

3. Scientific Evidence Supports the Bible's Accuracy. Archaeological findings have supported many of the complex historical passages found in the Bible. In addition, the Bible has greater documented accuracy than any other ancient literary work [see Norman L. Geisler & William E. Nix, *A General Introduction to the Bible* (Chicago: Moody Press, Moody Bible Institute, 1986)].

In spite of the evidence, God's Word must be accepted by faith. You, as an individual, must come to recognize that the words of the Lord are perfect, trustworthy, and right (see Hebrews 11:7-12). Your belief in and practice of the truths found in this book—God's message to us—will make the most profound impact on your life for time and eternity.

BIG QUESTIONS

69 He has sent us a mighty Savior
from the royal line of his servant David,
70 just as he promised
through his holy prophets long ago.
71 Now we will be saved from our enemies
and from all who hate us.
72 He has been merciful to our ancestors
by remembering his sacred covenant
with them,
73 the covenant he gave to our ancestor
Abraham.
74 We have been rescued from our enemies,
so we can serve God without fear,
75 in holiness and righteousness forever.

76 "And you, my little son,
will be called the prophet of the Most
High,
because you will prepare the way for the
Lord.
77 You will tell his people how to find
salvation
through forgiveness of their sins.
78 Because of God's tender mercy,
the light from heaven is about to break
upon us,
79 to give light to those who sit in darkness
and in the shadow of death,
and to guide us to the path of peace."

80John grew up and became strong in spirit.
Then he lived out in the wilderness until he
began his public ministry to Israel.

CHAPTER 2

The Birth of Jesus

At that time the Roman emperor, Augustus, de-
creed that a census should be taken throughout
the Roman Empire. 2(This was the first census
taken when Quirinius was governor of Syria.)
3All returned to their own towns to register for
this census. 4And because Joseph was a descendant of King David, he had to go to Bethlehem
in Judea, David's ancient home. He traveled
there from the village of Nazareth in Galilee.
5He took with him Mary, his fiancée, who was
obviously pregnant by this time.

6And while they were there, the time came for
her baby to be born. 7She gave birth to her first
child, a son. She wrapped him snugly in strips of
cloth and laid him in a manger, because there
was no room for them in the village inn.

The Shepherds and Angels

8That night some shepherds were in the fields
outside the village, guarding their flocks of sheep.
9Suddenly, an angel of the Lord appeared among
them, and the radiance of the Lord's glory surrounded them. They were terribly frightened,
10but the angel reassured them. "Don't be afraid!"
he said. "I bring you good news of great joy for
everyone! 11The Savior—yes, the Messiah, the
Lord—has been born tonight in Bethlehem, the
city of David! 12And this is how you will recognize
him: You will find a baby lying in a manger,
wrapped snugly in strips of cloth!"

13Suddenly, the angel was joined by a vast host
of others—the armies of heaven—praising God:

14 "Glory to God in the highest heaven,
and peace on earth to all whom God
favors.*"

15When the angels had returned to heaven,
the shepherds said to each other, " Come on,
let's go to Bethlehem! Let's see this wonderful
thing that has happened, which the Lord has
told us about."

16They ran to the village and found Mary and
Joseph. And there was the baby, lying in the manger. 17Then the shepherds told everyone what had
happened and what the angel had said to them
about this child. 18All who heard the shepherds'
story were astonished, 19but Mary quietly trea-
sured these things in her heart and thought about
them often. 20The shepherds went back to their
fields and flocks, glorifying and praising God for
what the angels had told them, and because they
had seen the child, just as the angel had said.

Jesus Is Presented in the Temple

21Eight days later, when the baby was circumcised, he was named Jesus, the name given him
by the angel even before he was conceived.

22Then it was time for the purification offering, as required by the law of Moses after the
birth of a child; so his parents took him to
Jerusalem to present him to the Lord. 23The law
of the Lord says, "If a woman's first child is a
boy, he must be dedicated to the Lord."* 24So
they offered a sacrifice according to what was
required in the law of the Lord—"either a pair
of turtledoves or two young pigeons."*

The Prophecy of Simeon

25Now there was a man named Simeon who
lived in Jerusalem. He was a righteous man and
very devout. He was filled with the Holy Spirit,
and he eagerly expected the Messiah to come
and rescue Israel. 26The Holy Spirit had revealed
to him that he would not die until he had seen
the Lord's Messiah. 27That day the Spirit led him
to the Temple. So when Mary and Joseph came
to present the baby Jesus to the Lord as the law
required, 28Simeon was there. He took the child
in his arms and praised God, saying,

29 "Lord, now I can die in peace!
As you promised me,
30 I have seen the Savior
31 you have given to all people.
32 He is a light to reveal God to the nations,
and he is the glory of your people Israel!"

33Joseph and Mary were amazed at what was
being said about Jesus. 34Then Simeon blessed
them, and he said to Mary, "This child will be
rejected by many in Israel, and it will be their
undoing. But he will be the greatest joy to many
others. 35Thus, the deepest thoughts of many
hearts will be revealed. And a sword will pierce
your very soul."

The Prophecy of Anna

36Anna, a prophet, was also there in the Temple.
She was the daughter of Phanuel, of the tribe of
Asher, and was very old. She was a widow, for her

2:14 Or *and peace on earth for all those pleasing God.* Some manuscripts read *and peace on earth, goodwill among people.* 2:23 Exod 13:2. 2:24 Lev 12:8.

husband had died when they had been married
only seven years. 37She was now eighty-four
years old. She never left the Temple but stayed
there day and night, worshiping God with fasting and prayer. 38She came along just as Simeon
was talking with Mary and Joseph, and she began praising God. She talked about Jesus to
everyone who had been waiting for the promised King to come and deliver Jerusalem.

39When Jesus' parents had fulfilled all the
requirements of the law of the Lord, they returned home to Nazareth in Galilee. 40There the
child grew up healthy and strong. He was filled
with wisdom beyond his years, and God placed
his special favor upon him.

Jesus Speaks with the Teachers

41Every year Jesus' parents went to Jerusalem for
the Passover festival. 42When Jesus was twelve
years old, they attended the festival as usual.
43After the celebration was over, they started
home to Nazareth, but Jesus stayed behind in
Jerusalem. His parents didn't miss him at first,
44because they assumed he was with friends
among the other travelers. But when he didn't
show up that evening, they started to look for
him among their relatives and friends. 45When
they couldn't find him, they went back to Jerusalem to search for him there. 46Three days later
they finally discovered him. He was in the
Temple, sitting among the religious teachers,
discussing deep questions with them. 47And all
who heard him were amazed at his understanding and his answers.

48His parents didn't know what to think.
"Son!" his mother said to him. "Why have you
done this to us? Your father and I have been
frantic, searching for you everywhere."

49"But why did you need to search?" he
asked. "You should have known that I would be
in my Father's house."* 50But they didn't understand what he meant.

51Then he returned to Nazareth with them
and was obedient to them; and his mother
stored all these things in her heart. 52So Jesus
grew both in height and in wisdom, and he was
loved by God and by all who knew him.

CHAPTER 3

John the Baptist Prepares the Way

It was now the fifteenth year of the reign of
Tiberius, the Roman emperor. Pilate was governor over Judea; Herod Antipas was ruler* over
Galilee; his brother Philip was ruler* over Iturea
and Traconitis; Lysanias was ruler over Abilene.
2Annas and Caiaphas were the high priests. At
this time a message from God came to John son
of Zechariah, who was living out in the wilderness. 3Then John went from place to place on
both sides of the Jordan River, preaching that
people should be baptized to show that they
had turned from their sins and turned to God to
be forgiven.* 4Isaiah had spoken of John when
he said,

"He is a voice shouting in the wilderness:
'Prepare a pathway for the Lord's coming!
  Make a straight road for him!
5 Fill in the valleys,
  and level the mountains and hills!
Straighten the curves,
  and smooth out the rough places!
6 And then all people will see
  the salvation sent from God.'"*

7Here is a sample of John's preaching to the
crowds that came for baptism: "You brood of
snakes! Who warned you to flee God's coming
judgment? 8Prove by the way you live that you
have really turned from your sins and turned to
God. Don't just say, 'We're safe—we're the descendants of Abraham.' That proves nothing.
God can change these stones here into children
of Abraham. 9Even now the ax of God's judgment is poised, ready to sever your roots. Yes,
every tree that does not produce good fruit will
be chopped down and thrown into the fire."

10The crowd asked, "What should we do?"

11John replied, "If you have two coats, give
one to the poor. If you have food, share it with
those who are hungry."

12Even corrupt tax collectors came to be baptized and asked, "Teacher, what should we do?"

13"Show your honesty," he replied. "Make
sure you collect no more taxes than the Roman
government requires you to."

14"What should we do?" asked some soldiers.

John replied, "Don't extort money, and don't
accuse people of things you know they didn't
do. And be content with your pay."

15Everyone was expecting the Messiah to
come soon, and they were eager to know
whether John might be the Messiah. 16John answered their questions by saying, "I baptize
with* water; but someone is coming soon who
is greater than I am—so much greater that I am

2:49 Or *"Didn't you realize that I should be involved with my Father's affairs?"* 3:1a Greek *Herod was tetrarch.* Herod Antipas was a son of King Herod. 3:1b Greek *tetrarch;* also in 3:19. 3:3 Greek *preaching a baptism of repentance for the forgiveness of sins.* 3:4-6 Isa 40:3-5. 3:16a Or *in.*

Jesus Had a Specific Mission to Accomplish Read LUKE 4:16-21

Jesus quoted from Isaiah 61:1-2 to describe the purpose of his ministry. This portion of Scripture describes five goals of Jesus' personal ministry on earth:

1. Preach the Good News to the Poor. Jesus ministered to people from all walks of life—from the wealthy tax collectors, to the "blue collar" fishermen, to the beggars on the street. It was not people's financial status that he was concerned with. Rather, he looked beyond people's outward need to their inward need. He saw the poverty of their soul. And to those who will listen, Jesus offers the good news of the gospel.

2. Heal the Brokenhearted. When your heart is broken, you may feel as though no one understands or cares. Yet Jesus understands. He knows what it is like to be abandoned by friends. He has experienced what it is like to be let down. He understands the sting of death. For that reason, he wants to heal your broken heart.

3. Bring Deliverance to the Captives. The Bible teaches that before we give our lives to God, we are held captive by sin. If you find yourself a slave to some vice or sin that you just can't overcome, Jesus wants to release you from that spiritual bondage. Just admit your sinful condition and turn from it, and ask God to give you a new heart. Then begin to yield yourself to the help and power of the Holy Spirit, and you will know true freedom.

4. Give Sight to the Blind. The Bible also teaches that before we give our lives to Jesus Christ, we are spiritually blind: "Satan, the god of this evil world, has blinded the minds of those who don't believe, so they are unable to see the glorious light of the Good News that is shining upon them. They don't understand the message we preach about the glory of Christ, who is the exact likeness of God" (2 Corinthians 4:4). Jesus wants to open our eyes so that we can understand and respond to the gospel message.

5. Bring Liberty to the Oppressed. The word *downtrodden* can also be translated "those who are crushed with life." Jesus understands your worries and hurts, and he wants to lift those burdens from your shoulders.

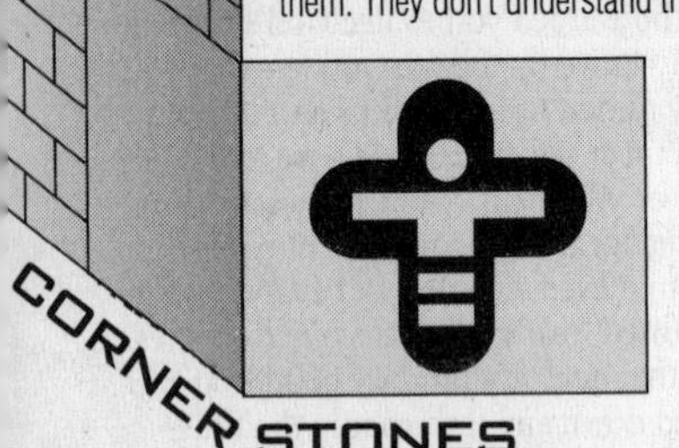

not even worthy to be his slave.* He will baptize
you with the Holy Spirit and with fire.* 17He is
ready to separate the chaff from the grain with
his winnowing fork. Then he will clean up the
threshing area, storing the grain in his barn but
burning the chaff with never-ending fire."
18John used many such warnings as he announced the Good News to the people.

19John also publicly criticized Herod Antipas,
ruler of Galilee, for marrying Herodias, his
brother's wife, and for many other wrongs he
had done. 20So Herod put John in prison, adding this sin to his many others.

The Baptism of Jesus

21One day when the crowds were being baptized,
Jesus himself was baptized. As he was praying, the
heavens opened, 22and the Holy Spirit descended
on him in the form of a dove. And a voice from
heaven said, "You are my beloved Son, and I am
fully pleased with you.*"

The Record of Jesus' Ancestors

23Jesus was about thirty years old when he began
his public ministry.

Jesus was known as the son of Joseph.
Joseph was the son of Heli.
24 Heli was the son of Matthat.
Matthat was the son of Levi.
Levi was the son of Melki.
Melki was the son of Jannai.
Jannai was the son of Joseph.
25 Joseph was the son of Mattathias.

3:16b Greek *to untie his sandals.* **3:16c** Or *in the Holy Spirit and in fire.* **3:22** Some manuscripts read *and today I have become your Father.*

Mattathias was the son of Amos.
Amos was the son of Nahum.
Nahum was the son of Esli.
Esli was the son of Naggai.
26 Naggai was the son of Maath.
Maath was the son of Mattathias.
Mattathias was the son of Semein.
Semein was the son of Josech.
Josech was the son of Joda.
27 Joda was the son of Joanan.
Joanan was the son of Rhesa.
Rhesa was the son of Zerubbabel.
Zerubbabel was the son of Shealtiel.
Shealtiel was the son of Neri.
28 Neri was the son of Melki.
Melki was the son of Addi.
Addi was the son of Cosam.
Cosam was the son of Elmadam.
Elmadam was the son of Er.
29 Er was the son of Joshua.
Joshua was the son of Eliezer.
Eliezer was the son of Jorim.
Jorim was the son of Matthat.
Matthat was the son of Levi.
30 Levi was the son of Simeon.
Simeon was the son of Judah.
Judah was the son of Joseph.
Joseph was the son of Jonam.
Jonam was the son of Eliakim.
31 Eliakim was the son of Melea.
Melea was the son of Menna.
Menna was the son of Mattatha.
Mattatha was the son of Nathan.
Nathan was the son of David.
32 David was the son of Jesse.
Jesse was the son of Obed.
Obed was the son of Boaz.
Boaz was the son of Salmon.*
Salmon was the son of Nahshon.
33 Nahshon was the son of Amminadab.
Amminadab was the son of Admin.
Admin was the son of Arni.*
Arni was the son of Hezron.
Hezron was the son of Perez.
Perez was the son of Judah.
34 Judah was the son of Jacob.
Jacob was the son of Isaac.
Isaac was the son of Abraham.
Abraham was the son of Terah.
Terah was the son of Nahor.
35 Nahor was the son of Serug.
Serug was the son of Reu.
Reu was the son of Peleg.
Peleg was the son of Eber.
Eber was the son of Shelah.
36 Shelah was the son of Cainan.
Cainan was the son of Arphaxad.
Arphaxad was the son of Shem.
Shem was the son of Noah.
Noah was the son of Lamech.
37 Lamech was the son of Methuselah.
Methuselah was the son of Enoch.
Enoch was the son of Jared.
Jared was the son of Mahalalel.
Mahalalel was the son of Kenan.
38 Kenan was the son of Enosh.*
Enosh was the son of Seth.
Seth was the son of Adam.
Adam was the son of God.

CHAPTER 4

The Temptation of Jesus

Then Jesus, full of the Holy Spirit, left the Jordan
River. He was led by the Spirit to go out into the
wilderness, 2where the Devil tempted him for forty
days. He ate nothing all that time and was very
hungry.

3Then the Devil said to him, "If you are the Son
of God, change this stone into a loaf of bread."

4But Jesus told him, "No! The Scriptures say,
'People need more than bread for their life.'* "

5Then the Devil took him up and revealed to
him all the kingdoms of the world in a moment
of time. 6The Devil told him, "I will give you the
glory of these kingdoms and authority over
them—because they are mine to give to anyone
I please. 7I will give it all to you if you will bow
down and worship me."

8Jesus replied, "The Scriptures say,

'You must worship the Lord your God;
serve only him.'* "

9Then the Devil took him to Jerusalem, to the
highest point of the Temple, and said, "If you are
the Son of God, jump off! 10For the Scriptures say,

'He orders his angels to protect and guard you.
11 And they will hold you with their hands
to keep you from striking your foot on a
stone.'* "

12Jesus responded, "The Scriptures also say,
'Do not test the Lord your God.'* "

13When the Devil had finished tempting
Jesus, he left him until the next opportunity
came.

3:32 Greek *Sala;* see Ruth 4:22. 3:33 *Arni* is the same person as Ram; see 1 Chr 2:9-10. 3:38 Greek *Enos;* see Gen 5:6. 4:4 Deut 8:3. 4:8 Deut 6:13. 4:10-11 Ps 91:11-12. 4:12 Deut 6:16.

Jesus Rejected at Nazareth

14 Then Jesus returned to Galilee, filled with the Holy Spirit's power. Soon he became well known throughout the surrounding country. 15 He taught in their synagogues and was praised by everyone.

16 When he came to the village of Nazareth, his boyhood home, he went as usual to the synagogue on the Sabbath and stood up to read the Scriptures. 17 The scroll containing the messages of Isaiah the prophet was handed to him, and he unrolled the scroll to the place where it says:

18 "The Spirit of the Lord is upon me,
for he has appointed me to preach Good
News to the poor.
He has sent me to proclaim
that captives will be released,
that the blind will see,
that the downtrodden will be freed from
their oppressors,
19 and that the time of the Lord's favor has
come.*"

20 He rolled up the scroll, handed it back to the attendant, and sat down. Everyone in the synagogue stared at him intently. 21 Then he said, "This Scripture has come true today before your very eyes!"

22 All who were there spoke well of him and were amazed by the gracious words that fell from his lips. "How can this be?" they asked. "Isn't this Joseph's son?"

23 Then he said, "Probably you will quote me that proverb, 'Physician, heal yourself'—meaning, 'Why don't you do miracles here in your hometown like those you did in Capernaum?' 24 But the truth is, no prophet is accepted in his own hometown.

25 "Certainly there were many widows in Israel who needed help in Elijah's time, when there was no rain for three and a half years and hunger stalked the land. 26 Yet Elijah was not sent to any of them. He was sent instead to a widow of Zarephath—a foreigner in the land of Sidon. 27 Or think of the prophet Elisha, who healed Naaman, a Syrian, rather than the many lepers in Israel who needed help."

28 When they heard this, the people in the synagogue were furious. 29 Jumping up, they mobbed him and took him to the edge of the hill on which the city was built. They intended to push him over the cliff, 30 but he slipped away through the crowd and left them.

Jesus Casts Out a Demon

31 Then Jesus went to Capernaum, a town in Galilee, and taught there in the synagogue every Sabbath day. 32 There, too, the people were amazed at the things he said, because he spoke with authority.

33 Once when he was in the synagogue, a man possessed by a demon began shouting at Jesus, 34 "Go away! Why are you bothering us, Jesus of Nazareth? Have you come to destroy us? I know who you are—the Holy One sent from God."

35 Jesus cut him short. "Be silent!" he told the demon. "Come out of the man!" The demon threw the man to the floor as the crowd watched; then it left him without hurting him further.

36 Amazed, the people exclaimed, "What authority and power this man's words possess! Even evil spirits obey him and flee at his command!" 37 The story of what he had done spread like wildfire throughout the whole region.

Jesus Heals Many People

38 After leaving the synagogue that day, Jesus went to Simon's home, where he found Simon's mother-in-law very sick with a high fever. "Please heal her," everyone begged. 39 Standing at her bedside, he spoke to the fever, rebuking it, and immediately her temperature returned to normal. She got up at once and prepared a meal for them.

40 As the sun went down that evening, people throughout the village brought sick family members to Jesus. No matter what their diseases were, the touch of his hand healed every one. 41 Some were possessed by demons; and the demons came out at his command, shouting, "You are the Son of God." But because they knew he was the Messiah, he stopped them and told them to be silent.

Jesus Continues to Preach

42 Early the next morning Jesus went out into the wilderness. The crowds searched everywhere for him, and when they finally found him, they begged him not to leave them. 43 But he replied, "I must preach the Good News of the Kingdom of God in other places, too, because that is why I was sent." 44 So he continued to travel around, preaching in synagogues throughout Judea.*

CHAPTER 5

The First Disciples

One day as Jesus was preaching on the shore of the Sea of Galilee,* great crowds pressed in on him to listen to the word of God. 2 He noticed two empty

4:18-19 Or *and to proclaim the acceptable year of the Lord.* Isa 61:1-2. **4:44** Some manuscripts read *Galilee.* **5:1** Greek *Lake Gennesaret,* another name for the Sea of Galilee.

boats at the water's edge, for the fishermen had left
them and were washing their nets. 3Stepping into
one of the boats, Jesus asked Simon,* its owner, to
push it out into the water. So he sat in the boat and
taught the crowds from there.

4When he had finished speaking, he said to
Simon, "Now go out where it is deeper and let
down your nets, and you will catch many fish."

5"Master," Simon replied, "we worked hard
all last night and didn't catch a thing. But if you
say so, we'll try again." 6And this time their nets
were so full they began to tear! 7A shout for help
brought their partners in the other boat, and
soon both boats were filled with fish and on the
verge of sinking.

8When Simon Peter realized what had happened, he fell to his knees before Jesus and said,
"Oh, Lord, please leave me—I'm too much of a
sinner to be around you." 9For he was awestruck
by the size of their catch, as were the others with
him. 10His partners, James and John, the sons of
Zebedee, were also amazed.

Jesus replied to Simon, "Don't be afraid!
From now on you'll be fishing for people!"
11And as soon as they landed, they left everything and followed Jesus.

Jesus Heals a Man with Leprosy

12In one of the villages, Jesus met a man with an
advanced case of leprosy. When the man saw
Jesus, he fell to the ground, face down in the
dust, begging to be healed. "Lord," he said, "if
you want to, you can make me well again."

13Jesus reached out and touched the man. "I
want to," he said. "Be healed!" And instantly the
leprosy disappeared. 14Then Jesus instructed
him not to tell anyone what had happened. He
said, "Go right to the priest and let him examine
you. Take along the offering required in the law
of Moses for those who have been healed of
leprosy, so everyone will have proof of your
healing." 15Yet despite Jesus' instructions, the
report of his power spread even faster, and vast
crowds came to hear him preach and to be
healed of their diseases. 16But Jesus often withdrew to the wilderness for prayer.

Jesus Heals a Paralyzed Man

17One day while Jesus was teaching, some Pharisees and teachers of religious law were sitting
nearby. (It seemed that these men showed up
from every village in all Galilee and Judea, as well
as from Jerusalem.) And the Lord's healing power
was strongly with Jesus. 18Some men came carrying a paralyzed man on a sleeping mat. They tried
to push through the crowd to Jesus, 19but they
couldn't reach him. So they went up to the roof,
took off some tiles, and lowered the sick man
down into the crowd, still on his mat, right in front
of Jesus. 20Seeing their faith, Jesus said to the man,
"Son, your sins are forgiven."

21"Who does this man think he is?" the Pharisees and teachers of religious law said to each
other. "This is blasphemy! Who but God can
forgive sins?"

22Jesus knew what they were thinking, so he
asked them, "Why do you think this is blasphemy? 23Is it easier to say, 'Your sins are forgiven' or 'Get up and walk'? 24I will prove that I,
the Son of Man, have the authority on earth to
forgive sins." Then Jesus turned to the paralyzed
man and said, "Stand up, take your mat, and go
on home, because you are healed!"

25And immediately, as everyone watched, the
man jumped to his feet, picked up his mat, and
went home praising God. 26Everyone was
gripped with great wonder and awe. And they
praised God, saying over and over again, "We
have seen amazing things today."

Jesus Calls Levi (Matthew)

27Later, as Jesus left the town, he saw a tax-collec-
tor named Levi sitting at his tax-collection booth.
"Come, be my disciple!" Jesus said to him. 28So
Levi got up, left everything, and followed him.

29Soon Levi held a banquet in his home with
Jesus as the guest of honor. Many of Levi's fellow
tax collectors and other guests were there. 30But
the Pharisees and their teachers of religious law
complained bitterly to Jesus' disciples, "Why do
you eat and drink with such scum*?"

31Jesus answered them, "Healthy people
don't need a doctor—sick people do. 32I have
come to call sinners to turn from their sins, not
to spend my time with those who think they are
already good enough."

A Discussion about Fasting

33The religious leaders complained that Jesus'
disciples were feasting instead of fasting. "John
the Baptist's disciples always fast and pray," they
declared, "and so do the disciples of the Pharisees. Why are yours always feasting?"

34Jesus asked, "Do wedding guests fast while
celebrating with the groom? 35Someday he will be
taken away from them, and then they will fast."

5:3 *Simon* is called *Peter* in 6:14 and thereafter. 5:30 Greek *with tax collectors and sinners.*

36Then Jesus gave them this illustration: "No
one tears a piece of cloth from a new garment
and uses it to patch an old garment. For then the
new garment would be torn, and the patch
wouldn't even match the old garment. 37And no
one puts new wine into old wineskins. The new
wine would burst the old skins, spilling the wine
and ruining the skins. 38New wine must be put
into new wineskins. 39But no one who drinks
the old wine seems to want the fresh and the
new. 'The old is better,' they say."

CHAPTER 6

A Discussion about the Sabbath

One Sabbath day as Jesus was walking through
some grainfields, his disciples broke off heads of
wheat, rubbed off the husks in their hands, and
ate the grains. 2But some Pharisees said, "You
shouldn't be doing that! It's against the law to
work by harvesting grain on the Sabbath."

3Jesus replied, "Haven't you ever read in the
Scriptures what King David did when he and his
companions were hungry? 4He went into the
house of God, ate the special bread reserved for
the priests alone, and then gave some to his
friends. That was breaking the law, too." 5And
Jesus added, "I, the Son of Man, am master even
of the Sabbath."

Jesus Heals on the Sabbath

6On another Sabbath day, a man with a deformed right hand was in the synagogue while
Jesus was teaching. 7The teachers of religious
law and the Pharisees watched closely to see
whether Jesus would heal the man on the Sabbath, because they were eager to find some legal
charge to bring against him. 8But Jesus knew
their thoughts. He said to the man with the
deformed hand, "Come and stand here where
everyone can see." So the man came forward.
9Then Jesus said to his critics, "I have a question
for you. Is it legal to do good deeds on the
Sabbath, or is it a day for doing harm? Is this a
day to save life or to destroy it?" 10He looked
around at them one by one and then said to the
man, "Reach out your hand." The man reached
out his hand, and it became normal again! 11At
this, the enemies of Jesus were wild with rage
and began to discuss what to do with him.

Jesus Chooses the Twelve Apostles

12One day soon afterward Jesus went to a mountain to pray, and he prayed to God all night. 13At
daybreak he called together all of his disciples
and chose twelve of them to be apostles. Here
are their names:

14 Simon (he also called him Peter),
Andrew (Peter's brother),
James,
John,
Philip,
Bartholomew,
15 Matthew,
Thomas,
James (son of Alphaeus),
Simon (the Zealot),
16 Judas (son of James),
Judas Iscariot (who later betrayed him).

Crowds Follow Jesus

17When they came down the slopes of the
mountain, the disciples stood with Jesus on a
large, level area, surrounded by many of his
followers and by the crowds. There were people
from all over Judea and from Jerusalem and
from as far north as the seacoasts of Tyre and
Sidon. 18They had come to hear him and to be
healed, and Jesus cast out many evil spirits.
19Everyone was trying to touch him, because
healing power went out from him, and they
were all cured.

The Beatitudes

20Then Jesus turned to his disciples and said,

"God blesses you who are poor,
for the Kingdom of God is given to you.
21 God blesses you who are hungry now,
for you will be satisfied.
God blesses you who weep now,
for the time will come when you will
laugh with joy.
22 God blesses you who are hated and
excluded and mocked and cursed
because you are identified with me, the
Son of Man.

23"When that happens, rejoice! Yes, leap for
joy! For a great reward awaits you in heaven.
And remember, the ancient prophets were also
treated that way by your ancestors.

Sorrows Foretold

24 "What sorrows await you who are rich,
for you have your only happiness now.
25 What sorrows await you who are satisfied
and prosperous now,
for a time of awful hunger is before you.

What sorrows await you who laugh
carelessly,
for your laughing will turn to mourning
and sorrow.
26 What sorrows await you who are praised by
the crowds,
for their ancestors also praised false
prophets.

Love for Enemies

27"But if you are willing to listen, I say, love your
enemies. Do good to those who hate you. 28Pray
for the happiness of those who curse you. Pray
for those who hurt you. 29If someone slaps you
on one cheek, turn the other cheek. If someone
demands your coat, offer your shirt also. 30Give
what you have to anyone who asks you for it;
and when things are taken away from you, don't
try to get them back. 31Do for others as you
would like them to do for you.

32"Do you think you deserve credit merely for
loving those who love you? Even the sinners do
that! 33And if you do good only to those who do
good to you, is that so wonderful? Even sinners do
that much! 34And if you lend money only to those
who can repay you, what good is that? Even sinners will lend to their own kind for a full return.

35"Love your enemies! Do good to them!
Lend to them! And don't be concerned that they
might not repay. Then your reward from heaven
will be very great, and you will truly be acting as
children of the Most High, for he is kind to the
unthankful and to those who are wicked. 36You
must be compassionate, just as your Father is
compassionate.

Don't Condemn Others

37"Stop judging others, and you will not be
judged. Stop criticizing others, or it will all come
back on you. If you forgive others, you will be
forgiven. 38If you give, you will receive. Your gift
will return to you in full measure, pressed down,
shaken together to make room for more, and
running over. Whatever measure you use in giving—large or small—it will be used to measure
what is given back to you."

39Then Jesus gave the following illustration:
"What good is it for one blind person to lead
another? The first one will fall into a ditch and
pull the other down also. 40A student is not
greater than the teacher. But the student who
works hard will become like the teacher.

41"And why worry about a speck in your
friend's eye* when you have a log in your own?
42How can you think of saying, 'Friend,* let me
help you get rid of that speck in your eye,' when
you can't see past the log in your own eye?
Hypocrite! First get rid of the log from your own
eye; then perhaps you will see well enough to
deal with the speck in your friend's eye.

The Tree and Its Fruit

43"A good tree can't produce bad fruit, and a bad
tree can't produce good fruit. 44A tree is identified by the kind of fruit it produces. Figs never
grow on thornbushes or grapes on bramble

6:41 Greek *your brother's eye;* also in 6:42. 6:42 Greek *Brother.*

Trials Test Our Foundation

Read LUKE 6:48-49

From all outward appearances, these homes probably looked alike. They may have even had similar floor plans. The only thing that set them apart was their foundation. This became apparent when the storm hit. In the same way, when the storms of life hit us, the true foundation of our lives will be revealed. Upon which foundation have you built your life?

The Faulty (or Nonexistent) Foundation. The person who builds upon this foundation is known as a "hearer." This individual may be quick to read, listen, or talk about what Jesus has to say in his Word but will fail to apply those teachings to his or her own life. When the storms of life come—and they will—this person will be spiritually weakened and will likely "throw in the towel" on his or her faith because he or she does not have a good foothold.

The Rock Solid Foundation. The person who builds upon this foundation is known as a "doer." This individual not only listens to Jesus' teachings, but follows them in his or her day-to-day life. Such a person will be able to withstand even the most devastating tempest, because he or she is grounded in the teachings of the Lord.

If you find yourself on the faulty foundation, you still have time to remodel. But you are the only architect who can make that change.

bushes. 45A good person produces good deeds from a good heart, and an evil person produces evil deeds from an evil heart. Whatever is in your heart determines what you say.

Building on a Solid Foundation

46"So why do you call me 'Lord,' when you won't obey me? 47I will show you what it's like when someone comes to me, listens to my teaching, and then obeys me. 48It is like a person who builds a house on a strong foundation laid upon the underlying rock. When the floodwaters rise and break against the house, it stands firm because it is well built. 49But anyone who listens and doesn't obey is like a person who builds a house without a foundation. When the floods sweep down against that house, it will crumble into a heap of ruins."

CHAPTER 7

Faith of the Roman Officer

When Jesus had finished saying all this, he went back to Capernaum. 2Now the highly valued slave of a Roman officer was sick and near death. 3When the officer heard about Jesus, he sent some respected Jewish leaders to ask him to come and heal his slave. 4So they earnestly begged Jesus to come with them and help the man. "If anyone deserves your help, it is he," they said, 5"for he loves the Jews and even built a synagogue for us."

6So Jesus went with them. But just before they arrived at the house, the officer sent some friends to say, "Lord, don't trouble yourself by coming to my home, for I am not worthy of such an honor. 7I am not even worthy to come and meet you. Just say the word from where you are, and my servant will be healed. 8I know because I am under the authority of my superior officers, and I have authority over my soldiers. I only need to say, 'Go,' and they go, or 'Come,' and they come. And if I say to my slaves, 'Do this or that,' they do it."

9When Jesus heard this, he was amazed. Turning to the crowd, he said, "I tell you, I haven't seen faith like this in all the land of Israel!" 10And when the officer's friends returned to his house, they found the slave completely healed.

Jesus Raises a Widow's Son

11Soon afterward Jesus went with his disciples to the village of Nain, with a great crowd following him. 12A funeral procession was coming out as he approached the village gate. The boy who had died was the only son of a widow, and many mourners from the village were with her. 13When the Lord saw her, his heart overflowed with compassion. "Don't cry!" he said. 14Then he walked over to the coffin and touched it, and the bearers stopped. "Young man," he said, "get up." 15Then the dead boy sat up and began to talk to those around him! And Jesus gave him back to his mother.

16Great fear swept the crowd, and they praised God, saying, "A mighty prophet has risen among us," and "We have seen the hand of God at work today." 17The report of what Jesus had done that day spread all over Judea and even out across its borders.

Jesus and John the Baptist

18The disciples of John the Baptist told John about everything Jesus was doing. So John called for two of his disciples, 19and he sent them to the Lord to ask him, "Are you the Messiah we've been expecting, or should we keep looking for someone else?"

20John's two disciples found Jesus and said to him, "John the Baptist sent us to ask, 'Are you the Messiah we've been expecting, or should we keep looking for someone else?'"

21At that very time, he cured many people of their various diseases, and he cast out evil spirits and restored sight to the blind. 22Then he told John's disciples, "Go back to John and tell him what you have seen and heard—the blind see, the lame walk, the lepers are cured, the deaf hear, the dead are raised to life, and the Good News is being preached to the poor. 23And tell him, 'God blesses those who are not offended by me.*'"

24After they left, Jesus talked to the crowd about John. "Who is this man in the wilderness that you went out to see? Did you find him weak as a reed, moved by every breath of wind? 25Or were you expecting to see a man dressed in expensive clothes? No, people who wear beautiful clothes and live in luxury are found in palaces, not in the wilderness. 26Were you looking for a prophet? Yes, and he is more than a prophet. 27John is the man to whom the Scriptures refer when they say,

'Look, I am sending my messenger before
you,
and he will prepare your way before
you.'*

7:23 Or *who don't fall away because of me.* 7:27 Mal 3:1.

28I tell you, of all who have ever lived, none is
greater than John. Yet even the most insignificant person in the Kingdom of God is greater
than he is!"
29When they heard this, all the people, including the unjust tax collectors, agreed that
God's plan was right,* for they had been baptized by John. 30But the Pharisees and experts in
religious law had rejected God's plan for them,
for they had refused John's baptism.
31"How shall I describe this generation?"
Jesus asked. "With what will I compare them?
32They are like a group of children playing a
game in the public square. They complain to
their friends, 'We played wedding songs, and
you weren't happy, so we played funeral songs,
but you weren't sad.' 33For John the Baptist
didn't drink wine and he often fasted, and you
say, 'He's demon possessed.' 34And I, the Son of
Man, feast and drink, and you say, 'He's a glut-
ton and a drunkard, and a friend of the worst
sort of sinners!' 35But wisdom is shown to be
right by the lives of those who follow it.*"

Jesus Anointed by a Sinful Woman

36One of the Pharisees asked Jesus to come to
his home for a meal, so Jesus accepted the invitation and sat down to eat. 37A certain immoral
woman heard he was there and brought a beautiful jar* filled with expensive perfume. 38Then
she knelt behind him at his feet, weeping. Her
tears fell on his feet, and she wiped them off
with her hair. Then she kept kissing his feet and
putting perfume on them.
39When the Pharisee who was the host saw
what was happening and who the woman was,
he said to himself, "This proves that Jesus is no
prophet. If God had really sent him, he would
know what kind of woman is touching him.
She's a sinner!"
40Then Jesus spoke up and answered his
thoughts. "Simon," he said to the Pharisee, "I
have something to say to you."
"All right, Teacher," Simon replied, "go ahead."
41Then Jesus told him this story: "A man
loaned money to two people—five hundred
pieces of silver* to one and fifty pieces to the
other. 42But neither of them could repay him, so
he kindly forgave them both, canceling their
debts. Who do you suppose loved him more
after that?"
43Simon answered, "I suppose the one for
whom he canceled the larger debt."
"That's right," Jesus said. 44Then he turned to
the woman and said to Simon, "Look at this
woman kneeling here. When I entered your home,
you didn't offer me water to wash the dust from
my feet, but she has washed them with her tears
and wiped them with her hair. 45You didn't give
me a kiss of greeting, but she has kissed my feet
again and again from the time I first came in.
46You neglected the courtesy of olive oil to anoint
my head, but she has anointed my feet with rare
perfume. 47I tell you, her sins—and they are
many—have been forgiven, so she has shown me
much love. But a person who is forgiven little
shows only little love." 48Then Jesus said to the
woman, "Your sins are forgiven."
49The men at the table said among themselves, "Who does this man think he is, going
around forgiving sins?"
50And Jesus said to the woman, "Your faith
has saved you; go in peace."

CHAPTER 8

Women Who Followed Jesus

Not long afterward Jesus began a tour of the
nearby cities and villages to announce the Good
News concerning the Kingdom of God. He took
his twelve disciples with him, 2along with some
women he had healed and from whom he had
cast out evil spirits. Among them were Mary
Magdalene, from whom he had cast out seven
demons; 3Joanna, the wife of Chuza, Herod's
business manager; Susanna; and many others
who were contributing from their own resources
to support Jesus and his disciples.

Story of the Farmer Scattering Seed

4One day Jesus told this story to a large crowd
that had gathered from many towns to hear him:
5"A farmer went out to plant some seed. As he
scattered it across his field, some seed fell on a
footpath, where it was stepped on, and the birds
came and ate it. 6Other seed fell on shallow soil
with underlying rock. This seed began to grow,
but soon it withered and died for lack of mois-
ture. 7Other seed fell among thorns that shot up
and choked out the tender blades. 8Still other
seed fell on fertile soil. This seed grew and produced a crop one hundred times as much as had
been planted." When he had said this, he called
out, "Anyone who is willing to hear should
listen and understand!"
9His disciples asked him what the story

7:29 Or *praised God.* 7:35 Or *But wisdom is justified by all her children.* 7:37 Greek *an alabaster jar.* 7:41 Greek *500 denarii.* A denarius was the equivalent of a full day's wage.

Perseverance Produces Results Read LUKE 8:15

In verses 4 through 8 of this chapter, Jesus tells the well-known parable of the sower to illustrate four different reactions to his message. The verses following that parable explain what those responses are.

The seed that falls on the roadside represents those who hear the gospel, but who do not allow it to penetrate their hearts and minds (verse 12). The seed that lands on the rocky soil depicts those who hear God's Word and initially receive it with joy, but their "commitment" is shown to be shallow and superficial through time (verse 13). The seed that lands among the thorns portrays those who appear to believe, but who let the cares of this life slowly choke out any growth (verse 14). The seed that falls on the fertile soil is the seed that actually takes root to produce spiritual fruit.

What is the difference between this group of individuals and the rest? The key to their success can be broken down into three steps: (1) They *listen* to God's Word; (2) they *obey* God's Word; and (3) they *persevere* to "produce a huge harvest."

Describing their perseverance in the faith, Jesus uses the Greek word *hupomone*, which speaks of "a patient enduring." It is this type of perseverance that produces spiritual fruit in the form of new believers.

By letting God's Word take root in your heart and life, you will not only grow stronger and be able to withstand the storms of life, but your life will help to draw many others to the Lord Jesus Christ.

meant. 10He replied, "You have been permitted
to understand the secrets of the Kingdom of
God. But I am using these stories to conceal
everything about it from outsiders, so that the
Scriptures might be fulfilled:

'They see what I do,
but they don't really see;
they hear what I say,
but they don't understand.'*

11"This is the meaning of the story: The seed
is God's message. 12The seed that fell on the
hard path represents those who hear the message, but then the Devil comes and steals it away
and prevents them from believing and being
saved. 13The rocky soil represents those who
hear the message with joy. But like young plants
in such soil, their roots don't go very deep. They
believe for a while, but they wilt when the hot
winds of testing blow. 14The thorny ground represents those who hear and accept the message,
but all too quickly the message is crowded out
by the cares and riches and pleasures of this life.
And so they never grow into maturity. 15But the
good soil represents honest, good-hearted
people who hear God's message, cling to it, and
steadily produce a huge harvest.

8:10 Isa 6:9.

Illustration of the Lamp

16"No one would light a lamp and then cover it
up or put it under a bed. No, lamps are mounted
in the open, where they can be seen by those
entering the house. 17For everything that is hidden
or secret will eventually be brought to light and
made plain to all. 18So be sure to pay attention to
what you hear. To those who are open to my
teaching, more understanding will be given. But
to those who are not listening, even what they
think they have will be taken away from them."

The True Family of Jesus

19Once when Jesus' mother and brothers came
to see him, they couldn't get to him because of
the crowds. 20Someone told Jesus, "Your mother
and your brothers are outside, and they want to
see you."

21Jesus replied, "My mother and my brothers
are all those who hear the message of God and
obey it."

Jesus Calms the Storm

22One day Jesus said to his disciples, "Let's cross
over to the other side of the lake." So they got
into a boat and started out. 23On the way across,
Jesus lay down for a nap, and while he was

sleeping the wind began to rise. A fierce storm
developed that threatened to swamp them, and
they were in real danger.

24The disciples woke him up, shouting,
"Master, Master, we're going to drown!"

So Jesus rebuked the wind and the raging
waves. The storm stopped and all was calm!
25Then he asked them, "Where is your faith?"

And they were filled with awe and amaze-
ment. They said to one another, "Who is this
man, that even the winds and waves obey him?"

Jesus Heals a Demon-Possessed Man

26So they arrived in the land of the Gerasenes,*
across the lake from Galilee. 27As Jesus was
climbing out of the boat, a man who was possessed by demons came out to meet him. Home-
less and naked, he had lived in a cemetery for a
long time. 28As soon as he saw Jesus, he shrieked
and fell to the ground before him, screaming,
"Why are you bothering me, Jesus, Son of the
Most High God? Please, I beg you, don't torture
me!" 29For Jesus had already commanded the
evil spirit to come out of him. This spirit had
often taken control of the man. Even when he
was shackled with chains, he simply broke them
and rushed out into the wilderness, completely
under the demon's power.

30"What is your name?" Jesus asked.

"Legion," he replied—for the man was filled
with many demons. 31The demons kept begging
Jesus not to send them into the Bottomless Pit.
32A large herd of pigs was feeding on the hillside
nearby, and the demons pleaded with him to let
them enter into the pigs. Jesus gave them permission. 33So the demons came out of the man
and entered the pigs, and the whole herd
plunged down the steep hillside into the lake,
where they drowned.

34When the herdsmen saw it, they fled to the
nearby city and the surrounding countryside,
spreading the news as they ran. 35A crowd soon
gathered around Jesus, for they wanted to see for
themselves what had happened. And they saw
the man who had been possessed by demons
sitting quietly at Jesus' feet, clothed and sane.
And the whole crowd was afraid. 36Then those
who had seen what happened told the others
how the demon-possessed man had been
healed. 37And all the people in that region
begged Jesus to go away and leave them alone,
for a great wave of fear swept over them.

So Jesus returned to the boat and left, crossing
back to the other side of the lake. 38The man
who had been demon possessed begged to go,
too, but Jesus said, 39"No, go back to your family and tell them all the wonderful things God
has done for you." So he went all through the
city telling about the great thing Jesus had done
for him.

Jesus Heals in Response to Faith

40On the other side of the lake the crowds received Jesus with open arms because they had
been waiting for him. 41And now a man named
Jairus, a leader of the local synagogue, came and
fell down at Jesus' feet, begging him to come
home with him. 42His only child was dying, a
little girl twelve years old.

As Jesus went with him, he was surrounded
by the crowds. 43And there was a woman in the
crowd who had had a hemorrhage for twelve
years. She had spent everything she had on doctors* and still could find no cure. 44She came up
behind Jesus and touched the fringe of his robe.
Immediately, the bleeding stopped.

45"Who touched me?" Jesus asked.

Everyone denied it, and Peter said, "Master,
this whole crowd is pressing up against you."

46But Jesus told him, "No, someone deliberately touched me, for I felt healing power go out
from me." 47When the woman realized that
Jesus knew, she began to tremble and fell to her
knees before him. The whole crowd heard her
explain why she had touched him and that she
had been immediately healed. 48"Daughter," he
said to her, "your faith has made you well. Go in
peace."

49While he was still speaking to her, a messenger arrived from Jairus's home with the message, "Your little girl is dead. There's no use
troubling the Teacher now."

50But when Jesus heard what had happened,
he said to Jairus, "Don't be afraid. Just trust me,
and she will be all right."

51When they arrived at the house, Jesus
wouldn't let anyone go in with him except Peter,
James, John, and the little girl's father and
mother. 52The house was filled with people
weeping and wailing, but he said, "Stop the
weeping! She isn't dead; she is only asleep."

53But the crowd laughed at him because they
all knew she had died. 54Then Jesus took her by
the hand and said in a loud voice, "Get up, my
child!" 55And at that moment her life returned,
and she immediately stood up! Then Jesus told

8:26 Some manuscripts read *Gadarenes;* other manuscripts read *Gergesenes.* See Matt 8:28; Mark 5:1. 8:43 Some manuscripts omit *She had spent everything she had on doctors.*

them to give her something to eat. 56Her parents
were overwhelmed, but Jesus insisted that they
not tell anyone what had happened.

CHAPTER 9

Jesus Sends Out the Twelve Apostles

One day Jesus called together his twelve apostles
and gave them power and authority to cast out
demons and to heal all diseases. 2Then he sent
them out to tell everyone about the coming of
the Kingdom of God and to heal the sick.
3"Don't even take along a walking stick," he
instructed them, "nor a traveler's bag, nor food,
nor money. Not even an extra coat. 4When you
enter each village, be a guest in only one home.
5If the people of the village won't receive your
message when you enter it, shake off its dust
from your feet as you leave. It is a sign that you
have abandoned that village to its fate."

6So they began their circuit of the villages,
preaching the Good News and healing the sick.

Herod's Confusion

7When reports of Jesus' miracles reached Herod
Antipas,* he was worried and puzzled because
some were saying, "This is John the Baptist
come back to life again." 8Others were saying,
"It is Elijah or some other ancient prophet risen
from the dead."

9"I beheaded John," Herod said, "so who is
this man about whom I hear such strange stories?" And he tried to see him.

Jesus Feeds Five Thousand

10When the apostles returned, they told Jesus
everything they had done. Then he slipped quietly away with them toward the town of Bethsaida. 11But the crowds found out where he was
going, and they followed him. And he welcomed them, teaching them about the Kingdom
of God and curing those who were ill. 12Late in
the afternoon the twelve disciples came to him
and said, "Send the crowds away to the nearby
villages and farms, so they can find food and
lodging for the night. There is nothing to eat
here in this deserted place."

13But Jesus said, "You feed them."

"Impossible!" they protested. "We have only
five loaves of bread and two fish. Or are you
expecting us to go and buy enough food for this
whole crowd?" 14For there were about five thousand men there.

"Just tell them to sit down on the ground in
groups of about fifty each," Jesus replied. 15So
the people all sat down. 16Jesus took the five
loaves and two fish, looked up toward heaven,
and asked God's blessing on the food. Breaking
the loaves into pieces, he kept giving the bread
and fish to the disciples to give to the people.
17They all ate as much as they wanted, and they
picked up twelve baskets of leftovers!

Peter's Declaration about Jesus

18One day as Jesus was alone, praying, he came
over to his disciples and asked them, "Who do
people say I am?"

19"Well," they replied, "some say John the
Baptist, some say Elijah, and others say you are
one of the other ancient prophets risen from the
dead."

20Then he asked them, "Who do you say I
am?"

Peter replied, "You are the Messiah sent from
God!"

Jesus Predicts His Death

21Jesus warned them not to tell anyone about
this. 22"For I, the Son of Man, must suffer many
terrible things," he said. "I will be rejected by the
leaders, the leading priests, and the teachers of
religious law. I will be killed, but three days later
I will be raised from the dead."

23Then he said to the crowd, "If any of you
wants to be my follower, you must put aside
your selfish ambition, shoulder your cross daily,
and follow me. 24If you try to keep your life for
yourself, you will lose it. But if you give up your
life for me, you will find true life. 25And how do
you benefit if you gain the whole world but lose
or forfeit your own soul in the process? 26If a
person is ashamed of me and my message, I, the
Son of Man, will be ashamed of that person
when I return in my glory and in the glory of the
Father and the holy angels. 27And I assure you
that some of you standing here right now will
not die before you see the Kingdom of God."

The Transfiguration

28About eight days later Jesus took Peter, James,
and John to a mountain to pray. 29And as he was
praying, the appearance of his face changed, and
his clothing became dazzling white. 30Then two
men, Moses and Elijah, appeared and began
talking with Jesus. 31They were glorious to see.
And they were speaking of how he was about to
fulfill God's plan by dying in Jerusalem.

32Peter and the others were very drowsy and

9:7 Greek *Herod the tetrarch*. He was a son of King Herod and was ruler over one of the four districts in Palestine.

had fallen asleep. Now they woke up and saw
Jesus' glory and the two men standing with him.
33As Moses and Elijah were starting to leave,
Peter, not even knowing what he was saying,
blurted out, "Master, this is wonderful! We will
make three shrines*—one for you, one for
Moses, and one for Elijah." 34But even as he was
saying this, a cloud came over them; and terror
gripped them as it covered them.
35Then a voice from the cloud said, "This is
my Son, my Chosen One.* Listen to him."
36When the voice died away, Jesus was there
alone. They didn't tell anyone what they had
seen until long after this happened.

Jesus Heals a Demon-Possessed Boy

37The next day, after they had come down the
mountain, a huge crowd met Jesus. 38A man in
the crowd called out to him, "Teacher, look at
my boy, who is my only son. 39An evil spirit
keeps seizing him, making him scream. It
throws him into convulsions so that he foams at
the mouth. It is always hitting and injuring him.
It hardly ever leaves him alone. 40I begged your
disciples to cast the spirit out, but they couldn't
do it."
41"You stubborn, faithless people," Jesus
said, "how long must I be with you and put up
with you? Bring him here." 42As the boy came
forward, the demon knocked him to the ground
and threw him into a violent convulsion. But
Jesus rebuked the evil spirit and healed the boy.
Then he gave him back to his father. 43Awe
gripped the people as they saw this display of
God's power.

Jesus Again Predicts His Death

While everyone was marveling over all the wonderful things he was doing, Jesus said to his
disciples, 44"Listen to me and remember what I
say. The Son of Man is going to be betrayed."
45But they didn't know what he meant. Its significance was hidden from them, so they could
not understand it, and they were afraid to ask
him about it.

The Greatest in the Kingdom

46Then there was an argument among them as
to which of them would be the greatest. 47But
Jesus knew their thoughts, so he brought a little
child to his side. 48Then he said to them, "Anyone who welcomes a little child like this on my
behalf welcomes me, and anyone who

9:33 Or *shelters;* Greek reads *tabernacles.* 9:35 Some manuscripts read *This is my beloved Son.*

A Disciple Takes Up His or Her Cross and Follows Christ

Read LUKE 9:23-25

Choosing to be a disciple of Jesus Christ takes more than just some verbal affirmation. It takes daily sacrifice and commitment. But when you follow Christ's guidelines for discipleship, you will find that the end result is far better than you could ever have imagined. Here are three things a true disciple of Christ should do:

1. Your Desires Must Take a Backseat to His Desires for Your Life. Being a disciple means recognizing that God's plans for your life are ultimately better than your own. That may mean making some sacrifices in your life, such as spending more of your time in God's Word than in the newspaper, volunteering your services for teaching children's Sunday school, or putting off that vacation to work on a ministry project. Yet, in relinquishing your own plans, you will find yourself drawn closer to the Lord.

2. You Must Take Up Your Cross Daily. Jesus is not simply referring to a religious symbol. At this time in history, a cross symbolized the cruelest of deaths. Anyone seen carrying a cross was headed for a horrible death. Some have misunderstood this statement by Jesus to mean that your cross is your personal inconvenience or problem. In this passage, however, Jesus is talking about the act of dying to yourself. In essence, he wants you to lay yourself at his feet and say, "I want your will more than my own." Once you have taken up that cross, you will experience the abundant life that Jesus promises to those who follow him.

3. You Must Lose Yourself to Save Yourself. Verse 24 may sound like a contradiction when you first read it. Yet, if you truly want to find happiness and fulfillment, you must relinquish full control of your life to Jesus Christ. Paul wrote, "I myself no longer live, but Christ lives in me" (Galatians 2:20). Taking up the cross is no more a burden to the disciple than wings are to a bird, or sails are to a ship. A surrendered life holds the key to a fulfilling walk.

Though it is true that it costs to be a disciple, it is also true that it costs a lot more not to be!

What Makes Demons Powerless? Read LUKE 10:1-20

Some Christians cower in fear of Satan and his army of demons. Yet every person who has put his or her faith and trust in Jesus Christ comes under God's protection. In fact, Scripture says that God has given us weapons to break down Satan's strongholds (2 Corinthians 10:4-5, p. 225). So even though demons have real powers, we do not have to be paralyzed at their presence in this world. In fact, we need to recognize the power Christ has given us in the face of our enemy.

As Jesus' disciples found out, demons are drastically limited in their power before the true follower of Christ (verse 17). The power they had was not of themselves but from God. And Jesus was quick to warn them not to rejoice in the power they had been given over demons. Rather, Jesus told them to rejoice that their names were "registered as citizens of heaven" (verse 20).

Today you may find people who allege to have "conversations" with demons and reminding them how powerless they are. Yet even Michael the archangel, when arguing with Satan about Moses' body, did not taunt the devil, but simply said, "The Lord rebuke you" (see Jude 1:9, p. 329). Our focus should not be upon the power we have been given but on the Giver of that power.

CORNERSTONES

welcomes me welcomes my Father who sent me. Whoever is the least among you is the greatest."

Using the Name of Jesus

49John said to Jesus, "Master, we saw someone using your name to cast out demons. We tried to stop him because he isn't in our group."

50But Jesus said, "Don't stop him! Anyone who is not against you is for you."

Opposition from Samaritans

51As the time drew near for his return to heaven,
Jesus resolutely set out for Jerusalem. 52He sent
messengers ahead to a Samaritan village to prepare for his arrival. 53But they were turned away.
The people of the village refused to have anything to do with Jesus because he had resolved
to go to Jerusalem. 54When James and John
heard about it, they said to Jesus, "Lord, should
we order down fire from heaven to burn them
up*?" 55But Jesus turned and rebuked them.*
56So they went on to another village.

The Cost of Following Jesus

57As they were walking along someone said to Jesus, "I will follow you no matter where you go."

58But Jesus replied, "Foxes have dens to live in, and birds have nests, but I, the Son of Man, have no home of my own, not even a place to lay my head."

59He said to another person, "Come, be my disciple."

The man agreed, but he said, "Lord, first let me return home and bury my father."

60Jesus replied, "Let those who are spiritually dead care for their own dead.* Your duty is to go and preach the coming of the Kingdom of God."

61Another said, "Yes, Lord, I will follow you, but first let me say good-bye to my family."

62But Jesus told him, "Anyone who puts a hand to the plow and then looks back is not fit for the Kingdom of God."

CHAPTER **10**

Jesus Sends Out His Disciples

The Lord now chose seventy-two* other disciples
and sent them on ahead in pairs to all the towns
and villages he planned to visit. 2These were his
instructions to them: "The harvest is so great, but
the workers are so few. Pray to the Lord who is in
charge of the harvest, and ask him to send out
more workers for his fields. 3Go now, and remember that I am sending you out as lambs among
wolves. 4Don't take along any money, or a traveler's bag, or even an extra pair of sandals. And don't
stop to greet anyone on the road.

5"Whenever you enter a home, give it your
blessing. 6If those who live there are worthy, the
blessing will stand; if they are not, the blessing

9:54 Some manuscripts add *as Elijah did.* 9:55 Some manuscripts add *And he said, "You don't realize what your hearts are like. 56For the Son of Man has not come to destroy men's lives, but to save them."* 9:60 Greek *Let the dead bury their own dead.* 10:1 Some manuscripts read *70;* also in 10:17.

will return to you. 7When you enter a town, don't move around from home to home. Stay in one place, eating and drinking what they provide you. Don't hesitate to accept hospitality, because those who work deserve their pay.

8"If a town welcomes you, eat whatever is set before you 9and heal the sick. As you heal them, say, 'The Kingdom of God is near you now.' 10But if a town refuses to welcome you, go out into its streets and say, 11'We wipe the dust of your town from our feet as a public announcement of your doom. And don't forget the Kingdom of God is near!' 12The truth is, even wicked Sodom will be better off than such a town on the judgment day.

13"What horrors await you, Korazin and Bethsaida! For if the miracles I did in you had been done in wicked Tyre and Sidon, their people would have sat in deep repentance long ago, clothed in sackcloth and throwing ashes on their heads to show their remorse. 14Yes, Tyre and Sidon will be better off on the judgment day than you. 15And you people of Capernaum, will you be exalted to heaven? No, you will be brought down to the place of the dead.*"

16Then he said to the disciples, "Anyone who accepts your message is also accepting me. And anyone who rejects you is rejecting me. And anyone who rejects me is rejecting God who sent me."

17When the seventy-two disciples returned, they joyfully reported to him, "Lord, even the demons obey us when we use your name!"

18"Yes," he told them, "I saw Satan falling from heaven as a flash of lightning! 19And I have given you authority over all the power of the enemy, and you can walk among snakes and scorpions and crush them. Nothing will injure you. 20But don't rejoice just because evil spirits obey you; rejoice because your names are registered as citizens of heaven."

Jesus' Prayer of Thanksgiving

21Then Jesus was filled with the joy of the Holy Spirit and said, "O Father, Lord of heaven and earth, thank you for hiding the truth from those who think themselves so wise and clever, and for revealing it to the childlike. Yes, Father, it pleased you to do it this way.

22"My Father has given me authority over everything. No one really knows the Son except the Father, and no one really knows the Father except the Son and those to whom the Son chooses to reveal him."

23Then when they were alone, he turned to the disciples and said, "How privileged you are to see what you have seen. 24I tell you, many prophets and kings have longed to see and hear what you have seen and heard, but they could not."

The Most Important Commandment

25One day an expert in religious law stood up to test Jesus by asking him this question: "Teacher, what must I do to receive eternal life?"

26Jesus replied, "What does the law of Moses say? How do you read it?"

27The man answered, " 'You must love the Lord your God with all your heart, all your soul, all your strength, and all your mind.' And, 'Love your neighbor as yourself.' "*

28"Right!" Jesus told him. "Do this and you will live!"

29The man wanted to justify his actions, so he asked Jesus, "And who is my neighbor?"

Story of the Good Samaritan

30Jesus replied with an illustration: "A Jewish man was traveling on a trip from Jerusalem to Jericho, and he was attacked by bandits. They stripped him of his clothes and money, beat him up, and left him half dead beside the road.

31"By chance a Jewish priest came along; but when he saw the man lying there, he crossed to the other side of the road and passed him by. 32A Temple assistant* walked over and looked at him lying there, but he also passed by on the other side.

33"Then a despised Samaritan came along, and when he saw the man, he felt deep pity. 34Kneeling beside him, the Samaritan soothed his wounds with medicine and bandaged them. Then he put the man on his own donkey and took him to an inn, where he took care of him. 35The next day he handed the innkeeper two pieces of silver* and told him to take care of the man. 'If his bill runs higher than that,' he said, 'I'll pay the difference the next time I am here.'

36"Now which of these three would you say was a neighbor to the man who was attacked by bandits?" Jesus asked.

37The man replied, "The one who showed him mercy."

Then Jesus said, "Yes, now go and do the same."

10:15 Greek *to Hades.* **10:27** Deut 6:5; Lev 19:18. **10:32** Greek *A Levite.* **10:35** Greek *2 denarii.* A denarius was the equivalent of a full day's wage.

LUKE 11 ▸▸▸ page 84

Jesus Visits Martha and Mary

38As Jesus and the disciples continued on their way to Jerusalem, they came to a village where a woman named Martha welcomed them into her home. 39Her sister, Mary, sat at the Lord's feet, listening to what he taught. 40But Martha was worrying over the big dinner she was preparing. She came to Jesus and said, "Lord, doesn't it seem unfair to you that my sister just sits here while I do all the work? Tell her to come and help me."

41But the Lord said to her, "My dear Martha, you are so upset over all these details! 42There is really only one thing worth being concerned about. Mary has discovered it—and I won't take it away from her."

CHAPTER 11

Teaching about Prayer

Once when Jesus had been out praying, one of his disciples came to him as he finished and said, "Lord, teach us to pray, just as John taught his disciples."

2He said, "This is how you should pray:

"Father, may your name be honored.
  May your Kingdom come soon.
3 Give us our food day by day.
4 And forgive us our sins—
  just as we forgive those who have sinned
    against us.
  And don't let us yield to temptation.*"

5Then, teaching them more about prayer, he used this illustration: "Suppose you went to a friend's house at midnight, wanting to borrow three loaves of bread. You would say to him, 6'A friend of mine has just arrived for a visit, and I have nothing for him to eat.' 7He would call out from his bedroom, 'Don't bother me. The door is locked for the night, and we are all in bed. I can't help you this time.' 8But I tell you this—though he won't do it as a friend, if you keep knocking long enough, he will get up and give you what you want so his reputation won't be damaged.*

9"And so I tell you, keep on asking, and you will be given what you ask for. Keep on looking, and you will find. Keep on knocking, and the door will be opened. 10For everyone who asks, receives. Everyone who seeks, finds. And the door is opened to everyone who knocks.

11"You fathers—if your children ask* for a fish, do you give them a snake instead? 12Or if they ask for an egg, do you give them a scorpion? Of course not! 13If you sinful people know how to give good gifts to your children, how much more will your heavenly Father give the Holy Spirit to those who ask him."

Jesus and the Prince of Demons

14One day Jesus cast a demon out of a man who couldn't speak, and the man's voice returned to him. The crowd was amazed, 15but some said, "No wonder he can cast out demons. He gets his power from Satan,* the prince of demons!" 16Trying to test Jesus, others asked for a miraculous sign from heaven to see if he was from God.

17He knew their thoughts, so he said, "Any kingdom at war with itself is doomed. A divided home is also doomed. 18You say I am empowered by the prince of demons.* But if Satan is fighting against himself by empowering me to cast out his demons, how can his kingdom survive? 19And if I am empowered by

11:2-4 Some manuscripts add additional portions of the Lord's Prayer as it reads in Matt 6:9-13. **11:8** Greek *in order to avoid shame,* or *because of [your] persistence.* **11:11** Some manuscripts add *for bread, do you give them a stone? Or if they ask.* **11:15** Greek *Beelzeboul.* **11:18** Greek *by Beelzeboul;* also in 11:19.

OFF AND RUNNING

Balance Christian Service with Worship Read LUKE 10:38-42

It is easy to lose sight of Jesus in the midst of all our activity for him. This story shows the necessity of balancing our work with our worship. Here we see two personalities, represented by Martha and Mary.

Martha: the Doer. Martha was a practical type of person who wanted to get things done. Deep down, she probably wanted to please the Lord, but she made the common mistake of offering work for worship. She received Jesus into her house, then neglected Jesus in the process. Jesus wanted her attention, and she offered him a flurry of activity. As a result, she felt tired and overworked. Like Martha, we can become weary in our work for the Lord when we fail to take time to sit at his feet and draw from the spiritual resources available to us.

Mary: the Worshiper. Mary had a balanced life. She recognized that there was a time to work and a time to

the prince of demons, what about your own followers? They cast out demons, too, so they will judge you for what you have said. 20But if I am casting out demons by the power of God, then the Kingdom of God has arrived among you. 21For when Satan,* who is completely armed, guards his palace, it is safe—22until someone who is stronger attacks and overpowers him, strips him of his weapons, and carries off his belongings.

23"Anyone who isn't helping me opposes me, and anyone who isn't working with me is actually working against me.

24"When an evil spirit leaves a person, it goes into the desert, searching for rest. But when it finds none, it says, 'I will return to the person I came from.' 25So it returns and finds that its former home is all swept and clean. 26Then the spirit finds seven other spirits more evil than itself, and they all enter the person and live there. And so that person is worse off than before."

27As he was speaking, a woman in the crowd called out, "God bless your mother—the womb from which you came, and the breasts that nursed you!"

28He replied, "But even more blessed are all who hear the word of God and put it into practice."

The Sign of Jonah

29As the crowd pressed in on Jesus, he said, "These are evil times, and this evil generation keeps asking me to show them a miraculous sign. But the only sign I will give them is the sign of the prophet Jonah. 30What happened to him was a sign to the people of Nineveh that God had sent him. What happens to me will be a sign that God has sent me, the Son of Man, to these people.

31"The queen of Sheba* will rise up against this generation on judgment day and condemn it, because she came from a distant land to hear the wisdom of Solomon. And now someone greater than Solomon is here—and you refuse to listen to him. 32The people of Nineveh, too, will rise up against this generation on judgment day and condemn it, because they repented at the preaching of Jonah. And now someone greater than Jonah is here—and you refuse to repent.

Receiving the Light

33"No one lights a lamp and then hides it or puts it under a basket. Instead, it is put on a lampstand to give light to all who enter the room. 34Your eye is a lamp for your body. A pure eye lets sunshine into your soul. But an evil eye shuts out the light and plunges you into darkness. 35Make sure that the light you think you have is not really darkness. 36If you are filled with light, with no dark corners, then your whole life will be radiant, as though a floodlight is shining on you."

Jesus Criticizes the Religious Leaders

37As Jesus was speaking, one of the Pharisees invited him home for a meal. So he went in and took his place at the table. 38His host was amazed to see that he sat down to eat without first performing the ceremonial washing required by Jewish custom. 39Then the Lord said to him, "You Pharisees are so careful to clean the outside of the cup and the dish, but inside you are still filthy—full of greed and wickedness! 40Fools! Didn't God make the inside as well as the outside? 41So give to the needy

11:21 Greek *the strong one.* 11:31 Greek *the queen of the south.*

---

worship, a time to do and a time to pray. She knew when it was time to take off the apron and converse with this most honored guest. While Martha essentially wanted to "get the dishes done," Mary wanted to seize this wonderful moment to sit at the feet of the Creator of the universe.

Few things are as damaging to the Christian life as trying to work for Christ without taking time to commune with him. In his letter to young Timothy, the apostle Paul writes, "Hardworking farmers are the first to enjoy the fruit of their labor" (2 Timothy 2:6). In other words, you can't effectively feed others until you yourself have been fed.

What we do *with* Christ is far more important than what we do *for* Christ. Those who strike a balance between work and worship will keep themselves from spiritual burnout and will become more effective in their service to the Lord.

what you greedily possess, and you will be clean all over.

42"But how terrible it will be for you Pharisees! For you are careful to tithe even the tiniest part of your income,* but you completely forget about justice and the love of God. You should tithe, yes, but you should not leave undone the more important things.

43"How terrible it will be for you Pharisees! For how you love the seats of honor in the synagogues and the respectful greetings from everyone as you walk through the markets! 44Yes, how terrible it will be for you. For you are like hidden graves in a field. People walk over them without knowing the corruption they are stepping on."

45"Teacher," said an expert in religious law, "you have insulted us, too, in what you just said."

46"Yes," said Jesus, "how terrible it will be for you experts in religious law! For you crush people beneath impossible religious demands, and you never lift a finger to help ease the burden. 47How terrible it will be for you! For you build tombs for the very prophets your ancestors killed long ago. 48Murderers! You agree with your ancestors that what they did was right. You would have done the same yourselves. 49This is what God in his wisdom said about you:* 'I will send prophets and apostles to them, and they will kill some and persecute the others.'

50"And you of this generation will be held responsible for the murder of all God's prophets from the creation of the world—51from the murder of Abel to the murder of Zechariah, who was killed between the altar and the sanctuary. Yes, it will surely be charged against you.

52"How terrible it will be for you experts in religious law! For you hide the key to knowledge from the people. You don't enter the Kingdom yourselves, and you prevent others from entering."

53As Jesus finished speaking, the Pharisees and teachers of religious law were furious. From that time on they grilled him with many hostile questions, 54trying to trap him into saying something they could use against him.

CHAPTER 12

A Warning against Hypocrisy

Meanwhile, the crowds grew until thousands were milling about and crushing each other. Jesus turned first to his disciples and warned them, "Beware of the yeast of the Pharisees—beware of their hypocrisy. 2The time is coming when everything will be revealed; all that is secret will be made public. 3Whatever you have said in the dark will be heard in the light, and what you have whispered behind closed doors will be shouted from the housetops for all to hear!

4"Dear friends, don't be afraid of those who want to kill you. They can only kill the body; they cannot do any more to you. 5But I'll tell you whom to fear. Fear God, who has the power to kill people and then throw them into hell.

6"What is the price of five sparrows? A couple of pennies? Yet God does not forget a single one of them. 7And the very hairs on your head are all numbered. So don't be afraid; you are more valuable to him than a whole flock of sparrows.

8"And I assure you of this: If anyone acknowledges me publicly here on earth, I, the Son of Man, will openly acknowledge that person in the presence of God's angels. 9But if anyone denies me here on earth, I will deny that person before God's angels. 10Yet those who speak against the Son of Man may be forgiven, but anyone who speaks blasphemies against the Holy Spirit will never be forgiven.

11"And when you are brought to trial in the synagogues and before rulers and authorities, don't worry about what to say in your defense, 12for the Holy Spirit will teach you what needs to be said even as you are standing there."

11:42 Greek *to tithe the mint and the rue and every herb.* 11:49 Greek *Therefore, the wisdom of God said.*

OFF AND RUNNING

Don't Neglect Your Spiritual Health Read LUKE 12:16-21

As this parable illustrates, it is easy to allow other pursuits to cloud our spiritual vision. We have to make enough money to get that new car, buy that house, or take that dream vacation. Sometimes we can get so caught up in chasing after money and success that we leave God out of the equation altogether.

Story of the Rich Fool

13Then someone called from the crowd, "Teacher, please tell my brother to divide our father's estate with me."

14Jesus replied, "Friend, who made me a judge over you to decide such things as that?" 15Then he said, "Beware! Don't be greedy for what you don't have. Real life is not measured by how much we own."

16And he gave an illustration: "A rich man had a fertile farm that produced fine crops. 17In fact, his barns were full to overflowing. 18So he said, 'I know! I'll tear down my barns and build bigger ones. Then I'll have room enough to store everything. 19And I'll sit back and say to myself, My friend, you have enough stored away for years to come. Now take it easy! Eat, drink, and be merry!'

20"But God said to him, 'You fool! You will die this very night. Then who will get it all?'

21"Yes, a person is a fool to store up earthly wealth but not have a rich relationship with God."

Teaching about Money and Possessions

22Then turning to his disciples, Jesus said, "So I tell you, don't worry about everyday life—whether you have enough food to eat or clothes to wear. 23For life consists of far more than food and clothing. 24Look at the ravens. They don't need to plant or harvest or put food in barns because God feeds them. And you are far more valuable to him than any birds! 25Can all your worries add a single moment to your life? Of course not! 26And if worry can't do little things like that, what's the use of worrying over bigger things?

27"Look at the lilies and how they grow. They don't work or make their clothing, yet Solomon in all his glory was not dressed as beautifully as they are. 28And if God cares so wonderfully for flowers that are here today and gone tomorrow, won't he more surely care for you? You have so little faith! 29And don't worry about food—what to eat and drink. Don't worry whether God will provide it for you. 30These things dominate the thoughts of most people, but your Father already knows your needs. 31He will give you all you need from day to day if you make the Kingdom of God your primary concern.

32"So don't be afraid, little flock. For it gives your Father great happiness to give you the Kingdom.

33"Sell what you have and give to those in need. This will store up treasure for you in heaven! And the purses of heaven have no holes in them. Your treasure will be safe—no thief can steal it and no moth can destroy it. 34Wherever your treasure is, there your heart and thoughts will also be.

Be Ready for the Lord's Coming

35"Be dressed for service and well prepared, 36as though you were waiting for your master to return from the wedding feast. Then you will be ready to open the door and let him in the moment he arrives and knocks. 37There will be special favor for those who are ready and waiting for his return. I tell you, he himself will seat them, put on an apron, and serve them as they sit and eat! 38He may come in the middle of the night or just before dawn.* But whenever he comes, there will be special favor for his servants who are ready!

39"Know this: A homeowner who knew exactly when a burglar was coming would not permit the house to be broken into. 40You must be ready all the time, for the Son of Man will come when least expected."

41Peter asked, "Lord, is this illustration just for us or for everyone?"

42And the Lord replied, "I'm talking to any faithful, sensible servant to whom the master gives the responsibility of managing his household and feeding his family. 43If the master returns and finds that the servant has done a good job, there will be a reward. 44I assure you, the master will put that servant in charge of all he

12:38 Greek *in the second or third watch.*

God's answer to this dilemma is for us to seek first his reign and will in our lives. Then everything else will come into balance. It is simple. The more you channel your energy, your ambition, and your life into this one, holy pursuit, the less obsessed you will be with the cares and concerns of this world. For the sake of your spiritual health, seek God's kingdom in all that you do. Failure to do so will only guarantee confusion, failure, emptiness, and dissatisfaction.

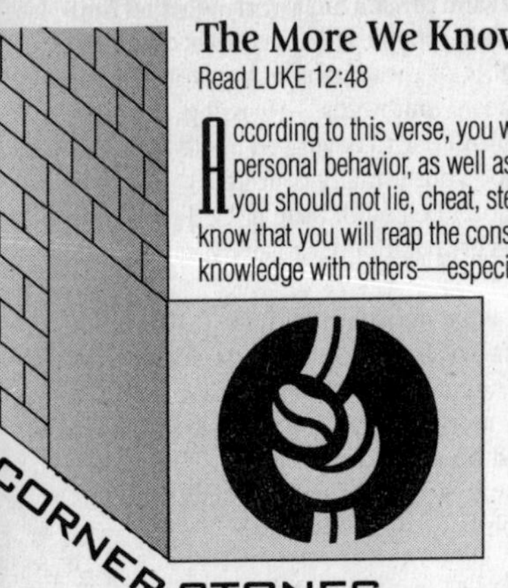

The More We Know, the Greater Our Responsibility Will Be

Read LUKE 12:48

According to this verse, you will be held accountable for what you know. This can refer to your personal behavior, as well as the work you do for God's Kingdom. For instance, you now know that you should not lie, cheat, steal, or live an immoral lifestyle. If you disregard God's commands, you know that you will reap the consequences. On the other hand, you must also share your spiritual knowledge with others—especially those who are on their way to spending eternity in hell. Our attitude should be as Paul's, who wrote, "For we speak as messengers who have been approved by God to be entrusted with the Good News. Our purpose is to please God, not people. He is the one who examines the motives of our hearts" (1 Thessalonians 2:4).

What are you doing with the spiritual knowledge and insight God has given you? Are you using it to his glory?

owns. 45But if the servant thinks, 'My master
won't be back for a while,' and begins oppressing the other servants, partying, and getting
drunk—46well, the master will return unannounced and unexpected. He will tear the servant apart and banish him with the unfaithful.
47The servant will be severely punished, for
though he knew his duty, he refused to do it.

48"But people who are not aware that they are
doing wrong will be punished only lightly.
Much is required from those to whom much is
given, and much more is required from those to
whom much more is given.

Jesus Causes Division

49"I have come to bring fire to the earth, and I
wish that my task were already completed!
50There is a terrible baptism ahead of me, and I
am under a heavy burden until it is accomplished. 51Do you think I have come to bring
peace to the earth? No, I have come to bring
strife and division! 52From now on families will
be split apart, three in favor of me, and two
against—or the other way around. 53There will
be a division between father and son, mother
and daughter, mother-in-law and daughter-in-
law."

54Then Jesus turned to the crowd and said,
"When you see clouds beginning to form in the
west, you say, 'Here comes a shower.' And you
are right. 55When the south wind blows, you say,
'Today will be a scorcher.' And it is. 56You hypocrites! You know how to interpret the appearance of the earth and the sky, but you can't
interpret these present times.

57"Why can't you decide for yourselves what
is right? 58If you are on the way to court and you
meet your accuser, try to settle the matter before
it reaches the judge, or you may be sentenced
and handed over to an officer and thrown in jail.
59And if that happens, you won't be free again
until you have paid the last penny."

CHAPTER 13

A Call to Repentance

About this time Jesus was informed that Pilate
had murdered some people from Galilee as they
were sacrificing at the Temple in Jerusalem.
2"Do you think those Galileans were worse sinners than other people from Galilee?" he asked.
"Is that why they suffered? 3Not at all! And you
will also perish unless you turn from your evil
ways and turn to God. 4And what about the
eighteen men who died when the Tower of Siloam fell on them? Were they the worst sinners
in Jerusalem? 5No, and I tell you again that
unless you repent, you will also perish."

Illustration of the Barren Fig Tree

6Then Jesus used this illustration: "A man
planted a fig tree in his garden and came again
and again to see if there was any fruit on it, but
he was always disappointed. 7Finally, he said to
his gardener, 'I've waited three years, and there
hasn't been a single fig! Cut it down. It's taking
up space we can use for something else.'

8"The gardener answered, 'Give it one more

chance. Leave it another year, and I'll give it special attention and plenty of fertilizer. 9If we get figs next year, fine. If not, you can cut it down.'"

Jesus Heals on the Sabbath

10One Sabbath day as Jesus was teaching in a synagogue, 11he saw a woman who had been crippled by an evil spirit. She had been bent double for eighteen years and was unable to stand up straight. 12When Jesus saw her, he called her over and said, "Woman, you are healed of your sickness!" 13Then he touched her, and instantly she could stand straight. How she praised and thanked God!

14But the leader in charge of the synagogue was indignant that Jesus had healed her on the Sabbath day. "There are six days of the week for working," he said to the crowd. "Come on those days to be healed, not on the Sabbath."

15But the Lord replied, "You hypocrite! You work on the Sabbath day! Don't you untie your ox or your donkey from their stalls on the Sabbath and lead them out for water? 16Wasn't it necessary for me, even on the Sabbath day, to free this dear woman* from the bondage in which Satan has held her for eighteen years?" 17This shamed his enemies. And all the people rejoiced at the wonderful things he did.

Illustration of the Mustard Seed

18Then Jesus said, "What is the Kingdom of God like? How can I illustrate it? 19It is like a tiny mustard seed planted in a garden; it grows and becomes a tree, and the birds come and find shelter among its branches."

Illustration of the Yeast

20He also asked, "What else is the Kingdom of God like? 21It is like yeast used by a woman making bread. Even though she used a large amount* of flour, the yeast permeated every part of the dough."

The Narrow Door

22Jesus went through the towns and villages, teaching as he went, always pressing on toward Jerusalem. 23Someone asked him, "Lord, will only a few be saved?"

He replied, 24"The door to heaven is narrow. Work hard to get in, because many will try to enter, 25but when the head of the house has locked the door, it will be too late. Then you will stand outside knocking and pleading, 'Lord, open the door for us!' But he will reply, 'I do not know you.' 26You will say, 'But we ate and drank with you, and you taught in our streets.' 27And he will reply, 'I tell you, I don't know you. Go away, all you who do evil.'

28"And there will be great weeping and gnashing of teeth, for you will see Abraham, Isaac, Jacob, and all the prophets within the Kingdom of God, but you will be thrown out. 29Then people will come from all over the world to take their places in the Kingdom of God. 30And note this: Some who are despised now will be greatly honored then; and some who are greatly honored now will be despised then.*"

Jesus Grieves over Jerusalem

31A few minutes later some Pharisees said to him, "Get out of here if you want to live, because Herod Antipas wants to kill you!"

32Jesus replied, "Go tell that fox that I will keep on casting out demons and doing miracles of healing today and tomorrow; and the third day I will accomplish my purpose. 33Yes, today, tomorrow, and the next day I must proceed on my way. For it wouldn't do for a prophet of God to be killed except in Jerusalem!

34"O Jerusalem, Jerusalem, the city that kills the prophets and stones God's messengers! How often I have wanted to gather your children together as a hen protects her chicks beneath her wings, but you wouldn't let me. 35And now look, your house is left to you empty. And you will never see me again until you say, 'Bless the one who comes in the name of the Lord!'* "

CHAPTER 14

Jesus Heals on the Sabbath

One Sabbath day Jesus was in the home of a leader of the Pharisees. The people were watching him closely, 2because there was a man there whose arms and legs were swollen.* 3Jesus asked the Pharisees and experts in religious law, "Well, is it permitted in the law to heal people on the Sabbath day, or not?" 4When they refused to answer, Jesus touched the sick man and healed him and sent him away. 5Then he turned to them and asked, "Which of you doesn't work on the Sabbath? If your son* or your cow falls into a pit, don't you proceed at once to get him out?" 6Again they had no answer.

13:16 Greek *this woman, a daughter of Abraham.* 13:21 Greek *3 measures.* 13:30 Greek *Some are last who will be first, and some are first who will be last.* 13:35 Ps 118:26. 14:2 Traditionally translated *who had dropsy.* 14:5 Some manuscripts read *donkey.*

Jesus Teaches about Humility

7When Jesus noticed that all who had come to
the dinner were trying to sit near the head of the
table, he gave them this advice: 8"If you are
invited to a wedding feast, don't always head for
the best seat. What if someone more respected
than you has also been invited? 9The host will
say, 'Let this person sit here instead.' Then you
will be embarrassed and will have to take whatever seat is left at the foot of the table!

10"Do this instead—sit at the foot of the
table. Then when your host sees you, he will
come and say, 'Friend, we have a better place
than this for you!' Then you will be honored in
front of all the other guests. 11For the proud will
be humbled, but the humble will be honored."

12Then he turned to his host. "When you put
on a luncheon or a dinner," he said, "don't
invite your friends, brothers, relatives, and rich
neighbors. For they will repay you by inviting
you back. 13Instead, invite the poor, the crippled, the lame, and the blind. 14Then at the
resurrection of the godly, God will reward you
for inviting those who could not repay you."

Story of the Great Feast

15Hearing this, a man sitting at the table with
Jesus exclaimed, "What a privilege it would be
to have a share in the Kingdom of God!"

16Jesus replied with this illustration: "A man
prepared a great feast and sent out many invitations. 17When all was ready, he sent his servant
around to notify the guests that it was time for
them to come. 18But they all began making
excuses. One said he had just bought a field and
wanted to inspect it, so he asked to be excused.
19Another said he had just bought five pair of
oxen and wanted to try them out. 20Another had
just been married, so he said he couldn't come.

21"The servant returned and told his master
what they had said. His master was angry and
said, 'Go quickly into the streets and alleys of the
city and invite the poor, the crippled, the lame,
and the blind.' 22After the servant had done this,
he reported, 'There is still room for more.' 23So
his master said, 'Go out into the country lanes
and behind the hedges and urge anyone you find
to come, so that the house will be full. 24For none
of those I invited first will get even the smallest
taste of what I had prepared for them.'"

The Cost of Being a Disciple

25Great crowds were following Jesus. He turned
around and said to them, 26"If you want to be
my follower you must love me more than* your
own father and mother, wife and children,
brothers and sisters—yes, more than your own
life. Otherwise, you cannot be my disciple.
27And you cannot be my disciple if you do not
carry your own cross and follow me.

28"But don't begin until you count the cost.
For who would begin construction of a building
without first getting estimates and then checking
to see if there is enough money to pay the bills?
29Otherwise, you might complete only the foundation before running out of funds. And then
how everyone would laugh at you! 30They
would say, 'There's the person who started that
building and ran out of money before it was
finished!'

31"Or what king would ever dream of going
to war without first sitting down with his
counselors and discussing whether his army of
ten thousand is strong enough to defeat the
twenty thousand soldiers who are marching
against him? 32If he is not able, then while the
enemy is still far away, he will send a delegation to discuss terms of peace. 33So no one can
become my disciple without giving up everything for me.

34"Salt is good for seasoning. But if it loses its
flavor, how do you make it salty again? 35Flavorless salt is good neither for the soil nor for
fertilizer. It is thrown away. Anyone who is willing to hear should listen and understand!"

CHAPTER 15

Story of the Lost Sheep

Tax collectors and other notorious sinners often
came to listen to Jesus teach. 2This made the
Pharisees and teachers of religious law complain
that he was associating with such despicable
people—even eating with them!

3So Jesus used this illustration: 4"If you had
one hundred sheep, and one of them strayed
away and was lost in the wilderness, wouldn't
you leave the ninety-nine others to go and
search for the lost one until you found it? 5And
then you would joyfully carry it home on your
shoulders. 6When you arrived, you would call
together your friends and neighbors to rejoice
with you because your lost sheep was found. 7In
the same way, heaven will be happier over one
lost sinner who returns to God than over ninety-nine others who are righteous and haven't
strayed away!

14:26 Greek *you must hate.*

Story of the Lost Coin

8"Or suppose a woman has ten valuable silver
coins* and loses one. Won't she light a lamp and
look in every corner of the house and sweep
every nook and cranny until she finds it? 9And
when she finds it, she will call in her friends and
neighbors to rejoice with her because she has
found her lost coin. 10In the same way, there is
joy in the presence of God's angels when even
one sinner repents."

Story of the Lost Son

11To illustrate the point further, Jesus told them
this story: "A man had two sons. 12The younger
son told his father, 'I want my share of your
estate now, instead of waiting until you die.' So
his father agreed to divide his wealth between
his sons.

13"A few days later this younger son packed
all his belongings and took a trip to a distant
land, and there he wasted all his money on wild
living. 14About the time his money ran out, a
great famine swept over the land, and he began
to starve. 15He persuaded a local farmer to hire
him to feed his pigs. 16The boy became so hungry that even the pods he was feeding the pigs
looked good to him. But no one gave him anything.

17"When he finally came to his senses, he
said to himself, 'At home even the hired men
have food enough to spare, and here I am, dying
of hunger! 18I will go home to my father and say,
"Father, I have sinned against both heaven and
you, 19and I am no longer worthy of being called
your son. Please take me on as a hired man." '

20"So he returned home to his father. And
while he was still a long distance away, his father
saw him coming. Filled with love and compassion, he ran to his son, embraced him, and
kissed him. 21His son said to him, 'Father, I have
sinned against both heaven and you, and I am
no longer worthy of being called your son.*'

22"But his father said to the servants, 'Quick!
Bring the finest robe in the house and put it on
him. Get a ring for his finger, and sandals for his
feet. 23And kill the calf we have been fattening
in the pen. We must celebrate with a feast, 24for
this son of mine was dead and has now returned
to life. He was lost, but now he is found.' So the
party began.

25"Meanwhile, the older son was in the fields
working. When he returned home, he heard
music and dancing in the house, 26and he asked
one of the servants what was going on. 27'Your
brother is back,' he was told, 'and your father has
killed the calf we were fattening and has prepared a great feast. We are celebrating because of
his safe return.'

28"The older brother was angry and wouldn't
go in. His father came out and begged him, 29but
he replied, 'All these years I've worked hard for
you and never once refused to do a single thing
you told me to. And in all that time you never
gave me even one young goat for a feast with my
friends. 30Yet when this son of yours comes back

15:8 Greek *10 drachmas.* A drachma was the equivalent of a full day's wage. 15:21 Some manuscripts add *Please take me on as a hired man.*

A Disciple Counts the Cost

Read LUKE 14:25-33

At the time Jesus said these words, he had become quite a popular figure. Crowds flocked around him wherever he went. But they did not always do so for the right reasons. Consequently, Jesus directed his solemn and searching words to those people who followed him for selfish purposes or because it was the thing to do.

Likewise, Jesus doesn't want you to follow him only when it is convenient or socially acceptable. He wants you to be his disciple for the long haul—regardless of how easy or difficult it might be. That is why you must count the cost of being a true disciple of Jesus Christ. What does it mean to count the cost? The following four questions will give you a concrete idea:

- Do you love Jesus more than anyone or anything else in your life?
- Do you love Jesus and desire his will for your life over your own?
- Are you willing to accept ridicule and sacrifice for the cause of Christ?
- Will you commit to following Jesus, whether or not it is popular or expedient?

If you have carefully examined your heart, counted the cost, and can truthfully answer yes to these questions, then you are on the road to discipleship and are now ready to spend the rest of your life as his disciple and friend.

Jesus is not looking for half-hearted followers. He wants wholehearted commitment.

What Is Hell Like? Read LUKE 16:19-31

Jesus gave us a rare glimpse of life in hell in this parable. Here is what he revealed about this dark place of punishment.

People's Lifestyles on Earth Will Not Be the Same in Eternity. Things dramatically changed for the rich man when he passed into eternity. Because he did not have a personal relationship with God, he immediately entered into the dark torment of hell, penniless and in agony. Those whose hearts are not right with God face the same future as the rich man in this story. After death they will be held in hell until they are brought before God at what is called the Great White Throne Judgment (see "Why Would a Good God Send Anyone to Hell?" p. 287).

Hell Is a Place of Flames and Torment. The rich man in this parable experienced unrelenting heat and an unquenchable thirst. He was in so much agony that he called out to Abraham to have Lazarus come and dip his finger in water to cool his (the rich man's) tongue. If you have ever been badly burned, then you have an idea of the torment that awaits those who will spend eternity in hell. Add to that darkness and isolation, and you have an incredibly bleak scenario.

People Do Not "Have a Good Time" in Hell. Some people say, "I want to go to hell. All of my friends will be there." That may be true. But hell holds no parties. As this parable states, the rich man is so alarmed by his situation that he wants Lazarus to go and warn his brothers, so that they will not join him in torment.

If you want to know about the reality of hell, you don't need some tabloid account of someone who has supposedly had an out-of-body experience. You can study the words of the living God, who died and rose again, and who can tell you exactly what to expect in eternity. Our acceptance or rejection of his words determines on which side of the divide we will spend the rest of our lives.

CORNER STONES

after squandering your money on prostitutes, you celebrate by killing the finest calf we have.'

31"His father said to him, 'Look, dear son, you and I are very close, and everything I have is yours. 32We had to celebrate this happy day. For your brother was dead and has come back to life! He was lost, but now he is found!'"

CHAPTER 16

Story of the Shrewd Manager

Jesus told this story to his disciples: "A rich man hired a manager to handle his affairs, but soon a rumor went around that the manager was thoroughly dishonest. 2So his employer called him in and said, 'What's this I hear about your stealing from me? Get your report in order, because you are going to be dismissed.'

3"The manager thought to himself, 'Now what? I'm through here, and I don't have the strength to go out and dig ditches, and I'm too proud to beg. 4I know just the thing! And then I'll have plenty of friends to take care of me when I leave!'

5"So he invited each person who owed money to his employer to come and discuss the situation. He asked the first one, 'How much do you owe him?' 6The man replied, 'I owe him eight hundred gallons of olive oil.' So the manager told him, 'Tear up that bill and write another one for four hundred gallons.*'

7" 'And how much do you owe my employer?' he asked the next man. 'A thousand bushels of wheat,' was the reply. 'Here,' the manager said, 'take your bill and replace it with one for only eight hundred bushels.*'

8"The rich man had to admire the dishonest rascal for being so shrewd. And it is true that the citizens of this world are more shrewd than the godly are. 9I tell you, use your worldly resources to

16:6 Greek *100 baths . . . 50 [baths]*. 16:7 Greek *100 korous . . . 80 [korous]*.

benefit others and make friends. In this way, your
generosity stores up a reward for you in heaven.*
10"Unless you are faithful in small matters,
you won't be faithful in large ones. If you cheat
even a little, you won't be honest with greater
responsibilities. 11And if you are untrustworthy
about worldly wealth, who will trust you with
the true riches of heaven? 12And if you are not
faithful with other people's money, why should
you be trusted with money of your own?
13"No one can serve two masters. For you will
hate one and love the other, or be devoted to one
and despise the other. You cannot serve both
God and money."
14The Pharisees, who dearly loved their
money, naturally scoffed at all this. 15Then he
said to them, "You like to look good in public,
but God knows your evil hearts. What this world
honors is an abomination in the sight of God.
16"Until John the Baptist began to preach, the
laws of Moses and the messages of the prophets
were your guides. But now the Good News of the
Kingdom of God is preached, and eager multitudes are forcing their way in. 17But that doesn't
mean that the law has lost its force in even the
smallest point. It is stronger and more permanent than heaven and earth.
18"Anyone who divorces his wife and marries
someone else commits adultery, and anyone who
marries a divorced woman commits adultery."

The Rich Man and Lazarus

19Jesus said, "There was a certain rich man who
was splendidly clothed and who lived each day
in luxury. 20At his door lay a diseased beggar
named Lazarus. 21As Lazarus lay there longing
for scraps from the rich man's table, the dogs
would come and lick his open sores. 22Finally,
the beggar died and was carried by the angels to
be with Abraham.* The rich man also died and
was buried, 23and his soul went to the place of
the dead.* There, in torment, he saw Lazarus in
the far distance with Abraham.
24"The rich man shouted, 'Father Abraham,
have some pity! Send Lazarus over here to dip
the tip of his finger in water and cool my tongue,
because I am in anguish in these flames.'
25"But Abraham said to him, 'Son, remember
that during your lifetime you had everything you
wanted, and Lazarus had nothing. So now he is
here being comforted, and you are in anguish.
26And besides, there is a great chasm separating
us. Anyone who wanted to cross over to you
from here is stopped at its edge, and no one
there can cross over to us.'
27"Then the rich man said, 'Please, Father
Abraham, send him to my father's home. 28For
I have five brothers, and I want him to warn
them about this place of torment so they won't
have to come here when they die.'
29"But Abraham said, 'Moses and the prophets have warned them. Your brothers can read
their writings anytime they want to.'
30"The rich man replied, 'No, Father Abraham! But if someone is sent to them from the
dead, then they will turn from their sins.'
31"But Abraham said, 'If they won't listen to
Moses and the prophets, they won't listen even
if someone rises from the dead.'"

CHAPTER 17

Teachings about Forgiveness and Faith

One day Jesus said to his disciples, "There will
always be temptations to sin, but how terrible it
will be for the person who does the tempting. 2It
would be better to be thrown into the sea with a
large millstone tied around the neck than to face
the punishment in store for harming one of
these little ones. 3I am warning you! If another
believer* sins, rebuke him; then if he repents,
forgive him. 4Even if he wrongs you seven times
a day and each time turns again and asks forgiveness, forgive him."
5One day the apostles said to the Lord, "We
need more faith; tell us how to get it."
6"Even if you had faith as small as a mustard
seed," the Lord answered, "you could say to this
mulberry tree, 'May God uproot you and throw
you into the sea,' and it would obey you!
7"When a servant comes in from plowing or
taking care of sheep, he doesn't just sit down
and eat. 8He must first prepare his master's meal
and serve him his supper before eating his own.
9And the servant is not even thanked, because he
is merely doing what he is supposed to do. 10In
the same way, when you obey me you should
say, 'We are not worthy of praise. We are servants
who have simply done our duty.'"

Ten Healed of Leprosy

11As Jesus continued on toward Jerusalem, he
reached the border between Galilee and Samaria. 12As he entered a village there, ten lepers
stood at a distance, 13crying out, "Jesus, Master,
have mercy on us!"

16:9 Or *Then when you run out at the end of this life, your friends will welcome you into eternal homes.* 16:22 Greek *into Abraham's bosom.*
16:23 Greek *to Hades.* 17:3 Greek *your brother.*

14He looked at them and said, "Go show yourselves to the priests." And as they went, their leprosy disappeared.

15One of them, when he saw that he was healed, came back to Jesus, shouting, "Praise God, I'm healed!" 16He fell face down on the ground at Jesus' feet, thanking him for what he had done. This man was a Samaritan.

17Jesus asked, "Didn't I heal ten men? Where are the other nine? 18Does only this foreigner return to give glory to God?" 19And Jesus said to the man, "Stand up and go. Your faith has made you well."

The Coming of the Kingdom

20One day the Pharisees asked Jesus, "When will the Kingdom of God come?"

Jesus replied, "The Kingdom of God isn't ushered in with visible signs.* 21You won't be able to say, 'Here it is!' or 'It's over there!' For the Kingdom of God is among you.*"

22Later he talked again about this with his disciples. "The time is coming when you will long to share in the days of the Son of Man, but you won't be able to," he said. 23"Reports will reach you that the Son of Man has returned and that he is in this place or that. Don't believe such reports or go out to look for him. 24For when the Son of Man returns, you will know it beyond all doubt. It will be as evident as the lightning that flashes across the sky. 25But first the Son of Man must suffer terribly* and be rejected by this generation.

26"When the Son of Man returns, the world will be like the people were in Noah's day. 27In those days before the flood, the people enjoyed banquets and parties and weddings right up to the time Noah entered his boat and the flood came to destroy them all.

28"And the world will be as it was in the days of Lot. People went about their daily business—eating and drinking, buying and selling, farming and building—29until the morning Lot left Sodom. Then fire and burning sulfur rained down from heaven and destroyed them all. 30Yes, it will be 'business as usual' right up to the hour when the Son of Man returns.* 31On that day a person outside the house* must not go into the house to pack. A person in the field must not return to town. 32Remember what happened to Lot's wife! 33Whoever clings to this life will lose it, and whoever loses this life will save it. 34That night two people will be asleep in one bed; one will be taken away, and the other will be left. 35Two women will be grinding flour together at the mill; one will be taken, the other left.*"

37"Lord, where will this happen?" the disciples asked.

Jesus replied, "Just as the gathering of vultures shows there is a carcass nearby, so these signs indicate that the end is near."*

CHAPTER 18

Story of the Persistent Widow

One day Jesus told his disciples a story to illustrate their need for constant prayer and to show them that they must never give up. 2"There was a judge in a certain city," he said, "who was a godless man with great contempt for everyone. 3A widow of that city came to him repeatedly, appealing for justice against someone who had harmed her. 4The judge ignored her for a while, but eventually she wore him out. 'I fear neither God nor man,' he said to himself, 5'but this woman is driving me crazy. I'm going to see that she gets justice, because she is wearing me out with her constant requests!'"

6Then the Lord said, "Learn a lesson from this evil judge. 7Even he rendered a just decision

17:20 Or *by your speculations.* 17:21 Or *within you.* 17:25 Or *suffer many things.* 17:30 Or *on the day the Son of Man is revealed.* 17:31 Greek *on the roof.* 17:35 Some manuscripts add verse 36, *Two men will be working in the field; one will be taken, the other left.* 17:37 Greek *Wherever the carcass is, the vultures gather.*

OFF AND RUNNING

Pray Persistently
Read LUKE 18:1-8

This parable illustrates the need for persistence in prayer. Interestingly enough, Jesus chose two unlikely characters for this parable: a poor, widowed woman, and a corrupt judge. These characters hardly seem like the proper comparison for describing our relationship with God, but Jesus wants us to focus upon several important contrasts in this story:

- The widow had to go to a corrupt judge. . . . We can go to our heavenly Father (see Ephesians 3:14, p. 239).
- The widow was a stranger. . . . We are God's children (see John 1:12, p. 107).

in the end, so don't you think God will surely
give justice to his chosen people who plead with
him day and night? Will he keep putting them
off? 8I tell you, he will grant justice to them
quickly! But when I, the Son of Man, return,
how many will I find who have faith?"

Story of the Pharisee and Tax Collector

9Then Jesus told this story to some who had
great self-confidence and scorned everyone else:
10"Two men went to the Temple to pray. One
was a Pharisee, and the other was a dishonest tax
collector. 11The proud Pharisee stood by himself
and prayed this prayer: 'I thank you, God, that I
am not a sinner like everyone else, especially like
that tax collector over there! For I never cheat, I
don't sin, I don't commit adultery, 12I fast twice
a week, and I give you a tenth of my income.'

13"But the tax collector stood at a distance and
dared not even lift his eyes to heaven as he
prayed. Instead, he beat his chest in sorrow, saying, 'O God, be merciful to me, for I am a sinner.'
14I tell you, this sinner, not the Pharisee, returned
home justified before God. For the proud will be
humbled, but the humble will be honored."

Jesus Blesses the Children

15One day some parents brought their little children to Jesus so he could touch them and bless
them, but the disciples told them not to bother
him. 16Then Jesus called for the children and
said to the disciples, "Let the children come to
me. Don't stop them! For the Kingdom of God
belongs to such as these. 17I assure you, anyone
who doesn't have their kind of faith will never
get into the Kingdom of God."

The Rich Man

18Once a religious leader asked Jesus this question: "Good teacher, what should I do to get
eternal life?"

19"Why do you call me good?" Jesus asked
him. "Only God is truly good. 20But as for your
question, you know the commandments: 'Do
not commit adultery. Do not murder. Do not
steal. Do not testify falsely. Honor your father
and mother.'* "

21The man replied, "I've obeyed all these
commandments since I was a child."

22"There is still one thing you lack," Jesus said.
"Sell all you have and give the money to the poor,
and you will have treasure in heaven. Then come,
follow me." 23But when the man heard this, he
became sad because he was very rich.

24Jesus watched him go and then said to his
disciples, "How hard it is for rich people to get
into the Kingdom of God! 25It is easier for a
camel to go through the eye of a needle than for
a rich person to enter the Kingdom of God!"

26Those who heard this said, "Then who in
the world can be saved?"

27He replied, "What is impossible from a
human perspective is possible with God."

28Peter said, "We have left our homes and
followed you."

29"Yes," Jesus replied, "and I assure you,
everyone who has given up house or wife or
brothers or parents or children, for the sake of
the Kingdom of God, 30will be repaid many
times over in this life, as well as receiving eternal
life in the world to come."

Jesus Again Predicts His Death

31Gathering the twelve disciples around him,
Jesus told them, "As you know, we are going to
Jerusalem. And when we get there, all the predictions of the ancient prophets concerning the Son
of Man will come true. 32He will be handed over
to the Romans to be mocked, treated shamefully, and spit upon. 33They will whip him and
kill him, but on the third day he will rise again."

34But they didn't understand a thing he said.

18:20 Exod 20:12-16; Deut 5:16-20.

- The widow had no access to the judge. . . . We have constant access to God (see Hebrews 10:19, p. 293).
- The widow came to the court of law. . . . We come to the throne of grace (see Hebrews 4:16, p. 288).
- The widow had no lawyer. . . . We have Jesus as our advocate (see 1 John 2:1, p. 317).
- The widow had to wear down the judge before he really listened. . . . We already know that God hears our requests (see Matthew 7:7-11, p. 11).

If this poor woman received what she deserved from a corrupt judge, how much more will we receive from our loving heavenly Father. As Jesus illustrated, persistence pays off. Keep on praying!

We Need to Invest Our Abilities and Resources in God's Kingdom Read LUKE 19:11-26

This parable explains what Jesus expects of us as we await his return to earth. The nobleman in this story represents Christ. The servants refer to us, his followers. In essence, the crux of the parable is that we are to work diligently on his behalf until he returns.

In this parable, each man was given ten pounds of silver. Likewise, every believer has been given equal opportunity to invest his or her life in God's Kingdom, a common responsibility. It is the simple commission to proclaim the gospel to the world and make disciples. We then see three levels of investment.

1. The Servant with Tremendous Gain. This ambitious servant gave the king back ten times the amount he originally had been given. This type of person is truly a disciple. He or she actively shares his or her faith with one person after another, then takes these individuals under his or her wing to help them mature in their faith.

2. The Servant with Splendid Gain. The second servant was a little less ambitious than the first, but he did make some gain. This type of person seems somewhat satisfied with the status quo. He or she gets the gospel out slowly but surely, but he or she doesn't see the same results as the first type of person. This person fails to use all of the resources God has given him or her, so he or she always falls a little short of his or her full potential.

3. The Servant with No Gain. The third servant wanted to "play it safe," so he buried his money. He did so because he had a false perception of his master. He claimed that his master was hard and unfair. In the same way, this person is often motivated out of fear of God rather than a love for God. He or she sees witnessing as a duty rather than a privilege. That is why Paul tells us that Christ's love needs to be the motivating force in all that we do (see 2 Corinthians 5:14, pp. 220-221). We can only give out what we ourselves have taken in. And this person knows little of the Savior he or she serves.

CORNERSTONES

In the Kingdom of God, God expects investment as well as results. Don't take this sacred trust he has given to you and bury it in the ground. Use it. Multiply it. Remember, God isn't asking you to work *for* him. He is asking to work *through* you. Yield to the power of the Holy Spirit and ask God for directions as to how you can be used by him. Then you will see results.

Its significance was hidden from them, and they failed to grasp what he was talking about.

Jesus Heals a Blind Beggar

35As they approached Jericho, a blind beggar was
sitting beside the road. 36When he heard the noise
of a crowd going past, he asked what was happening. 37They told him that Jesus of Nazareth was
going by. 38So he began shouting, "Jesus, Son of
David, have mercy on me!" 39The crowds ahead of
Jesus tried to hush the man, but he only shouted
louder, "Son of David, have mercy on me!"
40When Jesus heard him, he stopped and
ordered that the man be brought to him. 41Then
Jesus asked the man, "What do you want me to
do for you?"
"Lord," he pleaded, "I want to see!"
42And Jesus said, "All right, you can see! Your
faith has healed you." 43Instantly the man could
see, and he followed Jesus, praising God. And all
who saw it praised God, too.

CHAPTER **19**

Jesus and Zacchaeus

Jesus entered Jericho and made his way through
the town. 2There was a man there named Zacchaeus. He was one of the most influential Jews
in the Roman tax-collecting business, and he
had become very rich. 3He tried to get a look at
Jesus, but he was too short to see over the
crowds. 4So he ran ahead and climbed a syca-

more tree beside the road, so he could watch
from there.
5When Jesus came by, he looked up at Zacchaeus and called him by name. "Zacchaeus!"
he said. "Quick, come down! For I must be a
guest in your home today."
6Zacchaeus quickly climbed down and took
Jesus to his house in great excitement and joy.
7But the crowds were displeased. "He has gone
to be the guest of a notorious sinner," they
grumbled.
8Meanwhile, Zacchaeus stood there and said
to the Lord, "I will give half my wealth to the
poor, Lord, and if I have overcharged people on
their taxes, I will give them back four times as
much!"
9Jesus responded, "Salvation has come to this
home today, for this man has shown himself to
be a son of Abraham. 10And I, the Son of Man,
have come to seek and save those like him who
are lost."

Story of the Ten Servants

11The crowd was listening to everything Jesus
said. And because he was nearing Jerusalem,
he told a story to correct the impression that
the Kingdom of God would begin right away.
12He said, "A nobleman was called away to a
distant empire to be crowned king and then
return. 13Before he left, he called together ten
servants and gave them ten pounds of silver*
to invest for him while he was gone. 14But his
people hated him and sent a delegation after
him to say they did not want him to be their
king.
15"When he returned, the king called in the
servants to whom he had given the money. He
wanted to find out what they had done with the
money and what their profits were. 16The first
servant reported a tremendous gain—ten times
as much as the original amount! 17'Well done!'
the king exclaimed. 'You are a trustworthy servant. You have been faithful with the little I
entrusted to you, so you will be governor of ten
cities as your reward.'
18"The next servant also reported a good
gain—five times the original amount. 19'Well
done!' the king said. 'You can be governor over
five cities.'
20"But the third servant brought back only
the original amount of money and said, 'I hid it
and kept it safe. 21I was afraid because you are a
hard man to deal with, taking what isn't yours
and harvesting crops you didn't plant.'
22" 'You wicked servant!' the king roared.
'Hard, am I? If you knew so much about me and
how tough I am, 23why didn't you deposit the
money in the bank so I could at least get some
interest on it?' 24Then turning to the others
standing nearby, the king ordered, 'Take the
money from this servant, and give it to the one
who earned the most.'
25" 'But, master,' they said, 'that servant has
enough already!'
26" 'Yes,' the king replied, 'but to those who
use well what they are given, even more will be
given. But from those who are unfaithful,* even
what little they have will be taken away. 27And
now about these enemies of mine who didn't
want me to be their king—bring them in and
execute them right here in my presence.' "

The Triumphal Entry

28After telling this story, Jesus went on toward
Jerusalem, walking ahead of his disciples. 29As
they came to the towns of Bethphage and Bethany, on the Mount of Olives, he sent two disciples ahead. 30"Go into that village over there,"
he told them, "and as you enter it, you will see
a colt tied there that has never been ridden.
Untie it and bring it here. 31If anyone asks what
you are doing, just say, 'The Lord needs it.' "
32So they went and found the colt, just as
Jesus had said. 33And sure enough, as they were
untying it, the owners asked them, "Why are you
untying our colt?"
34And the disciples simply replied, "The Lord
needs it." 35So they brought the colt to Jesus and
threw their garments over it for him to ride on.
36Then the crowds spread out their coats on
the road ahead of Jesus. 37As they reached the
place where the road started down from the
Mount of Olives, all of his followers began to
shout and sing as they walked along, praising
God for all the wonderful miracles they had seen.

38 "Bless the King who comes in the name of
the Lord!
Peace in heaven
and glory in highest heaven!"*

39But some of the Pharisees among the crowd
said, "Teacher, rebuke your followers for saying
things like that!"
40He replied, "If they kept quiet, the stones
along the road would burst into cheers!"

19:13 Greek *10 minas;* 1 mina was worth about 3 months' wages. 19:26 Or *who have nothing.* 19:38 Pss 118:26; 148:1.

Jesus Weeps over Jerusalem

41But as they came closer to Jerusalem and Jesus saw the city ahead, he began to cry. 42"I wish that even today you would find the way of peace. But now it is too late, and peace is hidden from you. 43Before long your enemies will build ramparts against your walls and encircle you and close in on you. 44They will crush you to the ground, and your children with you. Your enemies will not leave a single stone in place, because you have rejected the opportunity God offered you."

Jesus Clears the Temple

45Then Jesus entered the Temple and began to drive out the merchants from their stalls. 46He told them, "The Scriptures declare, 'My Temple will be a place of prayer,' but you have turned it into a den of thieves."*

47After that, he taught daily in the Temple, but the leading priests, the teachers of religious law, and the other leaders of the people began planning how to kill him. 48But they could think of nothing, because all the people hung on every word he said.

CHAPTER 20

The Authority of Jesus Challenged

One day as Jesus was teaching and preaching the Good News in the Temple, the leading priests and teachers of religious law and other leaders came up to him. 2They demanded, "By whose authority did you drive out the merchants from the Temple?* Who gave you such authority?"

3"Let me ask you a question first," he replied. 4"Did John's baptism come from heaven, or was it merely human?"

5They talked it over among themselves. "If we say it was from heaven, he will ask why we didn't believe him. 6But if we say it was merely human, the people will stone us, because they are convinced he was a prophet." 7Finally they replied, "We don't know."

8And Jesus responded, "Then I won't answer your question either."

Story of the Evil Farmers

9Now Jesus turned to the people again and told them this story: "A man planted a vineyard, leased it out to tenant farmers, and moved to another country to live for several years. 10At grape-picking time, he sent one of his servants to collect his share of the crop. But the farmers attacked the servant, beat him up, and sent him back empty-handed. 11So the owner sent another servant, but the same thing happened; he was beaten up and treated shamefully, and he went away empty-handed. 12A third man was sent and the same thing happened. He, too, was wounded and chased away.

13" 'What will I do?' the owner asked himself. 'I know! I'll send my cherished son. Surely they will respect him.'

14"But when the farmers saw his son, they said to each other, 'Here comes the heir to this estate. Let's kill him and get the estate for ourselves!' 15So they dragged him out of the vineyard and murdered him.

"What do you suppose the owner of the vineyard will do to those farmers?" Jesus asked. 16"I'll tell you—he will come and kill them all and lease the vineyard to others."

"But God forbid that such a thing should ever happen," his listeners protested.

17Jesus looked at them and said, "Then what do the Scriptures mean?

'The stone rejected by the builders
has now become the cornerstone.'*

18All who stumble over that stone will be broken to pieces, and it will crush anyone on whom it falls."

19When the teachers of religious law and the leading priests heard this story, they wanted to arrest Jesus immediately because they realized he was pointing at them—that they were the farmers in the story. But they were afraid there would be a riot if they arrested him.

Taxes for Caesar

20Watching for their opportunity, the leaders sent secret agents pretending to be honest men. They tried to get Jesus to say something that could be reported to the Roman governor so he would arrest Jesus. 21They said, "Teacher, we know that you speak and teach what is right and are not influenced by what others think. You sincerely teach the ways of God. 22Now tell us—is it right to pay taxes to the Roman government or not?"

23He saw through their trickery and said, 24"Show me a Roman coin.* Whose picture and title are stamped on it?"

"Caesar's," they replied.

25"Well then," he said, "give to Caesar what belongs to him. But everything that belongs to

19:46 Isa 56:7; Jer 7:11. 20:2 Or *By whose authority do you do these things?* 20:17 Ps 118:22. 20:24 Greek *a denarius.*

God must be given to God." 26So they failed to
trap him in the presence of the people. Instead,
they were amazed by his answer, and they were
silenced.

Discussion about Resurrection

27Then some Sadducees stepped forward—a
group of Jews who say there is no resurrection
after death. 28They posed this question:
"Teacher, Moses gave us a law that if a man dies,
leaving a wife but no children, his brother
should marry the widow and have a child who
will be the brother's heir.* 29Well, there were
seven brothers. The oldest married and then
died without children. 30His brother married
the widow, but he also died. Still no children.
31And so it went, one after the other, until each
of the seven had married her and died, leaving
no children. 32Finally, the woman died, too.
33So tell us, whose wife will she be in the resurrection? For all seven were married to her!"

34Jesus replied, "Marriage is for people here
on earth. 35But that is not the way it will be in the
age to come. For those worthy of being raised
from the dead won't be married then. 36And they
will never die again. In these respects they are like
angels. They are children of God raised up to new
life. 37But now, as to whether the dead will be
raised—even Moses proved this when he wrote
about the burning bush. Long after Abraham,
Isaac, and Jacob had died, he referred to the
Lord* as 'the God of Abraham, the God of Isaac,
and the God of Jacob.'* 38So he is the God of the
living, not the dead. They are all alive to him."

39"Well said, Teacher!" remarked some of the
teachers of religious law who were standing
there. 40And that ended their questions; no one
dared to ask any more.

Whose Son Is the Messiah?

41Then Jesus presented them with a question.
"Why is it," he asked, "that the Messiah is said
to be the son of David? 42For David himself
wrote in the book of Psalms:

'The LORD said to my Lord,
Sit in honor at my right hand
43 until I humble your enemies,
making them a footstool under your
feet.'*

44Since David called him Lord, how can he be
his son at the same time?"

45Then, with the crowds listening, he turned
to his disciples and said, 46"Beware of these
teachers of religious law! For they love to parade
in flowing robes and to have everyone bow to
them as they walk in the marketplaces. And how
they love the seats of honor in the synagogues
and at banquets. 47But they shamelessly cheat
widows out of their property, and then, to cover
up the kind of people they really are, they make
long prayers in public. Because of this, their
punishment will be the greater."

CHAPTER 21

The Widow's Offering

While Jesus was in the Temple, he watched the
rich people putting their gifts into the collection
box. 2Then a poor widow came by and dropped
in two pennies.* 3"I assure you," he said, "this
poor widow has given more than all the rest of
them. 4For they have given a tiny part of their
surplus, but she, poor as she is, has given everything she has."

Jesus Foretells the Future

5Some of his disciples began talking about the
beautiful stonework of the Temple and the me-
morial decorations on the walls. But Jesus said,
6"The time is coming when all these things will
be so completely demolished that not one stone
will be left on top of another."

7"Teacher," they asked, "when will all this
take place? And will there be any sign ahead of
time?"

8He replied, "Don't let anyone mislead you.
For many will come in my name, claiming to be
the Messiah* and saying, 'The time has come!'
But don't believe them. 9And when you hear of
wars and insurrections, don't panic. Yes, these
things must come, but the end won't follow
immediately." 10Then he added, "Nations and
kingdoms will proclaim war against each other.
11There will be great earthquakes, and there will
be famines and epidemics in many lands, and
there will be terrifying things and great miraculous signs in the heavens.

12"But before all this occurs, there will be a
time of great persecution. You will be dragged
into synagogues and prisons, and you will be
accused before kings and governors of being my
followers. 13This will be your opportunity to tell
them about me. 14So don't worry about how to
answer the charges against you, 15for I will give
you the right words and such wisdom that none

20:28 Deut 25:5-6. **20:37a** Greek *when he wrote about the bush. He referred to the Lord.* **20:37b** Exod 3:6. **20:42-43** Ps 110:1. **21:2** Greek *2 lepta.* **21:8** Greek *name, saying, 'I am.'*

of your opponents will be able to reply! 16Even those closest to you—your parents, brothers, relatives, and friends—will betray you. And some of you will be killed. 17And everyone will hate you because of your allegiance to me. 18But not a hair of your head will perish! 19By standing firm, you will win your souls.

20"And when you see Jerusalem surrounded by armies, then you will know that the time of its destruction has arrived. 21Then those in Judea must flee to the hills. Let those in Jerusalem escape, and those outside the city should not enter it for shelter. 22For those will be days of God's vengeance, and the prophetic words of the Scriptures will be fulfilled. 23How terrible it will be for pregnant women and for mothers nursing their babies. For there will be great distress in the land and wrath upon this people. 24They will be brutally killed by the sword or sent away as captives to all the nations of the world. And Jerusalem will be conquered and trampled down by the Gentiles until the age of the Gentiles comes to an end.

25"And there will be strange events in the skies—signs in the sun, moon, and stars. And down here on earth the nations will be in turmoil, perplexed by the roaring seas and strange tides. 26The courage of many people will falter because of the fearful fate they see coming upon the earth, because the stability of the very heavens will be broken up. 27Then everyone will see the Son of Man arrive on the clouds with power and great glory.* 28So when all these things begin to happen, stand straight and look up, for your salvation is near!"

29Then he gave them this illustration: "Notice the fig tree, or any other tree. 30When the leaves come out, you know without being told that summer is near. 31Just so, when you see the events I've described taking place, you can be sure that the Kingdom of God is near. 32I assure you, this generation* will not pass from the scene until all these events have taken place. 33Heaven and earth will disappear, but my words will remain forever.

34"Watch out! Don't let me find you living in careless ease and drunkenness, and filled with the worries of this life. Don't let that day catch you unaware, 35as in a trap. For that day will come upon everyone living on the earth. 36Keep a constant watch. And pray that, if possible, you may escape these horrors and stand before the Son of Man."

37Every day Jesus went to the Temple to teach, and each evening he returned to spend the night on the Mount of Olives. 38The crowds gathered early each morning to hear him.

CHAPTER 22

Judas Agrees to Betray Jesus

The Festival of Unleavened Bread, which begins with the Passover celebration, was drawing near. 2The leading priests and teachers of religious law were actively plotting Jesus' murder. But they wanted to kill him without starting a riot, a possibility they greatly feared.

3Then Satan entered into Judas Iscariot, who was one of the twelve disciples, 4and he went over to the leading priests and captains of the Temple guard to discuss the best way to betray Jesus to them. 5They were delighted that he was ready to help them, and they promised him a reward. 6So he began looking for an opportunity to betray Jesus so they could arrest him quietly when the crowds weren't around.

The Last Supper

7Now the Festival of Unleavened Bread arrived, when the Passover lambs were sacrificed. 8Jesus sent Peter and John ahead and said, "Go and prepare the Passover meal, so we can eat it together."

9"Where do you want us to go?" they asked him.

10He replied, "As soon as you enter Jerusalem, a man carrying a pitcher of water will meet you. Follow him. At the house he enters, 11say to the owner, 'The Teacher asks, Where is the guest room where I can eat the Passover meal with my disciples?' 12He will take you upstairs to a large room that is already set up. That is the place. Go ahead and prepare our supper there." 13They went off to the city and found everything just as Jesus had said, and they prepared the Passover supper there.

14Then at the proper time Jesus and the twelve apostles sat down together at the table. 15Jesus said, "I have looked forward to this hour with deep longing, anxious to eat this Passover meal with you before my suffering begins. 16For I tell you now that I won't eat it again until it comes to fulfillment in the Kingdom of God."

17Then he took a cup of wine, and when he had given thanks for it, he said, "Take this and share it among yourselves. 18For I will not drink wine again until the Kingdom of God has come."

21:27 See Dan 7:13. **21:32** Or *this age,* or *this nation.*

19Then he took a loaf of bread; and when he had thanked God for it, he broke it in pieces and gave it to the disciples, saying, "This is my body, given for you. Do this in remembrance of me." 20After supper he took another cup of wine and said, "This wine is the token of God's new covenant to save you—an agreement sealed with the blood I will pour out for you.*

21"But here at this table, sitting among us as a friend, is the man who will betray me. 22For I, the Son of Man, must die since it is part of God's plan. But how terrible it will be for my betrayer!" 23Then the disciples began to ask each other which of them would ever do such a thing.

24And they began to argue among themselves as to who would be the greatest in the coming Kingdom. 25Jesus told them, "In this world the kings and great men order their people around, and yet they are called 'friends of the people.' 26But among you, those who are the greatest should take the lowest rank, and the leader should be like a servant. 27Normally the master sits at the table and is served by his servants. But not here! For I am your servant. 28You have remained true to me in my time of trial. 29And just as my Father has granted me a Kingdom, I now grant you the right 30to eat and drink at my table in that Kingdom. And you will sit on thrones, judging the twelve tribes of Israel.

Jesus Predicts Peter's Denial

31"Simon, Simon, Satan has asked to have all of you, to sift you like wheat. 32But I have pleaded in prayer for you, Simon, that your faith should not fail. So when you have repented and turned to me again, strengthen and build up your brothers."

33Peter said, "Lord, I am ready to go to prison with you, and even to die with you."

34But Jesus said, "Peter, let me tell you something. The rooster will not crow tomorrow morning until you have denied three times that you even know me."

35Then Jesus asked them, "When I sent you out to preach the Good News and you did not have money, a traveler's bag, or extra clothing, did you lack anything?"

"No," they replied.

36"But now," he said, "take your money and a traveler's bag. And if you don't have a sword, sell your clothes and buy one! 37For the time has come for this prophecy about me to be fulfilled: 'He was counted among those who were rebels.'* Yes, everything written about me by the prophets will come true."

38"Lord," they replied, "we have two swords among us."

"That's enough," he said.

Jesus Prays on the Mount of Olives

39Then, accompanied by the disciples, Jesus left the upstairs room and went as usual to the Mount of Olives. 40There he told them, "Pray that you will not be overcome by temptation."

41He walked away, about a stone's throw, and knelt down and prayed, 42"Father, if you are willing, please take this cup of suffering away from me. Yet I want your will, not mine." 43Then an angel from heaven appeared and strengthened him. 44He prayed more fervently, and he was in such agony of spirit that his sweat fell to the ground like great drops of blood.* 45At last he stood up again and returned to the disciples, only to find them asleep, exhausted from grief. 46"Why are you sleeping?" he asked. "Get up and pray. Otherwise temptation will overpower you."

Jesus Is Betrayed and Arrested

47But even as he said this, a mob approached, led by Judas, one of his twelve disciples. Judas walked over to Jesus and greeted him with a kiss. 48But Jesus said, "Judas, how can you betray me, the Son of Man, with a kiss?"

49When the other disciples saw what was about to happen, they exclaimed, "Lord, should we fight? We brought the swords!" 50And one of them slashed at the high priest's servant and cut off his right ear.

51But Jesus said, "Don't resist anymore." And he touched the place where the man's ear had been and healed him. 52Then Jesus spoke to the leading priests and captains of the Temple guard and the other leaders who headed the mob. "Am I some dangerous criminal," he asked, "that you have come armed with swords and clubs to arrest me? 53Why didn't you arrest me in the Temple? I was there every day. But this is your moment, the time when the power of darkness reigns."

Peter Denies Jesus

54So they arrested him and led him to the high priest's residence, and Peter was following far behind. 55The guards lit a fire in the courtyard and sat around it, and Peter joined them there.

22:19-20 Some manuscripts omit 22:19b-20, *given for you . . . I will pour out for you.* 22:37 Isa 53:12. 22:43-44 These verses are not included in many ancient manuscripts.

56A servant girl noticed him in the firelight and
began staring at him. Finally she said, "This man
was one of Jesus' followers!"
57Peter denied it. "Woman," he said, "I don't
even know the man!"
58After a while someone else looked at him
and said, "You must be one of them!"
"No, man, I'm not!" Peter replied.
59About an hour later someone else insisted,
"This must be one of Jesus' disciples because he
is a Galilean, too."
60But Peter said, "Man, I don't know what
you are talking about." And as soon as he said
these words, the rooster crowed. 61At that moment the Lord turned and looked at Peter. Then
Peter remembered that the Lord had said, "Before the rooster crows tomorrow morning, you
will deny me three times." 62And Peter left the
courtyard, crying bitterly.
63Now the guards in charge of Jesus began
mocking and beating him. 64They blindfolded
him; then they hit him and asked, "Who hit you
that time, you prophet?" 65And they threw all
sorts of terrible insults at him.

Jesus before the Council

66At daybreak all the leaders of the people assembled, including the leading priests and the
teachers of religious law. Jesus was led before
this high council,* 67and they said, "Tell us if
you are the Messiah."
But he replied, "If I tell you, you won't believe
me. 68And if I ask you a question, you won't
answer. 69But the time is soon coming when I,
the Son of Man, will be sitting at God's right
hand in the place of power."*
70They all shouted, "Then you claim you are
the Son of God?"
And he replied, "You are right in saying that I
am."
71"What need do we have for other
witnesses?" they shouted. "We ourselves heard
him say it."

CHAPTER 23

Jesus' Trial before Pilate

Then the entire council took Jesus over to Pilate,
the Roman governor. 2They began at once to
state their case: "This man has been leading our
people to ruin by telling them not to pay their
taxes to the Roman government and by claiming
he is the Messiah, a king."
3So Pilate asked him, "Are you the King of the
Jews?"
Jesus replied, "Yes, it is as you say."
4Pilate turned to the leading priests and to
the crowd and said, "I find nothing wrong with
this man!"
5Then they became desperate. "But he is
causing riots everywhere he goes, all over Judea,
from Galilee to Jerusalem!"
6"Oh, is he a Galilean?" Pilate asked. 7When
they answered that he was, Pilate sent him to
Herod Antipas, because Galilee was under Herod's jurisdiction, and Herod happened to be in
Jerusalem at the time.
8Herod was delighted at the opportunity to
see Jesus, because he had heard about him and
had been hoping for a long time to see him
perform a miracle. 9He asked Jesus question
after question, but Jesus refused to answer.
10Meanwhile, the leading priests and the teachers of religious law stood there shouting their
accusations. 11Now Herod and his soldiers began mocking and ridiculing Jesus. Then they put
a royal robe on him and sent him back to Pilate.
12Herod and Pilate, who had been enemies before, became friends that day.
13Then Pilate called together the leading
priests and other religious leaders, along with
the people, 14and he announced his verdict.
"You brought this man to me, accusing him of
leading a revolt. I have examined him thoroughly on this point in your presence and find
him innocent. 15Herod came to the same conclusion and sent him back to us. Nothing this
man has done calls for the death penalty. 16So I
will have him flogged, but then I will release
him."*
18Then a mighty roar rose from the crowd,
and with one voice they shouted, "Kill him, and
release Barabbas to us!" 19(Barabbas was in
prison for murder and for taking part in an
insurrection in Jerusalem against the government.) 20Pilate argued with them, because he
wanted to release Jesus. 21But they shouted,
"Crucify him! Crucify him!"
22For the third time he demanded, "Why?
What crime has he committed? I have found no
reason to sentence him to death. I will therefore
flog him and let him go."
23But the crowd shouted louder and louder
for Jesus' death, and their voices prevailed. 24So
Pilate sentenced Jesus to die as they demanded.
25As they had requested, he released Barabbas,

22:66 Greek *before their Sanhedrin.* 22:69 See Ps 110:1. 23:16 Some manuscripts add verse 17, *For it was necessary for him to release one [prisoner] for them during the feast.*

What Is Backsliding? Read LUKE 22:31-62

As believers we have been given a "new nature"—a part of us that spiritually hungers after God, a supernatural inclination to do what is right. Unfortunately, being human, we also have an "old nature"—a natural inclination to do wrong. Sometimes Christians begin to fall back spiritually or "backslide."

Perhaps the best way to understand the dangers of backsliding is to examine the biblical account of how one believer fell into this trap. He was none other than Simon Peter, one of Jesus' closest disciples. In Luke 22 we are given the account of his spiritual regression. His story serves as a warning that even the most mature believers have the potential to fall if they let their guard down.

BIG QUESTIONS

Self-Confidence and False Security. Not only did Peter reveal his unfounded confidence in himself (his claim that he would "die" with Jesus), but he also directly contradicted the Lord's prediction that he would fall (verse 34). He denied his own weakness to sin. The Bible warns, "If you think you are standing strong, be careful, for you, too, may fall into the same sin" (1 Corinthians 10:12).

Prayerlessness. Even after Jesus specifically instructed Peter to pray, he decided to sleep instead. In Matthew's account of this incident, Jesus had even warned them, "For though the spirit is willing enough, the body is weak!" (Matthew 26:41). Yet he felt no weakness and saw no need to be prayerful and watchful. Prayerlessness is as much a sin as directly breaking a commandment, for throughout Scripture God has specifically instructed us to pray.

Following God at a Distance. A lack of closeness and fellowship with the Lord will always be at the foundation of all spiritual regression. Although Peter was still following Jesus, he wasn't following as closely as he could have been. There are some Christians who want to try to live in both worlds. They want to be believers, but they don't want to be too committed. You endanger yourself when you live this way.

Warming Up at the Enemies' Fire. Following in the distance, Peter became cold and was attracted to the fire. Peter hoped to go unnoticed in the larger crowd, so he settled in with the very people who were responsible for arresting his Lord. The Bible tells us, "Oh, the joys of those who do not follow the advice of the wicked, or stand around with sinners, or join in with scoffers" (Psalm 1:1). Tragically, Peter was doing exactly the opposite. When that spiritual passion in our heart begins to die, that fire for Jesus Christ will grow cold, and we will look elsewhere for warmth.

Denial and Disassociations. Peter reached this final step of spiritual regression when he denied knowing or ever being with Jesus. Matthew's Gospel tells us that he began to curse and swear, which means that he took an oath, saying, "May God kill and damn me if I am not speaking the truth (26:74)." Peter had lost all sense of reality and seemingly all awareness of God.

Despite Peter's fall, he was restored. In verse 61, his eyes met those of Jesus, and Peter cried bitterly. As he grieved over his sin, Jesus saw his heart. The Bible says, "God can use sorrow in our lives to help us turn away from sin and seek salvation" (2 Corinthians 7:10). Interestingly enough, three days later, after Jesus' resurrection, the angel at the tomb specifically told Mary, "Now go and give this message to his disciples, *including Peter:* 'Jesus is going ahead of you to Galilee. You will see him there" (Mark 16:7, emphasis added). Jesus wanted Peter to know that he still loved him.

As Christians we will sin. Scripture says, "If we say that we have no sin, we are only fooling ourselves and refusing to accept the truth" (1 John 1:8). But the Holy Spirit will lovingly convict us of that sin and lead us back to the cross, where we can confess it and turn from it. Remember, when we sin we should run to—not away from—the Lord.

the man in prison for insurrection and murder. But he delivered Jesus over to them to do as they wished.

The Crucifixion

26As they led Jesus away, Simon of Cyrene,* who was coming in from the country just then, was forced to follow Jesus and carry his cross. 27Great crowds trailed along behind, including many grief-stricken women. 28But Jesus turned and said to them, "Daughters of Jerusalem, don't weep for me, but weep for yourselves and for your children. 29For the days are coming when they will say, 'Fortunate indeed are the women who are childless, the wombs that have not borne a child and the breasts that have never nursed.' 30People will beg the mountains to fall on them and the hills to bury them. 31For if these things are done when the tree is green, what will happen when it is dry?*"

32Two others, both criminals, were led out to be executed with him. 33Finally, they came to a place called The Skull.* All three were crucified there—Jesus on the center cross, and the two criminals on either side.

34Jesus said, "Father, forgive these people, because they don't know what they are doing."* And the soldiers gambled for his clothes by throwing dice.*

35The crowd watched, and the leaders laughed and scoffed. "He saved others," they said, "let him save himself if he is really God's Chosen One, the Messiah." 36The soldiers mocked him, too, by offering him a drink of sour wine. 37They called out to him, "If you are the King of the Jews, save yourself!" 38A signboard was nailed to the cross above him with these words: "This is the King of the Jews."

39One of the criminals hanging beside him scoffed, "So you're the Messiah, are you? Prove it by saving yourself—and us, too, while you're at it!"

40But the other criminal protested, "Don't you fear God even when you are dying? 41We deserve to die for our evil deeds, but this man hasn't done anything wrong." 42Then he said, "Jesus, remember me when you come into your Kingdom."

43And Jesus replied, "I assure you, today you will be with me in paradise."

The Death of Jesus

44By this time it was noon, and darkness fell across the whole land until three o'clock. 45The light from the sun was gone. And suddenly, the thick veil hanging in the Temple was torn apart. 46Then Jesus shouted, "Father, I entrust my spirit into your hands!"* And with those words he breathed his last.

47When the captain of the Roman soldiers handling the executions saw what had happened, he praised God and said, "Surely this man was innocent.*" 48And when the crowd that came to see the crucifixion saw all that had happened, they went home in deep sorrow.* 49But Jesus' friends, including the women who had followed him from Galilee, stood at a distance watching.

The Burial of Jesus

50Now there was a good and righteous man named Joseph. He was a member of the Jewish high council, 51but he had not agreed with the decision and actions of the other religious leaders. He was from the town of Arimathea in Judea, and he had been waiting for the Kingdom of God to come. 52He went to Pilate and asked for Jesus' body. 53Then he took the body down from the cross and wrapped it in a long linen cloth and laid it in a new tomb that had been carved out of rock. 54This was done late on Friday afternoon, the day of preparation* for the Sabbath.

55As his body was taken away, the women from Galilee followed and saw the tomb where they placed his body. 56Then they went home and prepared spices and ointments to embalm him. But by the time they were finished it was the Sabbath, so they rested all that day as required by the law.

CHAPTER 24

The Resurrection

But very early on Sunday morning* the women came to the tomb, taking the spices they had prepared. 2They found that the stone covering the entrance had been rolled aside. 3So they went in, but they couldn't find the body of the Lord Jesus. 4They were puzzled, trying to think what could have happened to it. Suddenly, two men appeared to them, clothed in dazzling robes. 5The women were terrified and bowed

23:26 *Cyrene* was a city in northern Africa. 23:31 Or *If these things are done to me, the living tree, what will happen to you, the dry tree?* 23:33 Sometimes rendered *Calvary,* which comes from the Latin word for "skull." 23:34a This sentence is not included in many ancient manuscripts. 23:34b Greek *by casting lots.* See Ps 22:18. 23:46 Ps 31:5. 23:47 Or *righteous.* 23:48 Greek *beating their breasts.* 23:54 Greek *on the day of preparation.* 24:1 Greek *But on the first day of the week, very early in the morning.*

low before them. Then the men asked, "Why are
you looking in a tomb for someone who is alive?
6He isn't here! He has risen from the dead!
Don't you remember what he told you back in
Galilee, 7that the Son of Man must be betrayed
into the hands of sinful men and be crucified,
and that he would rise again the third day?"

8Then they remembered that he had said this.
9So they rushed back to tell his eleven disciples—and everyone else—what had happened.
10The women who went to the tomb were Mary
Magdalene, Joanna, Mary the mother of James,
and several others. They told the apostles what
had happened, 11but the story sounded like
nonsense, so they didn't believe it. 12However,
Peter ran to the tomb to look. Stooping, he
peered in and saw the empty linen wrappings;
then he went home again, wondering what had
happened.*

The Walk to Emmaus

13That same day two of Jesus' followers were
walking to the village of Emmaus, seven miles*
out of Jerusalem. 14As they walked along they
were talking about everything that had happened. 15Suddenly, Jesus himself came along
and joined them and began walking beside
them. 16But they didn't know who he was, because God kept them from recognizing him.

17"You seem to be in a deep discussion about
something," he said. "What are you so concerned about?"

They stopped short, sadness written across
their faces. 18Then one of them, Cleopas, replied, "You must be the only person in Jerusalem who hasn't heard about all the things that
have happened there the last few days."

19"What things?" Jesus asked.

"The things that happened to Jesus, the man
from Nazareth," they said. "He was a prophet
who did wonderful miracles. He was a mighty
teacher, highly regarded by both God and all the
people. 20But our leading priests and other religious leaders arrested him and handed him over
to be condemned to death, and they crucified
him. 21We had thought he was the Messiah who
had come to rescue Israel. That all happened
three days ago. 22Then some women from our
group of his followers were at his tomb early this
morning, and they came back with an amazing
report. 23They said his body was missing, and
they had seen angels who told them Jesus is
alive! 24Some of our men ran out to see, and
sure enough, Jesus' body was gone, just as the
women had said."

25Then Jesus said to them, "You are such
foolish people! You find it so hard to believe all
that the prophets wrote in the Scriptures.
26Wasn't it clearly predicted by the prophets that
the Messiah would have to suffer all these things
before entering his time of glory?" 27Then Jesus
quoted passages from the writings of Moses and
all the prophets, explaining what all the
Scriptures said about himself.

28By this time they were nearing Emmaus and
the end of their journey. Jesus would have gone
on, 29but they begged him to stay the night with
them, since it was getting late. So he went home
with them. 30As they sat down to eat, he took a
small loaf of bread, asked God's blessing on it,
broke it, then gave it to them. 31Suddenly, their
eyes were opened, and they recognized him.
And at that moment he disappeared!

32They said to each other, "Didn't our hearts
feel strangely warm as he talked with us on the
road and explained the Scriptures to us?" 33And
within the hour they were on their way back to
Jerusalem, where the eleven disciples and the
other followers of Jesus were gathered. When
they arrived, they were greeted with the report,
34"The Lord has really risen! He appeared to
Peter*!"

Jesus Appears to the Disciples

35Then the two from Emmaus told their story of
how Jesus had appeared to them as they were
walking along the road and how they had recognized him as he was breaking the bread. 36And
just as they were telling about it, Jesus himself
was suddenly standing there among them. He
said, "Peace be with you."* 37But the whole
group was terribly frightened, thinking they
were seeing a ghost! 38"Why are you frightened?" he asked. "Why do you doubt who I am?
39Look at my hands. Look at my feet. You can see
that it's really me. Touch me and make sure that
I am not a ghost, because ghosts don't have
bodies, as you see that I do!" 40As he spoke, he
held out his hands for them to see, and he
showed them his feet.*

41Still they stood there doubting, filled with
joy and wonder. Then he asked them, "Do you
have anything here to eat?" 42They gave him a
piece of broiled fish, 43and he ate it as they
watched.

44Then he said, "When I was with you before,

24:12 Some manuscripts do not include this verse. **24:13** Greek *60 stadia* [11.1 kilometers]. **24:34** Greek *Simon.* **24:36** Some manuscripts do not include *He said, "Peace be with you."* **24:40** Some manuscripts do not include this verse.

I told you that everything written about me by
Moses and the prophets and in the Psalms must
all come true." 45Then he opened their minds to
understand these many Scriptures. 46And he
said, "Yes, it was written long ago that the Messiah must suffer and die and rise again from the
dead on the third day. 47With my authority, take
this message of repentance to all the nations,
beginning in Jerusalem: 'There is forgiveness of
sins for all who turn to me.' 48You are witnesses
of all these things.

49"And now I will send the Holy Spirit, just
as my Father promised. But stay here in the city
until the Holy Spirit comes and fills you with
power from heaven."

The Ascension

50Then Jesus led them to Bethany, and lifting his
hands to heaven, he blessed them. 51While he
was blessing them, he left them and was taken
up to heaven.* 52They worshiped him and*
then returned to Jerusalem filled with great joy.
53And they spent all of their time in the Temple,
praising God.

24:51 Some manuscripts do not include *and was taken up to heaven.* 24:52 Some manuscripts do not include *worshiped him and.*

John

CHAPTER 1

Christ, the Eternal Word

In the beginning the Word already existed. He was with God, and he was God. 2He was in the beginning with God. 3He created everything there is. Nothing exists that he didn't make. 4Life itself was in him, and this life gives light to everyone. 5The light shines through the darkness, and the darkness can never extinguish it.

6God sent John the Baptist 7to tell everyone about the light so that everyone might believe because of his testimony. 8John himself was not the light; he was only a witness to the light. 9The one who is the true light, who gives light to everyone, was going to come into the world.

10But although the world was made through him, the world didn't recognize him when he came. 11Even in his own land and among his own people, he was not accepted. 12But to all who believed him and accepted him, he gave the right to become children of God. 13They are reborn! This is not a physical birth resulting from human passion or plan—this rebirth comes from God.

14So the Word became human and lived here on earth among us. He was full of unfailing love and faithfulness.* And we have seen his glory, the glory of the only Son of the Father.

15John pointed him out to the people. He shouted to the crowds, "This is the one I was talking about when I said, 'Someone is coming who is far greater than I am, for he existed long before I did.'"

16We have all benefited from the rich blessings he brought to us—one gracious blessing after another.* 17For the law was given through Moses; God's unfailing love and faithfulness came through Jesus Christ. 18No one has ever seen God. But his only Son, who is himself God,* is near to the Father's heart; he has told us about him.

The Testimony of John the Baptist

19This was the testimony of John when the Jewish leaders sent priests and Temple assistants* from Jerusalem to ask John whether he claimed to be the Messiah. 20He flatly denied it. "I am not the Messiah," he said.

21"Well then, who are you?" they asked. "Are you Elijah?"

"No," he replied.

"Are you the Prophet?"*

"No."

22"Then who are you? Tell us, so we can give an answer to those who sent us. What do you have to say about yourself?"

23John replied in the words of Isaiah:

"I am a voice shouting in the wilderness,
'Prepare a straight pathway for the Lord's
coming!'"*

24Then those who were sent by the Pharisees 25asked him, "If you aren't the Messiah or Elijah or the Prophet, what right do you have to baptize?"

26John told them, "I baptize with* water, but right here in the crowd is someone you do not know, 27who will soon begin his ministry. I am not even worthy to be his slave.*" 28This incident took place at Bethany, a village east of the Jordan River, where John was baptizing.

Jesus, the Lamb of God

29The next day John saw Jesus coming toward him and said, "Look! There is the Lamb of God who takes away the sin of the world! 30He is the one I was talking about when I said, 'Soon a

1:14 Greek *grace and truth;* also in 1:17. **1:16** Greek *grace upon grace.* **1:18** Some manuscripts read *his one and only Son.* **1:19** Greek *and Levites.* **1:21** See Deut 18:15, 18; Mal 4:5-6. **1:23** Isa 40:3. **1:26** Or *in;* also in 1:31, 33. **1:27** Greek *to untie his sandals.*

man is coming who is far greater than I am, for he existed long before I did.' [31]I didn't know he was the one, but I have been baptizing with water in order to point him out to Israel."

[32]Then John said, "I saw the Holy Spirit descending like a dove from heaven and resting upon him. [33]I didn't know he was the one, but when God sent me to baptize with water, he told me, 'When you see the Holy Spirit descending and resting upon someone, he is the one you are looking for. He is the one who baptizes with the Holy Spirit.' [34]I saw this happen to Jesus, so I testify that he is the Son of God.*"

The First Disciples

[35]The following day, John was again standing with two of his disciples. [36]As Jesus walked by, John looked at him and then declared, "Look! There is the Lamb of God!" [37]Then John's two disciples turned and followed Jesus.

[38]Jesus looked around and saw them following. "What do you want?" he asked them.

They replied, "Rabbi" (which means Teacher), "where are you staying?"

[39]"Come and see," he said. It was about four o'clock in the afternoon when they went with him to the place, and they stayed there the rest of the day.

[40]Andrew, Simon Peter's brother, was one of these men who had heard what John said and then followed Jesus. [41]The first thing Andrew did was to find his brother, Simon, and tell him, "We have found the Messiah" (which means the Christ).

[42]Then Andrew brought Simon to meet Jesus. Looking intently at Simon, Jesus said, "You are Simon, the son of John—but you will be called Cephas" (which means Peter*).

[43]The next day Jesus decided to go to Galilee. He found Philip and said to him, "Come, be my disciple." [44]Philip was from Bethsaida, Andrew and Peter's hometown.

[45]Philip went off to look for Nathanael and told him, "We have found the very person Moses and the prophets wrote about! His name is Jesus, the son of Joseph from Nazareth."

[46]"Nazareth!" exclaimed Nathanael. "Can anything good come from there?"

"Just come and see for yourself," Philip said.

[47]As they approached, Jesus said, "Here comes an honest man—a true son of Israel."

[48]"How do you know about me?" Nathanael asked.

And Jesus replied, "I could see you under the fig tree before Philip found you."

[49]Nathanael replied, "Teacher, you are the Son of God—the King of Israel!"

[50]Jesus asked him, "Do you believe all this just because I told you I had seen you under the fig tree? You will see greater things than this." [51]Then he said, "The truth is, you will all see heaven open and the angels of God going up and down upon the Son of Man."*

CHAPTER 2

The Wedding at Cana

The next day* Jesus' mother was a guest at a wedding celebration in the village of Cana in Galilee. [2]Jesus and his disciples were also invited to the celebration. [3]The wine supply ran out during the festivities, so Jesus' mother spoke to him about the problem. "They have no more wine," she told him.

[4]"How does that concern you and me?" Jesus asked. "My time has not yet come."

[5]But his mother told the servants, "Do whatever he tells you."

[6]Six stone waterpots were standing there; they were used for Jewish ceremonial purposes and held twenty to thirty gallons* each. [7]Jesus told the servants, "Fill the jars with water." When the jars had been filled to the brim, [8]he said, "Dip some out and take it to the master of ceremonies." So they followed his instructions.

[9]When the master of ceremonies tasted the water that was now wine, not knowing where it had come from (though, of course, the servants knew), he called the bridegroom over. [10]"Usually a host serves the best wine first," he said. "Then, when everyone is full and doesn't care, he brings out the less expensive wines. But you have kept the best until now!"

[11]This miraculous sign at Cana in Galilee was Jesus' first display of his glory. And his disciples believed in him.

[12]After the wedding he went to Capernaum for a few days with his mother, his brothers, and his disciples.

Jesus Clears the Temple

[13]It was time for the annual Passover celebration, and Jesus went to Jerusalem. [14]In the Temple area he saw merchants selling cattle, sheep, and doves for sacrifices; and he saw money changers behind their counters. [15]Jesus made a whip from some

1:34 Some manuscripts read *the chosen One of God.* 1:42 The names *Cephas* and *Peter* both mean "rock." 1:51 See Gen 28:10-17, the account of Jacob's ladder. 2:1 Greek *On the third day;* see 1:35, 43. 2:6 Greek *2 or 3 measures* [75 to 113 liters].

ropes and chased them all out of the Temple. He drove out the sheep and oxen, scattered the money changers' coins over the floor, and turned over their tables. 16Then, going over to the people who sold doves, he told them, "Get these things out of here. Don't turn my Father's house into a marketplace!"

17Then his disciples remembered this prophecy from the Scriptures: "Passion for God's house burns within me."*

18"What right do you have to do these things?" the Jewish leaders demanded. "If you have this authority from God, show us a miraculous sign to prove it."

19"All right," Jesus replied. "Destroy this temple, and in three days I will raise it up."

20"What!" they exclaimed. "It took forty-six years to build this Temple, and you can do it in three days?" 21But by "this temple," Jesus meant his body. 22After he was raised from the dead, the disciples remembered that he had said this. And they believed both Jesus and the Scriptures.

23Because of the miraculous signs he did in Jerusalem at the Passover celebration, many people were convinced that he was indeed the Messiah. 24But Jesus didn't trust them, because he knew what people were really like. 25No one needed to tell him about human nature.

CHAPTER 3

Jesus and Nicodemus

After dark one evening, a Jewish religious leader named Nicodemus, a Pharisee, 2came to speak with Jesus. "Teacher," he said, "we all know that God has sent you to teach us. Your miraculous signs are proof enough that God is with you."

3Jesus replied, "I assure you, unless you are born again,* you can never see the Kingdom of God."

4"What do you mean?" exclaimed Nicodemus. "How can an old man go back into his mother's womb and be born again?"

5Jesus replied, "The truth is, no one can enter the Kingdom of God without being born of water and the Spirit.* 6Humans can reproduce only human life, but the Holy Spirit gives new life from heaven. 7So don't be surprised at my statement that you* must be born again. 8Just as you can hear the wind but can't tell where it comes from or where it is going, so you can't explain how people are born of the Spirit."

9"What do you mean?" Nicodemus asked.

10Jesus replied, "You are a respected Jewish teacher, and yet you don't understand these things? 11I assure you, I am telling you what we know and have seen, and yet you won't believe us. 12But if you don't even believe me when I tell you about things that happen here on earth, how can you possibly believe if I tell you what is going on in heaven? 13For only I, the Son of Man,* have come to earth and will return to heaven again. 14And as Moses lifted up the bronze snake on a pole in the wilderness, so I, the Son of Man, must be lifted up on a pole,* 15so that everyone who believes in me will have eternal life.

16"For God so loved the world that he gave his only Son, so that everyone who believes in him will not perish but have eternal life. 17God did not send his Son into the world to condemn it, but to save it.

18"There is no judgment awaiting those who trust him. But those who do not trust him have already been judged for not believing in the only Son of God. 19Their judgment is based on this fact: The light from heaven came into the world, but they loved the darkness more than the light, for their actions were evil. 20They hate the light because they want to sin in the darkness. They stay away from the light for fear their sins will be exposed and they will be punished. 21But those who do what is right come to the light gladly, so everyone can see that they are doing what God wants."

John the Baptist Exalts Jesus

22Afterward Jesus and his disciples left Jerusalem, but they stayed in Judea for a while and baptized there.

23At this time John the Baptist was baptizing at Aenon, near Salim, because there was plenty of water there and people kept coming to him for baptism. 24This was before John was put into prison. 25At that time a certain Jew began an argument with John's disciples over ceremonial cleansing. 26John's disciples came to him and said, "Teacher, the man you met on the other side of the Jordan River, the one you said was the Messiah, is also baptizing people. And everybody is going over there instead of coming here to us."

27John replied, "God in heaven appoints each person's work. 28You yourselves know how plainly I told you that I am not the Messiah. I am here to prepare the way for him—that is all. 29The bride will go where the bridegroom is. A

2:17 Or *"Concern for God's house will be my undoing."* Ps 69:9. 3:3 Or *born from above;* also in 3:7. 3:5 Or *spirit.* The Greek word for *Spirit* can also be translated *wind;* see 3:8. 3:7 The Greek word for *you* is plural; also in 3:12. 3:13 Some manuscripts add *who lives in heaven.* 3:14 Greek *must be lifted up.*

bridegroom's friend rejoices with him. I am the
bridegroom's friend, and I am filled with joy at
his success. 30He must become greater and
greater, and I must become less and less.

31"He has come from above and is greater
than anyone else. I am of the earth, and my
understanding is limited to the things of earth,
but he has come from heaven.* 32He tells what
he has seen and heard, but how few believe what
he tells them! 33Those who believe him discover
that God is true. 34For he is sent by God. He
speaks God's words, for God's Spirit is upon him
without measure or limit. 35The Father loves his
Son, and he has given him authority over everything. 36And all who believe in God's Son have
eternal life. Those who don't obey the Son will
never experience eternal life, but the wrath of
God remains upon them."

CHAPTER 4

Jesus and the Samaritan Woman

Jesus* learned that the Pharisees had heard,
"Jesus is baptizing and making more disciples
than John" 2(though Jesus himself didn't baptize them—his disciples did). 3So he left Judea
to return to Galilee.

4He had to go through Samaria on the way.
5Eventually he came to the Samaritan village of
Sychar, near the parcel of ground that Jacob gave
to his son Joseph. 6Jacob's well was there; and
Jesus, tired from the long walk, sat wearily beside the well about noontime. 7Soon a Samaritan woman came to draw water, and Jesus said
to her, "Please give me a drink." 8He was alone
at the time because his disciples had gone into
the village to buy some food.

9The woman was surprised, for Jews refuse to
have anything to do with Samaritans. She said to
Jesus, "You are a Jew, and I am a Samaritan
woman. Why are you asking me for a drink?"

10Jesus replied, "If you only knew the gift
God has for you and who I am, you would ask
me, and I would give you living water."

11"But sir, you don't have a rope or a bucket,"
she said, "and this is a very deep well. Where
would you get this living water? 12And besides,
are you greater than our ancestor Jacob who gave
us this well? How can you offer better water than
he and his sons and his cattle enjoyed?"

13Jesus replied, "People soon become thirsty
again after drinking this water. 14But the water I
give them takes away thirst altogether. It becomes a perpetual spring within them, giving
them eternal life."

15"Please, sir," the woman said, "give me
some of that water! Then I'll never be thirsty
again, and I won't have to come here to haul
water."

16"Go and get your husband," Jesus told her.

17"I don't have a husband," the woman replied.

Jesus said, "You're right! You don't have a
husband—18for you have had five husbands,
and you aren't even married to the man you're
living with now."

19"Sir," the woman said, "you must be a
prophet. 20So tell me, why is it that you Jews
insist that Jerusalem is the only place of worship,
while we Samaritans claim it is here at Mount
Gerizim,* where our ancestors worshiped?"

21Jesus replied, "Believe me, the time is coming when it will no longer matter whether you
worship the Father here or in Jerusalem. 22You
Samaritans know so little about the one you
worship, while we Jews know all about him, for
salvation comes through the Jews. 23But the
time is coming and is already here when true
worshipers will worship the Father in spirit and
in truth. The Father is looking for anyone who
will worship him that way. 24For God is Spirit,
so those who worship him must worship in
spirit and in truth."

25The woman said, "I know the Messiah will
come—the one who is called Christ. When he
comes, he will explain everything to us."

26Then Jesus told her, "I am the Messiah!"*

27Just then his disciples arrived. They were
astonished to find him talking to a woman, but
none of them asked him why he was doing it or
what they had been discussing. 28The woman
left her water jar beside the well and went back
to the village and told everyone, 29"Come and
meet a man who told me everything I ever did!
Can this be the Messiah?" 30So the people came
streaming from the village to see him.

31Meanwhile, the disciples were urging Jesus
to eat. 32"No," he said, "I have food you don't
know about."

33"Who brought it to him?" the disciples
asked each other.

34Then Jesus explained: "My nourishment
comes from doing the will of God, who sent me,
and from finishing his work. 35Do you think the
work of harvesting will not begin until the summer ends four months from now? Look around

3:31 Some manuscripts omit *but he has come from heaven.* 4:1 Some manuscripts read *The Lord.* 4:20 Greek *on this mountain.* 4:26 Greek *"I am, the one speaking to you."*

you! Vast fields are ripening all around us and are ready now for the harvest. 36The harvesters are paid good wages, and the fruit they harvest is people brought to eternal life. What joy awaits both the planter and the harvester alike! 37You know the saying, 'One person plants and someone else harvests.' And it's true. 38I sent you to harvest where you didn't plant; others had already done the work, and you will gather the harvest."

Many Samaritans Believe

39Many Samaritans from the village believed in Jesus because the woman had said, "He told me everything I ever did!" 40When they came out to see him, they begged him to stay at their village. So he stayed for two days, 41long enough for many of them to hear his message and believe. 42Then they said to the woman, "Now we believe because we have heard him ourselves, not just because of what you told us. He is indeed the Savior of the world."

Jesus Heals an Official's Son

43At the end of the two days' stay, Jesus went on into Galilee. 44He had previously said, "A prophet is honored everywhere except in his own country." 45The Galileans welcomed him, for they had been in Jerusalem at the Passover celebration and had seen all his miraculous signs.

46In the course of his journey through Galilee, he arrived at the town of Cana, where he had turned the water into wine. There was a government official in the city of Capernaum whose son was very sick. 47When he heard that Jesus had come from Judea and was traveling in Galilee, he went over to Cana. He found Jesus and begged him to come to Capernaum with him to heal his son, who was about to die.

48Jesus asked, "Must I do miraculous signs and wonders before you people will believe in me?"

49The official pleaded, "Lord, please come now before my little boy dies."

50Then Jesus told him, "Go back home. Your son will live!" And the man believed Jesus' word and started home.

51While he was on his way, some of his servants met him with the news that his son was alive and well. 52He asked them when the boy had begun to feel better, and they replied, "Yesterday afternoon at one o'clock his fever suddenly disappeared!" 53Then the father realized it was the same time that Jesus had told him, "Your son will live." And the officer and his entire household believed in Jesus. 54This was Jesus' second miraculous sign in Galilee after coming from Judea.

CHAPTER 5

Jesus Heals a Lame Man

Afterward Jesus returned to Jerusalem for one of the Jewish holy days. 2Inside the city, near the Sheep Gate, was the pool of Bethesda,* with five covered porches. 3Crowds of sick people—blind, lame, or paralyzed—lay on the porches.* 5One of the men lying there had been sick for thirty-eight years. 6When Jesus saw him and knew how long he had been ill, he asked him, "Would you like to get well?"

7"I can't, sir," the sick man said, "for I have no one to help me into the pool when the water is stirred up. While I am trying to get there, someone else always gets in ahead of me."

8Jesus told him, "Stand up, pick up your sleeping mat, and walk!"

9Instantly, the man was healed! He rolled up the mat and began walking! But this miracle happened on the Sabbath day. 10So the Jewish leaders objected. They said to the man who was cured, "You can't work on the Sabbath! It's illegal to carry that sleeping mat!"

11He replied, "The man who healed me said to me, 'Pick up your sleeping mat and walk.' "

12"Who said such a thing as that?" they demanded.

13The man didn't know, for Jesus had disappeared into the crowd. 14But afterward Jesus found him in the Temple and told him, "Now you are well; so stop sinning, or something even worse may happen to you." 15Then the man went to find the Jewish leaders and told them it was Jesus who had healed him.

Jesus Claims to Be the Son of God

16So the Jewish leaders began harassing Jesus for breaking the Sabbath rules. 17But Jesus replied, "My Father never stops working, so why should I?" 18So the Jewish leaders tried all the more to kill him. In addition to disobeying the Sabbath rules, he had spoken of God as his Father, thereby making himself equal with God.

19Jesus replied, "I assure you, the Son can do nothing by himself. He does only what he sees the Father doing. Whatever the Father does, the Son also does. 20For the Father loves the Son and

5:2 Some manuscripts read *Beth-zatha;* other manuscripts read *Bethsaida.* 5:3 Some manuscripts add *waiting for a certain movement of the water, 4for an angel of the Lord came from time to time and stirred up the water. And the first person to step down into it afterward was healed.*

tells him everything he is doing, and the Son will
do far greater things than healing this man. You
will be astonished at what he does. 21He will
even raise from the dead anyone he wants to,
just as the Father does. 22And the Father leaves
all judgment to his Son, 23so that everyone will
honor the Son, just as they honor the Father. But
if you refuse to honor the Son, then you are
certainly not honoring the Father who sent him.

24"I assure you, those who listen to my message and believe in God who sent me have eternal
life. They will never be condemned for their sins,
but they have already passed from death into life.

25"And I assure you that the time is coming, in
fact it is here, when the dead will hear my voice—
the voice of the Son of God. And those who listen
will live. 26The Father has life in himself, and he
has granted his Son to have life in himself. 27And
he has given him authority to judge all mankind
because he is the Son of Man. 28Don't be so
surprised! Indeed, the time is coming when all
the dead in their graves will hear the voice of
God's Son, 29and they will rise again. Those who
have done good will rise to eternal life, and those
who have continued in evil will rise to judgment.
30But I do nothing without consulting the Father.
I judge as I am told. And my judgment is absolutely just, because it is according to the will of
God who sent me; it is not merely my own.

Witnesses to Jesus

31"If I were to testify on my own behalf, my
testimony would not be valid. 32But someone else
is also testifying about me, and I can assure you
that everything he says about me is true. 33In fact,
you sent messengers to listen to John the Baptist,
and he preached the truth. 34But the best testimony about me is not from a man, though I have
reminded you about John's testimony so you
might be saved. 35John shone brightly for a while,
and you benefited and rejoiced. 36But I have a
greater witness than John—my teachings and my
miracles. They have been assigned to me by the
Father, and they testify that the Father has sent me.
37And the Father himself has also testified about
me. You have never heard his voice or seen him
face to face, 38and you do not have his message in
your hearts, because you do not believe me—the
one he sent to you.

39"You search the Scriptures because you believe they give you eternal life. But the Scriptures
point to me! 40Yet you refuse to come to me so
that I can give you this eternal life.

41"Your approval or disapproval means nothing to me, 42because I know you don't have
God's love within you. 43For I have come to you
representing my Father, and you refuse to welcome me, even though you readily accept others
who represent only themselves. 44No wonder
you can't believe! For you gladly honor each
other, but you don't care about the honor that
comes from God alone.

45"Yet it is not I who will accuse you of this
before the Father. Moses will accuse you! Yes,
Moses, on whom you set your hopes. 46But if
you had believed Moses, you would have believed me because he wrote about me. 47And
since you don't believe what he wrote, how will
you believe what I say?"

CHAPTER 6

Jesus Feeds Five Thousand

After this, Jesus crossed over the Sea of Galilee,
also known as the Sea of Tiberias. 2And a huge
crowd kept following him wherever he went,
because they saw his miracles as he healed the
sick. 3Then Jesus went up into the hills and sat
down with his disciples around him. 4(It was
nearly time for the annual Passover celebration.)
5Jesus soon saw a great crowd of people climbing the hill, looking for him. Turning to Philip,
he asked, "Philip, where can we buy bread to
feed all these people?" 6He was testing Philip,
for he already knew what he was going to do.

7Philip replied, "It would take a small fortune* to feed them!"

8Then Andrew, Simon Peter's brother, spoke
up. 9"There's a young boy here with five barley
loaves and two fish. But what good is that with
this huge crowd?"

10"Tell everyone to sit down," Jesus ordered.
So all of them—the men alone numbered five
thousand—sat down on the grassy slopes.
11Then Jesus took the loaves, gave thanks to
God, and passed them out to the people. Afterward he did the same with the fish. And they all
ate until they were full. 12"Now gather the leftovers," Jesus told his disciples, "so that nothing
is wasted." 13There were only five barley loaves
to start with, but twelve baskets were filled with
the pieces of bread the people did not eat!

14When the people saw this miraculous sign,
they exclaimed, "Surely, he is the Prophet* we
have been expecting!" 15Jesus saw that they were
ready to take him by force and make him king,
so he went higher into the hills alone.

6:7 Greek *200 denarii.* A denarius was the equivalent of a full day's wage. 6:14 See Deut 18:15, 18.

Jesus Walks on Water

16That evening his disciples went down to the shore to wait for him. 17But as darkness fell and Jesus still hadn't come back, they got into the boat and headed out across the lake toward Capernaum. 18Soon a gale swept down upon them as they rowed, and the sea grew very rough. 19They were three or four miles* out when suddenly they saw Jesus walking on the water toward the boat. They were terrified, 20but he called out to them, "I am here! Don't be afraid." 21Then they were eager to let him in, and immediately the boat arrived at their destination!

Jesus, the Bread of Life

22The next morning, back across the lake, crowds began gathering on the shore, waiting to see Jesus. For they knew that he and his disciples had come over together and that the disciples had gone off in their boat, leaving him behind. 23Several boats from Tiberias landed near the place where the Lord had blessed the bread and the people had eaten. 24When the crowd saw that Jesus wasn't there, nor his disciples, they got into the boats and went across to Capernaum to look for him. 25When they arrived and found him, they asked, "Teacher, how did you get here?"

26Jesus replied, "The truth is, you want to be with me because I fed you, not because you saw the miraculous sign. 27But you shouldn't be so concerned about perishable things like food. Spend your energy seeking the eternal life that I, the Son of Man, can give you. For God the Father has sent me for that very purpose."

28They replied, "What does God want us to do?"

29Jesus told them, "This is what God wants you to do: Believe in the one he has sent."

30They replied, "You must show us a miraculous sign if you want us to believe in you. What will you do for us? 31After all, our ancestors ate manna while they journeyed through the wilderness! As the Scriptures say, 'Moses gave them bread from heaven to eat.'* "

32Jesus said, "I assure you, Moses didn't give them bread from heaven. My Father did. And now he offers you the true bread from heaven. 33The true bread of God is the one who comes down from heaven and gives life to the world."

34"Sir," they said, "give us that bread every day of our lives."

35Jesus replied, "I am the bread of life. No one who comes to me will ever be hungry again. Those who believe in me will never thirst. 36But you haven't believed in me even though you have seen me. 37However, those the Father has given me will come to me, and I will never reject them. 38For I have come down from heaven to do the will of God who sent me, not to do what I want. 39And this is the will of God, that I should not lose even one of all those he has given me, but that I should raise them to eternal life at the last day. 40For it is my Father's will that all who see his Son and believe in him should have eternal life—that I should raise them at the last day."

41Then the people* began to murmur in disagreement because he had said, "I am the bread from heaven." 42They said, "This is Jesus, the son of Joseph. We know his father and mother. How can he say, 'I came down from heaven'?"

43But Jesus replied, "Don't complain about what I said. 44For people can't come to me unless the Father who sent me draws them to me, and at the last day I will raise them from the dead. 45As it is written in the Scriptures, 'They will all be taught by God.'* Everyone who hears and learns from the Father comes to me. 46(Not that anyone has ever seen the Father; only I, who was sent from God, have seen him.)

47"I assure you, anyone who believes in me already has eternal life. 48Yes, I am the bread of life! 49Your ancestors ate manna in the wilderness, but they all died. 50However, the bread from heaven gives eternal life to everyone who eats it. 51I am the living bread that came down out of heaven. Anyone who eats this bread will live forever; this bread is my flesh, offered so the world may live."

52Then the people began arguing with each other about what he meant. "How can this man give us his flesh to eat?" they asked.

53So Jesus said again, "I assure you, unless you eat the flesh of the Son of Man and drink his blood, you cannot have eternal life within you. 54But those who eat my flesh and drink my blood have eternal life, and I will raise them at the last day. 55For my flesh is the true food, and my blood is the true drink. 56All who eat my flesh and drink my blood remain in me, and I in them. 57I live by the power of the living Father who sent me; in the same way, those who partake of me will live because of me. 58I am the true bread from heaven. Anyone who eats this bread will live forever and not die as your ancestors did, even though they ate the manna."

6:19 Greek *25 or 30 stadia* [4.6 or 5.5 kilometers]. 6:31 Exod 16:4; Ps 78:24. 6:41 Greek *Jewish people;* also in 6:52. 6:45 Isa 54:13.

59He said these things while he was teaching in the synagogue in Capernaum.

Many Disciples Desert Jesus

60Even his disciples said, "This is very hard to understand. How can anyone accept it?"

61Jesus knew within himself that his disciples were complaining, so he said to them, "Does this offend you? 62Then what will you think if you see me, the Son of Man, return to heaven again? 63It is the Spirit who gives eternal life. Human effort accomplishes nothing. And the very words I have spoken to you are spirit and life. 64But some of you don't believe me." (For Jesus knew from the beginning who didn't believe, and he knew who would betray him.) 65Then he said, "That is what I meant when I said that people can't come to me unless the Father brings them to me."

66At this point many of his disciples turned away and deserted him. 67Then Jesus turned to the Twelve and asked, "Are you going to leave, too?"

68Simon Peter replied, "Lord, to whom would we go? You alone have the words that give eternal life. 69We believe them, and we know you are the Holy One of God."

70Then Jesus said, "I chose the twelve of you, but one is a devil." 71He was speaking of Judas, son of Simon Iscariot, one of the Twelve, who would betray him.

CHAPTER 7

Jesus and His Brothers

After this, Jesus stayed in Galilee, going from village to village. He wanted to stay out of Judea where the Jewish leaders were plotting his death. 2But soon it was time for the Festival of Shelters, 3and Jesus' brothers urged him to go to Judea for the celebration. "Go where your followers can see your miracles!" they scoffed. 4"You can't become a public figure if you hide like this! If you can do such wonderful things, prove it to the world!" 5For even his brothers didn't believe in him.

6Jesus replied, "Now is not the right time for me to go. But you can go anytime, and it will make no difference. 7The world can't hate you, but it does hate me because I accuse it of sin and evil. 8You go on. I am not yet* ready to go to this festival, because my time has not yet come." 9So Jesus remained in Galilee.

Jesus Teaches Openly at the Temple

10But after his brothers had left for the festival, Jesus also went, though secretly, staying out of public view. 11The Jewish leaders tried to find him at the festival and kept asking if anyone had seen him. 12There was a lot of discussion about him among the crowds. Some said, "He's a wonderful man," while others said, "He's nothing but a fraud, deceiving the people." 13But no one had the courage to speak favorably about him in public, for they were afraid of getting in trouble with the Jewish leaders.

14Then, midway through the festival, Jesus went up to the Temple and began to teach. 15The Jewish leaders were surprised when they heard him. "How does he know so much when he hasn't studied everything we've studied?" they asked.

16So Jesus told them, "I'm not teaching my own ideas, but those of God who sent me. 17Anyone who wants to do the will of God will know whether my teaching is from God or is merely my own. 18Those who present their own ideas are looking for praise for themselves, but those who seek to honor the one who sent them are good and genuine. 19None of you obeys the law of Moses! In fact, you are trying to kill me."

20The crowd replied, "You're demon possessed! Who's trying to kill you?"

21Jesus replied, "I worked on the Sabbath by healing a man, and you were offended. 22But you work on the Sabbath, too, when you obey Moses' law of circumcision. (Actually, this tradition of circumcision is older than the law of Moses; it goes back to Abraham.) 23For if the correct time for circumcising your son falls on the Sabbath, you go ahead and do it, so as not to break the law of Moses. So why should I be condemned for making a man completely well on the Sabbath? 24Think this through and you will see that I am right."

Is Jesus the Messiah?

25Some of the people who lived there in Jerusalem said among themselves, "Isn't this the man they are trying to kill? 26But here he is, speaking in public, and they say nothing to him. Can it be that our leaders know that he really is the Messiah? 27But how could he be? For we know where this man comes from. When the Messiah comes, he will simply appear; no one will know where he comes from."

28While Jesus was teaching in the Temple, he called out, "Yes, you know me, and you know where I come from. But I represent one you don't know, and he is true. 29I know him be-

7:8 Some manuscripts omit *yet.*

cause I have come from him, and he sent me to you." [30]Then the leaders tried to arrest him; but no one laid a hand on him, because his time had not yet come.

[31]Many among the crowds at the Temple believed in him. "After all," they said, "would you expect the Messiah to do more miraculous signs than this man has done?"

[32]When the Pharisees heard that the crowds were murmuring such things, they and the leading priests sent Temple guards to arrest Jesus. [33]But Jesus told them, "I will be here a little longer. Then I will return to the one who sent me. [34]You will search for me but not find me. And you won't be able to come where I am."

[35]The Jewish leaders were puzzled by this statement. "Where is he planning to go?" they asked. "Maybe he is thinking of leaving the country and going to the Jews in other lands, or maybe even to the Gentiles! [36]What does he mean when he says, 'You will search for me but not find me,' and 'You won't be able to come where I am'?"

Jesus Promises Living Water

[37]On the last day, the climax of the festival, Jesus stood and shouted to the crowds, "If you are thirsty, come to me! [38]If you believe in me, come and drink! For the Scriptures declare that rivers of living water will flow out from within."* [39](When he said "living water," he was speaking of the Spirit, who would be given to everyone believing in him. But the Spirit had not yet been given, because Jesus had not yet entered into his glory.)

Division and Unbelief

[40]When the crowds heard him say this, some of them declared, "This man surely is the Prophet."* [41]Others said, "He is the Messiah." Still others said, "But he can't be! Will the Messiah come from Galilee? [42]For the Scriptures clearly state that the Messiah will be born of the royal line of David, in Bethlehem, the village where King David was born."* [43]So the crowd was divided in their opinion about him. [44]And some wanted him arrested, but no one touched him.

[45]The Temple guards who had been sent to arrest him returned to the leading priests and Pharisees. "Why didn't you bring him in?" they demanded.

[46]"We have never heard anyone talk like this!" the guards responded.

[47]"Have you been led astray, too?" the Pharisees mocked. [48]"Is there a single one of us rulers or Pharisees who believes in him? [49]These ignorant crowds do, but what do they know about it? A curse on them anyway!"

[50]Nicodemus, the leader who had met with Jesus earlier, then spoke up. [51]"Is it legal to convict a man before he is given a hearing?" he asked.

[52]They replied, "Are you from Galilee, too? Search the Scriptures and see for yourself—no prophet ever comes from Galilee!"

[*The most ancient Greek manuscripts do not include John 7:53–8:11.*]

[53]Then the meeting broke up and everybody went home.

CHAPTER 8

A Woman Caught in Adultery

Jesus returned to the Mount of Olives, [2]but early the next morning he was back again at the Temple. A crowd soon gathered, and he sat down and taught them. [3]As he was speaking, the teachers of religious law and Pharisees brought a woman they had caught in the act of adultery. They put her in front of the crowd.

[4]"Teacher," they said to Jesus, "this woman was caught in the very act of adultery. [5]The law of Moses says to stone her. What do you say?"

[6]They were trying to trap him into saying something they could use against him, but Jesus stooped down and wrote in the dust with his finger. [7]They kept demanding an answer, so he stood up again and said, "All right, stone her. But let those who have never sinned throw the first stones!" [8]Then he stooped down again and wrote in the dust.

[9]When the accusers heard this, they slipped away one by one, beginning with the oldest, until only Jesus was left in the middle of the crowd with the woman. [10]Then Jesus stood up again and said to her, "Where are your accusers? Didn't even one of them condemn you?"

[11]"No, Lord," she said.

And Jesus said, "Neither do I. Go and sin no more."

Jesus, the Light of the World

[12]Jesus said to the people, "I am the light of the world. If you follow me, you won't be stumbling through the darkness, because you will have the light that leads to life."

7:37-38 Or *"Let anyone who is thirsty come to me and drink. [38]For the Scriptures declare that rivers of living water will flow from the heart of those who believe in me."* 7:40 See Deut 18:15, 18. 7:42 See Mic 5:2.

13The Pharisees replied, "You are making
false claims about yourself!"

14Jesus told them, "These claims are valid even
though I make them about myself. For I know
where I came from and where I am going, but you
don't know this about me. 15You judge me with
all your human limitations,* but I am not judging
anyone. 16And if I did, my judgment would be
correct in every respect because I am not alone—I
have with me the Father who sent me. 17Your own
law says that if two people agree about something,
their witness is accepted as fact.* 18I am one witness, and my Father who sent me is the other."

19"Where is your father?" they asked.

Jesus answered, "Since you don't know who
I am, you don't know who my Father is. If you
knew me, then you would know my Father,
too." 20Jesus made these statements while he
was teaching in the section of the Temple known
as the Treasury. But he was not arrested, because
his time had not yet come.

The Unbelieving People Warned

21Later Jesus said to them again, "I am going
away. You will search for me and die in your sin.
You cannot come where I am going."

22The Jewish leaders asked, "Is he planning
to commit suicide? What does he mean, 'You
cannot come where I am going'?"

23Then he said to them, "You are from below;
I am from above. You are of this world; I am not.
24That is why I said that you will die in your sins;
for unless you believe that I am who I say I am,
you will die in your sins."

25"Tell us who you are," they demanded.

Jesus replied, "I am the one I have always
claimed to be.* 26I have much to say about you
and much to condemn, but I won't. For I say only
what I have heard from the one who sent me, and
he is true." 27But they still didn't understand that
he was talking to them about his Father.

28So Jesus said, "When you have lifted up the
Son of Man on the cross, then you will realize
that I am he and that I do nothing on my own,
but I speak what the Father taught me. 29And the
one who sent me is with me—he has not deserted me. For I always do those things that are
pleasing to him." 30Then many who heard him
say these things believed in him.

Jesus and Abraham

31Jesus said to the people* who believed in him,
"You are truly my disciples if you keep obeying
my teachings. 32And you will know the truth,
and the truth will set you free."

33"But we are descendants of Abraham," they
said. "We have never been slaves to anyone on
earth. What do you mean, 'set free'?"

34Jesus replied, "I assure you that everyone
who sins is a slave of sin. 35A slave is not a
permanent member of the family, but a son is
part of the family forever. 36So if the Son sets you
free, you will indeed be free. 37Yes, I realize that
you are descendants of Abraham. And yet some
of you are trying to kill me because my message
does not find a place in your hearts. 38I am telling
you what I saw when I was with my Father. But
you are following the advice of your father."

39"Our father is Abraham," they declared.

"No," Jesus replied, "for if you were children
of Abraham, you would follow his good example.* 40I told you the truth I heard from God,
but you are trying to kill me. Abraham wouldn't
do a thing like that. 41No, you are obeying your
real father when you act that way."

They replied, "We were not born out of wed-
lock! Our true Father is God himself."

42Jesus told them, "If God were your Father,
you would love me, because I have come to you
from God. I am not here on my own, but he sent
me. 43Why can't you understand what I am
saying? It is because you are unable to do so!
44For you are the children of your father the
Devil, and you love to do the evil things he does.
He was a murderer from the beginning and has
always hated the truth. There is no truth in him.
When he lies, it is consistent with his character;
for he is a liar and the father of lies. 45So when I
tell the truth, you just naturally don't believe
me! 46Which of you can truthfully accuse me of
sin? And since I am telling you the truth, why
don't you believe me? 47Anyone whose Father is
God listens gladly to the words of God. Since
you don't, it proves you aren't God's children."

48The people retorted, "You Samaritan devil!
Didn't we say all along that you were possessed
by a demon?"

49"No," Jesus said, "I have no demon in me.
For I honor my Father—and you dishonor me.
50And though I have no wish to glorify myself,
God wants to glorify me. Let him be the judge.
51I assure you, anyone who obeys my teaching
will never die!"

52The people said, "Now we know you are
possessed by a demon. Even Abraham and the
prophets died, but you say that those who obey

8:15 Or *judge me by human standards.* 8:17 See Deut 19:15. 8:25 Or *"Why do I speak to you at all?"* 8:31 Greek *Jewish people;* also in 8:48, 52, 57. 8:39 Some manuscripts read *if you are children of Abraham, follow his example.*

your teaching will never die! 53Are you greater
than our father Abraham, who died? Are you
greater than the prophets, who died? Who do
you think you are?"

54Jesus answered, "If I am merely boasting
about myself, it doesn't count. But it is my Father
who says these glorious things about me. You
say, 'He is our God,' 55but you do not even know
him. I know him. If I said otherwise, I would be
as great a liar as you! But it is true—I know him
and obey him. 56Your ancestor Abraham rejoiced as he looked forward to my coming. He
saw it and was glad."

57The people said, "You aren't even fifty years
old. How can you say you have seen Abraham?*"

58Jesus answered, "The truth is, I existed before Abraham was even born!"* 59At that point
they picked up stones to kill him. But Jesus hid
himself from them and left the Temple.

CHAPTER 9

Jesus Heals a Man Born Blind

As Jesus was walking along, he saw a man who
had been blind from birth. 2"Teacher," his disciples asked him, "why was this man born blind?
Was it a result of his own sins or those of his
parents?"

3"It was not because of his sins or his parents'
sins," Jesus answered. "He was born blind so the
power of God could be seen in him. 4All of us
must quickly carry out the tasks assigned us by
the one who sent me, because there is little time
left before the night falls and all work comes to
an end. 5But while I am still here in the world, I
am the light of the world."

6Then he spit on the ground, made mud with
the saliva, and smoothed the mud over the blind
man's eyes. 7He told him, "Go and wash in the
pool of Siloam" (Siloam means Sent). So the
man went and washed, and came back seeing!

8His neighbors and others who knew him as a
blind beggar asked each other, "Is this the same
man—that beggar?" 9Some said he was, and
others said, "No, but he surely looks like him!"

And the beggar kept saying, "I am the same
man!"

10They asked, "Who healed you? What happened?"

11He told them, "The man they call Jesus made
mud and smoothed it over my eyes and told me,
'Go to the pool of Siloam and wash off the mud.'
I went and washed, and now I can see!"

12"Where is he now?" they asked.

"I don't know," he replied.

13Then they took the man to the Pharisees.
14Now as it happened, Jesus had healed the man
on a Sabbath. 15The Pharisees asked the man all
about it. So he told them, "He smoothed the
mud over my eyes, and when it was washed
away, I could see!"

16Some of the Pharisees said, "This man Jesus
is not from God, for he is working on the Sabbath." Others said, "But how could an ordinary
sinner do such miraculous signs?" So there was
a deep division of opinion among them.

8:57 Some manuscripts read *How can you say Abraham has seen you?* 8:58 Or *"Truly, truly, before Abraham was, I am."*

You Don't Need Any Training to Share

Read JOHN 9:1-41

Perhaps one of the biggest reasons many Christians haven't shared their faith is that they feel God could never use them to draw people to himself. You might say, "I am not qualified to speak for God!" In reality, once you invite Jesus Christ into your life as Savior and Lord, you can begin to tell others about your newfound faith.

This passage tells the story of a blind man whose sight was restored when Jesus touched his eyes. After Jesus healed this man, certain religious rulers known as Pharisees challenged him, asking him some rather complex questions about Jesus. The man's response was classic. He said, "I know this: I was blind, and now I can see!"

In many ways, we as believers are like this formerly blind man. We, too, were once blinded by the power and deception of sin. Scripture tells us that "Satan, the god of this evil world" made us "blind" and "unable to see the glorious light of the Good News" (2 Corinthians 4:4). But one day God lovingly "opened our eyes" to see our real spiritual need, and we responded to the message of the Gospel.

Although we may not yet be great scholars of Scripture, we still know more about the gospel than many, and we can start with that. Like that blind man, we can, in a spiritual sense, say to others, "Once I was blind, but now I can see. . . ." As we study the Bible on a regular basis, we will be able to answer many of the questions people have about our faith.

17Then the Pharisees once again questioned the man who had been blind and demanded, "This man who opened your eyes—who do you say he is?"

The man replied, "I think he must be a prophet."

18The Jewish leaders wouldn't believe he had been blind, so they called in his parents. 19They asked them, "Is this your son? Was he born blind? If so, how can he see?"

20His parents replied, "We know this is our son and that he was born blind, 21but we don't know how he can see or who healed him. He is old enough to speak for himself. Ask him." 22They said this because they were afraid of the Jewish leaders, who had announced that anyone saying Jesus was the Messiah would be expelled from the synagogue. 23That's why they said, "He is old enough to speak for himself. Ask him."

24So for the second time they called in the man who had been blind and told him, "Give glory to God by telling the truth,* because we know Jesus is a sinner."

25"I don't know whether he is a sinner," the man replied. "But I know this: I was blind, and now I can see!"

26"But what did he do?" they asked. "How did he heal you?"

27"Look!" the man exclaimed. "I told you once. Didn't you listen? Why do you want to hear it again? Do you want to become his disciples, too?"

28Then they cursed him and said, "You are his disciple, but we are disciples of Moses. 29We know God spoke to Moses, but as for this man, we don't know anything about him."

30"Why, that's very strange!" the man replied. "He healed my eyes, and yet you don't know anything about him! 31Well, God doesn't listen to sinners, but he is ready to hear those who worship him and do his will. 32Never since the world began has anyone been able to open the eyes of someone born blind. 33If this man were not from God, he couldn't do it."

34"You were born in sin!" they answered. "Are you trying to teach us?" And they threw him out of the synagogue.

Spiritual Blindness

35When Jesus heard what had happened, he found the man and said, "Do you believe in the Son of Man*?"

36The man answered, "Who is he, sir, because I would like to."

37"You have seen him," Jesus said, "and he is speaking to you!"

38"Yes, Lord," the man said, "I believe!" And he worshiped Jesus.

39Then Jesus told him, "I have come to judge the world. I have come to give sight to the blind and to show those who think they see that they are blind."

40The Pharisees who were standing there heard him and asked, "Are you saying we are blind?"

41"If you were blind, you wouldn't be guilty," Jesus replied. "But you remain guilty because you claim you can see.

CHAPTER 10

The Good Shepherd and His Sheep

"I assure you, anyone who sneaks over the wall of a sheepfold, rather than going through the gate, must surely be a thief and a robber! 2For a shepherd enters through the gate. 3The gatekeeper opens the gate for him, and the sheep hear his voice and come to him. He calls his own sheep by name and leads them out. 4After he has gathered his own flock, he walks ahead of them, and they follow him because they recognize his voice. 5They won't follow a stranger; they will run from him because they don't recognize his voice."

6Those who heard Jesus use this illustration didn't understand what he meant, 7so he explained it to them. "I assure you, I am the gate for the sheep," he said. 8"All others who came before me were thieves and robbers. But the true sheep did not listen to them. 9Yes, I am the gate. Those who come in through me will be saved. Wherever they go, they will find green pastures. 10The thief's purpose is to steal and kill and destroy. My purpose is to give life in all its fullness.

11"I am the good shepherd. The good shepherd lays down his life for the sheep. 12A hired hand will run when he sees a wolf coming. He will leave the sheep because they aren't his and he isn't their shepherd. And so the wolf attacks them and scatters the flock. 13The hired hand runs away because he is merely hired and has no real concern for the sheep.

14"I am the good shepherd; I know my own sheep, and they know me, 15just as my Father knows me and I know the Father. And I lay down

9:24 Or *Give glory to God, not to Jesus;* Greek reads *Give glory to God.* 9:35 Some manuscripts read *the Son of God.*

my life for the sheep. 16I have other sheep, too,
that are not in this sheepfold. I must bring them
also, and they will listen to my voice; and there
will be one flock with one shepherd.
17"The Father loves me because I lay down
my life that I may have it back again. 18No one
can take my life from me. I lay down my life
voluntarily. For I have the right to lay it down
when I want to and also the power to take it
again. For my Father has given me this command."
19When he said these things, the people*
were again divided in their opinions about him.
20Some of them said, "He has a demon, or he's
crazy. Why listen to a man like that?" 21Others
said, "This doesn't sound like a man possessed
by a demon! Can a demon open the eyes of the
blind?"

Jesus Claims to Be the Son of God

22It was now winter, and Jesus was in Jerusalem
at the time of Hanukkah.* 23He was at the
Temple, walking through the section known as
Solomon's Colonnade. 24The Jewish leaders surrounded him and asked, "How long are you
going to keep us in suspense? If you are the
Messiah, tell us plainly."
25Jesus replied, "I have already told you, and
you don't believe me. The proof is what I do in
the name of my Father. 26But you don't believe
me because you are not part of my flock. 27My
sheep recognize my voice; I know them, and
they follow me. 28I give them eternal life, and
they will never perish. No one will snatch them
away from me, 29for my Father has given them
to me, and he is more powerful than anyone
else. So no one can take them from me. 30The
Father and I are one."
31Once again the Jewish leaders picked up
stones to kill him. 32Jesus said, "At my Father's
direction I have done many things to help the
people. For which one of these good deeds are
you killing me?"
33They replied, "Not for any good work, but
for blasphemy, because you, a mere man, have
made yourself God."
34Jesus replied, "It is written in your own law
that God said to certain leaders of the people, 'I
say, you are gods!'* 35And you know that the
Scriptures cannot be altered. So if those people,
who received God's message, were called 'gods,'
36why do you call it blasphemy when the Holy
One who was sent into the world by the Father
says, 'I am the Son of God'? 37Don't believe me
unless I carry out my Father's work. 38But if I do
his work, believe in what I have done, even if you
don't believe me. Then you will realize that the
Father is in me, and I am in the Father."
39Once again they tried to arrest him, but he got
away and left them. 40He went beyond the Jordan
River to stay near the place where John was first
baptizing. 41And many followed him. "John
didn't do miracles," they remarked to one another, "but all his predictions about this man have
come true." 42And many believed in him there.

CHAPTER 11

The Death of Lazarus

A man named Lazarus was sick. He lived in
Bethany with his sisters, Mary and Martha. 2This
is the Mary who poured the expensive perfume
on the Lord's feet and wiped them with her
hair.* Her brother, Lazarus, was sick. 3So the two
sisters sent a message to Jesus telling him, "Lord,
the one you love is very sick."
4But when Jesus heard about it he said, "Lazarus's sickness will not end in death. No, it is for
the glory of God. I, the Son of God, will receive
glory from this." 5Although Jesus loved Martha,
Mary, and Lazarus, 6he stayed where he was for
the next two days and did not go to them. 7Fi-
nally after two days, he said to his disciples,
"Let's go to Judea again."
8But his disciples objected. "Teacher," they
said, "only a few days ago the Jewish leaders in
Judea were trying to kill you. Are you going there
again?"
9Jesus replied, "There are twelve hours of
daylight every day. As long as it is light, people
can walk safely. They can see because they have
the light of this world. 10Only at night is there
danger of stumbling because there is no light."
11Then he said, "Our friend Lazarus has fallen
asleep, but now I will go and wake him up."
12The disciples said, "Lord, if he is sleeping,
that means he is getting better!" 13They thought
Jesus meant Lazarus was having a good night's
rest, but Jesus meant Lazarus had died.
14Then he told them plainly, "Lazarus is
dead. 15And for your sake, I am glad I wasn't
there, because this will give you another opportunity to believe in me. Come, let's go see him."
16Thomas, nicknamed the Twin,* said to his
fellow disciples, "Let's go, too—and die with
Jesus."

10:19 Greek *Jewish people.* **10:22** Or *the Festival of Dedication.* **10:34** Ps 82:6. **11:2** This incident is recorded in chapter 12. **11:16** Greek *the one who was called Didymus.*

17When Jesus arrived at Bethany, he was told that Lazarus had already been in his grave for four days. 18Bethany was only a few miles* down the road from Jerusalem, 19and many of the people* had come to pay their respects and console Martha and Mary on their loss. 20When Martha got word that Jesus was coming, she went to meet him. But Mary stayed at home. 21Martha said to Jesus, "Lord, if you had been here, my brother would not have died. 22But even now I know that God will give you whatever you ask."

23Jesus told her, "Your brother will rise again."

24"Yes," Martha said, "when everyone else rises, on resurrection day."

25Jesus told her, "I am the resurrection and the life.* Those who believe in me, even though they die like everyone else, will live again. 26They are given eternal life for believing in me and will never perish. Do you believe this, Martha?"

27"Yes, Lord," she told him. "I have always believed you are the Messiah, the Son of God, the one who has come into the world from God." 28Then she left him and returned to Mary. She called Mary aside from the mourners and told her, "The Teacher is here and wants to see you." 29So Mary immediately went to him.

30Now Jesus had stayed outside the village, at the place where Martha met him. 31When the people who were at the house trying to console Mary saw her leave so hastily, they assumed she was going to Lazarus's grave to weep. So they followed her there. 32When Mary arrived and saw Jesus, she fell down at his feet and said, "Lord, if you had been here, my brother would not have died."

33When Jesus saw her weeping and saw the other people wailing with her, he was moved with indignation and was deeply troubled. 34"Where have you put him?" he asked them.

They told him, "Lord, come and see." 35Then Jesus wept. 36The people who were standing nearby said, "See how much he loved him." 37But some said, "This man healed a blind man. Why couldn't he keep Lazarus from dying?"

Jesus Raises Lazarus from the Dead

38And again Jesus was deeply troubled. Then they came to the grave. It was a cave with a stone rolled across its entrance. 39"Roll the stone aside," Jesus told them.

But Martha, the dead man's sister, said, "Lord, by now the smell will be terrible because he has been dead for four days."

40Jesus responded, "Didn't I tell you that you will see God's glory if you believe?" 41So they rolled the stone aside. Then Jesus looked up to heaven and said, "Father, thank you for hearing me. 42You always hear me, but I said it out loud for the sake of all these people standing here, so they will believe you sent me." 43Then Jesus shouted, "Lazarus, come out!" 44And Lazarus came out, bound in graveclothes, his face wrapped in a headcloth. Jesus told them, "Unwrap him and let him go!"

The Plot to Kill Jesus

45Many of the people who were with Mary believed in Jesus when they saw this happen. 46But some went to the Pharisees and told them what Jesus had done. 47Then the leading priests and Pharisees called the high council* together to discuss the situation. "What are we going to do?" they asked each other. "This man certainly performs many miraculous signs. 48If we leave him alone, the whole nation will follow him, and then the Roman army will come and destroy both our Temple and our nation."

49And one of them, Caiaphas, who was high priest that year, said, "How can you be so stupid? 50Why should the whole nation be destroyed? Let this one man die for the people."

51This prophecy that Jesus should die for the entire nation came from Caiaphas in his position as high priest. He didn't think of it himself; he was inspired to say it. 52It was a prediction that Jesus' death would be not for Israel only, but for the gathering together of all the children of God scattered around the world.

53So from that time on the Jewish leaders began to plot Jesus' death. 54As a result, Jesus stopped his public ministry among the people and left Jerusalem. He went to a place near the wilderness, to the village of Ephraim, and stayed there with his disciples.

55It was now almost time for the celebration of Passover, and many people from the country arrived in Jerusalem several days early so they could go through the cleansing ceremony before the Passover began. 56They wanted to see Jesus, and as they talked in the Temple, they asked each other, "What do you think? Will he come for the Passover?" 57Meanwhile, the leading priests and Pharisees had publicly announced that anyone seeing Jesus must report him immediately so they could arrest him.

11:18 Greek *was about 15 stadia* [about 2.8 kilometers]. **11:19** Greek *Jewish people;* also 11:31, 33, 36, 45, 54. **11:25** Some manuscripts do not include *and the life.* **11:47** Greek *the Sanhedrin.*

CHAPTER 12

Jesus Anointed at Bethany

Six days before the Passover ceremonies began,
Jesus arrived in Bethany, the home of Lazarus—
the man he had raised from the dead. 2A dinner
was prepared in Jesus' honor. Martha served, and
Lazarus sat at the table with him. 3Then Mary took
a twelve-ounce jar* of expensive perfume made
from essence of nard, and she anointed Jesus' feet
with it and wiped his feet with her hair. And the
house was filled with fragrance.

4But Judas Iscariot, one of his disciples—the
one who would betray him—said, 5"That perfume was worth a small fortune.* It should have
been sold and the money given to the poor."
6Not that he cared for the poor—he was a thief
who was in charge of the disciples' funds, and he
often took some for his own use.

7Jesus replied, "Leave her alone. She did it in
preparation for my burial. 8You will always have
the poor among you, but I will not be here with
you much longer."

9When all the people* heard of Jesus' arrival,
they flocked to see him and also to see Lazarus,
the man Jesus had raised from the dead. 10Then
the leading priests decided to kill Lazarus, too,
11for it was because of him that many of the
people had deserted them and believed in Jesus.

The Triumphal Entry

12The next day, the news that Jesus was on the way
to Jerusalem swept through the city. A huge crowd
of Passover visitors 13took palm branches and
went down the road to meet him. They shouted,

"Praise God!*
Bless the one who comes in the name of the Lord!
Hail to the King of Israel!"*

14Jesus found a young donkey and sat on it,
fulfilling the prophecy that said:

15 "Don't be afraid, people of Israel.*
Look, your King is coming,
sitting on a donkey's colt."*

16His disciples didn't realize at the time that this
was a fulfillment of prophecy. But after Jesus
entered into his glory, they remembered that
these Scriptures had come true before their eyes.

17Those in the crowd who had seen Jesus call
Lazarus back to life were telling others all about it.
18That was the main reason so many went out to
meet him—because they had heard about this
mighty miracle. 19Then the Pharisees said to each
other, "We've lost. Look, the whole world has
gone after him!"

Jesus Predicts His Death

20Some Greeks who had come to Jerusalem to
attend the Passover 21paid a visit to Philip, who
was from Bethsaida in Galilee. They said, "Sir,
we want to meet Jesus." 22Philip told Andrew
about it, and they went together to ask Jesus.

23Jesus replied, "The time has come for the
Son of Man to enter into his glory. 24The truth is,
a kernel of wheat must be planted in the soil.
Unless it dies it will be alone—a single seed. But
its death will produce many new kernels—a
plentiful harvest of new lives. 25Those who love
their life in this world will lose it. Those who
despise their life in this world will keep it for
eternal life. 26All those who want to be my disciples must come and follow me, because my servants must be where I am. And if they follow me,
the Father will honor them. 27Now my soul is
deeply troubled. Should I pray, 'Father, save me
from what lies ahead'? But that is the very reason
why I came! 28Father, bring glory to your name."

Then a voice spoke from heaven, saying, "I
have already brought it glory, and I will do it
again." 29When the crowd heard the voice, some
thought it was thunder, while others declared an
angel had spoken to him.

30Then Jesus told them, "The voice was for your
benefit, not mine. 31The time of judgment for the
world has come, when the prince of this world*
will be cast out. 32And when I am lifted up on the
cross,* I will draw everyone to myself." 33He said
this to indicate how he was going to die.

34"Die?" asked the crowd. "We understood
from Scripture that the Messiah would live forever. Why are you saying the Son of Man will die?
Who is this Son of Man you are talking about?"

35Jesus replied, "My light will shine out for
you just a little while longer. Walk in it while you
can, so you will not stumble when the darkness
falls. If you walk in the darkness, you cannot see
where you are going. 36Believe in the light while
there is still time; then you will become children
of the light." After saying these things, Jesus
went away and was hidden from them.

The Unbelief of the People

37But despite all the miraculous signs he had
done, most of the people did not believe in him.

12:3 Greek *took 1 litra* [327 grams]. **12:5** Greek *300 denarii.* A denarius was equivalent to a full day's wage. **12:9** Greek *Jewish people;* also in 12:11. **12:13a** Greek *Hosanna,* an exclamation of praise that literally means "save now." **12:13b** Ps 118:25-26; Zeph 3:15. **12:15a** Greek *daughter of Zion.* **12:15b** Zech 9:9. **12:31** *The prince of this world* is a name for Satan. **12:32** Greek *lifted up from the earth.*

38This is exactly what Isaiah the prophet had predicted:

"Lord, who has believed our message?
To whom will the Lord reveal his saving power?"*

39But the people couldn't believe, for as Isaiah also said,

40 "The Lord has blinded their eyes
and hardened their hearts—
so their eyes cannot see,
and their hearts cannot understand,
and they cannot turn to me
and let me heal them."*

41Isaiah was referring to Jesus when he made this prediction, because he was given a vision of the Messiah's glory. 42Many people, including some of the Jewish leaders, believed in him. But they wouldn't admit it to anyone because of their fear that the Pharisees would expel them from the synagogue. 43For they loved human praise more than the praise of God.

44Jesus shouted to the crowds, "If you trust me, you are really trusting God who sent me. 45For when you see me, you are seeing the one who sent me. 46I have come as a light to shine in this dark world, so that all who put their trust in me will no longer remain in the darkness. 47If anyone hears me and doesn't obey me, I am not his judge—for I have come to save the world and not to judge it. 48But all who reject me and my message will be judged at the day of judgment by the truth I have spoken. 49I don't speak on my own authority. The Father who sent me gave me his own instructions as to what I should say. 50And I know his instructions lead to eternal life; so I say whatever the Father tells me to say!"

CHAPTER 13

Jesus Washes His Disciples' Feet

Before the Passover celebration, Jesus knew that his hour had come to leave this world and return to his Father. He now showed the disciples the full extent of his love.* 2It was time for supper, and the Devil had already enticed Judas, son of Simon Iscariot, to carry out his plan to betray Jesus. 3Jesus knew that the Father had given him authority over everything and that he had come from God and would return to God. 4So he got up from the table, took off his robe, wrapped a towel around his waist, 5and poured water into a basin. Then he began to wash the disciples' feet and to wipe them with the towel he had around him.

6When he came to Simon Peter, Peter said to him, "Lord, why are you going to wash my feet?"

7Jesus replied, "You don't understand now why I am doing it; someday you will."

8"No," Peter protested, "you will never wash my feet!"

Jesus replied, "But if I don't wash you, you won't belong to me."

9Simon Peter exclaimed, "Then wash my hands and head as well, Lord, not just my feet!"

10Jesus replied, "A person who has bathed all over does not need to wash, except for the feet,* to be entirely clean. And you are clean, but that isn't true of everyone here." 11For Jesus knew who would betray him. That is what he meant when he said, "Not all of you are clean."

12After washing their feet, he put on his robe again and sat down and asked, "Do you understand what I was doing? 13You call me 'Teacher' and 'Lord,' and you are right, because it is true. 14And since I, the Lord and Teacher, have washed your feet, you ought to wash each other's feet. 15I have given you an example to follow. Do as I have done to you. 16How true it is that a servant is not greater than the master. Nor are messengers more important than the one who sends them. 17You know these things—now do them! That is the path of blessing.

Jesus Predicts His Betrayal

18"I am not saying these things to all of you; I know so well each one of you I chose. The Scriptures declare, 'The one who shares my food has turned against me,'* and this will soon come true. 19I tell you this now, so that when it happens you will believe I am the Messiah. 20Truly, anyone who welcomes my messenger is welcoming me, and anyone who welcomes me is welcoming the Father who sent me."

21Now Jesus was in great anguish of spirit, and he exclaimed, "The truth is, one of you will betray me!"

22The disciples looked at each other, wondering whom he could mean. 23One of Jesus' disciples, the one Jesus loved, was sitting next to Jesus at the table.* 24Simon Peter motioned to him to ask who would do this terrible thing. 25Leaning toward Jesus, he asked, "Lord, who is it?"

26Jesus said, "It is the one to whom I give the bread dipped in the sauce." And when he had

12:38 Isa 53:1. 12:40 Isa 6:10. 13:1 Or *He loved his disciples to the very end.* 13:10 Some manuscripts do not include *except for the feet.* 13:18 Ps 41:9. 13:23 Greek *was reclining on Jesus' bosom.* The "disciple whom Jesus loved" was probably John.

dipped it, he gave it to Judas, son of Simon
Iscariot. 27As soon as Judas had eaten the bread,
Satan entered into him. Then Jesus told him,
"Hurry. Do it now." 28None of the others at the
table knew what Jesus meant. 29Since Judas was
their treasurer, some thought Jesus was telling
him to go and pay for the food or to give some
money to the poor. 30So Judas left at once, going
out into the night.

Jesus Predicts Peter's Denial

31As soon as Judas left the room, Jesus said, "The
time has come for me, the Son of Man, to enter
into my glory, and God will receive glory because of all that happens to me. 32And God will
bring* me into my glory very soon. 33Dear children, how brief are these moments before I must
go away and leave you! Then, though you search
for me, you cannot come to me—just as I told
the Jewish leaders. 34So now I am giving you a
new commandment: Love each other. Just as I
have loved you, you should love each other.
35Your love for one another will prove to the
world that you are my disciples."

36Simon Peter said, "Lord, where are you going?"

And Jesus replied, "You can't go with me now,
but you will follow me later."

37"But why can't I come now, Lord?" he
asked. "I am ready to die for you."

38Jesus answered, "Die for me? No, before
the rooster crows tomorrow morning, you will
deny three times that you even know me.

CHAPTER 14

Jesus, the Way to the Father

"Don't be troubled. You trust God, now trust in
me. 2There are many rooms in my Father's home,
and I am going to prepare a place for you. If this
were not so, I would tell you plainly. 3When everything is ready, I will come and get you, so that you
will always be with me where I am. 4And you
know where I am going and how to get there."

5"No, we don't know, Lord," Thomas said.
"We haven't any idea where you are going, so
how can we know the way?"

6Jesus told him, "I am the way, the truth, and
the life. No one can come to the Father except
through me. 7If you had known who I am, then
you would have known who my Father is.* From
now on you know him and have seen him!"

8Philip said, "Lord, show us the Father and
we will be satisfied."

9Jesus replied, "Philip, don't you even yet
know who I am, even after all the time I have

13:32 Some manuscripts read *And if God is glorified in him [the Son of Man], God will bring.* 14:7 Some manuscripts read *If you really have known me, you will know who my Father is.*

God Gives Hope to Our Troubled Hearts

Read JOHN 14:1-4

Have you ever felt troubled and uncertain about your future? Have you ever questioned whether God realizes that your world has turned upside down? The disciples may have been experiencing these feelings when Jesus gave them this message. He had just told them that he was going to leave them, and they were extremely concerned. Yet he tells them to not be troubled, then gives them three reasons why they should have peace in their hearts:

1. We Can Take God at His Word. When Jesus said, "You trust God, now trust in me," he was reminding his disciples to trust in God's Word (verse 1). Scripture had spoken not only of Jesus' impending crucifixion but also of his resurrection. Somehow they had missed that. Sometimes we forget to look at the whole picture when our circumstances seem overwhelming. But we must remember that the words found in these pages will "remain forever" (Matthew 24:35). We can always take God's promises at face value.

2. We Are Going to Heaven. The next time you face some kind of difficulty—be it an illness, a family problem, or an unexpected change in your life—remember that you are going to heaven (verse 2). That will help to keep everything in perspective. Your trials are only temporary. One day you will be in the presence of the Lord, and there will be no more fear, no more death, no more pain, and no more sorrow.

3. Jesus Is Coming Back for Us. Notice that Jesus says, "I will come and get you" (verse 3). The Lord is not merely going to send for us. He is going to personally escort us to the Father's house. The Bible tells us to *"comfort* and encourage each other with these words" (1 Thessalonians 4:18). In the midst of your trials, remember that God cares for you so much that he is coming back so that you can be with him forever.

FIRST STEPS

JOHN 15 ▸▸▸ page 124

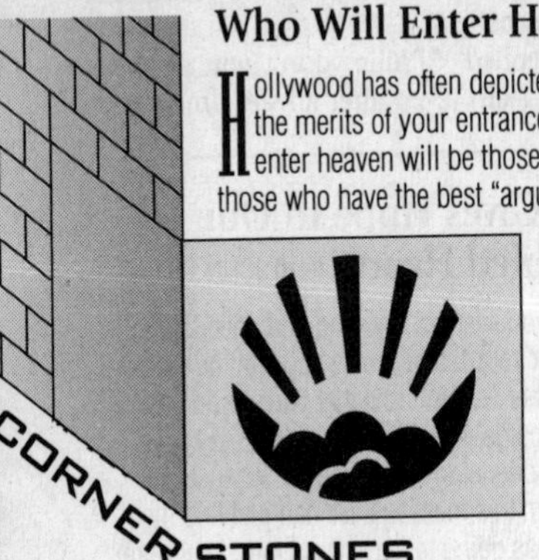

Who Will Enter Heaven? Read JOHN 14:2-6

Hollywood has often depicted the gates of heaven as the place where you "plead your case" for the merits of your entrance. In this passage, Jesus clearly explains that the only ones who will enter heaven will be those who have accepted him as the way, the truth, and the life—not those who have the best "arguments" or who have performed the greatest number of good deeds.

Heaven is not a court but a prepared place for prepared people. If you are a Christian, you can rest assured that your reservation for heaven was made the moment you received Christ. And when it comes to accommodations, you don't need to worry, for Jesus himself has promised to prepare a place for you.

The Bible tells us to prepare to meet our God. Is your reservation in place?

been with you? Anyone who has seen me has
seen the Father! So why are you asking to see
him? 10Don't you believe that I am in the Father
and the Father is in me? The words I say are not
my own, but my Father who lives in me does his
work through me. 11Just believe that I am in the
Father and the Father is in me. Or at least believe
because of what you have seen me do.
12"The truth is, anyone who believes in me
will do the same works I have done, and even
greater works, because I am going to be with the
Father. 13You can ask for anything in my name,
and I will do it, because the work of the Son
brings glory to the Father. 14Yes, ask anything in
my name, and I will do it!

Jesus Promises the Holy Spirit

15"If you love me, obey my commandments.
16And I will ask the Father, and he will give you
another Counselor,* who will never leave you.
17He is the Holy Spirit, who leads into all truth.
The world at large cannot receive him, because it
isn't looking for him and doesn't recognize him.
But you do, because he lives with you now and
later will be in you. 18No, I will not abandon you
as orphans—I will come to you. 19In just a little
while the world will not see me again, but you
will. For I will live again, and you will, too.
20When I am raised to life again, you will know
that I am in my Father, and you are in me, and I
am in you. 21Those who obey my commandments
are the ones who love me. And because they love
me, my Father will love them, and I will love them.
And I will reveal myself to each one of them."
22Judas (not Judas Iscariot, but the other disciple with that name) said to him, "Lord, why
are you going to reveal yourself only to us and
not to the world at large?"
23Jesus replied, "All those who love me will
do what I say. My Father will love them, and we
will come to them and live with them. 24Anyone
who doesn't love me will not do what I say. And
remember, my words are not my own. This message is from the Father who sent me. 25I am
telling you these things now while I am still with
you. 26But when the Father sends the Counselor
as my representative—and by the Counselor I
mean the Holy Spirit—he will teach you everything and will remind you of everything I myself
have told you.
27"I am leaving you with a gift—peace of
mind and heart. And the peace I give isn't like
the peace the world gives. So don't be troubled
or afraid. 28Remember what I told you: I am
going away, but I will come back to you again. If
you really love me, you will be very happy for
me, because now I can go to the Father, who is
greater than I am. 29I have told you these things
before they happen so that you will believe
when they do happen.
30"I don't have much more time to talk to you,
because the prince of this world approaches. He
has no power over me, 31but I will do what the
Father requires of me, so that the world will know
that I love the Father. Come, let's be going.

CHAPTER 15

Jesus, the True Vine

"I am the true vine, and my Father is the gardener. 2He cuts off every branch that doesn't

14:16 Or *Comforter,* or *Encourager,* or *Advocate.* Greek *Paraclete;* also in 14:26.

produce fruit, and he prunes the branches that
do bear fruit so they will produce even more.
3You have already been pruned for greater fruit-
fulness by the message I have given you. 4Re-
main in me, and I will remain in you. For a
branch cannot produce fruit if it is severed from
the vine, and you cannot be fruitful apart from
me.

5"Yes, I am the vine; you are the branches.
Those who remain in me, and I in them, will
produce much fruit. For apart from me you can
do nothing. 6Anyone who parts from me is
thrown away like a useless branch and withers.
Such branches are gathered into a pile to be
burned. 7But if you stay joined to me and my
words remain in you, you may ask any request
you like, and it will be granted! 8My true disciples produce much fruit. This brings great glory
to my Father.

9"I have loved you even as the Father has
loved me. Remain in my love. 10When you
obey me, you remain in my love, just as I obey
my Father and remain in his love. 11I have told
you this so that you will be filled with my joy.
Yes, your joy will overflow! 12I command you
to love each other in the same way that I love
you. 13And here is how to measure it—the
greatest love is shown when people lay down
their lives for their friends. 14You are my
friends if you obey me. 15I no longer call you
servants, because a master doesn't confide in
his servants. Now you are my friends, since I
have told you everything the Father told me.
16You didn't choose me. I chose you. I appointed you to go and produce fruit that will
last, so that the Father will give you whatever
you ask for, using my name. 17I command you
to love each other.

The World's Hatred

18"When the world hates you, remember it
hated me before it hated you. 19The world
would love you if you belonged to it, but you
don't. I chose you to come out of the world,
and so it hates you. 20Do you remember what
I told you? 'A servant is not greater than the
master.' Since they persecuted me, naturally
they will persecute you. And if they had listened to me, they would listen to you! 21The
people of the world will hate you because you
belong to me, for they don't know God who
sent me. 22They would not be guilty if I had
not come and spoken to them. But now they
have no excuse for their sin. 23Anyone who
hates me hates my Father, too. 24If I hadn't
done such miraculous signs among them that
no one else could do, they would not be
counted guilty. But as it is, they saw all that I

A Disciple Abides in Christ

Read JOHN 15:1-17

Jesus knows that his true followers desire to live productive, fulfilling, joy-filled lives. In this passage, he lays out four predominant characteristics of a growing disciple:

1. A Disciple Stays Close to the Master. Jesus encourages us to remain in him (verses 4-5). Another way to translate that is "to abide in him." The word *abide* signifies a permanence of position. It means that you sink your roots deep into your relationship with Jesus, allowing him to fill every part of your life and daily activities. If you maintain this unbroken fellowship with God, a changed lifestyle will result.

2. A Disciple Is Fruitful. Just as a branch can only be fruitful when attached to the vine, we can only be productive when we draw our strength from Jesus (verses 6, 16). The Bible describes the fruit Jesus is talking about as love, joy, peace, patience, kindness, goodness, faithfulness, gentleness, and self-control (see Galatians 5:22, p. 234).

3. A Disciple Obeys the Master. Another clear sign that you are Christ's disciple is your obedience to the principles and guidelines found in his Word, the Bible (verse 10). Then, and only then, will you discover what it means to live in God's love.

4. A Disciple Loves Others. Jesus gave us the ultimate example of love by laying down his life for us. He, in essence, is asking us to do nothing less. Although that may not mean actually dying for someone, it may mean placing someone else's needs before our own.

In verse 11 we find Jesus' reason for sharing these principles: He wants us to be filled with joy. If you try to find happiness by pursuing it in and of itself, it will elude you. The only way to find happiness is through the pursuit of God. If you prioritize your life as Jesus has laid out in these verses, then "your joy will overflow."

How the Holy Spirit Works in Our Lives Read JOHN 14:15-17

The Bible uses three different Greek prepositions in the New Testament to describe the different ways in which the Holy Spirit works in our lives. This verse shows two of these ways, and a third can be found elsewhere in Scripture:

1. He Works *with* Us as Nonbelievers (*para*). Prior to our conversion to faith in Jesus Christ, the Holy Spirit convicts us of our sin and reveals Christ as the answer (see John 16:8, p. 126). Some might dismiss his working as the prodding of one's personal conscience. Yet it is the Holy Spirit who opens our eyes to our terminally sinful condition, exposing our lack of righteousness so that we will see the need to turn our lives over to Jesus Christ.

2. He Comes *into* Our Lives When We Turn to Christ (*en*). Once we accept Jesus Christ as our Savior and invite him into our lives, the Holy Spirit moves into our lives and sets up residence, so to speak. First, he produces the process of salvation in our heart. As Jesus said, "No one can enter the Kingdom of God without being born of . . . the Spirit" (John 3:5). Second, he assures us that we have done the right thing. For Scripture tells us, "For his Holy Spirit speaks to us deep in our hearts and tells us that we are God's children" (Romans 8:16). He gives us the inner knowledge that Christ is living in us. Now he can begin changing us from the inside out and develop the new nature within us.

3. He Will Come *upon* Us to Empower Us as Believers (*epi*). This aspect of the Holy Spirit's work is described in Luke 24:49, where Jesus says, "And now I will send the Holy Spirit, just as my Father promised." Here Jesus describes the dynamic empowering of the Holy Spirit upon our lives. This is what the early Christians experienced in Acts chapter 2, and it dramatically emboldened their witness for Jesus Christ. This power is available to believers today, for Scripture says of the giving of his Spirit, "This promise is to you and your children, and even to the Gentiles—all who have been called by the Lord our God!" (Acts 2:39).

CORNERSTONES

did and yet hated both of us—me and my
Father. 25This has fulfilled what the Scriptures
said: 'They hated me without cause.'*
26"But I will send you the Counselor*—the
Spirit of truth. He will come to you from the
Father and will tell you all about me. 27And you
must also tell others about me because you have
been with me from the beginning.

CHAPTER 16

"I have told you these things so that you won't
fall away. 2For you will be expelled from the
synagogues, and the time is coming when those
who kill you will think they are doing God a
service. 3This is because they have never known
the Father or me. 4Yes, I'm telling you these things
now, so that when they happen, you will remember I warned you. I didn't tell you earlier because
I was going to be with you for a while longer.

The Work of the Holy Spirit

5"But now I am going away to the one who sent
me, and none of you has asked me where I am
going. 6Instead, you are very sad. 7But it is actually best for you that I go away, because if I don't,
the Counselor* won't come. If I do go away, he
will come because I will send him to you. 8And
when he comes, he will convince the world of its
sin, and of God's righteousness, and of the coming judgment. 9The world's sin is unbelief in me.
10Righteousness is available because I go to the
Father, and you will see me no more. 11Judgment
will come because the prince of this world has
already been judged.
12"Oh, there is so much more I want to tell
you, but you can't bear it now. 13When the Spirit
of truth comes, he will guide you into all truth.
He will not be presenting his own ideas; he will
be telling you what he has heard. He will tell you

15:25 Pss 35:19; 69:4. 15:26 Or *Comforter*, or *Encourager*, or *Advocate*. Greek *Paraclete*. 16:7 Or *Comforter*, or *Encourager*, or *Advocate*. Greek *Paraclete*.

about the future. 14He will bring me glory by
revealing to you whatever he receives from me.
15All that the Father has is mine; this is what I
mean when I say that the Spirit will reveal to you
whatever he receives from me.

Sadness Will Be Turned to Joy

16"In just a little while I will be gone, and you
won't see me anymore. Then, just a little while
after that, you will see me again."

17The disciples asked each other, "What does
he mean when he says, 'You won't see me, and
then you will see me'? And what does he mean
when he says, 'I am going to the Father'? 18And
what does he mean by 'a little while'? We don't
understand."

19Jesus realized they wanted to ask him, so he
said, "Are you asking yourselves what I meant? I
said in just a little while I will be gone, and you
won't see me anymore. Then, just a little while
after that, you will see me again. 20Truly, you will
weep and mourn over what is going to happen to
me, but the world will rejoice. You will grieve, but
your grief will suddenly turn to wonderful joy
when you see me again. 21It will be like a woman
experiencing the pains of labor. When her child
is born, her anguish gives place to joy because she
has brought a new person into the world. 22You
have sorrow now, but I will see you again; then
you will rejoice, and no one can rob you of that
joy. 23At that time you won't need to ask me for
anything. The truth is, you can go directly to the
Father and ask him, and he will grant your request because you use my name. 24You haven't
done this before. Ask, using my name, and you
will receive, and you will have abundant joy.

25"I have spoken of these matters in parables,
but the time will come when this will not be
necessary, and I will tell you plainly all about the
Father. 26Then you will ask in my name. I'm not
saying I will ask the Father on your behalf, 27for
the Father himself loves you dearly because you
love me and believe that I came from God. 28Yes,
I came from the Father into the world, and I will
leave the world and return to the Father."

29Then his disciples said, "At last you are
speaking plainly and not in parables. 30Now we
understand that you know everything and don't
need anyone to tell you anything.* From this we
believe that you came from God."

31Jesus asked, "Do you finally believe? 32But
the time is coming—in fact, it is already here—
when you will be scattered, each one going his

16:30 Or *don't need that anyone should ask you anything.*

Live in God's Love Read JOHN 15:9-11

This passage is a portion of Jesus' last message to his disciples before his death. In preparing them for his departure, he wanted to emphasize his love for them and how that love should affect their lives. He wanted them to realize that they could experience true and lasting joy in their walk with God—even if he could not personally be with them. For that reason this intimate message and command from Christ applies to us today as well. In this text Jesus gives four simple points that will enable us to live in his love:

1. Realize That You Have the Love of Jesus and Your Heavenly Father. Jesus is not simply some authoritative figure who demands our respect. He is a personal being who loved us so much that he died in our place. In return, he requires our obedience. Knowing that you are loved by Jesus frees you to love him in return. The best way to show your love for him is to obey his commands. Trying to obey his commands out of obligation rather than love can produce resentment toward him. That is because there is no joy in mere obligation. But obeying Jesus out of love produces joy.

2. Live within God's Love by Obeying His Commands. This is one of the earmarks of a true follower of Christ. It is easy to boast of our great love for God or the wonderful affection and devotion we feel toward him. But as the saying goes, The proof is in the pudding. If we really love God, we will obey him. If we do not obey him, it is questionable as to just how deep our love for him really is.

3. Follow Jesus' Example. Jesus is our perfect model of obedience. Pay careful attention to how Jesus obeyed his heavenly Father throughout the Gospels of Matthew, Mark, Luke, and John.

4. Experience the Reward of Obedience: Overflowing Joy. The obedient Christian is the happy Christian. If you want more joy in your life, make sure that you are following the guidelines God has given you in his Word.

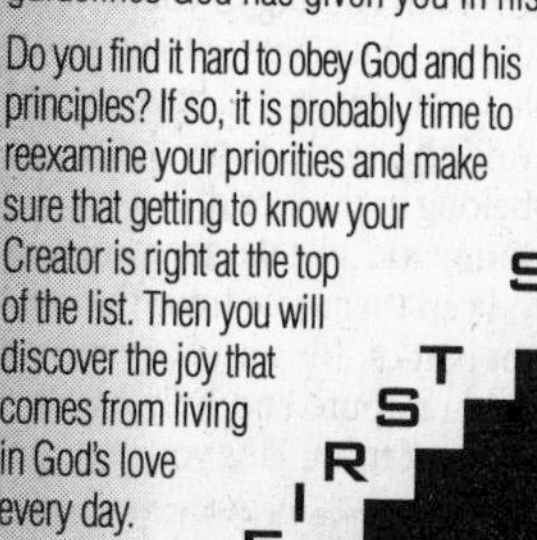
Do you find it hard to obey God and his principles? If so, it is probably time to reexamine your priorities and make sure that getting to know your Creator is right at the top of the list. Then you will discover the joy that comes from living in God's love every day.

own way, leaving me alone. Yet I am not alone
because the Father is with me. 33I have told you
all this so that you may have peace in me. Here
on earth you will have many trials and sorrows.
But take heart, because I have overcome the
world."

CHAPTER 17

The Prayer of Jesus

When Jesus had finished saying all these things,
he looked up to heaven and said, "Father, the
time has come. Glorify your Son so he can give
glory back to you. 2For you have given him
authority over everyone in all the earth. He gives
eternal life to each one you have given him.
3And this is the way to have eternal life—to
know you, the only true God, and Jesus Christ,
the one you sent to earth. 4I brought glory to you
here on earth by doing everything you told me
to do. 5And now, Father, bring me into the glory
we shared before the world began.

6"I have told these men about you. They were
in the world, but then you gave them to me.
Actually, they were always yours, and you gave
them to me; and they have kept your word.
7Now they know that everything I have is a gift
from you, 8for I have passed on to them the
words you gave me; and they accepted them and
know that I came from you, and they believe you
sent me.

9"My prayer is not for the world, but for those
you have given me, because they belong to you.
10And all of them, since they are mine, belong to
you; and you have given them back to me, so
they are my glory! 11Now I am departing the
world; I am leaving them behind and coming to
you. Holy Father, keep them and care for
them—all those you have given me—so that
they will be united just as we are. 12During my
time here, I have kept them safe.* I guarded
them so that not one was lost, except the one
headed for destruction, as the Scriptures foretold.

13"And now I am coming to you. I have told
them many things while I was with them so they
would be filled with my joy. 14I have given them
your word. And the world hates them because
they do not belong to the world, just as I do not.
15I'm not asking you to take them out of the
world, but to keep them safe from the evil one.
16They are not part of this world any more than
I am. 17Make them pure and holy by teaching
them your words of truth. 18As you sent me into
the world, I am sending them into the world.
19And I give myself entirely to you so they also
might be entirely yours.

20"I am praying not only for these disciples
but also for all who will ever believe in me
because of their testimony. 21My prayer for all of
them is that they will be one, just as you and I
are one, Father—that just as you are in me and I
am in you, so they will be in us, and the world
will believe you sent me.

22"I have given them the glory you gave me,
so that they may be one, as we are—23I in them
and you in me, all being perfected into one.
Then the world will know that you sent me and
will understand that you love them as much as
you love me. 24Father, I want these whom you've
given me to be with me, so they can see my glory.
You gave me the glory because you loved me
even before the world began!

25"O righteous Father, the world doesn't
know you, but I do; and these disciples know
you sent me. 26And I have revealed you to them
and will keep on revealing you. I will do this so
that your love for me may be in them and I in
them."

CHAPTER 18

Jesus Is Betrayed and Arrested

After saying these things, Jesus crossed the Kid-
ron Valley with his disciples and entered a grove
of olive trees. 2Judas, the betrayer, knew this
place, because Jesus had gone there many times
with his disciples. 3The leading priests and Pharisees had given Judas a battalion of Roman soldiers and Temple guards to accompany him.
Now with blazing torches, lanterns, and weapons, they arrived at the olive grove.

4Jesus fully realized all that was going to happen to him. Stepping forward to meet them, he
asked, "Whom are you looking for?"

5"Jesus of Nazareth," they replied.

"I am he,"* Jesus said. Judas was standing
there with them when Jesus identified himself.
6And as he said, "I am he," they all fell backward
to the ground! 7Once more he asked them,
"Whom are you searching for?"

And again they replied, "Jesus of Nazareth."

8"I told you that I am he," Jesus said. "And
since I am the one you want, let these others go."
9He did this to fulfill his own statement: "I have
not lost a single one of those you gave me."*

10Then Simon Peter drew a sword and
slashed off the right ear of Malchus, the high

17:12 Greek *I have kept in your name those whom you have given me.* 18:5 Greek *I am;* also in 18:6, 8. 18:9 See John 6:39 and 17:12.

priest's servant. 11But Jesus said to Peter, "Put
your sword back into its sheath. Shall I not drink
from the cup the Father has given me?"

Annas Questions Jesus

12So the soldiers, their commanding officer, and
the Temple guards arrested Jesus and tied him
up. 13First they took him to Annas, the father-in-
law of Caiaphas, the high priest that year. 14Cai-
aphas was the one who had told the other Jewish
leaders, "Better that one should die for all."

Peter's First Denial

15Simon Peter followed along behind, as did
another of the disciples. That other disciple was
acquainted with the high priest, so he was allowed to enter the courtyard with Jesus. 16Peter
stood outside the gate. Then the other disciple
spoke to the woman watching at the gate, and
she let Peter in. 17The woman asked Peter,
"Aren't you one of Jesus' disciples?"
"No," he said, "I am not."
18The guards and the household servants
were standing around a charcoal fire they had
made because it was cold. And Peter stood there
with them, warming himself.

The High Priest Questions Jesus

19Inside, the high priest began asking Jesus
about his followers and what he had been teaching them. 20Jesus replied, "What I teach is
widely known, because I have preached regularly in the synagogues and the Temple. I have
been heard by people* everywhere, and I teach
nothing in private that I have not said in public.
21Why are you asking me this question? Ask
those who heard me. They know what I said."
22One of the Temple guards standing there
struck Jesus on the face. "Is that the way to
answer the high priest?" he demanded.
23Jesus replied, "If I said anything wrong, you
must give evidence for it. Should you hit a man
for telling the truth?"
24Then Annas bound Jesus and sent him to
Caiaphas, the high priest.

Peter's Second and Third Denials

25Meanwhile, as Simon Peter was standing by
the fire, they asked him again, "Aren't you one
of his disciples?"
"I am not," he said.
26But one of the household servants of the
high priest, a relative of the man whose ear Peter
had cut off, asked, "Didn't I see you out there in
the olive grove with Jesus?" 27Again Peter denied
it. And immediately a rooster crowed.

Jesus' Trial before Pilate

28Jesus' trial before Caiaphas ended in the early
hours of the morning. Then he was taken to the
headquarters of the Roman governor. His accusers didn't go in themselves because it would

18:20 Greek *Jewish people;* also in 18:38.

God's Spirit Will Guide You

Read JOHN 16:13-15

The work of the Holy Spirit in the life of a Christian is multidimensional. We are told that, among other things, the Holy Spirit "speaks to us deep in our hearts and tells us that we are God's children" (Romans 8:16). In this passage, we see that the Holy Spirit serves as a teacher and a guide.

The Holy Spirit Will Help Us Understand the Bible. Before you became a Christian, understanding the Bible may have been like walking around with blinders on. But those "blinders" you once had were taken off, so to speak, when the Holy Spirit took up residence in your heart. The Holy Spirit teaches you the truth of the Scripture, helping you grasp hard-to-understand passages.

The Holy Spirit Will Reveal More and More about God and Jesus. The Bible makes it abundantly clear that one of the primary roles of the Holy Spirit is to glorify Christ. The moment you invited Jesus into your heart, God's Spirit began to help you grasp the awesome, praiseworthy attributes of Jesus. Those who do not have a personal relationship with Christ cannot see or understand the full glory of God, because they do not have the Holy Spirit's assistance.

The Holy Spirit wants to be actively involved in your life, helping you grow in the knowledge of God and his Word so that you can better understand God's will for your life.

Every time you open the Bible, pray for the Holy Spirit to show you how the passages you read can apply to your life.

defile them, and they wouldn't be allowed to
celebrate the Passover feast. 29So Pilate, the governor, went out to them and asked, "What is
your charge against this man?"
30"We wouldn't have handed him over to you
if he weren't a criminal!" they retorted.
31"Then take him away and judge him by
your own laws," Pilate told them.
"Only the Romans are permitted to execute
someone," the Jewish leaders replied. 32This
fulfilled Jesus' prediction about the way he
would die.*
33Then Pilate went back inside and called for
Jesus to be brought to him. "Are you the King of
the Jews?" he asked him.
34Jesus replied, "Is this your own question, or
did others tell you about me?"
35"Am I a Jew?" Pilate asked. "Your own
people and their leading priests brought you
here. Why? What have you done?"
36Then Jesus answered, "I am not an earthly
king. If I were, my followers would have fought
when I was arrested by the Jewish leaders. But
my Kingdom is not of this world."
37Pilate replied, "You are a king then?"
"You say that I am a king, and you are right,"
Jesus said. "I was born for that purpose. And I
came to bring truth to the world. All who love
the truth recognize that what I say is true."
38"What is truth?" Pilate asked. Then he went
out again to the people and told them, "He is
not guilty of any crime. 39But you have a custom
of asking me to release someone from prison
each year at Passover. So if you want me to, I'll
release the King of the Jews."
40But they shouted back, "No! Not this man,
but Barabbas!" (Barabbas was a criminal.)

CHAPTER 19

Jesus Sentenced to Death

Then Pilate had Jesus flogged with a lead-tipped
whip. 2The soldiers made a crown of long, sharp
thorns and put it on his head, and they put a royal
purple robe on him. 3"Hail! King of the Jews!"
they mocked, and they hit him with their fists.
4Pilate went outside again and said to the
people, "I am going to bring him out to you
now, but understand clearly that I find him not
guilty." 5Then Jesus came out wearing the crown
of thorns and the purple robe. And Pilate said,
"Here is the man!"
6When they saw him, the leading priests
and Temple guards began shouting, "Crucify!
Crucify!"
"You crucify him," Pilate said. "I find him not
guilty."
7The Jewish leaders replied, "By our laws he
ought to die because he called himself the Son
of God."
8When Pilate heard this, he was more frightened than ever. 9He took Jesus back into the
headquarters again and asked him, "Where are
you from?" But Jesus gave no answer. 10"You
won't talk to me?" Pilate demanded. "Don't you
realize that I have the power to release you or to
crucify you?"
11Then Jesus said, "You would have no power
over me at all unless it were given to you from
above. So the one who brought me to you has
the greater sin."
12Then Pilate tried to release him, but the
Jewish leaders told him, "If you release this
man, you are not a friend of Caesar. Anyone who
declares himself a king is a rebel against Caesar."
13When they said this, Pilate brought Jesus
out to them again. Then Pilate sat down on the
judgment seat on the platform that is called the
Stone Pavement (in Hebrew, *Gabbatha*). 14It was
now about noon of the day of preparation for
the Passover. And Pilate said to the people,*
"Here is your king!"
15"Away with him," they yelled. "Away with
him—crucify him!"
"What? Crucify your king?" Pilate asked.
"We have no king but Caesar," the leading
priests shouted back.
16Then Pilate gave Jesus to them to be crucified.

The Crucifixion

So they took Jesus and led him away. 17Carrying
the cross by himself, Jesus went to the place
called Skull Hill (in Hebrew, *Golgotha*). 18There
they crucified him. There were two others crucified with him, one on either side, with Jesus
between them. 19And Pilate posted a sign over
him that read, "Jesus of Nazareth, the King of
the Jews." 20The place where Jesus was crucified
was near the city; and the sign was written in
Hebrew, Latin, and Greek, so that many people
could read it.
21Then the leading priests said to Pilate,
"Change it from 'The King of the Jews' to 'He
said, I am King of the Jews.'"
22Pilate replied, "What I have written, I have
written. It stays exactly as it is."

18:32 See John 12:32-33. 19:14 Greek *Jewish people;* also in 19:20.

23When the soldiers had crucified Jesus, they divided his clothes among the four of them. They also took his robe, but it was seamless, woven in one piece from the top. 24So they said, "Let's not tear it but throw dice* to see who gets it." This fulfilled the Scripture that says, "They divided my clothes among themselves and threw dice for my robe."* 25So that is what they did.

Standing near the cross were Jesus' mother, and his mother's sister, Mary (the wife of Clopas), and Mary Magdalene. 26When Jesus saw his mother standing there beside the disciple he loved, he said to her, "Woman, he is your son." 27And he said to this disciple, "She is your mother." And from then on this disciple took her into his home.

The Death of Jesus

28Jesus knew that everything was now finished, and to fulfill the Scriptures he said, "I am thirsty."* 29A jar of sour wine was sitting there, so they soaked a sponge in it, put it on a hyssop branch, and held it up to his lips. 30When Jesus had tasted it, he said, "It is finished!" Then he bowed his head and gave up his spirit.

31The Jewish leaders didn't want the victims hanging there the next day, which was the Sabbath (and a very special Sabbath at that, because it was the Passover), so they asked Pilate to hasten their deaths by ordering that their legs be broken. Then their bodies could be taken down. 32So the soldiers came and broke the legs of the two men crucified with Jesus. 33But when they came to Jesus, they saw that he was dead already, so they didn't break his legs. 34One of the soldiers, however, pierced his side with a spear, and blood and water flowed out. 35This report is from an eyewitness giving an accurate account; it is presented so that you also can believe. 36These things happened in fulfillment of the Scriptures that say, "Not one of his bones will be broken,"* 37and "They will look on him whom they pierced."*

The Burial of Jesus

38Afterward Joseph of Arimathea, who had been a secret disciple of Jesus (because he feared the Jewish leaders), asked Pilate for permission to take Jesus' body down. When Pilate gave him permission, he came and took the body away. 39Nicodemus, the man who had come to Jesus at night, also came, bringing about seventy-five pounds* of embalming ointment made from myrrh and aloes. 40Together they wrapped Jesus' body in a long linen cloth with the spices, as is the Jewish custom of burial. 41The place of crucifixion was near a garden, where there was a new tomb, never used before. 42And so, because it was the day of preparation before the Passover and since the tomb was close at hand, they laid Jesus there.

CHAPTER 20

The Resurrection

Early Sunday morning,* while it was still dark, Mary Magdalene came to the tomb and found that the stone had been rolled away from the entrance. 2She ran and found Simon Peter and the other disciple, the one whom Jesus loved. She said, "They have taken the Lord's body out of the tomb, and I don't know where they have put him!"

3Peter and the other disciple ran to the tomb to see. 4The other disciple outran Peter and got there first. 5He stooped and looked in and saw the linen cloth lying there, but he didn't go in. 6Then Simon Peter arrived and went inside. He also noticed the linen wrappings lying there, 7while the cloth that had covered Jesus' head was folded up and lying to the side. 8Then the other disciple also went in, and he saw and believed—9for until then they hadn't realized that the Scriptures said he would rise from the dead. 10Then they went home.

Jesus Appears to Mary Magdalene

11Mary was standing outside the tomb crying, and as she wept, she stooped and looked in. 12She saw two white-robed angels sitting at the head and foot of the place where the body of Jesus had been lying. 13"Why are you crying?" the angels asked her.

"Because they have taken away my Lord," she replied, "and I don't know where they have put him."

14She glanced over her shoulder and saw someone standing behind her. It was Jesus, but she didn't recognize him. 15"Why are you crying?" Jesus asked her. "Who are you looking for?"

She thought he was the gardener. "Sir," she said, "if you have taken him away, tell me where you have put him, and I will go and get him."

16"Mary!" Jesus said.

She turned toward him and exclaimed, "Teacher!"*

17"Don't cling to me," Jesus said, "for I haven't

19:24a Greek *cast lots.* 19:24b Ps 22:18. 19:28 See Pss 22:15; 69:21. 19:36 Exod 12:46; Num 9:12; Ps 34:20. 19:37 Zech 12:10. 19:39 Greek *100 litras* [32.7 kilograms]. 20:1 Greek *On the first day of the week.* 20:16 Greek *and said in Hebrew, "Rabboni," which means "Teacher."*

Our Love for God Prepares Us for Service Read JOHN 21:15-17

Peter knew that he had let Jesus down by denying him three times prior to the Crucifixion. But Peter also knew that Jesus had forgiven him. So Jesus tested Peter by asking him the searching question, "Do you love me?" three times.

Peter's response to Jesus' questions has great significance in the original language of the text. When Jesus posed the questions, he had basically asked, "Peter, do you love me with a sacrificial, committed love?" Peter, however, responded with a different word for "love" than Jesus had suggested. Peter essentially said, "Lord, I like you. I love you as a friend."

At least Peter was being honest. He told Jesus the truth about his commitment. Interestingly enough, Jesus still enlisted Peter in his service, to feed and care for his sheep. Jesus just wanted Peter to affirm his devotion to the Lord before giving him his directions for ministry.

As this story implies, we must love God before we can serve him faithfully. Do you love God? Here are five ways to tell if you really love God and are growing in that love for him:

1. If You Love the Lord, You Will Long for Personal Communion with Him. Can you relate to the words of the psalmist, "As the deer pants for streams of water, so I long for you, O God" (Psalm 42:1)? When you really love God, you will delight in praising and worshiping him. That is because your praise and worship will overflow from a heart filled with love for God. And this love will cause you to look forward to spending time with him and his people.

2. If You Love God, You Will Love the Things He Loves. We know what God loves by what he has declared in his Word, the Bible. So if you love God, you will love his Word. Bible study will not be a drudgery, but a delight.

3. If You Love the Lord, You Will Hate What He Hates. As the Lord's nature becomes your nature, his likes and dislikes become your likes and dislikes. His outlook becomes your outlook. We know from his Word that he hates sin. If we love him, then we should also hate sin.

4. If You Love the Lord, You Will Long for His Return. Jesus described himself as a bridegroom (Mark 2:19). His bride is the church—the body of believers (Ephesians 5:23-29). When Jesus returns, he will be united with his bride. Therefore, if you love the Lord, you will long for his return as a bride and bridegroom long to be together.

5. If You Love the Lord, You Will Keep His Commandments. Jesus says, "If you love me, obey my commandments" (John 14:15). That does not mean that you will never sin. Though it is impossible for any of us who love God to go on an endless course of sin, it is quite possible to fall into individual sins. But if we love God, we will repent of those sins and seek his forgiveness, and our lifestyle will conform to the truths we find in his Word.

Do you love the Lord? Like Peter, you may be tempted to believe that you have no love for Jesus when you sin. Maybe you feel that God could never use you in his service again. Be honest with God; then start rebuilding that relationship by following the steps above. As you reaffirm your love for him, God will open up opportunities for you to serve him and share that love with others. A committed heart leads to committed service.

CORNERSTONES

yet ascended to the Father. But go find my brothers and tell them that I am ascending to my
Father and your Father, my God and your God."
18Mary Magdalene found the disciples and
told them, "I have seen the Lord!" Then she gave
them his message.

Jesus Appears to His Disciples

19That evening, on the first day of the week, the
disciples were meeting behind locked doors because they were afraid of the Jewish leaders.
Suddenly, Jesus was standing there among
them! "Peace be with you," he said. 20As he

spoke, he held out his hands for them to see, and
he showed them his side. They were filled with
joy when they saw their Lord! 21He spoke to
them again and said, "Peace be with you. As the
Father has sent me, so I send you." 22Then he
breathed on them and said to them, "Receive
the Holy Spirit. 23If you forgive anyone's sins,
they are forgiven. If you refuse to forgive them,
they are unforgiven."

Jesus Appears to Thomas

24One of the disciples, Thomas (nicknamed the
Twin*), was not with the others when Jesus
came. 25They told him, "We have seen the
Lord!" But he replied, "I won't believe it unless
I see the nail wounds in his hands, put my
fingers into them, and place my hand into the
wound in his side."

26Eight days later the disciples were together
again, and this time Thomas was with them. The
doors were locked; but suddenly, as before, Jesus
was standing among them. He said, "Peace be
with you." 27Then he said to Thomas, "Put your
finger here and see my hands. Put your hand
into the wound in my side. Don't be faithless
any longer. Believe!"

28"My Lord and my God!" Thomas exclaimed.

29Then Jesus told him, "You believe because
you have seen me. Blessed are those who haven't
seen me and believe anyway."

Purpose of the Book

30Jesus' disciples saw him do many other miraculous signs besides the ones recorded in
this book. 31But these are written so that you
may believe* that Jesus is the Messiah, the Son
of God, and that by believing in him you will
have life.

CHAPTER 21

Jesus Appears to Seven Disciples

Later Jesus appeared again to the disciples beside the Sea of Galilee.* This is how it happened.
2Several of the disciples were there—Simon Peter, Thomas (nicknamed the Twin*), Nathanael
from Cana in Galilee, the sons of Zebedee, and
two other disciples.

3Simon Peter said, "I'm going fishing."

"We'll come, too," they all said. So they went
out in the boat, but they caught nothing all
night.

4At dawn the disciples saw Jesus standing on
the beach, but they couldn't see who he was.
5He called out, "Friends, have you caught any
fish?"

"No," they replied.

6Then he said, "Throw out your net on the
right-hand side of the boat, and you'll get plenty
of fish!" So they did, and they couldn't draw in
the net because there were so many fish in it.

7Then the disciple whom Jesus loved said to
Peter, "It is the Lord!" When Simon Peter heard
that it was the Lord, he put on his tunic (for he
had stripped for work), jumped into the water,
and swam ashore. 8The others stayed with the
boat and pulled the loaded net to the shore, for
they were only out about three hundred feet.*
9When they got there, they saw that a charcoal
fire was burning and fish were frying over it, and
there was bread.

10"Bring some of the fish you've just caught,"
Jesus said. 11So Simon Peter went aboard and
dragged the net to the shore. There were 153
large fish, and yet the net hadn't torn.

12"Now come and have some breakfast!"
Jesus said. And no one dared ask him if he really
was the Lord because they were sure of it. 13Then
Jesus served them the bread and the fish. 14This
was the third time Jesus had appeared to his
disciples since he had been raised from the dead.

Jesus Challenges Peter

15After breakfast Jesus said to Simon Peter, "Simon son of John, do you love me more than
these?"

"Yes, Lord," Peter replied, "you know I love
you."

"Then feed my lambs," Jesus told him.

16Jesus repeated the question: "Simon son of
John, do you love me?"

"Yes, Lord," Peter said, "you know I love you."

"Then take care of my sheep," Jesus said.

17Once more he asked him, "Simon son of
John, do you love me?"

Peter was grieved that Jesus asked the question a third time. He said, "Lord, you know
everything. You know I love you."

Jesus said, "Then feed my sheep. 18The truth
is, when you were young, you were able to do as
you liked and go wherever you wanted to. But
when you are old, you will stretch out your
hands, and others will direct you and take you
where you don't want to go." 19Jesus said this to
let him know what kind of death he would die

20:24 Greek *the one who was called Didymus.* **20:31** Some manuscripts read *may continue to believe.* **21:1** Greek *Sea of Tiberias,* another name for the Sea of Galilee. **21:2** Greek *the one who was called Didymus.* **21:8** Greek *200 cubits* [90 meters].

to glorify God. Then Jesus told him, "Follow
me."
20Peter turned around and saw the disciple
Jesus loved following them—the one who had
leaned over to Jesus during supper and asked,
"Lord, who among us will betray you?" 21Peter
asked Jesus, "What about him, Lord?"
22Jesus replied, "If I want him to remain alive
until I return, what is that to you? You follow
me." 23So the rumor spread among the community of believers* that that disciple wouldn't die.
But that isn't what Jesus said at all. He only said,
"If I want him to remain alive until I return,
what is that to you?"

Conclusion

24This is that disciple who saw these events and
recorded them here. And we all know that his
account of these things is accurate.
25And I suppose that if all the other things
Jesus did were written down, the whole world
could not contain the books.

21:23 Greek *the brothers.*

Acts

CHAPTER 1

The Promise of the Holy Spirit

Dear Theophilus:

In my first book* I told you about everything Jesus began to do and teach 2until the day he ascended to heaven after giving his chosen apostles further instructions from the Holy Spirit. 3During the forty days after his crucifixion, he appeared to the apostles from time to time and proved to them in many ways that he was actually alive. On these occasions he talked to them about the Kingdom of God.

4In one of these meetings as he was eating a meal with them, he told them, "Do not leave Jerusalem until the Father sends you what he promised. Remember, I have told you about this before. 5John baptized with* water, but in just a few days you will be baptized with the Holy Spirit."

The Ascension of Jesus

6When the apostles were with Jesus, they kept asking him, "Lord, are you going to free Israel now and restore our kingdom?"

7"The Father sets those dates," he replied, "and they are not for you to know. 8But when the Holy Spirit has come upon you, you will receive power and will tell people about me everywhere—in Jerusalem, throughout Judea, in Samaria, and to the ends of the earth."

9It was not long after he said this that he was taken up into the sky while they were watching, and he disappeared into a cloud. 10As they were straining their eyes to see him, two white-robed men suddenly stood there among them. 11They said, "Men of Galilee, why are you standing here staring at the sky? Jesus has been taken away from you into heaven. And someday, just as you saw him go, he will return!"

Matthias Replaces Judas

12The apostles were at the Mount of Olives when this happened, so they walked the half mile* back to Jerusalem. 13Then they went to the upstairs room of the house where they were staying. Here is the list of those who were present:

Peter,
John,
James,
Andrew,
Philip,
Thomas,
Bartholomew,
Matthew,
James (son of Alphaeus),
Simon (the Zealot),
and Judas (son of James).

14They all met together continually for prayer, along with Mary the mother of Jesus, several other women, and the brothers of Jesus.

15During this time, on a day when about 120 believers* were present, Peter stood up and addressed them as follows:

16"Brothers, it was necessary for the Scriptures to be fulfilled concerning Judas, who guided the Temple police to arrest Jesus. This was predicted long ago by the Holy Spirit, speaking through King David. 17Judas was one of us, chosen to share in the ministry with us."

18(Judas bought a field with the money he received for his treachery, and falling there, he burst open, spilling out his intestines. 19The news of his death spread rapidly among all the people of Jerusalem, and they gave the place the Aramaic name *Akeldama,* which means "Field of Blood.")

1:1 The reference is to the book of Luke. 1:5 Or *in;* also in 1:5b. 1:12 Greek *a Sabbath day's journey.* 1:15 Greek *brothers.*

Who the Holy Spirit Helps Read ACTS 2:1-41

Who is the Holy Spirit here to help? The Holy Spirit has been given to all believers to deepen their spiritual walk and to enable them to make an impact upon their world for Jesus Christ. This passage illustrates three aspects of the Holy Spirit's unique work in the lives of believers:

1. The Holy Spirit Fills All Believers. In the Old Testament, the Holy Spirit was given only to a select few to perform specific tasks. This chapter indicates a change in that pattern. The Holy Spirit was poured out on all the believers in the house that day (verse 4), and he continued to be present in each of their lives from that day forward. This outpouring of the Holy Spirit was used by God to establish the church—and to spread the message of the gospel around the world (see verse 39).

2. The Holy Spirit Draws Attention to the Savior. Notice that Peter did not focus on the unique happening that had just taken place but turned the crowd's attention to the message of Jesus Christ and their need for repentance. Likewise, the Holy Spirit does not draw attention to himself but to the Savior. And when he fills your life, he radically increases your ability to share the gospel with others.

3. The Holy Spirit Inspired Peter's Message. Peter's sermon, inspired by the Holy Spirit, led many in the crowd to a point of decision: "What should we do?"(verse 37). The people were not attracted to Peter but to his message. As stated in point 2 above, one of the primary roles of the Holy Spirit is to draw people to God. As stated above, the Holy Spirit worked powerfully this day, and three thousand people responded to the message.

The Holy Spirit is promised to all who repent and receive Jesus Christ into their lives. Many people fail to understand who the Holy Spirit is and what dimension of power is available to them through him. It may help to examine what took place after the disciples received the filling of the Holy Spirit that Jesus had promised (see Acts 1:8, p. 135).

CORNERSTONES

20Peter continued, "This was predicted in the
book of Psalms, where it says, 'Let his home become desolate, with no one living in it.' And again, 'Let his position be given to someone else.'*
21"So now we must choose another man to
take Judas's place. It must be someone who has been with us all the time that we were with the Lord Jesus—22from the time he was baptized by
John until the day he was taken from us into heaven. Whoever is chosen will join us as a witness of Jesus' resurrection."
23So they nominated two men: Joseph called
Barsabbas (also known as Justus) and Matthias.
24Then they all prayed for the right man to be
chosen. "O Lord," they said, "you know every heart. Show us which of these men you have chosen 25as an apostle to replace Judas the trai-
tor in this ministry, for he has deserted us and gone where he belongs." 26Then they cast lots,
and in this way Matthias was chosen and became an apostle with the other eleven.

CHAPTER 2

The Holy Spirit Comes

On the day of Pentecost, seven weeks after Jesus' resurrection,* the believers were meeting together in one place. 2Suddenly, there was a
sound from heaven like the roaring of a mighty windstorm in the skies above them, and it filled the house where they were meeting. 3Then,
what looked like flames or tongues of fire appeared and settled on each of them. 4And every-
one present was filled with the Holy Spirit and began speaking in other languages,* as the Holy Spirit gave them this ability.
5Godly Jews from many nations were living
in Jerusalem at that time. 6When they heard this
sound, they came running to see what it was all

1:20 Pss 69:25; 109:8. 2:1 Greek *When the day of Pentecost arrived.* This annual celebration came 50 days after the Passover ceremonies. See Lev 23:16. 2:4 Or *in other tongues.*

about, and they were bewildered to hear their
own languages being spoken by the believers.
7They were beside themselves with wonder.
"How can this be?" they exclaimed. "These
people are all from Galilee, 8and yet we hear
them speaking the languages of the lands where
we were born! 9Here we are—Parthians, Medes,
Elamites, people from Mesopotamia, Judea, Cappadocia, Pontus, the province of Asia, 10Phrygia,
Pamphylia, Egypt, and the areas of Libya toward
Cyrene, visitors from Rome (both Jews and converts to Judaism), 11Cretans, and Arabians. And
we all hear these people speaking in our own
languages about the wonderful things God has
done!" 12They stood there amazed and perplexed. "What can this mean?" they asked each
other. 13But others in the crowd were mocking.
"They're drunk, that's all!" they said.

Peter Preaches to a Crowd

14Then Peter stepped forward with the eleven
other apostles and shouted to the crowd, "Listen
carefully, all of you, fellow Jews and residents of
Jerusalem! Make no mistake about this. 15Some
of you are saying these people are drunk. It isn't
true! It's much too early for that. People don't
get drunk by nine o'clock in the morning. 16No,
what you see this morning was predicted centuries ago by the prophet Joel:

17 'In the last days, God said,
I will pour out my Spirit upon all people.
Your sons and daughters will prophesy,
your young men will see visions,
and your old men will dream dreams.
18 In those days I will pour out my Spirit
upon all my servants, men and women
alike,
and they will prophesy.
19 And I will cause wonders in the heavens
above
and signs on the earth below—
blood and fire and clouds of smoke.
20 The sun will be turned into darkness,
and the moon will turn bloodred,
before that great and glorious day of the
Lord arrives.
21 And anyone who calls on the name of the
Lord
will be saved.'*

22"People of Israel, listen! God publicly en-
dorsed Jesus of Nazareth by doing wonderful
miracles, wonders, and signs through him, as

2:17-21 Joel 2:28-32.

you well know. 23But you followed God's prearranged plan. With the help of lawless Gentiles,
you nailed him to the cross and murdered him.
24However, God released him from the horrors
of death and raised him back to life again, for
death could not keep him in its grip. 25King
David said this about him:

'I know the Lord is always with me.
I will not be shaken, for he is right beside
me.
26 No wonder my heart is filled with joy,
and my mouth shouts his praises!
My body rests in hope.
27 For you will not leave my soul among the
dead*

2:27 Greek *in Hades;* also in 2:31.

God's Spirit Will Empower Your Witness Read ACTS 1:8

One of the greatest things the Holy Spirit wants to do in the life of the believer is empower his or her witness. The word for *power* in this verse comes from the Greek word *dunamis*, from which we get the words *dynamite*, *dynamic*, and *dynamo*. God didn't give us the power of the Holy Spirit to *feel* something, but to *accomplish* something.

Sometimes the Holy Spirit's power acts like dynamite in our lives, blasting us with zeal, jolting us out of complacency, and motivating us to greater spiritual growth. At other times God's Spirit is like a dynamic, generating power that will help us live from day to day at a level we could not achieve on our own. We need to remember the encouraging words the apostle Paul gave to young Timothy: "For God has not given us a spirit of fear and timidity, but of power, love, and self-discipline" (2 Timothy 1:7).

Are you timid in your witness for Christ? Is it hard for you to speak up for what you believe? Then you need to tap in to that power he has made available to you through his Spirit. God's Holy Spirit will give you an added dimension of boldness, power, and persuasiveness in your witness that you have never experienced before.

or allow your Holy One to rot in the
grave.
28 You have shown me the way of life,
and you will give me wonderful joy in
your presence.'*

29 "Dear brothers, think about this! David
wasn't referring to himself when he spoke these
words I have quoted, for he died and was buried,
and his tomb is still here among us. 30 But he was
a prophet, and he knew God had promised with
an oath that one of David's own descendants
would sit on David's throne as the Messiah.
31 David was looking into the future and predict-
ing the Messiah's resurrection. He was saying
that the Messiah would not be left among the
dead and that his body would not rot in the
grave.
32 "This prophecy was speaking of Jesus,
whom God raised from the dead, and we all are
witnesses of this. 33 Now he sits on the throne of
highest honor in heaven, at God's right hand.
And the Father, as he had promised, gave him
the Holy Spirit to pour out upon us, just as you
see and hear today. 34 For David himself never
ascended into heaven, yet he said,

'The LORD said to my Lord,
Sit in honor at my right hand
35 until I humble your enemies,
making them a footstool under your
feet.'*

36 So let it be clearly known by everyone in Israel
that God has made this Jesus whom you crucified to be both Lord and Messiah!"
37 Peter's words convicted them deeply, and
they said to him and to the other apostles,
"Brothers, what should we do?"
38 Peter replied, "Each of you must turn from
your sins and turn to God, and be baptized in
the name of Jesus Christ for the forgiveness of
your sins. Then you will receive the gift of the
Holy Spirit. 39 This promise is to you and to your
children, and even to the Gentiles*—all who
have been called by the Lord our God." 40 Then
Peter continued preaching for a long time,
strongly urging all his listeners, "Save yourselves
from this generation that has gone astray!"
41 Those who believed what Peter said were
baptized and added to the church—about three
thousand in all. 42 They joined with the other
believers and devoted themselves to the apostles' teaching and fellowship, sharing in the
Lord's Supper and in prayer.

The Believers Meet Together

43 A deep sense of awe came over them all, and
the apostles performed many miraculous signs
and wonders. 44 And all the believers met together constantly and shared everything they
had. 45 They sold their possessions and shared
the proceeds with those in need. 46 They worshiped together at the Temple each day, met in
homes for the Lord's Supper, and shared their
meals with great joy and generosity—47 all the
while praising God and enjoying the goodwill of
all the people. And each day the Lord added to
their group those who were being saved.

CHAPTER 3

Peter Heals a Crippled Beggar

Peter and John went to the Temple one afternoon to take part in the three o'clock prayer
service. 2 As they approached the Temple, a man
lame from birth was being carried in. Each day
he was put beside the Temple gate, the one
called the Beautiful Gate, so he could beg from
the people going into the Temple. 3 When he saw
Peter and John about to enter, he asked them for
some money.
4 Peter and John looked at him intently, and
Peter said, "Look at us!" 5 The lame man looked
at them eagerly, expecting a gift. 6 But Peter said,
"I don't have any money for you. But I'll give
you what I have. In the name of Jesus Christ of
Nazareth, get up and walk!"
7 Then Peter took the lame man by the right
hand and helped him up. And as he did, the
man's feet and anklebones were healed and
strengthened. 8 He jumped up, stood on his feet,
and began to walk! Then, walking, leaping, and
praising God, he went into the Temple with
them.
9 All the people saw him walking and heard
him praising God. 10 When they realized he was
the lame beggar they had seen so often at the
Beautiful Gate, they were absolutely astounded!
11 They all rushed out to Solomon's Colonnade,
where he was holding tightly to Peter and John.
Everyone stood there in awe of the wonderful
thing that had happened.

Peter Preaches in the Temple

12 Peter saw his opportunity and addressed the
crowd. "People of Israel," he said, "what is so
astounding about this? And why look at us as
though we had made this man walk by our own
power and godliness? 13 For it is the God of

2:25-28 Ps 16:8-11. 2:34-35 Ps 110:1. 2:39 Greek *to those far away.*

Abraham, the God of Isaac, the God of Jacob,
the God of all our ancestors who has brought
glory to his servant Jesus by doing this. This is
the same Jesus whom you handed over and
rejected before Pilate, despite Pilate's decision to
release him. 14You rejected this holy, righteous
one and instead demanded the release of a murderer. 15You killed the author of life, but God
raised him to life. And we are witnesses of this
fact!

16"The name of Jesus has healed this man—
and you know how lame he was before. Faith in
Jesus' name has caused this healing before your
very eyes.

17"Friends,* I realize that what you did to
Jesus was done in ignorance; and the same can
be said of your leaders. 18But God was fulfilling
what all the prophets had declared about the
Messiah beforehand—that he must suffer all
these things. 19Now turn from your sins and
turn to God, so you can be cleansed of your sins.
20Then wonderful times of refreshment will
come from the presence of the Lord, and he will
send Jesus your Messiah to you again. 21For he
must remain in heaven until the time for the
final restoration of all things, as God promised
long ago through his prophets. 22Moses said,
'The Lord your God will raise up a Prophet like
me from among your own people. Listen carefully to everything he tells you.'* 23Then Moses
said, 'Anyone who will not listen to that Prophet
will be cut off from God's people and utterly
destroyed.'*

24"Starting with Samuel, every prophet spoke
about what is happening today. 25You are the
children of those prophets, and you are included
in the covenant God promised to your ancestors.
For God said to Abraham, 'Through your descendants all the families on earth will be blessed.'*
26When God raised up his servant, he sent him
first to you people of Israel, to bless you by
turning each of you back from your sinful ways."

CHAPTER 4

Peter and John before the Council

While Peter and John were speaking to the
people, the leading priests, the captain of the
Temple guard, and some of the Sadducees came
over to them. 2They were very disturbed that
Peter and John were claiming, on the authority
of Jesus, that there is a resurrection of the dead.
3They arrested them and, since it was already

3:17 Greek *Brothers.* 3:22 Deut 18:15. 3:23 Deut 18:19; Lev 23:29. 3:25 Gen 22:18.

What to Look for in a Church

Read ACTS 2:42, 44-47

The first-century church turned the world upside down with its message (see Acts 17:6, p. 159). What made the early church so dynamic was the commitment of its members to follow Christ wholeheartedly. When you look for a church to attend, make sure it has these five characteristics of a healthy church:

1. Look for a Church That Meets Together Regularly. The early believers did not view church as a social club, but as a place for devoted fellowship and valuable instruction. We miss out on a tremendous blessing when we neglect meeting together with God's people. When we are spiritually weak, we should not run *from* church but *to* church!

2. Look for a Church That Places a High Priority on Bible Study. The first-century Christians "devoted themselves to the apostles' teaching." The apostles' teachings on the life and ministry of Jesus eventually became the Gospel portion of the New Testament. Studying the Bible is important to every Christian's spiritual growth. Without Bible study, Christians cannot know and understand God's commands and truth.

3. Look for a Church That Is a Place of Corporate Worship and Prayer. The early church recognized the importance of corporate worship and prayer. Corporate worship focused their attention on the praiseworthy character of God and gave them an opportunity to express their thanks to God. Corporate prayer allowed them to express their thanks to God as well, but it was also an opportunity to seek God together and present their requests before him as a body.

4. Look for a Church That Looks after Its Members. The early believers shared food, clothing, and housing with each other. The Bible reminds us to care for fellow believers who are in need (see 2 Corinthians 9:1-15).

5. Look for a Church That Is Growing. Church growth is not our responsibility but God's. If we do our part as a church, God will do his. We see proof of this in verse 47.

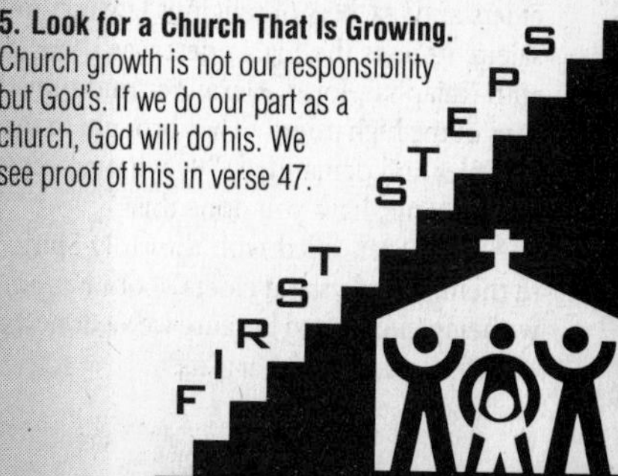

Jesus Has Great Power to Transform People Read ACTS 4:1-13

The entire book of Acts is a testimony to the transformation that takes place in the life of a true follower of Jesus Christ. Consider the case of Peter and John. Immediately after Christ's crucifixion, Peter and John went into hiding. In fact, Peter denied knowing Jesus three times before Jesus even died! These men were far from bold. Yet when Jesus came back to life, met with them, and told them to wait for the promised Holy Spirit once he returned to heaven, everything changed.

Why were Peter and John so bold? What made their witness so effective, and how can our lives be so dramatically transformed?

Peter and John Spent Time with Jesus. For three years Peter and John followed Jesus throughout Israel. During this time they saw Jesus perform many miracles. They also listened to his teaching and observed his lifestyle. But they weren't just casual observers. They talked with Jesus and shared their lives with him. In doing so, they made Jesus a significant part of their lives. Even though we did not walk alongside Jesus during his time on earth, we can invite him into our hearts. In addition, we have his teachings to study and the ability to spend time with him in prayer. In other words, we don't have to live in Bible times to have a relationship with Jesus.

Peter and John Modeled Their Lives after Jesus' Life and Teachings. Christ's life and resurrection had such an impact on Peter and John that they began to imitate Jesus in their behavior. We can see the impact Jesus made on these two disciples in the first few chapters of Acts. Here Peter and John speak boldly for Jesus in public, heal a crippled beggar, and endure persecution for Jesus. Their actions prove an important point: We need to put into practice what we have learned from spending time with Jesus.

Peter and John Put Their Confidence in Christ, Not in Their Own Abilities. Remember, Peter and John were common fishermen. They had no impressive credentials to flash in front of these people. They simply relied upon Jesus to guide them and help them through any obstacles, and that gave them all the confidence they needed. We should do no less.

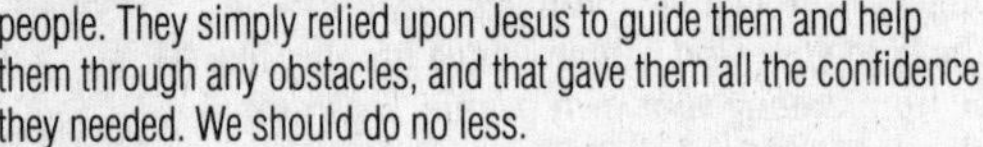

If you want to see the power of Jesus Christ in action today, take a look at some of the lives he has turned around. Some of the greatest evidence for Jesus Christ today consists of the countless lives that have been dramatically changed by his touch.

evening, jailed them until morning. [4]But many
of the people who heard their message believed
it, so that the number of believers totaled about
five thousand men, not counting women and
children.*

[5]The next day the council of all the rulers and
elders and teachers of religious law met in Jerusalem. [6]Annas the high priest was there, along
with Caiaphas, John, Alexander, and other relatives of the high priest. [7]They brought in the two
disciples and demanded, "By what power, or in
whose name, have you done this?"

[8]Then Peter, filled with the Holy Spirit, said
to them, "Leaders and elders of our nation, [9]are
we being questioned because we've done a good
deed for a crippled man? Do you want to know
how he was healed? [10]Let me clearly state to you
and to all the people of Israel that he was healed
in the name and power of Jesus Christ from
Nazareth, the man you crucified, but whom
God raised from the dead. [11]For Jesus is the one
referred to in the Scriptures, where it says,

'The stone that you builders rejected
has now become the cornerstone.'*

[12]There is salvation in no one else! There is no
other name in all of heaven for people to call on
to save them."

[13]The members of the council were amazed
when they saw the boldness of Peter and John,

4:4 Greek *5,000 adult males.* 4:11 Ps 118:22.

Why Is Jesus Christ the Only Way to God? Read ACTS 4:12

One of the most common criticisms of Christianity is that it is too narrow. Many people just cannot believe that there is only one way to heaven.

Because Christians have championed this truth, they have been criticized for implying that they are better than those who do not believe in Jesus Christ. But it is important to note that the reason Christians believe Jesus Christ is the only way to heaven is because he himself said it. Jesus said, "I am the way, the truth, and the life. No one can come to the Father except through me" (John 14:6).

If humankind could have reached God any other way, Jesus would not have had to die. His voluntary death on the cross clearly illustrates the fact that there is no other way. Those who reject his loving offer of forgiveness—which is extended to all of humankind—do so at their own peril.

for they could see that they were ordinary men who had had no special training. They also recognized them as men who had been with Jesus. 14But since the man who had been healed was standing right there among them, the council had nothing to say. 15So they sent Peter and John out of the council chamber* and conferred among themselves.

16"What should we do with these men?" they asked each other. "We can't deny they have done a miraculous sign, and everybody in Jerusalem knows about it. 17But perhaps we can stop them from spreading their propaganda. We'll warn them not to speak to anyone in Jesus' name again." 18So they called the apostles back in and told them never again to speak or teach about Jesus.

19But Peter and John replied, "Do you think God wants us to obey you rather than him? 20We cannot stop telling about the wonderful things we have seen and heard."

21The council then threatened them further, but they finally let them go because they didn't know how to punish them without starting a riot. For everyone was praising God 22for this miraculous sign—the healing of a man who had been lame for more than forty years.

The Believers Pray for Courage

23As soon as they were freed, Peter and John found the other believers and told them what the leading priests and elders had said. 24Then all the believers were united as they lifted their voices in prayer: "O Sovereign Lord, Creator of heaven and earth, the sea, and everything in them—25you spoke long ago by the Holy Spirit through our ancestor King David, your servant, saying,

'Why did the nations rage?
 Why did the people waste their time with
  futile plans?
26 The kings of the earth prepared for battle;
 the rulers gathered together
against the Lord
 and against his Messiah.'*

27"That is what has happened here in this city! For Herod Antipas, Pontius Pilate the governor, the Gentiles, and the people of Israel were all united against Jesus, your holy servant, whom you anointed. 28In fact, everything they did occurred according to your eternal will and plan. 29And now, O Lord, hear their threats, and give your servants great boldness in their preaching. 30Send your healing power; may miraculous signs and wonders be done through the name of your holy servant Jesus."

31After this prayer, the building where they were meeting shook, and they were all filled with the Holy Spirit. And they preached God's message with boldness.

4:15 Greek *the Sanhedrin.* 4:25-26 Ps 2:1-2.

When the Holy Spirit Can Be Sinned Against Read ACTS 5:1-10

One way Scripture supports the concept that the Holy Spirit is a person rather than a force is by showing how one can sin against him. It is important to understand that the Holy Spirit is indeed *God* at work and that to commit a sin against him is to commit a sin against God. In this passage we see one way in which we can sin against the Holy Spirit. But other passages inform us of at least five additional ways in which a person can sin against the Spirit.

1. Lying to the Holy Spirit. Ananias and Sapphira lied to the Holy Spirit by pretending to be thoroughly devoted to God when they really were not. One way people continue to do this today is by "going through the [spiritual] motions" without really meaning it in their hearts.

2. Grieving the Holy Spirit. Only believers can grieve the Holy Spirit (see Ephesians 4:30, p. 242). We grieve the Holy Spirit when we carry anger in our heart, slander others, or do things that we know go against the new nature that is inside of us.

3. Quenching the Holy Spirit. When the Holy Spirit convicts us of something we need to change in our life and we ignore his promptings, we are extinguishing his power in our life (1 Thessalonians 5:19). He is still in our life, but we are holding back from giving him complete control.

4. Resisting the Holy Spirit. When Stephen, the first recorded Christian martyr, spoke to his persecutors, he shared the message of Jesus Christ but closed with the words: "You stubborn people! . . . Must you forever resist the Holy Spirit?" (Acts 7:51). People who commit this sin may know that the Holy Spirit is trying to bring them to Jesus, but their pride keeps them from acknowledging Christ as Savior and Lord. The danger with this sin is that every time a person resists God's Spirit, he or she makes it more difficult for him or herself to come to Christ.

5. Insulting the Holy Spirit. To insult the Holy Spirit means to treat "the blood of the covenant as if it were common and unholy" (Hebrews 10:29). The person who commits this sin essentially dismisses the great price that Jesus paid for him or her at the cross of Calvary. This person has refused to accept the tremendous gift of salvation that God has offered to him or her.

6. Blaspheming the Holy Spirit. The two sins listed above, resisting and insulting the Holy

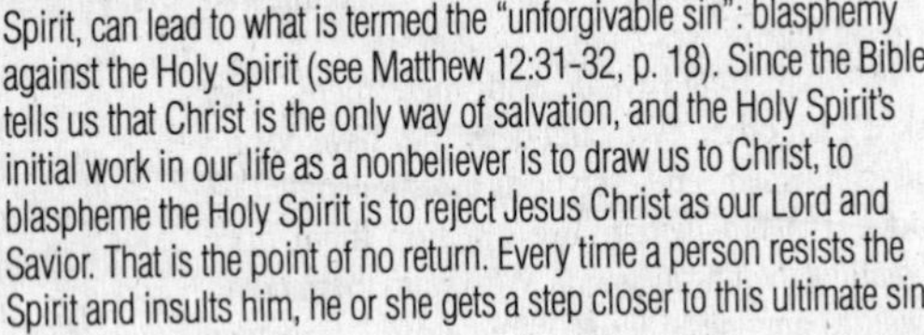

Spirit, can lead to what is termed the "unforgivable sin": blasphemy against the Holy Spirit (see Matthew 12:31-32, p. 18). Since the Bible tells us that Christ is the only way of salvation, and the Holy Spirit's initial work in our life as a nonbeliever is to draw us to Christ, to blaspheme the Holy Spirit is to reject Jesus Christ as our Lord and Savior. That is the point of no return. Every time a person resists the Spirit and insults him, he or she gets a step closer to this ultimate sin.

CORNERSTONES

The Believers Share Their Possessions
32All the believers were of one heart and mind,
and they felt that what they owned was not their
own; they shared everything they had. 33And the
apostles gave powerful witness to the resurrection of the Lord Jesus, and God's great favor was
upon them all. 34There was no poverty among
them, because people who owned land or
houses sold them 35and brought the money to
the apostles to give to others in need.
36For instance, there was Joseph, the one the
apostles nicknamed Barnabas (which means
"Son of Encouragement"). He was from the
tribe of Levi and came from the island of Cyprus.
37He sold a field he owned and brought the
money to the apostles for those in need.

CHAPTER **5**

Ananias and Sapphira
There was also a man named Ananias who, with
his wife, Sapphira, sold some property. 2He
brought part of the money to the apostles, but
he claimed it was the full amount. His wife had
agreed to this deception.
3Then Peter said, "Ananias, why has Satan
filled your heart? You lied to the Holy Spirit, and

Aren't Other Religions Just As Good As Christianity? Read ACTS 4:12

BIG QUESTIONS

Some people say that all religions basically say and teach the same thing, so they must all be "true." To quote another well-used phrase, "If a person is really sincere in what he or she believes, he or she will get to heaven."

In reality, all belief systems cannot be true, because they contradict one another. Many would like to think that all religions blend together beautifully, but they do not. Look at the differences between what the followers of three major world religions believe compared with what Christians believe.

The Existence of a Personal God.

- Buddhists deny the existence of a personal God.
- Hindus believe in two major gods, Vishnu and Siva, as well as in millions of lesser gods.
- Muslims believe in one God named Allah.
- Christians believe that God is a being who created humans in his own image and who loves them and wants to have a personal relationship with them.

The Subject of Salvation.

- Buddhists believe salvation is by self-effort only.
- Hindus believe you achieve salvation by devotion, works, and self-control.
- Muslims believe that people earn their own salvation and pay for their own sins.
- Christians believe that Jesus Christ died for their sins. If people turn from their sins and follow Jesus, they can be forgiven and have the hope of being with Jesus in heaven.

The Person of Jesus Christ.

- Buddhists believe that Jesus Christ was a good teacher, though less important then Buddha.
- Hindus believe that Jesus was just one of many incarnations—or sons —of God. Yet they also assert that Christ was not the unique Son of God. He was no more divine then any other man, and he did not die for people's sins.
- Muslims believe that Jesus Christ was the greatest of the prophets below Muhammad. In addition, they do not believe that Christ died for people's sin.
- Christians believe that Jesus is God as well as man, that he was sinless, and that he died to redeem humankind.

As you can see, you cannot believe in all of the major religious beliefs. That is because each religion eventually contradicts the claims of Christianity [Fritz Ridenour, *So What's the Difference?* (Glendale: Gospel Light Publications, 1967)].

you kept some of the money for yourself. 4The property was yours to sell or not sell, as you wished. And after selling it, the money was yours to give away. How could you do a thing like this? You weren't lying to us but to God."

5As soon as Ananias heard these words, he fell to the floor and died. Everyone who heard about it was terrified. 6Then some young men wrapped him in a sheet and took him out and buried him.

7About three hours later his wife came in, not knowing what had happened. 8Peter asked her, "Was this the price you and your husband received for your land?"

"Yes," she replied, "that was the price."

9And Peter said, "How could the two of you even think of doing a thing like this—conspiring together to test the Spirit of the Lord? Just outside that door are the young men who buried your husband, and they will carry you out, too."

10Instantly, she fell to the floor and died. When the young men came in and saw that she was dead, they carried her out and buried her beside her husband. 11Great fear gripped the entire church and all others who heard what had happened.

The Apostles Heal Many

12Meanwhile, the apostles were performing many miraculous signs and wonders among the people. And the believers were meeting regularly at the Temple in the area known as Solomon's Colonnade. 13No one else dared to join them, though everyone had high regard for them. 14And more and more people believed and were brought to the Lord—crowds of both men and women. 15As a result of the apostles' work, sick people were brought out into the streets on beds and mats so that Peter's shadow might fall across some of them as he went by. 16Crowds came in from the villages around Jerusalem, bringing their sick and those possessed by evil spirits, and they were all healed.

The Apostles Meet Opposition

17The high priest and his friends, who were Sadducees, reacted with violent jealousy. 18They arrested the apostles and put them in the jail. 19But an angel of the Lord came at night, opened the gates of the jail, and brought them out. Then he told them, 20"Go to the Temple and give the people this message of life!" 21So the apostles entered the Temple about daybreak and immediately began teaching.

When the high priest and his officials arrived, they convened the high council,* along with all the elders of Israel. Then they sent for the apostles to be brought for trial. 22But when the Temple guards went to the jail, the men were gone. So they returned to the council and reported, 23"The jail was locked, with the guards standing outside, but when we opened the gates, no one was there!"

24When the captain of the Temple guard and the leading priests heard this, they were perplexed, wondering where it would all end. 25Then someone arrived with the news that the men they had jailed were out in the Temple, teaching the people.

26The captain went with his Temple guards and arrested them, but without violence, for they were afraid the people would kill them if they treated the apostles roughly. 27Then they brought the apostles in before the council. 28"Didn't we tell you never again to teach in this man's name?" the high priest demanded. "Instead, you have filled all Jerusalem with your teaching about Jesus, and you intend to blame us for his death!"

29But Peter and the apostles replied, "We must obey God rather than human authority. 30The God of our ancestors raised Jesus from the dead after you killed him by crucifying him. 31Then God put him in the place of honor at his right hand as Prince and Savior. He did this to give the people of Israel an opportunity to turn from their sins and turn to God so their sins would be forgiven. 32We are witnesses of these things and so is the Holy Spirit, who is given by God to those who obey him."

33At this, the high council was furious and decided to kill them. 34But one member had a different perspective. He was a Pharisee named Gamaliel, who was an expert on religious law and was very popular with the people. He stood up and ordered that the apostles be sent outside the council chamber for a while. 35Then he addressed his colleagues as follows: "Men of Israel, take care what you are planning to do to these men! 36Some time ago there was that fellow Theudas, who pretended to be someone great. About four hundred others joined him, but he was killed, and his followers went their various ways. The whole movement came to nothing. 37After him, at the time of the census, there was Judas of Galilee. He got some people to follow him, but he was killed, too, and all his followers were scattered.

38"So my advice is, leave these men alone. If they are teaching and doing these things merely on their own, it will soon be overthrown. 39But if it is of God, you will not be able to stop them. You may even find yourselves fighting against God."

40The council accepted his advice. They called in the apostles and had them flogged. Then they ordered them never again to speak in the name of Jesus, and they let them go. 41The apostles left the high council rejoicing that God had counted them worthy to suffer dishonor for the name of Jesus. 42And every day, in the Temple and in their homes,* they continued to teach and preach this message: "The Messiah you are looking for is Jesus."

CHAPTER 6

Seven Men Chosen to Serve

But as the believers* rapidly multiplied, there were rumblings of discontent. Those who spoke Greek complained against those who spoke Hebrew, saying that their widows were being discriminated against in the daily distribution of food. 2So the Twelve called a meeting of all the believers.

"We apostles should spend our time preaching and teaching the word of God, not adminis-

5:21 Greek *Sanhedrin;* also in 5:27, 41. 5:42 Greek *from house to house.* 6:1 Greek *disciples;* also in 6:2, 7.

tering a food program," they said. 3"Now look around among yourselves, brothers, and select seven men who are well respected and are full of the Holy Spirit and wisdom. We will put them in charge of this business. 4Then we can spend our time in prayer and preaching and teaching the word."

5This idea pleased the whole group, and they chose the following: Stephen (a man full of faith and the Holy Spirit), Philip, Procorus, Nicanor, Timon, Parmenas, and Nicolas of Antioch (a Gentile convert to the Jewish faith, who had now become a Christian). 6These seven were presented to the apostles, who prayed for them as they laid their hands on them.

7God's message was preached in ever-widening circles. The number of believers greatly increased in Jerusalem, and many of the Jewish priests were converted, too.

Stephen Is Arrested

8Stephen, a man full of God's grace and power, performed amazing miracles and signs among the people. 9But one day some men from the Synagogue of Freed Slaves, as it was called, started to debate with him. They were Jews from Cyrene, Alexandria, Cilicia, and the province of Asia. 10None of them was able to stand against the wisdom and Spirit by which Stephen spoke.

11So they persuaded some men to lie about Stephen, saying, "We heard him blaspheme Moses, and even God." 12Naturally, this roused the crowds, the elders, and the teachers of religious law. So they arrested Stephen and brought him before the high council.* 13The lying witnesses said, "This man is always speaking against the Temple and against the law of Moses. 14We have heard him say that this Jesus of Nazareth will destroy the Temple and change the customs Moses handed down to us." 15At this point everyone in the council stared at Stephen because his face became as bright as an angel's.

CHAPTER 7

Stephen Addresses the Council

Then the high priest asked Stephen, "Are these accusations true?"

2This was Stephen's reply: "Brothers and honorable fathers, listen to me. Our glorious God appeared to our ancestor Abraham in Mesopotamia before he moved to Haran.* 3God told him, 'Leave your native land and your relatives, and come to the land that I will show you.'* 4So Abraham left the land of the Chaldeans and lived in Haran until his father died. Then God brought him here to the land where you now live. 5But God gave him no inheritance here, not even one square foot of land. God did promise, however, that eventually the whole country would belong to Abraham and his descendants—though he had no children yet. 6But God also told him that his descendants would live in a foreign country where they would be mistreated as slaves for four hundred years. 7'But I will punish the nation that enslaves them,' God told him, 'and in the end they will come out and worship me in this place.'* 8God also gave Abraham the covenant of circumcision at that time. And so Isaac, Abraham's son, was circumcised when he was eight days old. Isaac became the father of Jacob, and Jacob was the father of the twelve patriarchs of the Jewish nation.

9"These sons of Jacob were very jealous of their brother Joseph, and they sold him to be a slave in Egypt. But God was with him 10and delivered him from his anguish. And God gave him favor before Pharaoh, king of Egypt. God also gave Joseph unusual wisdom, so that Pharaoh appointed him governor over all of Egypt and put him in charge of all the affairs of the palace.

11"But a famine came upon Egypt and Canaan. There was great misery for our ancestors, as they ran out of food. 12Jacob heard that there was still grain in Egypt, so he sent his sons* to buy some. 13The second time they went, Joseph revealed his identity to his brothers, and they were introduced to Pharaoh. 14Then Joseph sent for his father, Jacob, and all his relatives to come to Egypt, seventy-five persons in all. 15So Jacob went to Egypt. He died there, as did all his sons. 16All of them were taken to Shechem and buried in the tomb Abraham had bought from the sons of Hamor in Shechem.

17"As the time drew near when God would fulfill his promise to Abraham, the number of our people in Egypt greatly increased. 18But then a new king came to the throne of Egypt who knew nothing about Joseph. 19This king plotted against our people and forced parents to abandon their newborn babies so they would die.

20"At that time Moses was born—a beautiful child in God's eyes. His parents cared for him at home for three months. 21When at last they had to abandon him, Pharaoh's daughter found him

6:12 Greek *Sanhedrin;* also in 6:15. 7:2 *Mesopotamia* was the region now called Iraq. *Haran* was a city in what is now called Syria. 7:3 Gen 12:1. 7:5-7 Gen 12:7; 15:13-14; Exod 3:12. 7:12 Greek *our fathers;* also in 7:15.

and raised him as her own son. 22Moses was
taught all the wisdom of the Egyptians, and he
became mighty in both speech and action.

23"One day when he was forty years old, he
decided to visit his relatives, the people of Israel.
24During this visit, he saw an Egyptian mistreat-
ing a man of Israel. So Moses came to his defense and avenged him, killing the Egyptian.
25Moses assumed his brothers would realize
that God had sent him to rescue them, but they
didn't.

26"The next day he visited them again and
saw two men of Israel fighting. He tried to be a
peacemaker. 'Men,' he said, 'you are brothers.
Why are you hurting each other?'

27"But the man in the wrong pushed Moses
aside and told him to mind his own business.
'Who made you a ruler and judge over us?' he
asked. 28'Are you going to kill me as you killed
that Egyptian yesterday?' 29When Moses heard
that, he fled the country and lived as a foreigner
in the land of Midian, where his two sons were
born.

30"Forty years later, in the desert near Mount
Sinai, an angel appeared to Moses in the flame
of a burning bush. 31Moses saw it and wondered
what it was. As he went to see, the voice of the
Lord called out to him, 32'I am the God of your
ancestors—the God of Abraham, Isaac, and
Jacob.' Moses shook with terror and dared not
look.

33"And the Lord said to him, 'Take off your
sandals, for you are standing on holy ground.
34You can be sure that I have seen the misery of
my people in Egypt. I have heard their cries. So
I have come to rescue them. Now go, for I will
send you to Egypt.'* 35And so God sent back the
same man his people had previously rejected by
demanding, 'Who made you a ruler and judge
over us?' Through the angel who appeared to
him in the burning bush, Moses was sent to be
their ruler and savior. 36And by means of many
miraculous signs and wonders, he led them out
of Egypt, through the Red Sea, and back and
forth through the wilderness for forty years.

37"Moses himself told the people of Israel,
'God will raise up a Prophet like me from
among your own people.'* 38Moses was with
the assembly of God's people in the wilderness.
He was the mediator between the people of
Israel and the angel who gave him life-giving
words on Mount Sinai to pass on to us.

39"But our ancestors rejected Moses and
wanted to return to Egypt. 40They told Aaron,
'Make us some gods who can lead us, for we
don't know what has become of this Moses, who
brought us out of Egypt.' 41So they made an idol
shaped like a calf, and they sacrificed to it and
rejoiced in this thing they had made. 42Then
God turned away from them and gave them up
to serve the sun, moon, and stars as their gods!
In the book of the prophets it is written,

'Was it to me you were bringing sacrifices
  during those forty years in the
    wilderness, Israel?
43 No, your real interest was in your pagan
    gods—
  the shrine of Molech,
  the star god Rephan,
  and the images you made to worship
    them.
So I will send you into captivity
  far away in Babylon.'*

44"Our ancestors carried the Tabernacle*
with them through the wilderness. It was con-
structed in exact accordance with the plan
shown to Moses by God. 45Years later, when
Joshua led the battles against the Gentile nations that God drove out of this land, the Tabernacle was taken with them into their new
territory. And it was used there until the time of
King David.

46"David found favor with God and asked for
the privilege of building a permanent Temple
for the God of Jacob.* 47But it was Solomon
who actually built it. 48However, the Most High
doesn't live in temples made by human hands.
As the prophet says,

49 'Heaven is my throne,
    and the earth is my footstool.
  Could you ever build me a temple as good
      as that?'
    asks the Lord.
  'Could you build a dwelling place for me?
50 Didn't I make everything in heaven and
      earth?'*

51"You stubborn people! You are heathen at
heart and deaf to the truth. Must you forever
resist the Holy Spirit? But your ancestors did,
and so do you! 52Name one prophet your ancestors didn't persecute! They even killed the ones
who predicted the coming of the Righteous
One—the Messiah whom you betrayed and

7:31-34 Exod 3:5-10. 7:37 Deut 18:15. 7:42-43 Amos 5:25-27. 7:44 Greek *the tent of witness.* 7:46 Some manuscripts read *the house of Jacob.* 7:49-50 Isa 66:1-2.

murdered. 53You deliberately disobeyed God's
law, though you received it from the hands of
angels.*"
54The Jewish leaders were infuriated by Stephen's accusation, and they shook their fists in
rage.* 55But Stephen, full of the Holy Spirit,
gazed steadily upward into heaven and saw the
glory of God, and he saw Jesus standing in the
place of honor at God's right hand. 56And he
told them, "Look, I see the heavens opened and
the Son of Man standing in the place of honor
at God's right hand!"
57Then they put their hands over their ears,
and drowning out his voice with their shouts,
they rushed at him. 58They dragged him out of
the city and began to stone him. The official
witnesses took off their coats and laid them at
the feet of a young man named Saul.*
59And as they stoned him, Stephen prayed,
"Lord Jesus, receive my spirit." 60And he fell to
his knees, shouting, "Lord, don't charge them
with this sin!" And with that, he died.

CHAPTER 8

Saul was one of the official witnesses at the
killing of Stephen.

Persecution Scatters the Believers

A great wave of persecution began that day,
sweeping over the church in Jerusalem, and all
the believers except the apostles fled into Judea
and Samaria. 2(Some godly men came and
buried Stephen with loud weeping.) 3Saul was
going everywhere to devastate the church. He
went from house to house, dragging out both
men and women to throw them into jail.

Philip Preaches in Samaria

4But the believers who had fled Jerusalem went
everywhere preaching the Good News about
Jesus. 5Philip, for example, went to the city of
Samaria and told the people there about the
Messiah. 6Crowds listened intently to what he
had to say because of the miracles he did. 7Many
evil spirits were cast out, screaming as they left
their victims. And many who had been paralyzed or lame were healed. 8So there was great
joy in that city.
9A man named Simon had been a sorcerer
there for many years, claiming to be someone
great. 10The Samaritan people, from the least to

7:53 Greek *received the Law as it was ordained by angels.* 7:54 Greek *they were grinding their teeth against him.* 7:58 *Saul* is later called Paul; see 13:9.

Be Open to God's Leading

Read ACTS 8:4-8, 26-38

This text shows two forms of evangelism. In the beginning of this passage, we see Philip engaged in "mass evangelism" (verses 4-8). Toward the end of the chapter, we see Philip taking part in personal, "one-on-one evangelism" with the Ethiopian (verses 26-38). The text also gives us three principles to follow for effective evangelism:

1. Philip Was Led by God's Spirit. This principle (verse 29) can make all the difference in sharing one's faith. This leading will often come in the form of an "impression" or a burden—such as a compelling desire to talk to someone about your faith (see Acts 17:16-31, pp. 159–160). Like Philip, we should simply be open and available to what God would have us to do.

2. Philip Obeyed God's Leading. Philip did exactly what the Lord told him to do without delay (verse 27). Jesus said, "My sheep recognize my voice; I know them, and they follow me" (John 10:27). So when God said, "Go," Philip went! Likewise, we need to be on duty at all times, ready to "preach the word of God" (2 Timothy 4:2).

3. Philip Knew Scripture. Philip used the Scripture this man was reading as a starting point. Then he used a number of other passages to tell the Ethiopian about Jesus (verse 35). Knowing God's Word is essential for any person who wants to lead others to Jesus Christ. Arguments will not have nearly the impact that God's Word will when we share our faith with others.

The same God who led Philip in his evangelistic work also wants to direct your steps. You might start each day with a prayer like the prophet Isaiah: "Lord, I'll go! Send me" (Isaiah 6:8). Remember, God is not looking so much for a person's ability as his or her availability. God is not looking for "strong" people to be his witnesses so much as he is looking for people through whom he can show his strength.

the greatest, often spoke of him as "the Great One—the Power of God." 11He was very influential because of the magic he performed. 12But now the people believed Philip's message of Good News concerning the Kingdom of God and the name of Jesus Christ. As a result, many men and women were baptized. 13Then Simon himself believed and was baptized. He began following Philip wherever he went, and he was amazed by the great miracles and signs Philip performed.

14When the apostles back in Jerusalem heard that the people of Samaria had accepted God's message, they sent Peter and John there. 15As soon as they arrived, they prayed for these new Christians to receive the Holy Spirit. 16The Holy Spirit had not yet come upon any of them, for they had only been baptized in the name of the Lord Jesus. 17Then Peter and John laid their hands upon these believers, and they received the Holy Spirit.

18When Simon saw that the Holy Spirit was given when the apostles placed their hands upon people's heads, he offered money to buy this power. 19"Let me have this power, too," he exclaimed, "so that when I lay my hands on people, they will receive the Holy Spirit!"

20But Peter replied, "May your money perish with you for thinking God's gift can be bought! 21You can have no part in this, for your heart is not right before God. 22Turn from your wickedness and pray to the Lord. Perhaps he will forgive your evil thoughts, 23for I can see that you are full of bitterness and held captive by sin."

24"Pray to the Lord for me," Simon exclaimed, "that these terrible things won't happen to me!"

25After testifying and preaching the word of the Lord in Samaria, Peter and John returned to Jerusalem. And they stopped in many Samaritan villages along the way to preach the Good News to them, too.

Philip and the Ethiopian Eunuch

26As for Philip, an angel of the Lord said to him, "Go south* down the desert road that runs from Jerusalem to Gaza." 27So he did, and he met the treasurer of Ethiopia, a eunuch of great authority under the queen of Ethiopia.* The eunuch had gone to Jerusalem to worship, 28and he was now returning. Seated in his carriage, he was reading aloud from the book of the prophet Isaiah.

29The Holy Spirit said to Philip, "Go over and walk along beside the carriage."

30Philip ran over and heard the man reading from the prophet Isaiah; so he asked, "Do you understand what you are reading?"

31The man replied, "How can I, when there is no one to instruct me?" And he begged Philip to come up into the carriage and sit with him. 32The passage of Scripture he had been reading was this:

"He was led as a sheep to the slaughter.
And as a lamb is silent before the shearers,
he did not open his mouth.
33 He was humiliated and received no justice.
Who can speak of his descendants?
For his life was taken from the earth."*

34The eunuch asked Philip, "Was Isaiah talking about himself or someone else?" 35So Philip began with this same Scripture and then used many others to tell him the Good News about Jesus.

36As they rode along, they came to some water, and the eunuch said, "Look! There's some water! Why can't I be baptized?"* 38He ordered the carriage to stop, and they went down into the water, and Philip baptized him.

39When they came up out of the water, the Spirit of the Lord caught Philip away. The eunuch never saw him again but went on his way rejoicing. 40Meanwhile, Philip found himself farther north at the city of Azotus! He preached the Good News there and in every city along the way until he came to Caesarea.

CHAPTER 9

Saul's Conversion

Meanwhile, Saul was uttering threats with every breath. He was eager to destroy the Lord's followers,* so he went to the high priest. 2He requested letters addressed to the synagogues in Damascus, asking their cooperation in the arrest of any followers of the Way he found there. He wanted to bring them—both men and women—back to Jerusalem in chains.

3As he was nearing Damascus on this mission, a brilliant light from heaven suddenly beamed down upon him! 4He fell to the ground and heard a voice saying to him, "Saul! Saul! Why are you persecuting me?"

8:26 Or *Go at noon.* 8:27 Greek *under the Candace, the queen of Ethiopia.* 8:32-33 Isa 53:7-8. 8:36 Some manuscripts add verse 37, *"You can," Philip answered, "if you believe with all your heart." And the eunuch replied, "I believe that Jesus Christ is the Son of God."* 9:1 Greek *disciples.*

5 "Who are you, sir?" Saul asked.

And the voice replied, "I am Jesus, the one you are persecuting! 6 Now get up and go into the city, and you will be told what you are to do."

7 The men with Saul stood speechless with surprise, for they heard the sound of someone's voice, but they saw no one! 8 As Saul picked himself up off the ground, he found that he was blind. 9 So his companions led him by the hand to Damascus. He remained there blind for three days. And all that time he went without food and water.

10 Now there was a believer* in Damascus named Ananias. The Lord spoke to him in a vision, calling, "Ananias!"

"Yes, Lord!" he replied.

11 The Lord said, "Go over to Straight Street, to the house of Judas. When you arrive, ask for Saul of Tarsus. He is praying to me right now. 12 I have shown him a vision of a man named Ananias coming in and laying his hands on him so that he can see again."

13 "But Lord," exclaimed Ananias, "I've heard about the terrible things this man has done to the believers in Jerusalem! 14 And we hear that he is authorized by the leading priests to arrest every believer in Damascus."

15 But the Lord said, "Go and do what I say. For Saul is my chosen instrument to take my message to the Gentiles and to kings, as well as to the people of Israel. 16 And I will show him how much he must suffer for me."

17 So Ananias went and found Saul. He laid his hands on him and said, "Brother Saul, the Lord Jesus, who appeared to you on the road, has sent me so that you may get your sight back and be filled with the Holy Spirit." 18 Instantly something like scales fell from Saul's eyes, and he regained his sight. Then he got up and was baptized. 19 Afterward he ate some food and was strengthened.

Saul in Damascus and Jerusalem

Saul stayed with the believers* in Damascus for a few days. 20 And immediately he began preaching about Jesus in the synagogues, saying, "He is indeed the Son of God!"

21 All who heard him were amazed. "Isn't this the same man who persecuted Jesus' followers with such devastation in Jerusalem?" they asked. "And we understand that he came here to arrest them and take them in chains to the leading priests."

22 Saul's preaching became more and more powerful, and the Jews in Damascus couldn't refute his proofs that Jesus was indeed the Messiah. 23 After a while the Jewish leaders decided to kill him. 24 But Saul was told about their plot, and that they were watching for him day and night at the city gate so they could murder him. 25 So during the night, some of the other believers* let him down in a large basket through an opening in the city wall.

26 When Saul arrived in Jerusalem, he tried to meet with the believers, but they were all afraid of him. They thought he was only pretending to be a believer! 27 Then Barnabas brought him to the apostles and told them how Saul had seen the Lord on the way to Damascus. Barnabas also told them what the Lord had said to Saul and how he boldly preached in the name of Jesus in Damascus. 28 Then the apostles accepted Saul, and after that he was constantly with them in Jerusalem, preaching boldly in the name of the Lord. 29 He debated with some Greek-speaking Jews, but they plotted to murder him. 30 When the believers* heard about it, however, they took him to Caesarea and sent him on to his hometown of Tarsus.

31 The church then had peace throughout Judea, Galilee, and Samaria, and it grew in strength and numbers. The believers were walking in the fear of the Lord and in the comfort of the Holy Spirit.

Peter Heals Aeneas and Raises Dorcas

32 Peter traveled from place to place to visit the believers, and in his travels he came to the Lord's people in the town of Lydda. 33 There he met a man named Aeneas, who had been paralyzed and bedridden for eight years. 34 Peter said to him, "Aeneas, Jesus Christ heals you! Get up and make your bed!" And he was healed instantly. 35 Then the whole population of Lydda and Sharon turned to the Lord when they saw Aeneas walking around.

36 There was a believer in Joppa named Tabitha (which in Greek is Dorcas*). She was always doing kind things for others and helping the poor. 37 About this time she became ill and died. Her friends prepared her for burial and laid her in an upstairs room. 38 But they had heard that Peter was nearby at Lydda, so they sent two men to beg him, "Please come as soon as possible!"

9:10 Greek *disciple;* also in 9:36. 9:19 Greek *disciples;* also in 9:26. 9:25 Greek *his disciples.* 9:30 Greek *brothers.* 9:36 The names *Tabitha* in Aramaic and *Dorcas* in Greek both mean "gazelle."

39So Peter returned with them; and as soon as he arrived, they took him to the upstairs room. The room was filled with widows who were weeping and showing him the coats and other garments Dorcas had made for them. 40But Peter asked them all to leave the room; then he knelt and prayed. Turning to the body he said, "Get up, Tabitha." And she opened her eyes! When she saw Peter, she sat up! 41He gave her his hand and helped her up. Then he called in the widows and all the believers, and he showed them that she was alive.

42The news raced through the whole town, and many believed in the Lord. 43And Peter stayed a long time in Joppa, living with Simon, a leatherworker.

CHAPTER 10

Cornelius Calls for Peter

In Caesarea there lived a Roman army officer named Cornelius, who was a captain of the Italian Regiment. 2He was a devout man who feared the God of Israel, as did his entire household. He gave generously to charity and was a man who regularly prayed to God. 3One afternoon about three o'clock, he had a vision in which he saw an angel of God coming toward him. "Cornelius!" the angel said.

4Cornelius stared at him in terror. "What is it, sir?" he asked the angel.

And the angel replied, "Your prayers and gifts to the poor have not gone unnoticed by God! 5Now send some men down to Joppa to find a man named Simon Peter. 6He is staying with Simon, a leatherworker who lives near the shore. Ask him to come and visit you."

7As soon as the angel was gone, Cornelius called two of his household servants and a devout soldier, one of his personal attendants. 8He told them what had happened and sent them off to Joppa.

Peter Visits Cornelius

9The next day as Cornelius's messengers were nearing the city, Peter went up to the flat roof to pray. It was about noon, 10and he was hungry. But while lunch was being prepared, he fell into a trance. 11He saw the sky open, and something like a large sheet was let down by its four corners. 12In the sheet were all sorts of animals, reptiles, and birds. 13Then a voice said to him, "Get up, Peter; kill and eat them."

14"Never, Lord," Peter declared. "I have never in all my life eaten anything forbidden by our Jewish laws.*"

15The voice spoke again, "If God says something is acceptable, don't say it isn't."* 16The same vision was repeated three times. Then the sheet was pulled up again to heaven.

17Peter was very perplexed. What could the vision mean? Just then the men sent by Cornelius found the house and stood outside at the gate. 18They asked if this was the place where Simon Peter was staying. 19Meanwhile, as Peter was puzzling over the vision, the Holy Spirit said to him, "Three men have come looking for you. 20Go down and go with them without hesitation. All is well, for I have sent them."

21So Peter went down and said, "I'm the man you are looking for. Why have you come?"

22They said, "We were sent by Cornelius, a Roman officer. He is a devout man who fears the God of Israel and is well respected by all the Jews. A holy angel instructed him to send for you so you can go to his house and give him a message." 23So Peter invited the men to be his guests for the night. The next day he went with them, accompanied by some other believers* from Joppa.

24They arrived in Caesarea the following day. Cornelius was waiting for him and had called together his relatives and close friends to meet Peter. 25As Peter entered his home, Cornelius fell to the floor before him in worship. 26But Peter pulled him up and said, "Stand up! I'm a human being like you!" 27So Cornelius got up, and they talked together and went inside where the others were assembled.

28Peter told them, "You know it is against the Jewish laws for me to come into a Gentile home like this. But God has shown me that I should never think of anyone as impure. 29So I came as soon as I was sent for. Now tell me why you sent for me."

30Cornelius replied, "Four days ago I was praying in my house at three o'clock in the afternoon. Suddenly, a man in dazzling clothes was standing in front of me. 31He told me, 'Cornelius, your prayers have been heard, and your gifts to the poor have been noticed by God! 32Now send some men to Joppa and summon Simon Peter. He is staying in the home of Simon, a leatherworker who lives near the shore.' 33So I sent for you at once, and it was good of you to come. Now here we are, waiting before God to hear the message the Lord has given you."

10:14 Greek *anything common and unclean.* **10:15** Greek *"What God calls clean you must not call unclean."* **10:23** Greek *brothers.*

The Gentiles Hear the Good News

[34]Then Peter replied, "I see very clearly that God doesn't show partiality. [35]In every nation he accepts those who fear him and do what is right. [36]I'm sure you have heard about the Good News for the people of Israel—that there is peace with God through Jesus Christ, who is Lord of all. [37]You know what happened all through Judea, beginning in Galilee after John the Baptist began preaching. [38]And no doubt you know that God anointed Jesus of Nazareth with the Holy Spirit and with power. Then Jesus went around doing good and healing all who were oppressed by the Devil, for God was with him.

[39]"And we apostles are witnesses of all he did throughout Israel and in Jerusalem. They put him to death by crucifying him, [40]but God raised him to life three days later. Then God allowed him to appear, [41]not to the general public,* but to us whom God had chosen beforehand to be his witnesses. We were those who ate and drank with him after he rose from the dead. [42]And he ordered us to preach everywhere and to testify that Jesus is ordained of God to be the judge of all—the living and the dead. [43]He is the one all the prophets testified about, saying that everyone who believes in him will have their sins forgiven through his name."

The Gentiles Receive the Holy Spirit

[44]Even as Peter was saying these things, the Holy Spirit fell upon all who had heard the message. [45]The Jewish believers who came with Peter were amazed that the gift of the Holy Spirit had been poured out upon the Gentiles, too. [46]And there could be no doubt about it, for they heard them speaking in tongues and praising God.

Then Peter asked, [47]"Can anyone object to their being baptized, now that they have received the Holy Spirit just as we did?" [48]So he gave orders for them to be baptized in the name of Jesus Christ. Afterward Cornelius asked him to stay with them for several days.

CHAPTER **11**

Peter Explains His Actions

Soon the news reached the apostles and other believers* in Judea that the Gentiles had received the word of God. [2]But when Peter arrived back in Jerusalem, some of the Jewish believers* criticized him. [3]"You entered the home of Gentiles* and even ate with them!" they said.

[4]Then Peter told them exactly what had happened. [5]"One day in Joppa," he said, "while I was praying, I went into a trance and saw a vision. Something like a large sheet was let down by its four corners from the sky. And it came right down to me. [6]When I looked inside the sheet, I saw all sorts of small animals, wild animals, reptiles, and birds that we are not allowed to eat. [7]And I heard a voice say, 'Get up, Peter; kill and eat them.'

[8]" 'Never, Lord,' I replied. 'I have never eaten anything forbidden by our Jewish laws.*'

[9]"But the voice from heaven came again, 'If God says something is acceptable, don't say it isn't.'*

[10]"This happened three times before the sheet and all it contained was pulled back up to heaven. [11]Just then three men who had been sent from Caesarea arrived at the house where I was staying. [12]The Holy Spirit told me to go with them and not to worry about their being Gentiles. These six brothers here accompanied me, and we soon arrived at the home of the man who had sent for us. [13]He told us how an angel had appeared to him in his home and had told him, 'Send messengers to Joppa to find Simon Peter. [14]He will tell you how you and all your household will be saved!'

[15]"Well, I began telling them the Good News, but just as I was getting started, the Holy Spirit fell on them, just as he fell on us at the beginning. [16]Then I thought of the Lord's words when he said, 'John baptized with* water, but you will be baptized with the Holy Spirit.' [17]And since God gave these Gentiles the same gift he gave us when we believed in the Lord Jesus Christ, who was I to argue?"

[18]When the others heard this, all their objections were answered and they began praising God. They said, "God has also given the Gentiles the privilege of turning from sin and receiving eternal life."

The Church in Antioch of Syria

[19]Meanwhile, the believers who had fled from Jerusalem during the persecution after Stephen's death traveled as far as Phoenicia, Cyprus, and Antioch of Syria. They preached the Good News, but only to Jews. [20]However, some of the believers who went to Antioch from Cyprus and Cyrene began preaching to Gentiles* about the

10:41 Greek *the people.* 11:1 Greek *brothers.* 11:2 Greek *those of the circumcision.* 11:3 Greek *of uncircumcised men.* 11:8 Greek *anything common or unclean.* 11:9 Greek *'What God calls clean you must not call unclean.'* 11:16 Or *in;* also in 11:16b. 11:20 Greek *the Greeks;* other manuscripts read *the Hellenists.*

Lord Jesus. 21The power of the Lord was upon them, and large numbers of these Gentiles believed and turned to the Lord.

22When the church at Jerusalem heard what had happened, they sent Barnabas to Antioch. 23When he arrived and saw this proof of God's favor, he was filled with joy, and he encouraged the believers to stay true to the Lord. 24Barnabas was a good man, full of the Holy Spirit and strong in faith. And large numbers of people were brought to the Lord.

25Then Barnabas went on to Tarsus to find Saul. 26When he found him, he brought him back to Antioch. Both of them stayed there with the church for a full year, teaching great numbers of people. (It was there at Antioch that the believers* were first called Christians.)

27During this time, some prophets traveled from Jerusalem to Antioch. 28One of them named Agabus stood up in one of the meetings to predict by the Spirit that a great famine was coming upon the entire Roman world. (This was fulfilled during the reign of Claudius.) 29So the believers in Antioch decided to send relief to the brothers and sisters* in Judea, everyone giving as much as they could. 30This they did, entrusting their gifts to Barnabas and Saul to take to the elders of the church in Jerusalem.

CHAPTER 12

James Is Killed and Peter Is Imprisoned

About that time King Herod Agrippa* began to persecute some believers in the church. 2He had the apostle James (John's brother) killed with a sword. 3When Herod saw how much this pleased the Jewish leaders, he arrested Peter during the Passover celebration* 4and imprisoned him, placing him under the guard of four squads of four soldiers each. Herod's intention was to bring Peter out for public trial after the Passover. 5But while Peter was in prison, the church prayed very earnestly for him.

Peter's Miraculous Escape from Prison

6The night before Peter was to be placed on trial, he was asleep, chained between two soldiers, with others standing guard at the prison gate. 7Suddenly, there was a bright light in the cell, and an angel of the Lord stood before Peter. The angel tapped him on the side to awaken him and said, "Quick! Get up!" And the chains fell off his wrists. 8Then the angel told him, "Get dressed and put on your sandals." And he did. "Now put on your coat and follow me," the angel ordered.

9So Peter left the cell, following the angel. But all the time he thought it was a vision. He didn't realize it was really happening. 10They passed the first and second guard posts and came to the iron gate to the street, and this opened to them all by itself. So they passed through and started walking down the street, and then the angel suddenly left him.

11Peter finally realized what had happened. "It's really true!" he said to himself. "The Lord has sent his angel and saved me from Herod and from what the Jews were hoping to do to me!"

12After a little thought, he went to the home of Mary, the mother of John Mark, where many were gathered for prayer. 13He knocked at the door in the gate, and a servant girl named Rhoda

11:26 Greek *disciples;* also in 11:29. 11:29 Greek *the brothers.* 12:1 Greek *Herod the king.* He was the nephew of Herod Antipas and a grandson of Herod the Great. 12:3 Greek *the days of unleavened bread.*

OFF AND RUNNING

Pray Effectively Read ACTS 12:1-17

This Bible story vividly illustrates how God works in response to the prayers of his people. Though all appeared hopeless for Peter, the body of believers did all that they could for him—they called on God. What made the prayers of these believers so effective? Their secret is found in verse 5. There we see the three basic steps these Christians took in response to what appeared to be a hopeless situation:

1. They Directed Their Prayer to God. Ironically, many times our prayers often contain little thought of God himself. We fill our mind with thoughts about our own needs instead of our heavenly Father. But Jesus himself encouraged us to respectfully consider whom we are praying to when he gave us the Lord's Prayer (see Matthew 6:9-13, p. 9). This will allow you to take your eyes off of your dilemma and to place them on Jesus, and it will also help to align your will or desire with his.

2. They Prayed Earnestly. These believers offered constant, fervent prayer on Peter's behalf. Another way

came to open it. [14]When she recognized Peter's voice, she was so overjoyed that, instead of opening the door, she ran back inside and told everyone, "Peter is standing at the door!"

[15]"You're out of your mind," they said. When she insisted, they decided, "It must be his angel."

[16]Meanwhile, Peter continued knocking. When they finally went out and opened the door, they were amazed. [17]He motioned for them to quiet down and told them what had happened and how the Lord had led him out of jail. "Tell James and the other brothers what happened," he said. And then he went to another place.

[18]At dawn, there was a great commotion among the soldiers about what had happened to Peter. [19]Herod Agrippa ordered a thorough search for him. When he couldn't be found, Herod interrogated the guards and sentenced them to death. Afterward Herod left Judea to stay in Caesarea for a while.

The Death of Herod Agrippa

[20]Now Herod was very angry with the people of Tyre and Sidon. So they sent a delegation to make peace with him because their cities were dependent upon Herod's country for their food. They made friends with Blastus, Herod's personal assistant, [21]and an appointment with Herod was granted. When the day arrived, Herod put on his royal robes, sat on his throne, and made a speech to them. [22]The people gave him a great ovation, shouting, "It is the voice of a god, not of a man!"

[23]Instantly, an angel of the Lord struck Herod with a sickness, because he accepted the people's worship instead of giving the glory to God. So he was consumed with worms and died.

[24]But God's Good News was spreading rapidly, and there were many new believers.

[25]When Barnabas and Saul had finished their mission in Jerusalem, they returned to Antioch, taking John Mark with them.

CHAPTER 13

Barnabas and Saul Are Sent Out

Among the prophets and teachers of the church at Antioch of Syria were Barnabas, Simeon (called "the black man"*), Lucius (from Cyrene), Manaen (the childhood companion of King Herod Antipas*), and Saul. [2]One day as these men were worshiping the Lord and fasting, the Holy Spirit said, "Dedicate Barnabas and Saul for the special work I have for them." [3]So after more fasting and prayer, the men laid their hands on them and sent them on their way.

Paul's First Missionary Journey

[4]Sent out by the Holy Spirit, Saul and Barnabas went down to the seaport of Seleucia and then sailed for the island of Cyprus. [5]There, in the town of Salamis, they went to the Jewish synagogues and preached the word of God. (John Mark went with them as their assistant.)

[6]Afterward they preached from town to town across the entire island until finally they reached Paphos, where they met a Jewish sorcerer, a false prophet named Bar-Jesus. [7]He had attached himself to the governor, Sergius Paulus, a man of considerable insight and understanding. The governor invited Barnabas and Saul to visit him, for he wanted to hear the word of God. [8]But

13:1a Greek *who was called Niger.* **13:1b** Greek *Herod the tetrarch.*

to translate this verse is, "They prayed with agony." It is the same phrase used to describe the way Jesus prayed in the garden of Gethsemane. Their prayers had intensity. Many of our prayers have no power because they have little or no heart in them. If we put so little heart into our prayers, we cannot expect God to put much heart into answering them.

3. They Prayed as a Body. There is power in united prayer. Jesus said in Matthew 18:19, "I also tell you this: If two of you agree down here on earth concerning anything you ask, my Father in heaven will do it for you." What Jesus meant is that if two or more people who share the same God-given burden are sure of God's will and are in agreement with the Spirit of God and one another as they pray—they will see dynamic results.

Someone once said, "Satan trembles when he sees the weakest saint upon his knees." If you are in a bleak situation today, consider how God worked through the prayers of these early Christians. Don't give up. If you follow these principles, you will see results done God's way and in God's timing.

Elymas, the sorcerer (as his name means in
Greek), interfered and urged the governor to pay
no attention to what Saul and Barnabas said. He
was trying to turn the governor away from the
Christian faith.

9Then Saul, also known as Paul, filled with
the Holy Spirit, looked the sorcerer in the eye
and said, 10"You son of the Devil, full of every
sort of trickery and villainy, enemy of all that is
good, will you never stop perverting the true
ways of the Lord? 11And now the Lord has laid
his hand of punishment upon you, and you will
be stricken awhile with blindness." Instantly
mist and darkness fell upon him, and he began
wandering around begging for someone to take
his hand and lead him. 12When the governor
saw what had happened, he believed and was
astonished at what he learned about the Lord.

Paul Preaches in Antioch of Pisidia

13Now Paul and those with him left Paphos by
ship for Pamphylia,* landing at the port town of
Perga. There John Mark left them and returned
to Jerusalem. 14But Barnabas and Paul traveled
inland to Antioch of Pisidia.*

On the Sabbath they went to the synagogue
for the services. 15After the usual readings from
the books of Moses and from the Prophets,
those in charge of the service sent them this
message: "Brothers, if you have any word of
encouragement for us, come and give it!"

16So Paul stood, lifted his hand to quiet
them, and started speaking. "People of Israel,"
he said, "and you devout Gentiles who fear the
God of Israel, listen to me.

17"The God of this nation of Israel chose our
ancestors and made them prosper in Egypt.
Then he powerfully led them out of their slavery.
18He put up with them* through forty years of
wandering around in the wilderness. 19Then he
destroyed seven nations in Canaan and gave
their land to Israel as an inheritance. 20All this
took about 450 years. After that, judges ruled
until the time of Samuel the prophet. 21Then the
people begged for a king, and God gave them
Saul son of Kish, a man of the tribe of Benjamin,
who reigned for forty years. 22But God removed
him from the kingship and replaced him with
David, a man about whom God said, 'David son
of Jesse is a man after my own heart, for he will
do everything I want him to.'*

23"And it is one of King David's descendants,
Jesus, who is God's promised Savior of Israel!
24But before he came, John the Baptist preached
the need for everyone in Israel to turn from sin
and turn to God and be baptized. 25As John was
finishing his ministry he asked, 'Do you think I
am the Messiah? No! But he is coming soon—
and I am not even worthy to be his slave.*'

26"Brothers—you sons of Abraham, and also
all of you devout Gentiles who fear the God of
Israel—this salvation is for us! 27The people in
Jerusalem and their leaders fulfilled prophecy by
condemning Jesus to death. They didn't recognize him or realize that he is the one the prophets had written about, though they hear the
prophets' words read every Sabbath. 28They
found no just cause to execute him, but they
asked Pilate to have him killed anyway.

29"When they had fulfilled all the prophecies
concerning his death, they took him down from
the cross and placed him in a tomb. 30But God
raised him from the dead! 31And he appeared
over a period of many days to those who had
gone with him from Galilee to Jerusalem—
these are his witnesses to the people of Israel.

32"And now Barnabas and I are here to bring
you this Good News. God's promise to our ancestors has come true in our own time, 33in that
God raised Jesus. This is what the second psalm
is talking about when it says concerning Jesus,

'You are my Son.
Today I have become your Father.*'

34For God had promised to raise him from the
dead, never again to die. This is stated in the
Scripture that says, 'I will give you the sacred
blessings I promised to David.'* 35Another
psalm explains more fully, saying, 'You will not
allow your Holy One to rot in the grave.'*
36Now this is not a reference to David, for after
David had served his generation according to
the will of God, he died and was buried, and his
body decayed. 37No, it was a reference to someone else—someone whom God raised and
whose body did not decay.

38"Brothers, listen! In this man Jesus there is
forgiveness for your sins. 39Everyone who believes in him is freed from all guilt and declared
right with God—something the Jewish law
could never do. 40Be careful! Don't let the
prophets' words apply to you. For they said,

41 'Look you mockers,

13:13-14 *Pamphylia* and *Pisidia* were districts in the land now called Turkey. 13:18 Other manuscripts read *He cared for them;* compare Deut 1:31. 13:22 1 Sam 13:14. 13:25 Greek *to untie his sandals.* 13:33 Or *Today I reveal you as my Son.* Ps 2:7. 13:34 Isa 55:3. 13:35 Ps 16:10.

be amazed and die!
For I am doing something in your own day,
something you wouldn't believe
even if someone told you about it.'* "

42As Paul and Barnabas left the synagogue
that day, the people asked them to return again
and speak about these things the next week.
43Many Jews and godly converts to Judaism who
worshiped at the synagogue followed Paul and
Barnabas, and the two men urged them, "By
God's grace, remain faithful."

Paul Turns to the Gentiles

44The following week almost the entire city
turned out to hear them preach the word of the
Lord. 45But when the Jewish leaders saw the
crowds, they were jealous; so they slandered
Paul and argued against whatever he said.
46Then Paul and Barnabas spoke out boldly
and declared, "It was necessary that this Good
News from God be given first to you Jews. But
since you have rejected it and judged yourselves
unworthy of eternal life—well, we will offer it to
Gentiles. 47For this is as the Lord commanded us
when he said,

'I have made you a light to the Gentiles,
to bring salvation to the farthest corners
of the earth.'* "

48When the Gentiles heard this, they were
very glad and thanked the Lord for his message;
and all who were appointed to eternal life became believers. 49So the Lord's message spread
throughout that region.
50Then the Jewish leaders stirred up both the
influential religious women and the leaders of
the city, and they incited a mob against Paul and
Barnabas and ran them out of town. 51But they
shook off the dust of their feet against them and
went to the city of Iconium. 52And the believers*
were filled with joy and with the Holy Spirit.

CHAPTER 14

Paul and Barnabas in Iconium

In Iconium,* Paul and Barnabas went together
to the synagogue and preached with such
power that a great number of both Jews and
Gentiles believed. 2But the Jews who spurned
God's message stirred up distrust among the
Gentiles against Paul and Barnabas, saying all
sorts of evil things about them. 3The apostles
stayed there a long time, preaching boldly
about the grace of the Lord. The Lord proved
their message was true by giving them power
to do miraculous signs and wonders. 4But the
people of the city were divided in their opinion about them. Some sided with the Jews, and
some with the apostles.
5A mob of Gentiles and Jews, along with their
leaders, decided to attack and stone them.
6When the apostles learned of it, they fled for
their lives. They went to the region of Lycaonia,
to the cities of Lystra and Derbe and the surrounding area, 7and they preached the Good
News there.

Paul and Barnabas in Lystra and Derbe

8While they were at Lystra, Paul and Barnabas
came upon a man with crippled feet. He had
been that way from birth, so he had never
walked. 9He was listening as Paul preached, and
Paul noticed him and realized he had faith to be
healed. 10So Paul called to him in a loud voice,
"Stand up!" And the man jumped to his feet and
started walking.
11When the listening crowd saw what Paul
had done, they shouted in their local dialect,
"These men are gods in human bodies!" 12They
decided that Barnabas was the Greek god Zeus
and that Paul, because he was the chief speaker,
was Hermes. 13The temple of Zeus was located
on the outskirts of the city. The priest of the
temple and the crowd brought oxen and wreaths
of flowers, and they prepared to sacrifice to the
apostles at the city gates.
14But when Barnabas and Paul heard what
was happening, they tore their clothing in dis-
may and ran out among the people, shouting,
15"Friends,* why are you doing this? We are
merely human beings like yourselves! We have
come to bring you the Good News that you
should turn from these worthless things to the
living God, who made heaven and earth, the sea,
and everything in them. 16In earlier days he
permitted all the nations to go their own ways,
17but he never left himself without a witness.
There were always his reminders, such as sending you rain and good crops and giving you food
and joyful hearts." 18But even so, Paul and Barnabas could scarcely restrain the people from
sacrificing to them.
19Now some Jews arrived from Antioch and
Iconium and turned the crowds into a murder-
ous mob. They stoned Paul and dragged him out
of the city, apparently dead. 20But as the believ-

13:41 Hab 1:5. 13:47 Isa 49:6. 13:52 Greek *the disciples.* 14:1 *Iconium,* as well as *Lystra* and *Derbe* (14:6), were cities in the land now called Turkey. 14:15 Greek *Men.*

ers* stood around him, he got up and went back
into the city. The next day he left with Barnabas
for Derbe.

Paul and Barnabas Return to Antioch of Syria

21After preaching the Good News in Derbe and
making many disciples, Paul and Barnabas returned again to Lystra, Iconium, and Antioch of
Pisidia, 22where they strengthened the believers.
They encouraged them to continue in the faith,
reminding them that they must enter into the
Kingdom of God through many tribulations.
23Paul and Barnabas also appointed elders in
every church and prayed for them with fasting,
turning them over to the care of the Lord, in
whom they had come to trust. 24Then they traveled back through Pisidia to Pamphylia. 25They
preached again in Perga, then went on to Attalia.

26Finally, they returned by ship to Antioch of
Syria, where their journey had begun and where
they had been committed to the grace of God for
the work they had now completed. 27Upon arriv-
ing in Antioch, they called the church together
and reported about their trip, telling all that God
had done and how he had opened the door of
faith to the Gentiles, too. 28And they stayed there
with the believers in Antioch for a long time.

CHAPTER 15

The Council at Jerusalem

While Paul and Barnabas were at Antioch of
Syria, some men from Judea arrived and began
to teach the Christians*: "Unless you keep the
ancient Jewish custom of circumcision taught by
Moses, you cannot be saved." 2Paul and Barnabas, disagreeing with them, argued forcefully
and at length. Finally, Paul and Barnabas were
sent to Jerusalem, accompanied by some local
believers, to talk to the apostles and elders about
this question. 3The church sent the delegates to
Jerusalem, and they stopped along the way in
Phoenicia and Samaria to visit the believers.*
They told them—much to everyone's joy—that
the Gentiles, too, were being converted.

4When they arrived in Jerusalem, Paul and
Barnabas were welcomed by the whole church,
including the apostles and elders. They reported
on what God had been doing through their ministry. 5But then some of the men who had been
Pharisees before their conversion stood up and
declared that all Gentile converts must be circumcised and be required to follow the law of Moses.

6So the apostles and church elders got together to decide this question. 7At the meeting,
after a long discussion, Peter stood and addressed them as follows: "Brothers, you all know
that God chose me from among you some time
ago to preach to the Gentiles so that they could
hear the Good News and believe. 8God, who
knows people's hearts, confirmed that he accepts Gentiles by giving them the Holy Spirit,
just as he gave him to us. 9He made no distinction between us and them, for he also cleansed
their hearts through faith. 10Why are you now
questioning God's way by burdening the Gentile
believers* with a yoke that neither we nor our
ancestors were able to bear? 11We believe that we
are all saved the same way, by the special favor
of the Lord Jesus."

12There was no further discussion, and everyone listened as Barnabas and Paul told about the
miraculous signs and wonders God had done
through them among the Gentiles.

13When they had finished, James stood and
said, "Brothers, listen to me. 14Peter* has told
you about the time God first visited the Gentiles
to take from them a people for himself. 15And
this conversion of Gentiles agrees with what the
prophets predicted. For instance, it is written:

16 'Afterward I will return,
and I will restore the fallen kingdom of David.
From the ruins I will rebuild it,
and I will restore it,
17 so that the rest of humanity might find the Lord,
including the Gentiles—
all those I have called to be mine.
This is what the Lord says,
18 he who made these things known long ago.'*

19And so my judgment is that we should stop
troubling the Gentiles who turn to God, 20ex-
cept that we should write to them and tell them
to abstain from eating meat sacrificed to idols,
from sexual immorality, and from consuming
blood or eating the meat of strangled animals.
21For these laws of Moses have been preached in
Jewish synagogues in every city on every Sabbath
for many generations."

The Letter for Gentile Believers

22Then the apostles and elders and the whole
church in Jerusalem chose delegates, and they

14:20 Greek *disciples;* also in 14:22, 28. 15:1 Greek *brothers;* also in 15:32, 33. 15:3 Greek *brothers;* also in 15:23, 36, 40. 15:10 Greek *disciples.* 15:14 Greek *Simon.* 15:16-18 Amos 9:11-12; Isa 45:21.

sent them to Antioch of Syria with Paul and
Barnabas to report on this decision. The men
chosen were two of the church leaders*—Judas
(also called Barsabbas) and Silas. 23This is the
letter they took along with them:

"This letter is from the apostles and elders,
your brothers in Jerusalem. It is written to
the Gentile believers in Antioch, Syria, and
Cilicia. Greetings!

24"We understand that some men from
here have troubled you and upset you with
their teaching, but they had no such
instructions from us. 25So it seemed good
to us, having unanimously agreed on our
decision, to send you these official
representatives, along with our beloved
Barnabas and Paul, 26who have risked their
lives for the sake of our Lord Jesus Christ.
27So we are sending Judas and Silas to tell
you what we have decided concerning your
question.

28"For it seemed good to the Holy Spirit
and to us to lay no greater burden on you
than these requirements: 29You must
abstain from eating food offered to idols,
from consuming blood or eating the meat
of strangled animals, and from sexual
immorality. If you do this, you will do well.
Farewell."

30The four messengers went at once to Antioch, where they called a general meeting of the
Christians and delivered the letter. 31And there
was great joy throughout the church that day as
they read this encouraging message.

32Then Judas and Silas, both being prophets,
spoke extensively to the Christians, encouraging
and strengthening their faith. 33They stayed for
a while, and then Judas and Silas were sent back
to Jerusalem, with the blessings of the Christians, to those who had sent them.* 35Paul and
Barnabas stayed in Antioch to assist many others
who were teaching and preaching the word of
the Lord there.

Paul and Barnabas Separate

36After some time Paul said to Barnabas, "Let's
return to each city where we previously preached
the word of the Lord, to see how the new believers are getting along." 37Barnabas agreed and
wanted to take along John Mark. 38But Paul
disagreed strongly, since John Mark had deserted
them in Pamphylia and had not shared in their
work. 39Their disagreement over this was so
sharp that they separated. Barnabas took John
Mark with him and sailed for Cyprus. 40Paul
chose Silas, and the believers sent them off,
entrusting them to the Lord's grace. 41So they
traveled throughout Syria and Cilicia to
strengthen the churches there.

CHAPTER 16

Paul's Second Missionary Journey

Paul and Silas went first to Derbe and then on to
Lystra. There they met Timothy, a young disciple
whose mother was a Jewish believer, but whose
father was a Greek. 2Timothy was well thought of
by the believers* in Lystra and Iconium, 3so Paul
wanted him to join them on their journey. In
deference to the Jews of the area, he arranged for
Timothy to be circumcised before they left, for
everyone knew that his father was a Greek. 4Then
they went from town to town, explaining the
decision regarding the commandments that were
to be obeyed, as decided by the apostles and elders
in Jerusalem. 5So the churches were strengthened
in their faith and grew daily in numbers.

A Call from Macedonia

6Next Paul and Silas traveled through the area of
Phrygia and Galatia, because the Holy Spirit had
told them not to go into the province of Asia at
that time. 7Then coming to the borders of Mysia,
they headed for the province of Bithynia,* but
again the Spirit of Jesus did not let them go. 8So
instead, they went on through Mysia to the city
of Troas.

9That night Paul had a vision. He saw a man
from Macedonia in northern Greece, pleading
with him, "Come over here and help us." 10So
we* decided to leave for Macedonia at once, for
we could only conclude that God was calling us
to preach the Good News there.

Lydia of Philippi Believes in Jesus

11We boarded a boat at Troas and sailed straight
across to the island of Samothrace, and the next
day we landed at Neapolis. 12From there we
reached Philippi, a major city of the district of
Macedonia and a Roman colony; we stayed there
several days.

13On the Sabbath we went a little way outside
the city to a riverbank, where we supposed that
some people met for prayer, and we sat down to

15:22 Greek *were leaders among the brothers.* 15:33 Some manuscripts add verse 34, *But Silas decided to stay there.* 16:2 Greek *brothers;* also in 16:40. 16:6-7 *Phrygia, Galatia, Asia, Mysia,* and *Bithynia* were all districts in the land now called Turkey. 16:10 Luke, the writer of this book, here joined Paul and accompanied him on his journey.

speak with some women who had come together. 14One of them was Lydia from Thyatira,
a merchant of expensive purple cloth. She was a
worshiper of God. As she listened to us, the Lord
opened her heart, and she accepted what Paul
was saying. 15She was baptized along with other
members of her household, and she asked us to
be her guests. "If you agree that I am faithful to
the Lord," she said, "come and stay at my
home." And she urged us until we did.

Paul and Silas in Prison

16One day as we were going down to the place
of prayer, we met a demon-possessed slave girl.
She was a fortune-teller who earned a lot of
money for her masters. 17She followed along
behind us shouting, "These men are servants of
the Most High God, and they have come to tell
you how to be saved."

18This went on day after day until Paul got so
exasperated that he turned and spoke to the
demon within her. "I command you in the
name of Jesus Christ to come out of her," he
said. And instantly it left her.

19Her masters' hopes of wealth were now
shattered, so they grabbed Paul and Silas and
dragged them before the authorities at the marketplace. 20"The whole city is in an uproar because of these Jews!" they shouted. 21"They are
teaching the people to do things that are against
Roman customs."

22A mob quickly formed against Paul and
Silas, and the city officials ordered them
stripped and beaten with wooden rods. 23They
were severely beaten, and then they were thrown
into prison. The jailer was ordered to make sure
they didn't escape. 24So he took no chances but
put them into the inner dungeon and clamped
their feet in the stocks.

25Around midnight, Paul and Silas were praying and singing hymns to God, and the other
prisoners were listening. 26Suddenly, there was a
great earthquake, and the prison was shaken to
its foundations. All the doors flew open, and the
chains of every prisoner fell off! 27The jailer
woke up to see the prison doors wide open. He
assumed the prisoners had escaped, so he drew
his sword to kill himself. 28But Paul shouted to
him, "Don't do it! We are all here!"

29Trembling with fear, the jailer called for
lights and ran to the dungeon and fell down
before Paul and Silas. 30He brought them out
and asked, "Sirs, what must I do to be saved?"

31They replied, "Believe on the Lord Jesus and
you will be saved, along with your entire household." 32Then they shared the word of the Lord
with him and all who lived in his household.
33That same hour the jailer washed their
wounds, and he and everyone in his household
were immediately baptized. 34Then he brought
them into his house and set a meal before them.
He and his entire household rejoiced because
they all believed in God.

35The next morning the city officials sent the
police to tell the jailer, "Let those men go!" 36So
the jailer told Paul, "You and Silas are free to
leave. Go in peace."

37But Paul replied, "They have publicly
beaten us without trial and jailed us—and we
are Roman citizens. So now they want us to leave
secretly? Certainly not! Let them come themselves to release us!"

38When the police made their report, the city
officials were alarmed to learn that Paul and Silas
were Roman citizens. 39They came to the jail and
apologized to them. Then they brought them out
and begged them to leave the city. 40Paul and
Silas then returned to the home of Lydia, where
they met with the believers and encouraged them
once more before leaving town.

OFF AND RUNNING

Make Sure Your Children Hear the Gospel Message

Read ACTS 16:29-34

In this wonderful story, we see how one man looked out for the spiritual welfare of his family. He took the opportunity at hand to expose his family to the message of Christ through the testimony of Paul and Silas.

We, too, need to take advantage of every opportunity to share Christ with our family—and particularly our children. They are never too young (or too old) to be taught about the things of God. Here are four suggestions to help you share the gospel with your family:

1. Set Aside Time for Family Devotions. Study the Bible, pray together, and share how God has been working in your life.

CHAPTER 17

Paul Preaches in Thessalonica

Now Paul and Silas traveled through the towns
of Amphipolis and Apollonia and came to Thessalonica, where there was a Jewish synagogue.
2As was Paul's custom, he went to the synagogue
service, and for three Sabbaths in a row he inter-
preted the Scriptures to the people. 3He was
explaining and proving the prophecies about
the sufferings of the Messiah and his rising from
the dead. He said, "This Jesus I'm telling you
about is the Messiah." 4Some who listened were
persuaded and became converts, including a
large number of godly Greek men and also
many important women of the city.*

5But the Jewish leaders were jealous, so they
gathered some worthless fellows from the streets
to form a mob and start a riot. They attacked the
home of Jason, searching for Paul and Silas so
they could drag them out to the crowd.* 6Not
finding them there, they dragged out Jason and
some of the other believers* instead and took
them before the city council. "Paul and Silas
have turned the rest of the world upside down,
and now they are here disturbing our city," they
shouted. 7"And Jason has let them into his
home. They are all guilty of treason against Caesar, for they profess allegiance to another king,
Jesus."

8The people of the city, as well as the city
officials, were thrown into turmoil by these reports. 9But the officials released Jason and the
other believers after they had posted bail.

Paul and Silas in Berea

10That very night the believers sent Paul and
Silas to Berea. When they arrived there, they
went to the synagogue. 11And the people of Berea were more open-minded than those in Thessalonica, and they listened eagerly to Paul's message. They searched the Scriptures day after day
to check up on Paul and Silas, to see if they were
really teaching the truth. 12As a result, many Jews
believed, as did some of the prominent Greek
women and many men.

13But when some Jews in Thessalonica
learned that Paul was preaching the word of
God in Berea, they went there and stirred up
trouble. 14The believers acted at once, sending
Paul on to the coast, while Silas and Timothy
remained behind. 15Those escorting Paul went
with him to Athens; then they returned to Berea
with a message for Silas and Timothy to hurry
and join him.

Paul Preaches in Athens

16While Paul was waiting for them in Athens, he
was deeply troubled by all the idols he saw
everywhere in the city. 17He went to the synagogue to debate with the Jews and the God-fear-
ing Gentiles, and he spoke daily in the public
square to all who happened to be there.

18He also had a debate with some of the
Epicurean and Stoic philosophers. When he told
them about Jesus and his resurrection, they said,
"This babbler has picked up some strange
ideas." Others said, "He's pushing some foreign
religion."

19Then they took him to the Council of Philosophers.* "Come and tell us more about this
new religion," they said. 20"You are saying some
rather startling things, and we want to know
what it's all about." 21(It should be explained
that all the Athenians as well as the foreigners in
Athens seemed to spend all their time discussing
the latest ideas.)

17:4 Some manuscripts read *many of the wives of the leading men.* 17:5 Or *the city council.* 17:6 Greek *brothers;* also in 17:10, 14. 17:19 Greek *the Areopagus.*

---

2. Invite Other Believers to Your Home. This jailer invited Paul and Silas over for dinner, and we read how the whole household rejoiced because all were now believers. This type of fellowship can be an enriching time for your family.

3. Bring Your Children to Church with You. Your children will probably learn lessons here that they will carry with them the rest of their lives. If they are young enough, bring them. If they are older, strongly encourage them to join you.

4. Pray for Your Children Daily. As a parent, you cannot "make" your children Christians, but you can pray that their hearts will be sensitive and open to the gospel message.

Use God's Word to Evaluate Someone's Teachings

Read ACTS 17:11

The group of people in this passage—the Bereans—actually searched the written Word of God to see if Paul's words were true. In the original Greek, the word for "searched" could also be translated "scrutinized." They did this because they knew that they could trust God's Word and use it as the standard against which to evaluate others' teachings.

The same is true for us today. Everything we need to know about God is found in the pages of Scripture. Applying ourselves in the study of his Word helps us determine whether someone's teachings are true or false. If we fail to study the Bible, we may be lured into believing false teachings. But if we consistently study God's Word, it—along with the illumination of the Holy Spirit—will enable us to distinguish truth from error.

Here is a trustworthy saying to keep in mind: If someone says they "have a new 'word' or 'revelation' from the Lord," rest assured that it is not true. If it is true, it is not new. If it is new, it is not true! If it is not in the Word, it is not of the Lord.

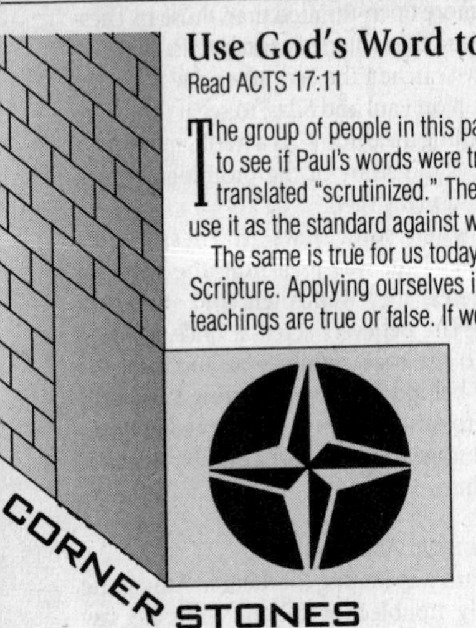

22So Paul, standing before the Council,* addressed them as follows: "Men of Athens, I notice that you are very religious, 23for as I was
walking along I saw your many altars. And one
of them had this inscription on it—'To an Unknown God.' You have been worshiping him
without knowing who he is, and now I wish to
tell you about him.
24"He is the God who made the world and
everything in it. Since he is Lord of heaven and
earth, he doesn't live in man-made temples,
25and human hands can't serve his needs—for
he has no needs. He himself gives life and breath
to everything, and he satisfies every need there
is. 26From one man he created all the nations
throughout the whole earth. He decided beforehand which should rise and fall, and he determined their boundaries.
27"His purpose in all of this was that the
nations should seek after God and perhaps feel
their way toward him and find him—though he
is not far from any one of us. 28For in him we
live and move and exist. As one of your own
poets says, 'We are his offspring.' 29And since
this is true, we shouldn't think of God as an idol
designed by craftsmen from gold or silver or
stone. 30God overlooked people's former ignorance about these things, but now he commands
everyone everywhere to turn away from idols
and turn to him.* 31For he has set a day for
judging the world with justice by the man he has
appointed, and he proved to everyone who this
is by raising him from the dead."
32When they heard Paul speak of the resurrection of a person who had been dead, some
laughed, but others said, "We want to hear more
about this later." 33That ended Paul's discussion
with them, 34but some joined him and became
believers. Among them were Dionysius, a member of the Council,* a woman named Damaris,
and others.

CHAPTER 18

Paul Meets Priscilla and Aquila in Corinth

Then Paul left Athens and went to Corinth.*
2There he became acquainted with a Jew named
Aquila, born in Pontus, who had recently arrived
from Italy with his wife, Priscilla. They had been
expelled from Italy as a result of Claudius Caesar's order to deport all Jews from Rome. 3Paul
lived and worked with them, for they were tent-
makers* just as he was.
4Each Sabbath found Paul at the synagogue,
trying to convince the Jews and Greeks alike.
5And after Silas and Timothy came down from
Macedonia, Paul spent his full time preaching
and testifying to the Jews, telling them, "The
Messiah you are looking for is Jesus." 6But when
the Jews opposed him and insulted him, Paul

17:22 Or *in the middle of Mars Hill;* Greek reads *in the middle of the Areopagus.* 17:30 Greek *everywhere to repent.* 17:34 Greek *an Areopagite.* 18:1 *Athens* and *Corinth* were major cities in Achaia, the region on the southern end of the Greek peninsula. 18:3 Or *leatherworkers.*

shook the dust from his robe and said, "Your blood be upon your own heads—I am innocent. From now on I will go to the Gentiles."

7After that he stayed with Titius Justus, a Gentile who worshiped God and lived next door to the synagogue. 8Crispus, the leader of the synagogue, and all his household believed in the Lord. Many others in Corinth also became believers and were baptized.

9One night the Lord spoke to Paul in a vision and told him, "Don't be afraid! Speak out! Don't be silent! 10For I am with you, and no one will harm you because many people here in this city belong to me." 11So Paul stayed there for the next year and a half, teaching the word of God.

12But when Gallio became governor of Achaia, some Jews rose in concerted action against Paul and brought him before the governor for judgment. 13They accused Paul of "persuading people to worship God in ways that are contrary to the law." 14But just as Paul started to make his defense, Gallio turned to Paul's accusers and said, "Listen, you Jews, if this were a case involving some wrongdoing or a serious crime, I would be obliged to listen to you. 15But since it is merely a question of words and names and your Jewish laws, you take care of it. I refuse to judge such matters." 16And he drove them out of the courtroom. 17The mob had grabbed Sosthenes, the leader of the synagogue, and had beaten him right there in the courtroom. But Gallio paid no attention.

Paul Returns to Antioch of Syria

18Paul stayed in Corinth for some time after that and then said good-bye to the brothers and sisters* and sailed for the coast of Syria, taking Priscilla and Aquila with him. (Earlier, at Cenchrea, Paul had shaved his head according to Jewish custom, for he had taken a vow.) 19When they arrived at the port of Ephesus, Paul left the others behind. But while he was there, he went to the synagogue to debate with the Jews. 20They asked him to stay longer, but he declined. 21So he left, saying, "I will come back later,* God willing." Then he set sail from Ephesus. 22The next stop was at the port of Caesarea. From there he went up and visited the church at Jerusalem* and then went back to Antioch.

23After spending some time in Antioch, Paul went back to Galatia and Phrygia, visiting all the believers,* encouraging them and helping them to grow in the Lord.

Apollos Instructed at Ephesus

24Meanwhile, a Jew named Apollos, an eloquent speaker who knew the Scriptures well, had just arrived in Ephesus from Alexandria in Egypt. 25He had been taught the way of the Lord and talked to others with great enthusiasm and accuracy about Jesus. However, he knew only about John's baptism. 26When Priscilla and Aquila heard him preaching boldly in the synagogue, they took him aside and explained the way of God more accurately.

27Apollos had been thinking about going to Achaia, and the brothers and sisters in Ephesus encouraged him in this. They wrote to the believers in Achaia, asking them to welcome him. When he arrived there, he proved to be of great benefit to those who, by God's grace, had believed. 28He refuted all the Jews with powerful arguments in public debate. Using the Scriptures, he explained to them, "The Messiah you are looking for is Jesus."

CHAPTER 19

Paul's Third Missionary Journey

While Apollos was in Corinth, Paul traveled through the interior provinces. Finally, he came to Ephesus, where he found several believers.* 2"Did you receive the Holy Spirit when you believed?" he asked them.

"No," they replied, "we don't know what you mean. We haven't even heard that there is a Holy Spirit."

3"Then what baptism did you experience?" he asked.

And they replied, "The baptism of John."

4Paul said, "John's baptism was to demonstrate a desire to turn from sin and turn to God. John himself told the people to believe in Jesus, the one John said would come later."

5As soon as they heard this, they were baptized in the name of the Lord Jesus. 6Then when Paul laid his hands on them, the Holy Spirit came on them, and they spoke in other tongues and prophesied. 7There were about twelve men in all.

Paul Ministers in Ephesus

8Then Paul went to the synagogue and preached boldly for the next three months, arguing persuasively about the Kingdom of God. 9But some rejected his message and publicly spoke against the Way, so Paul left the synagogue and took the believers with him. Then he began preaching

18:18 Greek *brothers;* also in 18:27. **18:21** Some manuscripts read *"I must by all means be at Jerusalem for the upcoming festival, but I will come back later."* **18:22** Greek *the church.* **18:23** Greek *disciples;* also in 18:27. **19:1** Greek *disciples;* also in 19:9, 30.

God Is Personal Read ACTS 17:22-33

Paul's audience in this passage included people of two different beliefs. There were those who did not believe in life after death and lived only for pleasure. They were known as the Epicureans. There were also those who believed that God existed in every material object and strived to be at peace with the world. These people were known as the Stoics. In speaking to these two groups, Paul showed them how their philosophies fell short of grasping the true nature of God. He did this by bringing out the following truths about who God is.

God Is the All-Powerful Creator

- God made heaven and earth, and every living creature.
- God is too great to be housed in man-made temples or shrines.
- God created all the people of the world from one man.
- God is the architect behind the world stage.

God Is the Personal Supreme Being

- His purpose behind creation was to draw people to himself.
- He is concerned about people's needs.
- He is not far from any of us.
- He makes it easy for us to know him personally (salvation through Jesus Christ).
- He can and will judge every thought and motive on Judgment Day.

The people who listened to Paul speak responded in one of three ways: (1) Some mocked him; (2) some procrastinated and said they would make a decision after listening to him again later; and (3) some believed him and accepted Jesus as their Savior. People today react to the gospel message in much the same way. However, if someone really wants to know the powerful God who created him or her and who is personally interested in his or her life, only the last response will do.

CORNER STONES

daily at the lecture hall of Tyrannus. 10This went on for the next two years, so that people throughout the province of Asia—both Jews and Greeks—heard the Lord's message.

11God gave Paul the power to do unusual miracles, 12so that even when handkerchiefs or cloths that had touched his skin were placed on sick people, they were healed of their diseases, and any evil spirits within them came out.

13A team of Jews who were traveling from town to town casting out evil spirits tried to use the name of the Lord Jesus. The incantation they used was this: "I command you by Jesus, whom Paul preaches, to come out!" 14Seven sons of Sceva, a leading priest, were doing this. 15But when they tried it on a man possessed by an evil spirit, the spirit replied, "I know Jesus, and I know Paul. But who are you?" 16And he leaped on them and attacked them with such violence that they fled from the house, naked and badly injured.

17The story of what happened spread quickly all through Ephesus, to Jews and Greeks alike. A solemn fear descended on the city, and the name of the Lord Jesus was greatly honored. 18Many who became believers confessed their sinful practices. 19A number of them who had been practicing magic brought their incantation books and burned them at a public bonfire. The value of the books was several million dollars.* 20So the message about the Lord spread widely and had a powerful effect.

The Riot in Ephesus

21Afterward Paul felt impelled by the Holy Spirit* to go over to Macedonia and Achaia before returning to Jerusalem. "And after that," he said, "I must go on to Rome!" 22He sent his two assistants, Timothy and Erastus, on ahead to Macedonia while he stayed awhile longer in the province of Asia.

23But about that time, serious trouble developed in Ephesus concerning the Way. 24It began

19:19 Greek *50,000 pieces of silver,* each of which was the equivalent of a day's wage. 19:21 Or *purposed in his spirit.*

with Demetrius, a silversmith who had a large
business manufacturing silver shrines of the
Greek goddess Artemis.* He kept many craftsmen busy. 25He called the craftsmen together,
along with others employed in related trades,
and addressed them as follows:

"Gentlemen, you know that our wealth
comes from this business. 26As you have seen
and heard, this man Paul has persuaded many
people that handmade gods aren't gods at all.
And this is happening not only here in Ephesus
but throughout the entire province! 27Of course,
I'm not just talking about the loss of public
respect for our business. I'm also concerned that
the temple of the great goddess Artemis will lose
its influence and that Artemis—this magnificent
goddess worshiped throughout the province of
Asia and all around the world—will be robbed
of her prestige!"

28At this their anger boiled, and they began
shouting, "Great is Artemis of the Ephesians!"
29A crowd began to gather, and soon the city was
filled with confusion. Everyone rushed to the
amphitheater, dragging along Gaius and Aristarchus, who were Paul's traveling companions
from Macedonia. 30Paul wanted to go in, but the
believers wouldn't let him. 31Some of the officials of the province, friends of Paul, also sent a
message to him, begging him not to risk his life
by entering the amphitheater.

32Inside, the people were all shouting, some
one thing and some another. Everything was in
confusion. In fact, most of them didn't even
know why they were there. 33Alexander was
thrust forward by some of the Jews, who encouraged him to explain the situation. He motioned
for silence and tried to speak in defense. 34But
when the crowd realized he was a Jew, they
started shouting again and kept it up for two
hours: "Great is Artemis of the Ephesians! Great
is Artemis of the Ephesians!"

35At last the mayor was able to quiet them
down enough to speak. "Citizens of Ephesus,"
he said. "Everyone knows that Ephesus is the
official guardian of the temple of the great
Artemis, whose image fell down to us from
heaven. 36Since this is an indisputable fact, you
shouldn't be disturbed, no matter what is said.
Don't do anything rash. 37You have brought
these men here, but they have stolen nothing
from the temple and have not spoken against
our goddess. 38If Demetrius and the craftsmen
have a case against them, the courts are in session and the judges can take the case at once. Let
them go through legal channels. 39And if there
are complaints about other matters, they can be
settled in a legal assembly. 40I am afraid we are
in danger of being charged with rioting by the
Roman government, since there is no cause for
all this commotion. And if Rome demands an
explanation, we won't know what to say."
41Then he dismissed them, and they dispersed.

CHAPTER 20

Paul Goes to Macedonia and Greece

When it was all over, Paul sent for the believers*
and encouraged them. Then he said good-bye
and left for Macedonia. 2Along the way, he encouraged the believers in all the towns he passed
through. Then he traveled down to Greece,
3where he stayed for three months. He was preparing to sail back to Syria when he discovered
a plot by some Jews against his life, so he decided to return through Macedonia.

4Several men were traveling with him. They
were Sopater of Berea, the son of Pyrrhus; Aristarchus and Secundus, from Thessalonica; Gaius, from Derbe; Timothy; and Tychicus and
Trophimus, who were from the province of Asia.
5They went ahead and waited for us at Troas. 6As
soon as the Passover season* ended, we boarded
a ship at Philippi in Macedonia and five days
later arrived in Troas, where we stayed a week.

Paul's Final Visit to Troas

7On the first day of the week, we gathered to
observe the Lord's Supper.* Paul was preaching;
and since he was leaving the next day, he talked
until midnight. 8The upstairs room where we
met was lighted with many flickering lamps. 9As
Paul spoke on and on, a young man named
Eutychus, sitting on the windowsill, became very
drowsy. Finally, he sank into a deep sleep and
fell three stories to his death below. 10Paul went
down, bent over him, and took him into his
arms. "Don't worry," he said, "he's alive!"
11Then they all went back upstairs and ate the
Lord's Supper together.* And Paul continued
talking to them until dawn; then he left.
12Meanwhile, the young man was taken home
unhurt, and everyone was greatly relieved.

Paul Meets the Ephesian Elders

13Paul went by land to Assos, where he had
arranged for us to join him, and we went on

19:24 *Artemis* is otherwise known as Diana. 20:1 Greek *disciples.* 20:6 Greek *the days of unleavened bread.* 20:7 Greek *to break bread.* 20:11 Greek *broke the bread.*

Can Demons Personally Harm You? Read ACTS 19:13-20

While Christians have the promise of angelic protection over their lives, non-Christians are open targets for the Devil and his demon forces. As this passage relates, demons will only respond to or avoid the "genuine" believer. They will not answer to someone who simply uses the name of Jesus without really knowing who Jesus is. Religion will not keep them away, nor will symbols like a crucifix. Certainly the Devil hates what Jesus did on the literal cross, but wearing a cross will not drive these evil spirits away.

The only thing that will secure you from the Devil's domination—and even possession—of your soul is the presence of Jesus Christ in your life. Once you trust in him, you come under divine protection and become his property. He said that you are his sheep and that no one can take you out of his hand (see John 10:27-29, p. 119). But if you are not a Christian, you are open game that the Devil can take at his will.

CORNERSTONES

ahead by ship. 14He joined us there and we
sailed together to Mitylene. 15The next day we
passed the island of Kios. The following day, we
crossed to the island of Samos. And a day later
we arrived at Miletus.

16Paul had decided against stopping at Ephesus this time because he didn't want to spend
further time in the province of Asia. He was
hurrying to get to Jerusalem, if possible, for the
Festival of Pentecost. 17But when we landed at
Miletus, he sent a message to the elders of the
church at Ephesus, asking them to come down
to meet him.

18When they arrived he declared, "You know
that from the day I set foot in the province of
Asia until now 19I have done the Lord's work
humbly—yes, and with tears. I have endured the
trials that came to me from the plots of the Jews.
20Yet I never shrank from telling you the truth,
either publicly or in your homes. 21I have had
one message for Jews and Gentiles alike—the
necessity of turning from sin and turning to
God, and of faith in our Lord Jesus.

22"And now I am going to Jerusalem, drawn
there irresistibly by the Holy Spirit,* not knowing
what awaits me, 23except that the Holy Spirit has
told me in city after city that jail and suffering lie
ahead. 24But my life is worth nothing unless I use
it for doing the work assigned me by the Lord
Jesus—the work of telling others the Good News
about God's wonderful kindness and love.

25"And now I know that none of you to
whom I have preached the Kingdom will ever
see me again. 26Let me say plainly that I have
been faithful. No one's damnation can be
blamed on me,* 27for I didn't shrink from declaring all that God wants for you.

28"And now beware! Be sure that you feed
and shepherd God's flock—his church, purchased with his blood—over whom the Holy
Spirit has appointed you as elders.* 29I know
full well that false teachers, like vicious wolves,
will come in among you after I leave, not sparing
the flock. 30Even some of you will distort the
truth in order to draw a following. 31Watch out!
Remember the three years I was with you—my
constant watch and care over you night and day,
and my many tears for you.

32"And now I entrust you to God and the
word of his grace—his message that is able to
build you up and give you an inheritance with
all those he has set apart for himself.

33"I have never coveted anyone's money or
fine clothing. 34You know that these hands of
mine have worked to pay my own way, and I have
even supplied the needs of those who were with
me. 35And I have been a constant example of how
you can help the poor by working hard. You
should remember the words of the Lord Jesus: 'It
is more blessed to give than to receive.' "

36When he had finished speaking, he knelt
and prayed with them. 37They wept aloud as
they embraced him in farewell, 38sad most of all
because he had said that they would never see
him again. Then they accompanied him down
to the ship.

20:22 Or *by my spirit,* or *by an inner compulsion;* Greek reads *by the spirit.* 20:26 Greek *I am innocent of the blood of all.* 20:28 Greek *overseers.*

CHAPTER 21

Paul's Journey to Jerusalem
After saying farewell to the Ephesian elders, we
sailed straight to the island of Cos. The next day
we reached Rhodes and then went to Patara.
2There we boarded a ship sailing for the Syrian
province of Phoenicia. 3We sighted the island of
Cyprus, passed it on our left, and landed at the
harbor of Tyre, in Syria, where the ship was to
unload. 4We went ashore, found the local believers,* and stayed with them a week. These disciples prophesied through the Holy Spirit that
Paul should not go on to Jerusalem. 5When we
returned to the ship at the end of the week, the
entire congregation, including wives and children, came down to the shore with us. There we
knelt, prayed, 6and said our farewells. Then we
went aboard, and they returned home.

7The next stop after leaving Tyre was Ptole-
mais, where we greeted the brothers and sisters*
but stayed only one day. 8Then we went on to
Caesarea and stayed at the home of Philip the
Evangelist, one of the seven men who had been
chosen to distribute food. 9He had four unmarried daughters who had the gift of prophecy.

10During our stay of several days, a man
named Agabus, who also had the gift of prophecy, arrived from Judea. 11When he visited us, he
took Paul's belt and bound his own feet and
hands with it. Then he said, "The Holy Spirit
declares, 'So shall the owner of this belt be
bound by the Jewish leaders in Jerusalem and
turned over to the Romans.'" 12When we heard
this, we who were traveling with him, as well as
the local believers, begged Paul not to go on to
Jerusalem.

13But he said, "Why all this weeping? You are
breaking my heart! For I am ready not only to be
jailed at Jerusalem but also to die for the sake of
the Lord Jesus." 14When it was clear that we
couldn't persuade him, we gave up and said,
"The will of the Lord be done."

Paul Arrives at Jerusalem
15Shortly afterward we packed our things and
left for Jerusalem. 16Some believers from Caesarea accompanied us, and they took us to the
home of Mnason, a man originally from Cyprus
and one of the early disciples. 17All the brothers
and sisters in Jerusalem welcomed us cordially.

18The next day Paul went in with us to meet
with James, and all the elders of the Jerusalem
church were present. 19After greetings were ex-
changed, Paul gave a detailed account of the
things God had accomplished among the Gentiles through his ministry.

20After hearing this, they praised God. But
then they said, "You know, dear brother, how
many thousands of Jews have also believed, and
they all take the law of Moses very seriously.
21Our Jewish Christians here at Jerusalem have
been told that you are teaching all the Jews living
in the Gentile world to turn their backs on the
laws of Moses. They say that you teach people
not to circumcise their children or follow other
Jewish customs. 22Now what can be done? For
they will certainly hear that you have come.

23"Here's our suggestion. We have four men
here who have taken a vow and are preparing to
shave their heads. 24Go with them to the Temple
and join them in the purification ceremony, and
pay for them to have their heads shaved. Then
everyone will know that the rumors are all false
and that you yourself observe the Jewish laws.

25"As for the Gentile Christians, all we ask of
them is what we already told them in a letter:
They should not eat food offered to idols, nor
consume blood, nor eat meat from strangled
animals, and they should stay away from all
sexual immorality."

Paul Is Arrested
26So Paul agreed to their request, and the next
day he went through the purification ritual with
the men and went to the Temple. Then he publicly announced the date when their vows would
end and sacrifices would be offered for each of
them.

27The seven days were almost ended when
some Jews from the province of Asia saw Paul in
the Temple and roused a mob against him. They
grabbed him, 28yelling, "Men of Israel! Help!
This is the man who teaches against our people
and tells everybody to disobey the Jewish laws.
He speaks against the Temple—and he even
defiles it by bringing Gentiles in!" 29(For earlier
that day they had seen him in the city with
Trophimus, a Gentile from Ephesus,* and they
assumed Paul had taken him into the Temple.)

30The whole population of the city was
rocked by these accusations, and a great riot
followed. Paul was dragged out of the Temple,
and immediately the gates were closed behind
him. 31As they were trying to kill him, word
reached the commander of the Roman regiment that all Jerusalem was in an uproar. 32He

21:4 Greek *disciples;* also in 21:16. 21:7 Greek *brothers;* also in 21:17. 21:29 Greek *Trophimus, the Ephesian.*

immediately called out his soldiers and officers
and ran down among the crowd. When the
mob saw the commander and the troops coming, they stopped beating Paul. 33The commander arrested him and ordered him bound
with two chains. Then he asked the crowd who
he was and what he had done. 34Some shouted
one thing and some another. He couldn't find
out the truth in all the uproar and confusion,
so he ordered Paul to be taken to the fortress.
35As they reached the stairs, the mob grew so
violent the soldiers had to lift Paul to their
shoulders to protect him. 36And the crowd followed behind shouting, "Kill him, kill him!"

Paul Speaks to the Crowd

37As Paul was about to be taken inside, he said to
the commander, "May I have a word with you?"
"Do you know Greek?" the commander
asked, surprised. 38"Aren't you the Egyptian
who led a rebellion some time ago and took
four thousand members of the Assassins out
into the desert?"
39"No," Paul replied, "I am a Jew from Tarsus
in Cilicia, which is an important city. Please, let
me talk to these people." 40The commander
agreed, so Paul stood on the stairs and motioned to the people to be quiet. Soon a deep
silence enveloped the crowd, and he addressed
them in their own language, Aramaic.*

CHAPTER 22

"Brothers and esteemed fathers," Paul said,
"listen to me as I offer my defense." 2When they
heard him speaking in their own language,* the
silence was even greater. 3"I am a Jew, born in
Tarsus, a city in Cilicia, and I was brought up and
educated here in Jerusalem under Gamaliel. At
his feet I learned to follow our Jewish laws and
customs very carefully. I became very zealous to
honor God in everything I did, just as all of you
are today. 4And I persecuted the followers of the
Way, hounding some to death, binding and delivering both men and women to prison. 5The
high priest and the whole council of leaders can
testify that this is so. For I received letters from
them to our Jewish brothers in Damascus, au-
thorizing me to bring the Christians from there
to Jerusalem, in chains, to be punished.
6"As I was on the road, nearing Damascus,
about noon a very bright light from heaven
suddenly shone around me. 7I fell to the ground
and heard a voice saying to me, 'Saul, Saul, why
are you persecuting me?'
8" 'Who are you, sir?' I asked. And he replied,
'I am Jesus of Nazareth, the one you are persecuting.' 9The people with me saw the light but
didn't hear the voice.
10"I said, 'What shall I do, Lord?' And the
Lord told me, 'Get up and go into Damascus,
and there you will be told all that you are to do.'
11"I was blinded by the intense light and had
to be led into Damascus by my companions. 12A
man named Ananias lived there. He was a godly
man in his devotion to the law, and he was well
thought of by all the Jews of Damascus. 13He
came to me and stood beside me and said,
'Brother Saul, receive your sight.' And that very
hour I could see him!
14"Then he told me, 'The God of our ancestors has chosen you to know his will and to see
the Righteous One and hear him speak. 15You
are to take his message everywhere, telling the
whole world what you have seen and heard.
16And now, why delay? Get up and be baptized,
and have your sins washed away, calling on the
name of the Lord.'
17"One day after I returned to Jerusalem, I
was praying in the Temple, and I fell into a
trance. 18I saw a vision of Jesus saying to me,
'Hurry! Leave Jerusalem, for the people here
won't believe you when you give them your
testimony about me.'
19" 'But Lord,' I argued, 'they certainly know
that I imprisoned and beat those in every synagogue who believed on you. 20And when your
witness Stephen was killed, I was standing there
agreeing. I kept the coats they laid aside as they
stoned him.'
21"But the Lord said to me, 'Leave Jerusalem,
for I will send you far away to the Gentiles!' "
22The crowd listened until Paul came to that
word; then with one voice they shouted, "Away
with such a fellow! Kill him! He isn't fit to live!"
23They yelled, threw off their coats, and tossed
handfuls of dust into the air.

Paul Reveals His Roman Citizenship

24The commander brought Paul inside and ordered him lashed with whips to make him confess his crime. He wanted to find out why the
crowd had become so furious. 25As they tied
Paul down to lash him, Paul said to the officer
standing there, "Is it legal for you to whip a
Roman citizen who hasn't even been tried?"

21:40 Or *Hebrew.* 22:2 Greek *in Aramaic.*

26The officer went to the commander and asked, "What are you doing? This man is a Roman citizen!"

27So the commander went over and asked Paul, "Tell me, are you a Roman citizen?"

"Yes, I certainly am," Paul replied.

28"I am, too," the commander muttered, "and it cost me plenty!"

"But I am a citizen by birth!"

29The soldiers who were about to interrogate Paul quickly withdrew when they heard he was a Roman citizen, and the commander was frightened because he had ordered him bound and whipped.

Paul before the High Council

30The next day the commander freed Paul from his chains and ordered the leading priests into session with the Jewish high council.* He had Paul brought in before them to try to find out what the trouble was all about.

CHAPTER 23

Gazing intently at the high council,* Paul began: "Brothers, I have always lived before God in all good conscience!"

2Instantly Ananias the high priest commanded those close to Paul to slap him on the mouth. 3But Paul said to him, "God will slap you, you whitewashed wall! What kind of judge are you to break the law yourself by ordering me struck like that?"

4Those standing near Paul said to him, "Is that the way to talk to God's high priest?"

5"I'm sorry, brothers. I didn't realize he was the high priest," Paul replied, "for the Scriptures say, 'Do not speak evil of anyone who rules over you.'* "

6Paul realized that some members of the high council were Sadducees and some were Pharisees, so he shouted, "Brothers, I am a Pharisee, as were all my ancestors! And I am on trial because my hope is in the resurrection of the dead!"

7This divided the council—the Pharisees against the Sadducees—8for the Sadducees say there is no resurrection or angels or spirits, but the Pharisees believe in all of these. 9So a great clamor arose. Some of the teachers of religious law who were Pharisees jumped up to argue that Paul was all right. "We see nothing wrong with him," they shouted. "Perhaps a spirit or an angel spoke to him." 10The shouting grew louder and louder, and the men were tugging at Paul from both sides, pulling him this way and that. Finally, the commander, fearing they would tear him apart, ordered his soldiers to take him away from them and bring him back to the fortress.

11That night the Lord appeared to Paul and said, "Be encouraged, Paul. Just as you have told the people about me here in Jerusalem, you must preach the Good News in Rome."

The Plan to Kill Paul

12The next morning a group of Jews got together and bound themselves with an oath to neither eat nor drink until they had killed Paul. 13There were more than forty of them. 14They went to the leading priests and other leaders and told them what they had done. "We have bound ourselves under oath to neither eat nor drink until we have killed Paul. 15You and the high council should tell the commander to bring Paul back to the council again," they requested. "Pretend you want to examine his case more fully. We will kill him on the way."

16But Paul's nephew heard of their plan and went to the fortress and told Paul. 17Paul called one of the officers and said, "Take this young man to the commander. He has something important to tell him."

18So the officer did, explaining, "Paul, the prisoner, called me over and asked me to bring this young man to you because he has something to tell you."

19The commander took him by the arm, led him aside, and asked, "What is it you want to tell me?"

20Paul's nephew told him, "Some Jews are going to ask you to bring Paul before the Jewish high council tomorrow, pretending they want to get some more information. 21But don't do it! There are more than forty men hiding along the way ready to jump him and kill him. They have vowed not to eat or drink until they kill him. They are ready, expecting you to agree to their request."

22"Don't let a soul know you told me this," the commander warned the young man as he sent him away.

Paul Is Sent to Caesarea

23Then the commander called two of his officers and ordered, "Get two hundred soldiers ready to leave for Caesarea at nine o'clock tonight. Also take two hundred spearmen and

22:30 Greek *Sanhedrin.* 23:1 Greek *Sanhedrin;* also in 23:6, 15, 20, 28. 23:5 Exod 22:28.

seventy horsemen. 24Provide horses for Paul
to ride, and get him safely to Governor Felix."
25Then he wrote this letter to the governor:

> 26"From Claudius Lysias, to his Excellency,
> Governor Felix. Greetings! 27This man was
> seized by some Jews, and they were about
> to kill him when I arrived with the troops.
> When I learned that he was a Roman
> citizen, I removed him to safety. 28Then I
> took him to their high council to try to find
> out what he had done. 29I soon discovered
> it was something regarding their religious
> law—certainly nothing worthy of
> imprisonment or death. 30But when I was
> informed of a plot to kill him, I
> immediately sent him on to you. I have
> told his accusers to bring their charges
> before you."

31So that night, as ordered, the soldiers took
Paul as far as Antipatris. 32They returned to the
fortress the next morning, while the horsemen
took him on to Caesarea. 33When they arrived
in Caesarea, they presented Paul and the letter to
Governor Felix. 34He read it and then asked Paul
what province he was from. "Cilicia," Paul answered.

35"I will hear your case myself when your
accusers arrive," the governor told him. Then the
governor ordered him kept in the prison at Herod's headquarters.

CHAPTER 24

Paul Appears before Felix

Five days later Ananias, the high priest, arrived
with some of the Jewish leaders and the lawyer*
Tertullus, to press charges against Paul. 2When
Paul was called in, Tertullus laid charges against
Paul in the following address to the governor:

"Your Excellency, you have given peace to us
Jews and have enacted reforms for us. 3And for
all of this we are very grateful to you. 4But lest I
bore you, kindly give me your attention for only
a moment as I briefly outline our case against
this man. 5For we have found him to be a trou-
blemaker, a man who is constantly inciting the
Jews throughout the world to riots and rebel-
lions against the Roman government. He is a
ringleader of the sect known as the Nazarenes.
6Moreover he was trying to defile the Temple
when we arrested him.* 8You can find out the
truth of our accusations by examining him yourself." 9Then the other Jews chimed in, declaring
that everything Tertullus said was true.

10Now it was Paul's turn. The governor motioned for him to rise and speak. Paul said, "I
know, sir, that you have been a judge of Jewish
affairs for many years, and this gives me confidence as I make my defense. 11You can quickly
discover that it was no more than twelve days
ago that I arrived in Jerusalem to worship at the
Temple. 12I didn't argue with anyone in the
Temple, nor did I incite a riot in any synagogue
or on the streets of the city. 13These men certainly cannot prove the things they accuse me
of doing.

14"But I admit that I follow the Way, which
they call a sect. I worship the God of our
ancestors, and I firmly believe the Jewish law
and everything written in the books of prophecy. 15I have hope in God, just as these men
do, that he will raise both the righteous and
the ungodly. 16Because of this, I always try to
maintain a clear conscience before God and
everyone else.

17"After several years away, I returned to Jerusalem with money to aid my people and to offer
sacrifices to God. 18My accusers saw me in the
Temple as I was completing a purification ritual.
There was no crowd around me and no rioting.
19But some Jews from the province of Asia were
there—and they ought to be here to bring
charges if they have anything against me! 20Ask
these men here what wrongdoing the Jewish
high council* found in me, 21except for one
thing I said when I shouted out, 'I am on trial
before you today because I believe in the resurrection of the dead!'"

22Felix, who was quite familiar with the Way,
adjourned the hearing and said, "Wait until Lysias, the garrison commander, arrives. Then I will
decide the case." 23He ordered an officer to keep
Paul in custody but to give him some freedom
and allow his friends to visit him and take care
of his needs.

24A few days later Felix came with his wife,
Drusilla, who was Jewish. Sending for Paul, they
listened as he told them about faith in Christ
Jesus. 25As he reasoned with them about righteousness and self-control and the judgment to
come, Felix was terrified. "Go away for now," he
replied. "When it is more convenient, I'll call for
you again." 26He also hoped that Paul would
bribe him, so he sent for him quite often and
talked with him.

24:1 Greek *some elders and an orator.* **24:6** Some manuscripts add *We would have judged him by our law, 7but Lysias, the commander of the garrison, came and took him violently away from us, 8commanding his accusers to come before you.* **24:20** Greek *Sanhedrin.*

27Two years went by in this way; then Felix
was succeeded by Porcius Festus. And because
Felix wanted to gain favor with the Jewish leaders, he left Paul in prison.

CHAPTER 25

Paul Appears before Festus

Three days after Festus arrived in Caesarea to
take over his new responsibilities, he left for
Jerusalem, 2where the leading priests and other
Jewish leaders met with him and made their
accusations against Paul. 3They asked Festus as
a favor to transfer Paul to Jerusalem. (Their plan
was to waylay and kill him.) 4But Festus replied
that Paul was at Caesarea and he himself would
be returning there soon. 5So he said, "Those of
you in authority can return with me. If Paul has
done anything wrong, you can make your accusations."

6Eight or ten days later he returned to Caesarea, and on the following day Paul's trial began.
7On Paul's arrival in court, the Jewish leaders
from Jerusalem gathered around and made
many serious accusations they couldn't prove.
8Paul denied the charges. "I am not guilty," he
said. "I have committed no crime against the
Jewish laws or the Temple or the Roman government."

9Then Festus, wanting to please the Jews,
asked him, "Are you willing to go to Jerusalem
and stand trial before me there?"

10But Paul replied, "No! This is the official
Roman court, so I ought to be tried right here.
You know very well I am not guilty. 11If I have
done something worthy of death, I don't refuse
to die. But if I am innocent, neither you nor
anyone else has a right to turn me over to these
men to kill me. I appeal to Caesar!"

12Festus conferred with his advisers and then
replied, "Very well! You have appealed to Caesar,
and to Caesar you shall go!"

13A few days later King Agrippa arrived with
his sister, Bernice,* to pay their respects to Festus. 14During their stay of several days, Festus
discussed Paul's case with the king. "There is a
prisoner here," he told him, "whose case was left
for me by Felix. 15When I was in Jerusalem, the
leading priests and other Jewish leaders pressed
charges against him and asked me to sentence
him. 16Of course, I quickly pointed out to them
that Roman law does not convict people without
a trial. They are given an opportunity to defend
themselves face to face with their accusers.
17"When they came here for the trial, I called
the case the very next day and ordered Paul
brought in. 18But the accusations made against
him weren't at all what I expected. 19It was
something about their religion and about someone called Jesus who died, but whom Paul insists is alive. 20I was perplexed as to how to
conduct an investigation of this kind, and I
asked him whether he would be willing to stand
trial on these charges in Jerusalem. 21But Paul
appealed to the emperor. So I ordered him back
to jail until I could arrange to send him to
Caesar."

22"I'd like to hear the man myself," Agrippa
said.

And Festus replied, "You shall—tomorrow!"

Paul Speaks to Agrippa

23So the next day Agrippa and Bernice arrived at
the auditorium with great pomp, accompanied
by military officers and prominent men of the
city. Festus ordered that Paul be brought in.
24Then Festus said, "King Agrippa and all present, this is the man whose death is demanded
both by the local Jews and by those in Jerusalem.
25But in my opinion he has done nothing worthy of death. However, he appealed his case to
the emperor, and I decided to send him. 26But
what shall I write the emperor? For there is no
real charge against him. So I have brought him
before all of you, and especially you, King
Agrippa, so that after we examine him, I might
have something to write. 27For it doesn't seem
reasonable to send a prisoner to the emperor
without specifying the charges against him!"

CHAPTER 26

Then Agrippa said to Paul, "You may speak in
your defense."

So Paul, with a gesture of his hand, started his
defense: 2"I am fortunate, King Agrippa, that
you are the one hearing my defense against all
these accusations made by the Jewish leaders,
3for I know you are an expert on Jewish customs
and controversies. Now please listen to me patiently!

4"As the Jewish leaders are well aware, I was
given a thorough Jewish training from my earliest childhood among my own people and in
Jerusalem. 5If they would admit it, they know
that I have been a member of the Pharisees, the
strictest sect of our religion. 6Now I am on trial
because I am looking forward to the fulfillment

25:13 Greek *Agrippa the king and Bernice arrived.*

of God's promise made to our ancestors. 7In
fact, that is why the twelve tribes of Israel worship God night and day, and they share the same
hope I have. Yet, O king, they say it is wrong for
me to have this hope! 8Why does it seem incredible to any of you that God can raise the dead?

9"I used to believe that I ought to do everything I could to oppose the followers of Jesus of
Nazareth.* 10Authorized by the leading priests,
I caused many of the believers in Jerusalem to be
sent to prison. And I cast my vote against them
when they were condemned to death. 11Many
times I had them whipped in the synagogues to
try to get them to curse Christ. I was so violently
opposed to them that I even hounded them in
distant cities of foreign lands.

12"One day I was on such a mission to Damascus, armed with the authority and commission of the leading priests. 13About noon, Your
Majesty, a light from heaven brighter than the
sun shone down on me and my companions.
14We all fell down, and I heard a voice saying to
me in Aramaic,* 'Saul, Saul, why are you persecuting me? It is hard for you to fight against my
will.*'

15" 'Who are you, sir?' I asked.

"And the Lord replied, 'I am Jesus, the one
you are persecuting. 16Now stand up! For I have
appeared to you to appoint you as my servant
and my witness. You are to tell the world about
this experience and about other times I will
appear to you. 17And I will protect you from
both your own people and the Gentiles. Yes, I
am going to send you to the Gentiles, 18to open
their eyes so they may turn from darkness to
light, and from the power of Satan to God. Then
they will receive forgiveness for their sins and be
given a place among God's people, who are set
apart by faith in me.'

19"And so, O King Agrippa, I was not disobedient to that vision from heaven. 20I preached
first to those in Damascus, then in Jerusalem
and throughout all Judea, and also to the Gentiles, that all must turn from their sins and turn
to God—and prove they have changed by the
good things they do. 21Some Jews arrested me in
the Temple for preaching this, and they tried to
kill me. 22But God protected me so that I am still
alive today to tell these facts to everyone, from
the least to the greatest. I teach nothing except
what the prophets and Moses said would happen—23that the Messiah would suffer and be
the first to rise from the dead as a light to Jews
and Gentiles alike."

24Suddenly, Festus shouted, "Paul, you are
insane. Too much study has made you crazy!"

25But Paul replied, "I am not insane, Most
Excellent Festus. I am speaking the sober truth.
26And King Agrippa knows about these things. I
speak frankly, for I am sure these events are all
familiar to him, for they were not done in a
corner! 27King Agrippa, do you believe the
prophets? I know you do—"

28Agrippa interrupted him. "Do you think
you can make me a Christian so quickly?"*

29Paul replied, "Whether quickly or not, I
pray to God that both you and everyone here in
this audience might become the same as I am,
except for these chains."

30Then the king, the governor, Bernice, and
all the others stood and left. 31As they talked it
over they agreed, "This man hasn't done anything worthy of death or imprisonment." 32And
Agrippa said to Festus, "He could be set free if
he hadn't appealed to Caesar!"

CHAPTER 27

Paul Sails for Rome

When the time came, we set sail for Italy. Paul
and several other prisoners were placed in the
custody of an army officer named Julius, a captain of the Imperial Regiment. 2And Aristarchus,
a Macedonian from Thessalonica, was also with
us. We left on a boat whose home port was
Adramyttium; it was scheduled to make several
stops at ports along the coast of the province of
Asia.

3The next day when we docked at Sidon,
Julius was very kind to Paul and let him go
ashore to visit with friends so they could provide
for his needs. 4Putting out to sea from there, we
encountered headwinds that made it difficult to
keep the ship on course, so we sailed north of
Cyprus between the island and the mainland.
5We passed along the coast of the provinces of
Cilicia and Pamphylia, landing at Myra, in the
province of Lycia. 6There the officer found an
Egyptian ship from Alexandria that was bound
for Italy, and he put us on board.

7We had several days of rough sailing, and
after great difficulty we finally neared Cnidus. But
the wind was against us, so we sailed down to the
leeward side of Crete, past the cape of Salmone.
8We struggled along the coast with great difficulty

26:9 Greek *oppose the name of Jesus the Nazarene.* **26:14a** Or *Hebrew.* **26:14b** Greek *It is hard for you to kick against the oxgoads.* **26:28** Or *"A little more, and your arguments would make me a Christian."*

and finally arrived at Fair Havens, near the city of Lasea. 9We had lost a lot of time. The weather was becoming dangerous for long voyages by then because it was so late in the fall,* and Paul spoke to the ship's officers about it.

10"Sirs," he said, "I believe there is trouble ahead if we go on—shipwreck, loss of cargo, injuries, and danger to our lives." 11But the officer in charge of the prisoners listened more to the ship's captain and the owner than to Paul. 12And since Fair Havens was an exposed harbor—a poor place to spend the winter—most of the crew wanted to go to Phoenix, farther up the coast of Crete, and spend the winter there. Phoenix was a good harbor with only a southwest and northwest exposure.

The Storm at Sea

13When a light wind began blowing from the south, the sailors thought they could make it. So they pulled up anchor and sailed along close to shore. 14But the weather changed abruptly, and a wind of typhoon strength (a "northeaster," they called it) caught the ship and blew it out to sea. 15They couldn't turn the ship into the wind, so they gave up and let it run before the gale.

16We sailed behind a small island named Cauda,* where with great difficulty we hoisted aboard the lifeboat that was being towed behind us. 17Then we banded the ship with ropes to strengthen the hull. The sailors were afraid of being driven across to the sandbars of Syrtis off the African coast, so they lowered the sea anchor and were thus driven before the wind.

18The next day, as gale-force winds continued to batter the ship, the crew began throwing the cargo overboard. 19The following day they even threw out the ship's equipment and anything else they could lay their hands on. 20The terrible storm raged unabated for many days, blotting out the sun and the stars, until at last all hope was gone.

21No one had eaten for a long time. Finally, Paul called the crew together and said, "Men, you should have listened to me in the first place and not left Fair Havens. You would have avoided all this injury and loss. 22But take courage! None of you will lose your lives, even though the ship will go down. 23For last night an angel of the God to whom I belong and whom I serve stood beside me, 24and he said, 'Don't be afraid, Paul, for you will surely stand trial before Caesar! What's more, God in his goodness has granted safety to everyone sailing with you.' 25So take courage! For I believe God. It will be just as he said. 26But we will be shipwrecked on an island."

The Shipwreck

27About midnight on the fourteenth night of the storm, as we were being driven across the Sea of Adria,* the sailors sensed land was near. 28They took soundings and found the water was only 120 feet deep. A little later they sounded again and found only 90 feet.* 29At this rate they were

27:9 Greek *because the fast was now already gone by.* This fast happened on the Day of Atonement (*Yom Kippur*), which occurred in late September or early October. 27:16 Some manuscripts read *Claudà.*

27:27 The *Sea of Adria* is in the central Mediterranean; it is not to be confused with the Adriatic Sea. 27:28 Greek *20 fathoms . . . 15 fathoms* [37 meters . . . 27 meters].

Share Your Own Story

Read ACTS 26:1-23

Another useful tool in our "evangelistic toolbox" is the story, or testimony, of how we came to personally know Jesus Christ. Paul used this method effectively when he appeared before King Agrippa. As was often his style, he began his presentation of the gospel by explaining how he had personally come into a relationship with Christ. Then he segued into the proclamation of the gospel message (verses 19-23).

Every believer has a testimony. Some may be more dramatic than others. Such was the case with Paul, formerly the notorious Saul of Tarsus, an aggressive persecutor of the church. Regardless of how incredible your testimony may seem, your personal salvation story will help you find common ground with a nonbeliever. You can tell him or her of your former life and attitude before coming to Christ, then explain the changes that came afterward. When a nonbeliever sees that you can relate to his or her own life, he or she may be more open to what you have to say.

Why don't you take a moment to think about the changes that have taken place in your life now that you are a Christian? You may even want to write down your testimony so that you will be ready to share it at the next opportunity.

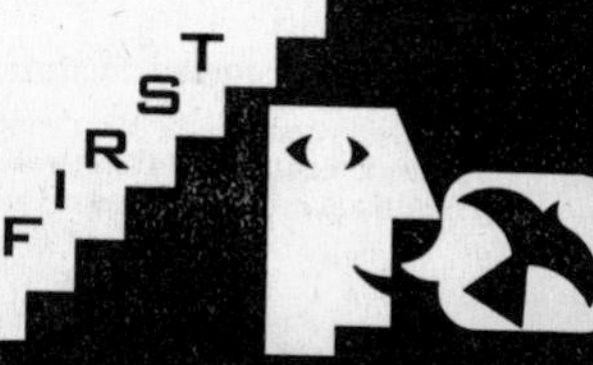

afraid we would soon be driven against the rocks
along the shore, so they threw out four anchors
from the stern and prayed for daylight. 30Then
the sailors tried to abandon the ship; they lowered the lifeboat as though they were going to
put out anchors from the prow. 31But Paul said
to the commanding officer and the soldiers,
"You will all die unless the sailors stay aboard."
32So the soldiers cut the ropes and let the boat
fall off.

33As the darkness gave way to the early morning light, Paul begged everyone to eat. "You
haven't touched food for two weeks," he said.
34"Please eat something now for your own
good. For not a hair of your heads will perish."
35Then he took some bread, gave thanks to God
before them all, and broke off a piece and ate it.
36Then everyone was encouraged, 37and all 276
of us began eating—for that is the number we
had aboard. 38After eating, the crew lightened
the ship further by throwing the cargo of wheat
overboard.

39When morning dawned, they didn't recognize the coastline, but they saw a bay with a
beach and wondered if they could get between
the rocks and get the ship safely to shore. 40So
they cut off the anchors and left them in the sea.
Then they lowered the rudders, raised the fore-
sail, and headed toward shore. 41But the ship hit
a shoal and ran aground. The bow of the ship
stuck fast, while the stern was repeatedly
smashed by the force of the waves and began to
break apart.

42The soldiers wanted to kill the prisoners to
make sure they didn't swim ashore and escape.
43But the commanding officer wanted to spare
Paul, so he didn't let them carry out their plan.
Then he ordered all who could swim to jump
overboard first and make for land, 44and he told
the others to try for it on planks and debris from
the broken ship. So everyone escaped safely
ashore!

CHAPTER 28

Paul on the Island of Malta

Once we were safe on shore, we learned that we
were on the island of Malta. 2The people of the
island were very kind to us. It was cold and rainy,
so they built a fire on the shore to welcome us
and warm us.

3As Paul gathered an armful of sticks and was
laying them on the fire, a poisonous snake,
driven out by the heat, fastened itself onto his
hand. 4The people of the island saw it hanging
there and said to each other, "A murderer, no
doubt! Though he escaped the sea, justice will
not permit him to live." 5But Paul shook off the
snake into the fire and was unharmed. 6The
people waited for him to swell up or suddenly
drop dead. But when they had waited a long
time and saw no harm come to him, they
changed their minds and decided he was a god.

7Near the shore where we landed was an
estate belonging to Publius, the chief official of
the island. He welcomed us courteously and fed
us for three days. 8As it happened, Publius's
father was ill with fever and dysentery. Paul went
in and prayed for him, and laying his hands on
him, he healed him. 9Then all the other sick
people on the island came and were cured. 10As
a result we were showered with honors, and
when the time came to sail, people put on board
all sorts of things we would need for the trip.

Paul Arrives at Rome

11It was three months after the shipwreck that we
set sail on another ship that had wintered at the
island—an Alexandrian ship with the twin
gods* as its figurehead. 12Our first stop was
Syracuse,* where we stayed three days. 13From
there we sailed across to Rhegium.* A day later
a south wind began blowing, so the following
day we sailed up the coast to Puteoli. 14There we
found some believers,* who invited us to stay
with them seven days. And so we came to Rome.

15The brothers and sisters* in Rome had
heard we were coming, and they came to meet
us at the Forum* on the Appian Way. Others
joined us at The Three Taverns.* When Paul saw
them, he thanked God and took courage.

16When we arrived in Rome, Paul was permitted to have his own private lodging, though he
was guarded by a soldier.

Paul Preaches at Rome under Guard

17Three days after Paul's arrival, he called together the local Jewish leaders. He said to them,
"Brothers, I was arrested in Jerusalem and
handed over to the Roman government, even
though I had done nothing against our people
or the customs of our ancestors. 18The Romans
tried me and wanted to release me, for they
found no cause for the death sentence. 19But

28:11 The *twin gods* were the Roman gods Castor and Pollux. 28:12 *Syracuse* was on the island of Sicily. 28:13 *Rhegium* was on the southern tip of Italy. 28:14 Greek *brothers*. 28:15a Greek *brothers*. 28:15b *The Forum* was about 43 miles (70 kilometers) from Rome. 28:15c *The Three Taverns* was about 35 miles (57 kilometers) from Rome.

when the Jewish leaders protested the decision,
I felt it necessary to appeal to Caesar, even
though I had no desire to press charges against
my own people. 20I asked you to come here
today so we could get acquainted and so I could
tell you that I am bound with this chain because
I believe that the hope of Israel—the Messiah—
has already come."

21They replied, "We have heard nothing
against you. We have had no letters from Judea
or reports from anyone who has arrived here.
22But we want to hear what you believe, for the
only thing we know about these Christians* is
that they are denounced everywhere."

23So a time was set, and on that day a large
number of people came to Paul's house. He told
them about the Kingdom of God and taught
them about Jesus from the Scriptures—from the
five books of Moses and the books of the prophets. He began lecturing in the morning and went
on into the evening. 24Some believed and some
didn't. 25But after they had argued back and
forth among themselves, they left with this final
word from Paul: "The Holy Spirit was right
when he said to our ancestors through Isaiah the
prophet,

26 'Go and say to my people,
You will hear my words,
but you will not understand;
you will see what I do,
but you will not perceive its meaning.
27 For the hearts of these people are hardened,
and their ears cannot hear,
and they have closed their eyes—
so their eyes cannot see,
and their ears cannot hear,
and their hearts cannot understand,
and they cannot turn to me
and let me heal them.'*

28So I want you to realize that this salvation
from God is also available to the Gentiles, and
they will accept it."*

30For the next two years, Paul lived in his own
rented house.* He welcomed all who visited
him, 31proclaiming the Kingdom of God with all
boldness and teaching about the Lord Jesus
Christ. And no one tried to stop him.

28:22 Greek *this sect.* **28:26-27** Isa 6:9-10. **28:28** Some manuscripts add verse 29, *And when he had said these words, the Jews departed, greatly disagreeing with each other.* **28:30** Or *at his own expense.*

Romans

CHAPTER 1

Greetings from Paul

This letter is from Paul, Jesus Christ's slave, chosen by God to be an apostle and sent out to
preach his Good News. 2This Good News was
promised long ago by God through his prophets
in the holy Scriptures. 3It is the Good News
about his Son, Jesus, who came as a man, born
into King David's royal family line. 4And Jesus
Christ our Lord was shown to be the Son of God
when God powerfully raised him from the dead
by means of the Holy Spirit.* 5Through Christ,
God has given us the privilege and authority to
tell Gentiles everywhere what God has done for
them, so that they will believe and obey him,
bringing glory to his name.

6You are among those who have been called
to belong to Jesus Christ, 7dear friends in Rome.
God loves you dearly, and he has called you to
be his very own people.

May grace and peace be yours from God our
Father and the Lord Jesus Christ.

God's Good News

8Let me say first of all that your faith in God
is becoming known throughout the world.
How I thank God through Jesus Christ for
each one of you. 9God knows how often I
pray for you. Day and night I bring you and
your needs in prayer to God, whom I serve
with all my heart* by telling others the Good
News about his Son.

10One of the things I always pray for is the
opportunity, God willing, to come at last to see
you. 11For I long to visit you so I can share a
spiritual blessing with you that will help you
grow strong in the Lord. 12I'm eager to encourage you in your faith, but I also want to be
encouraged by yours. In this way, each of us will
be a blessing to the other.

13I want you to know, dear brothers and sisters,* that I planned many times to visit you, but
I was prevented until now. I want to work among
you and see good results, just as I have done
among other Gentiles. 14For I have a great sense
of obligation to people in our culture and to
people in other cultures,* to the educated and
uneducated alike. 15So I am eager to come to
you in Rome, too, to preach God's Good News.

16For I am not ashamed of this Good News
about Christ. It is the power of God at work,
saving everyone who believes—Jews first and
also Gentiles. 17This Good News tells us how
God makes us right in his sight. This is accomplished from start to finish by faith. As the
Scriptures say, "It is through faith that a righteous person has life."*

God's Anger at Sin

18But God shows his anger from heaven against
all sinful, wicked people who push the truth
away from themselves.* 19For the truth about
God is known to them instinctively.* God has
put this knowledge in their hearts. 20From the
time the world was created, people have seen the
earth and sky and all that God made. They can
clearly see his invisible qualities—his eternal
power and divine nature. So they have no excuse
whatsoever for not knowing God.

21Yes, they knew God, but they wouldn't worship him as God or even give him thanks. And
they began to think up foolish ideas of what
God was like. The result was that their minds
became dark and confused. 22Claiming to be
wise, they became utter fools instead. 23And
instead of worshiping the glorious, ever-living

1:4 Or *the Spirit of holiness.* 1:9 Or *in my spirit.* 1:13 Greek *brothers.* 1:14 Greek *to Greeks and to barbarians.* 1:17 Hab 2:4. 1:18 Or *who prevent the truth from being known.* 1:19 Greek *is manifest in them.*

God, they worshiped idols made to look like mere people, or birds and animals and snakes.

24So God let them go ahead and do whatever shameful things their hearts desired. As a result, they did vile and degrading things with each other's bodies. 25Instead of believing what they knew was the truth about God, they deliberately chose to believe lies. So they worshiped the things God made but not the Creator himself, who is to be praised forever. Amen.

26That is why God abandoned them to their shameful desires. Even the women turned against the natural way to have sex and instead indulged in sex with each other. 27And the men, instead of having normal sexual relationships with women, burned with lust for each other. Men did shameful things with other men and, as a result, suffered within themselves the penalty they so richly deserved.

28When they refused to acknowledge God, he abandoned them to their evil minds and let them do things that should never be done. 29Their lives became full of every kind of wickedness, sin, greed, hate, envy, murder, fighting, deception, malicious behavior, and gossip. 30They are backstabbers, haters of God, insolent, proud, and boastful. They are forever inventing new ways of sinning and are disobedient to their parents. 31They refuse to understand, break their promises, and are heartless and unforgiving. 32They are fully aware of God's death penalty for those who do these things, yet they go right ahead and do them anyway. And, worse yet, they encourage others to do them, too.

CHAPTER 2

God's Judgment of Sin

You may be saying, "What terrible people you have been talking about!" But you are just as bad, and you have no excuse! When you say they are wicked and should be punished, you are condemning yourself, for you do these very same things. 2And we know that God, in his justice, will punish anyone who does such things. 3Do you think that God will judge and condemn others for doing them and not judge you when you do them, too? 4Don't you realize how kind, tolerant, and patient God is with you? Or don't you care? Can't you see how kind he has been in giving you time to turn from your sin?

5But no, you won't listen. So you are storing up terrible punishment for yourself because of your stubbornness in refusing to turn from your sin. For there is going to come a day of judgment when God, the just judge of all the world, 6will judge all people according to what they have done. 7He will give eternal life to those who persist in doing what is good, seeking after the glory and honor and immortality that God offers. 8But he will pour out his anger and wrath on those who live for themselves, who refuse to obey the truth and practice evil deeds. 9There will be trouble and calamity for everyone who keeps on sinning—for the Jew first and also for the Gentile. 10But there will be glory and honor and peace from God for all who do good—for the Jew first and also for the Gentile. 11For God does not show favoritism.

12God will punish the Gentiles when they sin, even though they never had God's written law. And he will punish the Jews when they sin, for they do have the law. 13For it is not merely knowing the law that brings God's approval. Those who obey the law will be declared right in God's sight. 14Even when Gentiles, who do not have God's written law, instinctively follow what the law says, they show that in their hearts they know right from wrong. 15They demonstrate that God's law is written within them, for their own consciences either accuse them or tell them they are doing what is right. 16The day will surely come when God, by Jesus Christ, will judge everyone's secret life. This is my message.

The Jews and the Law

17If you are a Jew, you are relying on God's law for your special relationship with him. You boast that all is well between yourself and God. 18Yes, you know what he wants; you know right from wrong because you have been taught his law. 19You are convinced that you are a guide for the blind and a beacon light for people who are lost in darkness without God. 20You think you can instruct the ignorant and teach children the ways of God. For you are certain that in God's law you have complete knowledge and truth.

21Well then, if you teach others, why don't you teach yourself? You tell others not to steal, but do you steal? 22You say it is wrong to commit adultery, but do you do it? You condemn idolatry, but do you steal from pagan temples? 23You are so proud of knowing the law, but you dishonor God by breaking it. 24No wonder the Scriptures say, "The world blasphemes the name of God because of you."*

2:24 Isa 52:5.

What Happens to Those Who Have Never Heard the Gospel?

Read ROMANS 1:18-20

Sometimes the person who asks this question is not so much concerned about those who have never heard the gospel. Rather, this person may be more concerned about trying to put up a "smoke screen" to keep you—the Christian—from showing his or her need for God. We might remind that person that God is loving and compassionate, and that he will deal fairly and justly with those who have never heard the gospel. But the person who asks you this question needs to recognize that knowledge brings responsibility. Those who know the truth of the gospel will be held accountable.

As we know from the Bible, God will judge us according to what we know of him (see Luke 12:48, p. 88). We will not be held accountable for what we do not know. Still, that does not excuse us from all responsibility. Otherwise we might say, "Ignorance is bliss." But this is not to say that the person who has not heard of Jesus will never know of him.

We, as humans, no matter where we live on God's earth, were born with a soul, an emptiness, a sense that life should have meaning and purpose. In spite of that spiritual longing, we have disregarded God and his Word. But if we are truly seeking God, he will reveal himself to us. We find proof of this in Acts 10:1-48 (pp. 150–151). There, a man named Cornelius—a religious man who constantly prayed to God—asked the Lord to reveal himself to him. Although Cornelius may have heard of Jesus Christ, he did not know God's plan for salvation. But that did not stop God from answering his prayer by sending the apostle Peter to preach the gospel to him. When Cornelius heard that wonderful message, he believed!

The Bible tells us that God is unchanging (see James 1:17, p. 299). He is the same yesterday, today, and tomorrow. If he heard Cornelius's prayer, he will also hear the prayers of those who do not know him but desire to.

BIG QUESTIONS

25The Jewish ceremony of circumcision is
worth something only if you obey God's law. But
if you don't obey God's law, you are no better off
than an uncircumcised Gentile. 26And if the
Gentiles obey God's law, won't God give them
all the rights and honors of being his own
people? 27In fact, uncircumcised Gentiles who
keep God's law will be much better off than you
Jews who are circumcised and know so much
about God's law but don't obey it.
28For you are not a true Jew just because you
were born of Jewish parents or because you have
gone through the Jewish ceremony of circumcision. 29No, a true Jew is one whose heart is right
with God. And true circumcision is not a cutting
of the body but a change of heart produced by
God's Spirit. Whoever has that kind of change
seeks praise from God, not from people.

CHAPTER **3**

God Remains Faithful

Then what's the advantage of being a Jew? Is
there any value in the Jewish ceremony of circumcision? 2Yes, being a Jew has many advan-
tages. First of all, the Jews were entrusted with
the whole revelation of God.*
3True, some of them were unfaithful; but just
because they broke their promises, does that
mean God will break his promises? 4Of course
not! Though everyone else in the world is a liar,
God is true. As the Scriptures say, "He will be
proved right in what he says, and he will win his
case in court."*
5"But," some say, "our sins serve a good purpose, for people will see God's goodness when
he declares us sinners to be innocent. Isn't it
unfair, then, for God to punish us?" (That is
actually the way some people talk.) 6Of course
not! If God is not just, how is he qualified to
judge the world? 7"But," some might still argue,
"how can God judge and condemn me as a
sinner if my dishonesty highlights his truthfulness and brings him more glory?" 8If you follow
that kind of thinking, however, you might as

3:2 Greek *the oracles of God.* 3:4 Ps 51:4.

well say that the more we sin the better it is! Those who say such things deserve to be condemned, yet some slander me by saying this is what I preach!

All People Are Sinners

[9]Well then, are we Jews better than others?* No, not at all, for we have already shown that all people, whether Jews or Gentiles, are under the power of sin. [10]As the Scriptures say,

"No one is good—
not even one.
11 No one has real understanding;
no one is seeking God.
12 All have turned away from God;
all have gone wrong.
No one does good,
not even one."*
13 "Their talk is foul, like the stench from an open grave.
Their speech is filled with lies."
"The poison of a deadly snake drips from their lips."*
14 "Their mouths are full of cursing and bitterness."*
15 "They are quick to commit murder.
16 Wherever they go, destruction and misery follow them.
17 They do not know what true peace is."*
18 "They have no fear of God to restrain them."*

[19]Obviously, the law applies to those to whom it was given, for its purpose is to keep people from having excuses and to bring the entire world into judgment before God. [20]For no one can ever be made right in God's sight by doing what his law commands. For the more we know God's law, the clearer it becomes that we aren't obeying it.

Christ Took Our Punishment

[21]But now God has shown us a different way of being right in his sight—not by obeying the law but by the way promised in the Scriptures long ago. [22]We are made right in God's sight when we trust in Jesus Christ to take away our sins. And we all can be saved in this same way, no matter who we are or what we have done.

[23]For all have sinned; all fall short of God's glorious standard. [24]Yet now God in his gracious kindness declares us not guilty. He has done this through Christ Jesus, who has freed us by taking away our sins. [25]For God sent Jesus to take the punishment for our sins and to satisfy God's anger against us. We are made right with God when we believe that Jesus shed his blood, sacrificing his life for us. God was being entirely fair and just when he did not punish those who sinned in former times. [26]And he is entirely fair and just in this present time when he declares sinners to be right in his sight because they believe in Jesus.

[27]Can we boast, then, that we have done anything to be accepted by God? No, because our acquittal is not based on our good deeds. It is based on our faith. [28]So we are made right with God through faith and not by obeying the law.

[29]After all, God is not the God of the Jews only, is he? Isn't he also the God of the Gentiles? Of course he is. [30]There is only one God, and there is only one way of being accepted by him. He makes people right with himself only by faith, whether they are Jews or Gentiles. [31]Well then, if we emphasize faith, does this mean that we can forget about the law? Of course not! In fact, only when we have faith do we truly fulfill the law.

CHAPTER 4

The Faith of Abraham

Abraham was, humanly speaking, the founder of our Jewish nation. What were his experiences concerning this question of being saved by faith? [2]Was it because of his good deeds that God accepted him? If so, he would have had something to boast about. But from God's point of view Abraham had no basis at all for pride. [3]For the Scriptures tell us, "Abraham believed God, so God declared him to be righteous."*

[4]When people work, their wages are not a gift. Workers earn what they receive. [5]But people are declared righteous because of their faith, not because of their work.

[6]King David spoke of this, describing the happiness of an undeserving sinner who is declared to be righteous:

7 "Oh, what joy for those whose disobedience is forgiven,
whose sins are put out of sight.
8 Yes, what joy for those
whose sin is no longer counted against them by the Lord."*

3:9 Greek *Are we better?* 3:10-12 Pss 14:1-3; 53:1-3. 3:13 Pss 5:9; 140:3. 3:14 Ps 10:7. 3:15-17 Isa 59:7-8. 3:18 Ps 36:1. 4:3 Gen 15:6. 4:7-8 Ps 32:1-2.

If God Is So Good, Why Do Bad Things Happen to His People? Read ROMANS 5:1-5

Sickness, war, accidents, natural disasters, tragedies—they come to the just and the unjust, the Christian and the non-Christian, the moral and the immoral. Yet, if God is so good and all-powerful, why doesn't he just wipe out evil things in this world? This question often arises after any tragedy, but especially when it affects people who you would think should be "immune" to such things.

In addressing this question, it is important to remember that God originally created the world perfect. But he also gave man the freedom to obey or disobey. When Adam sinned, death and suffering became an inevitable part of life (verse 12). Yet, as the Christian thinker C. S. Lewis observed, it is idle for us to speculate about the *origin* of evil. The problem we all face is the *fact* of evil. The only *solution* to the fact of evil is God's solution, Jesus Christ [Paul Little, *How to Give Away Your Faith* (Downers Grove, Ill.: InterVarsity Press, 1966), p. 72].

How is Jesus Christ the solution to the fact of evil? The moment you surrendered your life to Jesus Christ, you entered into the master plan that God has for you. Though it is true that you may not know what the future holds, you know who holds the future. And he has promised that all things work together for good to those that love God (see Romans 8:28, p. 185). Not just the good things, but all things.

That is easy to say when things are going smoothly. But when something unexpected comes into the picture, we may wonder if God is paying attention. That is when we need to realize that God is painting on a large canvas. He is looking at the big picture. We only see what is in front of us at the given moment.

God will allow many events to come into our life—good things, bad things, things that make sense, things that make no sense at all. But every one of these incidents in our lives serves as a part of his plan for us. Tragedy in itself is not good. But God can take tragedy and hardship and use them for his glory. As God's children, we know that everything that happens to us first goes through his screen of protection. And he will never give us more than we can handle (see 1 Corinthians 10:13, p. 208). For that reason we can follow the advice in verse 3 and rejoice. We have the assurance that God is working in our lives to strengthen and develop our character. More important, he will never leave our side (see Hebrews 13:5, p. 298).

BIG QUESTIONS ?

[9]Now then, is this blessing only for the Jews, or is it for Gentiles, too? Well, what about Abraham? We have been saying he was declared righteous by God because of his faith. [10]But how did his faith help him? Was he declared righteous only after he had been circumcised, or was it before he was circumcised? The answer is that God accepted him first, and then he was circumcised later!

[11]The circumcision ceremony was a sign that Abraham already had faith and that God had already accepted him and declared him to be righteous—even before he was circumcised. So Abraham is the spiritual father of those who have faith but have not been circumcised. They are made right with God by faith. [12]And Abraham is also the spiritual father of those who have been circumcised, but only if they have the same kind of faith Abraham had before he was circumcised.

[13]It is clear, then, that God's promise to give the whole earth to Abraham and his descendants was not based on obedience to God's law, but on the new relationship with God that comes by faith. [14]So if you claim that God's promise is for those who obey God's law and think they are "good enough" in God's sight, then you are saying that faith is useless. And in that case, the promise is also meaningless. [15]But the law brings punishment on those who try to obey it. (The only way to avoid breaking the law is to have no law to break!)

[16]So that's why faith is the key! God's promise is given to us as a free gift. And we are certain to receive it, whether or not we follow Jewish

customs, if we have faith like Abraham's. For
Abraham is the father of all who believe. 17That
is what the Scriptures mean when God told him,
"I have made you the father of many nations."*
This happened because Abraham believed in the
God who brings the dead back to life and who
brings into existence what didn't exist before.

18When God promised Abraham that he
would become the father of many nations, Abraham believed him. God had also said, "Your
descendants will be as numerous as the stars,"*
even though such a promise seemed utterly impossible! 19And Abraham's faith did not
weaken, even though he knew that he was too
old to be a father at the age of one hundred and
that Sarah, his wife, had never been able to have
children.

20Abraham never wavered in believing God's
promise. In fact, his faith grew stronger, and in
this he brought glory to God. 21He was absolutely convinced that God was able to do anything he promised. 22And because of Abraham's
faith, God declared him to be righteous.

23Now this wonderful truth—that God declared him to be righteous—wasn't just for
Abraham's benefit. 24It was for us, too, assuring
us that God will also declare us to be righteous
if we believe in God, who brought Jesus our
Lord back from the dead. 25He was handed over
to die because of our sins, and he was raised
from the dead to make us right with God.

CHAPTER 5

Faith Brings Joy

Therefore, since we have been made right in
God's sight by faith, we have peace with God
because of what Jesus Christ our Lord has done
for us. 2Because of our faith, Christ has brought
us into this place of highest privilege where we
now stand, and we confidently and joyfully look
forward to sharing God's glory.

3We can rejoice, too, when we run into problems and trials, for we know that they are good
for us—they help us learn to endure. 4And endurance develops strength of character in us,
and character strengthens our confident expectation of salvation. 5And this expectation will
not disappoint us. For we know how dearly God
loves us, because he has given us the Holy Spirit
to fill our hearts with his love.

6When we were utterly helpless, Christ came
at just the right time and died for us sinners.
7Now, no one is likely to die for a good person,
though someone might be willing to die for a
person who is especially good. 8But God
showed his great love for us by sending Christ to
die for us while we were still sinners. 9And since
we have been made right in God's sight by the
blood of Christ, he will certainly save us from
God's judgment. 10For since we were restored to
friendship with God by the death of his Son
while we were still his enemies, we will certainly
be delivered from eternal punishment by his
life. 11So now we can rejoice in our wonderful
new relationship with God—all because of what
our Lord Jesus Christ has done for us in making
us friends of God.

Adam and Christ Contrasted

12When Adam sinned, sin entered the entire
human race. Adam's sin brought death, so
death spread to everyone, for everyone sinned.
13Yes, people sinned even before the law was
given. And though there was no law to break,
since it had not yet been given, 14they all died
anyway—even though they did not disobey an
explicit commandment of God, as Adam did.
What a contrast between Adam and Christ,
who was yet to come! 15And what a difference
between our sin and God's generous gift of
forgiveness. For this one man, Adam, brought
death to many through his sin. But this other
man, Jesus Christ, brought forgiveness to
many through God's bountiful gift. 16And the
result of God's gracious gift is very different
from the result of that one man's sin. For
Adam's sin led to condemnation, but we have
the free gift of being accepted by God, even
though we are guilty of many sins. 17The sin of
this one man, Adam, caused death to rule over
us, but all who receive God's wonderful, gracious gift of righteousness will live in triumph
over sin and death through this one man, Jesus
Christ.

18Yes, Adam's one sin brought condemnation
upon everyone, but Christ's one act of righteousness makes all people right in God's sight and
gives them life. 19Because one person disobeyed
God, many people became sinners. But because
one other person obeyed God, many people will
be made right in God's sight.

20God's law was given so that all people could
see how sinful they were. But as people sinned
more and more, God's wonderful kindness became more abundant. 21So just as sin ruled over
all people and brought them to death, now

4:17 Gen 17:5. 4:18 Gen 15:5.

God's wonderful kindness rules instead, giving
us right standing with God and resulting in eternal life through Jesus Christ our Lord.

CHAPTER 6

Sin's Power Is Broken

Well then, should we keep on sinning so that
God can show us more and more kindness and
forgiveness? 2Of course not! Since we have
died to sin, how can we continue to live in it?
3Or have you forgotten that when we became
Christians and were baptized to become one
with Christ Jesus, we died with him? 4For we
died and were buried with Christ by baptism.
And just as Christ was raised from the dead by
the glorious power of the Father, now we also
may live new lives.

5Since we have been united with him in his
death, we will also be raised as he was. 6Our old
sinful selves were crucified with Christ so that
sin might lose its power in our lives. We are no
longer slaves to sin. 7For when we died with
Christ, we were set free from the power of sin.
8And since we died with Christ, we know we will
also share his new life. 9We are sure of this
because Christ rose from the dead, and he will
never die again. Death no longer has any power
over him. 10He died once to defeat sin, and now
he lives for the glory of God. 11So you should
consider yourselves dead to sin and able to live
for the glory of God through Christ Jesus.

12Do not let sin control the way you live;* do
not give in to its lustful desires. 13Do not let any
part of your body become a tool of wickedness,
to be used for sinning. Instead, give yourselves
completely to God since you have been given
new life. And use your whole body as a tool to
do what is right for the glory of God. 14Sin is no
longer your master, for you are no longer subject
to the law, which enslaves you to sin. Instead,
you are free by God's grace.

Freedom to Obey God

15So since God's grace has set us free from the
law, does this mean we can go on sinning? Of
course not! 16Don't you realize that whatever
you choose to obey becomes your master? You
can choose sin, which leads to death, or you
can choose to obey God and receive his approval. 17Thank God! Once you were slaves of
sin, but now you have obeyed with all your
heart the new teaching God has given you.
18Now you are free from sin, your old master,
and you have become slaves to your new master, righteousness.

19I speak this way, using the illustration of
slaves and masters, because it is easy to understand.
Before, you let yourselves be slaves of impurity

6:12 Or *Do not let sin reign in your body, which is subject to death.*

God's Spirit Will Help You Overcome Sin

Read ROMANS 8:9-14

This powerful passage of Scripture contains some critical truths we need to know about letting the Holy Spirit lead our lives. Remember, once you became a Christian, God gave you his Holy Spirit to help you live out your faith, guide your steps, empower your witness, and, as this passage attests, overcome sin. Look at four key points the apostle Paul makes here:

1. You Are Controlled by a New Nature. Your old, sinful nature will still try to get a hand on the steering wheel. But now your new nature is in the driver's seat, and your old nature has become like an annoying backseat driver. You can either give in to your old nature's nagging and bad directions, or you can ignore it and let the Holy Spirit direct your path.

2. Even Though You Will Face Physical Death, You Will Not Face Spiritual Death. As a believer, physical death is simply a transition to eternal life in heaven. You have been spared from spiritual death, which leads to everlasting torment and hell (see Revelation 21:8, p. 347). This important fact should reassure you when the devil tries to throw doubts your way.

3. The Same Spirit of God That Raised Jesus from the Dead Resides in *You*. Did you catch that? The Holy Spirit, who had the power to raise Jesus from the dead, now lives in you! If that is indeed true—and God's Word says it is—just think of the supernatural power you now have in your life to resist sin!

4. We Do Not Have to Give In to Our Sinful Nature and Urges. Paul wasn't talking about New Year's resolutions here. If we try to live a morally upright, godly life in our own strength, we will fail—and fail miserably. But, if we rely on the power of the Holy Spirit to help us, we will be overcomers.

Our Lives Should Show That God Is at Work in Our Hearts

Read ROMANS 7:4

While we still live on this side of heaven, we will always struggle between the desire to obey God and the desire to follow our sinful instincts. Even the apostle Paul knew what it was like to struggle with sin. In the verses surrounding this text, he describes the six keys to winning this battle and living a life that not only pleases God, but shows that God is working in our heart:

1. Admit the Power of Sin in Your Life (see Romans 7:14, p. 183). Recognize that you have that "combustible nature" within you, a vulnerability to the enticements of sin. If we fail to see our potential weaknesses, we are even more vulnerable to fall to them. The Bible warns against such an attitude, saying, "If you think you are standing strong, be careful, for you too may fall into the same sin" (1 Corinthians 10:12).

2. Realize That You Are Powerless to Change on Your Own (see Romans 7:18, p. 183). Your sinful nature is the source of the problem. You will never "master" sin and live a life pleasing to God on your own. Apart from God, you can do nothing.

3. Become "Fed Up" with Your Condition and Cry for Help (see Romans 7:24, p. 183). You cannot control evil in your life by simply determining to do so. You have to come to the end of yourself and ask for God's help in this struggle.

4. Accept Your Freedom (see Romans 7:25, p. 183). Take the hand of help that is offered to you by Jesus.

5. Accept God's Forgiveness and Lack of Condemnation (see Romans 8:1-2, pp. 183–184). Because of your unique union with Christ, God will forgive you—not condemn you—when you acknowledge your failures, struggles, and broken commitments.

6. Cut the Instinctive Actions of Your Sinful Nature (see Romans 8:3-8, p. 184). The only way to stop committing instinctive sinful actions is to stop living by your sinful nature and start

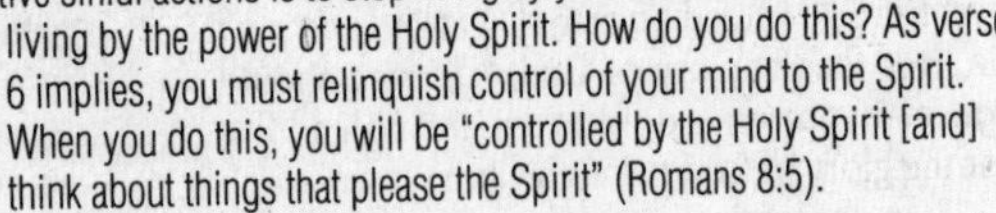

living by the power of the Holy Spirit. How do you do this? As verse 6 implies, you must relinquish control of your mind to the Spirit. When you do this, you will be "controlled by the Holy Spirit [and] think about things that please the Spirit" (Romans 8:5).

You will always have the potential to sin. But God has given you the power to overcome sin through his Holy Spirit. The key to drawing on his power is to be obedient to the Holy Spirit.

and lawlessness. Now you must choose to be
slaves of righteousness so that you will become
holy.
[20]In those days, when you were slaves of sin,
you weren't concerned with doing what was
right. [21]And what was the result? It was not
good, since now you are ashamed of the things
you used to do, things that end in eternal doom.
[22]But now you are free from the power of sin
and have become slaves of God. Now you do
those things that lead to holiness and result in
eternal life. [23]For the wages of sin is death, but
the free gift of God is eternal life through Christ
Jesus our Lord.

CHAPTER 7

No Longer Bound to the Law

Now, dear brothers and sisters*—you who are
familiar with the law—don't you know that the
law applies only to a person who is still living?
[2]Let me illustrate. When a woman marries, the
law binds her to her husband as long as he is
alive. But if he dies, the laws of marriage no
longer apply to her. [3]So while her husband is
alive, she would be committing adultery if she
married another man. But if her husband dies,
she is free from that law and does not commit
adultery when she remarries.
[4]So this is the point: The law no longer holds

7:1 Greek *brothers.*

you in its power, because you died to its power
when you died with Christ on the cross. And now
you are united with the one who was raised from
the dead. As a result, you can produce good fruit,
that is, good deeds for God. 5When we were
controlled by our old nature, sinful desires were
at work within us, and the law aroused these evil
desires that produced sinful deeds, resulting in
death. 6But now we have been released from the
law, for we died with Christ, and we are no longer
captive to its power. Now we can really serve God,
not in the old way by obeying the letter of the law,
but in the new way, by the Spirit.

God's Law Reveals Our Sin

7Well then, am I suggesting that the law of God
is evil? Of course not! The law is not sinful, but
it was the law that showed me my sin. I would
never have known that coveting is wrong if the
law had not said, "Do not covet."* 8But sin took
advantage of this law and aroused all kinds of
forbidden desires within me! If there were no
law, sin would not have that power.

9I felt fine when I did not understand what
the law demanded. But when I learned the truth,
I realized I had broken the law and was a sinner,
doomed to die. 10So the good law, which was
supposed to show me the way of life, instead
gave me the death penalty. 11Sin took advantage
of the law and fooled me; it took the good law
and used it to make me guilty of death. 12But
still, the law itself is holy and right and good.

13But how can that be? Did the law, which is
good, cause my doom? Of course not! Sin used
what was good to bring about my condemnation.
So we can see how terrible sin really is. It
uses God's good commandment for its own evil
purposes.

Struggling with Sin

14The law is good, then. The trouble is not with
the law but with me, because I am sold into
slavery, with sin as my master. 15I don't understand myself at all, for I really want to do what
is right, but I don't do it. Instead, I do the very
thing I hate. 16I know perfectly well that what I
am doing is wrong, and my bad conscience
shows that I agree that the law is good. 17But I
can't help myself, because it is sin inside me that
makes me do these evil things.

18I know I am rotten through and through so
far as my old sinful nature is concerned. No
matter which way I turn, I can't make myself do
right. I want to, but I can't. 19When I want to do
good, I don't. And when I try not to do wrong, I
do it anyway. 20But if I am doing what I don't
want to do, I am not really the one doing it; the
sin within me is doing it.

21It seems to be a fact of life that when I want
to do what is right, I inevitably do what is wrong.
22I love God's law with all my heart. 23But there
is another law at work within me that is at war
with my mind. This law wins the fight and
makes me a slave to the sin that is still within
me. 24Oh, what a miserable person I am! Who
will free me from this life that is dominated by
sin?* 25Thank God! The answer is in Jesus Christ
our Lord. So you see how it is: In my mind I
really want to obey God's law, but because of my
sinful nature I am a slave to sin.

CHAPTER 8

Life in the Spirit

So now there is no condemnation for those who
belong to Christ Jesus. 2For the power* of the
life-giving Spirit has freed you* through Christ Jesus

7:7 Exod 20:17; Deut 5:21.

7:24 Greek *from this body of death?* 8:2a Greek *the law;* also in 8:2b.

Prayer Is Not a Solitary Experience Read ROMANS 8:26-27

Have you ever wondered what to say to God? Perhaps you have a sick friend that you don't know how to pray for. Or maybe you are unsure of how to pray for your spiritual needs. This portion of Scripture will encourage you. From the moment you asked Jesus to be your personal Lord and Savior, you received a resident guest in your heart: the Holy Spirit.

One of the many things he does is to help you in prayer—especially at those times when you don't know what to pray. As you realize how intimately God is involved in your prayers, you will begin to feel a unique closeness to your Father in heaven. You may even discover a freshness in your prayer life that you never had before.

The next time you don't know what to pray for, ask the Holy Spirit to help you voice your concerns and needs to God.

Live to Please God Read ROMANS 8:5-8

Living to please God may seem like a daunting task. And for some, it is. They struggle to live up to a list of do's and don'ts. They try to obtain God's favor through acts of kindness and compassion. They attempt to "appease" God for their sinful behavior by going to church or making a "confession." But this passage—in fact, this entire chapter in Romans—lets you know that it *is* possible to live a life that is pure and pleasing to God.

The beginning verses of this chapter explain that once we enter into a relationship with Jesus Christ, God frees us from the "vicious circle" of sin and death through the power of his Holy Spirit. This terminology illustrates the basis of our freedom: In essence, the Holy Spirit you received by accepting Jesus Christ into your life has made you a "slave" of Jesus Christ—not a "slave" of your sinful nature.

The apostle Paul often identified himself as a slave of Jesus Christ in his writings. He used the word *doulos*, which means "servant by choice." This word was readily understood by those in the Roman culture. A "doulos," or "bondslave," was a slave who had been granted freedom by his master, but who loved his master so deeply that he voluntarily chose to continue on as that master's servant. Likewise, Paul was not a slave to Christ because he had to be; he was a slave to Christ because he *wanted* to be. He had totally surrendered himself to his Master.

The only way to be free from sin is to be "bound" to Jesus. Unless you completely surrender your life to the Lord, all of your efforts to lead a pure life will be futile. That old sinful nature will continue to rear its ugly head and influence your thoughts and actions. But if you are a bondslave

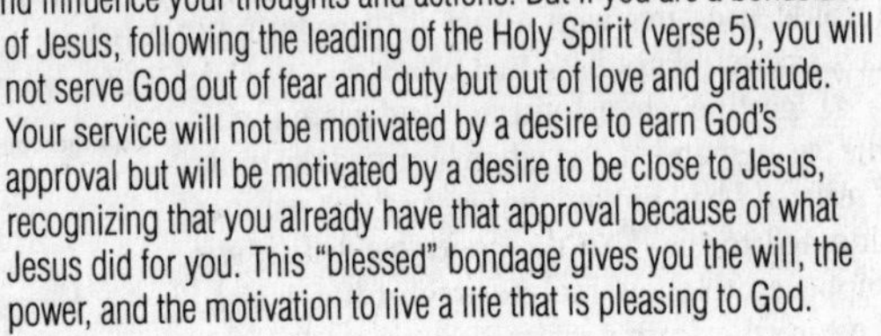

of Jesus, following the leading of the Holy Spirit (verse 5), you will not serve God out of fear and duty but out of love and gratitude. Your service will not be motivated by a desire to earn God's approval but will be motivated by a desire to be close to Jesus, recognizing that you already have that approval because of what Jesus did for you. This "blessed" bondage gives you the will, the power, and the motivation to live a life that is pleasing to God.

CORNERSTONES

from the power of sin that leads to death. 3The law
of Moses could not save us, because of our sinful
nature. But God put into effect a different plan to
save us. He sent his own Son in a human body like
ours, except that ours are sinful. God destroyed sin's
control over us by giving his Son as a sacrifice for our
sins. 4He did this so that the requirement of the law
would be fully accomplished for us* who no longer
follow our sinful nature but instead follow the
Spirit.
5Those who are dominated by the sinful
nature think about sinful things, but those who
are controlled by the Holy Spirit think about
things that please the Spirit. 6If your sinful
nature controls your mind, there is death. But
if the Holy Spirit controls your mind, there is
life and peace. 7For the sinful nature is always
hostile to God. It never did obey God's laws,
and it never will. 8That's why those who are still
under the control of their sinful nature can
never please God.
9But you are not controlled by your sinful
nature. You are controlled by the Spirit if you
have the Spirit of God living in you. (And remember
that those who do not have the Spirit of
Christ living in them are not Christians at all.)
10Since Christ lives within you, even though your
body will die because of sin, your spirit is alive*
because you have been made right with God.
11The Spirit of God, who raised Jesus from the
dead, lives in you. And just as he raised Christ
from the dead, he will give life to your mortal
body by this same Spirit living within you.
12So, dear brothers and sisters,* you have no
obligation whatsoever to do what your sinful
nature urges you to do. 13For if you keep on
following it, you will perish. But if through the
power of the Holy Spirit you turn from it* and

8:2b Some manuscripts read *me.* 8:4 Or *accomplished by us.* 8:10 Or *the Spirit will bring you eternal life.* 8:12 Greek *brothers;* also in 8:29. 8:13 Greek *put it to death.*

its evil deeds, you will live. 14For all who are led
by the Spirit of God are children* of God.
15So you should not be like cowering, fearful
slaves. You should behave instead like God's
very own children, adopted into his family*—
calling him "Father, dear Father."* 16For his
Holy Spirit speaks to us deep in our hearts and
tells us that we are God's children. 17And since
we are his children, we will share his treasures—
for everything God gives to his Son, Christ, is
ours, too. But if we are to share his glory, we
must also share his suffering.

The Future Glory

18Yet what we suffer now is nothing compared to
the glory he will give us later. 19For all creation is
waiting eagerly for that future day when God will
reveal who his children really are. 20Against its
will, everything on earth was subjected to God's
curse. 21All creation anticipates the day when it
will join God's children in glorious freedom from
death and decay. 22For we know that all creation
has been groaning as in the pains of childbirth
right up to the present time. 23And even we Christians, although we have the Holy Spirit within us
as a foretaste of future glory, also groan to be
released from pain and suffering. We, too, wait
anxiously for that day when God will give us our
full rights as his children,* including the new
bodies he has promised us. 24Now that we are
saved, we eagerly look forward to this freedom.
For if you already have something, you don't need
to hope for it. 25But if we look forward to something we don't have yet, we must wait patiently
and confidently.
26And the Holy Spirit helps us in our distress.
For we don't even know what we should pray
for, nor how we should pray. But the Holy Spirit
prays for us with groanings that cannot be expressed in words. 27And the Father who knows
all hearts knows what the Spirit is saying, for the
Spirit pleads for us believers in harmony with
God's own will. 28And we know that God causes
everything to work together* for the good of
those who love God and are called according to
his purpose for them. 29For God knew his
people in advance, and he chose them to become like his Son, so that his Son would be the
firstborn, with many brothers and sisters. 30And
having chosen them, he called them to come to

8:14 Greek *sons;* also in 8:19. 8:15a Greek *You received a spirit of sonship.* 8:15b Greek *"Abba, Father." Abba* is an Aramaic term for "father." 8:23 Greek *wait anxiously for sonship.* 8:28 Some manuscripts read *And we know that everything works together.*

Unconditionally Surrender Your Life Read ROMANS 12:1-2

This passage of Scripture is what we call a conditional promise. The last part of verse 2 contains the promise. Yet if we want to discover God's perfect will for our lives, we must meet the three conditions mentioned at the beginning of these verses.

1. We Must Present Ourselves to God as Living Sacrifices. We need to recognize that we, as Christians, belong to God. The Bible tells us that we no longer own our bodies because Christ paid for them when he died on the cross (see 1 Corinthians 6:19b-20, p. 204). Because our bodies belong to him, we must refrain from sinning. This is what is meant by living sacrifice—putting aside our own will and replacing it with God's.

2. We Must Not Be Conformed to This World. The next step to prepare our hearts to know the will of God is to keep from copying "the behavior and customs of this world." When the Bible speaks of the "world," it is not referring to the earth. Rather it is speaking of the mentality and thinking of the times—the spiritually bankrupt mind-set that is hostile toward the things of God and primarily focuses on mankind's own selfish desires.

3. We Must Be Transformed by the Renewing of Our Minds. One of the best ways to become "a new and different person" is to literally saturate your mind and heart with those things that spiritually build you up. You can do this by studying God's Word, singing hymns and praises, spending time in prayer, and fellowshiping with other believers. As the apostle Paul tells us, "Fix your thoughts on what is true and honorable and right. Think about things that are pure and lovely and admirable. Think about things that are excellent and worthy of praise" (Philippians 4:8).

As we take these preliminary steps, we will be able to more accurately discern the will of God for our lives.

him. And he gave them right standing with himself, and he promised them his glory.

Nothing Can Separate Us from God's Love
31What can we say about such wonderful things
as these? If God is for us, who can ever be against
us? 32Since God did not spare even his own Son
but gave him up for us all, won't God, who gave
us Christ, also give us everything else?

33Who dares accuse us whom God has chosen for his own? Will God? No! He is the one
who has given us right standing with himself.
34Who then will condemn us? Will Christ Jesus?
No, for he is the one who died for us and was
raised to life for us and is sitting at the place of
highest honor next to God, pleading for us.

35Can anything ever separate us from Christ's
love? Does it mean he no longer loves us if we
have trouble or calamity, or are persecuted, or
are hungry or cold or in danger or threatened
with death? 36(Even the Scriptures say, "For your
sake we are killed every day; we are being slaughtered like sheep."*) 37No, despite all these
things, overwhelming victory is ours through
Christ, who loved us.

38And I am convinced that nothing can ever
separate us from his love. Death can't, and life
can't. The angels can't, and the demons can't.
Our fears for today, our worries about tomorrow,
and even the powers of hell can't keep God's love
away. 39Whether we are high above the sky or in
the deepest ocean, nothing in all creation will
ever be able to separate us from the love of God
that is revealed in Christ Jesus our Lord.

CHAPTER 9

God's Selection of Israel
In the presence of Christ, I speak with utter
truthfulness—I do not lie—and my conscience
and the Holy Spirit confirm that what I am
saying is true. 2My heart is filled with bitter
sorrow and unending grief 3for my people, my
Jewish brothers and sisters.* I would be willing
to be forever cursed—cut off from Christ!—if
that would save them. 4They are the people of
Israel, chosen to be God's special children.*
God revealed his glory to them. He made covenants with them and gave his law to them. They
have the privilege of worshiping him and receiving his wonderful promises. 5Their ancestors
were great people of God, and Christ himself
was a Jew as far as his human nature is concerned. And he is God, who rules over everything and is worthy of eternal praise! Amen.*

6Well then, has God failed to fulfill his promise to the Jews? No, for not everyone born into a
Jewish family is truly a Jew! 7Just the fact that
they are descendants of Abraham doesn't make
them truly Abraham's children. For the
Scriptures say, "Isaac is the son through whom
your descendants will be counted,"* though
Abraham had other children, too. 8This means
that Abraham's physical descendants are not
necessarily children of God. It is the children of
the promise who are considered to be Abraham's children. 9For God had promised, "Next
year I will return, and Sarah will have a son."*

10This son was our ancestor Isaac. When he
grew up, he married Rebekah, who gave birth to
twins. 11But before they were born, before they
had done anything good or bad, she received a
message from God. (This message proves that
God chooses according to his own plan, 12not
according to our good or bad works.) She was
told, "The descendants of your older son will
serve the descendants of your younger son."*
13In the words of the Scriptures, "I loved Jacob,
but I rejected Esau."*

8:36 Ps 44:22. 9:3 Greek *my brothers.* 9:4 Greek *chosen for sonship.* 9:5 Or *May God, who rules over everything, be praised forever. Amen.* 9:7 Gen 21:12. 9:9 Gen 18:10, 14. 9:12 Gen 25:23. 9:13 Mal 1:2-3.

OFF AND RUNNING

Keep Your Spiritual Zeal Alive Read ROMANS 12:11

This verse not only encourages us to keep our zeal for God alive, but it commands us to do so. Another meaning of the phrase "serve the Lord enthusiastically" is to have a burning heart for God. The importance of this is seen in the book of Revelation. There Jesus warned the church in Laodicea that they were in danger of being "spit . . . out of [his] mouth" because they were lukewarm (Revelation 3:15-16). In essence, they had lost the fire of their spiritual zeal and were an offense to Christ. Therefore, Jesus told them to repent or he would reject them.

So what can be done to keep our spiritual zeal alive? We can keep our spiritual fire fueled by spending time

14What can we say? Was God being unfair? Of course not! 15For God said to Moses,

"I will show mercy to anyone I choose,
and I will show compassion to anyone I choose."*

16So receiving God's promise is not up to us. We can't get it by choosing it or working hard for it. God will show mercy to anyone he chooses.

17For the Scriptures say that God told Pharaoh, "I have appointed you for the very purpose of displaying my power in you, and so that my fame might spread throughout the earth."* 18So you see, God shows mercy to some just because he wants to, and he chooses to make some people refuse to listen.

19Well then, you might say, "Why does God blame people for not listening? Haven't they simply done what he made them do?"

20No, don't say that. Who are you, a mere human being, to criticize God? Should the thing that was created say to the one who made it, "Why have you made me like this?" 21When a potter makes jars out of clay, doesn't he have a right to use the same lump of clay to make one jar for decoration and another to throw garbage into? 22God has every right to exercise his judgment and his power, but he also has the right to be very patient with those who are the objects of his judgment and are fit only for destruction. 23He also has the right to pour out the riches of his glory upon those he prepared to be the objects of his mercy—24even upon us, whom he selected, both from the Jews and from the Gentiles.

25Concerning the Gentiles, God says in the prophecy of Hosea,

"Those who were not my people,
I will now call my people.
And I will love those
whom I did not love before."*

26And,

"Once they were told,
'You are not my people.'
But now he will say,
'You are children of the living God.'*"

27Concerning Israel, Isaiah the prophet cried out,

"Though the people of Israel are as numerous as the sand on the seashore,
only a small number will be saved.
28 For the Lord will carry out his sentence upon the earth
quickly and with finality."*

29And Isaiah said in another place,

"If the Lord Almighty
had not spared a few of us,
we would have been wiped out
as completely as Sodom and Gomorrah."*

Israel's Unbelief

30Well then, what shall we say about these things? Just this: The Gentiles have been made right with God by faith, even though they were not seeking him. 31But the Jews, who tried so hard to get right with God by keeping the law, never succeeded. 32Why not? Because they were trying to get right with God by keeping the law and being good instead of by depending on faith. They stumbled over the great rock in their path. 33God warned them of this in the Scriptures when he said,

9:15 Exod 33:19. 9:17 Exod 9:16. 9:25 Hos 2:23. 9:26 Greek *You are sons of the living God.* Hos 1:10. 9:27-28 Isa 10:22-23. 9:29 Isa 1:9.

with God's people in fellowship and prayer. We can also feed the fire with constant input from God's Word. As two discouraged disciples realized, listening to the words of Jesus can rekindle a person's zeal for God: "They said to each other, 'Didn't our hearts feel strangely warm as he talked with us on the road and explained the Scriptures to us?'" (Luke 24:32).

What is your spiritual temperature? Are you passionate about the Lord you serve? Do you make the most of every opportunity to tell others about Jesus? The English evangelist John Wesley once said, "Give me a hundred men who love God with all of their hearts and fear nothing but sin, and I will move the world." If you are aglow with the Spirit, serving the Lord with zeal and enthusiasm, your life *will* make a difference.

Our Peace Continues As We Follow the Holy Spirit Read ROMANS 8:5-8

Even if you are a Christian, you still must struggle with your sinful nature. However, if you allow God's Holy Spirit to control your life, that struggle will be much less intense. For, as this passage says, you will want to live to please God.

If you follow your old evil desires, you "can never please God" (verse 8). Your life—whether you realize it or not—will be empty. But if you live the Spirit-controlled life, you will experience "life and peace" (verse 6). To enter into the Spirit-controlled life, follow the advice of the apostle Paul, "Let heaven fill your thoughts. Do not think only about things down here on earth. For you died when Christ died, and your real life is hidden with Christ in God" (Colossians 3:2-3).

"I am placing a stone in Jerusalem* that
causes people to stumble,
and a rock that makes them fall.*
But anyone who believes in him
will not be disappointed.*"

CHAPTER **10**

Dear brothers and sisters,* the longing of my heart
and my prayer to God is that the Jewish people
might be saved. 2I know what enthusiasm they
have for God, but it is misdirected zeal. 3For they
don't understand God's way of making people
right with himself. Instead, they are clinging to
their own way of getting right with God by trying
to keep the law. They won't go along with God's
way. 4For Christ has accomplished the whole purpose* of the law. All who believe in him are made
right with God.

Salvation Is for Everyone

5For Moses wrote that the law's way of making a
person right with God requires obedience to all
of its commands.* 6But the way of getting right
with God through faith says, "You don't need to
go to heaven" (to find Christ and bring him
down to help you). 7And it says, "You don't
need to go to the place of the dead" (to bring
Christ back to life again). 8Salvation that comes
from trusting Christ—which is the message we
preach—is already within easy reach. In fact, the
Scriptures say, "The message is close at hand; it
is on your lips and in your heart."*

9For if you confess with your mouth that
Jesus is Lord and believe in your heart that God
raised him from the dead, you will be saved.
10For it is by believing in your heart that you are
made right with God, and it is by confessing
with your mouth that you are saved. 11As the
Scriptures tell us, "Anyone who believes in him
will not be disappointed.*" 12Jew and Gentile
are the same in this respect. They all have the
same Lord, who generously gives his riches to all
who ask for them. 13For "Anyone who calls on
the name of the Lord will be saved."*

14But how can they call on him to save them
unless they believe in him? And how can they
believe in him if they have never heard about
him? And how can they hear about him unless
someone tells them? 15And how will anyone go
and tell them without being sent? That is what
the Scriptures mean when they say, "How beautiful are the feet of those who bring good news!"*

16But not everyone welcomes the Good
News, for Isaiah the prophet said, "Lord, who
has believed our message?"* 17Yet faith comes
from listening to this message of good news—
the Good News about Christ.

18But what about the Jews? Have they actually heard the message? Yes, they have:

"The message of God's creation has gone
out to everyone,
and its words to all the world."*

19But did the people of Israel really understand?
Yes, they did, for even in the time of Moses, God
had said,

"I will rouse your jealousy by blessing other
nations.
I will make you angry by blessing the
foolish Gentiles."*

9:33a Greek *in Zion.* **9:33b** Isa 8:14. **9:33c** Or *will not be put to shame.* Isa 28:16. **10:1** Greek *Brothers.* **10:4** Or *the end.* **10:5** Lev 18:5. **10:6-8** Deut 30:12-14. **10:11** Or *will not be put to shame.* Isa 28:16. **10:13** Joel 2:32. **10:15** Isa 52:7. **10:16** Isa 53:1. **10:18** Ps 19:4. **10:19** Deut 32:21.

How Should I View Authority? Read ROMANS 13:1-2

When dealing with the subject of authority—particularly how one should act toward those in the government—the Bible gives us some important things to consider.

God Raises Up Rulers. It is true that not every government official has been obedient to God. In fact, far too many have directly violated his Word. Yet God has allowed certain people to rule for his purposes. In the Old Testament God often allowed certain "evil" countries to come to power in order to punish Israel for their wrongdoing and to remind them of their need to return to God. Therefore, we need to respect those in authority, since God has divinely appointed them.

God Uses Those in Government Who Fear Him. While God is ultimately in control of every event that takes place in the world, he still uses his people in strategic positions of power. When Queen Esther, a Jew, faced the prospect of seeing her people put to death, her Uncle Mordecai challenged her with these words: "If you keep quiet at a time like this, deliverance for the Jews will arise from some other place, but you and your relatives will die. What's more, who can say but that you have been elevated to the palace for just such a time as this" (Esther 4:14)? Certainly, God does not forbid us to be part of the political process. Sometimes he will even use Christians in government to accomplish his purposes.

We Are to Be a Witness to Those in Authority. Your obedience to the laws of the land serves as a witness to the God you serve. Peter, addressing the early Christians who were suffering persecution under the cruel tyranny of Nero, still challenged believers to be law-abiding citizens (see 1 Peter 2:13-15, p. 307).

BIG QUESTION.

Our Allegiance to God Should Always Come First. What about those times when a law or government does something that directly contradicts God's law? We are accountable to a higher authority. In the Old Testament we read how Daniel defied the king's decree that forbade people to pray to anyone but him (Daniel 6:1-28). Daniel knew that God had said to worship him alone, so he obeyed God's law instead of man's. As you may recall, he was sent to the lions' den, but God spared his life by shutting the lions' mouths. In the New Testament, Peter told the high priest, when he had been warned not to talk about Jesus, "We must obey God rather than human authority" (Acts 5:29). In more recent times, Christians in Communist and Muslim countries continue to share Christ and distribute Bibles, despite laws that make such actions illegal.

Perhaps the best approach to those in authority over us is to follow the advice found in 1 Peter 2:17: "Fear God. Show respect for the king." Here we see a perfect balance, for as we fear God in our daily lives, we will live above reproach and be examples to those in authority. At the same time, we will be able to discern when human laws contradict the divine laws established by God.

---

20 And later Isaiah spoke boldly for God:

"I was found by people
who were not looking for me.
I showed myself to those
who were not asking for me."*

21 But regarding Israel, God said,

"All day long I opened my arms to them,
but they kept disobeying me and arguing
with me."*

10:20 Isa 65:1. 10:21 Isa 65:2.

CHAPTER 11

God's Mercy on Israel

I ask, then, has God rejected his people, the
Jews? Of course not! Remember that I myself am
a Jew, a descendant of Abraham and a member
of the tribe of Benjamin.
2 No, God has not rejected his own people,
whom he chose from the very beginning. Do you
remember what the Scriptures say about this?
Elijah the prophet complained to God about the

people of Israel and said, 3 "Lord, they have killed
your prophets and torn down your altars. I alone
am left, and now they are trying to kill me, too."*
4 And do you remember God's reply? He said,
"You are not the only one left. I have seven thousand
others who have never bowed down to Baal!"*
5 It is the same today, for not all the Jews have
turned away from God. A few* are being saved
as a result of God's kindness in choosing them.
6 And if they are saved by God's kindness, then it
is not by their good works. For in that case,
God's wonderful kindness would not be what it
really is—free and undeserved.
7 So this is the situation: Most of the Jews have
not found the favor of God they are looking for
so earnestly. A few have—the ones God has
chosen—but the rest were made unresponsive.
8 As the Scriptures say,

"God has put them into a deep sleep.
To this very day he has shut their eyes so
they do not see,
and closed their ears so they do not hear."*

9 David spoke of this same thing when he said,

"Let their bountiful table become a snare,
a trap that makes them think all is well.
Let their blessings cause them to stumble.
10 Let their eyes go blind so they cannot see,
and let their backs grow weaker and
weaker."*

11 Did God's people stumble and fall beyond
recovery? Of course not! His purpose was to
make his salvation available to the Gentiles, and
then the Jews would be jealous and want it for
themselves. 12 Now if the Gentiles were enriched
because the Jews turned down God's offer of
salvation, think how much greater a blessing the
world will share when the Jews finally accept it.
13 I am saying all of this especially for you
Gentiles. God has appointed me as the apostle
to the Gentiles. I lay great stress on this, 14 for I
want to find a way to make the Jews want what
you Gentiles have, and in that way I might save
some of them. 15 For since the Jews' rejection
meant that God offered salvation to the rest of
the world, how much more wonderful their acceptance will be. It will be life for those who
were dead! 16 And since Abraham and the other
patriarchs were holy, their children will also be
holy.* For if the roots of the tree are holy, the
branches will be, too.
17 But some of these branches from Abraham's tree, some of the Jews, have been broken
off. And you Gentiles, who were branches from
a wild olive tree, were grafted in. So now you
also receive the blessing God has promised
Abraham and his children, sharing in God's rich
nourishment of his special olive tree. 18 But you
must be careful not to brag about being grafted
in to replace the branches that were broken off.
Remember, you are just a branch, not the root.
19 "Well," you may say, "those branches were
broken off to make room for me." 20 Yes, but
remember—those branches, the Jews, were broken off because they didn't believe God, and you
are there because you do believe. Don't think
highly of yourself, but fear what could happen.
21 For if God did not spare the branches he put
there in the first place, he won't spare you either.
22 Notice how God is both kind and severe.
He is severe to those who disobeyed, but kind to
you as you continue to trust in his kindness. But
if you stop trusting, you also will be cut off.
23 And if the Jews turn from their unbelief, God
will graft them back into the tree again. He has the
power to do it.
24 For if God was willing to take you who were,
by nature, branches from a wild olive tree and
graft you into his own good tree—a very unusual
thing to do—he will be far more eager to graft the
Jews back into the tree where they belong.

God's Mercy Is for Everyone

25 I want you to understand this mystery, dear
brothers and sisters,* so that you will not feel
proud and start bragging. Some of the Jews have
hard hearts, but this will last only until the
complete number of Gentiles comes to Christ.
26 And so all Israel will be saved. Do you remember what the prophets said about this?

"A Deliverer will come from Jerusalem,*
and he will turn Israel* from all ungodliness.
27 And then I will keep my covenant with them
and take away their sins."*

28 Many of the Jews are now enemies of the
Good News. But this has been to your benefit, for
God has given his gifts to you Gentiles. Yet the Jews
are still his chosen people because of his promises
to Abraham, Isaac, and Jacob. 29 For God's gifts and
his call can never be withdrawn. 30 Once, you Gentiles were rebels against God, but when the Jews
refused his mercy, God was merciful to you instead.

11:3 1 Kgs 19:10, 14. **11:4** 1 Kgs 19:18. **11:5** Greek *A remnant.* **11:8** Deut 29:4; Isa 29:10. **11:9-10** Ps 69:22-23. **11:16** Greek *If the dough offered as firstfruits is holy, so is the whole lump.* **11:25** Greek *brothers.* **11:26a** Greek *from Zion.* **11:26b** Greek *Jacob.* **11:26-27** Isa 59:20-21.

31And now, in the same way, the Jews are the rebels,
and God's mercy has come to you. But someday
they,* too, will share in God's mercy. 32For God has
imprisoned all people in their own disobedience so
he could have mercy on everyone.
33Oh, what a wonderful God we have! How
great are his riches and wisdom and knowledge!
How impossible it is for us to understand his
decisions and his methods! 34For who can know
what the Lord is thinking? Who knows enough
to be his counselor?* 35And who could ever give
him so much that he would have to pay it back?
36For everything comes from him; everything
exists by his power and is intended for his glory.
To him be glory evermore. Amen.

CHAPTER 12

A Living Sacrifice to God

12 And so, dear brothers and sisters,* I plead with
you to give your bodies to God. Let them be a
living and holy sacrifice—the kind he will accept. When you think of what he has done for
you, is this too much to ask? 2Don't copy the
behavior and customs of this world, but let God
transform you into a new person by changing
the way you think. Then you will know what
God wants you to do, and you will know how
good and pleasing and perfect his will really is.
3As God's messenger, I give each of you this
warning: Be honest in your estimate of yourselves,
measuring your value by how much faith God has
given you. 4Just as our bodies have many parts and
each part has a special function, 5so it is with
Christ's body. We are all parts of his one body, and
each of us has different work to do. And since we
are all one body in Christ, we belong to each other,
and each of us needs all the others.
6God has given each of us the ability to do
certain things well. So if God has given you the
ability to prophesy, speak out when you have
faith that God is speaking through you. 7If your
gift is that of serving others, serve them well. If
you are a teacher, do a good job of teaching. 8If
your gift is to encourage others, do it! If you have
money, share it generously. If God has given you
leadership ability, take the responsibility seriously. And if you have a gift for showing kindness to others, do it gladly.
9Don't just pretend that you love others.
Really love them. Hate what is wrong. Stand on
the side of the good. 10Love each other with
genuine affection,* and take delight in honoring
each other. 11Never be lazy in your work, but
serve the Lord enthusiastically.
12Be glad for all God is planning for you. Be
patient in trouble, and always be prayerful.
13When God's children are in need, be the one
to help them out. And get into the habit of
inviting guests home for dinner or, if they need
lodging, for the night.
14If people persecute you because you are a
Christian, don't curse them; pray that God will

11:31 Some manuscripts read *But now they;* other manuscripts read *But they.* 11:34 See Isa 40:13. 12:1 Greek *brothers.* 12:10 Greek *with brotherly love.*

Put on God's Armor

Read ROMANS 13:11-14

Another way the last verse of this text has been translated is "Be Christ's men from head to foot, and give no chances to the flesh to have its fling." In other words, we need to "clothe ourselves" with Christ. To do this, you need to let him be a part of everything that you do. Let him go with you everywhere you go. Let him act through you in every decision you make. Remember these three simple truths as you strive to obey Christ:

1. Time Is Short. Jesus Christ will return soon, and we need to be the best possible witness for him that we can be.

2. Live in the Light. As Ephesians 5:8 says, "For though your hearts were once full of darkness, now you are full of light from the Lord, and your behavior should show it!" The more you live in God's light, the less you will want to be influenced by the darkness of the world around you.

3. Rely upon Christ for Your Strength. You will never be able to stand against the temptations of life on your own. As you follow Christ and his example, you will find it much easier to avoid spiritual pitfalls. As it has been said, "The best defense is a good offense."

Some people want to put God in a little compartment. They will worship God from nine to eleven on Sunday morning, but the rest of the week is theirs. That is not the Christian life. As true followers of Jesus Christ, we need to be identified with our Master twenty-four hours a day, seven days a week, for the rest of our lives.

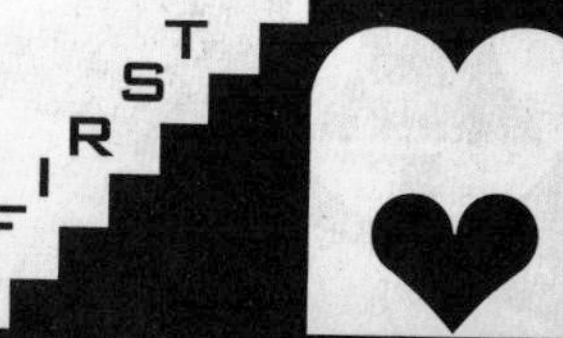

bless them. [15]When others are happy, be happy with them. If they are sad, share their sorrow. [16]Live in harmony with each other. Don't try to act important, but enjoy the company of ordinary people. And don't think you know it all!

[17]Never pay back evil for evil to anyone. Do things in such a way that everyone can see you are honorable. [18]Do your part to live in peace with everyone, as much as possible.

[19]Dear friends, never avenge yourselves. Leave that to God. For it is written,

"I will take vengeance;
I will repay those who deserve it,"*
says the Lord.

[20]Instead, do what the Scriptures say:

"If your enemies are hungry, feed them.
If they are thirsty, give them something to drink,
and they will be ashamed of what they have done to you."*

[21]Don't let evil get the best of you, but conquer evil by doing good.

CHAPTER 13

Respect for Authority

Obey the government, for God is the one who put it there. All governments have been placed in power by God. [2]So those who refuse to obey the laws of the land are refusing to obey God, and punishment will follow. [3]For the authorities do not frighten people who are doing right, but they frighten those who do wrong. So do what they say, and you will get along well. [4]The authorities are sent by God to help you. But if you are doing something wrong, of course you should be afraid, for you will be punished. The authorities are established by God for that very purpose, to punish those who do wrong. [5]So you must obey the government for two reasons: to keep from being punished and to keep a clear conscience.

[6]Pay your taxes, too, for these same reasons. For government workers need to be paid so they can keep on doing the work God intended them to do. [7]Give to everyone what you owe them: Pay your taxes and import duties, and give respect and honor to all to whom it is due.

Love Fulfills God's Requirements

[8]Pay all your debts, except the debt of love for others. You can never finish paying that! If you love your neighbor, you will fulfill all the requirements of God's law. [9]For the commandments against adultery and murder and stealing and coveting—and any other commandment—are all summed up in this one commandment: "Love your neighbor as yourself."* [10]Love does no wrong to anyone, so love satisfies all of God's requirements.

[11]Another reason for right living is that you know how late it is; time is running out. Wake up, for the coming of our salvation is nearer now than when we first believed. [12]The night is almost gone; the day of salvation will soon be here. So don't live in darkness. Get rid of your evil deeds. Shed them like dirty clothes. Clothe yourselves with the armor of right living, as those who live in the light. [13]We should be decent and true in everything we do, so that everyone can approve of our behavior. Don't participate in wild parties and getting drunk, or in adultery and immoral living, or in fighting and jealousy. [14]But let the Lord Jesus Christ take control of you, and don't think of ways to indulge your evil desires.

CHAPTER 14

The Danger of Criticism

Accept Christians who are weak in faith, and don't argue with them about what they think is right or wrong. [2]For instance, one person believes it is all right to eat anything. But another believer who has a sensitive conscience will eat only vegetables. [3]Those who think it is all right to eat anything must not look down on those who won't. And those who won't eat certain foods must not condemn those who do, for God

12:19 Deut 32:35. **12:20** Greek *and you will heap burning coals on their heads.* Prov 25:21-22. **13:9** Lev 19:18.

OFF AND RUNNING

Could This Activity Cause Other Christians to Stumble in Their Faith? Read ROMANS 14:15

Don't do anything that will bring criticism against yourself, even if you know that a certain activity is all right. What we do and become has a direct effect on others—not only for our

has accepted them. 4Who are you to condemn God's servants? They are responsible to the Lord, so let him tell them whether they are right or wrong. The Lord's power will help them do as they should.

5In the same way, some think one day is more holy than another day, while others think every day is alike. Each person should have a personal conviction about this matter. 6Those who have a special day for worshiping the Lord are trying to honor him. Those who eat all kinds of food do so to honor the Lord, since they give thanks to God before eating. And those who won't eat everything also want to please the Lord and give thanks to God. 7For we are not our own masters when we live or when we die. 8While we live, we live to please the Lord. And when we die, we go to be with the Lord. So in life and in death, we belong to the Lord. 9Christ died and rose again for this very purpose, so that he might be Lord of those who are alive and of those who have died.

10So why do you condemn another Christian*? Why do you look down on another Christian? Remember, each of us will stand personally before the judgment seat of God. 11For the Scriptures say,

" 'As surely as I live,' says the Lord,
'every knee will bow to me
and every tongue will confess allegiance
to God.' "*

12Yes, each of us will have to give a personal account to God. 13So don't condemn each other anymore. Decide instead to live in such a way that you will not put an obstacle in another Christian's path.

14I know and am perfectly sure on the authority of the Lord Jesus that no food, in and of itself, is wrong to eat. But if someone believes it is wrong, then for that person it is wrong. 15And if another Christian is distressed by what you eat, you are not acting in love if you eat it. Don't let your eating ruin someone for whom Christ died. 16Then you will not be condemned for doing something you know is all right.

17For the Kingdom of God is not a matter of what we eat or drink, but of living a life of goodness and peace and joy in the Holy Spirit. 18If you serve Christ with this attitude, you will please God. And other people will approve of you, too. 19So then, let us aim for harmony in the church and try to build each other up.

20Don't tear apart the work of God over what you eat. Remember, there is nothing wrong with these things in themselves. But it is wrong to eat anything if it makes another person stumble. 21Don't eat meat or drink wine or do anything else if it might cause another Christian to stumble. 22You may have the faith to believe that there is nothing wrong with what you are doing, but keep it between yourself and God. Blessed are those who do not condemn themselves by doing something they know is all right. 23But if people have doubts about whether they should eat something, they shouldn't eat it. They would be condemned for not acting in faith before God. If you do anything you believe is not right, you are sinning.

CHAPTER 15

Living to Please Others

We may know that these things make no difference, but we cannot just go ahead and do them to please ourselves. We must be considerate of the doubts and fears of those who think these things are wrong. 2We should please others. If we do what helps them, we will build them up in the Lord. 3For even Christ didn't please himself. As the Scriptures say, "Those who insult you are also insulting me."* 4Such things were written in the Scriptures long ago to teach us. They give us hope and encouragement as we wait patiently for God's promises.

5May God, who gives this patience and encouragement, help you live in complete harmony with each other—each with the attitude of Christ Jesus toward the other. 6Then all of you can join

14:10 Greek *your brother;* also in 14:10b, 13, 15, 21. **14:11** Isa 45:23. **15:3** Ps 69:9.

life here on this earth, but also for eternity. We not only need to live our lives conscious of God's opinion, but we also need to live our lives with consideration for others. We do not want to do anything that has the potential of causing another Christian brother or sister to stumble or fall.

together with one voice, giving praise and glory
to God, the Father of our Lord Jesus Christ.
7So accept each other just as Christ has accepted
you; then God will be glorified. 8Remember that
Christ came as a servant to the Jews to show that
God is true to the promises he made to their ancestors. 9And he came so the Gentiles might also give
glory to God for his mercies to them. That is what
the psalmist meant when he wrote:

"I will praise you among the Gentiles;
I will sing praises to your name."*

10And in another place it is written,

"Rejoice, O you Gentiles,
along with his people, the Jews."*

11And yet again,

"Praise the Lord, all you Gentiles;
praise him, all you people of the earth."*

12And the prophet Isaiah said,

"The heir to David's throne* will come,
and he will rule over the Gentiles.
They will place their hopes on him."*

13So I pray that God, who gives you hope, will
keep you happy and full of peace as you believe
in him. May you overflow with hope through
the power of the Holy Spirit.

Paul's Reason for Writing

14I am fully convinced, dear brothers and sisters,*
that you are full of goodness. You know these
things so well that you are able to teach others all
about them. 15Even so, I have been bold enough
to emphasize some of these points, knowing that
all you need is this reminder from me. For I am,
by God's grace, 16a special messenger from Christ
Jesus to you Gentiles. I bring you the Good News
and offer you up as a fragrant sacrifice to God so
that you might be pure and pleasing to him by the
Holy Spirit. 17So it is right for me to be enthusiastic about all Christ Jesus has done through me in
my service to God. 18I dare not boast of anything
else. I have brought the Gentiles to God by my
message and by the way I lived before them. 19I
have won them over by the miracles done through
me as signs from God—all by the power of God's
Spirit. In this way, I have fully presented the Good
News of Christ all the way from Jerusalem clear
over into Illyricum.*
20My ambition has always been to preach the
Good News where the name of Christ has never
been heard, rather than where a church has
already been started by someone else. 21I have
been following the plan spoken of in the
Scriptures, where it says,

"Those who have never been told about
him will see,
and those who have never heard of him
will understand."*

22In fact, my visit to you has been delayed so long
because I have been preaching in these places.

Paul's Travel Plans

23But now I have finished my work in these
regions, and after all these long years of waiting,
I am eager to visit you. 24I am planning to go to
Spain, and when I do, I will stop off in Rome.
And after I have enjoyed your fellowship for a
little while, you can send me on my way again.
25But before I come, I must go down to Jerusalem to take a gift to the Christians there. 26For
you see, the believers in Greece* have eagerly
taken up an offering for the Christians in Jerusalem, who are going through such hard times.
27They were very glad to do this because they
feel they owe a real debt to them. Since the
Gentiles received the wonderful spiritual blessings of the Good News from the Jewish Christians, they feel the least they can do in return is
help them financially. 28As soon as I have deliv-

15:9 Ps 18:49. 15:10 Deut 32:43. 15:11 Ps 117:1. 15:12a Greek *The root of Jesse.* 15:12b Isa 11:10. 15:14 Greek *brothers;* also in 15:30. 15:19 *Illyricum* was a region northeast of Italy. 15:21 Isa 52:15. 15:26 Greek *Macedonia and Achaia,* the northern and southern regions of Greece.

OFF AND RUNNING

Do I Have an Uneasy Conscience about This Activity?

Read ROMANS 14:23

When it comes to participating in questionable activities, it is easy to rationalize joining in because others are doing it. Yet this verse places the responsibility of your choice squarely on your shoulders. You may protest and say, "Well, so-and-so is doing it!" But you are not that person. You must be obedient to what God tells *you* to do.

ered this money and completed this good deed of theirs, I will come to see you on my way to Spain. 29And I am sure that when I come, Christ will give me a great blessing for you.

30Dear brothers and sisters, I urge you in the name of our Lord Jesus Christ to join me in my struggle by praying to God for me. Do this because of your love for me, given to you by the Holy Spirit. 31Pray that I will be rescued from those in Judea who refuse to obey God. Pray also that the Christians there will be willing to accept the donation I am bringing them. 32Then, by the will of God, I will be able to come to you with a happy heart, and we will be an encouragement to each other.

33And now may God, who gives us his peace, be with you all. Amen.

CHAPTER 16

Paul Greets His Friends

Our sister Phoebe, a deacon in the church in Cenchrea, will be coming to see you soon. 2Receive her in the Lord, as one who is worthy of high honor. Help her in every way you can, for she has helped many in their needs, including me.

3Greet Priscilla and Aquila. They have been co-workers in my ministry for Christ Jesus. 4In fact, they risked their lives for me. I am not the only one who is thankful to them; so are all the Gentile churches. 5Please give my greetings to the church that meets in their home.

Greet my dear friend Epenetus. He was the very first person to become a Christian in the province of Asia. 6Give my greetings to Mary, who has worked so hard for your benefit. 7Then there are Andronicus and Junia,* my relatives,* who were in prison with me. They are respected among the apostles and became Christians before I did. Please give them my greetings. 8Say hello to Ampliatus, whom I love as one of the Lord's own children, 9and Urbanus, our co-worker in Christ, and beloved Stachys.

10Give my greetings to Apelles, a good man whom Christ approves. And give my best regards to the members of the household of Aristobulus. 11Greet Herodion, my relative.* Greet the Christians in the household of Narcissus. 12Say hello to Tryphena and Tryphosa, the Lord's workers, and to dear Persis, who has worked so hard for the Lord. 13Greet Rufus, whom the Lord picked out to be his very own; and also his dear mother, who has been a mother to me.

14And please give my greetings to Asyncritus, Phlegon, Hermes, Patrobas, Hermas, and the brothers and sisters* who are with them. 15Give my greetings to Philologus, Julia, Nereus and his sister, and to Olympas and all the other believers who are with them. 16Greet each other in Christian love.* All the churches of Christ send you their greetings.

Paul's Final Instructions

17And now I make one more appeal, my dear brothers and sisters. Watch out for people who cause divisions and upset people's faith by teaching things that are contrary to what you have been taught. Stay away from them. 18Such people are not serving Christ our Lord; they are serving their own personal interests. By smooth talk and glowing words they deceive innocent people. 19But everyone knows that you are obedient to the Lord. This makes me very happy. I want you to see clearly what is right and to stay innocent of any wrong. 20The God of peace will soon crush Satan under your feet. May the grace of our Lord Jesus Christ be with you.

21Timothy, my fellow worker, and Lucius, Jason, and Sosipater, my relatives, send you their good wishes.

22I, Tertius, the one who is writing this letter for Paul, send my greetings, too, as a Christian brother.

16:7a Or *Junias;* some manuscripts read *Julia.* **16:7b** Or *compatriots;* also in 16:21. **16:11** Or *compatriot.* **16:14** Greek *brothers;* also in 16:17. **16:16** Greek *with a sacred kiss.*

How do you know when you should not participate in a certain activity? God's Holy Spirit will often give you an uneasy conscience about something you should not be doing. For example, you may have a sense that you are in the wrong place, with the wrong people, about to do the wrong thing. Or, you may have a lack of peace in your heart about an activity in which you are participating. When this happens, it is up to you to pay attention to your conscience and follow through by being obedient to God.

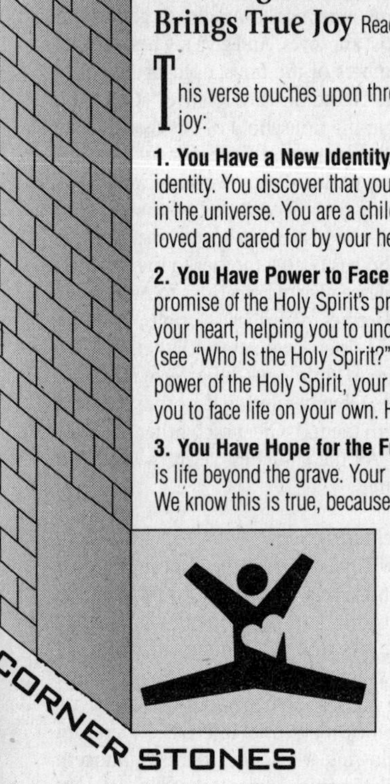

Knowing Whom You Belong to and What the Future Holds Brings True Joy Read ROMANS 15:13

This verse touches upon three important facets of the Christian life that should give you great joy:

1. You Have a New Identity. When you accept Jesus Christ into your life, God gives you a new identity. You discover that you are not merely some product of random chance. You are not a speck in the universe. You are a child of God. And as God's child you can rest assured that you will be loved and cared for by your heavenly Father.

2. You Have Power to Face Life. With that new identity and hope in Christ, you also have the promise of the Holy Spirit's presence and power in your life. The Holy Spirit works constantly in your heart, helping you to understand God's Word and to transform your attitudes and behavior (see "Who Is the Holy Spirit?" p. A12). An expanded translation of this verse says that by the power of the Holy Spirit, your whole life and outlook will be "radiant with hope." God has not left you to face life on your own. He has promised to guide and strengthen you with his Spirit.

3. You Have Hope for the Future. As a Christian, you have the hope and knowledge that there is life beyond the grave. Your last breath on earth will be followed by your first breath in heaven. We know this is true, because God has promised it in his Word (see "What Is Heaven?" p. A5). This verse asserts that your belief in Jesus and his promises to us as his followers will fill you with joy and peace.

The world offers many roads to happiness: sex, money, power, personal success. But they are all cheap and worthless substitutes in comparison to knowing that you are God's child and that you have the hope of heaven. This is the only road to lasting—indeed, eternal—joy.

23Gaius says hello to you. I am his guest, and
the church meets here in his home. Erastus, the
city treasurer, sends you his greetings, and so
does Quartus, a Christian brother.*
25God is able to make you strong, just as the
Good News says. It is the message about Jesus
Christ and his plan for you Gentiles, a plan kept
secret from the beginning of time. 26But now as
the prophets* foretold and as the eternal God
has commanded, this message is made known
to all Gentiles everywhere, so that they might
believe and obey Christ. 27To God, who alone is
wise, be the glory forever through Jesus Christ.
Amen.

16:23 Some manuscripts add verse 24, *May the grace of our Lord Jesus Christ be with you all. Amen.* 16:26 Greek *the prophetic writings.*

I Corinthians

CHAPTER 1

Greetings from Paul

This letter is from Paul, chosen by the will of
God to be an apostle of Christ Jesus, and from
our brother Sosthenes.
2We are writing to the church of God in Corinth, you who have been called by God to be his
own holy people. He made you holy by means
of Christ Jesus, just as he did all Christians everywhere—whoever calls upon the name of Jesus
Christ, our Lord and theirs.
3May God our Father and the Lord Jesus
Christ give you his grace and peace.

Paul Gives Thanks to God

4I can never stop thanking God for all the generous gifts he has given you, now that you belong
to Christ Jesus. 5He has enriched your church
with the gifts of eloquence and every kind of
knowledge. 6This shows that what I told you
about Christ is true. 7Now you have every spiritual gift you need as you eagerly wait for the
return of our Lord Jesus Christ. 8He will keep
you strong right up to the end, and he will keep
you free from all blame on the great day when
our Lord Jesus Christ returns. 9God will surely
do this for you, for he always does just what he
says, and he is the one who invited you into this
wonderful friendship with his Son, Jesus Christ
our Lord.

Divisions in the Church

10Now, dear brothers and sisters,* I appeal to
you by the authority of the Lord Jesus Christ to
stop arguing among yourselves. Let there be real
harmony so there won't be divisions in the
church. I plead with you to be of one mind,
united in thought and purpose. 11For some
members of Chloe's household have told me
about your arguments, dear brothers and sisters.
12Some of you are saying, "I am a follower of
Paul." Others are saying, "I follow Apollos," or
"I follow Peter,*" or "I follow only Christ."
13Can Christ be divided into pieces?
Was I, Paul, crucified for you? Were any of you
baptized in the name of Paul? 14I thank God
that I did not baptize any of you except Crispus
and Gaius, 15for now no one can say they were
baptized in my name. 16(Oh yes, I also baptized
the household of Stephanas. I don't remember
baptizing anyone else.) 17For Christ didn't send
me to baptize, but to preach the Good News—
and not with clever speeches and high-sounding
ideas, for fear that the cross of Christ would lose
its power.

The Wisdom of God

18I know very well how foolish the message of
the cross sounds to those who are on the road to
destruction. But we who are being saved recognize this message as the very power of God. 19As
the Scriptures say,

> "I will destroy human wisdom
> and discard their most brilliant ideas."*

20So where does this leave the philosophers, the
scholars, and the world's brilliant debaters? God
has made them all look foolish and has shown
their wisdom to be useless nonsense. 21Since
God in his wisdom saw to it that the world
would never find him through human wisdom,
he has used our foolish preaching to save all
who believe. 22God's way seems foolish to the
Jews because they want a sign from heaven to
prove it is true. And it is foolish to the Greeks
because they believe only what agrees with their
own wisdom. 23So when we preach that Christ

1:10 Greek *brothers;* also in 1:11, 26. 1:12 Greek *Cephas.* 1:19 Isa 29:14.

Overlooking Petty Issues Frees Us to Experience Joy

Read 1 CORINTHIANS 1:10-17

In Paul's first letter to the Corinthians, he addressed several problems the church of Corinth was experiencing. One of the church's problems was that the believers were dividing the church by aligning themselves under the teachings of one apostle or another, rather than focusing on the joy of their salvation. Paul, therefore, rebuked the Corinthians for dividing the church over such a petty issue, reminding them that it is Christ they follow and serve, not Apollos, Paul, or Peter.

Like the Corinthians, we can get bogged down in issues that not only divide the church but really don't matter. When we immerse ourselves in petty issues, we rob ourselves of experiencing the joy that Christ has given us. That is because advocating these issues can become more important to us than salvation itself. It is then that we can become obsessed with others' adherence to our point of view rather than their faith in Christ. However, ignoring petty issues is liberating. It frees us to focus on our own salvation and experience the joy of Christ's forgiveness.

How do we do this? Here are four ways to overlook petty issues and experience joy in Christ:

1. Be Single-Minded in Purpose. The purpose of our life is to serve Christ (see Philippians 1:21, p. 247).

2. Adopt God's Priorities As Your Own. Put God first, others second, and yourself third (see Philippians 2:5-6, p. 248).

3. Keep Moving Forward Spiritually. Acknowledge that you haven't "arrived" spiritually, and keep pressing on to know God more (see Philippians 3:13-14, p. 250).

4. Have a Rejoicing Mind. Don't rejoice in circumstances, but rejoice in God and his faithfulness (see Philippians 4:4-5, p. 250).

Failure to maintain the joy of the Lord in our personal lives leads to spiritual breakdown. Failure to keep the joy of the Lord in our churches cripples the cause of Christ. Let his joy overflow from your life.

was crucified, the Jews are offended, and the
Gentiles say it's all nonsense. 24But to those
called by God to salvation, both Jews and Gentiles,* Christ is the mighty power of God and the
wonderful wisdom of God. 25This "foolish"
plan of God is far wiser than the wisest of human plans, and God's weakness is far stronger
than the greatest of human strength.
26Remember, dear brothers and sisters, that
few of you were wise in the world's eyes, or
powerful, or wealthy when God called you. 27In-
stead, God deliberately chose things the world
considers foolish in order to shame those who
think they are wise. And he chose those who are
powerless to shame those who are powerful.
28God chose things despised by the world,
things counted as nothing at all, and used them
to bring to nothing what the world considers
important, 29so that no one can ever boast in the
presence of God.
30God alone made it possible for you to be in
Christ Jesus. For our benefit God made Christ to
be wisdom itself. He is the one who made us
acceptable to God. He made us pure and holy,
and he gave himself to purchase our freedom.
31As the Scriptures say,

"The person who wishes to boast
should boast only of what the Lord has
done."*

CHAPTER 2

Paul Preaches Wisdom

Dear brothers and sisters,* when I first came to
you I didn't use lofty words and brilliant ideas
to tell you God's message.* 2For I decided to
concentrate only on Jesus Christ and his death
on the cross. 3I came to you in weakness—timid
and trembling. 4And my message and my
preaching were very plain. I did not use wise and

1:24 Greek *Greeks.* 1:31 Jer 9:24. 2:1a Greek *Brothers.* 2:1b Greek *mystery;* other manuscripts read *testimony.*

persuasive speeches, but the Holy Spirit was
powerful among you. 5I did this so that you
might trust the power of God rather than human
wisdom.

6Yet when I am among mature Christians, I
do speak with words of wisdom, but not the
kind of wisdom that belongs to this world, and
not the kind that appeals to the rulers of this
world, who are being brought to nothing. 7No,
the wisdom we speak of is the secret wisdom of
God,* which was hidden in former times,
though he made it for our benefit before the
world began. 8But the rulers of this world have
not understood it; if they had, they would never
have crucified our glorious Lord. 9That is what
the Scriptures mean when they say,

"No eye has seen, no ear has heard,
and no mind has imagined
what God has prepared
for those who love him."*

10But we know these things because God has
revealed them to us by his Spirit, and his Spirit
searches out everything and shows us even
God's deep secrets. 11No one can know what
anyone else is really thinking except that person
alone, and no one can know God's thoughts
except God's own Spirit. 12And God has actually
given us his Spirit (not the world's spirit) so we
can know the wonderful things God has freely
given us. 13When we tell you this, we do not use
words of human wisdom. We speak words given
to us by the Spirit, using the Spirit's words to
explain spiritual truths.* 14But people who
aren't Christians can't understand these truths
from God's Spirit. It all sounds foolish to them
because only those who have the Spirit can understand what the Spirit means. 15We who have
the Spirit understand these things, but others
can't understand us at all. 16How could they?
For,

"Who can know what the Lord is thinking?
Who can give him counsel?"*

But we can understand these things, for we have
the mind of Christ.

CHAPTER 3

Paul and Apollos, Servants of Christ

Dear brothers and sisters,* when I was with you
I couldn't talk to you as I would to mature
Christians. I had to talk as though you belonged
to this world or as though you were infants in
the Christian life.* 2I had to feed you with milk
and not with solid food, because you couldn't
handle anything stronger. And you still aren't
ready, 3for you are still controlled by your own
sinful desires. You are jealous of one another
and quarrel with each other. Doesn't that prove
you are controlled by your own desires? You are
acting like people who don't belong to the Lord.

2:7 Greek *we speak God's wisdom in a mystery.* 2:9 Isa 64:4. 2:13 Or *explaining spiritual truths in spiritual language,* or *explaining spiritual truths to spiritual people.* 2:16 Isa 40:13. 3:1a Greek *Brothers.*

3:1b Greek *in Christ.*

Understand the Simplicity of the Gospel

Read 1 CORINTHIANS 2:1-5

Paul reminds us in this text that the heartbeat of the gospel message is the story of the life, death, and resurrection of Jesus Christ. The apostles emphasized this message in their preaching throughout the New Testament—especially in the book of Acts, which chronicles the start of the early church. As you share your faith with others, keep in mind these two points demonstrated in the apostles' own efforts to spread the gospel:

1. Remember the Simplicity of the Gospel. People need to know that they are sinners and that their sin separates them from God. But Jesus came to bring God and humankind together. When he died on the cross, the sins of humankind were placed upon him, and the penalty for those sins was paid in full. Three days after his crucifixion, he rose from the dead, proving that he was the true Son of God, the only one who could pay for our sins.

2. Recognize the Power of the Gospel. Although our message is simple, it is incredibly powerful. Paul wrote, "For I am not ashamed of this Good News about Christ. It is the power of God at work, saving everyone who believes" (Romans 1:16). The word Paul uses to describe the power of the gospel is the root for our English words *dynamite* and *dynamic.*

Remember there is power in the simple message of the life, death, and resurrecton of Jesus Christ. We should not be ashamed of it but boldly proclaim it.

The Value of Our Work on Earth Will Be Tested

Read 1 CORINTHIANS 3:10-15

The British preacher Alan Redpath once said, "It is possible to have a saved soul and a lost life." In other words, it is possible to be saved and forgiven of one's sin but to waste one's life by not serving the Lord.

That is what Paul warned the Corinthians about in this passage. Here Paul describes another judgment—besides the Great White Throne Judgment—specifically for believers. You might call it the Christian's award ceremony. Yet it won't be like any awards ceremony on earth. There the quality of our work for the Lord will be tested, as well as our motives for doing it. Our reward will reflect what we have or haven't done with the talents and abilities God has given us.

One day you are going to stand before Jesus. When you do, you want to be welcomed into the arms of Jesus and hear him say, "Well done, my good and faithful servant" (Matthew 25:21).

Be an "expert builder." Take the gifts and abilities God has given you—however insignificant they may seem to you—and use them for his glory. Then you will have a saved soul *and* an abundant life.

CORNER STONES

4When one of you says, "I am a follower of
Paul," and another says, "I prefer Apollos,"
aren't you acting like those who are not Christians?*
5Who is Apollos, and who is Paul, that we
should be the cause of such quarrels? Why, we're
only servants. Through us God caused you to
believe. Each of us did the work the Lord gave us.
6My job was to plant the seed in your hearts, and
Apollos watered it, but it was God, not we, who
made it grow. 7The ones who do the planting or
watering aren't important, but God is important
because he is the one who makes the seed grow.
8The one who plants and the one who waters
work as a team with the same purpose. Yet they
will be rewarded individually, according to their
own hard work. 9We work together as partners
who belong to God. You are God's field, God's
building—not ours.
10Because of God's special favor to me, I have
laid the foundation like an expert builder. Now
others are building on it. But whoever is building on this foundation must be very careful.
11For no one can lay any other foundation than
the one we already have—Jesus Christ. 12Now
anyone who builds on that foundation may use
gold, silver, jewels, wood, hay, or straw. 13But
there is going to come a time of testing at the
judgment day to see what kind of work each
builder has done. Everyone's work will be put
through the fire to see whether or not it keeps its
value. 14If the work survives the fire, that builder
will receive a reward. 15But if the work is burned
up, the builder will suffer great loss. The builders
themselves will be saved, but like someone es-
caping through a wall of flames.
16Don't you realize that all of you together
are the temple of God and that the Spirit of God
lives in* you? 17God will bring ruin upon anyone who ruins this temple. For God's temple is
holy, and you Christians are that temple.
18Stop fooling yourselves. If you think you
are wise by this world's standards, you will have
to become a fool so you can become wise by
God's standards. 19For the wisdom of this world
is foolishness to God. As the Scriptures say,

> "God catches those who think they are wise
> in their own cleverness."*

20And again,

> "The Lord knows the thoughts of the wise,
> that they are worthless."*

21So don't take pride in following a particular
leader. Everything belongs to you: 22Paul and
Apollos and Peter*; the whole world and life
and death; the present and the future. Everything belongs to you, 23and you belong to
Christ, and Christ belongs to God.

3:4 Greek *aren't you merely human?* 3:16 Or *among.* 3:19 Job 5:13. 3:20 Ps 94:11. 3:22 Greek *Cephas.*

Does God Approve of Alternative Lifestyles? Read 1 CORINTHIANS 6:9-10, 15-20

In this day and age we hear a lot of talk about "alternative lifestyles." But what does God have to say about homosexuality, living together as an unmarried couple, or being promiscuous? While some say that God is accepting of any relationship, the Bible paints a very different picture. Just because these relationships exist does not make them right. In fact, God clearly labels them as sin.

About Homosexuality. Saying that homosexuality is wrong is not a popular thing to do in our culture today. Yet God is not concerned with what is and what is not popular. He is concerned with people's salvation and their obedience to his Word. Just because homosexuality is viewed as an acceptable lifestyle does not mean that it is not a sin. God declared it to be just that when he gave his law to the Israelites (see Leviticus 18:22). Paul reiterated God's command on abstaining from homosexual sex in his letter to the Romans (see Romans 1:26-27, p. 176), as well as in some of his other letters to the early church.

About Living Together before Marriage and Premarital Sex. Have you ever thought that something was OK to do because "everybody is doing it"? Today, couples living together outside of marriage has become acceptable. In addition, it seems that premarital sex is the norm, rather than the exception. But God has not given his approval of these relationships (see Hebrews 13:4, p. 297). Although God created sex, he did not intend us to have it before marriage. That is because he created sex to be a means by which a husband and wife would grow closer in their relationship. He did not create sex to be something cheaply enjoyed outside the bonds of marital commitment, which is what living together and premarital sex are.

About Promiscuity. *Promiscuity* is a word that we do not hear as often today as we used to. The problem with promiscuity is that it involves having many sexual partners. We know from God's Word that he intended us to have one sexual partner—our spouse. When a person has more than one partner (with the exception of remarriage after a spouse's death or a divorce on solid biblical grounds), he or she is involved in sexual immorality, if not married, or adultery, if married (see Ephesians 5:3, p. 243, and Matthew 5:27-28, p. 7).

Some have questions about whether God's Word on these subjects still applies to us today, or if it was simply meant for the people of that particular time and culture. The Word of the Lord stands forever (see 1 Peter 1:25, p. 306). Consequently, these instructions apply just as much to us today as they did to their original audience centuries ago.

God gave us our sexual desires to enjoy within the bounds of marriage (see 1 Corinthians 7:1-5, p. 204). If you go against God's divinely instituted plan and do not repent, you will reap the consequences—not only in this life, but in eternity. For you cannot be close to God if you are engaged in any immoral behavior. At the same time, you won't be engaged in this type of behavior if you are truly close to God.

CHAPTER 4

Paul and the Corinthians

So look at Apollos and me as mere servants of
Christ who have been put in charge of explaining
God's secrets. 2Now, a person who is put in
charge as a manager must be faithful. 3What
about me? Have I been faithful? Well, it matters
very little what you or anyone else thinks. I don't
even trust my own judgment on this point. 4My
conscience is clear, but that isn't what matters. It
is the Lord himself who will examine me and
decide.

5So be careful not to jump to conclusions
before the Lord returns as to whether or not

someone is faithful. When the Lord comes, he will bring our deepest secrets to light and will reveal our private motives. And then God will give to everyone whatever praise is due.

6Dear brothers and sisters,* I have used Apollos and myself to illustrate what I've been saying. If you pay attention to the Scriptures,* you won't brag about one of your leaders at the expense of another. 7What makes you better than anyone else? What do you have that God hasn't given you? And if all you have is from God, why boast as though you have accomplished something on your own?

8You think you already have everything you need! You are already rich! Without us you have become kings! I wish you really were on your thrones already, for then we would be reigning with you! 9But sometimes I think God has put us apostles on display, like prisoners of war at the end of a victor's parade, condemned to die. We have become a spectacle to the entire world—to people and angels alike.

10Our dedication to Christ makes us look like fools, but you are so wise! We are weak, but you are so powerful! You are well thought of, but we are laughed at. 11To this very hour we go hungry and thirsty, without enough clothes to keep us warm. We have endured many beatings, and we have no homes of our own. 12We have worked wearily with our own hands to earn our living. We bless those who curse us. We are patient with those who abuse us. 13We respond gently when evil things are said about us. Yet we are treated like the world's garbage, like everybody's trash—right up to the present moment.

14I am not writing these things to shame you, but to warn you as my beloved children. 15For even if you had ten thousand others to teach you about Christ, you have only one spiritual father. For I became your father in Christ Jesus when I preached the Good News to you. 16So I ask you to follow my example and do as I do.

17That is the very reason I am sending Timothy—to help you do this. For he is my beloved and trustworthy child in the Lord. He will remind you of what I teach about Christ Jesus in all the churches wherever I go.

18I know that some of you have become arrogant, thinking I will never visit you again. 19But I will come—and soon—if the Lord will let me, and then I'll find out whether these arrogant people are just big talkers or whether they really have God's power. 20For the Kingdom of God is not just fancy talk; it is living by God's power. 21Which do you choose? Should I come with punishment and scolding, or should I come with quiet love and gentleness?

CHAPTER 5

Paul Condemns Spiritual Pride

I can hardly believe the report about the sexual immorality going on among you, something so evil that even the pagans don't do it. I am told that you have a man in your church who is living in sin with his father's wife. 2And you are so proud of yourselves! Why aren't you mourning in sorrow and shame? And why haven't you removed this man from your fellowship?

3Even though I am not there with you in person, I am with you in the Spirit.* Concerning the one who has done this, I have already passed judgment 4in the name of the Lord Jesus. You are to call a meeting of the church,* and I will be there in spirit, and the power of the Lord Jesus will be with you as you meet. 5Then you must cast this man out of the church and into Satan's hands, so that his sinful nature will be destroyed* and he himself* will be saved when the Lord returns.

6How terrible that you should boast about your spirituality, and yet you let this sort of thing

4:6a Greek *Brothers.* **4:6b** Or *You must learn not to go beyond "what is written," so that.* **5:3** Or *in spirit.* **5:4** Or *In the name of the Lord Jesus, you are to call a meeting of the church.* **5:5a** Or *so that he will die;* Greek reads *for the destruction of the flesh.* **5:5b** Greek *and the spirit.*

OFF AND RUNNING

Does This Activity Bring Me under Its Power?

Read 1 CORINTHIANS 6:12

Some have mistakenly assumed that following Christ means drudgingly obeying a list of "do's and don'ts." In reality, the Christian life, if lived according to Scripture, is one of joy and satisfaction. This verse serves as a case in point. To follow the principle laid out here is not overly restricting but truly liberating!

Some people are controlled by pleasure. For example, they may live for a certain sport and become so

go on. Don't you realize that if even one person is allowed to go on sinning, soon all will be affected? 7 Remove this wicked person from among you so that you can stay pure.* Christ, our Passover Lamb, has been sacrificed for us. 8 So let us celebrate the festival, not by eating the old bread* of wickedness and evil, but by eating the new bread* of purity and truth.

9 When I wrote to you before, I told you not to associate with people who indulge in sexual sin. 10 But I wasn't talking about unbelievers who indulge in sexual sin, or who are greedy or are swindlers or idol worshipers. You would have to leave this world to avoid people like that. 11 What I meant was that you are not to associate with anyone who claims to be a Christian* yet indulges in sexual sin, or is greedy, or worships idols, or is abusive, or a drunkard, or a swindler. Don't even eat with such people.

12 It isn't my responsibility to judge outsiders, but it certainly is your job to judge those inside the church who are sinning in these ways. 13 God will judge those on the outside; but as the Scriptures say, "You must remove the evil person from among you."*

CHAPTER 6

Avoiding Lawsuits with Christians

When you have something against another Christian, why do you file a lawsuit and ask a secular court to decide the matter, instead of taking it to other Christians to decide who is right? 2 Don't you know that someday we Christians are going to judge the world? And since you are going to judge the world, can't you decide these little things among yourselves? 3 Don't you realize that we Christians will judge angels? So you should surely be able to resolve ordinary disagreements here on earth. 4 If you have legal disputes about such matters, why do you go to outside judges who are not respected by the church? 5 I am saying this to shame you. Isn't there anyone in all the church who is wise enough to decide these arguments? 6 But instead, one Christian* sues another—right in front of unbelievers!

7 To have such lawsuits at all is a real defeat for you. Why not just accept the injustice and leave it at that? Why not let yourselves be cheated? 8 But instead, you yourselves are the ones who do wrong and cheat even your own Christian brothers and sisters.*

Avoiding Sexual Sin

9 Don't you know that those who do wrong will have no share in the Kingdom of God? Don't fool yourselves. Those who indulge in sexual sin, who are idol worshipers, adulterers, male prostitutes, homosexuals, 10 thieves, greedy people, drunkards, abusers, and swindlers—none of these will have a share in the Kingdom of God. 11 There was a time when some of you were just like that, but now your sins have been washed away,* and you have been set apart for God. You have been made right with God because of what the Lord Jesus Christ and the Spirit of our God have done for you.

12 You may say, "I am allowed to do anything." But I reply, "Not everything is good for you." And even though "I am allowed to do anything," I must not become a slave to anything. 13 You say, "Food is for the stomach, and the stomach is for food." This is true, though someday God will do away with both of them. But our bodies were not made for sexual immorality. They were made for the Lord, and the Lord cares about our bodies. 14 And God will raise our bodies from the dead by his marvelous power, just as he raised our Lord from the dead. 15 Don't you realize that your bodies are actually parts of Christ? Should a man take his body, which belongs to Christ, and join

5:6-7 Greek *Don't you realize that even a little leaven spreads quickly through the whole batch of dough? 7 Purge out the old leaven so that you can be a new batch of dough, just as you are already unleavened.* 5:8a Greek *not with old leaven.* 5:8b Greek *but with unleavened [bread].* 5:11 Greek *a brother.* 5:13 Deut 17:7. 6:6 Greek *one brother.* 6:8 Greek *brothers.* 6:11 Or *you have been cleansed.*

---

fanatical about it that it turns into an obsession. Others may be hooked on soap operas, food, or some particular habit that has them under its power. Yet, as a Christian, you should only want to be controlled by and under the power of Jesus Christ.

We need to so treasure our relationship with God—and the ensuing freedom from sin it has brought—that we jealously guard that relationship, wanting no thing or person to get in its way. As the Psalmist prayed, we, too, should pray, "Search me, O God, and know my heart; test me and know my thoughts. Point out anything in me that offends you, and lead me along the path of everlasting life" (Psalm 139:23-24).

it to a prostitute? Never! 16And don't you know
that if a man joins himself to a prostitute, he
becomes one body with her? For the Scriptures
say, "The two are united into one."* 17But the
person who is joined to the Lord becomes one
spirit with him.
18Run away from sexual sin! No other sin so
clearly affects the body as this one does. For
sexual immorality is a sin against your own
body. 19Or don't you know that your body is the
temple of the Holy Spirit, who lives in you and
was given to you by God? You do not belong to
yourself, 20for God bought you with a high
price. So you must honor God with your body.

CHAPTER 7

Instruction on Marriage

Now about the questions you asked in your
letter. Yes, it is good to live a celibate life. 2But
because there is so much sexual immorality,
each man should have his own wife, and each
woman should have her own husband.
3The husband should not deprive his wife of
sexual intimacy, which is her right as a married
woman, nor should the wife deprive her husband. 4The wife gives authority over her body to
her husband, and the husband also gives authority over his body to his wife. 5So do not
deprive each other of sexual relations. The only
exception to this rule would be the agreement of
both husband and wife to refrain from sexual
intimacy for a limited time, so they can give
themselves more completely to prayer. Afterward they should come together again so that
Satan won't be able to tempt them because of
their lack of self-control. 6This is only my suggestion. It's not meant to be an absolute rule. 7I
wish everyone could get along without marrying, just as I do. But we are not all the same. God
gives some the gift of marriage, and to others he
gives the gift of singleness.
8Now I say to those who aren't married and
to widows—it's better to stay unmarried, just as
I am. 9But if they can't control themselves, they
should go ahead and marry. It's better to marry
than to burn with lust.
10Now, for those who are married I have a
command that comes not from me, but from the
Lord.* A wife must not leave her husband. 11But
if she does leave him, let her remain single or
else go back to him. And the husband must not
leave his wife.
12Now, I will speak to the rest of you, though
I do not have a direct command from the Lord. If
a Christian man* has a wife who is an unbeliever
and she is willing to continue living with him, he
must not leave her. 13And if a Christian woman
has a husband who is an unbeliever, and he is
willing to continue living with her, she must not
leave him. 14For the Christian wife brings holiness to her marriage, and the Christian husband
brings holiness to his marriage. Otherwise, your
children would not have a godly influence, but
now they are set apart for him. 15(But if the
husband or wife who isn't a Christian insists on
leaving, let them go. In such cases the Christian
husband or wife is not required to stay with
them, for God wants his children to live in
peace.) 16You wives must remember that your
husbands might be converted because of you.
And you husbands must remember that your
wives might be converted because of you.

6:16 Gen 2:24. **7:10** See Matt 5:32; 19:9; Mark 10:11-12; Luke 16:18. **7:12** Greek *a brother.*

OFF AND RUNNING

Marriage Is Not for Everyone Read 1 CORINTHIANS 7:1-40

Contrary to what popular opinion suggests, God has given some the ability to remain "happily unmarried." Verse 35 of this passage reminds us that, when it comes to marrying, it is vitally important to make sure that your decision "will help you serve the Lord best."

If you are contemplating marriage, here are four important things to consider:

1. Take Time Getting to Know One Another. Don't rush into marriage. If you are really in love with someone, you will want to build your friendship with that person as well. That is the foundation of your marriage. As Benjamin Franklin humorously said, "Keep your eyes wide open before marriage and half shut afterwards"—not the other way around!

2. Test the Depth of Your Love. Love is more than some gooey emotion. It is a commitment. In the Greek language, love was described in three different ways: *eros* (physical attraction), *philos* (love between friends), and *agape* (unconditional love). Marriages that are simply based upon *eros* or *phileo* love are destined for

[17]You must accept whatever situation the Lord has put you in, and continue on as you were when God first called you. This is my rule for all the churches. [18]For instance, a man who was circumcised before he became a believer should not try to reverse it. And the man who was uncircumcised when he became a believer should not be circumcised now. [19]For it makes no difference whether or not a man has been circumcised. The important thing is to keep God's commandments.

[20]You should continue on as you were when God called you. [21]Are you a slave? Don't let that worry you—but if you get a chance to be free, take it. [22]And remember, if you were a slave when the Lord called you, the Lord has now set you free from the awful power of sin. And if you were free when the Lord called you, you are now a slave of Christ. [23]God purchased you at a high price. Don't be enslaved by the world.* [24]So, dear brothers and sisters,* whatever situation you were in when you became a believer, stay there in your new relationship with God.

[25]Now, about the young women who are not yet married. I do not have a command from the Lord for them. But the Lord in his kindness has given me wisdom that can be trusted, and I will share it with you. [26]Because of the present crisis,* I think it is best to remain just as you are. [27]If you have a wife, do not end the marriage. If you do not have a wife, do not get married. [28]But if you do get married, it is not a sin. And if a young woman gets married, it is not a sin. However, I am trying to spare you the extra problems that come with marriage.

[29]Now let me say this, dear brothers and sisters: The time that remains is very short, so husbands should not let marriage be their major concern. [30]Happiness or sadness or wealth should not keep anyone from doing God's work. [31]Those in frequent contact with the things of the world should make good use of them without becoming attached to them, for this world and all it contains will pass away. [32]In everything you do, I want you to be free from the concerns of this life. An unmarried man can spend his time doing the Lord's work and thinking how to please him. [33]But a married man can't do that so well. He has to think about his earthly responsibilities and how to please his wife. [34]His interests are divided. In the same way, a woman who is no longer married or has never been married can be more devoted to the Lord in body and in spirit, while the married woman must be concerned about her earthly responsibilities and how to please her husband.

[35]I am saying this for your benefit, not to place restrictions on you. I want you to do whatever will help you serve the Lord best, with as few distractions as possible. [36]But if a man thinks he ought to marry his fiancée because he has trouble controlling his passions and time is passing, it is all right; it is not a sin. Let them marry. [37]But if he has decided firmly not to marry and there is no urgency and he can control his passion, he does well not to marry. [38]So the person who marries does well, and the person who doesn't marry does even better.

[39]A wife is married to her husband as long as he lives. If her husband dies, she is free to marry whomever she wishes, but this must be a marriage acceptable to the Lord.* [40]But in my opinion it

7:23 Greek *don't become slaves of people.* 7:24 Greek *brothers;* also in 7:29. 7:26 Or *pressures of life.* 7:39 Or *but only to a Christian;* Greek reads *but only in the Lord.*

---

trouble, but marriages built around the *agape* love that Christ displayed will last. Emotions will come and go, but true love is far more than that. The Bible says, "Many waters cannot quench love; neither can rivers drown it" (Song of Songs 8:7).

3. Make Sure of Your Commitment. Ask yourself the following questions: Are you ready to spend the rest of your life with this person? Can you see yourselves going through parenthood together? Are you willing to make sacrifices in relationships, hobbies, and even your career for the sake of your marriage?

4. Consider Your Witness for Christ. If this other person is not a believer, don't even consider marriage. Scripture gives stern warnings against being teamed with those who are unbelievers (2 Corinthians 6:14, p. 222). You need to also consider the spiritual implications of this relationship. Will the two of you together be a more effective and powerful witness for Christ than the two of you apart?

Whether you marry or remain single, learn to be content in whatever situation the Lord places you. Then you will possess one of the keys to true happiness.

will be better for her if she doesn't marry again,
and I think I am giving you counsel from God's
Spirit when I say this.

CHAPTER 8

Food Sacrificed to Idols

Now let's talk about food that has been sacrificed to idols. You think that everyone should
agree with your perfect knowledge. While
knowledge may make us feel important, it is
love that really builds up the church. 2Anyone
who claims to know all the answers doesn't
really know very much. 3But the person who
loves God is the one God knows and cares for.

4So now, what about it? Should we eat meat
that has been sacrificed to idols? Well, we all
know that an idol is not really a god and that
there is only one God and no other. 5According
to some people, there are many so-called gods
and many lords, both in heaven and on earth.
6But we know that there is only one God, the
Father, who created everything, and we exist for
him. And there is only one Lord, Jesus Christ,
through whom God made everything and
through whom we have been given life.

7However, not all Christians realize this.
Some are accustomed to thinking of idols as
being real, so when they eat food that has been
offered to idols, they think of it as the worship
of real gods, and their weak consciences are
violated. 8It's true that we can't win God's approval by what we eat. We don't miss out on
anything if we don't eat it, and we don't gain
anything if we do. 9But you must be careful with
this freedom of yours. Do not cause a brother or
sister with a weaker conscience to stumble.

10You see, this is what can happen: Weak
Christians who think it is wrong to eat this food
will see you eating in the temple of an idol. You
know there's nothing wrong with it, but they
will be encouraged to violate their conscience by
eating food that has been dedicated to the idol.
11So because of your superior knowledge, a weak
Christian,* for whom Christ died, will be destroyed. 12And you are sinning against Christ
when you sin against other Christians* by encouraging them to do something they believe is
wrong. 13If what I eat is going to make another
Christian sin, I will never eat meat again as long
as I live—for I don't want to make another
Christian stumble.

CHAPTER 9

Paul Gives Up His Rights

Do I not have as much freedom as anyone else?*
Am I not an apostle? Haven't I seen Jesus our
Lord with my own eyes? Isn't it because of my
hard work that you are in the Lord? 2Even if
others think I am not an apostle, I certainly am
to you, for you are living proof that I am the
Lord's apostle.

3This is my answer to those who question my
authority as an apostle.* 4Don't we have the
right to live in your homes and share your
meals? 5Don't we have the right to bring a Christian wife* along with us as the other disciples
and the Lord's brothers and Peter* do? 6Or is it
only Barnabas and I who have to work to support ourselves? 7What soldier has to pay his own
expenses? And have you ever heard of a farmer
who harvests his crop and doesn't have the right
to eat some of it? What shepherd takes care of a
flock of sheep and isn't allowed to drink some
of the milk? 8And this isn't merely human opinion. Doesn't God's law say the same thing? 9For
the law of Moses says, "Do not keep an ox from
eating as it treads out the grain."* Do you suppose God was thinking only about oxen when

8:11 Greek *brother;* also in 8:13. 8:12 Greek *brothers.* 9:1 Greek *Am I not free?* 9:3 Greek *those who examine me.* 9:5a Greek *a sister, a wife.* 9:5b Greek *Cephas.* 9:9 Deut 25:4.

OFF AND RUNNING

A Christian Should Not Leave a Non-Christian Spouse

Read 1 CORINTHIANS 7:12-16

While it is easy to rationalize leaving an unbelieving spouse who does not support or encourage your faith, it is not biblical. As Paul reiterates here, divorce is not God's intent for married couples. In the case of a Christian and non-Christian spouse, there are two additional reasons to remain married:

1. A Christian Spouse Serves as a Witness to an Unbelieving Spouse. A Christian may play an important role in winning his or her spouse to the Lord. Scripture says that the Christian wife of a nonbelieving husband can have a powerful influence on her spouse through her godly actions and

he said this? 10Wasn't he also speaking to us? Of course he was. Just as farm workers who plow fields and thresh the grain expect a share of the harvest, Christian workers should be paid by those they serve.

11We have planted good spiritual seed among you. Is it too much to ask, in return, for mere food and clothing? 12If you support others who preach to you, shouldn't we have an even greater right to be supported? Yet we have never used this right. We would rather put up with anything than put an obstacle in the way of the Good News about Christ.

13Don't you know that those who work in the Temple get their meals from the food brought to the Temple as offerings? And those who serve at the altar get a share of the sacrificial offerings. 14In the same way, the Lord gave orders that those who preach the Good News should be supported by those who benefit from it. 15Yet I have never used any of these rights. And I am not writing this to suggest that I would like to start now. In fact, I would rather die than lose my distinction of preaching without charge. 16For preaching the Good News is not something I can boast about. I am compelled by God to do it. How terrible for me if I didn't do it!

17If I were doing this of my own free will, then I would deserve payment. But God has chosen me and given me this sacred trust, and I have no choice. 18What then is my pay? It is the satisfaction I get from preaching the Good News without expense to anyone, never demanding my rights as a preacher.

19This means I am not bound to obey people just because they pay me, yet I have become a servant of everyone so that I can bring them to Christ. 20When I am with the Jews, I become one of them so that I can bring them to Christ. When I am with those who follow the Jewish laws, I do the same, even though I am not subject to the law, so that I can bring them to Christ. 21When I am with the Gentiles who do not have the Jewish law,* I fit in with them as much as I can. In this way, I gain their confidence and bring them to Christ. But I do not discard the law of God; I obey the law of Christ.

22When I am with those who are oppressed, I share their oppression so that I might bring them to Christ. Yes, I try to find common ground with everyone so that I might bring them to Christ. 23I do all this to spread the Good News, and in doing so I enjoy its blessings.

24Remember that in a race everyone runs, but only one person gets the prize. You also must run in such a way that you will win. 25All athletes practice strict self-control. They do it to win a prize that will fade away, but we do it for an eternal prize. 26So I run straight to the goal with purpose in every step. I am not like a boxer who misses his punches.* 27I discipline my body like an athlete, training it to do what it should. Otherwise, I fear that after preaching to others I myself might be disqualified.

CHAPTER 10

Warnings against Idolatry

I don't want you to forget, dear brothers and sisters,* what happened to our ancestors in the wilderness long ago. God guided all of them by sending a cloud that moved along ahead of them, and he brought them all safely through the waters of the sea on dry ground. 2As followers of Moses, they were all baptized in the cloud and the sea. 3And all of them ate the same miraculous* food, 4and all of them drank the same miraculous water. For they all drank from the miraculous rock that traveled with them, and that rock was Christ. 5Yet after all this, God

9:21 Greek *those without the law.* 9:26 Or *I am not just shadowboxing.* 10:1 Greek *brothers.* 10:3 Greek *spiritual;* also in 10:4.

example, which may encourage him to come to faith in Christ (see 1 Peter 3:1-2, p. 308). The same is true for Christian husbands.

2. A Christian Spouse Can Influence the Couple's Children for Christ. If you separate, as Paul states, there is a good chance your children may not come to faith. It will help them to see your faith in the context of a united family.

If, however, your unbelieving spouse abandons you, and you have done everything you could to keep the marriage together, God will not hold you to that relationship. This is one of the few marriage "release clauses" found in Scripture. God will not force you to stay married to an unbelieving partner who doesn't want to stay married to you.

was not pleased with most of them, and he
destroyed them in the wilderness.
6These events happened as a warning to us,
so that we would not crave evil things as they did
7or worship idols as some of them did. For the
Scriptures say, "The people celebrated with
feasting and drinking, and they indulged themselves in pagan revelry."* 8And we must not
engage in sexual immorality as some of them
did, causing 23,000 of them to die in one day.
9Nor should we put Christ* to the test, as some
of them did and then died from snakebites.
10And don't grumble as some of them did, for
that is why God sent his angel of death to destroy them. 11All these events happened to them
as examples for us. They were written down to
warn us, who live at the time when this age is
drawing to a close.
12If you think you are standing strong, be
careful, for you, too, may fall into the same sin.
13But remember that the temptations that come
into your life are no different from what others
experience. And God is faithful. He will keep the
temptation from becoming so strong that you
can't stand up against it. When you are tempted,
he will show you a way out so that you will not
give in to it.
14So, my dear friends, flee from the worship
of idols. 15You are reasonable people. Decide for
yourselves if what I am about to say is true.
16When we bless the cup at the Lord's Table,
aren't we sharing in the benefits of the blood of
Christ? And when we break the loaf of bread,
aren't we sharing in the benefits of the body of
Christ? 17And we all eat from one loaf, showing
that we are one body. 18And think about the
nation of Israel; all who eat the sacrifices are
united by that act.
19What am I trying to say? Am I saying that
the idols to whom the pagans bring sacrifices are
real gods and that these sacrifices are of some
value? 20No, not at all. What I am saying is that
these sacrifices are offered to demons, not to
God. And I don't want any of you to be partners
with demons. 21You cannot drink from the cup
of the Lord and from the cup of demons, too.
You cannot eat at the Lord's Table and at the
table of demons, too. 22What? Do you dare to
rouse the Lord's jealousy as Israel did? Do you
think we are stronger than he is?
23You say, "I am allowed to do anything"—
but not everything is helpful. You say, "I am
allowed to do anything"—but not everything is
beneficial. 24Don't think only of your own
good. Think of other Christians and what is best
for them.
25Here's what you should do. You may eat
any meat that is sold in the marketplace. Don't
ask whether or not it was offered to idols, and
then your conscience won't be bothered. 26For
"the earth is the Lord's, and everything in it."*
27If someone who isn't a Christian asks you
home for dinner, go ahead; accept the invitation
if you want to. Eat whatever is offered to you and
don't ask any questions about it. Your conscience should not be bothered by this. 28But
suppose someone warns you that this meat has
been offered to an idol. Don't eat it, out of
consideration for the conscience of the one who
told you. 29It might not be a matter of conscience for you, but it is for the other person.
Now, why should my freedom be limited by
what someone else thinks? 30If I can thank God
for the food and enjoy it, why should I be condemned for eating it? 31Whatever you eat or
drink or whatever you do, you must do all for
the glory of God. 32Don't give offense to Jews or
Gentiles or the church of God. 33That is the plan
I follow, too. I try to please everyone in everything I do. I don't just do what I like or what is
best for me, but what is best for them so they
may be saved.

CHAPTER 11

And you should follow my example, just as I
follow Christ's.

Instructions for Public Worship

2I am so glad, dear friends, that you always keep
me in your thoughts and you are following the
Christian teaching I passed on to you. 3But there
is one thing I want you to know: A man is
responsible to Christ, a woman is responsible to
her husband, and Christ is responsible to God.
4A man dishonors Christ* if he covers his head
while praying or prophesying. 5But a woman
dishonors her husband* if she prays or prophesies without a covering on her head, for this is
the same as shaving her head. 6Yes, if she refuses
to wear a head covering, she should cut off all
her hair. And since it is shameful for a woman to
have her hair cut or her head shaved, then she
should wear a covering.* 7A man should not
wear anything on his head when worshiping, for
man is God's glory, made in God's own image,

10:7 Exod 32:6. **10:9** Some manuscripts read *the Lord.* **10:26** Ps 24:1. **11:4** Greek *his head.* **11:5** Greek *her head.* **11:6** Or *then she should have long hair.*

but woman is the glory of man. 8For the first man didn't come from woman, but the first woman came from man. 9And man was not made for woman's benefit, but woman was made for man. 10So a woman should wear a covering on her head as a sign of authority because the angels are watching.

11But in relationships among the Lord's people, women are not independent of men, and men are not independent of women. 12For although the first woman came from man, all men have been born from women ever since, and everything comes from God.

13What do you think about this? Is it right for a woman to pray to God in public without covering her head? 14Isn't it obvious that it's disgraceful for a man to have long hair? 15And isn't it obvious that long hair is a woman's pride and joy? For it has been given to her as a covering. 16But if anyone wants to argue about this, all I can say is that we have no other custom than this, and all the churches of God feel the same way about it.

Order at the Lord's Supper

17But now when I mention this next issue, I cannot praise you. For it sounds as if more harm than good is done when you meet together. 18First of all, I hear that there are divisions among you when you meet as a church, and to some extent I believe it. 19But, of course, there must be divisions among you so that those of you who are right will be recognized!

20It's not the Lord's Supper you are concerned about when you come together. 21For I am told that some of you hurry to eat your own meal without sharing with others. As a result, some go hungry while others get drunk. 22What? Is this really true? Don't you have your own homes for eating and drinking? Or do you really want to disgrace the church of God and shame the poor? What am I supposed to say about these things? Do you want me to praise you? Well, I certainly do not!

23For this is what the Lord himself said, and I pass it on to you just as I received it. On the night when he was betrayed, the Lord Jesus took a loaf of bread, 24and when he had given thanks, he broke it and said, "This is my body, which is given* for you. Do this in remembrance of me." 25In the same way, he took the cup of wine after supper, saying, "This cup is the new covenant between God and you, sealed by the shedding of my blood. Do this in remembrance of me as often as you drink it." 26For every time you eat this bread and drink this cup, you are announcing the Lord's death until he comes again.

27So if anyone eats this bread or drinks this cup of the Lord unworthily, that person is guilty of sinning against the body and the blood of the Lord. 28That is why you should examine yourself before eating the bread and drinking from the cup. 29For if you eat the bread or drink the cup unworthily, not honoring the body of Christ,* you are eating and drinking God's judgment upon yourself. 30That is why many of you are weak and sick and some have even died.

11:24 Some manuscripts read *broken*.

11:29 Greek *the body;* some manuscripts read *the Lord's body.*

Rejoice Because Victory Is Yours in Christ Jesus

Read 1 CORINTHIANS 10:13

God realizes that we as humans will be tempted by one thing or another in this world. Fortunately for us, God cares so deeply about us that he has taken action to help us through times of temptation. This verse provides two rays of hope for you when you are tempted:

1. Jesus Understands Your Situation. Any temptation you are facing or will face has been faced before. Better yet, Jesus understands what it is like to be tempted, for the Bible teaches that he can sympathize with us, for he "faced all of the same temptations we do, yet he did not sin" (Hebrews 4:15).

2. God Will Always Give You the Strength to Get Through the Temptation. When you face temptation, God will always give you the power to resist it or give you a way to escape it. Sometimes the way out of temptation is literal. For instance, if you are at the movie theater and an explicit sexual scene appears on the screen, the way of escape means walking out of the theater. At other times, it may mean relying on God's Holy Spirit to give you the power to resist.

The next time you are tempted or tested, remember this: God will allow hardship in the life of the Christian, but it will always be filtered through the screen of his love. He will never give you more than you can handle.

31But if we examine ourselves, we will not be
examined by God and judged in this way. 32But
when we are judged and disciplined by the Lord,
we will not be condemned with the world. 33So,
dear brothers and sisters,* when you gather for
the Lord's Supper, wait for each other. 34If you
are really hungry, eat at home so you won't bring
judgment upon yourselves when you meet together.

I'll give you instructions about the other matters after I arrive.

CHAPTER 12

Spiritual Gifts

And now, dear brothers and sisters,* I will write
about the special abilities the Holy Spirit gives
to each of us, for I must correct your misunder-
standings about them. 2You know that when
you were still pagans you were led astray and
swept along in worshiping speechless idols. 3So
I want you to know how to discern what is truly
from God: No one speaking by the Spirit of God
can curse Jesus, and no one is able to say, "Jesus
is Lord," except by the Holy Spirit.

4Now there are different kinds of spiritual
gifts, but it is the same Holy Spirit who is the
source of them all. 5There are different kinds of
service in the church, but it is the same Lord we
are serving. 6There are different ways God works
in our lives, but it is the same God who does the
work through all of us. 7A spiritual gift is given
to each of us as a means of helping the entire
church.

8To one person the Spirit gives the ability to
give wise advice; to another he gives the gift of
special knowledge. 9The Spirit gives special faith
to another, and to someone else he gives the
power to heal the sick. 10He gives one person the
power to perform miracles, and to another the
ability to prophesy. He gives someone else the
ability to know whether it is really the Spirit of
God or another spirit that is speaking. Still another person is given the ability to speak in
unknown languages,* and another is given the
ability to interpret what is being said. 11It is the
one and only Holy Spirit who distributes these
gifts. He alone decides which gift each person
should have.

One Body with Many Parts

12The human body has many parts, but the
many parts make up only one body. So it is with
the body of Christ. 13Some of us are Jews, some
are Gentiles, some are slaves, and some are free.
But we have all been baptized into Christ's body
by one Spirit, and we have all received the same
Spirit.*

14Yes, the body has many different parts, not
just one part. 15If the foot says, "I am not a part
of the body because I am not a hand," that does
not make it any less a part of the body. 16And if
the ear says, "I am not part of the body because
I am only an ear and not an eye," would that
make it any less a part of the body? 17Suppose
the whole body were an eye—then how would
you hear? Or if your whole body were just one
big ear, how could you smell anything?

18But God made our bodies with many parts,
and he has put each part just where he wants it.
19What a strange thing a body would be if it had
only one part! 20Yes, there are many parts, but
only one body. 21The eye can never say to the
hand, "I don't need you." The head can't say to
the feet, "I don't need you."

22In fact, some of the parts that seem weakest
and least important are really the most necessary. 23And the parts we regard as less honorable
are those we clothe with the greatest care. So we
carefully protect from the eyes of others those
parts that should not be seen, 24while other
parts do not require this special care. So God has
put the body together in such a way that extra
honor and care are given to those parts that have
less dignity. 25This makes for harmony among

11:33 Greek *brothers.* 12:1 Greek *brothers.* 12:10 Or *in tongues;* also in 12:28, 30. 12:13 Greek *we were all given one Spirit to drink.*

OFF AND RUNNING

Does This Activity Build Me Up Spiritually?

Read 1 CORINTHIANS 10:23

This verse tackles the issue of whether certain activities will be spiritually constructive in your life—even if it falls into a so-called "gray" area. A more literal translation of that verse is "All things are permissible, but not all things promote growth in Christian character."

The next time you question whether you should be seeing a certain movie, participating in a specific activity, or engaging in a certain habit, ask yourself the following questions:

the members, so that all the members care for each other equally. 26If one part suffers, all the parts suffer with it, and if one part is honored, all the parts are glad.

27Now all of you together are Christ's body, and each one of you is a separate and necessary part of it. 28Here is a list of some of the members that God has placed in the body of Christ:

first are apostles,
second are prophets,
third are teachers,
then those who do miracles,
those who have the gift of healing,
those who can help others,
those who can get others to work together,
those who speak in unknown languages.

29Is everyone an apostle? Of course not. Is everyone a prophet? No. Are all teachers? Does everyone have the power to do miracles? 30Does everyone have the gift of healing? Of course not. Does God give all of us the ability to speak in unknown languages? Can everyone interpret unknown languages? No! 31And in any event, you should desire the most helpful gifts.

Love Is the Greatest

First, however, let me tell you about something else that is better than any of them!

CHAPTER 13

If I could speak in any language in heaven or on earth* but didn't love others, I would only be making meaningless noise like a loud gong or a clanging cymbal. 2If I had the gift of prophecy, and if I knew all the mysteries of the future and knew everything about everything, but didn't love others, what good would I be? And if I had the gift of faith so that I could speak to a mountain and make it move, without love I would be no good to anybody. 3If I gave everything I have to the poor and even sacrificed my body, I could boast about it;* but if I didn't love others, I would be of no value whatsoever.

4Love is patient and kind. Love is not jealous or boastful or proud 5or rude. Love does not demand its own way. Love is not irritable, and it keeps no record of when it has been wronged. 6It is never glad about injustice but rejoices whenever the truth wins out. 7Love never gives up, never loses faith, is always hopeful, and endures through every circumstance.

8Love will last forever, but prophecy and speaking in unknown languages* and special knowledge will all disappear. 9Now we know only a little, and even the gift of prophecy reveals little! 10But when the end comes, these special gifts will all disappear.

11It's like this: When I was a child, I spoke and thought and reasoned as a child does. But when I grew up, I put away childish things. 12Now we see things imperfectly as in a poor mirror, but then we will see everything with perfect clarity.* All that I know now is partial and incomplete, but then I will know everything completely, just as God knows me now.

13There are three things that will endure—faith, hope, and love—and the greatest of these is love.

CHAPTER 14

The Gifts of Tongues and Prophecy

Let love be your highest goal, but also desire the special abilities the Spirit gives, especially the gift of prophecy. 2For if your gift is the ability to speak in tongues,* you will be talking to God but not to people, since they won't be able to understand you. You will be speaking by the power of the Spirit, but it will all be mysterious. 3But one who prophesies is helping others grow in the Lord, encouraging and comforting them. 4A person who speaks in tongues is strength-

13:1 Greek *in tongues of people and angels.* 13:3 Some manuscripts read *and even gave my body to be burned.* 13:8 Or *in tongues.* 13:12 Greek *see face to face.* 14:2 Or *in unknown languages;* also in 14:4, 5, 13, 14, 18, 22, 28, 39.

- Will this activity make the things of this world more appealing than the things of God?
- Will it keep me from prayer?
- Will it diminish my hunger for God's Word?
- Will it spiritually tear me down by pulling me away from other Christian believers?

You do not have time for anything that would make this world more attractive, dull your desire for prayer, take away your appetite for Bible study, or keep you from Christian fellowship. Instead, look for things that will benefit and build your Christian character.

ened personally in the Lord, but one who speaks a word of prophecy strengthens the entire church.

5I wish you all had the gift of speaking in tongues, but even more I wish you were all able to prophesy. For prophecy is a greater and more useful gift than speaking in tongues, unless someone interprets what you are saying so that the whole church can get some good out of it.

6Dear brothers and sisters,* if I should come to you talking in an unknown language,* how would that help you? But if I bring you some revelation or some special knowledge or some prophecy or some teaching—that is what will help you. 7Even musical instruments like the flute or the harp, though they are lifeless, are examples of the need for speaking in plain language. For no one will recognize the melody unless the notes are played clearly. 8And if the bugler doesn't sound a clear call, how will the soldiers know they are being called to battle? 9And it's the same for you. If you talk to people in a language they don't understand, how will they know what you mean? You might as well be talking to an empty room.

10There are so many different languages in the world, and all are excellent for those who understand them, 11but to me they mean nothing. I will not understand people who speak those languages, and they will not understand me. 12Since you are so eager to have spiritual gifts, ask God for those that will be of real help to the whole church.

13So anyone who has the gift of speaking in tongues should pray also for the gift of interpretation in order to tell people plainly what has been said. 14For if I pray in tongues, my spirit is praying, but I don't understand what I am saying.

15Well then, what shall I do? I will do both. I will pray in the spirit,* and I will pray in words I understand. I will sing in the spirit, and I will sing in words I understand. 16For if you praise God only in the spirit, how can those who don't understand you praise God along with you? How can they join you in giving thanks when they don't understand what you are saying? 17You will be giving thanks very nicely, no doubt, but it doesn't help the other people present.

18I thank God that I speak in tongues more than all of you. 19But in a church meeting I would much rather speak five understandable words that will help others than ten thousand words in an unknown language.

20Dear brothers and sisters, don't be childish in your understanding of these things. Be innocent as babies when it comes to evil, but be mature and wise in understanding matters of this kind. 21It is written in the Scriptures,*

"I will speak to my own people
  through unknown languages
  and through the lips of foreigners.
But even then, they will not listen to me,"*
  says the Lord.

22So you see that speaking in tongues is a sign, not for believers, but for unbelievers; prophecy, however, is for the benefit of believers, not unbelievers. 23Even so, if unbelievers or people who don't understand these things come into your meeting and hear everyone talking in an unknown language, they will think you are crazy. 24But if all of you are prophesying, and unbelievers or people who don't understand these things come into your meeting, they will be convicted of sin, and they will be condemned by what you say. 25As they listen, their secret thoughts will be laid bare, and they will fall down on their knees and worship God, declaring, "God is really here among you."

A Call to Orderly Worship

26Well, my brothers and sisters, let's summarize what I am saying. When you meet, one will sing, another will teach, another will tell some special revelation God has given, one will speak in an unknown language, while another will interpret what is said. But everything that is done must be useful to all and build them up in the Lord. 27No more than two or three should speak in an unknown language. They must speak one at a time, and someone must be ready to interpret what they are saying. 28But if no one is present who can interpret, they must be silent in your church meeting and speak in tongues to God privately.

29Let two or three prophesy, and let the others evaluate what is said. 30But if someone is prophesying and another person receives a revelation from the Lord, the one who is speaking must stop. 31In this way, all who prophesy will have a turn to speak, one after the other, so that everyone will learn and be encouraged. 32Remember that people who prophesy are in control of their spirit and can wait their turn.

14:6a Greek *brothers;* also in 14:20, 26, 39. **14:6b** Or *in tongues;* also in 14:19, 23, 26, 27. **14:15** Or *in the Spirit;* also in 14:15b, 16. **14:21a** Greek *in the law.* **14:21b** Isa 28:11-12.

33 For God is not a God of disorder but of peace,
as in all the other churches.*
34 Women should be silent during the church
meetings. It is not proper for them to speak.
They should be submissive, just as the law says.
35 If they have any questions to ask, let them ask
their husbands at home, for it is improper for
women to speak in church meetings.*
36 Do you think that the knowledge of God's
word begins and ends with you Corinthians?
Well, you are mistaken! 37 If you claim to be a
prophet or think you are very spiritual, you
should recognize that what I am saying is a
command from the Lord himself. 38 But if you
do not recognize this, you will not be recognized.*
39 So, dear brothers and sisters, be eager to
prophesy, and don't forbid speaking in tongues.
40 But be sure that everything is done properly
and in order.

CHAPTER 15

The Resurrection of Christ

1 Now let me remind you, dear brothers and sisters,* of the Good News I preached to you before. You welcomed it then and still do now, for
your faith is built on this wonderful message.
2 And it is this Good News that saves you if you
firmly believe it—unless, of course, you believed
something that was never true in the first place.
3 I passed on to you what was most important
and what had also been passed on to me—that
Christ died for our sins, just as the Scriptures
said. 4 He was buried, and he was raised from the
dead on the third day, as the Scriptures said. 5 He
was seen by Peter* and then by the twelve apostles. 6 After that, he was seen by more than five
hundred of his followers* at one time, most of
whom are still alive, though some have died by
now. 7 Then he was seen by James and later by all
the apostles. 8 Last of all, I saw him, too, long
after the others, as though I had been born at the
wrong time. 9 For I am the least of all the apostles, and I am not worthy to be called an apostle
after the way I persecuted the church of God.
10 But whatever I am now, it is all because God
poured out his special favor on me—and not
without results. For I have worked harder than
all the other apostles, yet it was not I but God
who was working through me by his grace. 11 So

14:33 The phrase *as in all the other churches* could be joined to the beginning of 14:34. 14:35 Some manuscripts place verses 34-35 after 14:40. 14:38 Some manuscripts read *If you are ignorant of this, stay in your ignorance.* 15:1 Greek *brothers;* also in 15:31, 50, 58. 15:5 Greek *Cephas.* 15:6 Greek *the brothers.*

You Have a Place in the Church

Read 1 CORINTHIANS 12:12-27

The apostle Paul used this illustration of the physical body to drive home an important point: Every single person has a vital role to play in the body of Christ. That means God has a specific purpose for *you* to carry out in your local church, and it is up to you to fill that purpose, with God's help. This passage explains why this is so important.

The Church Consists of Different People with Different Roles. When God designed the church, he did not intend for its members to be "Christian clones." Instead, he chose to use the various groups and spiritual gifts found throughout the church to bring attention to the person who unifies us: Jesus Christ (see Ephesians 3:10-11, p. 239). When the church operates as God intended, it serves as a powerful witness to a watching world.

No One Person Is More Valuable than Another. No gift of the Holy Spirit is "better" than another. Therefore, each individual has a special place of significance within the body of Christ. Even though your role may not seem as visible as others—for instance, God may be using you to visit convalescent homes while someone else leads a Bible study—your role is just as vital.

We Need One Another to Function as God Intended. If you fail to use the special gifts and abilities God has given you, you do a disservice to the church. God wants you to realize the importance of working together and building friendships with other committed Christians. One could liken the church to a group of coals burning brightly together. Each coal not only emanates its own heat, but also helps to keep the others hot, all the while benefiting from their warmth, as well. If you were to isolate one of those coals from the others, it would only be a matter of time until its heat dissipated. The same holds true for us as believers. We need one another to function as individuals and as the body of Christ.

FIRST STEPS

Love Surpasses All Spiritual Gifts Read 1 CORINTHIANS 13:1-13

This passage gives one of the most complete descriptions of love in the Bible. More importantly, it shows that love needs to be the one thing in life we seek more than anything else. For without it, whatever we do or say really has no lasting value. Compare the love described here with the superficial love found in this world:

- God says love should be directed toward others (verses 1-3).
  The world says love should be directed toward ourselves.
- God says love is patient and kind (verse 4).
  The world says love satisfies your immediate needs.
- God says love is never jealous or envious (verse 4).
  The world says love means that you deserve the "best."
- God says love is never boastful or proud (verse 4).
  The world says love isn't necessary to make people respect you.
- God says love is never rude (verse 5).
  The world says love lets you act as you please.
- God says love does not demand its own way (verse 5).
  The world says love gets in the way of what is in it for me.
- God says love is not irritable or touchy, and it holds no grudges (verse 5).
  The world says love takes a backseat when it comes to seeking revenge.
- God says love rejoices in justice and truth (verse 6).
  The world says love understands—even ignores—evil.
- God says love is loyal (verse 7).
  The world says love should be self-serving.

The kind of love God wants you to give others is impossible to "manufacture" on our own. You might say that it is a "supernatural" love. It is a natural outflow of God's presence in our lives. That is why the Bible says, "[God] has given us the Holy Spirit to fill our hearts with his love" (Romans 5:5).

If you feel your love for others is falling short of God's ideal, ask the Holy Spirit to strengthen you in this area. Your relationships with others will never be the same.

CORNER STONES

it makes no difference whether I preach or they
preach. The important thing is that you believed
what we preached to you.

The Resurrection of the Dead

12But tell me this—since we preach that Christ
rose from the dead, why are some of you saying there will be no resurrection of the dead?
13For if there is no resurrection of the dead,
then Christ has not been raised either. 14And if
Christ was not raised, then all our preaching is
useless, and your trust in God is useless. 15And
we apostles would all be lying about God, for
we have said that God raised Christ from the
grave, but that can't be true if there is no resurrection of the dead. 16If there is no resurrection of the dead, then Christ has not been
raised. 17And if Christ has not been raised,
then your faith is useless, and you are still
under condemnation for your sins. 18In that
case, all who have died believing in Christ have
perished! 19And if we have hope in Christ only
for this life, we are the most miserable people
in the world.

20But the fact is that Christ has been raised
from the dead. He has become the first of a great
harvest of those who will be raised to life again.

21So you see, just as death came into the
world through a man, Adam, now the resurrection from the dead has begun through another
man, Christ. 22Everyone dies because all of us
are related to Adam, the first man. But all who
are related to Christ, the other man, will be given
new life. 23But there is an order to this resurrec-

tion: Christ was raised first; then when Christ comes back, all his people will be raised.

24After that the end will come, when he will turn the Kingdom over to God the Father, having put down all enemies of every kind.* 25For Christ must reign until he humbles all his enemies beneath his feet. 26And the last enemy to be destroyed is death. 27For the Scriptures say, "God has given him authority over all things."* (Of course, when it says "authority over all things," it does not include God himself, who gave Christ his authority.) 28Then, when he has conquered all things, the Son will present himself to God, so that God, who gave his Son authority over all things, will be utterly supreme over everything everywhere.

29If the dead will not be raised, then what point is there in people being baptized for those who are dead? Why do it unless the dead will someday rise again?

30And why should we ourselves be continually risking our lives, facing death hour by hour? 31For I swear, dear brothers and sisters, I face death daily. This is as certain as my pride in what the Lord Jesus Christ has done in you. 32And what value was there in fighting wild beasts—those men of Ephesus*—if there will be no resurrection from the dead? If there is no resurrection,

"Let's feast and get drunk,
for tomorrow we die!"*

33Don't be fooled by those who say such things, for "bad company corrupts good character." 34Come to your senses and stop sinning. For to your shame I say that some of you don't even know God.

The Resurrection Body

35But someone may ask, "How will the dead be raised? What kind of bodies will they have?" 36What a foolish question! When you put a seed into the ground, it doesn't grow into a plant unless it dies first. 37And what you put in the ground is not the plant that will grow, but only a dry little seed of wheat or whatever it is you are planting. 38Then God gives it a new body—just the kind he wants it to have. A different kind of plant grows from each kind of seed. 39And just as there are different kinds of seeds and plants, so also there are different kinds of flesh—whether of humans, animals, birds, or fish.

40There are bodies in the heavens, and there are bodies on earth. The glory of the heavenly bodies is different from the beauty of the earthly bodies. 41The sun has one kind of glory, while the moon and stars each have another kind. And even the stars differ from each other in their beauty and brightness.

42It is the same way for the resurrection of the dead. Our earthly bodies, which die and decay, will be different when they are resurrected, for they will never die. 43Our bodies now disappoint us, but when they are raised, they will be full of glory. They are weak now, but when they are raised, they will be full of power. 44They are natural human bodies now, but when they are raised, they will be spiritual bodies. For just as there are natural bodies, so also there are spiritual bodies.

45The Scriptures tell us, "The first man, Adam, became a living person."* But the last Adam—that is, Christ—is a life-giving Spirit. 46What came first was the natural body, then the spiritual body comes later. 47Adam, the first man, was made from the dust of the earth, while Christ, the second man, came from heaven. 48Every human being has an earthly body just like Adam's, but our heavenly bodies will be just like Christ's. 49Just as we are now like Adam, the man of the earth, so we will someday be like Christ, the man from heaven.

50What I am saying, dear brothers and sisters, is that flesh and blood cannot inherit the Kingdom of God. These perishable bodies of ours are not able to live forever.

51But let me tell you a wonderful secret God has revealed to us. Not all of us will die, but we will all be transformed. 52It will happen in a moment, in the blinking of an eye, when the last trumpet is blown. For when the trumpet sounds, the Christians who have died* will be raised with transformed bodies. And then we who are living will be transformed so that we will never die. 53For our perishable earthly bodies must be transformed into heavenly bodies that will never die.

54When this happens—when our perishable earthly bodies have been transformed into heavenly bodies that will never die—then at last the Scriptures will come true:

"Death is swallowed up in victory.*
55 O death, where is your victory?
O death, where is your sting?"*

56For sin is the sting that results in death, and the law gives sin its power. 57How we thank God,

15:24 Greek *every ruler and every authority and power.* **15:27** Ps 8:6. **15:32a** Greek *fighting wild beasts in Ephesus.* **15:32b** Isa 22:13. **15:45** Gen 2:7. **15:52** Greek *the dead.* **15:54** Isa 25:8. **15:55** Hos 13:14.

who gives us victory over sin and death through
Jesus Christ our Lord!
58So, my dear brothers and sisters, be strong
and steady, always enthusiastic about the Lord's
work, for you know that nothing you do for the
Lord is ever useless.

CHAPTER 16

The Collection for Jerusalem

Now about the money being collected for the
Christians in Jerusalem: You should follow the
same procedures I gave to the churches in Galatia. 2On every Lord's Day,* each of you should
put aside some amount of money in relation to
what you have earned and save it for this offering. Don't wait until I get there and then try to
collect it all at once. 3When I come I will write
letters of recommendation for the messengers
you choose to deliver your gift to Jerusalem.
4And if it seems appropriate for me also to go
along, then we can travel together.

Paul's Final Instructions

5I am coming to visit you after I have been to
Macedonia, for I am planning to travel through
Macedonia. 6It could be that I will stay awhile
with you, perhaps all winter, and then you can
send me on my way to the next destination.
7This time I don't want to make just a short visit
and then go right on. I want to come and stay
awhile, if the Lord will let me. 8In the meantime,
I will be staying here at Ephesus until the Festival
of Pentecost, 9for there is a wide-open door for
a great work here, and many people are respond-
ing. But there are many who oppose me.
10When Timothy comes, treat him with respect. He is doing the Lord's work, just as I am.
11Don't let anyone despise him. Send him on his
way with your blessings when he returns to me.
I am looking forward to seeing him soon, along
with the other brothers.
12Now about our brother Apollos—I urged
him to join the other brothers when they visit
you, but he was not willing to come right now.
He will be seeing you later, when the time is right.
13Be on guard. Stand true to what you believe.
Be courageous. Be strong. 14And everything you
do must be done with love.
15You know that Stephanas and his household were the first to become Christians in
Greece,* and they are spending their lives in
service to other Christians. I urge you, dear
brothers and sisters,* 16to respect them fully and
others like them who serve with such real devotion. 17I am so glad that Stephanas, Fortunatus,
and Achaicus have come here. They have been
making up for the help you weren't here to give
me. 18They have been a wonderful encouragement to me, as they have been to you, too. You
must give proper honor to all who serve so well.

Paul's Final Greetings

19The churches here in the province of Asia*
greet you heartily in the Lord, along with Aquila
and Priscilla and all the others who gather in
their home for church meetings. 20All the brothers and sisters here have asked me to greet you
for them. Greet each other in Christian love.*
21Here is my greeting, which I write with my
own hand—PAUL.
22If anyone does not love the Lord, that person is cursed. Our Lord, come!*
23May the grace of the Lord Jesus be with you.
24My love to all of you in Christ Jesus.*

16:2 Greek *every first day of the week.* **16:15a** Greek *were the firstfruits in Achaia,* the southern region of the Greek peninsula. **16:15b** Greek *brothers;* also in 16:20. **16:19** *Asia* was a Roman province in what is now western Turkey. **16:20** Greek *with a sacred kiss.* **16:22** From Aramaic, *Marana tha.* **16:24** Some manuscripts add *Amen.*

2 Corinthians

CHAPTER 1

Greetings from Paul

This letter is from Paul, appointed by God to be
an apostle of Christ Jesus, and from our dear
brother Timothy.

We are writing to God's church in Corinth
and to all the Christians throughout Greece.*
2May God our Father and the Lord Jesus
Christ give you his grace and peace.

God Offers Comfort to All

3All praise to the God and Father of our Lord
Jesus Christ. He is the source* of every mercy
and the God who comforts us. 4He comforts
us in all our troubles so that we can comfort
others. When others are troubled, we will be
able to give them the same comfort God has
given us. 5You can be sure that the more we
suffer for Christ, the more God will shower us
with his comfort through Christ. 6So when we
are weighed down with troubles, it is for your
benefit and salvation! For when God comforts
us, it is so that we, in turn, can be an encouragement to you. Then you can patiently endure the same things we suffer. 7We are
confident that as you share in suffering, you
will also share God's comfort.

8I think you ought to know, dear brothers and
sisters,* about the trouble we went through in
the province of Asia. We were crushed and completely overwhelmed, and we thought we would
never live through it. 9In fact, we expected to die.
But as a result, we learned not to rely on ourselves, but on God who can raise the dead. 10And
he did deliver us from mortal danger. And we are
confident that he will continue to deliver us.
11He will rescue us because you are helping by
praying for us. As a result, many will give thanks
to God because so many people's prayers for our
safety have been answered.

Paul's Change of Plans

12We can say with confidence and a clear conscience that we have been honest* and sincere in
all our dealings. We have depended on God's
grace, not on our own earthly wisdom. That is
how we have acted toward everyone, and especially toward you. 13My letters have been
straightforward, and there is nothing written between the lines and nothing you can't understand. I hope someday you will fully understand
us, 14even if you don't fully understand us now.
Then on the day when our Lord Jesus comes
back again, you will be proud of us in the same
way we are proud of you.

15Since I was so sure of your understanding
and trust, I wanted to give you a double blessing.
16I wanted to stop and see you on my way to
Macedonia and again on my return trip. Then
you could send me on my way to Judea.

17You may be asking why I changed my plan.
Hadn't I made up my mind yet? Or am I like
people of the world who say yes when they really
mean no? 18As surely as God is true, I am not that
sort of person. My yes means yes 19because Jesus
Christ, the Son of God, never wavers between yes
and no. He is the one whom Timothy, Silas,* and
I preached to you, and he is the divine Yes—
God's affirmation. 20For all of God's promises
have been fulfilled in him. That is why we say
"Amen" when we give glory to God through
Christ. 21It is God who gives us, along with you,
the ability to stand firm for Christ.* He has com-
missioned us, 22and he has identified us as his
own by placing the Holy Spirit in our hearts as the
first installment of everything he will give us.

1:1 Greek *Achaia,* the southern region of the Greek peninsula. 1:3 Greek *the Father.* 1:8 Greek *brothers.* 1:12 Some manuscripts read *holy.* 1:19 Greek *Silvanus.* 1:21 Or *who has identified us and you as genuine Christians.*

23Now I call upon God as my witness that I am telling the truth. The reason I didn't return to Corinth was to spare you from a severe rebuke. 24But that does not mean we want to tell you exactly how to put your faith into practice.* We want to work together with you so you will be full of joy as you stand firm in your faith.

CHAPTER 2

So I said to myself, "No, I won't do it. I won't make them unhappy with another painful visit." 2For if I cause you pain and make you sad, who is going to make me glad? 3That is why I wrote as I did in my last letter, so that when I do come, I will not be made sad by the very ones who ought to give me the greatest joy. Surely you know that my happiness depends on your happiness. 4How painful it was to write that letter! Heartbroken, I cried over it. I didn't want to hurt you, but I wanted you to know how very much I love you.

Forgiveness for the Sinner

5I am not overstating it when I say that the man who caused all the trouble hurt your entire church more than he hurt me. 6He was punished enough when most of you were united in your judgment against him. 7Now it is time to forgive him and comfort him. Otherwise he may become so discouraged that he won't be able to recover. 8Now show him that you still love him.

9I wrote to you as I did to find out how far you would go in obeying me. 10When you forgive this man, I forgive him, too. And when I forgive him (for whatever is to be forgiven), I do so with Christ's authority for your benefit, 11so that Satan will not outsmart us. For we are very familiar with his evil schemes.

Ministers of the New Covenant

12Well, when I came to the city of Troas to preach the Good News of Christ, the Lord gave me tremendous opportunities. 13But I couldn't rest because my dear brother Titus hadn't yet arrived with a report from you. So I said good-bye and went on to Macedonia to find him.

14But thanks be to God, who made us his captives and leads us along in Christ's triumphal procession. Now wherever we go he uses us to tell others about the Lord and to spread the Good News like a sweet perfume. 15Our lives are a fragrance presented by Christ to God. But this fragrance is perceived differently by those being saved and by those perishing. 16To those who are perishing we are a fearful smell of death and doom. But to those who are being saved we are a life-giving perfume. And who is adequate for such a task as this? 17You see, we are not like those hucksters—and there are many of them—who preach just to make money. We preach God's message with sincerity and with Christ's authority. And we know that the God who sent us is watching us.

CHAPTER 3

Are we beginning again to tell you how good we are? Some people need to bring letters of recommendation with them or ask you to write letters of recommendation for them. 2But the only letter of recommendation we need is you yourselves! Your lives are a letter written in our* hearts, and everyone can read it and recognize our good work among you. 3Clearly, you are a letter from Christ prepared by us. It is written not with pen and ink, but with the Spirit of the living God. It is carved not on stone, but on human hearts.

4We are confident of all this because of our great trust in God through Christ. 5It is not that we think we can do anything of lasting value by ourselves. Our only power and success come from God. 6He is the one who has enabled us to represent his new covenant. This is a covenant, not of written laws, but of the Spirit. The old way ends in death; in the new way, the Holy Spirit gives life.

The Glory of the New Covenant

7That old system of law etched in stone led to death, yet it began with such glory that the people of Israel could not bear to look at Moses' face. For his face shone with the glory of God, even though the brightness was already fading away. 8Shouldn't we expect far greater glory when the Holy Spirit is giving life? 9If the old covenant, which brings condemnation, was glorious, how much more glorious is the new covenant, which makes us right with God! 10In fact, that first glory was not glorious at all compared with the overwhelming glory of the new covenant. 11So if the old covenant, which has been set aside, was full of glory, then the new covenant, which remains forever, has far greater glory.

12Since this new covenant gives us such confidence, we can be very bold. 13We are not like

1:24 Greek *want to lord it over your faith.* 3:2 Some manuscripts read *your.*

Moses, who put a veil over his face so the people
of Israel would not see the glory fading away.
14But the people's minds were hardened, and
even to this day whenever the old covenant is
being read, a veil covers their minds so they
cannot understand the truth. And this veil can
be removed only by believing in Christ. 15Yes,
even today when they read Moses' writings, their
hearts are covered with that veil, and they do not
understand.

16But whenever anyone turns to the Lord,
then the veil is taken away. 17Now, the Lord is
the Spirit, and wherever the Spirit of the Lord is,
he gives freedom. 18And all of us have had that
veil removed so that we can be mirrors that
brightly reflect* the glory of the Lord. And as the
Spirit of the Lord works within us, we become
more and more like him and reflect his glory
even more.

CHAPTER 4

Treasure in Perishable Containers

And so, since God in his mercy has given us this
wonderful ministry, we never give up. 2We reject
all shameful and underhanded methods. We do
not try to trick anyone, and we do not distort the
word of God. We tell the truth before God, and
all who are honest know that.

3If the Good News we preach is veiled from
anyone, it is a sign that they are perishing. 4Sa-
tan, the god of this evil world, has blinded the
minds of those who don't believe, so they are
unable to see the glorious light of the Good
News that is shining upon them. They don't
understand the message we preach about the
glory of Christ, who is the exact likeness of God.

5We don't go around preaching about ourselves; we preach Christ Jesus, the Lord. All we
say about ourselves is that we are your servants
because of what Jesus has done for us. 6For God,
who said, "Let there be light in the darkness,"
has made us understand that this light is the
brightness of the glory of God that is seen in the
face of Jesus Christ.

7But this precious treasure—this light and
power that now shine within us—is held in
perishable containers, that is, in our weak bodies.* So everyone can see that our glorious power
is from God and is not our own.

8We are pressed on every side by troubles, but
we are not crushed and broken. We are perplexed, but we don't give up and quit. 9We are
hunted down, but God never abandons us. We
get knocked down, but we get up again and keep
going. 10Through suffering, these bodies of ours
constantly share in the death of Jesus so that the
life of Jesus may also be seen in our bodies.

11Yes, we live under constant danger of death
because we serve Jesus, so that the life of Jesus
will be obvious in our dying bodies. 12So we live
in the face of death, but it has resulted in eternal
life for you.

13But we continue to preach because we have
the same kind of faith the psalmist had when he
said, "I believed in God, and so I speak."* 14We
know that the same God who raised our Lord
Jesus will also raise us with Jesus and present us
to himself along with you. 15All of these things
are for your benefit. And as God's grace brings
more and more people to Christ, there will be
great thanksgiving, and God will receive more
and more glory.

16That is why we never give up. Though our
bodies are dying, our spirits are* being renewed

3:18 Or *so that we can see in a mirror.* 4:7 Greek *But we have this treasure in earthen vessels.* 4:13 Ps 116:10. 4:16 Greek *our inner being is.*

Trials Help Us Comfort Others

Read 2 CORINTHIANS 1:3-7

The apostle Paul penned these words from personal experience. He had seen his share of suffering over the years—particularly for the sake of the gospel of Jesus Christ. He was thrown into prison on more than one occasion, but he continued to praise God and share his faith in Christ. He was shipwrecked, abandoned by former friends, pelted by stones, and left for dead. His faith, however, remained firm. Why? Because he learned to draw his comfort from the Lord. This then enabled him to be a greater source of comfort to those around him.

The next time someone ridicules or rejects you because of your commitment to Christ, remember Paul's words. You do not need to fear trials in your life. No matter how great a hardship you face, realize that Jesus *will* comfort and strengthen you. In turn, you will be better equipped to comfort those around you who suffer the same hardships.

What Are Satan's Abilities? Read 2 CORINTHIANS 4:3-4

Ever since Satan lost his privileges and was cast to this earth, he has been using his abilities to oppose the work that God has been seeking to accomplish. Paul's second letter to the Corinthians reveals at least three of Satan's abilities:

1. He Is the God of This World. This becomes more and more evident as you survey the increasing wickedness around you. While Christ conquered sin and death at the cross, this world is still flawed and evil. But Satan will lose his reign in this world when Christ returns to establish his Kingdom on earth.

2. He Blinds the Minds of Unbelievers. According to this text, Satan wants to keep those who do not have a relationship with God from coming to God. The unbelieving mind has a difficult time understanding the message of the gospel because Satan has darkened or blinded that person's mind. Yet Christ can break through that barrier (see 2 Timothy 2:24-26, p. 277).

3. He Is a Master Counterfeiter. One of Satan's greatest abilities is deception. He is good at deception because he makes lies look like truth. Paul describes Satan as someone who disguises himself as an angel of light (see 2 Corinthians 11:14, p. 226). That is, he fools people by making them think the lies he offers are truth. His lies take on various forms, such as cults and false doctrines. But we can discern the difference between truth and error when we test them against what is found in God's Word.

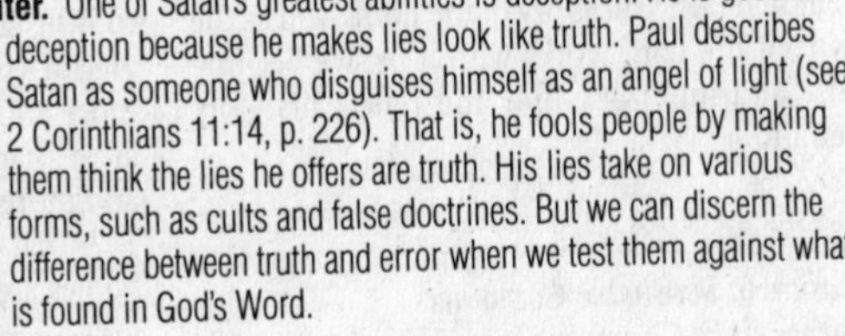

CORNERSTONES

every day. 17For our present troubles are quite
small and won't last very long. Yet they produce
for us an immeasurably great glory that will last
forever! 18So we don't look at the troubles we can
see right now; rather, we look forward to what we
have not yet seen. For the troubles we see will soon
be over, but the joys to come will last forever.

CHAPTER 5

New Bodies

For we know that when this earthly tent we live
in is taken down—when we die and leave these
bodies—we will have a home in heaven, an
eternal body made for us by God himself and
not by human hands. 2We grow weary in our
present bodies, and we long for the day when we
will put on our heavenly bodies like new clothing. 3For we will not be spirits without bodies,
but we will put on new heavenly bodies. 4Our
dying bodies make us groan and sigh, but it's
not that we want to die and have no bodies at
all. We want to slip into our new bodies so that
these dying bodies will be swallowed up by
everlasting life. 5God himself has prepared us
for this, and as a guarantee he has given us his
Holy Spirit.

6So we are always confident, even though we
know that as long as we live in these bodies we
are not at home with the Lord. 7That is why we
live by believing and not by seeing. 8Yes, we are
fully confident, and we would rather be away
from these bodies, for then we will be at home
with the Lord. 9So our aim is to please him
always, whether we are here in this body or away
from this body. 10For we must all stand before
Christ to be judged. We will each receive whatever we deserve for the good or evil we have
done in our bodies.

We Are God's Ambassadors

11It is because we know this solemn fear of the
Lord that we work so hard to persuade others.
God knows we are sincere, and I hope you know
this, too. 12Are we trying to pat ourselves on the
back again? No, we are giving you a reason to be
proud of us, so you can answer those who brag
about having a spectacular ministry rather than
having a sincere heart before God. 13If it seems
that we are crazy, it is to bring glory to God. And
if we are in our right minds, it is for your benefit.
14Whatever we do, it is because Christ's love
controls us.* Since we believe that Christ died

5:14a Or *urges us on.*

for everyone, we also believe that we have all
died to the old life we used to live.* 15He died
for everyone so that those who receive his new
life will no longer live to please themselves.
Instead, they will live to please Christ, who died
and was raised for them.
16So we have stopped evaluating others by
what the world thinks about them. Once I mistakenly thought of Christ that way, as though he
were merely a human being. How differently I
think about him now! 17What this means is that
those who become Christians become new persons. They are not the same anymore, for the old
life is gone. A new life has begun!
18All this newness of life is from God, who
brought us back to himself through what Christ
did. And God has given us the task of reconciling
people to him. 19For God was in Christ, reconciling the world to himself, no longer counting
people's sins against them. This is the wonderful
message he has given us to tell others. 20We are
Christ's ambassadors, and God is using us to
speak to you. We urge you, as though Christ
himself were here pleading with you, "Be reconciled to God!" 21For God made Christ, who
never sinned, to be the offering for our sin, so
that we could be made right with God through
Christ.

CHAPTER 6

As God's partners,* we beg you not to reject this
marvelous message of God's great kindness.
2For God says,

> "At just the right time, I heard you.
> On the day of salvation, I helped you."*

Indeed, God is ready to help you right now.
Today is the day of salvation.

Paul's Hardships

3We try to live in such a way that no one will be
hindered from finding the Lord by the way we
act, and so no one can find fault with our ministry. 4In everything we do we try to show that we
are true ministers of God. We patiently endure
troubles and hardships and calamities of every
kind. 5We have been beaten, been put in jail,
faced angry mobs, worked to exhaustion, endured sleepless nights, and gone without food.
6We have proved ourselves by our purity, our
understanding, our patience, our kindness, our
sincere love, and the power of the Holy Spirit.*

5:14b Greek *Since one died on behalf of all, then all died.* **6:1** Or *As we work together.* **6:2** Isa 49:8. **6:6** Or *the holiness of spirit.*

Trials Are Survivable

Read 2 CORINTHIANS 4:7-18

When we face trials in our lives, we can do one of two things. We can either become self-absorbed with our problems and say, "Look at how tough things are!" Or we can keep our eyes on Jesus and say, "This is only temporary." The apostle Paul was able to focus on the temporary nature of his problems because he accepted five important facts:

1. Our Bodies Are Weak and Mortal. Paul wasn't the type to be caught up in his bodily aches and pains. He didn't strive for the perfect body or the perfect image because he knew his body was a "perishable container." The Bible does not teach that we should neglect our bodies, but it does say that spiritual exercise is more important and beneficial (see 1 Timothy 4:8, p. 272).

2. God's Power Is Displayed in Our Weakness. If we become overly obsessed with ourselves, we will never give God the chance to work through our lives. Paul recognized that God's glory shines through our weaknesses.

3. God Does Not Abandon Us. Even though we may be "crushed" and "perplexed," we have the hope that God will protect and strengthen us through these trials.

4. Trials Can Be Witnessing Opportunities. When people see the inner strength we have in Christ, they will take notice. This is well illustrated in the story of Paul and Silas, who were put in prison for preaching the gospel (see Acts 16:16-36, p. 158). Though they had been whipped and had their legs clamped in stocks in a damp, dark dungeon, they began to pray and worship the Lord in song. In an unusual string of events, these men were able to lead their jailer, as well as his entire family, to the Lord. Paul and Silas's godly attitude, which enabled them to rejoice in such a time of trouble, prepared the soil of this man's heart, opening him up to the gospel they preached.

5. We Have the Hope of Heaven. These trials are only a momentary blink in time compared to the eternal joys and blessings of heaven.

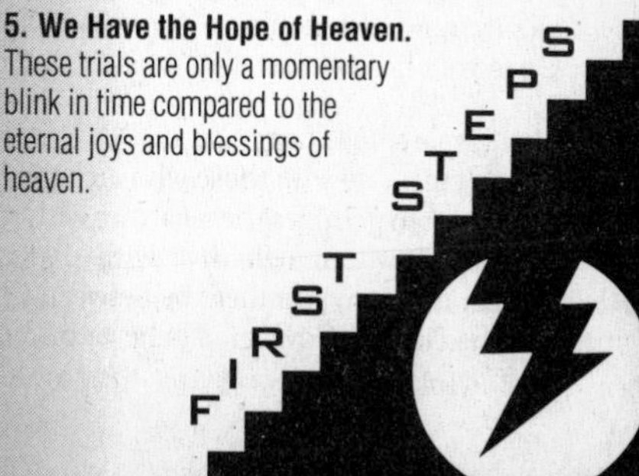

When Does a Christian Enter Heaven? Read 2 CORINTHIANS 5:6-9

Some people teach that when we die we go into a state of suspended animation. Then later on we are called into the presence of God. But this passage clearly explains that when a believer dies, he or she will go directly to heaven to "be at home with the Lord." This is illustrated in at least two other instances in Scripture:

1. The Thief on the Cross. As Jesus was being crucified, a thief hanging on a cross next to him asked Jesus to remember him when Jesus entered his Kingdom. To this request, Jesus replied, "*Today* you will be with me in paradise" (Luke 23:40-43).

2. The Apostle Paul. The apostle Paul wrote, "I long to go and be with Christ" (Philippians 1:23). He didn't say, "I long to depart and be suspended in a soul sleep for a few thousand years." Paul understood better than most this truth about entering heaven, because he had already had a glimpse of heaven. It is probable that when Paul had been stoned, he died and entered the presence of the Lord. But God still had work for Paul to do on earth. So he sent Paul back to earth to carry out God's work (see 2 Corinthians 12:2-4, p. 227).

The moment you take your last breath on earth, you will take your first breath in heaven. So don't be afraid of death. Instead, enjoy your life in Christ on earth, and spend the rest of your time here introducing others to the one with whom you will spend eternity.

CORNERSTONES

7We have faithfully preached the truth. God's
power has been working in us. We have righteousness as our weapon, both to attack and to
defend ourselves. 8We serve God whether
people honor us or despise us, whether they
slander us or praise us. We are honest, but they
call us impostors. 9We are well known, but we
are treated as unknown. We live close to death,
but here we are, still alive. We have been beaten
within an inch of our lives. 10Our hearts ache,
but we always have joy. We are poor, but we give
spiritual riches to others. We own nothing, and
yet we have everything.
11Oh, dear Corinthian friends! We have spoken honestly with you. Our hearts are open to
you. 12If there is a problem between us, it is not
because of a lack of love on our part, but because
you have withheld your love from us. 13I am
talking now as I would to my own children.
Open your hearts to us!

The Temple of the Living God

14Don't team up with those who are unbelievers. How can goodness be a partner with wickedness? How can light live with darkness?
15What harmony can there be between Christ
and the Devil*? How can a believer be a partner with an unbeliever? 16And what union can
there be between God's temple and idols? For
we are the temple of the living God. As God
said:

"I will live in them
 and walk among them.
I will be their God,
 and they will be my people.*
17 Therefore, come out from them
 and separate yourselves from them, says
  the Lord.
Don't touch their filthy things,
 and I will welcome you.*
18 And I will be your Father,
 and you will be my sons and daughters,
 says the Lord Almighty.*"

CHAPTER 7

Because we have these promises, dear friends, let
us cleanse ourselves from everything that can
defile our body or spirit. And let us work toward
complete purity because we fear God.

Paul's Joy at the Church's Repentance

2Please open your hearts to us. We have not
done wrong to anyone. We have not led anyone

6:15 Greek *and Beliar.* 6:16 Lev 26:12; Ezek 37:27. 6:17 Isa 52:11; Ezek 20:34. 6:18 2 Sam 7:14.

astray. We have not taken advantage of anyone. 3I'm not saying this to condemn you, for I said before that you are in our hearts forever. We live or die together with you. 4I have the highest confidence in you, and my pride in you is great. You have greatly encouraged me; you have made me happy despite all our troubles.

5When we arrived in Macedonia there was no rest for us. Outside there was conflict from every direction, and inside there was fear. 6But God, who encourages those who are discouraged, encouraged us by the arrival of Titus. 7His presence was a joy, but so was the news he brought of the encouragement he received from you. When he told me how much you were looking forward to my visit, and how sorry you were about what had happened, and how loyal your love is for me, I was filled with joy!

8I am no longer sorry that I sent that letter to you, though I was sorry for a time, for I know that it was painful to you for a little while. 9Now I am glad I sent it, not because it hurt you, but because the pain caused you to have remorse and change your ways. It was the kind of sorrow God wants his people to have, so you were not harmed by us in any way. 10For God can use sorrow in our lives to help us turn away from sin and seek salvation. We will never regret that kind of sorrow. But sorrow without repentance is the kind that results in death.

11Just see what this godly sorrow produced in you! Such earnestness, such concern to clear yourselves, such indignation, such alarm, such longing to see me, such zeal, and such a readiness to punish the wrongdoer. You showed that you have done everything you could to make things right. 12My purpose was not to write about who did the wrong or who was wronged. I wrote to you so that in the sight of God you could show how much you really do care for us. 13We have been encouraged by this.

In addition to our own encouragement, we were especially delighted to see how happy Titus was at the way you welcomed him and set his mind at ease. 14I had told him how proud I was of you—and you didn't disappoint me. I have always told you the truth, and now my boasting to Titus has also proved true! 15Now he cares for you more than ever when he remembers the way you listened to him and welcomed him with such respect and deep concern. 16I am very happy now because I have complete confidence in you.

CHAPTER 8

A Call to Generous Giving

Now I want to tell you, dear brothers and sisters,* what God in his kindness has done for the churches in Macedonia. 2Though they have been going through much trouble and hard times, their wonderful joy and deep poverty have overflowed in rich generosity. 3For I can testify that they gave not only what they could

8:1 Greek *brothers.*

Recognize That You Are a New Creation Read 2 CORINTHIANS 5:14-17

Although outwardly you may appear to be the same person, when you received Christ you underwent a radical heart transplant. You literally became a "new person" (or "creation") inside. This short passage of Scripture highlights some encouraging points as you endeavor to be obedient to God.

- As "new creations," Christ's love compels us to please God rather than ourselves.
- As "new creations," we can look beyond the "packaging" of a person to what is inside.
- As "new creations," we have become altogether different people.
- As "new creations," we have been given a clean slate, a fresh start, and a new nature.

The new nature you have received is like a tender little flower. It takes time and effort to cultivate. You may find it hard at times to obey God and leave certain old habits behind at first. But as you cultivate that new nature by spending more time with God through activities like prayer and Bible study, you will notice changes as the weeks, months, and years go by.

A man from India was heard to compare our new spiritual nature and our old selfish one to two dogs constantly fighting with each other. He went on to say that he could determine which dog would win. When asked how he determined which dog won, his response was, "The one I feed the most, of course." When you take time to "feed" your new spiritual nature (as you are doing right now), you give it the edge in this ongoing conflict between good and evil.

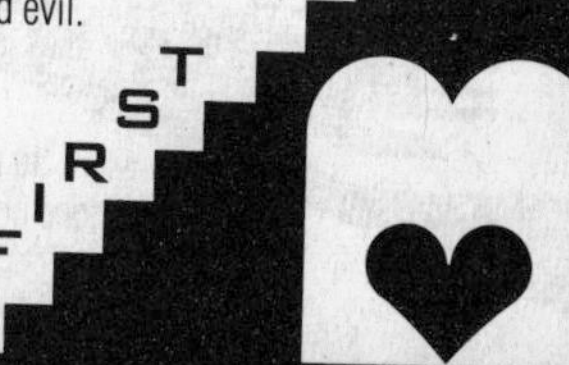

afford but far more. And they did it of their own
free will. 4They begged us again and again for
the gracious privilege of sharing in the gift for
the Christians in Jerusalem. 5Best of all, they
went beyond our highest hopes, for their first
action was to dedicate themselves to the Lord
and to us for whatever directions God might give
them.

6So we have urged Titus, who encouraged
your giving in the first place, to return to you and
encourage you to complete your share in this
ministry of giving. 7Since you excel in so many
ways—you have so much faith, such gifted
speakers, such knowledge, such enthusiasm,
and such love for us*—now I want you to excel
also in this gracious ministry of giving. 8I am not
saying you must do it, even though the other
churches are eager to do it. This is one way to
prove your love is real.

9You know how full of love and kindness our
Lord Jesus Christ was. Though he was very rich,
yet for your sakes he became poor, so that by his
poverty he could make you rich.

10I suggest that you finish what you started a
year ago, for you were the first to propose this
idea, and you were the first to begin doing something about it. 11Now you should carry this project through to completion just as
enthusiastically as you began it. Give whatever
you can according to what you have. 12If you are
really eager to give, it isn't important how much
you are able to give. God wants you to give what
you have, not what you don't have. 13Of course,
I don't mean you should give so much that you
suffer from having too little. I only mean that
there should be some equality. 14Right now you
have plenty and can help them. Then at some
other time they can share with you when you
need it. In this way, everyone's needs will be met.
15Do you remember what the Scriptures say
about this? "Those who gathered a lot had nothing left over, and those who gathered only a little
had enough."*

Titus and His Companions

16I am thankful to God that he has given Titus the
same enthusiasm for you that I have. 17He welcomed our request that he visit you again. In fact,
he himself was eager to go and see you. 18We are
also sending another brother with Titus. He is highly
praised in all the churches as a preacher of the
Good News. 19He was appointed by the churches to
accompany us as we take the offering to Jerusalem*—a service that glorifies the Lord and shows
our eagerness to help. 20By traveling together we
will guard against any suspicion, for we are anxious that no one should find fault with the way we
are handling this generous gift. 21We are careful to
be honorable before the Lord, but we also want
everyone else to know we are honorable.

22And we are also sending with them another
brother who has been thoroughly tested and has
shown how earnest he is on many occasions. He
is now even more enthusiastic because of his
increased confidence in you. 23If anyone asks
about Titus, say that he is my partner who works
with me to help you. And these brothers are
representatives* of the churches. They are splendid examples of those who bring glory to Christ.
24So show them your love, and prove to all the
churches that our boasting about you is justified.

CHAPTER 9

The Collection for Christians in Jerusalem

I really don't need to write to you about this gift
for the Christians in Jerusalem.* 2For I know
how eager you are to help, and I have been
boasting to our friends in Macedonia that you
Christians in Greece* were ready to send an
offering a year ago. In fact, it was your enthusiasm that stirred up many of them to begin helping. 3But I am sending these brothers just to be
sure that you really are ready, as I told them you
would be, with your money all collected. I don't
want it to turn out that I was wrong in my
boasting about you. 4I would be humiliated—

8:7 Some manuscripts read *love from us to you.* 8:15 Exod 16:18. 8:19 See 1 Cor 16:3-4. 8:23 Greek *apostles.* 9:1 Greek *about the offering for the saints.* 9:2 Greek *Achaia,* the southern region of the Greek peninsula.

OFF AND RUNNING

Avoid Relationships That Could Cause You to Sin

Read 2 CORINTHIANS 6:14–7:1

As a Christian, you should avoid anything that would compromise your relationship with Jesus. That includes entering into a relationship, business deal, or any other association that would tempt you to lower your standards or discredit your integrity. When you team up with someone who does not love and fear the Lord, that relationship can dramatically weaken you spiritually.

and so would you—if some Macedonian Christians came with me, only to find that you still weren't ready after all I had told them! 5So I thought I should send these brothers ahead of me to make sure the gift you promised is ready. But I want it to be a willing gift, not one given under pressure.

6Remember this—a farmer who plants only a few seeds will get a small crop. But the one who plants generously will get a generous crop. 7You must each make up your own mind as to how much you should give. Don't give reluctantly or in response to pressure. For God loves the person who gives cheerfully. 8And God will generously provide all you need. Then you will always have everything you need and plenty left over to share with others. 9As the Scriptures say,

> "Godly people give generously to the poor.
> Their good deeds will never be forgotten."*

10For God is the one who gives seed to the farmer and then bread to eat. In the same way, he will give you many opportunities to do good, and he will produce a great harvest of generosity* in you.

11Yes, you will be enriched so that you can give even more generously. And when we take your gifts to those who need them, they will break out in thanksgiving to God. 12So two good things will happen—the needs of the Christians in Jerusalem will be met, and they will joyfully express their thanksgiving to God. 13You will be glorifying God through your generous gifts. For your generosity to them will prove that you are obedient to the Good News of Christ. 14And they will pray for you with deep affection because of the wonderful grace of God shown through you.

15Thank God for his Son—a gift too wonderful for words!*

CHAPTER 10

Paul Defends His Authority

Now I, Paul, plead with you. I plead with the gentleness and kindness that Christ himself would use, even though some of you say I am bold in my letters but timid in person. 2I hope it won't be necessary, but when I come I may have to be very bold with those who think we act from purely human motives. 3We are human, but we don't wage war with human plans and methods. 4We use God's mighty weapons, not mere worldly weapons, to knock down the Devil's strongholds. 5With these weapons we break down every proud argument that keeps people from knowing God. With these weapons we conquer their rebellious ideas, and we teach them to obey Christ. 6And we will punish those who remained disobedient after the rest of you became loyal and obedient.

7The trouble with you is that you make your decisions on the basis of appearance.* You must recognize that we belong to Christ just as much as those who proudly declare that they belong to Christ. 8I may seem to be boasting too much about the authority given to us by the Lord. But this authority is to build you up, not to tear you down. And I will not be put to shame by having my work among you destroyed.

9Now this is not just an attempt to frighten you by my letters. 10For some say, "Don't worry about Paul. His letters are demanding and forceful, but in person he is weak, and his speeches are really bad!" 11The ones who say this must realize that we will be just as demanding and forceful in person as we are in our letters.

12Oh, don't worry; I wouldn't dare say that I am as wonderful as these other men who tell you how important they are! But they are only comparing themselves with each other, and measuring themselves by themselves. What foolishness!

13But we will not boast of authority we do not have. Our goal is to stay within the boundaries of God's plan for us, and this plan includes our working there with you. 14We are not going too far when we claim authority over you, for we were the first to travel all the way to you with the

9:9 Ps 112:9. 9:10 Greek *righteousness.* 9:15 Greek *Thank God for his indescribable gift.* 10:7 Or *Look at the obvious facts.*

God does not want us to avoid all interaction with nonbelievers. Jesus himself spent time with the "sinners" and social outcasts of his day in order to share the message of salvation. God just wants us to keep from being so closely connected to unbelievers that it ultimately affects our faith and behavior, tempting us to compromise our witness for and obedience to God.

Good News of Christ. 15Nor do we claim credit for the work someone else has done. Instead, we hope that your faith will grow and that our work among you will be greatly enlarged. 16Then we will be able to go and preach the Good News in other places that are far beyond you, where no one else is working. Then there will be no question about being in someone else's territory. 17As the Scriptures say,

"The person who wishes to boast
should boast only of what the Lord has done."*

18When people boast about themselves, it doesn't count for much. But when the Lord commends someone, that's different!

CHAPTER 11

Paul and the False Apostles

I hope you will be patient with me as I keep on talking like a fool. Please bear with me. 2I am jealous for you with the jealousy of God himself. For I promised you as a pure bride* to one husband, Christ. 3But I fear that somehow you will be led away from your pure and simple devotion to Christ, just as Eve was deceived by the serpent. 4You seem to believe whatever anyone tells you, even if they preach about a different Jesus than the one we preach, or a different Spirit than the one you received, or a different kind of gospel than the one you believed. 5But I don't think I am inferior to these "super apostles." 6I may not be a trained speaker, but I know what I am talking about. I think you realize this by now, for we have proved it again and again.

7Did I do wrong when I humbled myself and honored you by preaching God's Good News to you without expecting anything in return? 8I "robbed" other churches by accepting their contributions so I could serve you at no cost. 9And when I was with you and didn't have enough to live on, I did not ask you to help me. For the brothers who came from Macedonia brought me another gift. I have never yet asked you for any support, and I never will. 10As surely as the truth of Christ is in me, I will never stop boasting about this all over Greece.* 11Why? Because I don't love you? God knows I do.

12But I will continue doing this to cut the ground out from under the feet of those who boast that their work is just like ours. 13These people are false apostles. They have fooled you by disguising themselves as apostles of Christ. 14But I am not surprised! Even Satan can disguise himself as an angel of light. 15So it is no wonder his servants can also do it by pretending to be godly ministers. In the end they will get every bit of punishment their wicked deeds deserve.

Paul's Many Trials

16Once again, don't think that I have lost my wits to talk like this. But even if you do, listen to me, as you would to a foolish person, while I also boast a little. 17Such bragging is not something the Lord wants, but I am acting like a fool. 18And since others boast about their human achievements, I will, too. 19After all, you, who think you are so wise, enjoy listening to fools! 20You put up with it when they make you their slaves, take everything you have, take advantage of you, put on airs, and slap you in the face. 21I'm ashamed to say that we were not strong enough to do that!

But whatever they dare to boast about—I'm talking like a fool again—I can boast about it, too. 22They say they are Hebrews, do they? So am I. And they say they are Israelites? So am I. And they are descendants of Abraham? So am I. 23They say they serve Christ? I know I sound like a madman, but I have served him far more! I have worked harder, been put in jail more often, been whipped times without number, and faced death again and again. 24Five different times the Jews gave me thirty-nine lashes. 25Three times I was beaten with rods. Once I was stoned. Three times I was shipwrecked. Once I spent a whole night and a day adrift at sea. 26I have traveled many weary miles. I have faced danger from flooded rivers and from robbers. I have faced danger from my own people, the Jews, as well as from the Gentiles. I have faced danger in the cities, in the deserts, and on the stormy seas. And I have faced danger from men who claim to be Christians but are not.* 27I have lived with weariness and pain and sleepless nights. Often I have been hungry and thirsty and have gone without food. Often I have shivered with cold, without enough clothing to keep me warm.

28Then, besides all this, I have the daily burden of how the churches are getting along. 29Who is weak without my feeling that weakness? Who is led astray, and I do not burn with anger?

30If I must boast, I would rather boast about the things that show how weak I am. 31God, the

10:17 Jer 9:24. 11:2 Greek *a virgin.* 11:10 Greek *Achaia.* 11:26 Greek *from false brothers.*

Father of our Lord Jesus, who is to be praised
forever, knows I tell the truth. 32When I was in
Damascus, the governor under King Aretas kept
guards at the city gates to catch me. 33But I was
lowered in a basket through a window in the city
wall, and that's how I got away!

CHAPTER 12

Paul's Vision and His Thorn in the Flesh

This boasting is all so foolish, but let me go on.
Let me tell about the visions and revelations I
received from the Lord. 2I* was caught up into
the third heaven fourteen years ago. 3Whether
my body was there or just my spirit, I don't
know; only God knows. 4But I do know that I*
was caught up into paradise and heard things so
astounding that they cannot be told. 5That experience is something worth boasting about, but I
am not going to do it. I am going to boast only
about my weaknesses. 6I have plenty to boast
about and would be no fool in doing it, because
I would be telling the truth. But I won't do it. I
don't want anyone to think more highly of me
than what they can actually see in my life and
my message, 7even though I have received wonderful revelations from God. But to keep me
from getting puffed up, I was given a thorn in my
flesh, a messenger from Satan to torment me
and keep me from getting proud.

8Three different times I begged the Lord to
take it away. 9Each time he said, "My gracious
favor is all you need. My power works best in
your weakness." So now I am glad to boast
about my weaknesses, so that the power of
Christ may work through me. 10Since I know it
is all for Christ's good, I am quite content with
my weaknesses and with insults, hardships, persecutions, and calamities. For when I am weak,
then I am strong.

Paul's Concern for the Corinthians

11You have made me act like a fool—boasting
like this. You ought to be writing commenda-
tions for me, for I am not at all inferior to these
"super apostles," even though I am nothing at
all. 12When I was with you, I certainly gave you
every proof that I am truly an apostle, sent to you
by God himself. For I patiently did many signs
and wonders and miracles among you. 13The
only thing I didn't do, which I do in the other
churches, was to become a burden to you. Please
forgive me for this wrong!

14Now I am coming to you for the third time,

12:2 Greek *I know a man in Christ who.* 12:4 Greek *he.*

What Happens When You Give? Read 2 CORINTHIANS 9:6-14

One of Paul's goals in his ministry was to mend the division that existed between Jewish and Gentile believers. To do this, he took up a gift offering from the Gentile believers to be given to the needy Jewish believers in Jerusalem. Apparently the believers in Corinth were lagging behind in their giving. So Paul, in this portion of 2 Corinthians, wrote of the benefits of giving to God and the work of his church. Here are three important truths from this passage about our giving as believers:

1. Our Motives Are Important. The passage says that God prizes cheerful givers (verse 7). The word *cheerfully* could also be translated as "hilariously." We should give hilariously, joyfully—not out of mere duty or guilt. As Jesus said, it is truly "more blessed to give than to receive" (Acts 20:35).

2. As We Give, God Will Give to Us. You can't outgive God (verses 8, 10). As Jesus said, "If you give, you will receive. Your gift will return to you in full measure, pressed down, shaken together to make room for more, and running over. Whatever measure you use in giving—large or small—it will be used to measure what is given back to you" (Luke 6:38). Coming back to our motive for giving, we should not fall into the trap of "giving to get." We should give because God has so graciously and generously given to us.

3. Others Are Helped because of Our Financial Help. We should always be on the lookout to help Christian brothers and sisters who are in need. Paul was not speaking of the tithe you give, but an offering above and beyond your tithe (verses 11-14). Our tithe goes to the church. Our offerings go to other situations, like helping those in need. When these people receive our gifts, they see that our faith is deeper than mere words.

When you give to the Lord's work, that money, which really had no effect in any spiritual sense before, will be used to touch the lives of others for the glory of God. God is looking for openhanded people—people upon whom he can pour out his blessings, and who, in turn, will give it to others.

and I will not be a burden to you. I don't want
what you have; I want you. And anyway, little
children don't pay for their parents' food. It's
the other way around; parents supply food for
their children. 15I will gladly spend myself and
all I have for your spiritual good, even though
it seems that the more I love you, the less you
love me.

16Some of you admit I was not a burden to
you. But they still think I was sneaky and took
advantage of you by trickery. 17But how? Did
any of the men I sent to you take advantage of
you? 18When I urged Titus to visit you and sent
our other brother with him, did Titus take advantage of you? No, of course not! For we both
have the same Spirit and walk in each other's
steps, doing things the same way.

19Perhaps you think we are saying all this just
to defend ourselves. That isn't it at all. We tell
you this as Christ's servants, and we know that
God is listening. Everything we do, dear friends,
is for your benefit. 20For I am afraid that when I
come to visit you I won't like what I find, and
then you won't like my response. I am afraid
that I will find quarreling, jealousy, outbursts of
anger, selfishness, backstabbing, gossip, conceit,
and disorderly behavior. 21Yes, I am afraid that
when I come, God will humble me again because of you. And I will have to grieve because
many of you who sinned earlier have not repented of your impurity, sexual immorality, and
eagerness for lustful pleasure.

CHAPTER 13

Paul's Final Advice

This is the third time I am coming to visit you.
As the Scriptures say, "The facts of every case
must be established by the testimony of two or
three witnesses."* 2I have already warned those
who had been sinning when I was there on my
second visit. Now I again warn them and all
others, just as I did before, that this next time I
will not spare them.

3I will give you all the proof you want that
Christ speaks through me. Christ is not weak in
his dealings with you; he is a mighty power
among you. 4Although he died on the cross in
weakness, he now lives by the mighty power of
God. We, too, are weak, but we live in him and
have God's power—the power we use in dealing
with you.

5Examine yourselves to see if your faith is
really genuine. Test yourselves. If you cannot tell
that Jesus Christ is among you,* it means you
have failed the test. 6I hope you recognize that
we have passed the test and are approved by
God.

7We pray to God that you will not do anything wrong. We pray this, not to show that our
ministry to you has been successful, but because
we want you to do right even if we ourselves
seem to have failed. 8Our responsibility is never
to oppose the truth, but to stand for the truth at
all times. 9We are glad to be weak, if you are
really strong. What we pray for is your restoration to maturity.

10I am writing this to you before I come,
hoping that I won't need to deal harshly with
you when I do come. For I want to use the
authority the Lord has given me to build you up,
not to tear you down.

Paul's Final Greetings

11Dear brothers and sisters,* I close my letter with
these last words: Rejoice. Change your ways. Encourage each other. Live in harmony and peace.
Then the God of love and peace will be with you.

12Greet each other in Christian love.* All the
Christians here send you their greetings.

13May the grace of our Lord Jesus Christ, the
love of God, and the fellowship of the Holy
Spirit be with you all.*

13:1 Deut 19:15. 13:5 Or *in you.* 13:11 Greek *brothers.* 13:12 Greek *with a sacred kiss.* 13:12-13 Some English versions divide verse 12 into verses 12 and 13, and then verse 13 becomes verse 14.

Galatians

CHAPTER 1

Greetings from Paul

This letter is from Paul, an apostle. I was not appointed by any group or by human authority. My call is from Jesus Christ himself and from God the Father, who raised Jesus from the dead.

2All the brothers and sisters* here join me in sending greetings to the churches of Galatia.

3May grace and peace be yours from God our Father and from the Lord Jesus Christ. 4He died for our sins, just as God our Father planned, in order to rescue us from this evil world in which we live. 5That is why all glory belongs to God through all the ages of eternity. Amen.

There Is Only One Good News

6I am shocked that you are turning away so soon from God, who in his love and mercy called you to share the eternal life he gives through Christ. You are already following a different way 7that pretends to be the Good News but is not the Good News at all. You are being fooled by those who twist and change the truth concerning Christ.

8Let God's curse fall on anyone, including myself, who preaches any other message than the one we told you about. Even if an angel comes from heaven and preaches any other message, let him be forever cursed. 9I will say it again: If anyone preaches any other gospel than the one you welcomed, let God's curse fall upon that person.

10Obviously, I'm not trying to be a people pleaser! No, I am trying to please God. If I were still trying to please people, I would not be Christ's servant.

Paul's Message Comes from Christ

11Dear brothers and sisters, I solemnly assure you that the Good News of salvation which I preach is not based on mere human reasoning or logic. 12For my message came by a direct revelation from Jesus Christ himself. No one else taught me.

13You know what I was like when I followed the Jewish religion—how I violently persecuted the Christians.* I did my best to get rid of them. 14I was one of the most religious Jews of my own age, and I tried as hard as possible to follow all the old traditions of my religion.

15But then something happened! For it pleased God in his kindness to choose me and call me, even before I was born! What undeserved mercy! 16Then he revealed his Son to me* so that I could proclaim the Good News about Jesus to the Gentiles. When all this happened to me, I did not rush out to consult with anyone else; 17nor did I go up to Jerusalem to consult with those who were apostles before I was. No, I went away into Arabia and later returned to the city of Damascus. 18It was not until three years later that I finally went to Jerusalem for a visit with Peter* and stayed there with him for fifteen days. 19And the only other apostle I met at that time was James, our Lord's brother. 20You must believe what I am saying, for I declare before God that I am not lying. 21Then after this visit, I went north into the provinces of Syria and Cilicia. 22And still the Christians in the churches in Judea didn't know me personally. 23All they knew was that people were saying, "The one who used to persecute us now preaches the very faith he tried to destroy!" 24And they gave glory to God because of me.

CHAPTER 2

The Apostles Accept Paul

Then fourteen years later I went back to Jerusalem again, this time with Barnabas; and Titus

1:2 Greek *brothers;* also in 1:11. 1:13 Greek *the church of God.* 1:16 Or *in me.* 1:18 Greek *Cephas.*

Why Christians Need the Holy Spirit Read GALATIANS 5:16-26

This text lays out four important reasons we need to let the Holy Spirit have full control of our lives as believers:

1. The Holy Spirit Helps to Conquer Our Sin Nature. The Holy Spirit will help us make the right decisions if we listen to his advice.

2. The Holy Spirit Makes It Easier to Follow God's Guidelines. The Holy Spirit gives us the power to live by God's guidelines. If we listen to and follow the Holy Spirit's promptings, then we won't have to force ourselves to obey the Lord. That is because we will want to obey him.

3. The Holy Spirit Will Produce Godly Qualities in Our Lives. When we live by the Holy Spirit, he develops godly qualities (known as the fruit of the Spirit) in our lives.

4. The Holy Spirit Encourages Us to Seek God's Approval above Man's. We will seek God's glory above our own when we follow the Holy Spirit's leading.

In essence, the Holy Spirit enables Christians to live lives that are pleasing to God—something that is impossible to do on our own. He makes following Christ a joy rather than a duty.

CORNERSTONES

came along, too. 2I went there because God
revealed to me that I should go. While I was
there I talked privately with the leaders of the
church. I wanted them to understand what I
had been preaching to the Gentiles. I wanted
to make sure they did not disagree, or my
ministry would have been useless. 3And they
did agree. They did not even demand that my
companion Titus be circumcised, though he
was a Gentile.*

4Even that question wouldn't have come up
except for some so-called Christians there—
false ones, really*—who came to spy on us and
see our freedom in Christ Jesus. They wanted to
force us, like slaves, to follow their Jewish regulations. 5But we refused to listen to them for a
single moment. We wanted to preserve the truth
of the Good News for you.

6And the leaders of the church who were
there had nothing to add to what I was preaching. (By the way, their reputation as great leaders
made no difference to me, for God has no favorites.) 7They saw that God had given me the
responsibility of preaching the Good News to
the Gentiles, just as he had given Peter the responsibility of preaching to the Jews. 8For the
same God who worked through Peter for the
benefit of the Jews worked through me for the
benefit of the Gentiles. 9In fact, James, Peter,*
and John, who were known as pillars of the
church, recognized the gift God had given me,
and they accepted Barnabas and me as their
co-workers. They encouraged us to keep preaching to the Gentiles, while they continued their
work with the Jews. 10The only thing they suggested was that we remember to help the poor,
and I have certainly been eager to do that.

Paul Confronts Peter

11But when Peter came to Antioch, I had to
oppose him publicly, speaking strongly against
what he was doing, for it was very wrong.
12When he first arrived, he ate with the Gentile
Christians, who don't bother with circumcision.
But afterward, when some Jewish friends of
James came, Peter wouldn't eat with the Gentiles
anymore because he was afraid of what these
legalists would say. 13Then the other Jewish
Christians followed Peter's hypocrisy, and even
Barnabas was influenced to join them in their
hypocrisy.

14When I saw that they were not following
the truth of the Good News, I said to Peter in
front of all the others, "Since you, a Jew by birth,
have discarded the Jewish laws and are living
like a Gentile, why are you trying to make these

2:3 Greek *a Greek.* 2:4 Greek *some false brothers.* 2:9 Greek *Cephas;* also in 2:11, 14.

Gentiles obey the Jewish laws you abandoned? 15You and I are Jews by birth, not 'sinners' like the Gentiles. 16And yet we Jewish Christians know that we become right with God, not by doing what the law commands, but by faith in Jesus Christ. So we have believed in Christ Jesus, that we might be accepted by God because of our faith in Christ—and not because we have obeyed the law. For no one will ever be saved by obeying the law."*

17But what if we seek to be made right with God through faith in Christ and then find out that we are still sinners? Has Christ led us into sin? Of course not! 18Rather, I make myself guilty if I rebuild the old system I already tore down. 19For when I tried to keep the law, I realized I could never earn God's approval. So I died to the law so that I might live for God. I have been crucified with Christ. 20I myself no longer live, but Christ lives in me. So I live my life in this earthly body by trusting in the Son of God, who loved me and gave himself for me. 21I am not one of those who treats the grace of God as meaningless. For if we could be saved by keeping the law, then there was no need for Christ to die.

CHAPTER 3

The Law and Faith in Christ

Oh, foolish Galatians! What magician has cast an evil spell on you? For you used to see the meaning of Jesus Christ's death as clearly as though I had shown you a signboard with a picture of Christ dying on the cross. 2Let me ask you this one question: Did you receive the Holy Spirit by keeping the law? Of course not, for the Holy Spirit came upon you only after you believed the message you heard about Christ. 3Have you lost your senses? After starting your Christian lives in the Spirit, why are you now trying to become perfect by your own human effort? 4You have suffered so much for the Good News. Surely it was not in vain, was it? Are you now going to just throw it all away?

5I ask you again, does God give you the Holy Spirit and work miracles among you because you obey the law of Moses? Of course not! It is because you believe the message you heard about Christ.

6In the same way, "Abraham believed God, so God declared him righteous because of his faith."* 7The real children of Abraham, then, are all those who put their faith in God.

8What's more, the Scriptures looked forward to this time when God would accept the Gentiles, too, on the basis of their faith. God promised this good news to Abraham long ago when he said, "All nations will be blessed through you."* 9And so it is: All who put their faith in Christ share the same blessing Abraham received because of his faith.

10But those who depend on the law to make them right with God are under his curse, for the Scriptures say, "Cursed is everyone who does not observe and obey all these commands that are written in God's Book of the Law."* 11Consequently, it is clear that no one can ever be right with God by trying to keep the law. For the Scriptures say, "It is through faith that a righteous person has life."* 12How different from this way of faith is the way of law, which says, "If you wish to find life by obeying the law, you must obey all of its commands."* 13But Christ has rescued us from the curse pronounced by the law. When he was hung on the cross, he took upon himself the curse for our wrongdoing. For it is written in the Scriptures, "Cursed is everyone who is hung on a tree."* 14Through the work of Christ Jesus, God has blessed the Gentiles with the same blessing he promised to Abraham, and we Christians receive the promised Holy Spirit through faith.

The Law and God's Promises

15Dear brothers and sisters,* here's an example from everyday life. Just as no one can set aside or amend an irrevocable agreement, so it is in this case. 16God gave the promise to Abraham and his child.* And notice that it doesn't say the promise was to his children,* as if it meant many descendants. But the promise was to his child—and that, of course, means Christ. 17This is what I am trying to say: The agreement God made with Abraham could not be canceled 430 years later when God gave the law to Moses. God would be breaking his promise. 18For if the inheritance could be received only by keeping the law, then it would not be the result of accepting God's promise. But God gave it to Abraham as a promise.

19Well then, why was the law given? It was given to show people how guilty they are. But this system of law was to last only until the coming of the child to whom God's promise was made. And there is this further difference. God

2:16 Some translators hold that the quotation extends through verse 14; others through verse 16; and still others through verse 21.
3:6 Gen 15:6. **3:8** Gen 12:3; 18:18; 22:18. **3:10** Deut 27:26. **3:11** Hab 2:4. **3:12** Lev 18:5. **3:13** Deut 21:23. **3:15** Greek *Brothers.*
3:16a Greek *seed;* also in 3:16c, 19. See Gen 12:7. **3:16b** Greek *seeds.*

gave his laws to angels to give to Moses, who was
the mediator between God and the people.
20Now a mediator is needed if two people enter
into an agreement, but God acted on his own
when he made his promise to Abraham.
21Well then, is there a conflict between God's
law and God's promises? Absolutely not! If the
law could have given us new life, we could have
been made right with God by obeying it. 22But
the Scriptures have declared that we are all prisoners of sin, so the only way to receive God's
promise is to believe in Jesus Christ.
23Until faith in Christ was shown to us as the
way of becoming right with God, we were
guarded by the law. We were kept in protective
custody, so to speak, until we could put our faith
in the coming Savior.

God's Children through Faith

24Let me put it another way. The law was our
guardian and teacher to lead us until Christ came.
So now, through faith in Christ, we are made right
with God. 25But now that faith in Christ has come,
we no longer need the law as our guardian. 26So
you are all children* of God through faith in
Christ Jesus. 27And all who have been united with
Christ in baptism have been made like him.
28There is no longer Jew or Gentile,* slave or free,
male or female. For you are all Christians—you
are one in Christ Jesus. 29And now that you belong
to Christ, you are the true children of Abraham.
You are his heirs, and now all the promises God
gave to him belong to you.

CHAPTER 4

Think of it this way. If a father dies and leaves
great wealth for his young children, those children are not much better off than slaves until
they grow up, even though they actually own
everything their father had. 2They have to obey
their guardians until they reach whatever age
their father set.
3And that's the way it was with us before Christ
came. We were slaves to the spiritual powers of
this world. 4But when the right time came, God
sent his Son, born of a woman, subject to the law.
5God sent him to buy freedom for us who were
slaves to the law, so that he could adopt us as his
very own children.* 6And because you Gentiles
have become his children, God has sent the Spirit
of his Son into your hearts, and now you can call
God your dear Father.* 7Now you are no longer
a slave but God's own child.* And since you are
his child, everything he has belongs to you.

Paul's Concern for the Galatians

8Before you Gentiles knew God, you were slaves
to so-called gods that do not even exist. 9And now
that you have found God (or should I say, now
that God has found you), why do you want to go
back again and become slaves once more to the
weak and useless spiritual powers of this world?
10You are trying to find favor with God by what
you do or don't do on certain days or months or
seasons or years. 11I fear for you. I am afraid that
all my hard work for you was worth nothing.
12Dear brothers and sisters,* I plead with you to
live as I do in freedom from these things, for I have
become like you Gentiles were—free from the law.
You did not mistreat me when I first preached
to you. 13Surely you remember that I was sick
when I first brought you the Good News of
Christ. 14But even though my sickness was re-
volting to you, you did not reject me and turn
me away. No, you took me in and cared for me
as though I were an angel from God or even
Christ Jesus himself. 15Where is that joyful spirit

3:26 Greek *sons*. 3:28 Greek *Jew or Greek*. 4:5 Greek *sons;* also in 4:6. 4:6 Greek *into your hearts, crying, "Abba, Father." Abba* is an Aramaic term for "father." 4:7 Greek *son;* also in 4:7b. 4:12 Greek *brothers;* also in 4:28, 31.

OFF AND RUNNING

Find a Close Christian Friend Read GALATIANS 6:1-3

God never intended us to be "solo" Christians. That is why one of the first things you should do after becoming a Christian is find some good, solid Christian friends. Although God wants us to turn to him first in times of trouble, he also knows that we need Christian brothers and sisters here on earth to help us through our difficulties—and they need us, too. Here are three things to look for in a Christian friend:

1. A True Christian Friend Will Let You Know When You Sin. A true friend will care enough about your spiritual condition to tell you the truth. The Bible says, "Wounds from a friend are better than many kisses from an enemy" (Proverbs 27:6).

we felt together then? In those days, I know you would gladly have taken out your own eyes and given them to me if it had been possible. 16 Have I now become your enemy because I am telling you the truth?

17 Those false teachers who are so anxious to win your favor are not doing it for your good. They are trying to shut you off from me so that you will pay more attention to them. 18 Now it's wonderful if you are eager to do good, and especially when I am not with you. 19 But oh, my dear children! I feel as if I am going through labor pains for you again, and they will continue until Christ is fully developed in your lives. 20 How I wish I were there with you right now, so that I could be more gentle with you. But at this distance I frankly don't know what else to do.

Abraham's Two Children

21 Listen to me, you who want to live under the law. Do you know what the law really says? 22 The Scriptures say that Abraham had two sons, one from his slave-wife and one from his freeborn wife.* 23 The son of the slave-wife was born in a human attempt to bring about the fulfillment of God's promise. But the son of the freeborn wife was born as God's own fulfillment of his promise.

24 Now these two women serve as an illustration of God's two covenants. Hagar, the slave-wife, represents Mount Sinai where people first became enslaved to the law. 25 And now Jerusalem is just like Mount Sinai in Arabia, because she and her children live in slavery. 26 But Sarah, the free woman, represents the heavenly Jerusalem. And she is our mother. 27 That is what Isaiah meant when he prophesied,

"Rejoice, O childless woman!
Break forth into loud and joyful song,
even though you never gave birth to a child.
For the woman who could bear no children
now has more than all the other
women!"*

28 And you, dear brothers and sisters, are children of the promise, just like Isaac. 29 And we who are born of the Holy Spirit are persecuted by those who want us to keep the law, just as Isaac, the child of promise, was persecuted by Ishmael, the son of the slave-wife.

30 But what do the Scriptures say about that? "Get rid of the slave and her son, for the son of the slave woman will not share the family inheritance with the free woman's son."* 31 So, dear brothers and sisters, we are not children of the slave woman, obligated to the law. We are children of the free woman, acceptable to God because of our faith.

CHAPTER 5

Freedom in Christ

So Christ has really set us free. Now make sure that you stay free, and don't get tied up again in slavery to the law.

2 Listen! I, Paul, tell you this: If you are counting on circumcision to make you right with God, then Christ cannot help you. 3 I'll say it again. If you are trying to find favor with God by being circumcised, you must obey all of the regulations in the whole law of Moses. 4 For if you are trying to make yourselves right with God by keeping the law, you have been cut off from Christ! You have fallen away from God's grace.

5 But we who live by the Spirit eagerly wait to receive everything promised to us who are right with God through faith. 6 For when we place our faith in Christ Jesus, it makes no difference to God whether we are circumcised or not circumcised. What is important is faith expressing itself in love.

4:22 See Gen 16:15; 21:2-3. 4:27 Isa 54:1. 4:30 Gen 21:10.

---

2. A True Christian Friend Is Humble. If you fall spiritually, a friend who is a strong Christian can be counted upon to help restore you without spreading rumors. That is because this friend realizes that he or she is just as susceptible to sin as you are.

3. A True Christian Friend Will Help Carry Your Burdens. He will weep with you when you weep and rejoice with you when you rejoice (see Romans 12:15, p. 192).

Having a friend who is a strong Christian is not just a benefit—it is a necessity! And that is how Jesus wants it to be. Therefore, build your Christian friendships, and in so doing, you will help strengthen yourself and the body of Christ.

7You were getting along so well. Who has interfered with you to hold you back from following the truth? 8It certainly isn't God, for he is the one who called you to freedom. 9But it takes only one wrong person among you to infect all the others—a little yeast spreads quickly through the whole batch of dough! 10I am trusting the Lord to bring you back to believing as I do about these things. God will judge that person, whoever it is, who has been troubling and confusing you.

11Dear brothers and sisters,* if I were still preaching that you must be circumcised—as some say I do—why would the Jews persecute me? The fact that I am still being persecuted proves that I am still preaching salvation through the cross of Christ alone. 12I only wish that those troublemakers who want to mutilate you by circumcision would mutilate themselves.*

13For you have been called to live in freedom—not freedom to satisfy your sinful nature, but freedom to serve one another in love. 14For the whole law can be summed up in this one command: "Love your neighbor as yourself."* 15But if instead of showing love among yourselves you are always biting and devouring one another, watch out! Beware of destroying one another.

Living by the Spirit's Power

16So I advise you to live according to your new life in the Holy Spirit. Then you won't be doing what your sinful nature craves. 17The old sinful nature loves to do evil, which is just opposite from what the Holy Spirit wants. And the Spirit gives us desires that are opposite from what the sinful nature desires. These two forces are constantly fighting each other, and your choices are never free from this conflict. 18But when you are directed by the Holy Spirit, you are no longer subject to the law.

19When you follow the desires of your sinful nature, your lives will produce these evil results: sexual immorality, impure thoughts, eagerness for lustful pleasure, 20idolatry, participation in demonic activities, hostility, quarreling, jealousy, outbursts of anger, selfish ambition, divisions, the feeling that everyone is wrong except those in your own little group, 21envy, drunkenness, wild parties, and other kinds of sin. Let me tell you again, as I have before, that anyone living that sort of life will not inherit the Kingdom of God.

22But when the Holy Spirit controls our lives, he will produce this kind of fruit in us: love, joy, peace, patience, kindness, goodness, faithfulness, 23gentleness, and self-control. Here there is no conflict with the law.

24Those who belong to Christ Jesus have nailed the passions and desires of their sinful nature to his cross and crucified them there. 25If we are living now by the Holy Spirit, let us follow the Holy Spirit's leading in every part of our lives. 26Let us not become conceited, or irritate one another, or be jealous of one another.

CHAPTER 6

We Reap What We Sow

Dear brothers and sisters, if another Christian* is overcome by some sin, you who are godly should gently and humbly help that person back onto the right path. And be careful not to fall into the same temptation yourself. 2Share each other's troubles and problems, and in this way obey the law of Christ. 3If you think you are too important to help someone in need, you are only fooling yourself. You are really a nobody.

4Be sure to do what you should, for then you will enjoy the personal satisfaction of having done your work well, and you won't need to compare yourself to anyone else. 5For we are each responsible for our own conduct.

6Those who are taught the word of God should help their teachers by paying them.

7Don't be misled. Remember that you can't ignore God and get away with it. You will always reap what you sow! 8Those who live only to satisfy their own sinful desires will harvest the consequences of decay and death. But those who live to please the Spirit will harvest everlasting life from the Spirit. 9So don't get tired of doing what is good. Don't get discouraged and give up, for we will reap a harvest of blessing at the appropriate time. 10Whenever we have the opportunity, we should do good to everyone, especially to our Christian brothers and sisters.

Paul's Final Advice

11Notice what large letters I use as I write these closing words in my own handwriting. 12Those who are trying to force you to be circumcised are doing it for just one reason. They don't want to be persecuted for teaching that the cross of Christ alone can save. 13And even those who

5:11 Greek *Brothers.* 5:12 Or *castrate themselves;* Greek reads *cut themselves off.* 5:14 Lev 19:18. 6:1 Greek *Brothers, if a man.*

advocate circumcision don't really keep the whole law. They only want you to be circumcised so they can brag about it and claim you as their disciples.

14As for me, God forbid that I should boast about anything except the cross of our Lord Jesus Christ. Because of that cross,* my interest in this world died long ago, and the world's interest in me is also long dead. 15It doesn't make any difference now whether we have been circumcised or not. What counts is whether we really have been changed into new and different people. 16May God's mercy and peace be upon all those who live by this principle. They are the new people of God.*

17From now on, don't let anyone trouble me with these things. For I bear on my body the scars that show I belong to Jesus.

18My dear brothers and sisters,* may the grace of our Lord Jesus Christ be with you all. Amen.

6:14 Or *Because of him.* **6:16** Greek *the Israel of God.* **6:18** Greek *Brothers.*

Ephesians

CHAPTER 1

Greetings from Paul

This letter is from Paul, chosen by God to be an
apostle of Christ Jesus.
It is written to God's holy people in Ephesus,*
who are faithful followers of Christ Jesus.
2May grace and peace be yours, sent to you
from God our Father and Jesus Christ our Lord.

Spiritual Blessings

3How we praise God, the Father of our Lord
Jesus Christ, who has blessed us with every spiritual blessing in the heavenly realms because we
belong to Christ. 4Long ago, even before he
made the world, God loved us and chose us in
Christ to be holy and without fault in his eyes.
5His unchanging plan has always been to adopt
us into his own family by bringing us to himself
through Jesus Christ. And this gave him great
pleasure.
6So we praise God for the wonderful kindness
he has poured out on us because we belong to
his dearly loved Son. 7He is so rich in kindness
that he purchased our freedom through the
blood of his Son, and our sins are forgiven. 8He
has showered his kindness on us, along with all
wisdom and understanding.
9God's secret plan has now been revealed to
us; it is a plan centered on Christ, designed
long ago according to his good pleasure. 10And
this is his plan: At the right time he will bring
everything together under the authority of
Christ—everything in heaven and on earth.
11Furthermore, because of Christ, we have received an inheritance from God,* for he chose
us from the beginning, and all things happen
just as he decided long ago. 12God's purpose
was that we who were the first to trust in Christ
should praise our glorious God. 13And now
you also have heard the truth, the Good News
that God saves you. And when you believed in
Christ, he identified you as his own by giving
you the Holy Spirit, whom he promised long
ago. 14The Spirit is God's guarantee that he
will give us everything he promised and that
he has purchased us to be his own people. This
is just one more reason for us to praise our
glorious God.

Paul's Prayer for Spiritual Wisdom

15Ever since I first heard of your strong faith in
the Lord Jesus and your love for Christians everywhere, 16I have never stopped thanking God for
you. I pray for you constantly, 17asking God, the
glorious Father of our Lord Jesus Christ, to give
you spiritual wisdom and understanding, so
that you might grow in your knowledge of God.
18I pray that your hearts will be flooded with
light so that you can understand the wonderful
future he has promised to those he called. I want
you to realize what a rich and glorious inheritance he has given to his people.*
19I pray that you will begin to understand the
incredible greatness of his power for us who
believe him. This is the same mighty power
20that raised Christ from the dead and seated
him in the place of honor at God's right hand in
the heavenly realms. 21Now he is far above any
ruler or authority or power or leader or anything
else in this world or in the world to come. 22And
God has put all things under the authority of
Christ, and he gave him this authority for the
benefit of the church. 23And the church is his
body; it is filled by Christ, who fills everything
everywhere with his presence.

1:1 Some manuscripts do not include *in Ephesus.* 1:11 Or *we have become God's inheritance.* 1:18 Or *realize how much God has been honored by acquiring his people.*

Why God Gives Us the Holy Spirit Read EPHESIANS 1:13-14

You might say that the Holy Spirit is our "identifying mark" as a Christian. In this text we see three specific reasons God gives us his Holy Spirit:

1. The Holy Spirit Is a Promise. Once again, Scripture reminds us that God has promised to send the Holy Spirit to all those who have heard the good news of the gospel and trusted Christ as Savior.

2. The Holy Spirit Is a Seal. The Holy Spirit serves as a mark of ownership, showing that we belong to God.

3. The Holy Spirit Is a Guarantee. The Holy Spirit also represents God's pledge to bring us to our final spiritual inheritance. This word could also be translated as a "first installment" or "deposit," signifying that his sealing in our lives is a foretaste of much more to come!

God gives us the Holy Spirit not only to enable us to live out the Christian life but to prove that we are precious in his sight.

CORNER STONES

CHAPTER 2

Made Alive with Christ

Once you were dead, doomed forever because of
your many sins. 2You used to live just like the
rest of the world, full of sin, obeying Satan, the
mighty prince of the power of the air. He is the
spirit at work in the hearts of those who refuse
to obey God. 3All of us used to live that way,
following the passions and desires of our evil
nature. We were born with an evil nature, and we
were under God's anger just like everyone else.

4But God is so rich in mercy, and he loved us
so very much, 5that even while we were dead
because of our sins, he gave us life when he
raised Christ from the dead. (It is only by God's
special favor that you have been saved!) 6For he
raised us from the dead along with Christ, and
we are seated with him in the heavenly realms—
all because we are one with Christ Jesus. 7And so
God can always point to us as examples of the
incredible wealth of his favor and kindness toward us, as shown in all he has done for us
through Christ Jesus.

8God saved you by his special favor when you
believed. And you can't take credit for this; it is
a gift from God. 9Salvation is not a reward for
the good things we have done, so none of us can
boast about it. 10For we are God's masterpiece.
He has created us anew in Christ Jesus, so that
we can do the good things he planned for us
long ago.

Oneness and Peace in Christ

11Don't forget that you Gentiles used to be outsiders by birth. You were called "the uncircumcised ones" by the Jews, who were proud of their
circumcision, even though it affected only their
bodies and not their hearts. 12In those days you
were living apart from Christ. You were excluded
from God's people, Israel, and you did not know
the promises God had made to them. You lived
in this world without God and without hope.
13But now you belong to Christ Jesus. Though
you once were far away from God, now you have
been brought near to him because of the blood
of Christ.

14For Christ himself has made peace between
us Jews and you Gentiles by making us all one
people. He has broken down the wall of hostility
that used to separate us. 15By his death he ended
the whole system of Jewish law that excluded the
Gentiles. His purpose was to make peace between Jews and Gentiles by creating in himself
one new person from the two groups. 16To-
gether as one body, Christ reconciled both
groups to God by means of his death, and our
hostility toward each other was put to death.
17He has brought this Good News of peace to
you Gentiles who were far away from him, and
to us Jews who were near. 18Now all of us, both
Jews and Gentiles, may come to the Father
through the same Holy Spirit because of what
Christ has done for us.

A Temple for the Lord

19So now you Gentiles are no longer strangers and foreigners. You are citizens along with all of God's holy people. You are members of God's family. 20We are his house, built on the foundation of the apostles and the prophets. And the cornerstone is Christ Jesus himself. 21We who believe are carefully joined together, becoming a holy temple for the Lord. 22Through him you Gentiles are also joined together as part of this dwelling where God lives by his Spirit.

CHAPTER 3

God's Secret Plan Revealed

I, Paul, am a prisoner of Christ Jesus because of my preaching to you Gentiles. 2As you already know, God has given me this special ministry of announcing his favor to you Gentiles. 3As I briefly mentioned earlier in this letter, God himself revealed his secret plan to me. 4As you read what I have written, you will understand what I know about this plan regarding Christ. 5God did not reveal it to previous generations, but now he has revealed it by the Holy Spirit to his holy apostles and prophets.

6And this is the secret plan: The Gentiles have an equal share with the Jews in all the riches inherited by God's children. Both groups have believed the Good News, and both are part of the same body and enjoy together the promise of blessings through Christ Jesus. 7By God's special favor and mighty power, I have been given the wonderful privilege of serving him by spreading this Good News.

8Just think! Though I did nothing to deserve it, and though I am the least deserving Christian there is, I was chosen for this special joy of telling the Gentiles about the endless treasures available to them in Christ. 9I was chosen to explain to everyone this plan that God, the Creator of all things, had kept secret from the beginning.

10God's purpose was to show his wisdom in all its rich variety to all the rulers and authorities in the heavenly realms. They will see this when Jews and Gentiles are joined together in his church. 11This was his plan from all eternity, and it has now been carried out through Christ Jesus our Lord.

12Because of Christ and our faith in him, we can now come fearlessly into God's presence, assured of his glad welcome. 13So please don't despair because of what they are doing to me here. It is for you that I am suffering, so you should feel honored and encouraged.

Paul's Prayer for Spiritual Empowering

14When I think of the wisdom and scope of God's plan, I fall to my knees and pray to the Father,* 15the Creator of everything in heaven and on earth. 16I pray that from his glorious, unlimited resources he will give you mighty inner strength through his Holy Spirit. 17And I pray that Christ will be more and more at home in your hearts as you trust in him. May your roots go down deep into the soil of God's marvelous love. 18And may you have the power to under-

3:14 Some manuscripts read *the Father of our Lord Jesus Christ.*

Why the Church Needs You

Read EPHESIANS 4:11-16

Not only do you need the church, but the church needs you! As God's child, you are blessed with unique spiritual gifts and talents that can be used to benefit the body of Christ. You can use these gifts in at least two ways to benefit fellow believers:

1. The Gifts God Gives You Promote Spiritual Maturity. God wants you to grow spiritually. In order for this to happen, he has placed gifted people in the church to fulfill different aspects of ministry. If the pastor, teacher, evangelist, and others properly carry out their duties, this not only helps to promote your spiritual growth, but also equips you to do better work for him. For this to take place, however, you must be "fitted together perfectly," with "each part [doing] its own special work, [helping] the other parts grow."

2. The Gifts God Gives You Bless Others. Although you may not hold a prominent position in your church, you may be able to encourage others, care for the sick or those in need, financially support a ministry outreach, or even clean restrooms. If you fail to regularly fellowship in a church with other believers, you are neglecting a tremendous opportunity to use what God has given you.

God Saved Us for a Purpose Read EPHESIANS 2:10

As a nonbeliever, you had nothing to motivate you to live righteously. You may have searched for purpose and meaning in life but found nothing satisfying. As a believer, however, you are "God's workmanship," which means that his Spirit is working in your life to make you more like Christ and to give you a purpose for living.

This verse describes part of the purpose God has for your life as his child—to do good works by helping others. The amazing and wonderful truth about God's purpose for your life is that he had plans for you to do good works long before you even existed. He has already scheduled the days and events of your life with opportunities to tangibly share his love with others (see Ephesians 2:10, p. 238).

The next time you see a neighbor in trouble, hear about a friend struggling with a problem, notice a coworker in distress, or see a stranger who genuinely needs a helping hand—take hold of this opportunity God has placed in your path. Let your "light shine" (see Matthew 5:16, p. 7) because you are his child.

stand, as all God's people should, how wide,
how long, how high, and how deep his love
really is. 19May you experience the love of
Christ, though it is so great you will never fully
understand it. Then you will be filled with the
fullness of life and power that comes from God.
20Now glory be to God! By his mighty power
at work within us, he is able to accomplish
infinitely more than we would ever dare to ask
or hope. 21May he be given glory in the church
and in Christ Jesus forever and ever through
endless ages. Amen.

CHAPTER 4

Unity in the Body

Therefore I, a prisoner for serving the Lord, beg
you to lead a life worthy of your calling, for
you have been called by God. 2Be humble and
gentle. Be patient with each other, making allowance for each other's faults because of your
love. 3Always keep yourselves united in the
Holy Spirit, and bind yourselves together with
peace.
4We are all one body, we have the same Spirit,
and we have all been called to the same glorious
future. 5There is only one Lord, one faith, one
baptism, 6and there is only one God and Father,
who is over us all and in us all and living
through us all. 7However, he has given each one
of us a special gift according to the generosity of
Christ. 8That is why the Scriptures say,

"When he ascended to the heights,
he led a crowd of captives
and gave gifts to his people."*

9Notice that it says "he ascended." This means
that Christ first came down to the lowly world
in which we live.* 10The same one who came
down is the one who ascended higher than all
the heavens, so that his rule might fill the entire
universe.
11He is the one who gave these gifts to the
church: the apostles, the prophets, the evangelists, and the pastors and teachers. 12Their responsibility is to equip God's people to do his
work and build up the church, the body of
Christ, 13until we come to such unity in our faith
and knowledge of God's Son that we will be
mature and full grown in the Lord, measuring
up to the full stature of Christ.
14Then we will no longer be like children,
forever changing our minds about what we believe because someone has told us something
different or because someone has cleverly lied
to us and made the lie sound like the truth.
15Instead, we will hold to the truth in love,
becoming more and more in every way like
Christ, who is the head of his body, the church.
16Under his direction, the whole body is fitted
together perfectly. As each part does its own
special work, it helps the other parts grow, so
that the whole body is healthy and growing and
full of love.

4:8 Ps 68:18. 4:9 Or *to the lowest parts of the earth.*

What Are Spiritual Gifts? Read EPHESIANS 4:11-16

God has chosen people to do his work. He chose this course of action for reasons only he knows and understands. From a human perspective, we may wonder if this was the best decision. After all, "the sky was the limit" concerning what God could have done. He could have chosen to use angels to speak to lost humanity. He certainly used them on many significant occasions throughout Scripture. Or God could have created a special category of messengers that would never fail him—a "sin-proof" instrument that would faithfully proclaim his Word. For that matter, God himself could have simply poked his face through the heavens and said, "Hello, world! I'm God, and you're not!" But God has chosen men and women to do his work among humankind.

As we seek to follow and be used by Jesus Christ, we need to utilize all that he has made available to us. One of the great blessings Jesus has given to his church and to us as individuals is the gifts of the Spirit. Why has he given these gifts? The Bible has this to say about the vital role they play in the lives of believers:

Spiritual Gifts Enable Us to Grow in the Knowledge of Christ. Some people get sidetracked with spiritual gifts and become more obsessed with the gifts than with Jesus. Believers begin to follow signs and wonders, instead of signs and wonders following believers. This is a sign of spiritual immaturity. The Christian writer/preacher A. B. Simpson wrote these insightful words:

Once it was the blessing, now it is the Lord.
Once it was the feeling, now it is his Word.
Once his gifts I wanted, now the Giver own.
Once I sought for healing, now himself alone.

BIG QUESTIONS

Attaining spiritual gifts is not the goal—they are the gateway. They are not a hobby to play with—they are tools to build with, weapons to fight with. We will be more effective as we put them to use for God's glory and not our own.

Spiritual Gifts Are to Be Used. It is possible to let a gift go unused. In doing this, however, you disobey God and cheat the church of a blessing. For this reason, we must use those unique gifts he has given us. In fact, it must be insulting to God for us to demean some gift his Holy Spirit has instilled in our life by saying that it just isn't important enough to use.

Each Spiritual Gift Has a Special Place in the Body of Christ. Every gift that God has placed in the body of Christ, the church, is important. Some gifts such as preaching, teaching, and prophesying may seem more important than others such as hospitality or service. But God has given all of these gifts to build up his church. None of these gifts should be looked down upon or treated lightly.

Living as Children of Light

17With the Lord's authority let me say this:
Live no longer as the ungodly* do, for they are
hopelessly confused. 18Their closed minds are
full of darkness; they are far away from the life
of God because they have shut their minds and
hardened their hearts against him. 19They
don't care anymore about right and wrong,
and they have given themselves over to immoral ways. Their lives are filled with all kinds
of impurity and greed.
20But that isn't what you were taught when
you learned about Christ. 21Since you have
heard all about him and have learned the truth
that is in Jesus, 22throw off your old evil nature
and your former way of life, which is rotten
through and through, full of lust and deception. 23Instead, there must be a spiritual re-
newal of your thoughts and attitudes. 24You
must display a new nature because you are a
new person, created in God's likeness—righteous, holy, and true.
25So put away all falsehood and "tell your
neighbor the truth"* because we belong to each

4:17 Greek *Gentiles.* 4:25 Zech 8:16.

other. 26And "don't sin by letting anger gain
control over you."* Don't let the sun go down
while you are still angry, 27for anger gives a
mighty foothold to the Devil.

28If you are a thief, stop stealing. Begin using
your hands for honest work, and then give generously to others in need. 29Don't use foul or
abusive language. Let everything you say be
good and helpful, so that your words will be an
encouragement to those who hear them.

30And do not bring sorrow to God's Holy
Spirit by the way you live. Remember, he is the
one who has identified you as his own, guaranteeing that you will be saved on the day of
redemption.

31Get rid of all bitterness, rage, anger, harsh
words, and slander, as well as all types of malicious behavior. 32Instead, be kind to each other,
tenderhearted, forgiving one another, just as
God through Christ has forgiven you.

4:26 Ps 4:4.

CHAPTER 5

Living in the Light

Follow God's example in everything you do,
because you are his dear children. 2Live a life

OFF AND RUNNING

Husbands and Wives Have Distinct Roles in Marriage

Read EPHESIANS 5:21-33

The reason so many marriages fail is that husbands, wives, or both do not obey the standards God has laid out in Scripture. In this text, we find the specific roles God has given the husband and the wife.

God's Plan for the Husband.

• He is to be the head of his wife as Christ is the head of the church

True authority in the marriage relationship has been given by God to the husband. From the beginning, God designated the man as the leader in the marriage relationship (verse 23). Like Christ, a husband should be firm and decisive but also humble and unselfish. Before a husband can expect his wife to submit to him, though, he has to submit to Christ.

• He must love his wife as Christ loved the church

Jesus said, "I . . . came here not to be served but to serve others, and to give my life as a ransom for many" (Matthew 20:28). To love as Jesus loved means that a husband focuses primarily on his wife's needs, not his own (verse 25). The wife's submission hinges upon the husband's fulfillment of this role. Just as the church loves Jesus because of his incredible display of love for it, so the wife will love and submit to her husband as she sees his demonstration of love toward her. One heart burning with love sets another on fire.

• He must encourage his wife's spiritual growth

One of the husband's first priorities is to make sure his wife has a good relationship with God (verse 26). He is to encourage his wife's spiritual growth, recognizing that it affects her personal happiness as a woman, wife, and mother.

• He must love his wife as he loves himself

A husband must recognize that he and his wife are actually "one." Therefore, he must do for his wife what he would do for himself. He should give her needs as much attention as he would his own (verses 28-29).

God's Plan for the Wife.

• She must submit to her husband's leadership

Just as a wife submits to God, seeking his will above her own, so she must submit to her husband and his decisions (verses 21, 24).

These guidelines for the husband and the wife become much easier to follow if they respect the first code of conduct listed: "Submit to one another out of reverence for Christ" (verse 21). The word used for *submit* is a term that means "to arrange or rank under." In other words, we need to put the needs of our spouse before our own—in the fear of God. As we do that, our marriages will flourish as God intended—and you will be a living illustration of Christ's love for the church to an unbelieving world. For marriage is not so much *finding* the right person as it is *being* the right person.

filled with love for others, following the example of Christ, who loved you and gave himself as
a sacrifice to take away your sins. And God was
pleased, because that sacrifice was like sweet
perfume to him.
3Let there be no sexual immorality, impurity, or greed among you. Such sins have no
place among God's people. 4Obscene stories,
foolish talk, and coarse jokes—these are not
for you. Instead, let there be thankfulness to
God. 5You can be sure that no immoral, impure, or greedy person will inherit the Kingdom of Christ and of God. For a greedy person
is really an idolater who worships the things of
this world. 6Don't be fooled by those who try
to excuse these sins, for the terrible anger of
God comes upon all those who disobey him.
7Don't participate in the things these people
do. 8For though your hearts were once full of
darkness, now you are full of light from the
Lord, and your behavior should show it! 9For
this light within you produces only what is
good and right and true.
10Try to find out what is pleasing to the
Lord. 11Take no part in the worthless deeds of
evil and darkness; instead, rebuke and expose
them. 12It is shameful even to talk about the
things that ungodly people do in secret. 13But
when the light shines on them, it becomes
clear how evil these things are. 14And where
your light shines, it will expose their evil
deeds. This is why it is said,

"Awake, O sleeper,
rise up from the dead,
and Christ will give you light."

Living by the Spirit's Power

15So be careful how you live, not as fools but
as those who are wise. 16Make the most of
every opportunity for doing good in these evil
days. 17Don't act thoughtlessly, but try to understand what the Lord wants you to do.
18Don't be drunk with wine, because that will
ruin your life. Instead, let the Holy Spirit fill
and control you. 19Then you will sing psalms
and hymns and spiritual songs among yourselves, making music to the Lord in your
hearts. 20And you will always give thanks for
everything to God the Father in the name of
our Lord Jesus Christ.

Spirit-Guided Relationships: Wives and Husbands

21And further, you will submit to one another
out of reverence for Christ. 22You wives will
submit to your husbands as you do to the Lord.
23For a husband is the head of his wife as Christ
is the head of his body, the church; he gave his
life to be her Savior. 24As the church submits to
Christ, so you wives must submit to your husbands in everything.
25And you husbands must love your wives

Realize Who Is Tempting You

Read EPHESIANS 6:10-12

In the Bible, the Christian life is not simply compared to a war—it is actually called a war! As in any battle, it helps to know your enemy. In this case, our enemy is the same one who faced off against Christ in the wilderness: the devil. He is incensed that you have surrendered your life to Christ, and he also sees you as a potential threat to his kingdom. But the encouraging news is that the devil is not as powerful as he would like you to think. Here are two things the devil doesn't want you to know:

1. The Devil Was Conquered by Jesus. When Jesus Christ died on the cross, he disarmed the devil and his demon powers. They could no longer control and condemn people for their sin. In addition, they could no longer keep the penalty of death hanging above people's heads (see Colossians 2:13-15, p. 255; Hebrews 2:14, p. 287; 1 John 3:8-9, pp. 319–320). The fact that Jesus defeated the devil does not mean that the devil has no power today. But it does mean that he does not have the upper hand.

2. The Devil Has Definite Limitations. Satan would love to have us think that he is God's equal, but God has given us power to defeat him (see James 4:7, p. 303). Most important, before he can bring one temptation or hardship our way, he has to go through the protective hedge of Jesus Christ.

Temptation will come your way in the Christian life. But if you are wise, you will cling to the Lord that much tighter when the devil comes with his enticements. Then, once you have stood through the temptation, you will be stronger. As Martin Luther once said, "One Christian who has been tempted is worth a thousand who haven't."

Christ's Love Sets the Standard Read EPHESIANS 5:2

Think back for a moment to when you were a child. What if your parents had never demonstrated how to use a fork and spoon. Then one day they placed you at a table with these utensils and said, "Eat!" You would have had no idea how to use them to get food into your mouth. Consequently, you would have made a mess.

Fortunately, when it comes to loving others, God has given us the greatest example: Jesus Christ. He knew that the best way to teach us how to love was to show us how it is done, and throughout the Gospels, we can see Jesus' love in action. Of course the greatest display of Christ's love for us was when he took the punishment we deserved by dying on the cross. Because of that tremendous sacrifice, we are obligated to love others. Scripture says, "Pay all your debts, except the debt of love for others. You can never finish paying that!" (Romans 13:8). Because we will never match the depth of love God has for us, we will never be able to fully repay the debt of love we owe him. That is why we have to keep giving out that same kind of love to others.

Perhaps you have grown up in a home where love was seldom expressed, or you have had a distorted view of love, and you feel that you are incapable of truly loving others. Take heart, for as this passage says, you can look to Jesus as your example.

When Christ becomes the standard of your love, you will understand what the apostle Paul meant when he said that Christ's love controls us (see 2 Corinthians 5:14, pp. 220–221).

CORNERSTONES

with the same love Christ showed the church.
He gave up his life for her 26to make her holy
and clean, washed by baptism and God's word.*
27He did this to present her to himself as a
glorious church without a spot or wrinkle or any
other blemish. Instead, she will be holy and
without fault. 28In the same way, husbands
ought to love their wives as they love their own
bodies. For a man is actually loving himself
when he loves his wife. 29No one hates his own
body but lovingly cares for it, just as Christ cares
for his body, which is the church. 30And we are
his body.
31As the Scriptures say, "A man leaves his
father and mother and is joined to his wife, and
the two are united into one."* 32This is a great
mystery, but it is an illustration of the way Christ
and the church are one. 33So again I say, each
man must love his wife as he loves himself, and
the wife must respect her husband.

CHAPTER 6

Children and Parents

Children, obey your parents because you belong
to the Lord, for this is the right thing to do.
2"Honor your father and mother." This is the
first of the Ten Commandments that ends with
a promise. 3And this is the promise: If you honor
your father and mother, "you will live a long life,
full of blessing."*
4And now a word to you fathers. Don't make
your children angry by the way you treat them.
Rather, bring them up with the discipline and
instruction approved by the Lord.

Slaves and Masters

5Slaves, obey your earthly masters with deep
respect and fear. Serve them sincerely as you
would serve Christ. 6Work hard, but not just to
please your masters when they are watching. As
slaves of Christ, do the will of God with all your
heart. 7Work with enthusiasm, as though you
were working for the Lord rather than for
people. 8Remember that the Lord will reward
each one of us for the good we do, whether we
are slaves or free.
9And in the same way, you masters must treat
your slaves right. Don't threaten them; remember, you both have the same Master in heaven,
and he has no favorites.

The Whole Armor of God

10A final word: Be strong with the Lord's mighty

5:26 Greek *having cleansed her by the washing of water with the word.* 5:31 Gen 2:24. 6:2-3 Exod 20:12; Deut 5:16.

power. 11Put on all of God's armor so that you will be able to stand firm against all strategies and tricks of the Devil. 12For we are not fighting against people made of flesh and blood, but against the evil rulers and authorities of the unseen world, against those mighty powers of darkness who rule this world, and against wicked spirits in the heavenly realms.

13Use every piece of God's armor to resist the enemy in the time of evil, so that after the battle you will still be standing firm. 14Stand your ground, putting on the sturdy belt of truth and the body armor of God's righteousness. 15For shoes, put on the peace that comes from the Good News, so that you will be fully prepared.* 16In every battle you will need faith as your shield to stop the fiery arrows aimed at you by Satan.* 17Put on salvation as your helmet, and take the sword of the Spirit, which is the word of God. 18Pray at all times and on every occasion in the power of the Holy Spirit. Stay alert and be persistent in your prayers for all Christians everywhere.

19And pray for me, too. Ask God to give me the right words as I boldly explain God's secret plan that the Good News is for the Gentiles, too.* 20I am in chains now for preaching this message as God's ambassador. But pray that I will keep on speaking boldly for him, as I should.

Final Greetings

21Tychicus, a much loved brother and faithful helper in the Lord's work, will tell you all about how I am getting along. 22I am sending him to you for just this purpose. He will let you know how we are, and he will encourage you.

23May God give you peace, dear brothers and sisters,* and love with faith, from God the Father and the Lord Jesus Christ. 24May God's grace be upon all who love our Lord Jesus Christ with an undying love.

6:15 Or *For shoes, put on the readiness to preach the Good News of peace with God.* 6:16 Greek *by the evil one.* 6:19 Greek *explain the mystery of the gospel.* 6:23 Greek *brothers.*

Philippians

CHAPTER 1

Greetings from Paul

This letter is from Paul and Timothy, slaves of
Christ Jesus.

It is written to all of God's people in Philippi,
who believe in Christ Jesus, and to the elders*
and deacons.

2May God our Father and the Lord Jesus
Christ give you grace and peace.

Paul's Thanksgiving and Prayer

3Every time I think of you, I give thanks to my
God. 4I always pray for you, and I make my
requests with a heart full of joy 5because you
have been my partners in spreading the Good
News about Christ from the time you first heard
it until now. 6And I am sure that God, who
began the good work within you, will continue
his work until it is finally finished on that day
when Christ Jesus comes back again.

7It is right that I should feel as I do about
all of you, for you have a very special place in
my heart. We have shared together the blessings of God, both when I was in prison and
when I was out, defending the truth and telling others the Good News. 8God knows how
much I love you and long for you with the
tender compassion of Christ Jesus. 9I pray
that your love for each other will overflow
more and more, and that you will keep on
growing in your knowledge and understanding. 10For I want you to understand what
really matters, so that you may live pure and
blameless lives until Christ returns. 11May you
always be filled with the fruit of your salvation*—those good things that are produced
in your life by Jesus Christ—for this will bring
much glory and praise to God.

Paul's Joy That Christ Is Preached

12And I want you to know, dear brothers and
sisters,* that everything that has happened to
me here has helped to spread the Good News.
13For everyone here, including all the soldiers in
the palace guard, knows that I am in chains
because of Christ. 14And because of my imprisonment, many of the Christians* here have
gained confidence and become more bold in
telling others about Christ.

15Some are preaching out of jealousy and
rivalry. But others preach about Christ with
pure motives. 16They preach because they love
me, for they know the Lord brought me here to
defend the Good News. 17Those others do not
have pure motives as they preach about Christ.
They preach with selfish ambition, not sincerely, intending to make my chains more
painful to me. 18But whether or not their motives are pure, the fact remains that the message about Christ is being preached, so I
rejoice. And I will continue to rejoice. 19For I
know that as you pray for me and as the Spirit
of Jesus Christ helps me, this will all turn out
for my deliverance.

Paul's Life for Christ

20For I live in eager expectation and hope that I
will never do anything that causes me shame, but
that I will always be bold for Christ, as I have been
in the past, and that my life will always honor
Christ, whether I live or I die. 21For to me, living is
for Christ, and dying is even better. 22Yet if I live,
that means fruitful service for Christ. I really don't
know which is better. 23I'm torn between two
desires: Sometimes I want to live, and sometimes
I long to go and be with Christ. That would be far
better for me, 24but it is better for you that I live.

1:1 Greek *overseers.* 1:11 Greek *the fruit of righteousness.* 1:12 Greek *brothers.* 1:14 Greek *brothers in the Lord.*

Jesus Is Human Read PHILIPPIANS 2:5-11

This passage of Scripture paints a touching portrait of the Savior while letting us in on some key truths concerning Christ's divinity and humanity. In essence, it shows why we should worship and emulate Jesus in our lives.

Jesus Veiled His Deity without Voiding It. There was never a moment in the life of Jesus when he suddenly "became" God. He was God before he entered this world as a little baby. And he remained God after he became man. When the Scripture says that "made himself nothing," it does not mean that he ceased being God. He simply veiled his deity. But he never voided it. He always was and always will be God.

Jesus Experienced Our Experiences. Another way of saying that Jesus took the disguise of a slave is to say that "he emptied himself." Again, this does not mean that he emptied himself of his deity, but that he emptied himself of the privileges of deity. For instance, he never performed a miracle for his own benefit. He walked this earth as a man, not a spirit. He experienced human limitations. Jesus—God in human form—experienced hunger. He endured sorrow. He grew tired. He felt the sting of loneliness. He felt the pressure of temptation. For these reasons, we can be assured that our God understands what we are going through (see Hebrews 2:17-18, p. 287).

Jesus' Lordship Will Be Acknowledged by All. Regardless of what anyone thinks of Jesus now, in the end every knee will bow and every tongue will confess that Jesus Christ is Lord. The authority of the Bible backs this claim. Christ's divine nature, which he veiled at times during his time on earth, will then be clearly visible for all to see.

CORNERSTONES

25I am convinced of this, so I will continue
with you so that you will grow and experience
the joy of your faith. 26Then when I return to
you, you will have even more reason to boast
about what Christ Jesus has done for me.

Live as Citizens of Heaven

27But whatever happens to me, you must live
in a manner worthy of the Good News about
Christ, as citizens of heaven. Then, whether I
come and see you again or only hear about
you, I will know that you are standing side by
side, fighting together for the Good News.
28Don't be intimidated by your enemies. This
will be a sign to them that they are going to be
destroyed, but that you are going to be saved,
even by God himself. 29For you have been
given not only the privilege of trusting in
Christ but also the privilege of suffering for
him. 30We are in this fight together. You have
seen me suffer for him in the past, and you
know that I am still in the midst of this great
struggle.

CHAPTER 2

Unity through Humility

Is there any encouragement from belonging to
Christ? Any comfort from his love? Any fellowship together in the Spirit? Are your hearts tender and sympathetic? 2Then make me truly
happy by agreeing wholeheartedly with each
other, loving one another, and working together
with one heart and purpose.

3Don't be selfish; don't live to make a good
impression on others. Be humble, thinking of
others as better than yourself. 4Don't think only
about your own affairs, but be interested in
others, too, and what they are doing.

Christ's Humility and Exaltation

5Your attitude should be the same that Christ
Jesus had. 6Though he was God, he did not
demand and cling to his rights as God. 7He
made himself nothing;* he took the humble
position of a slave and appeared in human
form.* 8And in human form he obediently
humbled himself even further by dying a criminal's death on a cross. 9Because of this, God

2:7a Or *He laid aside his mighty power and glory.* **2:7b** Greek *and was born in the likeness of men and was found in appearance as a man.*

raised him up to the heights of heaven and gave
him a name that is above every other name, 10so
that at the name of Jesus every knee will bow, in
heaven and on earth and under the earth, 11and
every tongue will confess that Jesus Christ is
Lord, to the glory of God the Father.

Shine Brightly for Christ

12Dearest friends, you were always so careful to
follow my instructions when I was with you.
And now that I am away you must be even more
careful to put into action God's saving work in
your lives, obeying God with deep reverence and
fear. 13For God is working in you, giving you the
desire to obey him and the power to do what
pleases him.

14In everything you do, stay away from complaining and arguing, 15so that no one can speak
a word of blame against you. You are to live
clean, innocent lives as children of God in a dark
world full of crooked and perverse people. Let
your lives shine brightly before them. 16Hold
tightly to the word of life, so that when Christ
returns, I will be proud that I did not lose the
race and that my work was not useless. 17But
even if my life is to be poured out like a drink
offering to complete the sacrifice of your faithful
service (that is, if I am to die for you), I will
rejoice, and I want to share my joy with all of
you. 18And you should be happy about this and
rejoice with me.

Paul Commends Timothy

19If the Lord Jesus is willing, I hope to send
Timothy to you soon. Then when he comes
back, he can cheer me up by telling me how you
are getting along. 20I have no one else like Timothy, who genuinely cares about your welfare.
21All the others care only for themselves and not
for what matters to Jesus Christ. 22But you know
how Timothy has proved himself. Like a son
with his father, he has helped me in preaching
the Good News. 23I hope to send him to you just
as soon as I find out what is going to happen to
me here. 24And I have confidence from the Lord
that I myself will come to see you soon.

Paul Commends Epaphroditus

25Meanwhile, I thought I should send Epaphroditus back to you. He is a true brother, a faithful
worker, and a courageous soldier. And he was
your messenger to help me in my need. 26Now I
am sending him home again, for he has been
longing to see you, and he was very distressed
that you heard he was ill. 27And he surely was ill;
in fact, he almost died. But God had mercy on
him—and also on me, so that I would not have
such unbearable sorrow.

28So I am all the more anxious to send him
back to you, for I know you will be glad to see
him, and that will lighten all my cares. 29Wel-
come him with Christian love* and with great
joy, and be sure to honor people like him. 30For
he risked his life for the work of Christ, and he
was at the point of death while trying to do for
me the things you couldn't do because you were
far away.

CHAPTER 3

The Priceless Gain of Knowing Christ

Whatever happens, dear brothers and sisters,* may
the Lord give you joy. I never get tired of telling
you this. I am doing this for your own good.

2Watch out for those dogs, those wicked men
and their evil deeds, those mutilators who say
you must be circumcised to be saved. 3For we
who worship God in the Spirit* are the only
ones who are truly circumcised. We put no confidence in human effort. Instead, we boast about
what Christ Jesus has done for us.

4Yet I could have confidence in myself if anyone could. If others have reason for confidence
in their own efforts, I have even more! 5For I was
circumcised when I was eight days old, having
been born into a pure-blooded Jewish family
that is a branch of the tribe of Benjamin. So I am
a real Jew if there ever was one! What's more, I
was a member of the Pharisees, who demand the
strictest obedience to the Jewish law. 6And zealous? Yes, in fact, I harshly persecuted the church.
And I obeyed the Jewish law so carefully that I
was never accused of any fault.

7I once thought all these things were so very
important, but now I consider them worthless
because of what Christ has done. 8Yes, everything else is worthless when compared with the
priceless gain of knowing Christ Jesus my Lord.
I have discarded everything else, counting it all
as garbage, so that I may have Christ 9and become one with him. I no longer count on my
own goodness or my ability to obey God's law,
but I trust Christ to save me. For God's way of
making us right with himself depends on faith.
10As a result, I can really know Christ and experience the mighty power that raised him from
the dead. I can learn what it means to suffer with
him, sharing in his death, 11so that, somehow, I
can experience the resurrection from the dead!

2:29 Greek *in the Lord.* 3:1 Greek *brothers;* also in 3:13, 17. 3:3 Or *in spirit;* some manuscripts read *worship by the Spirit of God.*

Pressing toward the Goal

12I don't mean to say that I have already achieved
these things or that I have already reached perfection! But I keep working toward that day when I
will finally be all that Christ Jesus saved me for and
wants me to be. 13No, dear brothers and sisters, I
am still not all I should be,* but I am focusing all
my energies on this one thing: Forgetting the past
and looking forward to what lies ahead, 14I strain
to reach the end of the race and receive the prize
for which God, through Christ Jesus, is calling us
up to heaven.*

15I hope all of you who are mature Christians
will agree on these things. If you disagree on
some point, I believe God will make it plain to
you. 16But we must be sure to obey the truth we
have learned already.

17Dear brothers and sisters, pattern your lives
after mine, and learn from those who follow our
example. 18For I have told you often before, and I
say it again with tears in my eyes, that there are
many whose conduct shows they are really enemies of the cross of Christ. 19Their future is eternal
destruction. Their god is their appetite, they brag
about shameful things, and all they think about is
this life here on earth. 20But we are citizens of
heaven, where the Lord Jesus Christ lives. And we
are eagerly waiting for him to return as our Savior.
21He will take these weak mortal bodies of ours
and change them into glorious bodies like his
own, using the same mighty power that he will use
to conquer everything, everywhere.

CHAPTER 4

Dear brothers and sisters,* I love you and long to see
you, for you are my joy and the reward for my work.
So please stay true to the Lord, my dear friends.

Paul's Final Thoughts

2And now I want to plead with those two women,
Euodia and Syntyche. Please, because you belong
to the Lord, settle your disagreement. 3And I ask
you, my true teammate,* to help these women, for
they worked hard with me in telling others the
Good News. And they worked with Clement and
the rest of my co-workers, whose names are written in the Book of Life.

4Always be full of joy in the Lord. I say it
again—rejoice! 5Let everyone see that you are
considerate in all you do. Remember, the Lord is
coming soon.

6Don't worry about anything; instead, pray
about everything. Tell God what you need, and
thank him for all he has done. 7If you do this,
you will experience God's peace, which is far
more wonderful than the human mind can understand. His peace will guard your hearts and
minds as you live in Christ Jesus.

8And now, dear brothers and sisters, let me
say one more thing as I close this letter. Fix your
thoughts on what is true and honorable and
right. Think about things that are pure and
lovely and admirable. Think about things that
are excellent and worthy of praise. 9Keep putting into practice all you learned from me and

3:13 Some manuscripts read *I am not all I should be.* 3:14 Or *from heaven.* 4:1 Greek *brothers;* also in 4:8. 4:3 Greek *true yokefellow,* or *loyal Syzygus.*

OFF AND RUNNING

Place Christ before All Else Read PHILIPPIANS 3:4-8

As verses 4-6 attest, the apostle Paul was the epitome of a good Jew. He had been born a member of God's chosen people and had flawlessly kept God's laws. But when Paul met Jesus on the road to Damascus (see Acts 9:1-19, pp. 148–149), Paul realized that everything he was living for was taking him in the wrong direction. For that reason he counted everything else in life—his reputation, his achievements, his pursuits, his possessions—worthless, so that his sole pursuit would be in knowing and serving Jesus.

Do you, like Paul, place Christ above everything else in your life? If you are not sure, ask yourself the following questions: How do you spend your time? What dominates your thoughts? Where are your priorities? What motivates you? If the most important thing in your life is Jesus, then your life will revolve around getting to know him more and more. You will want to spend time learning about his nature, his will, and his purposes for you in his Word. And you will truly be able to say that you have discovered "the priceless gain of knowing Christ Jesus."

heard from me and saw me doing, and the God of peace will be with you.

Paul's Thanks for Their Gifts

10How grateful I am, and how I praise the Lord that you are concerned about me again. I know you have always been concerned for me, but for a while you didn't have the chance to help me.
11Not that I was ever in need, for I have learned how to get along happily whether I have much
or little. 12I know how to live on almost nothing or with everything. I have learned the secret of living in every situation, whether it is with a full stomach or empty, with plenty or little. 13For I
can do everything with the help of Christ who gives me the strength I need. 14But even so, you
have done well to share with me in my present difficulty.

15As you know, you Philippians were the only ones who gave me financial help when I brought you the Good News and then traveled on from Macedonia. No other church did this. 16Even
when I was in Thessalonica you sent help more than once. 17I don't say this because I want a gift
from you. What I want is for you to receive a well-earned reward because of your kindness.

18At the moment I have all I need—more than I need! I am generously supplied with the gifts you sent me with Epaphroditus. They are a sweet-smelling sacrifice that is acceptable to God and pleases him. 19And this same God who
takes care of me will supply all your needs from his glorious riches, which have been given to us in Christ Jesus. 20Now glory be to God our
Father forever and ever. Amen.

Paul's Final Greetings

21Give my greetings to all the Christians there. The brothers who are with me here send you their greetings. 22And all the other Christians
send their greetings, too, especially those who work in Caesar's palace.

23May the grace of the Lord Jesus Christ be with your spirit.

Prayer Helps Us Overcome Worry Read PHILIPPIANS 4:6-7

Have you ever been gripped by worry or fear? Worry is a completely unproductive emotion. It is the advance interest we pay on troubles that seldom come. But these verses give us the best antidote for worry—prayer. God wants to be the first one we turn to in times of worry or crisis. When we do, he promises a special blessing if we do the following four things:

1. Stop Worrying and Start Praying. Don't ever think that your need is too insignificant for God's attention. He wants us to pray about *everything*.

2. Tell God Your Needs. Even though God is all-knowing and is well aware of your situation, he desires that you verbalize your needs to him and place them in his hands.

3. Present Your Requests with Thanks. Instead of praying with feelings of doubt, we can thank God for his answers in advance because of the promises he has made to us in his Word.

4. Receive God's Peace. Once you do these things, verse 7 says that you will experience God's peace. In the original Greek text, this verse literally means that God's peace will "mount a guard or garrison" around your heart and mind to keep and protect you during those difficult times in your life.

The next time you are tempted to worry about something, channel into prayer all of the energy you would have put into worry. Say something like, "Lord, here is my problem. It looms ever larger in my path, so I am putting it into your hands. I am not going to worry, Lord. Instead, I am going to trust you. I am even going to thank you in advance for what you will do, because you know what you are doing." This may not always be an easy thing to do, but if you want to overcome worry and experience God's peace, it is something you must consciously do.

FIRST STEPS

Colossians

CHAPTER **1**

Greetings from Paul

This letter is from Paul, chosen by God to be an
apostle of Christ Jesus, and from our brother
Timothy.
2It is written to God's holy people in the city
of Colosse, who are faithful brothers and sisters*
in Christ.

May God our Father give you grace and peace.

Paul's Thanksgiving and Prayer

3We always pray for you, and we give thanks to
God the Father of our Lord Jesus Christ, 4for we
have heard that you trust in Christ Jesus and that
you love all of God's people. 5You do this because you are looking forward to the joys of
heaven—as you have been ever since you first
heard the truth of the Good News. 6This same
Good News that came to you is going out all
over the world. It is changing lives everywhere,
just as it changed yours that very first day you
heard and understood the truth about God's
great kindness to sinners.
7Epaphras, our much loved co-worker, was
the one who brought you the Good News. He is
Christ's faithful servant, and he is helping us in
your place.* 8He is the one who told us about
the great love for others that the Holy Spirit has
given you.
9So we have continued praying for you ever
since we first heard about you. We ask God to
give you a complete understanding of what he
wants to do in your lives, and we ask him to
make you wise with spiritual wisdom. 10Then
the way you live will always honor and please
the Lord, and you will continually do good, kind
things for others. All the while, you will learn to
know God better and better.
11We also pray that you will be strengthened
with his glorious power so that you will have all
the patience and endurance you need. May you
be filled with joy, 12always thanking the Father,
who has enabled you to share the inheritance
that belongs to God's holy people, who live in
the light. 13For he has rescued us from the one
who rules in the kingdom of darkness, and he
has brought us into the Kingdom of his dear
Son. 14God has purchased our freedom with his
blood* and has forgiven all our sins.

Christ Is Supreme

15Christ is the visible image of the invisible God.
He existed before God made anything at all and
is supreme over all creation.* 16Christ is the one
through whom God created everything in
heaven and earth. He made the things we can see
and the things we can't see—kings, kingdoms,
rulers, and authorities. Everything has been created through him and for him. 17He existed
before everything else began, and he holds all
creation together.
18Christ is the head of the church, which is his
body. He is the first of all who will rise from the
dead,* so he is first in everything. 19For God in
all his fullness was pleased to live in Christ,
20and by him God reconciled everything to himself. He made peace with everything in heaven
and on earth by means of his blood on the cross.
21This includes you who were once so far away
from God. You were his enemies, separated from
him by your evil thoughts and actions, 22yet
now he has brought you back as his friends. He
has done this through his death on the cross in
his own human body. As a result, he has brought
you into the very presence of God, and you are
holy and blameless as you stand before him

1:2 Greek *faithful brothers.* 1:7 Greek *he is ministering on your behalf;* other manuscripts read *he is ministering on our behalf.* 1:14 Some manuscripts do not include *with his blood.* 1:15 Greek *He is the firstborn of all creation.* 1:18 Greek *He is the beginning, the firstborn from the dead.*

Jesus Is Divine Read COLOSSIANS 1:15-20

The most crucial truth of the Christian faith is that Jesus Christ, though he came to earth as a man, was in fact God. This passage lays out six important details about Jesus' divinity and his work in heaven and on earth:

1. Jesus Is Eternal. Being God, Jesus never had a beginning, nor does he have an end (verse 15). The apostle John knew this. In John 1:1, he refers to Jesus as the Word and says that "in the beginning the Word already existed."

2. Jesus Is the Creator of All Things. This concept makes the whole idea of Jesus' coming as a Savior to this earth so amazing. He understood the way people acted and the hardness of humans' hearts because he created them (verse 16). Yet he loved people so much he was willing to come down to earth and die in order to redeem all humankind.

3. Jesus Holds Everything Together. Jesus has and always will be in control (verses 16-17). Our world is not in some chaotic state but has been created with a purpose in mind—to ultimately bring glory to Christ.

4. Jesus Is the Head of the Church. The church was not established by a group of people but by God himself. Although some leaders in the church may let us down at times, we must remember that Christ, the true head of this body of believers (verse 18), will never fail us.

5. Jesus Is the Leader of All Who Will Rise from the Dead. Christ was the first to actually defeat death and return to life in a resurrected body (verse 18). For that reason, we who follow him have the hope—and the evidence—that we, too, will one day rise again after death to spend eternity with him.

6. Jesus Is the Only Way to Peace with God. God was never surprised that man sinned in the Garden of Eden. The Bible even records that Jesus' sacrifice on the cross was known before "the world was made" (Revelation 13:8). That means that God had already made a provision for our sins long before Adam ate the forbidden fruit (verse 20).

Jesus was much more than a mere prophet, teacher, or messenger. In reality, Jesus was nothing less than God himself come to the earth. To deny this central truth is to deny the basis of the Christian faith. Remember, it was this truth that motivated the Christians of the first century to turn their world "upside down" for the sake of the gospel (see Acts 17:6, p. 159).

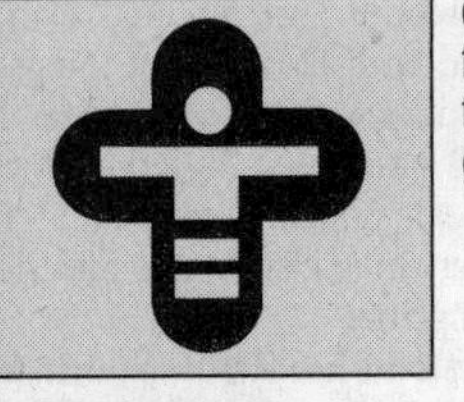

CORNER STONES

without a single fault. 23But you must continue
to believe this truth and stand in it firmly. Don't
drift away from the assurance you received when
you heard the Good News. The Good News has
been preached all over the world, and I, Paul,
have been appointed by God to proclaim it.

Paul's Work for the Church

24I am glad when I suffer for you in my body,
for I am completing what remains of Christ's
sufferings for his body, the church. 25God has
given me the responsibility of serving his
church by proclaiming his message in all its
fullness to you Gentiles. 26This message was
kept secret for centuries and generations past,
but now it has been revealed to his own holy
people. 27For it has pleased God to tell his
people that the riches and glory of Christ are
for you Gentiles, too. For this is the secret:
Christ lives in you, and this is your assurance
that you will share in his glory.

28So everywhere we go, we tell everyone
about Christ. We warn them and teach them
with all the wisdom God has given us, for we

want to present them to God, perfect* in their
relationship to Christ. 29I work very hard at this,
as I depend on Christ's mighty power that works
within me.

CHAPTER 2

I want you to know how much I have agonized
for you and for the church at Laodicea, and for
many other friends who have never known me
personally. 2My goal is that they will be encouraged and knit together by strong ties of
love. I want them to have full confidence because they have complete understanding of
God's secret plan, which is Christ himself. 3In
him lie hidden all the treasures of wisdom and
knowledge.

4I am telling you this so that no one will be
able to deceive you with persuasive arguments.
5For though I am far away from you, my heart is
with you. And I am very happy because you are
living as you should and because of your strong
faith in Christ.

Freedom from Rules and New Life in Christ

6And now, just as you accepted Christ Jesus as
your Lord, you must continue to live in obedience to him. 7Let your roots grow down into
him and draw up nourishment from him, so you
will grow in faith, strong and vigorous in the
truth you were taught. Let your lives overflow
with thanksgiving for all he has done.

8Don't let anyone lead you astray with empty
philosophy and high-sounding nonsense that
come from human thinking and from the evil
powers of this world,* and not from Christ. 9For
in Christ the fullness of God lives in a human
body,* 10and you are complete through your
union with Christ. He is the Lord over every ruler
and authority in the universe.

11When you came to Christ, you were "circumcised," but not by a physical procedure. It
was a spiritual procedure—the cutting away of
your sinful nature. 12For you were buried with
Christ when you were baptized. And with him
you were raised to a new life because you trusted
the mighty power of God, who raised Christ
from the dead.

13You were dead because of your sins and
because your sinful nature was not yet cut
away. Then God made you alive with Christ.
He forgave all our sins. 14He canceled the record that contained the charges against us. He
took it and destroyed it by nailing it to Christ's
cross. 15In this way, God disarmed the evil
rulers and authorities. He shamed them publicly by his victory over them on the cross of
Christ.

16So don't let anyone condemn you for
what you eat or drink, or for not celebrating
certain holy days or new-moon ceremonies or
Sabbaths. 17For these rules were only shadows
of the real thing, Christ himself. 18Don't let
anyone condemn you by insisting on self-denial. And don't let anyone say you must worship angels, even though they say they have
had visions about this. These people claim to
be so humble, but their sinful minds have

1:28 Or *mature.* 2:8 Or *from the basic principles of this world;* also in 2:20. 2:9 Greek *in him dwells all the fullness of the Godhead bodily.*

Let God Occupy Your Thoughts Read COLOSSIANS 3:2-4

A song in the church says, "Turn your eyes upon Jesus. Look full in his wonderful face. And the things of earth will grow strangely dim in the light of his glory and grace." These are good words to live by, for one of the strongest deterrents against returning to your old way of life is to focus upon your Savior and future. As a believer, you have been promised eternal life, the hope of heaven, and the assurance of spending eternity in the presence of God. When you think about that, the trappings of this world begin to lose their appeal.

The next time you feel inclined to dabble with your old life, or feel weighed down by the worries of this world, or fear that you won't make it as a Christian, remember to do these things:

- Keep your eyes on your final destination.
- Realize that worry should not be a part of your life.
- Picture yourself as dead to this world and alive in Christ.
- Remember that your Redeemer is returning.

If you allow these truths to occupy your thoughts, you will find it much easier to obey God and say no to the alluring, but damaging, enticements of this sinful world.

God's Peace Needs to Rule in Our Hearts Read COLOSSIANS 3:15

One of the most obvious identifying marks of a Christian is peace. As Paul points out in this verse, the peace a Christian has comes from Christ and "rules" in a Christian's heart. The Greek verb Paul uses for *rule* suggests that Christ's peace is to act as an "umpire" or a judge in our lives, deciding our outlook and mood in the midst of all circumstances.

What characterizes Christ's peace? Here are a few more biblical descriptions:

- It is not anxious about anything but trusts God (see Philippians 4:6-7, p. 250).
- It doesn't doubt that God is in control (see Mark 4:35-41, pp. 47–48).
- It doesn't forget God's blessings and answers to prayer (see Philippians 4:6, p. 250).
- It should be present in our relationships (see Romans 12:18, p. 192).
- It comes from Christ alone (see John 16:33, p. 128).
- It is produced by the Holy Spirit (see Galatians 5:22, p. 234).
- It promotes peace with others (see James 3:18, p. 302).

Does the peace of Christ rule in your life? If not, you are not living as Jesus really intends you to live. Give God your worries and concerns, and ask him to replace them with his peace. This peace will not only calm your heart, but it will also help encourage harmony between you and your Christian brothers and sisters.

CORNERSTONES

made them proud. 19But they are not connected to Christ, the head of the body. For we are joined together in his body by his strong sinews, and we grow only as we get our nourishment and strength from God.

20You have died with Christ, and he has set you free from the evil powers of this world. So why do you keep on following rules of the world, such as, 21"Don't handle, don't eat, don't touch." 22Such rules are mere human teaching about things that are gone as soon as we use them. 23These rules may seem wise because they require strong devotion, humility, and severe bodily discipline. But they have no effect when it comes to conquering a person's evil thoughts and desires.

CHAPTER **3**

Living the New Life

Since you have been raised to new life with Christ, set your sights on the realities of heaven, where Christ sits at God's right hand in the place of honor and power. 2Let heaven fill your thoughts. Do not think only about things down

OFF AND RUNNING

Avoid Aggravating Your Children Read COLOSSIANS 3:20-21

While discipline is necessary in the lives of children, it is equally necessary that discipline be tempered with love. This means that parents should not scold or nag their children, especially when disciplining them. Other words that have been used for scold and nag are *exasperate* and *aggravate*. The word *aggravate* means to irritate, enrage, harass, tease, and add fuel to the flame.

When discipline is administered in an aggravating manner, the consequences can be devastating. Children may not only be angry with their parents and resent them, but children may also disrespect and dishonor their parents. Even worse, they may one day end their relationship with their parents or act out violently against them.

If you really want your children to honor you as a parent, then you must discipline them with love, praise them when they obey, and train them in the instruction of the Lord.

here on earth. 3For you died when Christ died, and your real life is hidden with Christ in God. 4And when Christ, who is your* real life, is revealed to the whole world, you will share in all his glory.

5So put to death the sinful, earthly things lurking within you. Have nothing to do with sexual sin, impurity, lust, and shameful desires. Don't be greedy for the good things of this life, for that is idolatry. 6God's terrible anger will come upon those who do such things. 7You used to do them when your life was still part of this world. 8But now is the time to get rid of anger, rage, malicious behavior, slander, and dirty language. 9Don't lie to each other, for you have stripped off your old evil nature and all its wicked deeds. 10In its place you have clothed yourselves with a brand-new nature that is continually being renewed as you learn more and more about Christ, who created this new nature within you. 11In this new life, it doesn't matter if you are a Jew or a Gentile,* circumcised or uncircumcised, barbaric, uncivilized,* slave, or free. Christ is all that matters, and he lives in all of us.

12Since God chose you to be the holy people whom he loves, you must clothe yourselves with tenderhearted mercy, kindness, humility, gentleness, and patience. 13You must make allowance for each other's faults and forgive the person who offends you. Remember, the Lord forgave you, so you must forgive others. 14And the most important piece of clothing you must wear is love. Love is what binds us all together in perfect harmony. 15And let the peace that comes from Christ rule in your hearts. For as members of one body you are all called to live in peace. And always be thankful.

16Let the words of Christ, in all their richness, live in your hearts and make you wise. Use his words to teach and counsel each other. Sing psalms and hymns and spiritual songs to God with thankful hearts. 17And whatever you do or say, let it be as a representative of the Lord Jesus, all the while giving thanks through him to God the Father.

Instructions for Christian Households

18You wives must submit to your husbands, as is fitting for those who belong to the Lord. 19And you husbands must love your wives and never treat them harshly.

20You children must always obey your parents, for this is what pleases the Lord. 21Fathers, don't aggravate your children. If you do, they will become discouraged and quit trying.

22You slaves must obey your earthly masters in everything you do. Try to please them all the time, not just when they are watching you. Obey them willingly because of your reverent fear of the Lord. 23Work hard and cheerfully at whatever you do, as though you were working for the Lord rather than for people. 24Remember that the Lord will give you an inheritance as your reward, and the Master you are serving is Christ. 25But if you do what is wrong, you will be paid back for the wrong you have done. For God has no favorites who can get away with evil.

CHAPTER 4

You slave owners must be just and fair to your slaves. Remember that you also have a Master—in heaven.

An Encouragement for Prayer

2Devote yourselves to prayer with an alert mind and a thankful heart. 3Don't forget to pray for us, too, that God will give us many opportunities to preach about his secret plan—that Christ is also for you Gentiles. That is why I am here in chains. 4Pray that I will proclaim this message as clearly as I should.

5Live wisely among those who are not Christians, and make the most of every opportunity. 6Let your conversation be gracious and effective so that you will have the right answer for everyone.

Paul's Final Instructions and Greetings

7Tychicus, a much loved brother, will tell you how I am getting along. He is a faithful helper who serves the Lord with me. 8I have sent him on this special trip to let you know how we are doing and to encourage you. 9I am also sending Onesimus, a faithful and much loved brother, one of your own people. He and Tychicus will give you all the latest news.

10Aristarchus, who is in prison with me, sends you his greetings, and so does Mark, Barnabas's cousin. And as you were instructed before, make Mark welcome if he comes your way. 11Jesus (the one we call Justus) also sends his greetings. These are the only Jewish Christians among my co-workers; they are working with me here for the Kingdom of God. And what a comfort they have been!

12Epaphras, from your city, a servant of Christ Jesus, sends you his greetings. He always prays

3:4 Some manuscripts read *our.* 3:11a Greek *Greek.* 3:11b Greek *Barbarian, Scythian.*

OFF AND RUNNING

Work As If You Are Working for the Lord

Read COLOSSIANS 3:22-24

While the world says to work for the sake of your own welfare, Jesus says to work out of your desire to please him. While the world says to work hard to get ahead, Jesus says to work hard to show the world who you are really working for. When you work as though you are working for the Lord, your whole outlook changes.

Do you want to revolutionize your attitude toward your job? Then take this verse to heart. If you are a mother at home, tackle the dishes, laundry, and cooking as if you are serving the Lord, not just your family. If you work in an office, take care of your tasks and treat your co-workers as you would the Lord himself. Your work may be unappreciated and underpaid in this life, but God promises to give you your full reward in heaven (verse 24).

---

earnestly for you, asking God to make you
strong and perfect, fully confident of the whole
will of God. 13I can assure you that he has
agonized for you and also for the Christians in
Laodicea and Hierapolis.
14Dear Doctor Luke sends his greetings, and
so does Demas. 15Please give my greetings to our
Christian brothers and sisters* at Laodicea, and
to Nympha and those who meet in her house.
16After you have read this letter, pass it on to
the church at Laodicea so they can read it, too.
And you should read the letter I wrote to them.
17And say to Archippus, "Be sure to carry out the
work the Lord gave you."
18Here is my greeting in my own handwriting—PAUL.

Remember my chains.

May the grace of God be with you.

4:15 Greek *brothers.*

OFF AND RUNNING

Keep Your Conversation Gracious

Read COLOSSIANS 4:6

Witnessing to others about the Lord can be a bit intimidating at first. We never know what kind of response we will receive. But if you follow the three steps found in these verses, you will become much more effective at sharing your faith:

1. Tell the Good News. Center your conversation on the simple gospel message: (1) Man is separated from God by sin; (2) God sent his Son, Jesus Christ, to die on the cross and pay the price for our sin; and (3) if we will turn from that sin, embrace Christ as Savior and Lord, and follow him, we can be forgiven and have a relationship with God.

2. Be Wise When Sharing Your Faith. Use discernment. Don't push the subject of your faith if you sense the person is not interested. On the other hand, don't end the conversation if you feel the person is sincerely interested. Remember, God softens a person's heart. You simply present the message.

3. Let Your Conversation Be Gracious and Sensible. Don't rely upon sophisticated arguments to prove your point. Let Christ's love shine through you as you speak. Another translation adds that your conversation should also be "seasoned with salt." In other words, give the person a thirst to learn more about Christ.

Jesus communicated his message in a unique way to each individual. We must do the same. The more we share our faith, the easier that will become.

I Thessalonians

CHAPTER 1

Greetings from Paul

This letter is from Paul, Silas,* and Timothy.

It is written to the church in Thessalonica, you
who belong to God the Father and the Lord Jesus
Christ.

May his grace and peace be yours.

The Faith of the Thessalonian Believers

2We always thank God for all of you and pray for
you constantly. 3As we talk to our God and
Father about you, we think of your faithful work,
your loving deeds, and your continual anticipa-
tion of the return of our Lord Jesus Christ.
4We know that God loves you, dear brothers
and sisters,* and that he chose you to be his own
people. 5For when we brought you the Good
News, it was not only with words but also with
power, for the Holy Spirit gave you full assurance
that what we said was true. And you know that
the way we lived among you was further proof
of the truth of our message. 6So you received the
message with joy from the Holy Spirit in spite of
the severe suffering it brought you. In this way,
you imitated both us and the Lord. 7As a result,
you yourselves became an example to all the
Christians in Greece.* 8And now the word of the
Lord is ringing out from you to people everywhere, even beyond Greece, for wherever we go
we find people telling us about your faith in
God. We don't need to tell them about it, 9for
they themselves keep talking about the wonderful welcome you gave us and how you turned
away from idols to serve the true and living God.
10And they speak of how you are looking forward to the coming of God's Son from heaven—
Jesus, whom God raised from the dead. He is the
one who has rescued us from the terrors of the
coming judgment.

CHAPTER 2

Paul Remembers His Visit

You yourselves know, dear brothers and sisters,*
that our visit to you was not a failure. 2You know
how badly we had been treated at Philippi just
before we came to you and how much we suffered there. Yet our God gave us the courage to
declare his Good News to you boldly, even
though we were surrounded by many who opposed us. 3So you can see that we were not
preaching with any deceit or impure purposes or
trickery.
4For we speak as messengers who have been
approved by God to be entrusted with the Good
News. Our purpose is to please God, not people.
He is the one who examines the motives of our
hearts. 5Never once did we try to win you with
flattery, as you very well know. And God is our
witness that we were not just pretending to be
your friends so you would give us money! 6As
for praise, we have never asked for it from you or
anyone else. 7As apostles of Christ we certainly
had a right to make some demands of you, but
we were as gentle among you as a mother*
feeding and caring for her own children. 8We
loved you so much that we gave you not only
God's Good News but our own lives, too.
9Don't you remember, dear brothers and
sisters, how hard we worked among you?
Night and day we toiled to earn a living so that
our expenses would not be a burden to anyone
there as we preached God's Good News among

1:1 Greek *Silvanus.* 1:4 Greek *brothers.* 1:7 Greek *Macedonia and Achaia,* the northern and southern regions of Greece; also in 1:8.
2:1 Greek *brothers;* also in 2:9, 14, 17. 2:7 Some manuscripts read *we were as infants among you; we were as a mother.*

Our Love Should Grow

Read 1 THESSALONIANS 3:12-13

Too many of us think that love is some emotional thing that comes and goes. Yet this passage suggests that our love should not only remain steady but that it should also *grow.* This may seem like an impossible task on our own—and it is. That is why the apostle Paul says, "May the *Lord* make your love grow." You cannot manufacture sincere love. Christ's love must motivate and compel you (see 2 Corinthians 5:14, pp. 220-221). This love, in turn, will help to strengthen your heart, keep you from sin, and make you holy so that you can be guiltless when Christ returns.

If your love toward God and others seems stagnant, it is likely you have distanced yourself from the Source of that love. Return to the Lord and ask him to refill and refresh your love for him, then look for ways to share that love with others.

CORNER STONES

you. 10You yourselves are our witnesses—and
so is God—that we were pure and honest and
faultless toward all of you believers. 11And you
know that we treated each of you as a father
treats his own children. 12We pleaded with
you, encouraged you, and urged you to live
your lives in a way that God would consider
worthy. For he called you into his Kingdom to
share his glory.
13And we will never stop thanking God that
when we preached his message to you, you
didn't think of the words we spoke as being just
our own. You accepted what we said as the very
word of God—which, of course, it was. And this
word continues to work in you who believe.
14And then, dear brothers and sisters, you
suffered persecution from your own country-
men. In this way, you imitated the believers in
God's churches in Judea who, because of their
belief in Christ Jesus, suffered from their own
people, the Jews.
15For some of the Jews had killed their own
prophets, and some even killed the Lord Jesus.
Now they have persecuted us and driven us out.
They displease God and oppose everyone 16by
trying to keep us from preaching the Good News

OFF AND RUNNING

Encourage Your Children's Spiritual Growth

Read 1 THESSALONIANS 2:11-12

The apostle Paul compared his relationship with the Thessalonians to that of a father with his children. Although this passage doesn't necessarily deal with the father-child relationship, it does show three ways in which fathers play an important role in developing their children's faith:

1. **Fathers Encourage Children in Their Faith.** One way in which fathers can do this is to live out their faith before their children. Doing this will show children how one's faith affects the way a person lives.

2. **Fathers Comfort Children in Their Faith.** Be available for your children when they face challenges to their faith.

3. **Fathers Urge Children to Grow in Their Faith.** Set rules and boundaries that will help establish the moral foundation children need to live a life pleasing to God.

Fathers may not be able to be with their children twenty-four hours a day, but they can help build conviction in their children's lives so that their children will make the right choices. This is one of the most important investments fathers will ever make.

to the Gentiles, for fear some might be saved. By
doing this, they continue to pile up their sins. But
the anger of God has caught up with them at last.

Timothy's Good Report about the Church

17Dear brothers and sisters, after we were separated from you for a little while (though our
hearts never left you), we tried very hard to come
back because of our intense longing to see you
again. 18We wanted very much to come, and I,
Paul, tried again and again, but Satan prevented
us. 19After all, what gives us hope and joy, and
what is our proud reward and crown? It is you!
Yes, you will bring us much joy as we stand
together before our Lord Jesus when he comes
back again. 20For you are our pride and joy.

CHAPTER 3

Finally, when we could stand it no longer, we
decided that I should stay alone in Athens, 2and
we sent Timothy to visit you. He is our co-worker
for God and our brother in proclaiming the
Good News of Christ. We sent him to strengthen
you, to encourage you in your faith, 3and to
keep you from becoming disturbed by the
troubles you were going through. But, of course,
you know that such troubles are going to happen to us Christians. 4Even while we were with
you, we warned you that troubles would soon
come—and they did, as you well know.

5That is why, when I could bear it no longer,
I sent Timothy to find out whether your faith
was still strong. I was afraid that the Tempter had
gotten the best of you and that all our work had
been useless. 6Now Timothy has just returned,
bringing the good news that your faith and love
are as strong as ever. He reports that you remember our visit with joy and that you want to see us
just as much as we want to see you. 7So we have
been greatly comforted, dear brothers and sisters,* in all of our own crushing troubles and
suffering, because you have remained strong in
your faith. 8It gives us new life, knowing you
remain strong in the Lord.

9How we thank God for you! Because of you
we have great joy in the presence of God. 10Night
and day we pray earnestly for you, asking God to
let us see you again to fill up anything that may
still be missing in your faith.

11May God himself, our Father, and our Lord
Jesus make it possible for us to come to you very
soon. 12And may the Lord make your love grow
and overflow to each other and to everyone else,

3:7 Greek *brothers.*

Act upon What God Has Already Revealed in Scripture

Read 1 THESSALONIANS 4:1-5

We often wonder what God's will may be for us concerning a particular situation. Yet Scripture reveals certain things that are clearly the will of God for every believer—without exception. Here are four things Scripture reveals as God's will:

1. God Wants Us to Live under the Control of the Holy Spirit. God doesn't want us to fill our life with cheap substitutes, like alcohol, possessions, or worldly pursuits. Instead, he wants us to seek to live under the control of the Holy Spirit (see Ephesians 5:18, p. 243), who produces such attributes as love, joy, peace, patience, kindness, goodness, faithfulness, gentleness, and self-control in our lives. To be controlled by anything or anyone else is outside the will of God.

2. God Wants Us to Live a Pure and Holy Life. It is the clear will of God that we as Christians live sexually pure lives (verses 4-5). The only sexual relationship God will bless is that of a man and woman committed to each other in marriage. Premarital and extramarital sexual relationships are never the will of God for the believer, under any circumstances.

3. God Wants Us to Have an Attitude of Gratitude. No matter what happens, God wants us to be thankful, recognizing that he is in control of all the circumstances that surround our life (see 1 Thessalonians 5:18, p. 264). He has promised to work all things together for good in the life of the Christian. We can rejoice that he has a purpose in mind for whatever we are going through.

4. God Wants Everyone to Come to Repentance. God makes it clear that he desires to see more people come into a relationship with him (see 2 Peter 3:9, p. 315). For that reason, you should take advantage of every opportunity you have to pray for or witness to someone who needs Christ.

Avoid Adulterous Relationships Read 1 THESSALONIANS 4:1-8

This passage gives some strong reasons as to why we should avoid sexual immorality at all costs. Beyond that, there are at least six more damaging consequences the sin of adultery causes:

1. Adultery Inflicts Incredible Pain on the Adulterer's Spouse. A married adulterer violates the oneness with his or her mate by entering into this bond with another person. This sin is so serious that Jesus said it could be grounds for divorce (see Matthew 19:9, p. 27). While a marriage can survive the pain of adultery with God's help, the level of trust will never be the same.

2. Adultery Does Irreparable Damage to the Adulterer. Though God will forgive the person who commits this sin, others will not forgive this person so quickly. This person's reputation will be tarnished, and Satan will undoubtedly riddle him or her with guilt.

3. Adultery Tremendously Hurts the Adulterer's Children. A person who commits this sin may never fully regain his or her children's trust. Worse yet, the adulterer's children may even follow in his or her footsteps and fall to that same sin later in life.

4. Believers Who Commit Adultery Give the Church a Bad Reputation. Scripture teaches that when one part of the body of Christ suffers, we all suffer (see 1 Corinthians 12:26, p. 211). All Christians are representatives of the church. And when a Christian's sin is exposed, that person has hurt the reputation of the church—especially if that person is in a position of leadership.

5. Adultery Hurts the Cause of Christ. Such behavior hurts a Christian's witness and damages his or her credibility.

CORNERSTONES

6. Adultery Is a Sin against the Lord. This should be the primary motive for living a pure life.

As Paul reminds us in this text, God has given us his *Holy* Spirit to live in us. The more his Spirit fills and controls our life, the less likely we will be to give in to the temptation of adultery.

just as our love overflows toward you. [13]As a result, Christ will make your hearts strong, blameless, and holy when you stand before God our Father on that day when our Lord Jesus comes with all those who belong to him.

CHAPTER 4

Live to Please God

Finally, dear brothers and sisters,* we urge you in the name of the Lord Jesus to live in a way that pleases God, as we have taught you. You are

4:1 Greek *brothers;* also in 4:10, 13.

OFF AND RUNNING

Strive to Be Responsible Read 1 THESSALONIANS 4:11-12

As a Christian, you should strive to be the best worker you can be. If you don't, then you disgrace the Lord you serve by doing less than quality work. However, if you work hard and lead a responsible life, you will have many more opportunities to share your faith, because people will respect you.

Consider Joseph of the Old Testament. Although he had been sold into slavery by his own brothers, he worked diligently in every position he held. And his hard work made a difference. The Bible

doing this already, and we encourage you to do so more and more. 2For you remember what we taught you in the name of the Lord Jesus. 3God wants you to be holy, so you should keep clear of all sexual sin. 4Then each of you will control your body* and live in holiness and honor— 5not in lustful passion as the pagans do, in their ignorance of God and his ways.

6Never cheat a Christian brother in this matter by taking his wife, for the Lord avenges all such sins, as we have solemnly warned you before. 7God has called us to be holy, not to live impure lives. 8Anyone who refuses to live by these rules is not disobeying human rules but is rejecting God, who gives his Holy Spirit to you.

9But I don't need to write to you about the Christian love* that should be shown among God's people. For God himself has taught you to love one another. 10Indeed, your love is already strong toward all the Christians* in all of Macedonia. Even so, dear brothers and sisters, we beg you to love them more and more. 11This should be your ambition: to live a quiet life, minding your own business and working with your hands, just as we commanded you before. 12As a result, people who are not Christians will respect the way you live, and you will not need to depend on others to meet your financial needs.

The Hope of the Resurrection

13And now, brothers and sisters, I want you to know what will happen to the Christians who have died so you will not be full of sorrow like people who have no hope. 14For since we believe that Jesus died and was raised to life again, we also believe that when Jesus comes, God will bring back with Jesus all the Christians who have died.

15I can tell you this directly from the Lord: We who are still living when the Lord returns will not rise to meet him ahead of those who are in their graves. 16For the Lord himself will come down from heaven with a commanding shout, with the call of the archangel, and with the trumpet call of God. First, all the Christians who have died will rise from their graves. 17Then, together with them, we who are still alive and remain on the earth will be caught up in the clouds to meet the Lord in the air and remain with him forever. 18So comfort and encourage each other with these words.

CHAPTER 5

I really don't need to write to you about how and when all this will happen, dear brothers and sisters.* 2For you know quite well that the day of the Lord will come unexpectedly, like a thief in the night. 3When people are saying, "All is well; everything is peaceful and secure," then disaster will fall upon them as suddenly as a woman's birth pains begin when her child is about to be born. And there will be no escape.

4But you aren't in the dark about these things, dear brothers and sisters, and you won't be surprised when the day of the Lord comes like a thief. 5For you are all children of the light and of the day; we don't belong to darkness and night. 6So be on your guard, not asleep like the others. Stay alert and be sober. 7Night is the time for sleep and the time when people get drunk. 8But let us who live in the light think clearly, protected by the body armor of faith and love, and wearing as our helmet the confidence of our salvation. 9For God decided to save us through our Lord Jesus Christ, not to pour out his anger on us. 10He died for us so that we can live with him forever, whether we are dead or alive at the time of his return. 11So encourage each other and build each other up, just as you are already doing.

Paul's Final Advice

12Dear brothers and sisters, honor those who are your leaders in the Lord's work. They work hard

4:4 Or *will know how to take a wife for himself;* Greek reads *will know how to possess his own vessel.* 4:9 Greek *brotherly love.* 4:10 Greek *the brothers.* 5:1 Greek *brothers;* also in 5:4, 12, 14, 25, 26, 27.

---

records, "The LORD was with Joseph and blessed him greatly as he served in the home of his Egyptian master. Potiphar noticed this and realized that the LORD was with Joseph, giving him success in everything he did" (Genesis 39:2-3).

You can't expect others to take your message seriously if they don't see that you are serious in what you do. Don't draw attention to yourself by your laziness. Instead, draw attention to the Lord by your diligence. Your faithful, responsible lifestyle will be your greatest sermon.

among you and warn you against all that is
wrong. 13Think highly of them and give them
your wholehearted love because of their work.
And remember to live peaceably with each
other.
14Brothers and sisters, we urge you to warn
those who are lazy. Encourage those who are
timid. Take tender care of those who are weak.
Be patient with everyone.
15See that no one pays back evil for evil, but
always try to do good to each other and to
everyone else.
16Always be joyful. 17Keep on praying. 18No
matter what happens, always be thankful, for
this is God's will for you who belong to Christ
Jesus.
19Do not stifle the Holy Spirit. 20Do not scoff
at prophecies, 21but test everything that is said.
Hold on to what is good. 22Keep away from
every kind of evil.

Paul's Final Greetings

23Now may the God of peace make you holy in
every way, and may your whole spirit and soul
and body be kept blameless until that day when
our Lord Jesus Christ comes again. 24God, who
calls you, is faithful; he will do this.
25Dear brothers and sisters, pray for us.
26Greet all the brothers and sisters in Christian love.*
27I command you in the name of the Lord to
read this letter to all the brothers and sisters.
28And may the grace of our Lord Jesus Christ
be with all of you.

5:26 Greek *with a holy kiss.*

OFF AND RUNNING

Think of Ways to Encourage, Praise, and Build Up Others Read 1 THESSALONIANS 5:11

Do the words you use truly benefit and leave a positive impression upon those to whom you speak? In this passage Paul stresses the importance of speaking wholesomely. Below are three insights from this passage that will help you make your conversations more meaningful:

1. Do Not Use Bad Language. As Christians, our speech should be positive and uplifting, not vulgar and crude. Such speech draws attention away from Christ and does nothing to encourage others.

2. Listen before You Speak. Don't just pretend to be interested—*really* listen. You won't know what would be helpful to say to an individual unless you understand his or her needs, questions, and hurts. James instructs us to be quick to listen and slow to speak (see James 1:19, p. 299).

3. Strive to Honor Christ in What You Say. The greatest way we can bless or encourage others with our conversation is to point them to our Savior. This verse has also been translated to say that we should use "words suitable for the occasion, which God can use to help other people." For instance, when someone begins talking about a hurt in his or her life, take that opportunity to somehow bring the hope that Jesus Christ gives you into that discussion.

Unfortunately, with our busy, hectic lives, the quality of our conversations with others often suffers. Our discussions seem to revolve around "surface" issues like the weather, sports events, the latest headline, or our workday. Yet, as Christians, we should go the "extra mile" to make our conversations more meaningful so that those who listen to us will be encouraged and refreshed by what we say. Those who follow Paul's advice will not only develop deeper friendships, but will also be effective witnesses for the Lord.

2 Thessalonians

CHAPTER 1

Greetings from Paul

This letter is from Paul, Silas,* and Timothy.

It is written to the church in Thessalonica, you who belong to God our Father and the Lord Jesus Christ.

2May God our Father and the Lord Jesus Christ give you grace and peace.

Encouragement during Persecution

3Dear brothers and sisters,* we always thank God for you, as is right, for we are thankful that your faith is flourishing and you are all growing in love for each other. 4We proudly tell God's other churches about your endurance and faithfulness in all the persecutions and hardships you are suffering. 5But God will use this persecution to show his justice. For he will make you worthy of his Kingdom, for which you are suffering, 6and in his justice he will punish those who persecute you. 7And God will provide rest for you who are being persecuted and also for us when the Lord Jesus appears from heaven. He will come with his mighty angels, 8in flaming fire, bringing judgment on those who don't know God and on those who refuse to obey the Good News of our Lord Jesus. 9They will be punished with everlasting destruction, forever separated from the Lord and from his glorious power 10when he comes to receive glory and praise from his holy people. And you will be among those praising him on that day, for you believed what we testified about him.

11And so we keep on praying for you, that our God will make you worthy of the life to which he called you. And we pray that God, by his power, will fulfill all your good intentions and faithful deeds. 12Then everyone will give honor to the name of our Lord Jesus because of you, and you will be honored along with him. This is all made possible because of the undeserved favor of our God and Lord, Jesus Christ.*

CHAPTER 2

Events prior to the Lord's Second Coming

And now, brothers and sisters,* let us tell you about the coming again of our Lord Jesus Christ and how we will be gathered together to meet him. 2Please don't be so easily shaken and troubled by those who say that the day of the Lord has already begun. Even if they claim to have had a vision, a revelation, or a letter supposedly from us, don't believe them. 3Don't be fooled by what they say.

For that day will not come until there is a great rebellion against God and the man of lawlessness is revealed—the one who brings destruction.* 4He will exalt himself and defy every god there is and tear down every object of adoration and worship. He will position himself in the temple of God, claiming that he himself is God. 5Don't you remember that I told you this when I was with you? 6And you know what is holding him back, for he can be revealed only when his time comes.

7For this lawlessness is already at work secretly, and it will remain secret until the one who is holding it back steps out of the way. 8Then the man of lawlessness will be revealed, whom the Lord Jesus will consume with the breath of his mouth and destroy by the splendor of his coming. 9This evil man will come to do the work of Satan with counterfeit power and signs and miracles. 10He will use every kind of wicked

1:1 Greek *Silvanus.* 1:3 Greek *brothers.* 1:12 Or *of our God and the Lord Jesus Christ.* 2:1 Greek *brothers;* also in 2:13, 15. 2:3 Greek *the son of destruction.*

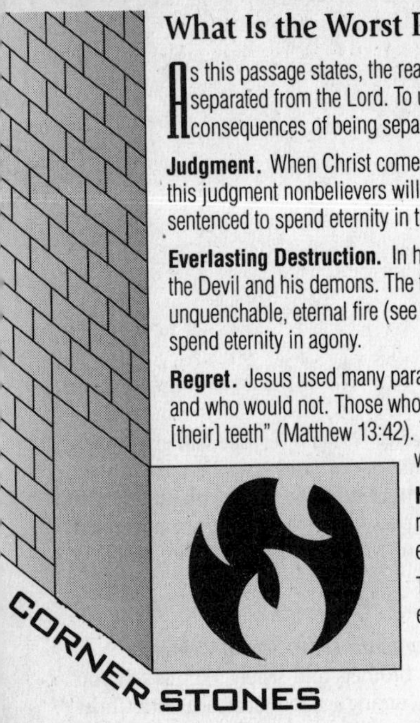

What Is the Worst Punishment of Hell? Read 2 THESSALONIANS 1:7-10

As this passage states, the real agony of those who go to hell is that they will be eternally separated from the Lord. To understand how terrible a punishment this is, examine the consequences of being separated from God's presence:

Judgment. When Christ comes back, nonbelievers will face a judgment that believers will not. At this judgment nonbelievers will have their deeds revealed before everyone and then will be sentenced to spend eternity in the lake of fire (see Revelation 20:11-15, p. 347).

Everlasting Destruction. In hell, nonbelievers will be doomed to exist in unending torment with the Devil and his demons. The torment that they will endure is described by Jesus as an unquenchable, eternal fire (see Matthew 18:8, p. 26, and Matthew 25:41, p. 36). Nonbelievers will spend eternity in agony.

Regret. Jesus used many parables to describe the Kingdom of Heaven—who would get into it, and who would not. Those who don't get into the Kingdom are pictured as "weeping and gnashing [their] teeth" (Matthew 13:42). Their response—weeping and gnashing of teeth—is one of regret when they realize what they will be missing out on for eternity.

Hopelessness. Because their punishment is everlasting, nonbelievers have no hope of their condition ever improving. Their existence is not only one of agony, but of despair.

Those who know Christ have much to gain. Those who do not, have everything to lose.

deception to fool those who are on their way to
destruction because they refuse to believe the
truth that would save them. 11So God will send
great deception upon them, and they will believe all these lies. 12Then they will be condemned for not believing the truth and for
enjoying the evil they do.

Believers Should Stand Firm

13As for us, we always thank God for you, dear
brothers and sisters loved by the Lord. We are
thankful that God chose you to be among the
first* to experience salvation, a salvation that
came through the Spirit who makes you holy and
by your belief in the truth. 14He called you to
salvation when we told you the Good News; now
you can share in the glory of our Lord Jesus Christ.

15With all these things in mind, dear brothers
and sisters, stand firm and keep a strong grip on
everything we taught you both in person and by
letter.

16May our Lord Jesus Christ and God our
Father, who loved us and in his special favor
gave us everlasting comfort and good hope,
17comfort your hearts and give you strength in
every good thing you do and say.

CHAPTER 3

Paul's Request for Prayer

Finally, dear brothers and sisters,* I ask you to
pray for us. Pray first that the Lord's message will
spread rapidly and be honored wherever it goes,
just as when it came to you. 2Pray, too, that we
will be saved from wicked and evil people, for
not everyone believes in the Lord. 3But the Lord
is faithful; he will make you strong and guard
you from the evil one.* 4And we are confident
in the Lord that you are practicing the things we
commanded you, and that you always will.
5May the Lord bring you into an ever deeper
understanding of the love of God and the endurance that comes from Christ.

An Exhortation to Proper Living

6And now, dear brothers and sisters, we give
you this command with the authority of our
Lord Jesus Christ: Stay away from any Christian* who lives in idleness and doesn't follow

2:13 Some manuscripts read *God chose you from the very beginning.* 3:1 Greek *brothers;* also in 3:6, 13. 3:3 Or *from evil.* 3:6 Greek *brother;* also in 3:15.

the tradition of hard work we gave you. 7For
you know that you ought to follow our example. We were never lazy when we were with
you. 8We never accepted food from anyone
without paying for it. We worked hard day and
night so that we would not be a burden to any
of you. 9It wasn't that we didn't have the right
to ask you to feed us, but we wanted to give
you an example to follow. 10Even while we
were with you, we gave you this rule: "Whoever does not work should not eat."

11Yet we hear that some of you are living idle
lives, refusing to work and wasting time med-
dling in other people's business. 12In the name
of the Lord Jesus Christ, we appeal to such
people—no, we command them: Settle down
and get to work. Earn your own living. 13And I
say to the rest of you, dear brothers and sisters,
never get tired of doing good.

14Take note of those who refuse to obey what
we say in this letter. Stay away from them so they
will be ashamed. 15Don't think of them as enemies, but speak to them as you would to a
Christian who needs to be warned.

Paul's Final Greetings

16May the Lord of peace himself always give you
his peace no matter what happens. The Lord be
with you all.

17Now here is my greeting, which I write with
my own hand—PAUL. I do this at the end of all
my letters to prove that they really are from me.

18May the grace of our Lord Jesus Christ be
with you all.

I Timothy

CHAPTER 1

Greetings from Paul

This letter is from Paul, an apostle of Christ Jesus, appointed by the command of God our Savior and by Christ Jesus our hope.

2It is written to Timothy, my true child in the faith.

May God our Father and Christ Jesus our Lord give you grace, mercy, and peace.

Warnings against False Teachings

3When I left for Macedonia, I urged you to stay there in Ephesus and stop those who are teaching wrong doctrine. 4Don't let people waste time in endless speculation over myths and spiritual pedigrees.* For these things only cause arguments; they don't help people live a life of faith in God.* 5The purpose of my instruction is that all the Christians there would be filled with love that comes from a pure heart, a clear conscience, and sincere faith.

6But some teachers have missed this whole point. They have turned away from these things and spend their time arguing and talking foolishness. 7They want to be known as teachers of the law of Moses, but they don't know what they are talking about, even though they seem so confident. 8We know these laws are good when they are used as God intended. 9But they were not made for people who do what is right. They are for people who are disobedient and rebellious, who are ungodly and sinful, who consider nothing sacred and defile what is holy, who murder their father or mother or other people. 10These laws are for people who are sexually immoral, for homosexuals and slave traders, for liars and oath breakers, and for those who do anything else that contradicts the right teaching 11that comes from the glorious Good News entrusted to me by our blessed God.

Paul's Gratitude for God's Mercy

12How thankful I am to Christ Jesus our Lord for considering me trustworthy and appointing me to serve him, 13even though I used to scoff at the name of Christ. I hunted down his people, harming them in every way I could. But God had mercy on me because I did it in ignorance and unbelief. 14Oh, how kind and gracious the Lord was! He filled me completely with faith and the love of Christ Jesus.

15This is a true saying, and everyone should believe it: Christ Jesus came into the world to save sinners—and I was the worst of them all. 16But that is why God had mercy on me, so that Christ Jesus could use me as a prime example of his great patience with even the worst sinners. Then others will realize that they, too, can believe in him and receive eternal life. 17Glory and honor to God forever and ever. He is the eternal King, the unseen one who never dies; he alone is God. Amen.

Timothy's Responsibility

18Timothy, my son, here are my instructions for you, based on the prophetic words spoken about you earlier. May they give you the confidence to fight well in the Lord's battles. 19Cling tightly to your faith in Christ, and always keep your conscience clear. For some people have deliberately violated their consciences; as a result, their faith has been shipwrecked. 20Hymenaeus and Alexander are two examples of this. I turned them over to Satan so they would learn not to blaspheme God.

1:4a Greek *in myths and endless genealogies, which cause speculation.* **1:4b** Greek *a stewardship of God in faith.*

Recognize Satan's Strategies Read 1 TIMOTHY 4:1-2

We must be on our guard against Satan's clever counterfeits, because, as this passage tells us, he will be at work in the last days (which we are in). In fact, we are warned that some in the church will fall prey to these aberrant ideas and teachings. Therefore, as you listen to various teachers and pastors today, remember this:

- Any so-called gospel that distorts the message of Jesus as found in the Bible by adding to it or taking away from it . . .
- Any so-called gospel that offers Christianity without Christ or the Cross . . .
- Any so-called gospel that promises forgiveness without repentance . . .
- Any so-called gospel that presents the hope of heaven without the reality of hell . . .

. . . is not the gospel, but a "watered-down" version that will give you a false assurance. Such teachings are extremely hazardous to your spiritual health. Stay away from them at all costs.

CORNERSTONES

CHAPTER 2
Instructions about Worship

I urge you, first of all, to pray for all people. As you make your requests, plead for God's mercy upon them, and give thanks. [2]Pray this way for kings and all others who are in authority, so that we can live in peace and quietness, in godliness and dignity. [3]This is good and pleases God our Savior, [4]for he wants everyone to be saved and to understand the truth. [5]For there is only one God and one Mediator who can reconcile God and people. He is the man Christ Jesus. [6]He gave his life to purchase freedom for everyone. This is the message that God gave to the world at the proper time. [7]And I have been chosen—this is the absolute truth—as a preacher and apostle to teach the Gentiles about faith and truth.

[8]So wherever you assemble, I want men to pray with holy hands lifted up to God, free from anger and controversy. [9]And I want women to be modest in their appearance. They should wear decent and appropriate clothing and not draw attention to themselves by the way they fix their hair or by wearing gold or pearls or expensive clothes. [10]For women who claim to be devoted to God should make themselves attractive by the good things they do.

[11]Women should listen and learn quietly and submissively. [12]I do not let women teach men or have authority over them. Let them listen quietly. [13]For God made Adam first, and afterward he made Eve. [14]And it was the woman, not Adam, who was deceived by Satan, and sin was the result. [15]But women will be saved through childbearing* and by continuing to live in faith, love, holiness, and modesty.

CHAPTER 3
Leaders in the Church

It is a true saying that if someone wants to be an elder,* he desires an honorable responsibility. [2]For an elder must be a man whose life cannot be spoken against. He must be faithful to his wife.* He must exhibit self-control, live wisely, and have a good reputation. He must enjoy having guests in his home and must be able to teach. [3]He must not be a heavy drinker or be violent. He must be gentle, peace loving, and not one who loves money. [4]He must manage his own family well, with children who respect and obey him. [5]For if a man cannot manage his own household, how can he take care of God's church?

[6]An elder must not be a new Christian, because he might be proud of being chosen so soon, and the Devil will use that pride to make him fall.* [7]Also, people outside the church must speak well of him so that he will not fall into the Devil's trap and be disgraced.

[8]In the same way, deacons must be people who are respected and have integrity. They must

2:15 Or *will be saved by accepting their role as mothers,* or *will be saved by the birth of the Child.* 3:1 Greek *overseer;* also in 3:2. 3:2 Greek *be the husband of one wife;* also in 3:12. 3:6 Or *he might fall into the same judgment as the Devil.*

not be heavy drinkers and must not be greedy for money. 9They must be committed to the revealed truths of the Christian faith and must live with a clear conscience. 10Before they are appointed as deacons, they should be given other responsibilities in the church as a test of their character and ability. If they do well, then they may serve as deacons.

11In the same way, their wives* must be respected and must not speak evil of others. They must exercise self-control and be faithful in everything they do.

12A deacon must be faithful to his wife, and he must manage his children and household well. 13Those who do well as deacons will be rewarded with respect from others and will have increased confidence in their faith in Christ Jesus.

The Truths of Our Faith

14I am writing these things to you now, even though I hope to be with you soon, 15so that if I can't come for a while, you will know how people must conduct themselves in the household of God. This is the church of the living God, which is the pillar and support of the truth.

16Without question, this is the great mystery of our faith:

Christ* appeared in the flesh
  and was shown to be righteous by the Spirit.*
He was seen by angels
  and was announced to the nations.
He was believed on in the world
  and was taken up into heaven.*

CHAPTER 4

Warnings against False Teachers

Now the Holy Spirit tells us clearly that in the last times some will turn away from what we believe; they will follow lying spirits and teachings that come from demons. 2These teachers are hypocrites and liars. They pretend to be religious, but their consciences are dead.*

3They will say it is wrong to be married and wrong to eat certain foods. But God created those foods to be eaten with thanksgiving by people who know and believe the truth. 4Since everything God created is good, we should not reject any of it. We may receive it gladly, with thankful hearts. 5For we know it is made holy by the word of God and prayer.

A Good Servant of Christ Jesus

6If you explain this to the brothers and sisters,* you will be doing your duty as a worthy servant of Christ Jesus, one who is fed by the message of faith and the true teaching you have followed. 7Do not waste time arguing over godless ideas and old

3:11 Or *the women deacons.* The Greek word can be translated *women or wives.* 3:16a Greek *Who;* some manuscripts read *God.* 3:16b Or *in his spirit.* 3:16c Greek *in glory.* 4:2 Greek *are seared.* 4:6 Greek *brothers.*

Can You Enjoy Wealth?

Read 1 TIMOTHY 6:17-19

The Lord can and may bless you with riches. They may not necessarily be the material kind. As verse 6 of this chapter says, "true religion with contentment is great wealth." Still, if God does bless you with material riches, he requires three things of you:

1. Do Not Be Arrogant or Put Your Ultimate Hope in Your Wealth. As verse 10 of this chapter says, "For the love of money is at the root of all kinds of evil. And some people, craving money, have wandered from the faith and pierced themselves with many sorrows." Wealth is not sinful. Wealth is not godly. It all depends on the heart of the wealthy person. There are godly people who are wealthy, and there are ungodly people who are poor—as well as vice versa. The question you must always ask yourself is, "Do I possess my possessions, or do my possessions possess me?"

2. Enjoy What God Has Given You. If God blesses you materially, don't feel guilty about it. Be thankful, realizing that he wants you to enjoy what you have.

3. Be Generous, Do Good, and Share Your Wealth with Others. With wealth comes responsibility. Recognize that you are a steward of what God has given you, and invest what you have in his work.

If you follow these three principles, they will help you be content with whatever you have. When you give God total control of this area of your life, you will never be controlled by your wealth—or by the wealth you wish you had.

wives' tales. Spend your time and energy in training yourself for spiritual fitness. 8Physical exercise
has some value, but spiritual exercise is much
more important, for it promises a reward in both
this life and the next. 9This is true, and everyone
should accept it. 10We work hard and suffer
much* in order that people will believe the truth,
for our hope is in the living God, who is the Savior
of all people, and particularly of those who believe.

11Teach these things and insist that everyone
learn them. 12Don't let anyone think less of you
because you are young. Be an example to all
believers in what you teach, in the way you live,
in your love, your faith, and your purity. 13Until
I get there, focus on reading the Scriptures to the
church, encouraging the believers, and teaching
them.

14Do not neglect the spiritual gift you received through the prophecies spoken to you
when the elders of the church laid their hands
on you. 15Give your complete attention to these
matters. Throw yourself into your tasks so that
everyone will see your progress. 16Keep a close
watch on yourself and on your teaching. Stay
true to what is right, and God will save you and
those who hear you.

CHAPTER 5

Never speak harshly to an older man,* but appeal to him respectfully as though he were your
own father. Talk to the younger men as you
would to your own brothers. 2Treat the older
women as you would your mother, and treat the
younger women with all purity as your own
sisters.

Advice about Widows, Elders, and Slaves

3The church should care for any widow who has
no one else to care for her. 4But if she has
children or grandchildren, their first responsibility is to show godliness at home and repay their
parents by taking care of them. This is something that pleases God very much.

5But a woman who is a true widow, one who
is truly alone in this world, has placed her hope
in God. Night and day she asks God for help and
spends much time in prayer. 6But the widow
who lives only for pleasure is spiritually dead.
7Give these instructions to the church so that the
widows you support* will not be criticized.

8But those who won't care for their own relatives, especially those living in the same household, have denied what we believe. Such people
are worse than unbelievers.

9A widow who is put on the list for support
must be a woman who is at least sixty years old
and was faithful to her husband.* 10She must be
well respected by everyone because of the good
she has done. Has she brought up her children
well? Has she been kind to strangers? Has she
served other Christians humbly?* Has she
helped those who are in trouble? Has she always
been ready to do good?

11The younger widows should not be on the
list, because their physical desires will overpower their devotion to Christ and they will
want to remarry. 12Then they would be guilty of
breaking their previous pledge. 13Besides, they
are likely to become lazy and spend their time
gossiping from house to house, getting into
other people's business and saying things they
shouldn't. 14So I advise these younger widows
to marry again, have children, and take care of
their own homes. Then the enemy will not be
able to say anything against them. 15For I am
afraid that some of them have already gone
astray and now follow Satan.

16If a Christian woman has relatives who are
widows, she must take care of them and not put
the responsibility on the church. Then the
church can care for widows who are truly alone.

17Elders who do their work well should be
paid well,* especially those who work hard at
both preaching and teaching. 18For the Scripture
says, "Do not keep an ox from eating as it treads
out the grain." And in another place, "Those
who work deserve their pay!"*

19Do not listen to complaints against an elder
unless there are two or three witnesses to accuse
him. 20Anyone who sins should be rebuked in
front of the whole church so that others will
have a proper fear of God.

21I solemnly command you in the presence of
God and Christ Jesus and the holy angels to
obey these instructions without taking sides or
showing special favor to anyone. 22Never be in a
hurry about appointing an elder. Do not participate in the sins of others. Keep yourself pure.

23Don't drink only water. You ought to drink
a little wine for the sake of your stomach because you are sick so often.

24Remember that some people lead sinful
lives, and everyone knows they will be judged.
But there are others whose sin will not be re-

4:10 Some manuscripts read *and strive.* 5:1 Or *an elder.* 5:7 Or *so the church;* Greek reads *so they.* 5:9 Greek *was the wife of one man.*
5:10 Greek *Has she washed the feet of saints?* 5:17 Greek *should be worthy of double honor.* 5:18 Deut 25:4; Luke 10:7.

vealed until later. [25]In the same way, everyone
knows how much good some people do, but
there are others whose good deeds won't be
known until later.

CHAPTER 6

Christians who are slaves should give their masters full respect so that the name of God and his
teaching will not be shamed. [2]If your master is a
Christian, that is no excuse for being disrespect-
ful. You should work all the harder because you
are helping another believer* by your efforts.

False Teaching and True Riches

Teach these truths, Timothy, and encourage
everyone to obey them. [3]Some false teachers
may deny these things, but these are the sound,
wholesome teachings of the Lord Jesus Christ,
and they are the foundation for a godly life.
[4]Anyone who teaches anything different is both
conceited and ignorant. Such a person has an
unhealthy desire to quibble over the meaning of
words. This stirs up arguments ending in jealousy, fighting, slander, and evil suspicions.
[5]These people always cause trouble. Their minds
are corrupt, and they don't tell the truth. To
them religion is just a way to get rich.

[6]Yet true religion with contentment is great
wealth. [7]After all, we didn't bring anything with
us when we came into the world, and we certainly cannot carry anything with us when we
die. [8]So if we have enough food and clothing, let
us be content. [9]But people who long to be rich
fall into temptation and are trapped by many
foolish and harmful desires that plunge them
into ruin and destruction. [10]For the love of
money is at the root of all kinds of evil. And
some people, craving money, have wandered
from the faith and pierced themselves with
many sorrows.

6:2 Greek *a brother.*

Paul's Final Instructions

[11]But you, Timothy, belong to God; so run from
all these evil things, and follow what is right and
good. Pursue a godly life, along with faith, love,
perseverance, and gentleness. [12]Fight the good
fight for what we believe. Hold tightly to the
eternal life that God has given you, which you
have confessed so well before many witnesses.
[13]And I command you before God, who gives
life to all, and before Christ Jesus, who gave a
good testimony before Pontius Pilate, [14]that you
obey his commands with all purity. Then no one
can find fault with you from now until our Lord
Jesus Christ returns. [15]For at the right time Christ
will be revealed from heaven by the blessed and
only almighty God, the King of kings and Lord
of lords. [16]He alone can never die, and he lives
in light so brilliant that no human can approach
him. No one has ever seen him, nor ever will. To
him be honor and power forever. Amen.

[17]Tell those who are rich in this world not to
be proud and not to trust in their money, which
will soon be gone. But their trust should be in
the living God, who richly gives us all we need
for our enjoyment. [18]Tell them to use their
money to do good. They should be rich in good
works and should give generously to those in
need, always being ready to share with others
whatever God has given them. [19]By doing this
they will be storing up their treasure as a good
foundation for the future so that they may take
hold of real life.

[20]Timothy, guard what God has entrusted to
you. Avoid godless, foolish discussions with
those who oppose you with their so-called
knowledge. [21]Some people have wandered from
the faith by following such foolishness.

May God's grace be with you all.

2 Timothy

CHAPTER 1

Greetings from Paul

This letter is from Paul, an apostle of Christ Jesus by God's will, sent out to tell others about the life he has promised through faith in Christ Jesus.

2It is written to Timothy, my dear son.

May God our Father and Christ Jesus our Lord give you grace, mercy, and peace.

Encouragement to Be Faithful

3Timothy, I thank God for you. He is the God I serve with a clear conscience, just as my ancestors did. Night and day I constantly remember you in my prayers. 4I long to see you again, for I remember your tears as we parted. And I will be filled with joy when we are together again.

5I know that you sincerely trust the Lord, for you have the faith of your mother, Eunice, and your grandmother, Lois. 6This is why I remind you to fan into flames the spiritual gift God gave you when I laid my hands on you. 7For God has not given us a spirit of fear and timidity, but of power, love, and self-discipline. 8So you must never be ashamed to tell others about our Lord. And don't be ashamed of me, either, even though I'm in prison for Christ. With the strength God gives you, be ready to suffer with me for the proclamation of the Good News.

9It is God who saved us and chose us to live a holy life. He did this not because we deserved it, but because that was his plan long before the world began—to show his love and kindness to us through Christ Jesus. 10And now he has made all of this plain to us by the coming of Christ Jesus, our Savior, who broke the power of death and showed us the way to everlasting life through the Good News. 11And God chose me to be a preacher, an apostle, and a teacher of this Good News.

12And that is why I am suffering here in prison. But I am not ashamed of it, for I know the one in whom I trust, and I am sure that he is able to guard what I have entrusted to him* until the day of his return.

13Hold on to the pattern of right teaching you learned from me. And remember to live in the faith and love that you have in Christ Jesus. 14With the help of the Holy Spirit who lives within us, carefully guard what has been entrusted to you.

15As you know, all the Christians who came here from the province of Asia have deserted me; even Phygelus and Hermogenes are gone. 16May the Lord show special kindness to Onesiphorus and all his family because he often visited and encouraged me. He was never ashamed of me because I was in prison. 17When he came to Rome, he searched everywhere until he found me. 18May the Lord show him special kindness on the day of Christ's return. And you know how much he helped me at Ephesus.

CHAPTER 2

A Good Soldier of Christ Jesus

Timothy, my dear son, be strong with the special favor God gives you in Christ Jesus. 2You have heard me teach many things that have been confirmed by many reliable witnesses. Teach these great truths to trustworthy people who are able to pass them on to others.

3Endure suffering along with me, as a good soldier of Christ Jesus. 4And as Christ's soldier, do not let yourself become tied up in the affairs of this life, for then you cannot satisfy the one

1:12 Or *what has been entrusted to me.*

Guard the Content of Your Thoughts Read 2 TIMOTHY 2:22

In Paul's second letter to Timothy, he gave Timothy helpful advice on how to live a pure life. This advice included (1) recognizing his potential to sin; (2) avoiding influences that could inspire youthful lust; (3) pursuing faith, love, and peace; and (4) spending time with other believers whose hearts are pure.

One of the more difficult challenges of living a pure life is guarding the content of our thoughts. It has been said, "You can't stop a bird from flying over your head, but you can stop it from building a nest in your hair." In the same way, we cannot stop an impure or wicked thought from "knocking" on the door of our imagination, but we certainly can keep that door closed and locked. If we don't, and we allow tempting thoughts to infiltrate our mind, we may fall, allowing our old nature to prevail.

The good news is that even though each one of us is still capable of falling, we don't have to. If we stay close to the Lord and follow Paul's advice in this verse, we will be building a strong "fortress" around our life—including our thoughts—and it will be harder for Satan's arrows of temptation to get through.

who has enlisted you in his army. 5Follow the
Lord's rules for doing his work, just as an athlete
either follows the rules or is disqualified and
wins no prize. 6Hardworking farmers are the
first to enjoy the fruit of their labor. 7Think
about what I am saying. The Lord will give you
understanding in all these things.

8Never forget that Jesus Christ was a man
born into King David's family and that he was
raised from the dead. This is the Good News I
preach. 9And because I preach this Good News,
I am suffering and have been chained like a
criminal. But the word of God cannot be
chained. 10I am willing to endure anything if it
will bring salvation and eternal glory in Christ
Jesus to those God has chosen.

11This is a true saying:

If we die with him,
  we will also live with him.
12 If we endure hardship,
  we will reign with him.
If we deny him,
  he will deny us.
13 If we are unfaithful,
  he remains faithful,
  for he cannot deny himself.

An Approved Worker

14Remind everyone of these things, and command them in God's name to stop fighting over
words. Such arguments are useless, and they can
ruin those who hear them. 15Work hard so God
can approve you. Be a good worker, one who
does not need to be ashamed and who correctly
explains the word of truth. 16Avoid godless,
foolish discussions that lead to more and more
ungodliness. 17This kind of talk spreads like
cancer. Hymenaeus and Philetus are examples
of this. 18They have left the path of truth,
preaching the lie that the resurrection of the
dead has already occurred; and they have under-
mined the faith of some.

19But God's truth stands firm like a foundation stone with this inscription: "The Lord
knows those who are his,"* and "Those who
claim they belong to the Lord must turn away
from all wickedness."*

20In a wealthy home some utensils are made
of gold and silver, and some are made of wood
and clay. The expensive utensils are used for
special occasions, and the cheap ones are for
everyday use. 21If you keep yourself pure, you
will be a utensil God can use for his purpose.
Your life will be clean, and you will be ready for
the Master to use you for every good work.

22Run from anything that stimulates youthful
lust. Follow anything that makes you want to do
right. Pursue faith and love and peace, and enjoy
the companionship of those who call on the
Lord with pure hearts.

23Again I say, don't get involved in foolish,

2:19a Num 16:5. 2:19b See Isa 52:11.

ignorant arguments that only start fights.
24The Lord's servants must not quarrel but
must be kind to everyone. They must be able
to teach effectively and be patient with difficult people. 25They should gently teach those
who oppose the truth. Perhaps God will
change those people's hearts, and they will
believe the truth. 26Then they will come to
their senses and escape from the Devil's trap.
For they have been held captive by him to do
whatever he wants.

CHAPTER 3

The Dangers of the Last Days

You should also know this, Timothy, that in the
last days there will be very difficult times. 2For
people will love only themselves and their
money. They will be boastful and proud, scoff-
ing at God, disobedient to their parents, and
ungrateful. They will consider nothing sacred.
3They will be unloving and unforgiving; they
will slander others and have no self-control; they
will be cruel and have no interest in what is
good. 4They will betray their friends, be reckless,
be puffed up with pride, and love pleasure rather
than God. 5They will act as if they are religious,
but they will reject the power that could make
them godly. You must stay away from people
like that.

6They are the kind who work their way into
people's homes and win the confidence of* vulnerable women who are burdened with the guilt
of sin and controlled by many desires. 7Such
women are forever following new teachings, but
they never understand the truth. 8And these
teachers fight the truth just as Jannes and Jambres fought against Moses. Their minds are de-
praved, and their faith is counterfeit. 9But they
won't get away with this for long. Someday
everyone will recognize what fools they are, just
as happened with Jannes and Jambres.

Paul's Charge to Timothy

10But you know what I teach, Timothy, and how I
live, and what my purpose in life is. You know my
faith and how long I have suffered. You know my
love and my patient endurance. 11You know how
much persecution and suffering I have endured.
You know all about how I was persecuted in Antioch, Iconium, and Lystra—but the Lord delivered
me from all of it. 12Yes, and everyone who wants
to live a godly life in Christ Jesus will suffer persecution. 13But evil people and impostors will flourish. They will go on deceiving others, and they
themselves will be deceived.

14But you must remain faithful to the things
you have been taught. You know they are true,
for you know you can trust those who taught
you. 15You have been taught the holy Scriptures
from childhood, and they have given you the
wisdom to receive the salvation that comes by
trusting in Christ Jesus. 16All Scripture is inspired by God and is useful to teach us what is
true and to make us realize what is wrong in our
lives. It straightens us out and teaches us to do

3:6 Greek *and take captive.*

Studying the Bible Is Necessary for Our Spiritual Growth Read 2 TIMOTHY 3:16-17

The primary reason we should study the Bible is because it was inspired by the Creator of the universe to guide us through this adventure called life. This passage of Scripture gives us three more reasons why we should make the Bible part of our day-to-day life:

1. The Bible Teaches Us What Is True. The Bible is the only book we need to discover the foundational truths of how to know and walk with God. Some aberrant religious groups or cults insist we need another book to help us interpret what the Bible says. But the Bible needs no outside interpretation. It speaks for itself. In fact, the best commentary on the Bible is the Bible.

2. The Bible Shows Us What Is Wrong in Our Lives. God's Word serves to reprove us or to make us aware when we are headed in the wrong direction.

3. The Bible Helps Us Do What Is Right. If we read and meditate on God's Word, we will be molded into the man or woman God wants us to be.

When we allow the Bible to teach us in these three areas, we are told that we will be prepared and equipped to do good to everyone (see 2 Timothy 3:14-16). Our foundation will be solid, our motives pure, and our character more refined. What better reasons are there to make a commitment to stick with Bible study!

what is right. 17 It is God's way of preparing us in
every way, fully equipped for every good thing
God wants us to do.

CHAPTER 4

And so I solemnly urge you before God and
before Christ Jesus—who will someday judge
the living and the dead when he appears to set
up his Kingdom: 2 Preach the word of God. Be
persistent, whether the time is favorable or not.
Patiently correct, rebuke, and encourage your
people with good teaching.

3 For a time is coming when people will no
longer listen to right teaching. They will follow
their own desires and will look for teachers who
will tell them whatever they want to hear. 4 They
will reject the truth and follow strange myths.

5 But you should keep a clear mind in every
situation. Don't be afraid of suffering for the
Lord. Work at bringing others to Christ. Complete the ministry God has given you.

Paul's Final Words

6 As for me, my life has already been poured out
as an offering to God. The time of my death is
near. 7 I have fought a good fight, I have finished
the race, and I have remained faithful. 8 And now
the prize awaits me—the crown of righteousness that the Lord, the righteous Judge, will give
me on that great day of his return. And the prize
is not just for me but for all who eagerly look
forward to his glorious return.

9 Please come as soon as you can. 10 Demas
has deserted me because he loves the things of
this life and has gone to Thessalonica. Crescens
has gone to Galatia, and Titus has gone to Dal-
matia. 11 Only Luke is with me. Bring Mark with
you when you come, for he will be helpful to
me. 12 I sent Tychicus to Ephesus. 13 When you
come, be sure to bring the coat I left with Carpus
at Troas. Also bring my books, and especially my
papers.*

14 Alexander the coppersmith has done me
much harm, but the Lord will judge him for
what he has done. 15 Be careful of him, for he
fought against everything we said.

16 The first time I was brought before the
judge, no one was with me. Everyone had abandoned me. I hope it will not be counted against
them. 17 But the Lord stood with me and gave me
strength, that I might preach the Good News in
all its fullness for all the Gentiles to hear. And he
saved me from certain death.* 18 Yes, and the
Lord will deliver me from every evil attack and
will bring me safely to his heavenly Kingdom. To
God be the glory forever and ever. Amen.

Paul's Final Greetings

19 Give my greetings to Priscilla and Aquila and
those living at the household of Onesiphorus.
20 Erastus stayed at Corinth, and I left Trophimus
sick at Miletus.

21 Hurry so you can get here before winter.
Eubulus sends you greetings, and so do Pudens,
Linus, Claudia, and all the brothers and sisters.*

22 May the Lord be with your spirit. Grace be
with you all.

4:13 Greek *especially the parchments.* 4:17 Greek *from the mouth of a lion.* 4:21 Greek *brothers.*

Titus

CHAPTER 1

Greetings from Paul

This letter is from Paul, a slave of God and an
apostle of Jesus Christ. I have been sent to bring
faith to those God has chosen and to teach them
to know the truth that shows them how to live
godly lives. 2This truth gives them the confidence of eternal life, which God promised them
before the world began—and he cannot lie.
3And now at the right time he has revealed this
Good News, and we announce it to everyone. It
is by the command of God our Savior that I have
been trusted to do this work for him.

4This letter is written to Titus, my true child
in the faith that we share.

May God the Father and Christ Jesus our
Savior give you grace and peace.

Titus's Work in Crete

5I left you on the island of Crete so you could
complete our work there and appoint elders in
each town as I instructed you. 6An elder must be
well thought of for his good life. He must be
faithful to his wife,* and his children must be
believers who are not wild or rebellious. 7An
elder* must live a blameless life because he is
God's minister. He must not be arrogant or
quick-tempered; he must not be a heavy drinker,
violent, or greedy for money. 8He must enjoy
having guests in his home and must love all that
is good. He must live wisely and be fair. He must
live a devout and disciplined life. 9He must have
a strong and steadfast belief in the trustworthy
message he was taught; then he will be able to
encourage others with right teaching and show
those who oppose it where they are wrong.

10For there are many who rebel against right
teaching; they engage in useless talk and deceive
people. This is especially true of those who insist
on circumcision for salvation. 11They must be
silenced. By their wrong teaching, they have already turned whole families away from the truth.
Such teachers only want your money. 12One of
their own men, a prophet from Crete, has said
about them, "The people of Crete are all liars;
they are cruel animals and lazy gluttons." 13This
is true. So rebuke them as sternly as necessary to
make them strong in the faith. 14They must stop
listening to Jewish myths and the commands of
people who have turned their backs on the truth.

15Everything is pure to those whose hearts are
pure. But nothing is pure to those who are corrupt and unbelieving, because their minds and
consciences are defiled. 16Such people claim
they know God, but they deny him by the way
they live. They are despicable and disobedient,
worthless for doing anything good.

CHAPTER 2

Promote Right Teaching

But as for you, promote the kind of living that
reflects right teaching. 2Teach the older men to
exercise self-control, to be worthy of respect, and
to live wisely. They must have strong faith and
be filled with love and patience.

3Similarly, teach the older women to live in a
way that is appropriate for someone serving the
Lord. They must not go around speaking evil of
others and must not be heavy drinkers. Instead,
they should teach others what is good. 4These
older women must train the younger women to
love their husbands and their children, 5to live
wisely and be pure, to take care of their homes,
to do good, and to be submissive to their husbands. Then they will not bring shame on the
word of God.

1:6 Or *have only one wife,* or *be married only once;* Greek reads *be the husband of one wife.* 1:7 Greek *overseer.*

We Need to Set an Example for Others Read TITUS 2:6-8

This passage gives some practical reasons and ways to live out your faith. Though these words were written to Titus, a leader in the early church, they apply to anyone whose life influences the lives of others. That is, the passage speaks to all of us! Take a moment to ponder these simple, yet useful, thoughts:

How Should We Behave?

- We need to be self-controlled and serious about life.
- We should do good deeds often as an example to others.
- We should love the truth.
- We should be earnest and serious in our pursuit of truth.
- We should think before we speak, making sure that our conversation is sound and sensible.

Why Should We Live Godly Lives?

- We represent God, who is holy.
- We are an example to others, particularly young people and new believers.
- Our behavior will silence our critics.

CORNER STONES

6In the same way, encourage the young men
to live wisely in all they do. 7And you yourself
must be an example to them by doing good
deeds of every kind. Let everything you do reflect
the integrity and seriousness of your teaching.
8Let your teaching be so correct that it can't be
criticized. Then those who want to argue will be
ashamed because they won't have anything bad
to say about us.
9Slaves must obey their masters and do their
best to please them. They must not talk back 10or
steal, but they must show themselves to be entirely trustworthy and good. Then they will
make the teaching about God our Savior attractive in every way.
11For the grace of God has been revealed,
bringing salvation to all people. 12And we are
instructed to turn from godless living and sinful
pleasures. We should live in this evil world with
self-control, right conduct, and devotion to

OFF AND RUNNING

Create a Spiritual Hunger in Those around You

Read TITUS 2:9-10

While we are not slaves, this verse could easily apply to workers and employees today—or to anyone who is asked to do something for someone else. Jesus gave a unique example of how this works when he told his disciples, "If a soldier demands that you carry his gear for a mile, carry it two miles" (Matthew 5:41). At that time, Roman law gave soldiers the right to retain private citizens to carry their pack for a mile. Yet Jesus told his disciples to go above and beyond that request. In so doing, they would have a "captive audience" for presenting the gospel.

Today, when everyone seems to be demanding his or her rights, this verse is a direct contradiction to the current wave of thinking. But it all comes back to our frame of reference as Christians: Our goal on earth is not to win our own rights, but to win people to our Lord.

Your work may be difficult. You may even think it is mundane and insignificant. But it is not. God has placed you in your place of employment for a reason—to let your light shine. Your dedicated work may be just the thing that wins your employer or supervisor to Christ. So look for opportunities to "go the extra mile."

God, [13]while we look forward to that wonderful event when the glory of our great God and Savior, Jesus Christ, will be revealed. [14]He gave his life to free us from every kind of sin, to cleanse us, and to make us his very own people, totally committed to doing what is right. [15]You must teach these things and encourage your people to do them, correcting them when necessary. You have the authority to do this, so don't let anyone ignore you or disregard what you say.

CHAPTER 3

Do What Is Good

Remind your people to submit to the government and its officers. They should be obedient, always ready to do what is good. [2]They must not speak evil of anyone, and they must avoid quarreling. Instead, they should be gentle and show true humility to everyone.

[3]Once we, too, were foolish and disobedient. We were misled by others and became slaves to many wicked desires and evil pleasures. Our lives were full of evil and envy. We hated others, and they hated us.

[4]But then God our Savior showed us his kindness and love. [5]He saved us, not because of the good things we did, but because of his mercy. He washed away our sins and gave us a new life through the Holy Spirit.* [6]He generously poured out the Spirit upon us because of what Jesus Christ our Savior did. [7]He declared us not guilty because of his great kindness. And now we know that we will inherit eternal life. [8]These things I have told you are all true. I want you to insist on them so that everyone who trusts in God will be careful to do good deeds all the time. These things are good and beneficial for everyone.

Paul's Final Remarks and Greetings

[9]Do not get involved in foolish discussions about spiritual pedigrees* or in quarrels and fights about obedience to Jewish laws. These kinds of things are useless and a waste of time. [10]If anyone is causing divisions among you, give a first and second warning. After that, have nothing more to do with that person. [11]For people like that have turned away from the truth. They are sinning, and they condemn themselves.

[12]I am planning to send either Artemas or Tychicus to you. As soon as one of them arrives, do your best to meet me at Nicopolis as quickly as you can, for I have decided to stay there for the winter. [13]Do everything you can to help Zenas the lawyer and Apollos with their trip. See that they are given everything they need. [14]For our people should not have unproductive lives. They must learn to do good by helping others who have urgent needs.

[15]Everybody here sends greetings. Please give my greetings to all of the believers who love us.

May God's grace be with you all.

3:5 Greek *He saved us through the washing of regeneration and renewing of the Holy Spirit.* 3:9 Greek *discussions and genealogies.*

Philemon

Greetings from Paul
This letter is from Paul, in prison for preaching
the Good News about Christ Jesus, and from our
brother Timothy.

It is written to Philemon, our much loved
co-worker, 2and to our sister Apphia and to
Archippus, a fellow soldier of the cross. I am also
writing to the church that meets in your house.

3May God our Father and the Lord Jesus
Christ give you grace and peace.

Paul's Thanksgiving and Prayer
4I always thank God when I pray for you, Philemon, 5because I keep hearing of your trust in the
Lord Jesus and your love for all of God's people.
6You are generous because of your faith. And I
am praying that you will really put your generosity to work, for in so doing you will come to
an understanding of all the good things we can
do for Christ. 7I myself have gained much joy
and comfort from your love, my brother, because your kindness has so often refreshed the
hearts of God's people.

Paul's Appeal for Onesimus
8That is why I am boldly asking a favor of you. I
could demand it in the name of Christ because
it is the right thing for you to do, 9but because
of our love, I prefer just to ask you. So take this
as a request from your friend Paul, an old man,
now in prison for the sake of Christ Jesus.

10My plea is that you show kindness to Onesimus. I think of him as my own son because he
became a believer as a result of my ministry here
in prison. 11Onesimus* hasn't been of much use
to you in the past, but now he is very useful to
both of us. 12I am sending him back to you, and
with him comes my own heart.

13I really wanted to keep him here with me
while I am in these chains for preaching the
Good News, and he would have helped me on
your behalf. 14But I didn't want to do anything
without your consent. And I didn't want you to
help because you were forced to do it but because you wanted to. 15Perhaps you could think
of it this way: Onesimus ran away for a little
while so you could have him back forever. 16He
is no longer just a slave; he is a beloved brother,
especially to me. Now he will mean much more
to you, both as a slave and as a brother in the
Lord.

17So if you consider me your partner, give
him the same welcome you would give me if I
were coming. 18If he has harmed you in any way
or stolen anything from you, charge me for it.
19I, Paul, write this in my own handwriting: "I
will repay it." And I won't mention that you owe
me your very soul!

20Yes, dear brother, please do me this favor for
the Lord's sake. Give me this encouragement in
Christ. 21I am confident as I write this letter that
you will do what I ask and even more!

22Please keep a guest room ready for me, for
I am hoping that God will answer your prayers
and let me return to you soon.

Paul's Final Greetings
23Epaphras, my fellow prisoner in Christ Jesus,
sends you his greetings. 24So do Mark, Aristarchus, Demas, and Luke, my co-workers.

25The grace of the Lord Jesus Christ be with
your spirit.

11 *Onesimus* means "useful."

Hebrews

CHAPTER 1

Jesus Christ Is God's Son

Long ago God spoke many times and in many
ways to our ancestors through the prophets.
2 But now in these final days, he has spoken to us
through his Son. God promised everything to
the Son as an inheritance, and through the Son
he made the universe and everything in it. 3 The
Son reflects God's own glory, and everything
about him represents God exactly. He sustains
the universe by the mighty power of his command. After he died to cleanse us from the stain
of sin, he sat down in the place of honor at the
right hand of the majestic God of heaven.

Christ Is Greater Than the Angels

4 This shows that God's Son is far greater than
the angels, just as the name God gave him is far
greater than their names. 5 For God never said to
any angel what he said to Jesus:

"You are my Son.
Today I have become your Father.*"

And again God said,

"I will be his Father,
and he will be my Son."*

6 And then, when he presented his honored*
Son to the world, God said, "Let all the angels of
God worship him."* 7 God calls his angels

"messengers swift as the wind,
and servants made of flaming fire."*

8 But to his Son he says,

"Your throne, O God, endures forever and ever.
Your royal power is expressed in righteousness.
9 You love what is right and hate what is wrong.
Therefore God, your God, has anointed you,
pouring out the oil of joy on you more than on anyone else."*

10 And,

"Lord, in the beginning you laid the foundation of the earth,
and the heavens are the work of your hands.
11 Even they will perish, but you remain forever.
They will wear out like old clothing.
12 You will roll them up like an old coat.
They will fade away like old clothing.
But you are always the same;
you will never grow old."*

13 And God never said to an angel, as he did to
his Son,

"Sit in honor at my right hand
until I humble your enemies,
making them a footstool under your feet."*

14 But angels are only servants. They are spirits
sent from God to care for those who will receive
salvation.

CHAPTER 2

A Warning against Drifting Away

So we must listen very carefully to the truth we
have heard, or we may drift away from it. 2 The

1:5a Or *Today I reveal you as my Son.* Ps 2:7. **1:5b** 2 Sam 7:14. **1:6a** Greek *firstborn.* **1:6b** Deut 32:43. **1:7** Ps 104:4. **1:8-9** Ps 45:6-7. **1:10-12** Ps 102:25-27. **1:13** Ps 110:1.

Why Did God Create Angels? Read HEBREWS 1:4-14

Throughout the ages, people have been fascinated with and awed by angels. Some have even tried to worship them. But it is important to understand that angels are distinctly different from God's Son, Jesus Christ. One significant area of distinction is creation. Angels are created beings, while Jesus is not. Because angels are created, it is wrong to worship them.

If they are not to be worshiped, then what did God create angels for? God created angels for several reasons, three of which are the following:

1. Angels Worship God. As verse 6 attests, one of the reasons God created angels was to worship him. Some people may think this is egotistical, but consider how many people worship professional athletes and other celebrities. These people by comparison have done nothing to earn or be worthy of the worship they receive. God, on the other hand, has created angels and humans and given them life. In addition, God is majestic beyond our understanding, so worshiping him is simply the natural response of being in his presence. For it is an incredible privilege to be in the presence of God. Only God is worthy of worship, and his creation, which includes angels, should worship him.

2. Angels Serve as God's Messengers. God uses angels to deliver messages to his followers on earth (verse 7). The Bible records a few instances of this. In Luke 1 God sent an angel to tell Mary that she would give birth to the Messiah. An angel was also sent to Jesus' tomb to tell his followers that he had risen from the dead (Matthew 28).

3. Angels Minister to God's Followers. God also created angels to minister to his followers (verse 14). In Acts 12, an angel freed Peter from prison before he was to be tried in public for being a follower of Christ.

While angels play a significant role in the lives of believers, we must be careful that we do not give them the honor and praise that should be reserved for Jesus Christ alone.

CORNERSTONES

message God delivered through angels has always
proved true, and the people were punished for
every violation of the law and every act of disobedience. 3What makes us think that we can escape
if we are indifferent to this great salvation that was
announced by the Lord Jesus himself? It was
passed on* to us by those who heard him speak,
4and God verified the message by signs and wonders and various miracles and by giving gifts of the
Holy Spirit whenever he chose to do so.

Jesus, the Man

5And furthermore, the future world we are talking about will not be controlled by angels. 6For
somewhere in the Scriptures it says,

"What is man that you should think of him,
and the son of man* that you should
care for him?
7 For a little while you made him lower than
the angels,
and you crowned him with glory and
honor.*
8 You gave him authority over all things."*

Now when it says "all things," it means nothing
is left out. But we have not yet seen all of this
happen. 9What we do see is Jesus, who "for a
little while was made lower than the angels" and
now is "crowned with glory and honor" because
he suffered death for us. Yes, by God's grace,
Jesus tasted death for everyone in all the world.
10And it was only right that God—who made
everything and for whom everything was
made—should bring his many children into
glory. Through the suffering of Jesus, God made
him a perfect leader, one fit to bring them into
their salvation.

2:3 Or *and confirmed.* 2:6 Or *Son of Man.* 2:7 Some manuscripts add *You put him in charge of everything you made.* 2:6-8 Ps 8:4-6.

Why Would a Good God Send Anyone to Hell? Read HEBREWS 2:2-3

If God loves people, why doesn't he just save everyone? Perhaps you have asked this question or know someone who has. While the question is good, it places the blame for people's damnation on the wrong person: God.

God does not want anyone to spend eternity in hell. In fact, he earnestly desires that everyone spend all eternity with him in heaven. Scripture tells us, "[God] does not want anyone to perish, so he is giving more time for everyone to repent" (2 Peter 3:9). Throughout the Bible we see God's loving and patient invitation for us to come to him:

BIG QUESTIONS

- "Come to me, all of you who are weary and carry heavy burdens, and I will give you rest." (Matthew 11:28)
- "'Come.' Let the thirsty ones come—anyone who wants to. Let them come and drink the water of life without charge." (Revelation 22:17)

The truth is that there are some things only God can do—such as cleanse us of our sin, forgive us, and justify us. At the same time, there are some things only we can do—such as come to him, believe in him, and repent of our sins. While God does indeed love everyone (see John 3:16, p. 109; and Romans 5:8, p. 180), he has given us a wonderful but dangerous gift. That gift is called "free will." It is the ability to choose between right and wrong, good and evil, God and Satan, and heaven and hell. God will not force his salvation and forgiveness upon our lives. It is our choice to say yes or no.

Anyone who ends up in hell is there because of his or her willful and deliberate decision to reject God's offer of forgiveness. As the famous British author C. S. Lewis put it, "The gates of hell are locked from the inside."

11So now Jesus and the ones he makes holy have the same Father. That is why Jesus is not ashamed to call them his brothers and sisters.*
12For he said to God,

"I will declare the wonder of your name to
my brothers and sisters.*
I will praise you among all your people."

13He also said, "I will put my trust in him." And in the same context he said, "Here I am—together with the children God has given me."*

14Because God's children are human beings—made of flesh and blood—Jesus also became flesh and blood by being born in human form. For only as a human being could he die, and only by dying could he break the power of the Devil, who had the power of death. 15Only in this way could he deliver those who have lived all their lives as slaves to the fear of dying.

16We all know that Jesus came to help the descendants of Abraham, not to help the angels.
17Therefore, it was necessary for Jesus to be in every respect like us, his brothers and sisters, so that he could be our merciful and faithful High Priest before God. He then could offer a sacrifice that would take away the sins of the people.
18Since he himself has gone through suffering and temptation, he is able to help us when we are being tempted.

CHAPTER 3

Jesus Is Greater Than Moses

And so, dear brothers and sisters who belong to God* and are bound for heaven, think about this Jesus whom we declare to be God's Messenger and High Priest. 2For he was faithful to God, who appointed him, just as Moses served faithfully and was entrusted with God's entire house. 3But Jesus deserves far more glory than Moses, just as a person who builds a fine house deserves more praise than the house itself. 4For every house has a builder, but God is the one who made everything.

5Moses was certainly faithful in God's house, but only as a servant. His work was an illustration of the truths God would reveal later. 6But Christ, the faithful Son, was in charge of the entire household. And we are God's household, if we keep up our courage and remain confident

2:11 Greek *his brothers;* also in 2:17. **2:12** Greek *my brothers.* Ps 22:22. **2:13** Isa 8:17-18. **3:1** Greek *And so, holy brothers.*

in our hope in Christ. 7That is why the Holy
Spirit says,

"Today you must listen to his voice.
8 Don't harden your hearts against him
as Israel did when they rebelled,
when they tested God's patience in the
wilderness.
9 There your ancestors tried my patience,
even though they saw my miracles for
forty years.
10 So I was angry with them, and I said,
'Their hearts always turn away from me.
They refuse to do what I tell them.'
11 So in my anger I made a vow:
'They will never enter my place of rest.'"*

12Be careful then, dear brothers and sisters.* Make
sure that your own hearts are not evil and unbelieving, turning you away from the living God.
13You must warn each other every day, as long as
it is called "today," so that none of you will be
deceived by sin and hardened against God. 14For
if we are faithful to the end, trusting God just as
firmly as when we first believed, we will share in
all that belongs to Christ. 15But never forget the
warning:

"Today you must listen to his voice.
Don't harden your hearts against him
as Israel did when they rebelled."*

16And who were those people who rebelled
against God, even though they heard his voice?
Weren't they the ones Moses led out of Egypt?
17And who made God angry for forty years?
Wasn't it the people who sinned, whose bodies
fell in the wilderness? 18And to whom was God
speaking when he vowed that they would never
enter his place of rest? He was speaking to those
who disobeyed him. 19So we see that they were not
allowed to enter his rest because of their unbelief.

CHAPTER 4

Promised Rest for God's People

God's promise of entering his place of rest still
stands, so we ought to tremble with fear that
some of you might fail to get there. 2For this
Good News—that God has prepared a place of
rest—has been announced to us just as it was to
them. But it did them no good because they
didn't believe what God told them.* 3For only
we who believe can enter his place of rest. As for
those who didn't believe, God said,

"In my anger I made a vow:
'They will never enter my place of rest,'"*

even though his place of rest has been ready
since he made the world. 4We know it is ready
because the Scriptures mention the seventh day,
saying, "On the seventh day God rested from all
his work."* 5But in the other passage God said,
"They will never enter my place of rest."* 6So
God's rest is there for people to enter. But those
who formerly heard the Good News failed to
enter because they disobeyed God. 7So God set
another time for entering his place of rest, and
that time is today. God announced this through
David a long time later in the words already
quoted:

"Today you must listen to his voice.
Don't harden your hearts against him."*

8This new place of rest was not the land of
Canaan, where Joshua led them. If it had been,
God would not have spoken later about another
day of rest. 9So there is a special rest* still waiting for the people of God. 10For all who enter
into God's rest will find rest from their labors,
just as God rested after creating the world. 11Let
us do our best to enter that place of rest. For
anyone who disobeys God, as the people of
Israel did, will fall.

12For the word of God is full of living power.
It is sharper than the sharpest knife, cutting deep
into our innermost thoughts and desires. It ex-
poses us for what we really are. 13Nothing in all
creation can hide from him. Everything is naked
and exposed before his eyes. This is the God to
whom we must explain all that we have done.

Christ Is Our High Priest

14That is why we have a great High Priest who
has gone to heaven, Jesus the Son of God. Let us
cling to him and never stop trusting him. 15This
High Priest of ours understands our weaknesses,
for he faced all of the same temptations we do,
yet he did not sin. 16So let us come boldly to the
throne of our gracious God. There we will receive his mercy, and we will find grace to help us
when we need it.

CHAPTER 5

Now a high priest is a man chosen to represent
other human beings in their dealings with God.
He presents their gifts to God and offers their
sacrifices for sins. 2And because he is human, he

3:7-11 Ps 95:7-11. 3:12 Greek *brothers*. 3:15 Ps 95:7-8. 4:2 Some manuscripts read *they didn't share the faith of those who listened [to God]*. 4:3 Ps 95:11. 4:4 Gen 2:2. 4:5 Ps 95:11. 4:7 Ps 95:7-8. 4:9 Or *Sabbath rest*.

is able to deal gently with the people, though
they are ignorant and wayward. For he is subject
to the same weaknesses they have. 3That is why
he has to offer sacrifices, both for their sins and
for his own sins. 4And no one can become a high
priest simply because he wants such an honor.
He has to be called by God for this work, just as
Aaron was.

5That is why Christ did not exalt himself to
become High Priest. No, he was chosen by God,
who said to him,

> "You are my Son.
> Today I have become your Father.*"

6And in another passage God said to him,

> "You are a priest forever
> in the line of Melchizedek."*

7While Jesus was here on earth, he offered
prayers and pleadings, with a loud cry and tears,
to the one who could deliver him out of death.
And God heard his prayers because of his reverence for God. 8So even though Jesus was God's
Son, he learned obedience from the things he
suffered. 9In this way, God qualified him as a
perfect High Priest, and he became the source of
eternal salvation for all those who obey him.
10And God designated him to be a High Priest in
the line of Melchizedek.

A Call to Spiritual Growth

11There is so much more we would like to say
about this. But you don't seem to listen, so it's
hard to make you understand. 12You have been
Christians a long time now, and you ought to be
teaching others. Instead, you need someone to
teach you again the basic things a beginner must
learn about the Scriptures.* You are like babies
who drink only milk and cannot eat solid food.
13And a person who is living on milk isn't very
far along in the Christian life and doesn't know
much about doing what is right. 14Solid food is
for those who are mature, who have trained
themselves to recognize the difference between
right and wrong and then do what is right.

CHAPTER 6

So let us stop going over the basics of Christianity* again and again. Let us go on instead and
become mature in our understanding. Surely we
don't need to start all over again with the importance of turning away from evil deeds and placing our faith in God. 2You don't need further
instruction about baptisms, the laying on of
hands, the resurrection of the dead, and eternal
judgment. 3And so, God willing, we will move
forward to further understanding.

4For it is impossible to restore to repentance
those who were once enlightened—those who
have experienced the good things of heaven and
shared in the Holy Spirit, 5who have tasted the
goodness of the word of God and the power of
the age to come—6and who then turn away
from God. It is impossible to bring such people
to repentance again because they are nailing the
Son of God to the cross again by rejecting him,
holding him up to public shame.

7When the ground soaks up the rain that falls
on it and bears a good crop for the farmer, it has
the blessing of God. 8But if a field bears thistles
and thorns, it is useless. The farmer will condemn that field and burn it.

9Dear friends, even though we are talking like
this, we really don't believe that it applies to you.
We are confident that you are meant for better
things, things that come with salvation. 10For
God is not unfair. He will not forget how hard
you have worked for him and how you have
shown your love to him by caring for other
Christians, as you still do. 11Our great desire is
that you will keep right on loving others as long
as life lasts, in order to make certain that what
you hope for will come true. 12Then you will not
become spiritually dull and indifferent. Instead,
you will follow the example of those who are
going to inherit God's promises because of their
faith and patience.

God's Promises Bring Hope

13For example, there was God's promise to Abraham. Since there was no one greater to swear by,
God took an oath in his own name, saying:

> 14 "I will certainly bless you richly,
> and I will multiply your descendants into
> countless millions."*

15Then Abraham waited patiently, and he received what God had promised.

16When people take an oath, they call on
someone greater than themselves to hold them
to it. And without any question that oath is
binding. 17God also bound himself with an
oath, so that those who received the promise
could be perfectly sure that he would never
change his mind. 18So God has given us both his
promise and his oath. These two things are un-

5:5 Or *Today I reveal you as my Son.* Ps 2:7. 5:6 Ps 110:4. 5:12 Or *about the oracles of God.* 6:1 Or *the basics about Christ.* 6:14 Gen 22:17.

changeable because it is impossible for God to lie. Therefore, we who have fled to him for refuge can take new courage, for we can hold on to his promise with confidence.

19This confidence is like a strong and trustworthy anchor for our souls. It leads us through the curtain of heaven into God's inner sanctuary. 20Jesus has already gone in there for us. He has become our eternal High Priest in the line of Melchizedek.

CHAPTER 7

Melchizedek Is Compared to Abraham

This Melchizedek was king of the city of Salem and also a priest of God Most High. When Abraham was returning home after winning a great battle against many kings, Melchizedek met him and blessed him. 2Then Abraham took a tenth of all he had won in the battle and gave it to Melchizedek. His name means "king of justice." He is also "king of peace" because *Salem* means "peace." 3There is no record of his father or mother or any of his ancestors—no beginning or end to his life. He remains a priest forever, resembling the Son of God.

4Consider then how great this Melchizedek was. Even Abraham, the great patriarch of Israel, recognized how great Melchizedek was by giving him a tenth of what he had taken in battle. 5Now the priests, who are descendants of Levi, are commanded in the law of Moses to collect a tithe from all the people, even though they are their own relatives.* 6But Melchizedek, who was not even related to Levi, collected a tenth from Abraham. And Melchizedek placed a blessing upon Abraham, the one who had already received the promises of God. 7And without question, the person who has the power to bless is always greater than the person who is blessed.

8In the case of Jewish priests, tithes are paid to men who will die. But Melchizedek is greater than they are, because we are told that he lives on. 9In addition, we might even say that Levi's descendants, the ones who collect the tithe, paid a tithe to Melchizedek through their ancestor Abraham. 10For although Levi wasn't born yet, the seed from which he came was in Abraham's loins when Melchizedek collected the tithe from him.

11And finally, if the priesthood of Levi could have achieved God's purposes—and it was that priesthood on which the law was based—why did God need to send a different priest from the line of Melchizedek, instead of from the line of Levi and Aaron?*

12And when the priesthood is changed, the law must also be changed to permit it. 13For the one we are talking about belongs to a different tribe, whose members do not serve at the altar. 14What I mean is, our Lord came from the tribe of Judah, and Moses never mentioned Judah in connection with the priesthood.

Christ Is like Melchizedek

15The change in God's law is even more evident from the fact that a different priest, who is like Melchizedek, has now come. 16He became a priest, not by meeting the old requirement of belonging to the tribe of Levi, but by the power of a life that cannot be destroyed. 17And the psalmist pointed this out when he said of Christ,

"You are a priest forever
  in the line of Melchizedek."*

18Yes, the old requirement about the priesthood was set aside because it was weak and useless. 19For the law made nothing perfect, and now a better hope has taken its place. And that is how we draw near to God.

20God took an oath that Christ would always be a priest, but he never did this for any other priest. 21Only to Jesus did he say,

"The Lord has taken an oath
  and will not break his vow:
'You are a priest forever.'"*

22Because of God's oath, it is Jesus who guarantees the effectiveness of this better covenant.

23Another difference is that there were many priests under the old system. When one priest died, another had to take his place. 24But Jesus remains a priest forever; his priesthood will never end. 25Therefore he is able, once and forever, to save* everyone who comes to God through him. He lives forever to plead with God on their behalf.

26He is the kind of high priest we need because he is holy and blameless, unstained by sin. He has now been set apart from sinners, and he has been given the highest place of honor in heaven. 27He does not need to offer sacrifices every day like the other high priests. They did this for their own sins first and then for the sins of the people. But Jesus did this once for all when he sacrificed himself on the cross. 28Those

7:5 Greek *their brothers, who are descendants of Abraham.* 7:11 Greek *according to the order of Aaron.* 7:17 Ps 110:4. 7:21 Ps 110:4. 7:25 Or *able to save completely.*

who were high priests under the law of Moses
were limited by human weakness. But after the
law was given, God appointed his Son with an
oath, and his Son has been made perfect forever.

CHAPTER 8

Christ Is Our High Priest

Here is the main point: Our High Priest sat
down in the place of highest honor in heaven, at
God's right hand. 2There he ministers in the
sacred tent, the true place of worship that was
built by the Lord and not by human hands.

3And since every high priest is required to
offer gifts and sacrifices, our High Priest must
make an offering, too. 4If he were here on earth,
he would not even be a priest, since there already are priests who offer the gifts required by
the law of Moses. 5They serve in a place of
worship that is only a copy, a shadow of the real
one in heaven. For when Moses was getting
ready to build the Tabernacle, God gave him this
warning: "Be sure that you make everything according to the design I have shown you here on
the mountain."* 6But our High Priest has been
given a ministry that is far superior to the ministry of those who serve under the old laws, for he
is the one who guarantees for us a better covenant with God, based on better promises.

7If the first covenant had been faultless, there
would have been no need for a second covenant
to replace it. 8But God himself found fault with
the old one when he said:

"The day will come, says the Lord,
when I will make a new covenant
with the people of Israel and Judah.
9 This covenant will not be like the one
I made with their ancestors
when I took them by the hand
and led them out of the land of Egypt.
They did not remain faithful to my
covenant,
so I turned my back on them, says the
Lord.
10 But this is the new covenant I will make
with the people of Israel on that day, says
the Lord:
I will put my laws in their minds
so they will understand them,
and I will write them on their hearts
so they will obey them.
I will be their God,
and they will be my people.
11 And they will not need to teach their
neighbors,
nor will they need to teach their family,
saying, 'You should know the Lord.'
For everyone, from the least to the greatest,
will already know me.
12 And I will forgive their wrongdoings,
and I will never again remember their
sins."*

13When God speaks of a new covenant, it means
he has made the first one obsolete. It is now out
of date and ready to be put aside.

CHAPTER 9

Old Rules about Worship

Now in that first covenant between God and
Israel, there were regulations for worship and a
sacred tent here on earth. 2There were two
rooms in this tent. In the first room were a
lampstand, a table, and loaves of holy bread on
the table. This was called the Holy Place. 3Then
there was a curtain, and behind the curtain was
the second room called the Most Holy Place. 4In
that room were a gold incense altar and a
wooden chest called the Ark of the Covenant,
which was covered with gold on all sides. Inside
the Ark were a gold jar containing some manna,
Aaron's staff that sprouted leaves, and the stone
tablets of the covenant with the Ten Commandments written on them. 5The glorious cherubim
were above the Ark. Their wings were stretched
out over the Ark's cover, the place of atonement.
But we cannot explain all of these things now.

6When these things were all in place, the
priests went in and out of the first room* regularly as they performed their religious duties.
7But only the high priest goes into the Most
Holy Place, and only once a year, and always
with blood, which he offers to God to cover his
own sins and the sins the people have committed in ignorance. 8By these regulations the Holy
Spirit revealed that the Most Holy Place was not
open to the people as long as the first room and
the entire system it represents were still in use.

9This is an illustration pointing to the present
time. For the gifts and sacrifices that the priests
offer are not able to cleanse the consciences of
the people who bring them. 10For that old system deals only with food and drink and ritual
washing—external regulations that are in effect
only until their limitations can be corrected.

8:5 Exod 25:40; 26:30. 8:8-12 Jer 31:31-34. 9:6 Greek *first tent;* also in 9:8.

Christ Is the Perfect Sacrifice

11So Christ has now become the High Priest over all the good things that have come. He has entered that great, perfect sanctuary in heaven, not made by human hands and not part of this created world. 12Once for all time he took blood into that Most Holy Place, but not the blood of goats and calves. He took his own blood, and with it he secured our salvation forever.

13Under the old system, the blood of goats and bulls and the ashes of a young cow could cleanse people's bodies from ritual defilement. 14Just think how much more the blood of Christ will purify our hearts from deeds that lead to death so that we can worship the living God. For by the power of the eternal Spirit, Christ offered himself to God as a perfect sacrifice for our sins. 15That is why he is the one who mediates the new covenant between God and people, so that all who are invited can receive the eternal inheritance God has promised them. For Christ died to set them free from the penalty of the sins they had committed under that first covenant.

16Now when someone dies and leaves a will, no one gets anything until it is proved that the person who wrote the will* is dead.* 17The will goes into effect only after the death of the person who wrote it. While the person is still alive, no one can use the will to get any of the things promised to them.

18That is why blood was required under the first covenant as a proof of death. 19For after Moses had given the people all of God's laws, he took the blood of calves and goats, along with water, and sprinkled both the book of God's laws and all the people, using branches of hyssop bushes and scarlet wool. 20Then he said, "This blood confirms the covenant God has made with you."* 21And in the same way, he sprinkled blood on the sacred tent and on everything used for worship. 22In fact, we can say that according to the law of Moses, nearly everything was purified by sprinkling with blood. Without the shedding of blood, there is no forgiveness of sins.

23That is why the earthly tent and everything in it—which were copies of things in heaven—had to be purified by the blood of animals. But the real things in heaven had to be purified with far better sacrifices than the blood of animals.

24For Christ has entered into heaven itself to appear now before God as our Advocate.* He did not go into the earthly place of worship, for that was merely a copy of the real Temple in heaven. 25Nor did he enter heaven to offer himself again and again, like the earthly high priest who enters the Most Holy Place year after year to offer the blood of an animal. 26If that had been necessary, he would have had to die again and again, ever since the world began. But no! He came once for all time, at the end of the age, to remove the power of sin forever by his sacrificial death for us.

27And just as it is destined that each person dies only once and after that comes judgment, 28so also Christ died only once as a sacrifice to take away the sins of many people. He will come again but not to deal with our sins again. This time he will bring salvation to all those who are eagerly waiting for him.

CHAPTER 10

Christ's Sacrifice Once for All

The old system in the law of Moses was only a shadow of the things to come, not the reality of the good things Christ has done for us. The sacrifices under the old system were repeated again and again, year after year, but they were never able to provide perfect cleansing for those who came to worship. 2If they could have provided perfect cleansing, the sacrifices would have stopped, for the worshipers would have been purified once for all time, and their feelings of guilt would have disappeared.

3But just the opposite happened. Those yearly sacrifices reminded them of their sins year after year. 4For it is not possible for the blood of bulls and goats to take away sins. 5That is why Christ, when he came into the world, said,

"You did not want animal sacrifices and
grain offerings.
But you have given me a body so that I
may obey you.
6 No, you were not pleased with animals
burned on the altar
or with other offerings for sin.
7 Then I said, 'Look, I have come to do your
will, O God—
just as it is written about me in the
Scriptures.'"*

8Christ said, "You did not want animal sacrifices or grain offerings or animals burned on the altar or other offerings for sin, nor were you pleased with them" (though they are required by the law

9:16a Or *covenant.* **9:16b** Or *Now when someone makes a covenant, it is necessary to ratify it with the death of a sacrifice.* **9:20** Exod 24:8. **9:24** Greek *on our behalf.* **10:5-7** Ps 40:6-8.

of Moses). 9Then he added, "Look, I have come
to do your will." He cancels the first covenant in
order to establish the second. 10And what God
wants is for us to be made holy by the sacrifice
of the body of Jesus Christ once for all time.

11Under the old covenant, the priest stands
before the altar day after day, offering sacrifices
that can never take away sins. 12But our High
Priest offered himself to God as one sacrifice for
sins, good for all time. Then he sat down at the
place of highest honor at God's right hand.
13There he waits until his enemies are humbled
as a footstool under his feet. 14For by that one
offering he perfected forever all those whom he
is making holy.

15And the Holy Spirit also testifies that this is
so. First he says,

16 "This is the new covenant I will make
with my people on that day, says the
Lord:
I will put my laws in their hearts
so they will understand them,
and I will write them on their minds
so they will obey them."

17Then he adds,

"I will never again remember
their sins and lawless deeds."*

18Now when sins have been forgiven, there is no
need to offer any more sacrifices.

A Call to Persevere

19And so, dear brothers and sisters,* we can
boldly enter heaven's Most Holy Place because
of the blood of Jesus. 20This is the new, life-giving way that Christ has opened up for us through
the sacred curtain, by means of his death for us.*

21And since we have a great High Priest who
rules over God's people, 22let us go right into the
presence of God, with true hearts fully trusting
him. For our evil consciences have been sprinkled with Christ's blood to make us clean, and
our bodies have been washed with pure water.

23Without wavering, let us hold tightly to the
hope we say we have, for God can be trusted to
keep his promise. 24Think of ways to encourage
one another to outbursts of love and good
deeds. 25And let us not neglect our meeting
together, as some people do, but encourage and
warn each other, especially now that the day of
his coming back again is drawing near.

26Dear friends, if we deliberately continue

10:16-17 Jer 31:33-34. **10:19** Greek *brothers*. **10:20** Greek *his flesh*.

Why We Need Fellowship with Other Believers

Read HEBREWS 10:25

Involvement in a local church is necessary for the spiritual growth of all Christians, and it is something we never outgrow. For the new believer, moreover, such interaction is critical for four reasons:

1. Fellowship Provides Us with Encouragement and Love. As Christians, we need a place where we can be encouraged in our faith and be reminded that we are a member of God's family. When we go to church, we are surrounded by others who share our love for Christ. Being in the presence of other believers can encourage us to live for Christ, as well as give us a sense of belonging and acceptance that we don't receive from the world.

2. Fellowship Allows Us to Learn from Spiritually Mature Christians. In the biblical account of the early church, we are told how the apostle Paul's friends, Priscilla and Aquila, took time to help another believer learn more about Jesus (see Acts 18:26, p. 161). Likewise, younger Christians in the church today will have the opportunity to gain spiritual wisdom and insight from more mature Christians.

3. Fellowship Helps Us Discern False Teachings. The Bible warns of false teachers and teachings, to which the young believer is especially susceptible because he or she lacks basic Bible understanding. A healthy, Bible-teaching church will encourage young believers in their growth and help them discern truth from error.

4. Fellowship Prepares Us for Christ's Return. As the day for Christ's return comes closer, we need to help each other through difficult times and keep our problems in perspective. We also need to encourage each other to live holy lives and to share God's Good News with others in the time that remains. God wants the body of Christ to stand out and be a light in these ever darkening days.

Christ Endured Great Pain for Us Read HEBREWS 12:1-3

Throughout the New Testament, the Christian life is compared to a race. With that in mind, we need to realize that it is not a short sprint, but a long-distance run. Sometimes, as we are participating in this race, we can grow discouraged by circumstances or by what others say to us. But just as a successful runner must "keep his eyes on the prize," we, too, must remember what this race is all about. We must bear in mind for whom and to whom we are running: Jesus Christ. In essence, we need to "keep our eyes on Jesus."

Corrie ten Boom, a Dutch Christian who survived the horrors of Hitler's concentration camps during World War II, often said, "Look within and be depressed. Look without and be distressed. Look at Jesus and be at rest."

God will see us through to the end. He has given us his word: "And I am sure that God, who began the good work within you, will continue his work until it is finally finished on that day when Christ Jesus comes back again" (Philippians 1:6).

CORNERSTONES

sinning after we have received a full knowledge
of the truth, there is no other sacrifice that will
cover these sins. 27There will be nothing to look
forward to but the terrible expectation of God's
judgment and the raging fire that will consume
his enemies. 28Anyone who refused to obey the
law of Moses was put to death without mercy on
the testimony of two or three witnesses. 29Think
how much more terrible the punishment will be
for those who have trampled on the Son of God
and have treated the blood of the covenant as if
it were common and unholy. Such people have
insulted and enraged the Holy Spirit who brings
God's mercy to his people.
30For we know the one who said,

"I will take vengeance.
I will repay those who deserve it."

He also said,

"The Lord will judge his own people."*

31It is a terrible thing to fall into the hands of the
living God.
32Don't ever forget those early days when you
first learned about Christ. Remember how you
remained faithful even though it meant terrible
suffering. 33Sometimes you were exposed to
public ridicule and were beaten, and sometimes
you helped others who were suffering the same
things. 34You suffered along with those who
were thrown into jail. When all you owned was
taken from you, you accepted it with joy. You
knew you had better things waiting for you in
eternity.
35Do not throw away this confident trust in
the Lord, no matter what happens. Remember
the great reward it brings you! 36Patient endurance is what you need now, so you will continue
to do God's will. Then you will receive all that
he has promised.

37 "For in just a little while,
the Coming One will come and not
delay.
38 And a righteous person will live by faith.
But I will have no pleasure in anyone
who turns away."*

39But we are not like those who turn their backs
on God and seal their fate. We have faith that
assures our salvation.

CHAPTER 11

Great Examples of Faith

What is faith? It is the confident assurance that
what we hope for is going to happen. It is the
evidence of things we cannot yet see. 2God gave
his approval to people in days of old because of
their faith.
3By faith we understand that the entire universe was formed at God's command, that what
we now see did not come from anything that can
be seen.

10:30 Deut 32:35-36. **10:37-38** Hab 2:3-4.

4It was by faith that Abel brought a more acceptable offering to God than Cain did. God accepted Abel's offering to show that he was a righteous man. And although Abel is long dead, he still speaks to us because of his faith.

5It was by faith that Enoch was taken up to heaven without dying—"suddenly he disappeared because God took him."* But before he was taken up, he was approved as pleasing to God. 6So, you see, it is impossible to please God without faith. Anyone who wants to come to him must believe that there is a God and that he rewards those who sincerely seek him.

7It was by faith that Noah built an ark to save his family from the flood. He obeyed God, who warned him about something that had never happened before. By his faith he condemned the rest of the world and was made right in God's sight.

8It was by faith that Abraham obeyed when God called him to leave home and go to another land that God would give him as his inheritance. He went without knowing where he was going. 9And even when he reached the land God promised him, he lived there by faith—for he was like a foreigner, living in a tent. And so did Isaac and Jacob, to whom God gave the same promise. 10Abraham did this because he was confidently looking forward to a city with eternal foundations, a city designed and built by God.

11It was by faith that Sarah together with Abraham was able to have a child, even though they were too old and Sarah was barren. Abraham believed that God would keep his promise.* 12And so a whole nation came from this one man, Abraham, who was too old to have any children—a nation with so many people that, like the stars of the sky and the sand on the seashore, there is no way to count them.

13All these faithful ones died without receiving what God had promised them, but they saw it all from a distance and welcomed the promises of God. They agreed that they were no more than foreigners and nomads here on earth. 14And obviously people who talk like that are looking forward to a country they can call their own. 15If they had meant the country they came from, they would have found a way to go back. 16But they were looking for a better place, a heavenly homeland. That is why God is not ashamed to be called their God, for he has prepared a heavenly city for them.

17It was by faith that Abraham offered Isaac as a sacrifice when God was testing him. Abraham, who had received God's promises, was ready to sacrifice his only son, Isaac, 18though God had promised him, "Isaac is the son through whom your descendants will be counted."* 19Abraham assumed that if Isaac died, God was able to bring him back to life again. And in a sense, Abraham did receive his son back from the dead.

20It was by faith that Isaac blessed his two sons, Jacob and Esau. He had confidence in what God was going to do in the future.

21It was by faith that Jacob, when he was old and dying, blessed each of Joseph's sons and bowed in worship as he leaned on his staff.

22And it was by faith that Joseph, when he was about to die, confidently spoke of God's bringing the people of Israel out of Egypt. He was so sure of it that he commanded them to carry his bones with them when they left!

23It was by faith that Moses' parents hid him for three months. They saw that God had given them an unusual child, and they were not afraid of what the king might do.

24It was by faith that Moses, when he grew up, refused to be treated as the son of Pharaoh's daughter. 25He chose to share the oppression of God's people instead of enjoying the fleeting pleasures of sin. 26He thought it was better to suffer for the sake of the Messiah than to own the treasures of Egypt, for he was looking ahead to the great reward that God would give him. 27It was by faith that Moses left the land of Egypt. He was not afraid of the king. Moses kept right on going because he kept his eyes on the one who is invisible. 28It was by faith that Moses commanded the people of Israel to keep the Passover and to sprinkle blood on the doorposts so that the angel of death would not kill their firstborn sons.

29It was by faith that the people of Israel went right through the Red Sea as though they were on dry ground. But when the Egyptians followed, they were all drowned.

30It was by faith that the people of Israel marched around Jericho seven days, and the walls came crashing down.

31It was by faith that Rahab the prostitute did not die with all the others in her city who refused to obey God. For she had given a friendly welcome to the spies.

32Well, how much more do I need to say? It would take too long to recount the stories of

11:5 Gen 5:24. **11:11** Some manuscripts read *It was by faith that Sarah was able to have a child, even though she was too old and barren. Sarah believed that God would keep his promise.* **11:18** Gen 21:12.

the faith of Gideon, Barak, Samson, Jephthah, David, Samuel, and all the prophets. 33By faith these people overthrew kingdoms, ruled with justice, and received what God had promised them. They shut the mouths of lions, 34quenched the flames of fire, and escaped death by the edge of the sword. Their weakness was turned to strength. They became strong in battle and put whole armies to flight. 35Women received their loved ones back again from death.

But others trusted God and were tortured, preferring to die rather than turn from God and be free. They placed their hope in the resurrection to a better life. 36Some were mocked, and their backs were cut open with whips. Others were chained in dungeons. 37Some died by stoning, and some were sawed in half; others were killed with the sword. Some went about in skins of sheep and goats, hungry and oppressed and mistreated. 38They were too good for this world. They wandered over deserts and mountains, hiding in caves and holes in the ground.

39All of these people we have mentioned received God's approval because of their faith, yet none of them received all that God had promised. 40For God had far better things in mind for us that would also benefit them, for they can't receive the prize at the end of the race until we finish the race.*

CHAPTER 12

God's Discipline Proves His Love

Therefore, since we are surrounded by such a huge crowd of witnesses to the life of faith, let us strip off every weight that slows us down, especially the sin that so easily hinders our progress. And let us run with endurance the race that God has set before us. 2We do this by keeping our eyes on Jesus, on whom our faith depends from start to finish.* He was willing to die a shameful death on the cross because of the joy he knew would be his afterward. Now he is seated in the place of highest honor beside God's throne in heaven. 3Think about all he endured when sinful people did such terrible things to him, so that you don't become weary and give up. 4After all, you have not yet given your lives in your struggle against sin.

11:40 Greek *for us, for they apart from us can't finish.* **12:2** Or *Jesus, the Originator and Perfecter of our faith.*

OFF AND RUNNING

Keeping Your Marriage Strong Read HEBREWS 13:4

Tragically, many people do not take marriage seriously today. They forget that their vows are made before God and include the words "till death do us part." So what steps can you take to keep from becoming another marriage "casualty"? Here are four principles that will help you to maintain a strong and flourishing marriage:

1. Walk with God. As you cultivate and deepen your fellowship with God, you will have the power, the will, and the resources to stand when temptation comes knocking.

2. Walk with Your Spouse. Keep the friendship and romance alive in your marriage. Remember what you did when you first started courting your spouse. Compliment one another. Spend time together. Be genuinely interested in one another's lives. Try your best to look attractive for each other. Treat your partner with respect. Take practical steps to keep that fire of love burning.

3. Don't Walk on Thin Ice. It is dangerous to form close relationships with those who do not love God as you do. You must avoid potentially dangerous and flirtatious relationships at all costs. Find Christian friends (of the same sex) who can be honest with you if they think you are heading into dangerous territory.

4. Count the Cost. Remember the price that comes with adultery and immorality. Are you ready to face the shame? Are you prepared for the disgrace and distrust you will bring upon your spouse and children—as well as the cause of Christ? A few moments of pleasure will result in a lifetime of regret.

An intense love for God and for your husband or wife will see you through the rough waters of sexual temptation. Don't be an easy target for Satan's arrows. Keep moving forward in your relationship with Christ and with your spouse.

5And have you entirely forgotten the encouraging words God spoke to you, his children? He said,

> "My child, don't ignore it when the Lord
> disciplines you,
> and don't be discouraged when he
> corrects you.
> 6 For the Lord disciplines those he loves,
> and he punishes those he accepts as his
> children."*

7As you endure this divine discipline, remember that God is treating you as his own children. Whoever heard of a child who was never disciplined? 8If God doesn't discipline you as he does all of his children, it means that you are illegitimate and are not really his children after all. 9Since we respect our earthly fathers who disciplined us, should we not all the more cheerfully submit to the discipline of our heavenly Father and live forever*?

10For our earthly fathers disciplined us for a few years, doing the best they knew how. But God's discipline is always right and good for us because it means we will share in his holiness. 11No discipline is enjoyable while it is happening—it is painful! But afterward there will be a quiet harvest of right living for those who are trained in this way.

12So take a new grip with your tired hands and stand firm on your shaky legs. 13Mark out a straight path for your feet. Then those who follow you, though they are weak and lame, will not stumble and fall but will become strong.

A Call to Listen to God

14Try to live in peace with everyone, and seek to live a clean and holy life, for those who are not holy will not see the Lord. 15Look after each other so that none of you will miss out on the special favor of God. Watch out that no bitter root of unbelief rises up among you, for whenever it springs up, many are corrupted by its poison. 16Make sure that no one is immoral or godless like Esau. He traded his birthright as the oldest son for a single meal. 17And afterward, when he wanted his father's blessing, he was rejected. It was too late for repentance, even though he wept bitter tears.

18You have not come to a physical mountain, to a place of flaming fire, darkness, gloom, and whirlwind, as the Israelites did at Mount Sinai when God gave them his laws. 19For they heard an awesome trumpet blast and a voice with a message so terrible that they begged God to stop speaking. 20They staggered back under God's command: "If even an animal touches the mountain, it must be stoned to death."* 21Moses himself was so frightened at the sight that he said, "I am terrified and trembling."*

22No, you have come to Mount Zion, to the city of the living God, the heavenly Jerusalem, and to thousands of angels in joyful assembly. 23You have come to the assembly of God's firstborn children, whose names are written in heaven. You have come to God himself, who is the judge of all people. And you have come to the spirits of the redeemed in heaven who have now been made perfect. 24You have come to Jesus, the one who mediates the new covenant between God and people, and to the sprinkled blood, which graciously forgives instead of crying out for vengeance as the blood of Abel did.

25See to it that you obey God, the one who is speaking to you. For if the people of Israel did not escape when they refused to listen to Moses, the earthly messenger, how terrible our danger if we reject the One who speaks to us from heaven! 26When God spoke from Mount Sinai his voice shook the earth, but now he makes another promise: "Once again I will shake not only the earth but the heavens also."* 27This means that the things on earth will be shaken, so that only eternal things will be left.

28Since we are receiving a kingdom that cannot be destroyed, let us be thankful and please God by worshiping him with holy fear and awe. 29For our God is a consuming fire.

CHAPTER 13

Concluding Words

Continue to love each other with true Christian love.* 2Don't forget to show hospitality to strangers, for some who have done this have entertained angels without realizing it! 3Don't forget about those in prison. Suffer with them as though you were there yourself. Share the sorrow of those being mistreated, as though you feel their pain in your own bodies.

4Give honor to marriage, and remain faithful to one another in marriage. God will surely judge people who are immoral and those who commit adultery.

12:5-6 Prov 3:11-12. 12:9 Or *really live.* 12:20 Exod 19:13. 12:21 Deut 9:19. 12:26 Hag 2:6. 13:1 Greek *with brotherly love.*

5Stay away from the love of money; be satisfied with what you have. For God has said,

"I will never fail you.
I will never forsake you."*

6That is why we can say with confidence,

"The Lord is my helper,
so I will not be afraid.
What can mere mortals do to me?"*

7Remember your leaders who first taught you the word of God. Think of all the good that has come from their lives, and trust the Lord as they do.

8Jesus Christ is the same yesterday, today, and forever. 9So do not be attracted by strange, new ideas. Your spiritual strength comes from God's special favor, not from ceremonial rules about food, which don't help those who follow them.

10We have an altar from which the priests in the Temple on earth have no right to eat. 11Under the system of Jewish laws, the high priest brought the blood of animals into the Holy Place as a sacrifice for sin, but the bodies of the animals were burned outside the camp. 12So also Jesus suffered and died outside the city gates in order to make his people holy by shedding his own blood. 13So let us go out to him outside the camp and bear the disgrace he bore. 14For this world is not our home; we are looking forward to our city in heaven, which is yet to come.

15With Jesus' help, let us continually offer our sacrifice of praise to God by proclaiming the glory of his name. 16Don't forget to do good and to share what you have with those in need, for such sacrifices are very pleasing to God.

17Obey your spiritual leaders and do what they say. Their work is to watch over your souls, and they know they are accountable to God. Give them reason to do this joyfully and not with sorrow. That would certainly not be for your benefit.

18Pray for us, for our conscience is clear and we want to live honorably in everything we do. 19I especially need your prayers right now so that I can come back to you soon.

20-21And now, may the God of peace, who brought again from the dead our Lord Jesus, equip you with all you need for doing his will. May he produce in you, through the power of Jesus Christ, all that is pleasing to him. Jesus is the great Shepherd of the sheep by an everlasting covenant, signed with his blood. To him be glory forever and ever. Amen.

22I urge you, dear brothers and sisters,* please listen carefully to what I have said in this brief letter.

23I want you to know that our brother Timothy is now out of jail. If he comes here soon, I will bring him with me to see you.

24Give my greetings to all your leaders and to the other believers there. The Christians from Italy send you their greetings.

25May God's grace be with you all.

13:5 Deut 31:6, 8. 13:6 Ps 118:6. 13:22 Greek *brothers*.

OFF AND RUNNING

Our Needs Must Come Last Read HEBREWS 13:11-13

Jesus gave us the ultimate example to follow in meekness. Jesus, who is God, came to this earth and humbled himself in an incredible way by becoming a man. It is important to note that he never at any time ceased being God. But he did lay aside the privileges of deity to experience genuine human conditions, such as sorrow, anger, weariness, and pain (see Philippians 2:3-11, pp. 248–249). Yet the most dramatic act of his meekness came when he went to a cross to be crucified. Although he was led away to die, no one took his life. That is because Jesus could have called down legions of angels to rescue him. But instead he "suffered and died" for us.

How should Christ's attitude affect the way we treat others? In short, we must put the needs of others before our own. During Jesus' earthly ministry, he always had time for others. We should follow his example. Here is a simple acrostic that will help you keep your priorities in order:

J is for Jesus.
O is for others.
Y is for yourself.

If you put the will of God first and the needs of others above your own, you will find joy.

James

CHAPTER **1**

Greetings from James

This letter is from James, a slave of God and of
the Lord Jesus Christ.

It is written to Jewish Christians scattered
among the nations.*

Greetings!

Faith and Endurance

2Dear brothers and sisters,* whenever trouble
comes your way, let it be an opportunity for
joy. 3For when your faith is tested, your endurance has a chance to grow. 4So let it grow, for
when your endurance is fully developed, you
will be strong in character and ready for anything.

5If you need wisdom—if you want to know
what God wants you to do—ask him, and he
will gladly tell you. He will not resent your
asking. 6But when you ask him, be sure that
you really expect him to answer, for a doubtful
mind is as unsettled as a wave of the sea that is
driven and tossed by the wind. 7People like
that should not expect to receive anything
from the Lord. 8They can't make up their
minds. They waver back and forth in everything they do.

9Christians who are* poor should be glad, for
God has honored them. 10And those who are
rich should be glad, for God has humbled them.
They will fade away like a flower in the field.
11The hot sun rises and dries up the grass; the
flower withers, and its beauty fades away. So
also, wealthy people will fade away with all of
their achievements.

12God blesses the people who patiently endure testing. Afterward they will receive the
crown of life that God has promised to those
who love him. 13And remember, no one who
wants to do wrong should ever say, "God is
tempting me." God is never tempted to do
wrong, and he never tempts anyone else either.
14Temptation comes from the lure of our own
evil desires. 15These evil desires lead to evil actions, and evil actions lead to death. 16So don't
be misled, my dear brothers and sisters.

17Whatever is good and perfect comes to us
from God above, who created all heaven's
lights.* Unlike them, he never changes or casts
shifting shadows. 18In his goodness he chose to
make us his own children by giving us his true
word. And we, out of all creation, became his
choice possession.

Listening and Doing

19My dear brothers and sisters, be quick to listen,
slow to speak, and slow to get angry. 20Your anger
can never make things right in God's sight.

21So get rid of all the filth and evil in your
lives, and humbly accept the message God has
planted in your hearts, for it is strong enough to
save your souls.

22And remember, it is a message to obey, not
just to listen to. If you don't obey, you are only
fooling yourself. 23For if you just listen and
don't obey, it is like looking at your face in a
mirror but doing nothing to improve your appearance. 24You see yourself, walk away, and
forget what you look like. 25But if you keep
looking steadily into God's perfect law—the law
that sets you free—and if you do what it says and
don't forget what you heard, then God will bless
you for doing it.

26If you claim to be religious but don't control your tongue, you are just fooling yourself,
and your religion is worthless. 27Pure and last-

1:1 Greek *To the twelve tribes in the dispersion.* 1:2 Greek *brothers;* also in 1:16, 19. 1:9 Greek *The brother who is.* 1:17 Greek *from above, from the Father of lights.*

Life's Trials Will Make You Stronger Read JAMES 1:2-4

One of the keys to growing and being able to effectively continue in the Christian life is enduring. A key aspect of endurance is patience. The word used for "endurance" in verse 3 is the Greek word *hupomone*, which means "a patient enduring."

This cheerful, enduring patience, which helps us to continue in our Christian walk, actually comes—and develops—in times of testing and hardship. During these trials or "storms of life," our spiritual roots grow deeper, thus strengthening our faith. If we had our way, most of us would probably try to avoid these difficult times in our lives. Yet God promises that he will never give us more than we can handle (see 1 Corinthians 10:13, p. 208).

These times of trial and testing will make us either better or bitter. It really is up to us and the outlook we choose to take. If we can learn to walk in our relationship with God on the basis of faith as opposed to mere feeling, we will grow stronger and, as this passage says, "be strong in character and ready for anything."

ing religion in the sight of God our Father
means that we must care for orphans and widows in their troubles, and refuse to let the world
corrupt us.

CHAPTER 2

A Warning against Prejudice

My dear brothers and sisters,* how can you
claim that you have faith in our glorious Lord
Jesus Christ if you favor some people more than
others?

2For instance, suppose someone comes into
your meeting* dressed in fancy clothes and expensive jewelry, and another comes in who is
poor and dressed in shabby clothes. 3If you give
special attention and a good seat to the rich
person, but you say to the poor one, "You can
stand over there, or else sit on the floor"—well,
4doesn't this discrimination show that you are
guided by wrong motives?

5Listen to me, dear brothers and sisters.
Hasn't God chosen the poor in this world to be
rich in faith? Aren't they the ones who will
inherit the kingdom God promised to those
who love him? 6And yet, you insult the poor
man! Isn't it the rich who oppress you and
drag you into court? 7Aren't they the ones who
slander Jesus Christ, whose noble name you
bear?

8Yes indeed, it is good when you truly obey
our Lord's royal command found in the
Scriptures: "Love your neighbor as yourself."*
9But if you pay special attention to the rich, you
are committing a sin, for you are guilty of breaking that law.

10And the person who keeps all of the laws
except one is as guilty as the person who has
broken all of God's laws. 11For the same God
who said, "Do not commit adultery," also said,
"Do not murder."* So if you murder someone,
you have broken the entire law, even if you do
not commit adultery.

12So whenever you speak, or whatever you
do, remember that you will be judged by the law
of love, the law that set you free. 13For there will
be no mercy for you if you have not been merciful to others. But if you have been merciful, then
God's mercy toward you will win out over his
judgment against you.

Faith without Good Deeds Is Dead

14Dear brothers and sisters, what's the use
of saying you have faith if you don't prove it
by your actions? That kind of faith can't save
anyone. 15Suppose you see a brother or sister who needs food or clothing, 16and you
say, "Well, good-bye and God bless you; stay
warm and eat well"—but then you don't
give that person any food or clothing. What
good does that do?

17So you see, it isn't enough just to have faith.
Faith that doesn't show itself by good deeds is
no faith at all—it is dead and useless.

2:1 Greek *brothers;* also in 2:5, 14. 2:2 Greek *synagogue.* 2:8 Lev 19:18. 2:11 Exod 20:13-14; Deut 5:17-18.

18Now someone may argue, "Some people
have faith; others have good deeds." I say, "I
can't see your faith if you don't have good deeds,
but I will show you my faith through my good
deeds."
19Do you still think it's enough just to believe
that there is one God? Well, even the demons
believe this, and they tremble in terror! 20Fool!
When will you ever learn that faith that does not
result in good deeds is useless?
21Don't you remember that our ancestor
Abraham was declared right with God because of what he did when he offered his
son Isaac on the altar? 22You see, he was
trusting God so much that he was willing to
do whatever God told him to do. His faith
was made complete by what he did—by his
actions. 23And so it happened just as the
Scriptures say: "Abraham believed God, so
God declared him to be righteous."* He was
even called "the friend of God."* 24So you
see, we are made right with God by what we
do, not by faith alone.
25Rahab the prostitute is another example of
this. She was made right with God by her actions—when she hid those messengers and sent
them safely away by a different road. 26Just as
the body is dead without a spirit, so also faith is
dead without good deeds.

CHAPTER 3

Controlling the Tongue

Dear brothers and sisters,* not many of you
should become teachers in the church, for we
who teach will be judged by God with greater
strictness.
2We all make many mistakes, but those
who control their tongues can also control
themselves in every other way. 3We can make
a large horse turn around and go wherever we
want by means of a small bit in its mouth.
4And a tiny rudder makes a huge ship turn
wherever the pilot wants it to go, even though
the winds are strong. 5So also, the tongue is a
small thing, but what enormous damage it
can do. A tiny spark can set a great forest on
fire. 6And the tongue is a flame of fire. It is full
of wickedness that can ruin your whole life. It
can turn the entire course of your life into a
blazing flame of destruction, for it is set on
fire by hell itself.
7People can tame all kinds of animals and
birds and reptiles and fish, 8but no one can tame
the tongue. It is an uncontrollable evil, full of
deadly poison. 9Sometimes it praises our Lord
and Father, and sometimes it breaks out into
curses against those who have been made in the
image of God. 10And so blessing and cursing
come pouring out of the same mouth. Surely,
my brothers and sisters, this is not right! 11Does
a spring of water bubble out with both fresh
water and bitter water? 12Can you pick olives
from a fig tree or figs from a grapevine? No, and
you can't draw fresh water from a salty pool.

True Wisdom Comes from God

13If you are wise and understand God's ways,
live a life of steady goodness so that only good
deeds will pour forth. And if you don't brag
about the good you do, then you will be truly

2:23a Gen 15:6. 2:23b See Isa 41:8. 3:1 Greek *brothers;* also in 3:10.

Prayer Allows Us to Voice Our Requests to God

Read JAMES 4:2-3

There may come a time in your life when you wonder why you are not growing in your faith. Or you might wonder why you don't ever have the opportunity to lead others to Christ. When you ask yourself these kinds of questions, you may be able to answer them with another question: "Have I asked God to help me in this area?"

Understand that this passage does not advocate that you "demand" things from God as though he were some "cosmic butler," prepared to answer your every beck and call. Yet it is equally wrong to fail to ask him to help meet your needs or to bless your life and spiritually strengthen you. God wants to bless you because you are his child. Unfortunately, many of us fail to receive what God has for us because we don't pray.

Take a moment to look at your own spiritual progress. Do you want to have a better understanding of the Bible? Are you looking for some Christian friends? Do you want the Lord to show you what your gifts and talents are? God wants to bless you, but he may be just waiting for your invitation to do so.

FIRST STEPS

CORNER STONES

We Must Live Out Our Faith Read JAMES 2:14-17

While you do not need to change your lifestyle before you come to Christ, once you do come to Christ, your lifestyle should show tangible changes. If it does not, then one could doubt whether Christ has really come into your life. The way you live should reflect what you believe. As John the Baptist said, "Prove by the way you live that you have really turned from your sins and turned to God" (Luke 3:8).

James brings out another important reason for backing up our faith with our actions in verses 15 and 16: It makes it easier to share our faith with others. When people see that we genuinely care about them as individuals, then they will be much more open to hearing about what motivates us.

Can people see Jesus in the way you live? If not, it is time to move Jesus into the "pilot seat" of your life.

wise! 14But if you are bitterly jealous and there
is selfish ambition in your hearts, don't brag
about being wise. That is the worst kind of lie.
15For jealousy and selfishness are not God's
kind of wisdom. Such things are earthly, un-
spiritual, and motivated by the Devil. 16For
wherever there is jealousy and selfish ambition, there you will find disorder and every
kind of evil.

17But the wisdom that comes from heaven is
first of all pure. It is also peace loving, gentle at
all times, and willing to yield to others. It is full
of mercy and good deeds. It shows no partiality
and is always sincere. 18And those who are
peacemakers will plant seeds of peace and reap
a harvest of goodness.

CHAPTER 4

Drawing Close to God

What is causing the quarrels and fights among
you? Isn't it the whole army of evil desires at war
within you? 2You want what you don't have, so
you scheme and kill to get it. You are jealous for
what others have, and you can't possess it, so
you fight and quarrel to take it away from them.
And yet the reason you don't have what you
want is that you don't ask God for it. 3And even
when you do ask, you don't get it because your
whole motive is wrong—you want only what
will give you pleasure.

4You adulterers! Don't you realize that
friendship with this world makes you an enemy
of God? I say it again, that if your aim is to enjoy

OFF AND RUNNING

Control Your Tongue Read JAMES 3:1-12

It has been said that "A lie is halfway around the world while truth is still putting its shoes on." This illustrates the power of malicious speech. One unfounded rumor, one careless remark, one morsel of gossip can cause the greatest devastation. How correct James was when he wrote that the tongue is a flame of fire and full of wickedness.

Unfortunately, it is the sins of the tongue—backbiting, gossip, and tearing down another person—that we often excuse. We think that because we do not murder, commit adultery, or steal we are basically good people. But James makes it clear that certain kinds of speech are wrong. The content of a Christian's conversation should reflect what has happened in his or her heart. After all, part of the fruit, or evidence, of the Holy Spirit's presence in our lives is self-control (see Galatians 5:22-23, p. 234). The person who has no control over his or her tongue is usually "out of control" in other areas of life. But the person who has discipline over this area of life has yielded to the control of the Holy Spirit and will undoubtedly be able to keep other areas of his or her life in check as well.

this world, you can't be a friend of God. 5What
do you think the Scriptures mean when they say
that the Holy Spirit, whom God has placed
within us, jealously longs for us to be faithful*?
6He gives us more and more strength to stand
against such evil desires. As the Scriptures say,

"God sets himself against the proud,
but he shows favor to the humble."*

7So humble yourselves before God. Resist the
Devil, and he will flee from you. 8Draw close to
God, and God will draw close to you. Wash your
hands, you sinners; purify your hearts, you hypocrites. 9Let there be tears for the wrong things
you have done. Let there be sorrow and deep
grief. Let there be sadness instead of laughter,
and gloom instead of joy. 10When you bow
down before the Lord and admit your depen-
dence on him, he will lift you up and give you
honor.

Warning against Judging Others

11Don't speak evil against each other, my dear
brothers and sisters.* If you criticize each other
and condemn each other, then you are criticizing and condemning God's law. But you are
not a judge who can decide whether the law is
right or wrong. Your job is to obey it. 12God
alone, who made the law, can rightly judge
among us. He alone has the power to save or
to destroy. So what right do you have to condemn your neighbor?

Warning about Self-Confidence

13Look here, you people who say, "Today or
tomorrow we are going to a certain town and
will stay there a year. We will do business there
and make a profit." 14How do you know what
will happen tomorrow? For your life is like the
morning fog—it's here a little while, then it's
gone. 15What you ought to say is, "If the Lord
wants us to, we will live and do this or that."
16Otherwise you will be boasting about your
own plans, and all such boasting is evil.

17Remember, it is sin to know what you ought
to do and then not do it.

CHAPTER 5

Warning to the Rich

Look here, you rich people, weep and groan with
anguish because of all the terrible troubles
ahead of you. 2Your wealth is rotting away, and
your fine clothes are moth-eaten rags. 3Your
gold and silver have become worthless. The very
wealth you were counting on will eat away your
flesh in hell.* This treasure you have accumulated will stand as evidence against you on the
day of judgment. 4For listen! Hear the cries of
the field workers whom you have cheated of

4:5 Or *the spirit that God placed within us tends to envy,* or *the Holy Spirit, whom God has placed within us, opposes our envy.* 4:6 Prov 3:34. 4:11 Greek *brothers.* 5:3 Or *will eat your flesh like fire.*

Resist the Devil Read JAMES 4:7-8

Satan recognizes the value of getting a foothold in the realm of our thoughts. He knows that sin is not merely a matter of actions and deeds, but something within the heart and the mind that eventually leads to the sinful action. Here are four practical and effective ways to "resist" the Devil and his temptations:

1. Submit Yourself to God. When you submit yourself to God, you are acknowledging his authority in your life. Because God is holy, which means pure and without sin, he will help you live a life that is pleasing to him. But in order to do this, you must submit to his authority.

2. Resist the Devil. To resist the Devil means to not give in to temptation when it presents itself. Giving in to temptation is an open invitation for the Devil and his demons to continually tempt you. But if you resist giving in to sin, the Devil will flee from you, meaning that he will give up tempting you for the time being.

3. Draw Close to God. The closer you get to God, the more you distance yourself from your old partner, the Devil. And the more time you spend with the Lord, through Bible study and prayer, the less likely you will be to fall. As Psalm 16:8 says, "I am always thinking of the LORD; and because he is so near, I never need to stumble or fall."

4. Wash Your Hands and Purify Your Hearts. This set of instructions is a call to repentance for all those who are harboring sin in their life. To harbor sin in your life is to give the Devil an opportunity to work in you and through you. But God is the one who should work in your life, not the Devil. If you are harboring sin in any area of your life, stop doing it, confess it to God, and ask him to forgive you and then work through you.

FIRST STEPS

What Do Demons Believe? Read JAMES 2:19

Believe it or not, in some ways demons are quite orthodox in their beliefs. They recognize that Jesus is indeed the Son of God. In Matthew's Gospel, the demons say to Jesus, "Why are you bothering us, Son of God? You have no right to torture us before God's appointed time!" (Matthew 8:29). Clearly the demons understand Jesus' awesome power—and they shudder in fear at the thought of him!

Interestingly enough, many people today do not even accept that Jesus is God's Son. Yet, even if you do believe in God, these verses show that it is not enough to keep you from going to hell. Belief without obedience is worthless. Those who settle for less than a total commitment to Christ may find themselves in the company of the demons at the time of judgment.

CORNER STONES

their pay. The wages you held back cry out against you. The cries of the reapers have reached the ears of the Lord Almighty.

5You have spent your years on earth in luxury, satisfying your every whim. Now your hearts are nice and fat, ready for the slaughter. 6You have condemned and killed good people who had no power to defend themselves against you.

Patience in Suffering

7Dear brothers and sisters,* you must be patient as you wait for the Lord's return. Consider the farmers who eagerly look for the rains in the fall and in the spring. They patiently wait for the precious harvest to ripen. 8You, too, must be patient. And take courage, for the coming of the Lord is near.

9Don't grumble about each other, my brothers and sisters, or God will judge you. For look! The great Judge is coming. He is standing at the door!

10For examples of patience in suffering, dear brothers and sisters, look at the prophets who spoke in the name of the Lord. 11We give great honor to those who endure under suffering. Job is an example of a man who endured patiently. From his experience we see how the Lord's plan finally ended in good, for he is full of tenderness and mercy.

12But most of all, my brothers and sisters, never take an oath, by heaven or earth or anything else. Just say a simple yes or no, so that you will not sin and be condemned for it.

The Power of Prayer

13Are any among you suffering? They should keep on praying about it. And those who have reason to be thankful should continually sing praises to the Lord.

14Are any among you sick? They should call for the elders of the church and have them pray over them, anointing them with oil in the name of the Lord. 15And their prayer offered in faith will heal the sick, and the Lord will make them well. And anyone who has committed sins will be forgiven.

16Confess your sins to each other and pray for each other so that you may be healed. The earnest prayer of a righteous person has great power and wonderful results. 17Elijah was as human as we are, and yet when he prayed earnestly that no rain would fall, none fell for the next three and a half years! 18Then he prayed for rain, and down it poured. The grass turned green, and the crops began to grow again.

Restore Wandering Believers

19My dear brothers and sisters, if anyone among you wanders away from the truth and is brought back again, 20you can be sure that the one who brings that person back will save that sinner from death and bring about the forgiveness of many sins.

5:7 Greek *brothers;* also in 5:9, 10, 12, 19.

1 Peter

CHAPTER 1

Greetings from Peter

This letter is from Peter, an apostle of Jesus Christ.

I am writing to God's chosen people who are living as foreigners in the lands of Pontus, Galatia, Cappadocia, the province of Asia, and Bithynia.
[2]God the Father chose you long ago, and the Spirit has made you holy. As a result, you have obeyed Jesus Christ and are cleansed by his blood.

May you have more and more of God's special favor and wonderful peace.

The Hope of Eternal Life

[3]All honor to the God and Father of our Lord Jesus Christ, for it is by his boundless mercy that God has given us the privilege of being born again. Now we live with a wonderful expectation because Jesus Christ rose again from the dead.
[4]For God has reserved a priceless inheritance for his children. It is kept in heaven for you, pure and undefiled, beyond the reach of change and
decay. [5]And God, in his mighty power, will protect you until you receive this salvation, because you are trusting him. It will be revealed on the
last day for all to see. [6]So be truly glad!* There is wonderful joy ahead, even though it is necessary for you to endure many trials for a while.

[7]These trials are only to test your faith, to show that it is strong and pure. It is being tested as fire tests and purifies gold—and your faith is far more precious to God than mere gold. So if your faith remains strong after being tried by fiery trials, it will bring you much praise and glory and honor on the day when Jesus Christ is revealed to the whole world.

[8]You love him even though you have never seen him. Though you do not see him, you trust him; and even now you are happy with a glorious, inexpressible joy.
[9]Your reward for trusting him will be the salvation of your souls.

[10]This salvation was something the prophets wanted to know more about. They prophesied about this gracious salvation prepared for you, even though they had many questions as to what
it all could mean. [11]They wondered what the Spirit of Christ within them was talking about when he told them in advance about Christ's suffering and his great glory afterward. They wondered when and to whom all this would happen.

[12]They were told that these things would not happen during their lifetime, but many years later, during yours. And now this Good News has been announced by those who preached to you in the power of the Holy Spirit sent from heaven. It is all so wonderful that even the angels are eagerly watching these things happen.

A Call to Holy Living

[13]So think clearly and exercise self-control. Look forward to the special blessings that will come to
you at the return of Jesus Christ. [14]Obey God because you are his children. Don't slip back into your old ways of doing evil; you didn't
know any better then. [15]But now you must be holy in everything you do, just as God—who
chose you to be his children—is holy. [16]For he himself has said, "You must be holy because I am holy."*

[17]And remember that the heavenly Father to whom you pray has no favorites when he judges. He will judge or reward you according to what you do. So you must live in reverent fear of him during your time as foreigners here on earth.
[18]For you know that God paid a ransom to save

1:6 Or *So you are truly glad.* 1:16 Lev 11:44-45; 19:2; 20:7.

How the Holy Spirit Works with the Father and the Son

Read 1 PETER 1:2

The Holy Spirit has the distinct honor of being one of the three members of the Trinity—the other two members being God the Father and Jesus Christ, his Son. This particular verse shows how the Holy Spirit works with the Father and the Son in the life of a believer:

- The Father chooses us and makes us his children.
- Jesus redeems us, having died for us while we were still sinners.
- The Holy Spirit draws us to the Lord and continues to work in our lives to make us pleasing to God.

As you can see, all three members of the Trinity work in concert to bring us into a relationship with God. For that reason, we see that the Holy Spirit is indeed an integral part of what has been called "the Godhead."

CORNER STONES

you from the empty life you inherited from your
ancestors. And the ransom he paid was not mere
gold or silver. 19He paid for you with the precious lifeblood of Christ, the sinless, spotless
Lamb of God. 20God chose him for this purpose
long before the world began, but now in these
final days, he was sent to the earth for all to see.
And he did this for you.

21 Through Christ you have come to trust in
God. And because God raised Christ from the
dead and gave him great glory, your faith and hope
can be placed confidently in God. 22Now you can
have sincere love for each other as brothers and
sisters* because you were cleansed from your
sins when you accepted the truth of the Good
News. So see to it that you really do love each
other intensely with all your hearts.*

23For you have been born again. Your new life
did not come from your earthly parents because
the life they gave you will end in death. But this
new life will last forever because it comes from
the eternal, living word of God. 24As the prophet
says,

"People are like grass that dies away;
their beauty fades as quickly as the
beauty of wildflowers.
The grass withers,
and the flowers fall away.
25 But the word of the Lord will last forever."*

And that word is the Good News that was preached to you.

CHAPTER 2

So get rid of all malicious behavior and deceit.
Don't just pretend to be good! Be done with
hypocrisy and jealousy and backstabbing. 2You
must crave pure spiritual milk so that you can
grow into the fullness of your salvation. Cry out
for this nourishment as a baby cries for milk, 3now
that you have had a taste of the Lord's kindness.

Living Stones for God's House

4Come to Christ, who is the living cornerstone
of God's temple. He was rejected by the people,
but he is precious to God who chose him.

5And now God is building you, as living
stones, into his spiritual temple. What's more,
you are God's holy priests, who offer the spiritual sacrifices that please him because of Jesus
Christ. 6As the Scriptures express it,

"I am placing a stone in Jerusalem,*
a chosen cornerstone,
and anyone who believes in him
will never be disappointed.*"

7Yes, he is very precious to you who believe. But
for those who reject him,

"The stone that was rejected by the builders
has now become the cornerstone."*

8And the Scriptures also say,

"He is the stone that makes people stumble,
the rock that will make them fall."*

1:22a Greek *can have brotherly love.* **1:22b** Some manuscripts read *with a pure heart.* **1:24-25** Isa 40:6-8. **2:6a** Greek *in Zion.* **2:6b** Or *will never be put to shame.* Isa 28:16. **2:7** Ps 118:22. **2:8** Isa 8:14.

They stumble because they do not listen to
God's word or obey it, and so they meet the fate
that has been planned for them.
9But you are not like that, for you are a chosen people. You are a kingdom of priests, God's
holy nation, his very own possession. This is so
you can show others the goodness of God, for he
called you out of the darkness into his wonderful light.

10 "Once you were not a people;
now you are the people of God.
Once you received none of God's mercy;
now you have received his mercy."*

11Dear brothers and sisters, you are foreigners and aliens here. So I warn you to keep away
from evil desires because they fight against
your very souls. 12Be careful how you live
among your unbelieving neighbors. Even if
they accuse you of doing wrong, they will see
your honorable behavior, and they will believe
and give honor to God when he comes to
judge the world.*

Respecting People in Authority

13For the Lord's sake, accept all authority—the
king as head of state, 14and the officials he has
appointed. For the king has sent them to punish
all who do wrong and to honor those who do
right.
15It is God's will that your good lives should
silence those who make foolish accusations
against you. 16You are not slaves; you are free.
But your freedom is not an excuse to do evil. You
are free to live as God's slaves. 17Show respect for
everyone. Love your Christian brothers and sisters.* Fear God. Show respect for the king.

Slaves

18You who are slaves must accept the authority
of your masters. Do whatever they tell you—not
only if they are kind and reasonable, but even if
they are harsh. 19For God is pleased with you
when, for the sake of your conscience, you patiently endure unfair treatment. 20Of course, you
get no credit for being patient if you are beaten
for doing wrong. But if you suffer for doing right
and are patient beneath the blows, God is
pleased with you.
21This suffering is all part of what God has
called you to. Christ, who suffered for you, is
your example. Follow in his steps. 22He never
sinned, and he never deceived anyone. 23He
did not retaliate when he was insulted. When
he suffered, he did not threaten to get even. He
left his case in the hands of God, who always
judges fairly. 24He personally carried away our
sins in his own body on the cross so we can be
dead to sin and live for what is right. You have
been healed by his wounds! 25Once you were
wandering like lost sheep. But now you have
turned to your Shepherd, the Guardian of your
souls.

2:10 Hos 1:6, 9; 2:23. 2:12 Or *on the day of visitation.* 2:17 Greek *Love the brotherhood.*

Trials Sharpen Our Faith

Read 1 PETER 1:3-7

God has selected you for a choice work. But before he can use you, he must toughen the grain of your life. He does this by allowing you to go through difficulties so that your faith can be tested and purified. While this process may not be enjoyable, this passage of Scripture gives us four insights into what we should remember during the testing of our faith, so that our faith will be stronger in the end:

1. **Remember *Whose* You Are.** You are God's child (verse 3).
2. **Remember *What* God Has Promised You.** God has promised you the priceless gift of eternal life (verse 4).
3. **Remember *Who* Will See You Through.** God will protect you until you reach your final destination: heaven (verses 5-6).
4. **Remember *Why* God Lets You Go through Trials.** God wants to test the genuineness of your faith so that your life will result in praise and glory when Jesus returns (verse 7).

Although it is great to spend time on a "spiritual mountaintop," so to speak, we cannot stay there forever. More often than not, at the bottom of that mountain lies cold, hard reality. Yet fruit grows best in the "valleys" (the hard times of life), not on the mountaintops (when everything is going well). Our greatest character development takes place when we take what we have learned on the mountaintop and put it into practice in the valley.

Knowing and Trusting God Is the Source of Inexpressible Joy
Read 1 PETER 1:8

Many people today are seeking joy and happiness but are not finding it. Perhaps they don't understand what happiness really is. At best, they will only find fleeting happiness from possessions, pleasures, or accomplishments. But the joy God gives is not merely some emotional feeling. It is not affected by our circumstances. In fact, it is an unchanging, natural by-product of our faith in Jesus Christ.

As you trust in Jesus and look forward to his return, you will be filled with an "inexpressible joy." It won't be just some sort of emotional high, but it will be a deep, supernatural experience of contentedness based upon the fact that your life is right with God. And this lasting joy and happiness will sustain you for the rest of your life.

CORNERSTONES

CHAPTER 3

Wives

In the same way, you wives must accept the authority of your husbands, even those who refuse
to accept the Good News. Your godly lives will
speak to them better than any words. They will be
won over 2by watching your pure, godly behavior.
3Don't be concerned about the outward beauty
that depends on fancy hairstyles, expensive jewelry, or beautiful clothes. 4You should be known
for the beauty that comes from within, the unfad-
ing beauty of a gentle and quiet spirit, which is so
precious to God. 5That is the way the holy women
of old made themselves beautiful. They trusted
God and accepted the authority of their husbands.
6For instance, Sarah obeyed her husband, Abraham, when she called him her master. You are her
daughters when you do what is right without fear
of what your husbands might do.

Husbands

7In the same way, you husbands must give
honor to your wives. Treat her with understanding as you live together. She may be
weaker than you are, but she is your equal
partner in God's gift of new life. If you don't
treat her as you should, your prayers will not
be heard.

All Christians

8Finally, all of you should be of one mind, full
of sympathy toward each other, loving one another with tender hearts and humble minds.
9Don't repay evil for evil. Don't retaliate when
people say unkind things about you. Instead,
pay them back with a blessing. That is what God
wants you to do, and he will bless you for it.
10For the Scriptures say,

"If you want a happy life and good days,
keep your tongue from speaking evil,
and keep your lips from telling lies.
11 Turn away from evil and do good.
Work hard at living in peace with others.
12 The eyes of the Lord watch over those who
do right,
and his ears are open to their prayers.

OFF AND RUNNING

Never Use Vulgar Speech
Read 1 PETER 3:10

One thing that should certainly change when we come to Christ is the way we talk. If we continue using God's name in vain or keep telling dirty jokes, something is not right. Ephesians 4:29 says, "Don't use foul or abusive language." When we become indifferent to the way we speak (or the way others speak around us), we are downplaying the destructiveness of sin and doing a disservice to the Lord.

But the Lord turns his face
against those who do evil."*

Suffering for Doing Good

13Now, who will want to harm you if you are eager to do good? 14But even if you suffer for doing what is right, God will reward you for it. So don't be afraid and don't worry. 15Instead, you must worship Christ as Lord of your life. And if you are asked about your Christian hope, always be ready to explain it. 16But you must do this in a gentle and respectful way. Keep your conscience clear. Then if people speak evil against you, they will be ashamed when they see what a good life you live because you belong to Christ. 17Remember, it is better to suffer for doing good, if that is what God wants, than to suffer for doing wrong!

18Christ also suffered when he died for our sins once for all time. He never sinned, but he died for sinners that he might bring us safely home to God. He suffered physical death, but he was raised to life in the Spirit.*

19So he went and preached to the spirits in prison—20those who disobeyed God long ago when God waited patiently while Noah was building his boat. Only eight people were saved from drowning in that terrible flood.* 21And this is a picture of baptism, which now saves you by the power of Jesus Christ's resurrection. Baptism is not a removal of dirt from your body; it is an appeal to God from* a clean conscience.

22Now Christ has gone to heaven. He is seated in the place of honor next to God, and all the angels and authorities and powers are bowing before him.

CHAPTER 4

Living for God

So then, since Christ suffered physical pain, you must arm yourselves with the same attitude he had, and be ready to suffer, too. For if you are willing to suffer for Christ, you have decided to stop sinning. 2And you won't spend the rest of your life chasing after evil desires, but you will be anxious to do the will of God. 3You have had enough in the past of the evil things that godless people enjoy—their immorality and lust, their feasting and drunkenness and wild parties, and their terrible worship of idols.

4Of course, your former friends are very surprised when you no longer join them in the wicked things they do, and they say evil things about you. 5But just remember that they will have to face God, who will judge everyone, both the living and the dead. 6That is why the Good News was preached even to those who have died—so that although their bodies were punished with death, they could still live in the spirit as God does.

7The end of the world is coming soon. Therefore, be earnest and disciplined in your prayers. 8Most important of all, continue to show deep love for each other, for love covers a multitude of sins. 9Cheerfully share your home with those who need a meal or a place to stay.

10God has given gifts to each of you from his great variety of spiritual gifts. Manage them well so that God's generosity can flow through you. 11Are you called to be a speaker? Then speak as though God himself were speaking through you. Are you called to help others? Do it with all the strength and energy that God supplies. Then God will be given glory in everything through Jesus Christ. All glory and power belong to him forever and ever. Amen.

Suffering for Being a Christian

12Dear friends, don't be surprised at the fiery trials you are going through, as if something strange were happening to you. 13Instead, be very glad—because these trials will make you partners with Christ in his suffering, and afterward you will have the wonderful joy of sharing his glory when it is displayed to all the world.

3:10-12 Ps 34:12-16. 3:18 Or *spirit.* 3:20 Greek *saved through water.* 3:21 Or *for.*

If you find that this area is a trouble spot for you, commit it to God, and he will begin by cleaning up your thoughts. Then consciously replace that coarse language with praise and thankfulness to God for his goodness. As you focus upon God's goodness, your mind will be less filled with the perverse and wicked thoughts of this world.

Our Conduct Should Cause Others to Glorify Christ

Read 1 PETER 2:9-12

Have you ever felt like your life wasn't really important in the grand scheme of things? Have you ever wondered if it was possible to make a difference in the world around you? These verses show that you can—and should—play a significant role in this world.

Remember Who You Are. First, think about who you are. Christians need to be different than those who do not know the Lord. Your godly lifestyle, priorities, and outlook should set you apart from nonbelievers.

Make a Difference. We are not to isolate ourselves from the world. God has placed us in this world so that our lives can have an impact on the people with whom we come into contact. Our Christian character and lifestyle will expose those who are living an ungodly life and confront them with the life-changing message of the gospel.

In many ways, the holiest moment of a church service is when God's people go out the doors of the church and into the world. That is when your godly living will cause people to ask, "What makes you different?"

Some people may criticize, ridicule, or persecute you for living a godly life. Others, however, may come to know Jesus as a result of your faithful obedience to God's Word. If they do, they will glorify God for your testimony and their newfound salvation.

CORNERSTONES

14Be happy if you are insulted for being a
Christian, for then the glorious Spirit of God will
come upon you. 15If you suffer, however, it must
not be for murder, stealing, making trouble, or
prying into other people's affairs. 16But it is no
shame to suffer for being a Christian. Praise God
for the privilege of being called by his wonderful
name! 17For the time has come for judgment,
and it must begin first among God's own children. And if even we Christians must be judged,
what terrible fate awaits those who have never
believed God's Good News? 18And

"If the righteous are barely saved,
what chance will the godless and sinners have?"*

19So if you are suffering according to God's will,
keep on doing what is right, and trust yourself to the God who made you, for he will never fail you.

CHAPTER **5**

Advice for Elders and Young Men

And now, a word to you who are elders in the churches. I, too, am an elder and a witness to the sufferings of Christ. And I, too, will share his glory and his honor when he returns. As a fellow elder,
this is my appeal to you: 2Care for the flock of God
entrusted to you. Watch over it willingly, not grudgingly—not for what you will get out of it,
but because you are eager to serve God. 3Don't
lord it over the people assigned to your care, but
lead them by your good example. 4And when the
head Shepherd comes, your reward will be a never-ending share in his glory and honor.

5You younger men, accept the authority of the elders. And all of you, serve each other in humility, for

"God sets himself against the proud,
but he shows favor to the humble."*

6So humble yourselves under the mighty power
of God, and in his good time he will honor you.
7Give all your worries and cares to God, for he cares about what happens to you.

8Be careful! Watch out for attacks from the Devil, your great enemy. He prowls around like a roaring lion, looking for some victim to devour. 9Take a firm stand against him, and be strong in your faith. Remember that your Christian brothers and sisters* all over the world are going through the same kind of suffering you are.

10In his kindness God called you to his eter-

4:18 Prov 11:31. 5:5 Prov 3:34. 5:9 Greek *your brothers.*

nal glory by means of Jesus Christ. After you have suffered a little while, he will restore, support, and strengthen you, and he will place you on a firm foundation. 11All power is his forever and ever. Amen.

Peter's Final Greetings

12I have written this short letter to you with the help of Silas,* whom I consider a faithful brother. My purpose in writing is to encourage you and assure you that the grace of God is with you no matter what happens.

13Your sister church here in Rome* sends you greetings, and so does my son Mark. 14Greet each other in Christian love.*

Peace be to all of you who are in Christ.

5:12 Greek *Silvanus.* 5:13 Greek *The elect one in Babylon.* Babylon was probably a code name for Rome. 5:14 Greek *with a kiss of love.*

2 Peter

CHAPTER 1

Greetings from Peter

This letter is from Simon* Peter, a slave and apostle of Jesus Christ.

I am writing to all of you who share the same precious faith we have, faith given to us by Jesus Christ, our God and Savior, who makes us right with God.

2May God bless you with his special favor and wonderful peace as you come to know Jesus, our God and Lord,* better and better.

Growing in the Knowledge of God

3As we know Jesus better, his divine power gives us everything we need for living a godly life. He has called us to receive his own glory and goodness! 4And by that same mighty power, he has given us all of his rich and wonderful promises. He has promised that you will escape the decadence all around you caused by evil desires and that you will share in his divine nature.

5So make every effort to apply the benefits of these promises to your life. Then your faith will produce a life of moral excellence. A life of moral excellence leads to knowing God better. 6Knowing God leads to self-control. Self-control leads to patient endurance, and patient endurance leads to godliness. 7Godliness leads to love for other Christians,* and finally you will grow to have genuine love for everyone. 8The more you grow like this, the more you will become productive and useful in your knowledge of our Lord Jesus Christ. 9But those who fail to develop these virtues are blind or, at least, very shortsighted. They have already forgotten that God has cleansed them from their old life of sin.

10So, dear brothers and sisters,* work hard to prove that you really are among those God has called and chosen. Doing this, you will never stumble or fall away. 11And God will open wide the gates of heaven for you to enter into the eternal Kingdom of our Lord and Savior Jesus Christ.

Paying Attention to Scripture

12I plan to keep on reminding you of these things—even though you already know them and are standing firm in the truth. 13Yes, I believe I should keep on reminding you of these things as long as I live. 14But the Lord Jesus Christ has shown me that my days here on earth are numbered and I am soon to die.* 15So I will work hard to make these things clear to you. I want you to remember them long after I am gone.

16For we were not making up clever stories when we told you about the power of our Lord Jesus Christ and his coming again. We have seen his majestic splendor with our own eyes. 17And he received honor and glory from God the Father when God's glorious, majestic voice called down from heaven, "This is my beloved Son; I am fully pleased with him." 18We ourselves heard the voice when we were there with him on the holy mountain.

19Because of that, we have even greater confidence in the message proclaimed by the prophets. Pay close attention to what they wrote, for their words are like a light shining in a dark place—until the day Christ appears and his brilliant light shines in your hearts.* 20Above all, you must understand that no prophecy in Scripture ever came from the prophets themselves* 21or because they wanted to prophesy. It was the Holy Spirit who moved the prophets to speak from God.

1:1 Greek *Simeon.* 1:2 Or *come to know God and Jesus our Lord.* 1:7 Greek *brotherly love.* 1:10 Greek *brothers.* 1:14 Greek *I must soon put off this earthly tent.* 1:19 Or *until the day dawns and the morning star rises in your hearts.* 1:20 Or *is a matter of one's own interpretation.*

2 PETER 2 ▸▸▸ page 314

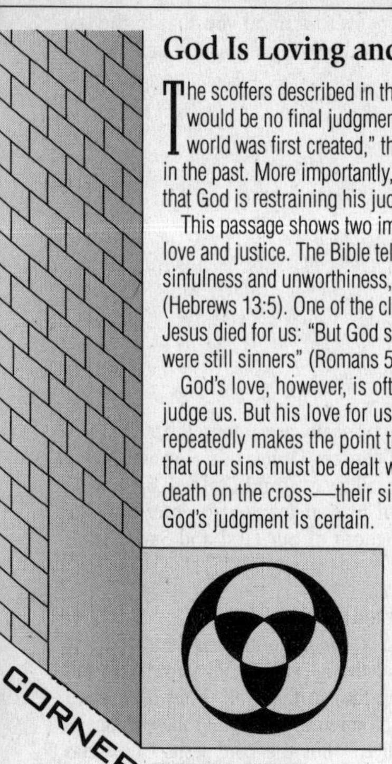

God Is Loving and Just Read 2 PETER 3:3-9

The scoffers described in this passage mistook Christ's delayed return to earth to mean that there would be no final judgment at all. Because everything "remained exactly the same since the world was first created," they not only doubted Christ's return but forgot about God's judgment in the past. More importantly, these scoffers overlooked God's love and mercy. It is for their sake that God is restraining his judgment because "he does not want anyone to perish."

This passage shows two important and seemingly contradictory aspects of God's character: love and justice. The Bible tells us that God is love. In spite of his extensive knowledge of our sinfulness and unworthiness, he has declared, "I will never fail you. I will never forsake you" (Hebrews 13:5). One of the clearest demonstrations of his love is found at the cross on which Jesus died for us: "But God showed his great love for us by sending Christ to die for us while we were still sinners" (Romans 5:8).

God's love, however, is often misunderstood. Many think that because he loves us, he won't judge us. But his love for us does not negate the fact that he is also just. Scripture clearly and repeatedly makes the point that only the godly will see his face. Therefore, we can be certain that our sins must be dealt with. For those who have accepted God's gift of salvation—Jesus' death on the cross—their sins have been forgiven. For those who haven't accepted this gift, God's judgment is certain.

Every day is another opportunity for nonbelievers to come to faith in Jesus Christ. It is also evidence of the tremendous love God has for his creation. In his holiness God is unapproachable, but in his love he approaches us. The next time you are tempted to doubt God's tender love for you, just take a long, hard look at the cross, and remember that it was not the nails that held Jesus there, but his love for you and others!

CHAPTER 2
The Danger of False Teachers

But there were also false prophets in Israel, just
as there will be false teachers among you. They
will cleverly teach their destructive heresies
about God and even turn against their Master
who bought them. Theirs will be a swift and
terrible end. 2Many will follow their evil teaching and shameful immorality. And because of
them, Christ and his true way will be slandered.
3In their greed they will make up clever lies to
get hold of your money. But God condemned
them long ago, and their destruction is on the
way.

4For God did not spare even the angels when
they sinned; he threw them into hell,* in
gloomy caves* and darkness until the judgment
day. 5And God did not spare the ancient
world—except for Noah and his family of
seven. Noah warned the world of God's righteous judgment. Then God destroyed the whole
world of ungodly people with a vast flood.
6Later, he turned the cities of Sodom and Gomorrah into heaps of ashes and swept them off
the face of the earth. He made them an example
of what will happen to ungodly people. 7But at
the same time, God rescued Lot out of Sodom
because he was a good man who was sick of all
the immorality and wickedness around him.
8Yes, he was a righteous man who was distressed by the wickedness he saw and heard day
after day.

9So you see, the Lord knows how to rescue
godly people from their trials, even while pun-
ishing the wicked right up until the day of
judgment. 10He is especially hard on those
who follow their own evil, lustful desires and
who despise authority. These people are proud
and arrogant, daring even to scoff at the glorious ones* without so much as trembling.
11But the angels, even though they are far
greater in power and strength than these false

2:4a Greek *Tartaros.* 2:4b Some manuscripts read *chains of gloom.* 2:10 *The glorious ones* are probably evil angels; also in 2:11.

teachers, never speak out disrespectfully against* the glorious ones.

12These false teachers are like unthinking animals, creatures of instinct, who are born to be caught and killed. They laugh at the terrifying powers they know so little about, and they will be destroyed along with them. 13Their destruction is their reward for the harm they have done. They love to indulge in evil pleasures in broad daylight. They are a disgrace and a stain among you. They revel in deceitfulness while they feast with you. 14They commit adultery with their eyes, and their lust is never satisfied. They make a game of luring unstable people into sin. They train themselves to be greedy; they are doomed and cursed. 15They have wandered off the right road and followed the way of Balaam son of Beor,* who loved to earn money by doing wrong. 16But Balaam was stopped from his mad course when his donkey rebuked him with a human voice.

17These people are as useless as dried-up springs of water or as clouds blown away by the wind—promising much and delivering nothing. They are doomed to blackest darkness. 18They brag about themselves with empty, foolish boasting. With lustful desire as their bait, they lure back into sin those who have just escaped from such wicked living. 19They promise freedom, but they themselves are slaves to sin and corruption. For you are a slave to whatever controls you. 20And when people escape from the wicked ways of the world by learning about our Lord and Savior Jesus Christ and then get tangled up with sin and become its slave again, they are worse off than before. 21It would be better if they had never known the right way to live than to know it and then reject the holy commandments that were given to them. 22They make these proverbs come true: "A dog returns to its vomit,"* and "A washed pig returns to the mud."

CHAPTER 3

The Day of the Lord Is Coming

This is my second letter to you, dear friends, and in both of them I have tried to stimulate your wholesome thinking and refresh your memory. 2I want you to remember and understand what the holy prophets said long ago and what our Lord and Savior commanded through your apostles.

3First, I want to remind you that in the last days there will be scoffers who will laugh at the truth and do every evil thing they desire. 4This will be their argument: "Jesus promised to come back, did he? Then where is he? Why, as far back as anyone can remember, everything has remained exactly the same since the world was first created."

5They deliberately forget that God made the heavens by the word of his command, and he brought the earth up from the water and surrounded it with water. 6Then he used the water to destroy the world with a mighty flood. 7And God has also commanded that the heavens and the earth will be consumed by fire on the day of judgment, when ungodly people will perish.

8But you must not forget, dear friends, that a day is like a thousand years to the Lord, and a thousand years is like a day. 9The Lord isn't really being slow about his promise to return, as some people think. No, he is being patient for your sake. He does not want anyone to perish, so he is giving more time for everyone to repent. 10But the day of the Lord will come as unexpectedly as a thief. Then the heavens will pass away with a terrible noise, and everything in them will disappear in fire, and the earth and everything on it will be exposed to judgment.*

11Since everything around us is going to melt away, what holy, godly lives you should be living! 12You should look forward to that day and hurry it along—the day when God will set the heavens on fire and the elements will melt away in the flames. 13But we are looking forward to the new heavens and new earth he has promised, a world where everyone is right with God.

14And so, dear friends, while you are waiting for these things to happen, make every effort to live a pure and blameless life. And be at peace with God.

15And remember, the Lord is waiting so that people have time to be saved. This is just as our beloved brother Paul wrote to you with the wisdom God gave him—16speaking of these things in all of his letters. Some of his comments are hard to understand, and those who are ignorant and unstable have twisted his letters around to mean something quite different from what he meant, just as they do the other parts of Scripture—and the result is disaster for them.

2:11 Greek *never bring blasphemous judgment from the Lord against.* **2:15** Other manuscripts read *Bosor.* **2:22** Prov 26:11. **3:10** Some manuscripts read *will be burned up.*

Keep an Eternal Perspective Read 2 PETER 3:10-11

If Jesus were to come today, would you be embarrassed by what you are doing? That is a good question to ask yourself each morning—and especially those times when immoral thoughts pop into your head. Jesus emphasized the importance of keeping a pure heart when he said, "God blesses those whose hearts are pure, for they shall see God" (Matthew 5:8).

A literal definition of the word *pure* is "without hypocrisy," or "single." In other words, Jesus says that we must have a singular, sincere devotion to him in order to see God.

The Bible reminds us that the hope of the coming return of Jesus Christ can have a spiritually purifying effect on our lives: "And all who believe this will keep themselves pure, just as Christ is pure" (1 John 3:3). As we recognize the holiness of God and his imminent return, we should pray along with the psalmist, "Teach me your ways, O LORD, that I may live according to your truth! Grant me purity of heart, that I may honor you" (Psalm 86:11).

Peter's Final Words

17I am warning you ahead of time, dear friends, so that you can watch out and not be carried away by the errors of these wicked people. I don't want you to lose your own secure footing. 18But grow in the special favor and knowledge of our Lord and Savior Jesus Christ.

To him be all glory and honor, both now and forevermore. Amen.

I John

CHAPTER 1

Introduction

The one who existed from the beginning* is the
one we have heard and seen. We saw him with our
own eyes and touched him with our own hands.
He is Jesus Christ, the Word of life. 2This one who
is life from God was shown to us, and we have
seen him. And now we testify and announce to
you that he is the one who is eternal life. He was
with the Father, and then he was shown to us. 3We
are telling you about what we ourselves have actually seen and heard, so that you may have fellowship with us. And our fellowship is with the Father
and with his Son, Jesus Christ.

4We are writing these things so that our* joy
will be complete.

Living in the Light

5This is the message he has given us to announce to
you: God is light and there is no darkness in him at
all. 6So we are lying if we say we have fellowship with
God but go on living in spiritual darkness. We are
not living in the truth. 7But if we are living in the
light of God's presence, just as Christ is, then we have
fellowship with each other, and the blood of Jesus,
his Son, cleanses us from every sin.

8If we say we have no sin, we are only fooling
ourselves and refusing to accept the truth. 9But
if we confess our sins to him, he is faithful and
just to forgive us and to cleanse us from every
wrong. 10If we claim we have not sinned, we are
calling God a liar and showing that his word has
no place in our hearts.

CHAPTER 2

My dear children, I am writing this to you so that
you will not sin. But if you do sin, there is
someone to plead for you before the Father. He
is Jesus Christ, the one who pleases God completely.* 2He is the sacrifice for our sins. He takes
away not only our sins but the sins of all the
world.

3And how can we be sure that we belong to
him? By obeying his commandments. 4If someone says, "I belong to God," but doesn't obey
God's commandments, that person is a liar and
does not live in the truth. 5But those who obey
God's word really do love him. That is the way
to know whether or not we live in him. 6Those
who say they live in God should live their lives
as Christ did.

A New Commandment

7Dear friends, I am not writing a new commandment, for it is an old one you have always had,
right from the beginning. This commandment—to love one another—is the same message you heard before. 8Yet it is also new. This
commandment is true in Christ and is true
among you, because the darkness is disappear-
ing and the true light is already shining.

9If anyone says, "I am living in the light,"
but hates a Christian brother or sister,* that
person is still living in darkness. 10Anyone
who loves other Christians* is living in the
light and does not cause anyone to stumble.
11Anyone who hates a Christian brother or
sister is living and walking in darkness. Such a
person is lost, having been blinded by the
darkness.

> 12I am writing to you, my dear children,
> because your sins have been forgiven
> because of Jesus.
>
> 13I am writing to you who are mature

1:1 Greek *What was from the beginning.* 1:4 Some manuscripts read *your.* 2:1 Greek *Jesus Christ, the righteous.* 2:9 Greek *his brother;* also in 2:11. 2:10 Greek *his brother.*

Our Love for Others Mirrors the Condition of Our Heart
Read 1 JOHN 2:9-11

Being a Christian involves more than just vocalizing our love to God. It also means demonstrating God's love to others. Humanly speaking, it is much easier to dislike someone than it is to love him or her. Grudges and resentment come easily. Yet bitterness toward others is a poison. Not only does it affect our relationships with other people, but it spiritually blinds us as well. Worse yet, harboring bitterness toward other people is a sin that can lead to other sins.

If you are having trouble loving others, then you need to learn how to walk "in the light." How do you do that? Verse 6 of this chapter says, "Those who say they live in God should live their lives as Christ did." Take a look at the way you treat the people in your life; then compare your relationships with Jesus' relationships in the Gospels (Matthew, Mark, Luke, and John). Here is a sampling of what you will find:

- Jesus reached out to the unlovable (see Luke 19:1-10, pp. 96–97).
- Jesus gave a second chance to a friend who had let him down (see John 18:25-27, p. 129, and John 21:15-19, pp. 133–134).
- Jesus showed patience toward those who questioned him (see John 20:24-28, p. 133).
- Jesus cared for the sick (see Luke 5:12-16, p. 73).
- Jesus initiated conversations with those whom others despised (see John 4:4-42, pp. 110–111).
- Jesus wept with those who grieved (see John 11:1-44, pp. 119–120).

Ask God to help you love as Jesus loved, and you will see some radical changes in your heart and your life.

CORNERSTONES

because you know Christ, the one who is from the beginning.

I am writing to you who are young because you have won your battle with Satan.

14I have written to you, children, because you have known the Father.

I have written to you who are mature because you know Christ, the one who is from the beginning.

I have written to you who are young because you are strong with God's word living in your hearts, and you have won your battle with Satan.

15Stop loving this evil world and all that it offers you, for when you love the world, you show that

OFF AND RUNNING

Make Sure Your Friendships Honor God
Read 1 JOHN 1:7

What is the key to having a friendship that honors God? First, make sure that you are walking in obedience to God, "living in the light of God's presence." If you are not committed to obeying God, then you will probably make friends with those who also lack this commitment. Any relationship that does not encourage you to live obediently to God and entices you to sin dishonors God.

On the other hand, if you are committed to obeying God, you will seek out friends who are also committed to him. As you walk with those who share the same love for the Lord as you have, you will be filled with joy and have greater impetus to keep from sinning. And your friendships will honor God.

you do not have the love of the Father in you. 16For the world offers only the lust for physical pleasure, the lust for everything we see, and pride in our possessions. These are not from the Father. They are from this evil world. 17And this world is fading away, along with everything it craves. But if you do the will of God, you will live forever.

18Dear children, the last hour is here. You have heard that the Antichrist is coming, and already many such antichrists have appeared. From this we know that the end of the world has come. 19These people left our churches because they never really belonged with us; otherwise they would have stayed with us. When they left us, it proved that they do not belong with us. 20But you are not like that, for the Holy Spirit has come upon you,* and all of you know the truth. 21So I am writing to you not because you don't know the truth but because you know the difference between truth and falsehood. 22And who is the great liar? The one who says that Jesus is not the Christ. Such people are antichrists, for they have denied the Father and the Son. 23Anyone who denies the Son doesn't have the Father either. But anyone who confesses the Son has the Father also.

24So you must remain faithful to what you have been taught from the beginning. If you do, you will continue to live in fellowship with the Son and with the Father. 25And in this fellowship we enjoy the eternal life he promised us.

26I have written these things to you because you need to be aware of those who want to lead you astray. 27But you have received the Holy Spirit,* and he lives within you, so you don't need anyone to teach you what is true. For the Spirit teaches you all things, and what he teaches is true—it is not a lie. So continue in what he has taught you, and continue to live in Christ.

28And now, dear children, continue to live in fellowship with Christ so that when he returns, you will be full of courage and not shrink back from him in shame. 29Since we know that God is always right, we also know that all who do what is right are his children.

CHAPTER 3

Living as Children of God

See how very much our heavenly Father loves us, for he allows us to be called his children, and we really are! But the people who belong to this world don't know God, so they don't understand that we are his children. 2Yes, dear friends, we are already God's children, and we can't even imagine what we will be like when Christ returns. But we do know that when he comes we will be like him, for we will see him as he really is. 3And all who believe this will keep themselves pure, just as Christ is pure.

4Those who sin are opposed to the law of God, for all sin opposes the law of God. 5And you know that Jesus came to take away our sins, for there is no sin in him. 6So if we continue to live in him, we won't sin either. But those who keep on sinning have never known him or understood who he is.

7Dear children, don't let anyone deceive you about this: When people do what is right, it is because they are righteous, even as Christ is righteous. 8But when people keep on sinning, it shows they belong to the Devil, who has been sinning since the beginning. But the Son of God came to destroy these works of the Devil. 9Those who have

2:20 Greek *But you have an anointing from the Holy One.*
2:27 Greek *the anointing.*

A Disciple Walks as Jesus Walked Read 1 JOHN 2:3-6

If you call yourself a disciple, you need to follow in Jesus' footsteps. As verse 6 says, you need to "live [your life] as Christ did." Another translation says that you should "walk as he walked."

Walking implies a steady motion—you put one foot in front of the other, and you keep moving. That is the way we should follow Christ. We need to stick with it and be consistent. How do you practically live as Christ did?

- Make time for God and his Word every single day.
- Spend time in prayer with the Lord throughout the day.
- Take time to be with God's people.

There is a tremendous benefit to the disciple who stays close to Christ. By walking as he walked, the Bible tells us we will have help to keep us from sinning (see 1 John 3:6, p. 319). For that reason, one of the greatest identifying marks of a disciple is that his or her walk resembles the Master's.

FIRST STEPS

Understand the Difference between the True Gospel and a False Gospel Read 1 JOHN 4:1-3

False teachings are not unique to our times. They cropped up in the days of the early church as well. When John wrote this passage, a teaching called Gnosticism (which means "to know") had become popular. It taught that Jesus was a mere human being, born by natural procreation. It also claimed that "the Christ" came upon Jesus at his baptism and left him before his crucifixion. This, of course, was false and unscriptural. Yet it is important to note that this heresy is still taught by some today.

As this text says, we need to "test" these teachings to see if they really come from God. Since false teachers don't carry ID cards, here are three simple questions to ask of anyone you may suspect of being a false teacher:

1. What Is Their Ultimate Hope? Some hope to make a better world. Mormons expect to be equal with God. They also hope that each Mormon couple will be given their own planet to populate. Jehovah's Witnesses believe God will come back to earth at the end of time and establish a paradise here. They hope to live in this paradise on earth. But the hope for the Christian is to spend eternity with Jesus Christ in heaven.

2. What Is the Basis for This Hope? Do they teach that you can only get to heaven by living a good life? Do they say that you obtain salvation by faith in Jesus Christ and by performing certain things or rituals, like baptism, keeping the Sabbath, or other works? You must beware of the "and's." The Bible says, "God saved you by his special favor when you believed. And you can't take credit for this; it is a gift from God. Salvation is not a reward for the good things we have done, so none of us can boast about it" (Ephesians 2:8-9).

3. How Do They View Jesus Christ? Another earmark of a false teacher preaching a false gospel is what he or she claims about the person of Jesus Christ. This is really the central and primary issue. Many cults seek to make their teachings more "palatable" to those in the church by including Jesus Christ in their teachings. They may even use terms like "saved" and "born again," and speak of Jesus dying on the cross. Interestingly enough, some teachings may pass the first two tests but fail this ultimate test, which is believing that Jesus was resurrected from the dead.

Any attempts to cast doubt upon the Bible's sufficiency should be rejected. Any "broadness" that would admit any other way to God outside of Christ is false. To say that Jesus is not the only way to God is to call Jesus a liar! Anytime Jesus, "the unique Son of God," is reduced to merely *"a* son of God" or one of many prophets from God, it is erroneous. The best way to know the false is to be familiar with the true: God's Word, the Bible.

CORNERSTONES

been born into God's family do not sin, because God's life is in them. So they can't keep on sinning, because they have been born of God. 10So now we can tell who are children of God and who are children of the Devil. Anyone who does not obey God's commands and does not love other Christians* does not belong to God.

Love One Another

11This is the message we have heard from the beginning: We should love one another. 12We must not be like Cain, who belonged to the evil one and killed his brother. And why did he kill him? Because Cain had been doing what was evil, and his brother had been doing what was right. 13So don't be surprised, dear brothers and sisters,* if the world hates you.

14If we love our Christian brothers and sisters, it proves that we have passed from death to eternal life. But a person who has no love is still dead. 15Anyone who hates another Christian* is really a murderer at heart. And you know that

3:10 Greek *his brother.* 3:13 Greek *brothers;* also in 3:14, 16. 3:15 Greek *his brother.*

How Can I Tell the Difference between True and False Teachings about God? Read 1 JOHN 4:1-2

The Bible tells us that we must be especially careful in these "last days," for the coming Antichrist and false prophet will perform signs and miracles and deceive many (see 2 Thessalonians 2:9-10, pp. 265–266).

So how does one tell the true gospel from a counterfeit or false gospel? Here are four tests you can apply to make sure the teachings you hear really come from God:

1. Does the Teaching Recognize Jesus Christ as the Son of God and the Only Way of Salvation? Proper teaching must agree that Jesus Christ is God's unique Son, and that he "became a human being" (verse 2). Most cults deny Christ's deity, recognizing him only as a great teacher or, as Jehovah's Witnesses claim, simply God's first created creature. So find out what this teaching has to say about Jesus.

2. Does the Teaching Agree with Scripture? The apostle Paul commended the Bereans because "they searched the Scriptures day after day to check up on [their statements] to see if they were really teaching the truth" (Acts 17:11). Don't simply take some pastor or teacher's word as gospel without examining it in the light of God's Word first.

3. If Miracles Are Involved, Do They Bring Glory to God or to Someone Else? Remember, God is not the only one who can do miracles. As mentioned above, the Antichrist will deceive many with his miraculous wonders. Satan is a great imitator. In the last days, "false messiahs and false prophets will rise up and perform great miraculous signs and wonders so as to deceive, if possible, even God's chosen ones" (Matthew 24:24). Do not accept any miracle at face value. Make sure that the person through whom the miracle comes has a strong personal relationship with Jesus Christ (see Matthew 7:21-23, p. 12). More important, be certain the miracle glorifies Jesus Christ and does not contradict what Scripture teaches.

4. Is the Teaching Widely Accepted by the World at Large? Contrary to conventional wisdom, the more popular a teaching is does not make it a more "correct" teaching. For instance, relativism, or the idea that each person can live the way he or she wants to as long as he or she is true to himself or herself, is a popular belief. However, we know that God's Word teaches differently. As shown in this passage, if the message is really from God, the world won't listen to it (1 John 4:6).

The more you study the "real thing"—God's Word—the more you will be able to quickly identify the counterfeits. And remember, "the Spirit who lives in you is greater than the spirit who lives in the world" (1 John 4:4).

BIG QUESTIONS

murderers don't have eternal life within them.
16We know what real love is because Christ gave
up his life for us. And so we also ought to give
up our lives for our Christian brothers and sisters. 17But if anyone has enough money to live
well and sees a brother or sister in need and
refuses to help—how can God's love be in that
person?

18Dear children, let us stop just saying we love
each other; let us really show it by our actions.
19It is by our actions that we know we are living
in the truth, so we will be confident when we
stand before the Lord, 20even if our hearts condemn us. For God is greater than our hearts, and
he knows everything.
21Dear friends, if our conscience is clear, we

can come to God with bold confidence. 22And
we will receive whatever we request because we
obey him and do the things that please him.
23And this is his commandment: We must believe in the name of his Son, Jesus Christ, and
love one another, just as he commanded us.
24Those who obey God's commandments live
in fellowship with him, and he with them. And
we know he lives in us because the Holy Spirit
lives in us.

CHAPTER 4

Discerning False Prophets

Dear friends, do not believe everyone who
claims to speak by the Spirit. You must test them
to see if the spirit they have comes from God. For
there are many false prophets in the world. 2This
is the way to find out if they have the Spirit of
God: If a prophet acknowledges that Jesus Christ
became a human being, that person has the
Spirit of God. 3If a prophet does not acknowledge Jesus, that person is not from God. Such a
person has the spirit of the Antichrist. You have
heard that he is going to come into the world,
and he is already here.

4But you belong to God, my dear children.
You have already won your fight with these false
prophets, because the Spirit who lives in you is
greater than the spirit who lives in the world.
5These people belong to this world, so they
speak from the world's viewpoint, and the world
listens to them. 6But we belong to God; that is
why those who know God listen to us. If they do
not belong to God, they do not listen to us. That
is how we know if someone has the Spirit of
truth or the spirit of deception.

Loving One Another

7Dear friends, let us continue to love one another, for love comes from God. Anyone who
loves is born of God and knows God. 8But anyone who does not love does not know God—for
God is love.

9God showed how much he loved us by sending his only Son into the world so that we might
have eternal life through him. 10This is real love. It
is not that we loved God, but that he loved us and
sent his Son as a sacrifice to take away our sins.

11Dear friends, since God loved us that much,
we surely ought to love each other. 12No one has
ever seen God. But if we love each other, God
lives in us, and his love has been brought to full
expression through us.

13And God has given us his Spirit as proof
that we live in him and he in us. 14Furthermore,
we have seen with our own eyes and now testify
that the Father sent his Son to be the Savior of
the world. 15All who proclaim that Jesus is the
Son of God have God living in them, and they
live in God. 16We know how much God loves us,
and we have put our trust in him.

God is love, and all who live in love live in
God, and God lives in them. 17And as we live in
God, our love grows more perfect. So we will not
be afraid on the day of judgment, but we can
face him with confidence because we are like
Christ here in this world.

18Such love has no fear because perfect love
expels all fear. If we are afraid, it is for fear of
judgment, and this shows that his love has not
been perfected in us. 19We love each other* as a
result of his loving us first.

20If someone says, "I love God," but hates a
Christian brother or sister,* that person is a liar;
for if we don't love people we can see, how can

4:19 Or *We love him;* Greek reads *We love.* 4:20 Greek *brother;* also in 4:21.

OFF AND RUNNING

Pray Expecting to Get Answers Read 1 JOHN 5:14-15

Prayer is not getting your will in heaven. It is getting God's will on earth. Prayer is not an argument with God in which you try to persuade him to move things your way. Prayer is an exercise in which his Spirit enables you to move yourself his way. Prayer is not overcoming God's reluctance. It is laying hold of his willingness.

We like to gravitate toward the latter part of these verses. But don't forget the first part: You have to first "stay in Christ" by maintaining a healthy, ongoing relationship with him. When that happens, you will see your will coming in line with his, and your requests will begin to mirror what Christ wants to do in your life and the lives of those around you. At that point, you can be assured that God is listening to you and will answer your prayers.

we love God, whom we have not seen? 21And
God himself has commanded that we must love
not only him but our Christian brothers and
sisters, too.

CHAPTER 5

Faith in the Son of God

Everyone who believes that Jesus is the Christ is a
child of God. And everyone who loves the Father
loves his children, too. 2We know we love God's
children if we love God and obey his commandments. 3Loving God means keeping his commandments, and really, that isn't difficult. 4For
every child of God defeats this evil world by trusting Christ to give the victory. 5And the ones who
win this battle against the world are the ones who
believe that Jesus is the Son of God.

6And Jesus Christ was revealed as God's Son
by his baptism in water and by shedding his
blood on the cross*—not by water only, but by
water and blood. And the Spirit also gives us the
testimony that this is true. 7So we have these
three witnesses*—8the Spirit, the water, and the
blood—and all three agree. 9Since we believe
human testimony, surely we can believe the testimony that comes from God. And God has
testified about his Son. 10All who believe in the
Son of God know that this is true. Those who
don't believe this are actually calling God a liar
because they don't believe what God has testified about his Son.

11And this is what God has testified: He has
given us eternal life, and this life is in his Son.
12So whoever has God's Son has life; whoever
does not have his Son does not have life.

Conclusion

13I write this to you who believe in the Son of
God, so that you may know you have eternal life.
14And we can be confident that he will listen to
us whenever we ask him for anything in line
with his will. 15And if we know he is listening
when we make our requests, we can be sure that
he will give us what we ask for.

16If you see a Christian brother or sister* sinning in a way that does not lead to death, you
should pray, and God will give that person life. But
there is a sin that leads to death, and I am not
saying you should pray for those who commit it.
17Every wrong is sin, but not all sin leads to death.

18We know that those who have become part
of God's family do not make a practice of sinning, for God's Son holds them securely, and the
evil one cannot get his hands on them. 19We
know that we are children of God and that the
world around us is under the power and control
of the evil one. 20And we know that the Son of
God has come, and he has given us understanding so that we can know the true God. And
now we are in God because we are in his Son,
Jesus Christ. He is the only true God, and he is
eternal life.

21Dear children, keep away from anything
that might take God's place in your hearts.*

5:6 Greek *This is he who came by water and blood.* 5:7 Some very late manuscripts add *in heaven—the Father, the Word, and the Holy Spirit, and these three are one. And we have three witnesses on earth.* 5:16 Greek *your brother.* 5:21 Greek *keep yourselves from idols.*

2 John

Greetings
This letter is from John the Elder.*
It is written to the chosen lady and to her
children,* whom I love in the truth, as does
everyone else who knows God's truth—2the
truth that lives in us and will be in our hearts
forever.
3May grace, mercy, and peace, which come
from God our Father and from Jesus Christ his
Son, be with us who live in truth and love.

Live in the Truth
4How happy I was to meet some of your children and find them living in the truth, just as we
have been commanded by the Father.
5And now I want to urge you, dear lady, that
we should love one another. This is not a new
commandment, but one we had from the beginning. 6Love means doing what God has
commanded us, and he has commanded us to
love one another, just as you heard from the
beginning.
7Many deceivers have gone out into the
world. They do not believe that Jesus Christ
came to earth in a real body. Such a person is a
deceiver and an antichrist. 8Watch out, so that
you do not lose the prize for which we* have
been working so hard. Be diligent so that you
will receive your full reward. 9For if you wander
beyond the teaching of Christ, you will not have
fellowship with God. But if you continue in the
teaching of Christ, you will have fellowship with
both the Father and the Son.
10If someone comes to your meeting and
does not teach the truth about Christ, don't
invite him into your house or encourage him in
any way. 11Anyone who encourages him becomes a partner in his evil work.

Conclusion
12Well, I have much more to say to you, but I
don't want to say it in a letter. For I hope to visit
you soon and to talk with you face to face. Then
our joy will be complete.
13Greetings from the children of your sister,*
chosen by God.

1a Greek *From the elder.* **1b** Or *the church God has chosen and her members,* or *the chosen Kyria and her children.* **8** Some manuscripts read *you.* **13** Or *from the members of your sister church.*

3 John

Greetings
This letter is from John the Elder.*
It is written to Gaius, my dear friend, whom I
love in the truth.
2Dear friend, I am praying that all is well with
you and that your body is as healthy as I know
your soul is. 3Some of the brothers recently
returned and made me very happy by telling me
about your faithfulness and that you are living
in the truth. 4I could have no greater joy than to
hear that my children live in the truth.

Caring for the Lord's Workers
5Dear friend, you are doing a good work for God
when you take care of the traveling teachers*
who are passing through, even though they are
strangers to you. 6They have told the church
here of your friendship and your loving deeds.
You do well to send them on their way in a
manner that pleases God. 7For they are traveling
for the Lord* and accept nothing from those
who are not Christians.* 8So we ourselves
should support them so that we may become
partners with them for the truth.
9I sent a brief letter to the church about this,
but Diotrephes, who loves to be the leader, does
not acknowledge our authority. 10When I come,
I will report some of the things he is doing and
the wicked things he is saying about us. He not
only refuses to welcome the traveling teachers,
he also tells others not to help them. And when
they do help, he puts them out of the church.
11Dear friend, don't let this bad example influence you. Follow only what is good. Remember that those who do good prove that they are
God's children, and those who do evil prove that
they do not know God. 12But everyone speaks
highly of Demetrius, even truth itself. We ourselves can say the same for him, and you know
we speak the truth.

Conclusion
13I have much to tell you, but I don't want to do
it in a letter. 14For I hope to see you soon, and
then we will talk face to face.
15May God's peace be with you.
Your friends here send you their greetings.
Please give my personal greetings to each of our
friends there.

1 Greek *From the elder.* 5 Greek *the brothers;* also in verse 10. 7a Greek *the Name.* 7b Greek *from Gentiles.*

Jude

Greetings from Jude

This letter is from Jude, a slave of Jesus Christ and a brother of James.

I am writing to all who are called to live in the love of God the Father and the care of Jesus Christ.

2May you receive more and more of God's mercy, peace, and love.

The Danger of False Teachers

3Dearly loved friends, I had been eagerly planning to write to you about the salvation we all share. But now I find that I must write about something else, urging you to defend the truth of the Good News.* God gave this unchanging truth once for all time to his holy people. 4I say this because some godless people have wormed their way in among you, saying that God's forgiveness allows us to live immoral lives. The fate of such people was determined long ago, for they have turned against our only Master and Lord, Jesus Christ.

5I must remind you—and you know it well—that even though the Lord* rescued the whole nation of Israel from Egypt, he later destroyed every one of those who did not remain faithful. 6And I remind you of the angels who did not stay within the limits of authority God gave them but left the place where they belonged. God has kept them chained in prisons of darkness, waiting for the day of judgment. 7And don't forget the cities of Sodom and Gomorrah and their neighboring towns, which were filled with sexual immorality and every kind of sexual perversion. Those cities were destroyed by fire and are a warning of the eternal fire that will punish all who are evil.

8Yet these false teachers, who claim authority from their dreams, live immoral lives, defy authority, and scoff at the power of the glorious ones.* 9But even Michael, one of the mightiest of the angels, did not dare accuse Satan of blasphemy, but simply said, "The Lord rebuke you." (This took place when Michael was arguing with Satan about Moses' body.) 10But these people mock and curse the things they do not understand. Like animals, they do whatever their instincts tell them, and they bring about their own destruction. 11How terrible it will be for them! For they follow the evil example of Cain, who killed his brother. Like Balaam, they will do anything for money. And like Korah, they will perish because of their rebellion.

12When these people join you in fellowship meals celebrating the love of the Lord, they are like dangerous reefs that can shipwreck you.* They are shameless in the way they care only about themselves. They are like clouds blowing over dry land without giving rain, promising much but producing nothing. They are like trees without fruit at harvesttime. They are not only dead but doubly dead, for they have been pulled out by the roots. 13They are like wild waves of the sea, churning up the dirty foam of their shameful deeds. They are wandering stars, heading for everlasting gloom and darkness.

14Now Enoch, who lived seven generations after Adam, prophesied about these people. He said,

"Look, the Lord is coming
with thousands of his holy ones.
15 He will bring the people of the world
to judgment.

3 Greek *to contend for the faith.* 5 Some manuscripts read *Jesus.* 8 *The glorious ones* are probably evil angels. 12 Or *they are contaminants among you,* or *they are stains.*

He will convict the ungodly of all the evil
things
they have done in rebellion
and of all the insults that godless sinners
have spoken against him."*

16These people are grumblers and complainers,
doing whatever evil they feel like. They are loud-
mouthed braggarts, and they flatter others to get
favors in return.

A Call to Remain Faithful

17But you, my dear friends, must remember
what the apostles of our Lord Jesus Christ told
you, 18that in the last times there would be
scoffers whose purpose in life is to enjoy themselves in every evil way imaginable. 19Now they
are here, and they are the ones who are creating
divisions among you. They live by natural instinct because they do not have God's Spirit
living in them.

20But you, dear friends, must continue to
build your lives on the foundation of your holy
faith. And continue to pray as you are directed
by the Holy Spirit.* 21Live in such a way that
God's love can bless you as you wait for the
eternal life that our Lord Jesus Christ in his
mercy is going to give you. 22Show mercy to
those whose faith is wavering. 23Rescue others
by snatching them from the flames of judgment.
There are still others to whom you need to show
mercy, but be careful that you aren't contami-
nated by their sins.*

A Prayer of Praise

24And now, all glory to God, who is able to keep
you from stumbling, and who will bring you
into his glorious presence innocent of sin and
with great joy. 25All glory to him, who alone is
God our Savior, through Jesus Christ our Lord.
Yes, glory, majesty, power, and authority belong
to him, in the beginning, now, and forevermore.
Amen.

14-15 The quotation comes from the Apocrypha: Enoch 1:9. **20** Greek *Pray in the Holy Spirit.* **23** Greek *mercy, hating even the clothing stained by the flesh.*

Revelation

CHAPTER 1

Prologue

This is a revelation from* Jesus Christ, which God gave him concerning the events that will happen soon. An angel was sent to God's servant John so that John could share the revelation with God's other servants. 2John faithfully reported the word of God and the testimony of Jesus Christ—everything he saw.

3God blesses the one who reads this prophecy to the church, and he blesses all who listen to it and obey what it says. For the time is near when these things will happen.

John's Greeting to the Seven Churches

4This letter is from John to the seven churches in the province of Asia. Grace and peace from the one who is, who always was, and who is still to come; from the sevenfold Spirit* before his throne; 5and from Jesus Christ, who is the faithful witness to these things, the first to rise from the dead, and the commander of all the rulers of the world.

All praise to him who loves us and has freed us from our sins by shedding his blood for us. 6He has made us his kingdom and his priests who serve before God his Father. Give to him everlasting glory! He rules forever and ever! Amen!

7Look! He comes with the clouds of heaven. And everyone will see him—even those who pierced him. And all the nations of the earth will weep because of him. Yes! Amen!

8"I am the Alpha and the Omega—the beginning and the end," says the Lord God. "I am the one who is, who always was, and who is still to come, the Almighty One."

Vision of the Son of Man

9I am John, your brother. In Jesus we are partners in suffering and in the Kingdom and in patient endurance. I was exiled to the island of Patmos for preaching the word of God and speaking about Jesus. 10It was the Lord's Day, and I was worshiping in the Spirit.* Suddenly, I heard a loud voice behind me, a voice that sounded like a trumpet blast. 11It said, "Write down what you see, and send it to the seven churches: Ephesus, Smyrna, Pergamum, Thyatira, Sardis, Philadelphia, and Laodicea."

12When I turned to see who was speaking to me, I saw seven gold lampstands. 13And standing in the middle of the lampstands was the Son of Man.* He was wearing a long robe with a gold sash across his chest. 14His head and his hair were white like wool, as white as snow. And his eyes were bright like flames of fire. 15His feet were as bright as bronze refined in a furnace, and his voice thundered like mighty ocean waves. 16He held seven stars in his right hand, and a sharp two-edged sword came from his mouth. And his face was as bright as the sun in all its brilliance.

17When I saw him, I fell at his feet as dead. But he laid his right hand on me and said, "Don't be afraid! I am the First and the Last. 18I am the living one who died. Look, I am alive forever and ever! And I hold the keys of death and the grave.* 19Write down what you have seen—both the things that are now happening and the things that will happen later. 20This is the meaning of the seven stars you saw in my right hand and the seven gold lampstands: The seven stars are the angels of* the seven churches, and the seven lampstands are the seven churches.

1:1 Or *of.* 1:4 Greek *the seven spirits.* 1:10 Or *in spirit.* 1:13 Or *one who looked like a man;* Greek reads *one like a son of man.* See Dan 7:13. 1:18 Greek *and Hades.* 1:20 Or *the messengers for.*

Jesus Has an Eternal Dominion Read REVELATION 1:4-8

This passage of Scripture confirms two important aspects about Jesus Christ: his majesty and dominion. Yet Jesus is distinctly different than any type of royalty or government we are familiar with. The following six points show that difference:

1. He Is the First to Rise from Death and Die No More. Christ gives us a glimpse of what will happen after we die.

2. He Is Greater than Any King in All the Earth. He is Lord over all creation—no earthly leader can make that claim.

3. He Loves Us and Demonstrated His Love by His Death. Rarely has someone in authority over others offered to die in their place.

4. He Has Set Us Free from Our Sins and Given Us a Place of Honor in His Kingdom. For those of us who have received Jesus into our lives, he has given us a place of tremendous privilege and access to the throne of God.

5. He Will Return Again in Triumph. This king will draw the attention of the entire universe with his return.

6. He Is Eternal. He always has been and always will be. No one else but God could make that claim.

Some people have a rather stereotypical view of Jesus. They picture him as most artists have, with long, flowing hair—perhaps a staff in his hand and a lamb wrapped around his neck. Yet the Bible never does give us a description of Jesus' physical appearance. If it did, we would undoubtedly worship the image instead of the Lord. This description of Christ in Revelation—though it does not give us a physical picture—allows us to see the glorified Christ. And this Christ is full of power and majesty.

CORNERSTONES

CHAPTER 2

The Message to the Church in Ephesus

"Write this letter to the angel of* the church in
Ephesus. This is the message from the one who
holds the seven stars in his right hand, the one
who walks among the seven gold lampstands:

2 "I know all the things you do. I have seen
your hard work and your patient
endurance. I know you don't tolerate evil
people. You have examined the claims of
those who say they are apostles but are not.
You have discovered they are liars. 3 You
have patiently suffered for me without
quitting. 4 But I have this complaint against
you. You don't love me or each other as you
did at first! 5 Look how far you have fallen
from your first love! Turn back to me again
and work as you did at first. If you don't, I
will come and remove your lampstand from
its place among the churches. 6 But there is
this about you that is good: You hate the
deeds of the immoral Nicolaitans, just as
I do.

7 "Anyone who is willing to hear should
listen to the Spirit and understand what the
Spirit is saying to the churches. Everyone
who is victorious will eat from the tree of
life in the paradise of God.

The Message to the Church in Smyrna

8 "Write this letter to the angel of the church in
Smyrna. This is the message from the one who
is the First and the Last, who died and is alive:

9 "I know about your suffering and your
poverty—but you are rich! I know the
slander of those opposing you. They say
they are Jews, but they really aren't because
theirs is a synagogue of Satan. 10 Don't be
afraid of what you are about to suffer. The
Devil will throw some of you into prison

2:1 Or *the messenger for;* also in 2:8, 12, 18.

and put you to the test. You will be
persecuted for 'ten days.' Remain faithful
even when facing death, and I will give you
the crown of life.
11"Anyone who is willing to hear should
listen to the Spirit and understand what the
Spirit is saying to the churches. Whoever is
victorious will not be hurt by the second
death.

The Message to the Church in Pergamum

12"Write this letter to the angel of the church in
Pergamum. This is the message from the one
who has a sharp two-edged sword:

13"I know that you live in the city where
that great throne of Satan is located, and yet
you have remained loyal to me. And you
refused to deny me even when Antipas, my
faithful witness, was martyred among you
by Satan's followers. 14And yet I have a few
complaints against you. You tolerate some
among you who are like Balaam, who
showed Balak how to trip up the people of
Israel. He taught them to worship idols
by eating food offered to idols and by
committing sexual sin. 15In the same way,
you have some Nicolaitans among
you—people who follow the same teaching
and commit the same sins. 16Repent, or I
will come to you suddenly and fight against
them with the sword of my mouth.
17"Anyone who is willing to hear should
listen to the Spirit and understand what the
Spirit is saying to the churches. Everyone
who is victorious will eat of the manna that
has been hidden away in heaven. And I will
give to each one a white stone, and on the
stone will be engraved a new name that no
one knows except the one who receives it.

The Message to the Church in Thyatira

18"Write this letter to the angel of the church in
Thyatira. This is the message from the Son of
God, whose eyes are bright like flames of fire,
whose feet are like polished bronze:

19"I know all the things you do—your love,
your faith, your service, and your patient
endurance. And I can see your constant
improvement in all these things. 20But I
have this complaint against you. You are
permitting that woman—that Jezebel who
calls herself a prophet—to lead my servants
astray. She is encouraging them to worship
idols, eat food offered to idols, and commit
sexual sin. 21I gave her time to repent,
but she would not turn away from her
immorality. 22Therefore, I will throw her
upon a sickbed, and she will suffer greatly
with all who commit adultery with her,
unless they turn away from all their evil
deeds. 23I will strike her children dead. And
all the churches will know that I am the one
who searches out the thoughts and
intentions of every person. And I will give
to each of you whatever you deserve. 24But I
also have a message for the rest of you in
Thyatira who have not followed this false
teaching ('deeper truths,' as they call
them—depths of Satan, really). I will ask
nothing more of you 25except that you hold
tightly to what you have until I come.
26"To all who are victorious, who obey
me to the very end, I will give authority over
all the nations. 27They will rule the nations
with an iron rod and smash them like clay
pots. 28They will have the same authority I
received from my Father, and I will also give
them the morning star! 29Anyone who is
willing to hear should listen to the Spirit
and understand what the Spirit is saying to
the churches.

CHAPTER 3

The Message to the Church in Sardis

"Write this letter to the angel of* the church in
Sardis. This is the message from the one who has
the sevenfold Spirit* of God and the seven stars:

"I know all the things you do, and that you
have a reputation for being alive—but you
are dead. 2Now wake up! Strengthen what
little remains, for even what is left is at the
point of death. Your deeds are far from right
in the sight of God. 3Go back to what you
heard and believed at first; hold to it firmly
and turn to me again. Unless you do, I will
come upon you suddenly, as unexpected as
a thief.
4"Yet even in Sardis there are some who
have not soiled their garments with evil
deeds. They will walk with me in white, for
they are worthy. 5All who are victorious will
be clothed in white. I will never erase their
names from the Book of Life, but I will
announce before my Father and his angels

3:1a Or *the messenger for;* also in 3:7, 14. **3:1b** Greek *the seven spirits.*

that they are mine. 6Anyone who is willing to hear should listen to the Spirit and understand what the Spirit is saying to the churches.

The Message to the Church in Philadelphia

7"Write this letter to the angel of the church in Philadelphia. This is the message from the one who is holy and true. He is the one who has the key of David. He opens doors, and no one can shut them; he shuts doors, and no one can open them.

8"I know all the things you do, and I have opened a door for you that no one can shut. You have little strength, yet you obeyed my word and did not deny me. 9Look! I will force those who belong to Satan—those liars who say they are Jews but are not—to come and bow down at your feet. They will acknowledge that you are the ones I love.

10"Because you have obeyed my command to persevere, I will protect you from the great time of testing that will come upon the whole world to test those who belong to this world. 11Look, I am coming quickly. Hold on to what you have, so that no one will take away your crown. 12All who are victorious will become pillars in the Temple of my God, and they will never have to leave it. And I will write my God's name on them, and they will be citizens in the city of my God—the new Jerusalem that comes down from heaven from my God. And they will have my new name inscribed upon them. 13Anyone who is willing to hear should listen to the Spirit and understand what the Spirit is saying to the churches.

The Message to the Church in Laodicea

14"Write this letter to the angel of the church in Laodicea. This is the message from the one who is the Amen—the faithful and true witness, the ruler* of God's creation:

15"I know all the things you do, that you are neither hot nor cold. I wish you were one or the other! 16But since you are like lukewarm water, I will spit you out of my mouth! 17You say, 'I am rich. I have everything I want. I don't need a thing!' And you don't realize that you are wretched and miserable and poor and blind and naked. 18I advise you to buy gold from me—gold that has been purified by fire. Then you will be rich. And also buy white garments so you will not be shamed by your nakedness. And buy ointment for your eyes so you will be able to see. 19I am the one who corrects and disciplines everyone I love. Be diligent and turn from your indifference.

20"Look! Here I stand at the door and knock. If you hear me calling and open the door, I will come in, and we will share a meal as friends. 21I will invite everyone who is victorious to sit with me on my throne, just as I was victorious and sat with my Father on his throne. 22Anyone who is willing to hear should listen to the Spirit and understand what the Spirit is saying to the churches."

CHAPTER 4

Worship in Heaven

Then as I looked, I saw a door standing open in heaven, and the same voice I had heard before spoke to me with the sound of a mighty trumpet blast. The voice said, "Come up here, and I will show you what must happen after these things." 2And instantly I was in the Spirit,* and I saw a throne in heaven and someone sitting on it! 3The one sitting on the throne was as brilliant as gemstones—jasper and carnelian. And the glow of an emerald circled his throne like a rainbow. 4Twenty-four thrones surrounded him, and twenty-four elders sat on them. They were all clothed in white and had gold crowns on their heads. 5And from the throne came flashes of lightning and the rumble of thunder. And in front of the throne were seven lampstands with burning flames. They are the seven spirits* of God. 6In front of the throne was a shiny sea of glass, sparkling like crystal.

In the center and around the throne were four living beings, each covered with eyes, front and back. 7The first of these living beings had the form of a lion; the second looked like an ox; the third had a human face; and the fourth had the form of an eagle with wings spread out as though in flight. 8Each of these living beings had six wings, and their wings were covered with eyes, inside and out. Day after day and night after night they keep on saying,

3:14 Or *the source.* 4:2 Or *in spirit.* 4:5 See 1:4 and 3:1, where the same expression is translated *the sevenfold Spirit.*

"Holy, holy, holy is the Lord God
Almighty—
the one who always was, who is, and
who is still to come."

9 Whenever the living beings give glory and
honor and thanks to the one sitting on the
throne, the one who lives forever and ever, 10 the
twenty-four elders fall down and worship the
one who lives forever and ever. And they lay
their crowns before the throne and say,

11 "You are worthy, O Lord our God,
to receive glory and honor and power.
For you created everything,
and it is for your pleasure that they exist
and were created."

CHAPTER 5

The Lamb Opens the Scroll

And I saw a scroll in the right hand of the one
who was sitting on the throne. There was writing
on the inside and the outside of the scroll, and
it was sealed with seven seals. 2 And I saw a
strong angel, who shouted with a loud voice:
"Who is worthy to break the seals on this scroll
and unroll it?" 3 But no one in heaven or on
earth or under the earth was able to open the
scroll and read it.

4 Then I wept because no one could be found
who was worthy to open the scroll and read it.
5 But one of the twenty-four elders said to me,
"Stop weeping! Look, the Lion of the tribe of
Judah, the heir to David's throne,* has conquered. He is worthy to open the scroll and
break its seven seals."

6 I looked and I saw a Lamb that had been
killed but was now standing between the throne
and the four living beings and among the
twenty-four elders. He had seven horns and
seven eyes, which are the seven spirits* of God
that are sent out into every part of the earth. 7 He
stepped forward and took the scroll from the
right hand of the one sitting on the throne. 8 And
as he took the scroll, the four living beings and
the twenty-four elders fell down before the
Lamb. Each one had a harp, and they held gold
bowls filled with incense—the prayers of God's
people!

9 And they sang a new song with these words:

"You are worthy to take the scroll
and break its seals and open it.
For you were killed, and your blood has
ransomed people for God
from every tribe and language and
people and nation.
10 And you have caused them to become
God's kingdom and his priests.
And they will reign* on the earth."

11 Then I looked again, and I heard the singing
of thousands and millions of angels around the
throne and the living beings and the elders.
12 And they sang in a mighty chorus:

"The Lamb is worthy—the Lamb who was
killed.
He is worthy to receive power and riches
and wisdom and strength
and honor and glory and blessing."

13 And then I heard every creature in heaven
and on earth and under the earth and in the sea.
They also sang:

"Blessing and honor and glory and power
belong to the one sitting on the throne
and to the Lamb forever and ever."

14 And the four living beings said, "Amen!"
And the twenty-four elders fell down and worshiped God and the Lamb.

CHAPTER 6

The Lamb Breaks the First Six Seals

As I watched, the Lamb broke the first of the
seven seals on the scroll. Then one of the four
living beings called out with a voice that
sounded like thunder, "Come!" 2 I looked up
and saw a white horse. Its rider carried a bow,
and a crown was placed on his head. He rode out
to win many battles and gain the victory.

3 When the Lamb broke the second seal, I
heard the second living being say, "Come!"
4 And another horse appeared, a red one. Its rider
was given a mighty sword and the authority to
remove peace from the earth. And there was war
and slaughter everywhere.

5 When the Lamb broke the third seal, I heard
the third living being say, "Come!" And I looked
up and saw a black horse, and its rider was
holding a pair of scales in his hand. 6 And a voice
from among the four living beings said, "A loaf
of wheat bread or three loaves of barley for a
day's pay.* And don't waste* the olive oil and
wine."

7 And when the Lamb broke the fourth seal, I

5:5 Greek *the root of David.* 5:6 See note on 4:5. 5:10 Some manuscripts read *they are reigning.* 6:6a Greek *A choinix of wheat for a denarius, and 3 choinix of barley for a denarius.* 6:6b Or *hurt.*

What Will Life in Heaven Be Like? Read REVELATION 7:13-17

The apostle Paul had a taste of heaven, either through a vision or by actually dying. He wrote about his experience in 2 Corinthians 12:2-4. Upon entering God's presence, he said, "I was caught up into paradise." The word *paradise* literally means "the royal garden of a king with all kinds of fruit and flowers." This passage of Scripture shows us four aspects of the life we will live in the wonderful place called paradise:

1. We Will Live a Life without Fear and Worry. Heaven is a place of protection (verse 15). We will have no reason to fear anything there. We won't find bars on windows, crime on the streets, or any other type of violence. God will be our shelter.

2. We Will Live a Life without Need. Heaven is a place of complete sufficiency (verse 16). Hunger and thirst will not be a part of our vocabulary there. That is because the Lord will feed us and quench our thirst.

3. We Will Live a Life without Pain. Heaven is a place of comfort (verse 16). Elsewhere, the Bible says that in heaven "there will be no more death or sorrow or crying or pain" (Revelation 21:4). Our heavenly bodies will not be subjected to the illnesses, aches, and pains that we know so well here on earth.

4. We Will Live a Life without Sorrow. Heaven is a place of joy (verse 17). Being in God's presence is a joyful and wonderful experience. Sorrow will not be found in heaven, and God will wipe away all of our tears.

While we can look forward to the glories of heaven, one thing far outweighs them all: the fact that we will be able to spend eternity with Jesus. Dwight L. Moody once wrote, "It is not the jeweled walls and pearly gates that are going to make heaven attractive. It is being with God." May that truth inspire you as you live out your life on this earth.

CORNERSTONES

heard the fourth living being say, "Come!" 8And
I looked up and saw a horse whose color was
pale green like a corpse. And Death was the
name of its rider, who was followed around by
the Grave.* They were given authority over one-
fourth of the earth, to kill with the sword and
famine and disease* and wild animals.
9And when the Lamb broke the fifth seal, I
saw under the altar the souls of all who had been
martyred for the word of God and for being
faithful in their witness. 10They called loudly to
the Lord and said, "O Sovereign Lord, holy and
true, how long will it be before you judge the
people who belong to this world for what they
have done to us? When will you avenge our
blood against these people?" 11Then a white
robe was given to each of them. And they were
told to rest a little longer until the full number
of their brothers and sisters*—their fellow servants of Jesus—had been martyred.

12I watched as the Lamb broke the sixth seal,
and there was a great earthquake. The sun became as dark as black cloth, and the moon
became as red as blood. 13Then the stars of the
sky fell to the earth like green figs falling from
trees shaken by mighty winds. 14And the sky
was rolled up like a scroll and taken away. And
all of the mountains and all of the islands
disappeared. 15Then the kings of the earth, the
rulers, the generals, the wealthy people, the
people with great power, and every slave and
every free person—all hid themselves in the
caves and among the rocks of the mountains.
16And they cried to the mountains and the
rocks, "Fall on us and hide us from the face of
the one who sits on the throne and from the
wrath of the Lamb. 17For the great day of their
wrath has come, and who will be able to survive?"

6:8a Greek *by Hades.* 6:8b Greek *death.* 6:11 Greek *their brothers.*

CHAPTER 7

God's People Will Be Preserved

Then I saw four angels standing at the four corners of the earth, holding back the four winds from blowing upon the earth. Not a leaf rustled in the trees, and the sea became as smooth as glass. 2And I saw another angel coming from the east, carrying the seal of the living God. And he shouted out to those four angels who had been given power to injure land and sea, 3"Wait! Don't hurt the land or the sea or the trees until we have placed the seal of God on the foreheads of his servants."

4And I heard how many were marked with the seal of God. There were 144,000 who were sealed from all the tribes of Israel:

5 from Judah 12,000
from Reuben 12,000
from Gad 12,000
6 from Asher 12,000
from Naphtali 12,000
from Manasseh 12,000
7 from Simeon 12,000
from Levi 12,000
from Issachar 12,000
8 from Zebulun 12,000
from Joseph 12,000
from Benjamin 12,000

Praise from the Great Multitude

9After this I saw a vast crowd, too great to count, from every nation and tribe and people and language, standing in front of the throne and before the Lamb. They were clothed in white and held palm branches in their hands. 10And they were shouting with a mighty shout, "Salvation comes from our God on the throne and from the Lamb!"

11And all the angels were standing around the throne and around the elders and the four living beings. And they fell face down before the throne and worshiped God. 12They said,

"Amen! Blessing and glory and wisdom
and thanksgiving and honor and power
and strength
belong to our God forever and forever.
Amen!"

13Then one of the twenty-four elders asked me, "Who are these who are clothed in white? Where do they come from?"

14And I said to him, "Sir, you are the one who knows."

Then he said to me, "These are the ones coming out of the great tribulation. They washed their robes in the blood of the Lamb and made them white. 15That is why they are standing in front of the throne of God, serving him day and night in his Temple. And he who sits on the throne will live among them and shelter them. 16They will never again be hungry or thirsty, and they will be fully protected from the scorching noontime heat. 17For the Lamb who stands in front of the throne will be their Shepherd. He will lead them to the springs of life-giving water. And God will wipe away all their tears."

CHAPTER 8

The Lamb Breaks the Seventh Seal

When the Lamb broke the seventh seal, there was silence throughout heaven for about half an hour. 2And I saw the seven angels who stand before God, and they were given seven trumpets.

3Then another angel with a gold incense burner came and stood at the altar. And a great quantity of incense was given to him to mix with the prayers of God's people, to be offered on the gold altar before the throne. 4The smoke of the incense, mixed with the prayers of the saints, ascended up to God from the altar where the angel had poured them out. 5Then the angel filled the incense burner with fire from the altar and threw it down upon the earth; and thunder crashed, lightning flashed, and there was a terrible earthquake.

The First Four Trumpets

6Then the seven angels with the seven trumpets prepared to blow their mighty blasts.

7The first angel blew his trumpet, and hail and fire mixed with blood were thrown down upon the earth, and one-third of the earth was set on fire. One-third of the trees were burned, and all the grass was burned.

8Then the second angel blew his trumpet, and a great mountain of fire was thrown into the sea. And one-third of the water in the sea became blood. 9And one-third of all things living in the sea died. And one-third of all the ships on the sea were destroyed.

10Then the third angel blew his trumpet, and a great flaming star fell out of the sky, burning like a torch. It fell upon one-third of the rivers and on the springs of water. 11The name of the star was Bitterness.* It made one-third of the

8:11 Greek *Wormwood.*

water bitter, and many people died because the water was so bitter.

12Then the fourth angel blew his trumpet, and one-third of the sun was struck, and one-third of the moon, and one-third of the stars, and they became dark. And one-third of the day was dark and one-third of the night also.

13Then I looked up. And I heard a single eagle crying loudly as it flew through the air, "Terror, terror, terror to all who belong to this world because of what will happen when the last three angels blow their trumpets."

CHAPTER 9

The Fifth Trumpet Brings the First Terror

Then the fifth angel blew his trumpet, and I saw a star that had fallen to earth from the sky, and he was given the key to the shaft of the bottomless pit. 2When he opened it, smoke poured out as though from a huge furnace, and the sunlight and air were darkened by the smoke.

3Then locusts came from the smoke and descended on the earth, and they were given power to sting like scorpions. 4They were told not to hurt the grass or plants or trees but to attack all the people who did not have the seal of God on their foreheads. 5They were told not to kill them but to torture them for five months with agony like the pain of scorpion stings. 6In those days people will seek death but will not find it. They will long to die, but death will flee away!

7The locusts looked like horses armed for battle. They had gold crowns on their heads, and they had human faces. 8Their hair was long like the hair of a woman, and their teeth were like the teeth of a lion. 9They wore armor made of iron, and their wings roared like an army of chariots rushing into battle. 10They had tails that stung like scorpions, with power to torture people. This power was given to them for five months. 11Their king is the angel from the bottomless pit; his name in Hebrew is *Abaddon,* and in Greek, *Apollyon*—the Destroyer.

12The first terror is past, but look, two more terrors are coming!

The Sixth Trumpet Brings the Second Terror

13Then the sixth angel blew his trumpet, and I heard a voice speaking from the four horns of the gold altar that stands in the presence of God. 14And the voice spoke to the sixth angel who held the trumpet: "Release the four angels who are bound at the great Euphrates River." 15And the four angels who had been prepared for this hour and day and month and year were turned loose to kill one-third of all the people on earth. 16They led an army of 200 million mounted troops—I heard an announcement of how many there were.

17And in my vision, I saw the horses and the riders sitting on them. The riders wore armor that was fiery red and sky blue and yellow. The horses' heads were like the heads of lions, and fire and smoke and burning sulfur billowed from their mouths. 18One-third of all the people on earth were killed by these three plagues—by the fire and the smoke and burning sulfur that came from the mouths of the horses. 19Their power was in their mouths, but also in their tails. For their tails had heads like snakes, with the power to injure people.

20But the people who did not die in these plagues still refused to turn from their evil deeds. They continued to worship demons and idols made of gold, silver, bronze, stone, and wood—idols that neither see nor hear nor walk! 21And they did not repent of their murders or their witchcraft or their immorality or their thefts.

CHAPTER 10

The Angel and the Small Scroll

Then I saw another mighty angel coming down from heaven, surrounded by a cloud, with a rainbow over his head. His face shone like the sun, and his feet were like pillars of fire. 2And in his hand was a small scroll, which he had unrolled. He stood with his right foot on the sea and his left foot on the land. 3And he gave a great shout, like the roar of a lion. And when he shouted, the seven thunders answered.

4When the seven thunders spoke, I was about to write. But a voice from heaven called to me: "Keep secret what the seven thunders said. Do not write it down."

5Then the mighty angel standing on the sea and on the land lifted his right hand to heaven. 6And he swore an oath in the name of the one who lives forever and ever, who created heaven and everything in it, the earth and everything in it, and the sea and everything in it. He said, "God will wait no longer. 7But when the seventh angel blows his trumpet, God's mysterious plan will be fulfilled. It will happen just as he announced it to his servants the prophets."

8Then the voice from heaven called to me again: "Go and take the unrolled scroll from the

angel who is standing on the sea and on the
land."
9So I approached him and asked him to give
me the little scroll. "Yes, take it and eat it," he
said. "At first it will taste like honey, but when
you swallow it, it will make your stomach sour!"
10So I took the little scroll from the hands of the
angel, and I ate it! It was sweet in my mouth, but
it made my stomach sour. 11Then he said to me,
"You must prophesy again about many peoples,
nations, languages, and kings."

CHAPTER 11

The Two Witnesses

Then I was given a measuring stick, and I was
told, "Go and measure the Temple of God and
the altar, and count the number of worshipers.
2But do not measure the outer courtyard, for it
has been turned over to the nations. They will
trample the holy city for 42 months. 3And I will
give power to my two witnesses, and they will be
clothed in sackcloth and will prophesy during
those 1,260 days."
4These two prophets are the two olive trees
and the two lampstands that stand before the
Lord of all the earth. 5If anyone tries to harm
them, fire flashes from the mouths of the prophets and consumes their enemies. This is how
anyone who tries to harm them must die. 6They
have power to shut the skies so that no rain will
fall for as long as they prophesy. And they have
the power to turn the rivers and oceans into
blood, and to send every kind of plague upon
the earth as often as they wish.
7When they complete their testimony, the
beast that comes up out of the bottomless pit
will declare war against them. He will conquer
them and kill them. 8And their bodies will lie in
the main street of Jerusalem,* the city which is
called "Sodom" and "Egypt," the city where
their Lord was crucified. 9And for three and a
half days, all peoples, tribes, languages, and nations will come to stare at their bodies. No one
will be allowed to bury them. 10All the people
who belong to this world will give presents to
each other to celebrate the death of the two
prophets who had tormented them.
11But after three and a half days, the spirit of
life from God entered them, and they stood up!
And terror struck all who were staring at them.
12Then a loud voice shouted from heaven,
"Come up here!" And they rose to heaven in a
cloud as their enemies watched.
13And in the same hour there was a terrible
earthquake that destroyed a tenth of the city.
Seven thousand people died in that earthquake.
And everyone who did not die was terrified and
gave glory to the God of heaven.
14The second terror is past, but look, now the
third terror is coming quickly.

The Seventh Trumpet Brings the Third Terror

15Then the seventh angel blew his trumpet, and
there were loud voices shouting in heaven: "The
whole world has now become the kingdom of
our Lord and of his Christ, and he will reign
forever and ever."
16And the twenty-four elders sitting on their
thrones before God fell on their faces and worshiped him. 17And they said,

"We give thanks to you, Lord God Almighty,
  the one who is and who always was,
for now you have assumed your great power
  and have begun to reign.
18 The nations were angry with you,
  but now the time of your wrath has come.
It is time to judge the dead and reward your
    servants.
You will reward your prophets and your
    holy people,
  all who fear your name, from the least to
    the greatest.
And you will destroy all who have caused
    destruction on the earth."

19Then, in heaven, the Temple of God was
opened and the Ark of his covenant could be
seen inside the Temple. Lightning flashed, thunder crashed and roared; there was a great hailstorm, and the world was shaken by a mighty
earthquake.

CHAPTER 12

The Woman and the Dragon

Then I witnessed in heaven an event of great
significance. I saw a woman clothed with the
sun, with the moon beneath her feet, and a
crown of twelve stars on her head. 2She was
pregnant, and she cried out in the pain of labor
as she awaited her delivery.
3Suddenly, I witnessed in heaven another significant event. I saw a large red dragon with
seven heads and ten horns, with seven crowns
on his heads. 4His tail dragged down one-third
of the stars, which he threw to the earth. He
stood before the woman as she was about to give

11:8 Greek *the great city.*

Who Can Thwart Satan's Agenda? Read REVELATION 12:10-12

God uses his faithful followers to ruin Satan's plans. Here we see three significant ways these martyrs for the gospel overcame the Devil's attacks:

1. They Overcame Him by the Blood of the Lamb. The Bible says, "Without the shedding of blood, there is no forgiveness of sins" (Hebrews 9:22). It is only through what Jesus did for us on the cross that we can approach God. These people knew that they could never go to heaven or overcome Satan's accusations on their own merit or ability. They realized that they had fallen short of God's ideal, but they also knew that the blood of Jesus "cleanses us from every sin" (1 John 1:7).

2. They Overcame Him by Their Testimony. The believers described in these verses had come to understand what God had done for them and were proclaiming it to others. They not only realized that they had unconditional access to God, but they also sought to "invade enemy territory" by reaching out to others with the message of the gospel.

3. They Overcame Him by Their Attitude toward Life. These believers did not love their lives more than Christ. They endured execution for their faith because they realized that a better life was awaiting them in heaven with Christ. As the apostle Paul said, "For to me, living is for Christ, and dying is even better" (Philippians 1:21).

History relates the story of a Christian who was persecuted by Rome for his faith. As he stood before the emperor, he was told, "Give up Christ. If you don't, I'll banish you."

The Christian replied, "You cannot banish me from Christ, for God says, 'I will never leave you or forsake you.'"

The ruler said, "I'll confiscate your property."

The Christian patiently responded, "My treasures are laid up in heaven. You can't touch them."

The emperor shot back, "I'll kill you!"

The Christian answered, "I've been dead to the world in Christ for forty years. My life is hid with Christ in God. You can't touch it."

The emperor turned to some of the members of his court and said in disgust, "What can you do with such a fanatic?"

May God give his church more men like this man.

CORNERSTONES

birth to her child, ready to devour the baby as soon as it was born.

5She gave birth to a boy who was to rule all nations with an iron rod. And the child was snatched away from the dragon and was caught up to God and to his throne. 6And the woman fled into the wilderness, where God had prepared a place to give her care for 1,260 days.

7Then there was war in heaven. Michael and the angels under his command fought the dragon and his angels. 8And the dragon lost the battle and was forced out of heaven. 9This great dragon—the ancient serpent called the Devil, or Satan, the one deceiving the whole world—was thrown down to the earth with all his angels.

10Then I heard a loud voice shouting across the heavens,

"It has happened at last—the salvation and power and kingdom of our God, and the authority of his Christ! For the Accuser has been thrown down to earth—the one who accused our brothers and sisters* before our God day and night. 11And they have defeated him because of the blood of the Lamb and because of their testimony. And they were not afraid to die. 12Rejoice, O heavens! And you who live in the heavens, rejoice! But terror will come on the earth and the sea. For the Devil has come down to you in great anger, and he knows that he has little time."

12:10 Greek *brothers*.

13And when the dragon realized that he had been thrown down to the earth, he pursued the woman who had given birth to the child. 14But she was given two wings like those of a great eagle. This allowed her to fly to a place prepared for her in the wilderness, where she would be cared for and protected from the dragon* for a time, times, and half a time.

15Then the dragon tried to drown the woman with a flood of water that flowed from its mouth. 16But the earth helped her by opening its mouth and swallowing the river that gushed out from the mouth of the dragon. 17Then the dragon became angry at the woman, and he declared war against the rest of her children—all who keep God's commandments and confess that they belong to Jesus.

The Beast out of the Sea

18Then he stood* waiting on the shore of the sea.

CHAPTER 13

And now in my vision I saw a beast rising up out of the sea. It had seven heads and ten horns, with ten crowns on its horns. And written on each head were names that blasphemed God. 2This beast looked like a leopard, but it had bear's feet and a lion's mouth! And the dragon gave him his own power and throne and great authority.

3I saw that one of the heads of the beast seemed wounded beyond recovery—but the fatal wound was healed! All the world marveled at this miracle and followed the beast in awe. 4They worshiped the dragon for giving the beast such power, and they worshiped the beast. "Is there anyone as great as the beast?" they exclaimed. "Who is able to fight against him?"

5Then the beast was allowed to speak great blasphemies against God. And he was given authority to do what he wanted for forty-two months. 6And he spoke terrible words of blasphemy against God, slandering his name and all who live in heaven, who are his temple. 7And the beast was allowed to wage war against God's holy people and to overcome them. And he was given authority to rule over every tribe and people and language and nation. 8And all the people who belong to this world worshiped the beast. They are the ones whose names were not written in the Book of Life, which belongs to the Lamb who was killed before the world was made.

9Anyone who is willing to hear should listen and understand. 10The people who are destined for prison will be arrested and taken away. Those who are destined for death will be killed. But do not be dismayed, for here is your opportunity to have endurance and faith.

The Beast out of the Earth

11Then I saw another beast come up out of the earth. He had two horns like those of a lamb, and he spoke with the voice of a dragon. 12He exercised all the authority of the first beast. And he required all the earth and those who belong to this world to worship the first beast, whose death-wound had been healed. 13He did astounding miracles, such as making fire flash down to earth from heaven while everyone was watching. 14And with all the miracles he was allowed to perform on behalf of the first beast, he deceived all the people who belong to this world. He ordered the people of the world to make a great statue of the first beast, who was fatally wounded and then came back to life. 15He was permitted to give life to this statue so that it could speak. Then the statue commanded that anyone refusing to worship it must die.

16He required everyone—great and small, rich and poor, slave and free—to be given a mark on the right hand or on the forehead. 17And no one could buy or sell anything without that mark, which was either the name of the beast or the number representing his name. 18Wisdom is needed to understand this. Let the one who has understanding solve the number of the beast, for it is the number of a man.* His number is 666.*

CHAPTER 14

The Lamb and the 144,000

Then I saw the Lamb standing on Mount Zion, and with him were 144,000 who had his name and his Father's name written on their foreheads. 2And I heard a sound from heaven like the roaring of a great waterfall or the rolling of mighty thunder. It was like the sound of many harpists playing together.

3This great choir sang a wonderful new song in front of the throne of God and before the four living beings and the twenty-four elders. And no one could learn this song except those 144,000 who had been redeemed from the earth. 4For they are spiritually undefiled, pure as virgins,*

12:14 Greek *the serpent;* also in 12:15. See 12:9. **12:18** Some manuscripts read *Then I stood,* and some translations put this entire sentence into 13:1. **13:18a** Or *of humanity.* **13:18b** Some manuscripts read *616.* **14:4a** Greek *they are virgins who have not defiled themselves with women.*

What Role Will Angels Play in the End Times? Read REVELATION 14:6-7

The Bible tells us that the last days are going to be spiritually dark. Many people will be deceived into believing "teachings that come from demons" (see 1 Timothy 4:1, p. 271), and people will become increasingly immoral, proud, and disobedient (see 2 Timothy 3:1-5, p. 277). We already see this beginning to happen. There is a fresh demand for psychics, an increasing amount of violent crime on the streets, and a blatant lack of values in much of entertainment today.

This text shows that during the Tribulation, which is generally recognized as the last seven years on earth before Christ's return, the demons will not be the only ones at work. The angels of God will fly through the heavens preaching the everlasting gospel to make sure that everyone throughout the world is aware of the upcoming judgment of God. In essence, it will be the final "wake-up call" for people to turn to Jesus Christ.

following the Lamb wherever he goes. They have
been purchased from among the people on the
earth as a special offering* to God and to the
Lamb. 5No falsehood can be charged against
them; they are blameless.

The Three Angels

6And I saw another angel flying through the
heavens, carrying the everlasting Good News to
preach to the people who belong to this
world—to every nation, tribe, language, and
people. 7"Fear God," he shouted. "Give glory to
him. For the time has come when he will sit as
judge. Worship him who made heaven and
earth, the sea, and all the springs of water."
8Then another angel followed him through
the skies, shouting, "Babylon is fallen—that
great city is fallen—because she seduced the
nations of the world and made them drink the
wine of her passionate immorality."
9Then a third angel followed them, shouting,
"Anyone who worships the beast and his statue
or who accepts his mark on the forehead or the
hand 10must drink the wine of God's wrath. It is
poured out undiluted into God's cup of wrath.
And they will be tormented with fire and burning sulfur in the presence of the holy angels and
the Lamb. 11The smoke of their torment rises
forever and ever, and they will have no relief day
or night, for they have worshiped the beast and
his statue and have accepted the mark of his
name. 12Let this encourage God's holy people to
endure persecution patiently and remain firm to
the end, obeying his commands and trusting in
Jesus."
13And I heard a voice from heaven saying,
"Write this down: Blessed are those who die in
the Lord from now on. Yes, says the Spirit, they
are blessed indeed, for they will rest from all
their toils and trials; for their good deeds follow
them!"

The Harvest of the Earth

14Then I saw the Son of Man* sitting on a white
cloud. He had a gold crown on his head and a
sharp sickle in his hand.
15Then an angel came from the Temple and
called out in a loud voice to the one sitting on
the cloud, "Use the sickle, for the time has come
for you to harvest; the crop is ripe on the earth."
16So the one sitting on the cloud swung his
sickle over the earth, and the whole earth was
harvested.
17After that, another angel came from the
Temple in heaven, and he also had a sharp
sickle. 18Then another angel, who has power to
destroy the world with fire, shouted to the angel
with the sickle, "Use your sickle now to gather
the clusters of grapes from the vines of the earth,
for they are fully ripe for judgment." 19So the
angel swung his sickle on the earth and loaded
the grapes into the great winepress of God's
wrath. 20And the grapes were trodden in the
winepress outside the city, and blood flowed
from the winepress in a stream about 180
miles* long and as high as a horse's bridle.

14:4b Greek *as firstfruits.* **14:14** Or *one who looked like a man;* Greek reads *one like a son of man.* **14:20** Greek *1,600 stadia* [296 kilometers].

CHAPTER 15

The Song of Moses and of the Lamb

Then I saw in heaven another significant event, and it was great and marvelous. Seven angels were holding the seven last plagues, which would bring God's wrath to completion. 2I saw before me what seemed to be a crystal sea mixed with fire. And on it stood all the people who had been victorious over the beast and his statue and the number representing his name. They were all holding harps that God had given them. 3And they were singing the song of Moses, the servant of God, and the song of the Lamb:

"Great and marvelous are your actions,
  Lord God Almighty.
Just and true are your ways,
  O King of the nations.*
4 Who will not fear, O Lord, and glorify your
    name?
  For you alone are holy.
All nations will come and worship before
    you,
  for your righteous deeds have been
    revealed."

The Seven Bowls of the Seven Plagues

5Then I looked and saw that the Temple in heaven, God's Tabernacle, was thrown wide open! 6The seven angels who were holding the bowls of the seven plagues came from the Temple, clothed in spotless white linen* with gold belts across their chests. 7And one of the four living beings handed each of the seven angels a gold bowl filled with the terrible wrath of God, who lives forever and forever. 8The Temple was filled with smoke from God's glory and power. No one could enter the Temple until the seven angels had completed pouring out the seven plagues.

CHAPTER 16

Then I heard a mighty voice shouting from the Temple to the seven angels, "Now go your ways and empty out the seven bowls of God's wrath on the earth."

2So the first angel left the Temple and poured out his bowl over the earth, and horrible, malignant sores broke out on everyone who had the mark of the beast and who worshiped his statue.

3Then the second angel poured out his bowl on the sea, and it became like the blood of a corpse. And everything in the sea died.

4Then the third angel poured out his bowl on the rivers and springs, and they became blood. 5And I heard the angel who had authority over all water saying, "You are just in sending this judgment, O Holy One, who is and who always was. 6For your holy people and your prophets have been killed, and their blood was poured out on the earth. So you have given their murderers blood to drink. It is their just reward." 7And I heard a voice from the altar saying, "Yes, Lord God Almighty, your punishments are true and just."

8Then the fourth angel poured out his bowl on the sun, causing it to scorch everyone with its fire. 9Everyone was burned by this blast of heat, and they cursed the name of God, who sent all of these plagues. They did not repent and give him glory.

10Then the fifth angel poured out his bowl on the throne of the beast, and his kingdom was plunged into darkness. And his subjects ground their teeth in anguish, 11and they cursed the God of heaven for their pains and sores. But they refused to repent of all their evil deeds.

12Then the sixth angel poured out his bowl on the great Euphrates River, and it dried up so that the kings from the east could march their armies westward without hindrance. 13And I saw three evil spirits that looked like frogs leap from the mouth of the dragon, the beast, and the false prophet. 14These miracle-working demons caused all the rulers of the world to gather for battle against the Lord on that great judgment day of God Almighty.

15"Take note: I will come as unexpectedly as a thief! Blessed are all who are watching for me, who keep their robes ready so they will not need to walk naked and ashamed."

16And they gathered all the rulers and their armies to a place called *Armageddon* in Hebrew.

17Then the seventh angel poured out his bowl into the air. And a mighty shout came from the throne of the Temple in heaven, saying, "It is finished!" 18Then the thunder crashed and rolled, and lightning flashed. And there was an earthquake greater than ever before in human history. 19The great city of Babylon split into three pieces, and cities around the world fell into heaps of rubble. And so God remembered all of Babylon's sins, and he made her drink the cup that was filled with the wine of his fierce wrath. 20And every island disappeared, and all the

15:3 Some manuscripts read *King of the ages;* other manuscripts read *King of the saints.* 15:6 Some manuscripts read *in bright and sparkling stone.*

mountains were leveled. 21There was a terrible hailstorm, and hailstones weighing seventy-five pounds* fell from the sky onto the people below. They cursed God because of the hailstorm, which was a very terrible plague.

CHAPTER 17

The Great Prostitute

One of the seven angels who had poured out the seven bowls came over and spoke to me. "Come with me," he said, "and I will show you the judgment that is going to come on the great prostitute, who sits on many waters. 2The rulers of the world have had immoral relations with her, and the people who belong to this world have been made drunk by the wine of her immorality."

3So the angel took me in spirit* into the wilderness. There I saw a woman sitting on a scarlet beast that had seven heads and ten horns, written all over with blasphemies against God. 4The woman wore purple and scarlet clothing and beautiful jewelry made of gold and precious gems and pearls. She held in her hand a gold goblet full of obscenities and the impurities of her immorality. 5A mysterious name was written on her forehead: "Babylon the Great, Mother of All Prostitutes and Obscenities in the World." 6I could see that she was drunk—drunk with the blood of God's holy people who were witnesses for Jesus. I stared at her completely amazed.

7"Why are you so amazed?" the angel asked. "I will tell you the mystery of this woman and of the beast with seven heads and ten horns. 8The beast you saw was alive but isn't now. And yet he will soon come up out of the bottomless pit and go to eternal destruction. And the people who belong to this world, whose names were not written in the Book of Life from before the world began, will be amazed at the reappearance of this beast who had died.

9"And now understand this: The seven heads of the beast represent the seven hills of the city where this woman rules. They also represent seven kings. 10Five kings have already fallen, the sixth now reigns, and the seventh is yet to come, but his reign will be brief. 11The scarlet beast that was alive and then died is the eighth king. He is like the other seven, and he, too, will go to his doom. 12His ten horns are ten kings who have not yet risen to power; they will be appointed to their kingdoms for one brief moment to reign with the beast. 13They will all agree to give their power and authority to him. 14Together they will wage war against the Lamb, but the Lamb will defeat them because he is Lord over all lords and King over all kings, and his people are the called and chosen and faithful ones."

15And the angel said to me, "The waters where the prostitute is sitting represent masses of people of every nation and language. 16The scarlet beast and his ten horns—which represent ten kings who will reign with him—all hate the prostitute. They will strip her naked, eat her flesh, and burn her remains with fire. 17For God has put a plan into their minds, a plan that will carry out his purposes. They will mutually agree to give their authority to the scarlet beast, and so the words of God will be fulfilled. 18And this woman you saw in your vision represents the great city that rules over the kings of the earth."

CHAPTER 18

The Fall of Babylon

After all this I saw another angel come down from heaven with great authority, and the earth grew bright with his splendor. 2He gave a mighty shout, "Babylon is fallen—that great city is fallen! She has become the hideout of demons and evil spirits, a nest for filthy buzzards, and a den for dreadful beasts. 3For all the nations have drunk the wine of her passionate immorality. The rulers of the world have committed adultery with her, and merchants throughout the world have grown rich as a result of her luxurious living."

4Then I heard another voice calling from heaven, "Come away from her, my people. Do not take part in her sins, or you will be punished with her. 5For her sins are piled as high as heaven, and God is ready to judge her for her evil deeds. 6Do to her as she has done to your people. Give her a double penalty for all her evil deeds. She brewed a cup of terror for others, so give her twice as much as she gave out. 7She has lived in luxury and pleasure, so match it now with torments and sorrows. She boasts, 'I am queen on my throne. I am no helpless widow. I will not experience sorrow.' 8Therefore, the sorrows of death and mourning and famine will overtake her in a single day. She will be utterly consumed by fire, for the Lord God who judges her is mighty."

9And the rulers of the world who took part in her immoral acts and enjoyed her great luxury will mourn for her as they see the smoke rising

16:21 Greek *1 talent* [34 kilograms]. **17:3** Or *in the Spirit.*

from her charred remains. 10They will stand at a
distance, terrified by her great torment. They will
cry out, "How terrible, how terrible for Babylon,
that great city! In one single moment God's
judgment came on her."

11The merchants of the world will weep and
mourn for her, for there is no one left to buy
their goods. 12She bought great quantities of
gold, silver, jewels, pearls, fine linen, purple dye,
silk, scarlet cloth, every kind of perfumed wood,
ivory goods, objects made of expensive wood,
bronze, iron, and marble. 13She also bought
cinnamon, spice, incense, myrrh, frankincense,
wine, olive oil, fine flour, wheat, cattle, sheep,
horses, chariots, and slaves—yes, she even
traded in human lives.

14"All the fancy things you loved so much are
gone," they cry. "The luxuries and splendor that
you prized so much will never be yours again.
They are gone forever."

15The merchants who became wealthy by
selling her these things will stand at a distance,
terrified by her great torment. They will weep
and cry. 16"How terrible, how terrible for that
great city! She was so beautiful—like a woman
clothed in finest purple and scarlet linens,
decked out with gold and precious stones and
pearls! 17And in one single moment all the
wealth of the city is gone!"

And all the shipowners and captains of the
merchant ships and their crews will stand at a
distance. 18They will weep as they watch the
smoke ascend, and they will say, "Where in all
the world is there another city like this?" 19And
they will throw dust on their heads to show their
great sorrow. And they will say, "How terrible,
how terrible for the great city! She made us all
rich from her great wealth. And now in a single
hour it is all gone."

20But you, O heaven, rejoice over her fate.
And you also rejoice, O holy people of God and
apostles and prophets! For at last God has
judged her on your behalf.

21Then a mighty angel picked up a boulder as
large as a great millstone. He threw it into the
ocean and shouted, "Babylon, the great city, will
be thrown down as violently as I have thrown
away this stone, and she will disappear forever.
22Never again will the sound of music be heard
there—no more harps, songs, flutes, or trumpets. There will be no industry of any kind, and
no more milling of grain. 23Her nights will be
dark, without a single lamp. There will be no
happy voices of brides and grooms. This will
happen because her merchants, who were the
greatest in the world, deceived the nations with
her sorceries. 24In her streets the blood of the
prophets was spilled. She was the one who
slaughtered God's people all over the world."

CHAPTER 19

Songs of Victory in Heaven

After this, I heard the sound of a vast crowd in
heaven shouting, "Hallelujah! Salvation is from
our God. Glory and power belong to him alone.
2His judgments are just and true. He has punished the great prostitute who corrupted the
earth with her immorality, and he has avenged
the murder of his servants." 3Again and again
their voices rang, "Hallelujah! The smoke from
that city ascends forever and forever!"

4Then the twenty-four elders and the four
living beings fell down and worshiped God,
who was sitting on the throne. They cried out,
"Amen! Hallelujah!"

5And from the throne came a voice that said,
"Praise our God, all his servants, from the least
to the greatest, all who fear him."

6Then I heard again what sounded like the
shout of a huge crowd, or the roar of mighty
ocean waves, or the crash of loud thunder: "Hallelujah! For the Lord our God, the Almighty,
reigns. 7Let us be glad and rejoice and honor
him. For the time has come for the wedding feast
of the Lamb, and his bride has prepared herself.
8She is permitted to wear the finest white linen."
(Fine linen represents the good deeds done by
the people of God.)

9And the angel said, "Write this: Blessed are
those who are invited to the wedding feast of the
Lamb." And he added, "These are true words
that come from God."

10Then I fell down at his feet to worship him,
but he said, "No, don't worship me. For I am a
servant of God, just like you and other brothers
and sisters* who testify of their faith in Jesus.
Worship God. For the essence of prophecy is to
give a clear witness for Jesus.*"

The Rider on the White Horse

11Then I saw heaven opened, and a white horse
was standing there. And the one sitting on the
horse was named Faithful and True. For he
judges fairly and then goes to war. 12His eyes
were bright like flames of fire, and on his head
were many crowns. A name was written on him,

19:10a Greek *brothers.* **19:10b** Or *is the message confirmed by Jesus.*

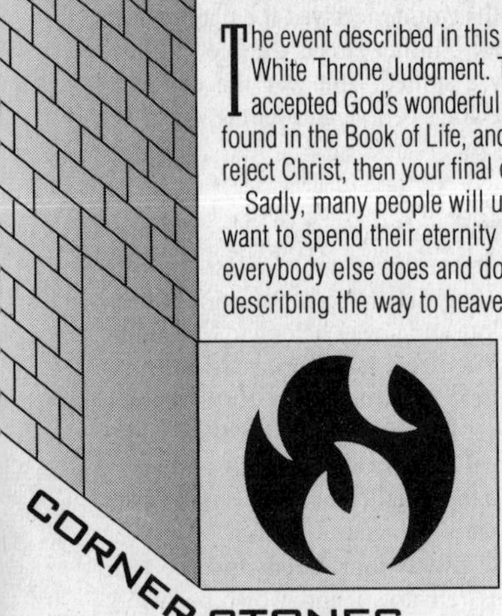

Who Will Go to Hell? Read REVELATION 20:11-15

The event described in this passage is the final judgment of humankind, also known as the Great White Throne Judgment. The standard by which you will be judged is simple. If you have accepted God's wonderful gift of salvation through his Son, Jesus Christ, your name will be found in the Book of Life, and you will spend eternity in heaven with God. If you have chosen to reject Christ, then your final destination will be the lake of fire. No arguments. Case closed.

Sadly, many people will unwittingly choose the latter option. They do so, not because they want to spend their eternity in agony, but because they just "go with the flow." They do what everybody else does and don't think for themselves. Jesus called this choice the "easy way." In describing the way to heaven and the way to hell, Jesus said, "You can enter God's Kingdom only through the narrow gate. The highway to hell is broad, and its gate is wide for the many who choose the easy way. But the gateway to life is small, and the road is narrow, and only a few ever find it" (Matthew 7:13-14). The only way to get off this broad road and "cancel" your reservation for hell is to make sure your name is entered into God's reservation book for heaven—the Book of Life.

and only he knew what it meant. 13He was
clothed with a robe dipped in blood, and his
title was the Word of God. 14The armies of
heaven, dressed in pure white linen, followed
him on white horses. 15From his mouth came a
sharp sword, and with it he struck down the
nations. He ruled them with an iron rod, and he
trod the winepress of the fierce wrath of almighty God. 16On his robe and thigh was written this title: King of kings and Lord of lords.

17Then I saw an angel standing in the sun,
shouting to the vultures flying high in the sky:
"Come! Gather together for the great banquet
God has prepared. 18Come and eat the flesh of
kings, captains, and strong warriors; of horses
and their riders; and of all humanity, both free
and slave, small and great."

19Then I saw the beast gathering the kings of
the earth and their armies in order to fight
against the one sitting on the horse and his
army. 20And the beast was captured, and with
him the false prophet who did mighty miracles
on behalf of the beast—miracles that deceived
all who had accepted the mark of the beast and
who worshiped his statue. Both the beast and
his false prophet were thrown alive into the lake
of fire that burns with sulfur. 21Their entire army
was killed by the sharp sword that came out of
the mouth of the one riding the white horse.
And all the vultures of the sky gorged themselves
on the dead bodies.

CHAPTER 20

The Thousand Years

Then I saw an angel come down from heaven
with the key to the bottomless pit and a heavy
chain in his hand. 2He seized the dragon—that
old serpent, the Devil, Satan—and bound him
in chains for a thousand years. 3The angel threw
him into the bottomless pit, which he then shut
and locked so Satan could not deceive the nations anymore until the thousand years were
finished. Afterward he would be released again
for a little while.

4Then I saw thrones, and the people sitting on
them had been given the authority to judge. And
I saw the souls of those who had been beheaded
for their testimony about Jesus, for proclaiming
the word of God. And I saw the souls of those
who had not worshiped the beast or his statue,
nor accepted his mark on their forehead or their
hands. They came to life again, and they reigned
with Christ for a thousand years. 5This is the first
resurrection. (The rest of the dead did not come
back to life until the thousand years had ended.)
6Blessed and holy are those who share in the first
resurrection. For them the second death holds no
power, but they will be priests of God and of
Christ and will reign with him a thousand years.

The Defeat of Satan

7When the thousand years end, Satan will be let
out of his prison. 8He will go out to deceive the

nations from every corner of the earth, which are
called Gog and Magog. He will gather them
together for battle—a mighty host, as number-
less as sand along the shore. [9]And I saw them as
they went up on the broad plain of the earth and
surrounded God's people and the beloved city.
But fire from heaven came down on the attack-
ing armies and consumed them.

[10]Then the Devil, who betrayed them, was
thrown into the lake of fire that burns with
sulfur, joining the beast and the false prophet.
There they will be tormented day and night
forever and ever.

The Final Judgment

[11]And I saw a great white throne, and I saw the
one who was sitting on it. The earth and sky fled
from his presence, but they found no place to
hide. [12]I saw the dead, both great and small,
standing before God's throne. And the books
were opened, including the Book of Life. And
the dead were judged according to the things
written in the books, according to what they had
done. [13]The sea gave up the dead in it, and death
and the grave* gave up the dead in them. They
were all judged according to their deeds. [14]And
death and the grave were thrown into the lake of
fire. This is the second death—the lake of fire.
[15]And anyone whose name was not found recorded in the Book of Life was thrown into the
lake of fire.

CHAPTER 21

The New Jerusalem

Then I saw a new heaven and a new earth, for the
old heaven and the old earth had disappeared.
And the sea was also gone. [2]And I saw the holy
city, the new Jerusalem, coming down from God
out of heaven like a beautiful bride prepared for
her husband.

[3]I heard a loud shout from the throne, saying,
"Look, the home of God is now among his
people! He will live with them, and they will be
his people. God himself will be with them.* [4]He
will remove all of their sorrows, and there will be
no more death or sorrow or crying or pain. For
the old world and its evils are gone forever."

[5]And the one sitting on the throne said,
"Look, I am making all things new!" And then
he said to me, "Write this down, for what I tell
you is trustworthy and true." [6]And he also said,
"It is finished! I am the Alpha and the Omega—
the Beginning and the End. To all who are thirsty
I will give the springs of the water of life without
charge! [7]All who are victorious will inherit all
these blessings, and I will be their God, and they
will be my children. [8]But cowards who turn
away from me, and unbelievers, and the corrupt,
and murderers, and the immoral, and those who
practice witchcraft, and idol worshipers, and all
liars—their doom is in the lake that burns with
fire and sulfur. This is the second death."

[9]Then one of the seven angels who held the
seven bowls containing the seven last plagues
came and said to me, "Come with me! I will
show you the bride, the wife of the Lamb."

[10]So he took me in spirit* to a great, high
mountain, and he showed me the holy city,
Jerusalem, descending out of heaven from God.
[11]It was filled with the glory of God and sparkled
like a precious gem, crystal clear like jasper. [12]Its
walls were broad and high, with twelve gates
guarded by twelve angels. And the names of the
twelve tribes of Israel were written on the gates.
[13]There were three gates on each side—east,
north, south, and west. [14]The wall of the city had
twelve foundation stones, and on them were
written the names of the twelve apostles of the
Lamb.

[15]The angel who talked to me held in his
hand a gold measuring stick to measure the city,
its gates, and its wall. [16]When he measured it, he
found it was a square, as wide as it was long. In
fact, it was in the form of a cube, for its length
and width and height were each 1,400 miles.*
[17]Then he measured the walls and found them
to be 216 feet thick* (the angel used a standard
human measure).

[18]The wall was made of jasper, and the city
was pure gold, as clear as glass. [19]The wall of the
city was built on foundation stones inlaid with
twelve gems: the first was jasper, the second
sapphire, the third agate, the fourth emerald,
[20]the fifth onyx, the sixth carnelian, the seventh
chrysolite, the eighth beryl, the ninth topaz, the
tenth chrysoprase, the eleventh jacinth, the
twelfth amethyst.

[21]The twelve gates were made of pearls—each
gate from a single pearl! And the main street was
pure gold, as clear as glass.

[22]No temple could be seen in the city, for the
Lord God Almighty and the Lamb are its temple.
[23]And the city has no need of sun or moon, for
the glory of God illuminates the city, and the
Lamb is its light. [24]The nations of the earth will

20:13 Greek *and Hades;* also in 20:14. **21:3** Some manuscripts read *God himself will be with them, their God.* **21:10** Or *in the Spirit.*
21:16 Greek *12,000 stadia* [2,220 kilometers]. **21:17** Greek *144 cubits* [65 meters].

walk in its light, and the rulers of the world will
come and bring their glory to it. 25Its gates never
close at the end of day because there is no night.
26And all the nations will bring their glory and
honor into the city. 27Nothing evil will be allowed to enter—no one who practices shameful
idolatry and dishonesty—but only those whose
names are written in the Lamb's Book of Life.

CHAPTER 22

And the angel showed me a pure river with the
water of life, clear as crystal, flowing from the
throne of God and of the Lamb, 2coursing down
the center of the main street. On each side of the
river grew a tree of life, bearing twelve crops of
fruit,* with a fresh crop each month. The leaves
were used for medicine to heal the nations.

3No longer will anything be cursed. For the
throne of God and of the Lamb will be there,
and his servants will worship him. 4And they
will see his face, and his name will be written on
their foreheads. 5And there will be no night
there—no need for lamps or sun—for the Lord
God will shine on them. And they will reign
forever and ever.

6Then the angel said to me, "These words are
trustworthy and true: 'The Lord God, who tells
his prophets what the future holds, has sent his
angel to tell you what will happen soon.'"

Jesus Is Coming

7"Look, I am coming soon! Blessed are
those who obey the prophecy written in
this scroll."

8I, John, am the one who saw and heard all
these things. And when I saw and heard these
things, I fell down to worship the angel who
showed them to me. 9But again he said, "No,
don't worship me. I am a servant of God, just
like you and your brothers the prophets, as well
as all who obey what is written in this scroll.
Worship God!"

10Then he instructed me, "Do not seal up the
prophetic words you have written, for the time
is near. 11Let the one who is doing wrong continue to do wrong; the one who is vile, continue
to be vile; the one who is good, continue to do
good; and the one who is holy, continue in
holiness."

12"See, I am coming soon, and my reward
is with me, to repay all according to their
deeds. 13I am the Alpha and the Omega,
the First and the Last, the Beginning and the
End."

14Blessed are those who wash their robes so
they can enter through the gates of the city and
eat the fruit from the tree of life. 15Outside the
city are the dogs—the sorcerers, the sexually
immoral, the murderers, the idol worshipers,
and all who love to live a lie.

16"I, Jesus, have sent my angel to give you
this message for the churches. I am both the
source of David and the heir to his throne.*
I am the bright morning star."

17The Spirit and the bride say, "Come." Let
each one who hears them say, "Come." Let the
thirsty ones come—anyone who wants to. Let
them come and drink the water of life without
charge. 18And I solemnly declare to everyone
who hears the prophetic words of this book: If
anyone adds anything to what is written here,
God will add to that person the plagues described in this book. 19And if anyone removes
any of the words of this prophetic book, God
will remove that person's share in the tree of life
and in the holy city that are described in this
book.

20He who is the faithful witness to all these
things says, "Yes, I am coming soon!"

Amen! Come, Lord Jesus!

21The grace of the Lord Jesus be with you all.

22:2 Or *12 kinds of fruit.* 22:16 Greek *I am the root and offspring of David.*

TOPICAL INDEX